THE MAITLAND QUARTO

The Scottish Text Society
Fifth Series
no. 13

THE MAITLAND QUARTO

A New Edition of
Cambridge, Magdalene College,
Pepys Library MS 1408

Edited by
Joanna M. Martin

The Scottish Text Society
2015

© The Scottish Text Society 2015

All Rights Reserved. Except as permitted under current legislation
no part of this work may be photocopied, stored in a retrieval system,
published, performed in public, adapted, broadcast,
transmitted, recorded or reproduced in any form or by any means,
without the prior permission of the copyright owner

First published 2015 by The Scottish Text Society

ISBN 978-1-89797-640-1

A Scottish Text Society publication
Published by The Boydell Press
an imprint of Boydell & Brewer Ltd
PO Box 9, Woodbridge, Suffolk IP12 3DF, UK
and of Boydell & Brewer Inc.
668 Mt Hope Avenue, Rochester, NY 14620–2731, USA
website: www.boydellandbrewer.com

The publisher has no responsibility for
the continued existence or accuracy of URLs for external or
third-party internet websites referred to in this book, and
does not guarantee that any content on such websites
is, or will remain, accurate or appropriate.

A CIP catalogue record for this book is available
from the British Library

This publication is printed on acid-free paper
Printed and bound in Great Britain by
TJ International Ltd, Padstow, Cornwall

Contents

Acknowledgements	vii
Abbreviations	viii
Introduction	1
The Evolution of Maitland's Poetry	3
Sources and Influences: Maitland and Sixteenth-century Literary Culture	12
MQ's Shaping of Maitland's Corpus	19
Order in Other MQ Texts	21
Alexander Arbuthnot	22
The Anonymous Verse in MQ	26
Women and the Culture of MQ	28
Varieties of Scripts	30
Textual Relationships	32
The Drummond and Reidpeth Manuscripts	35
About this Edition	37
Texts	41
Explanatory Notes	277
Appendix 1	457
Appendix 2	467
Glossary	471
Index of Names	511
Index of First Lines	515
Bibliography	519

Acknowledgements

I am grateful to the AHRC for the award of an Early Career Fellowship, in 2011–12, which enabled me to move closer to completing this edition. I am also grateful to the School of English, University of Nottingham, for a period of school research leave and teaching relief which allowed me dedicated research time for the project in 2010–11. I would like to thank the fellows of Magdalene College, Cambridge and the librarian of the Pepys Library, for allowing me to consult the manuscript on a number of occasions.

Particular thanks are due to Professor Alasdair MacDonald, my editorial advisor, for his generosity in reading various drafts of material from the edition, for his encouragement, and guidance on editorial matters and on 'Maitlandia' in general. Nicola Royan, president of the Scottish Text Society, has been a continuous source of advice, and has allowed herself to be a much-drawn-upon repository of wisdom on sixteenth-century Scottish literature and history. She was also sympathetic and uncomplaining when progress on the edition was slow. I am also grateful to Professor Tony Edwards, Professor David Parkinson, and Dr Máire ní Fhlathúin for reading drafts of the introduction to the edition, and to Dr Rhiannon Purdie for her extensive help with the glossary. Many other people have patiently listened to my thoughts on the contents of this manuscript, and answered many questions, and in particular, warm thanks in this respect are due to Dr Kate McClune, Professor Lynda Pratt, Professor Thorlac Turville-Petre, Professor Jenny Wormald, and Dr Emily Wingfield. I am also grateful to Dr Clare Wright and Erin Connelly for their help with proofreading the edition.

My last debt of gratitude is to my parents, and sister, and to my daughter Lucy, whose arrival coincided with the early stages of work on the project. The edition is dedicated to them.

Abbreviations

BL	British Library
BM	The Bannatyne Manuscript
Chaucer	*The Riverside Chaucer* (Benson, ed. 1987)
CPS	*Scotland Calendar Scottish Papers*, vol. 3 1569–71 (Edinburgh, 1903)
DIMEV	An Open Access, Digital Edition of the *Index of Middle English Verse* http://www.cddc.vt.edu/host/imev
DOST	*A Dictionary of the Older Scottish Tongue*, www.dsl.ac.uk
Dunbar	*The Poems of William Dunbar* (Bawcutt, ed. 1998)
EETS, OS	Early English, Text Society, Original Series
ESTC	*English Short Title Catalogue*, British Library http://estc.bl.uk
f. ff.	folio, folios
Geneva Bible 1560	*The Geneva Bible. A Facsimile of the 1560 Edition*, L.E. Berry, intro. (Madison, Milwaukee and London, 1969)
Henryson	*The Poems of Robert Henryson* (Fox, ed. 1980)
IMEV	*The Index of Middle English Verse*, C. Brown and R.H. Robbins (New York, 1943)
l. ll.	line, lines
Lyndsay	*The Works of David Lyndsay* (Hamer, ed. 1931–6)
MF	Maitland Folio Manuscript
Montgomerie	*The Poems of Alexander Montgomerie* (Parkinson, ed. 2000)
MQ	Maitland Quarto Manuscript
MS, MSS	manuscript, manuscripts
NAS	National Archives of Scotland
NIMEV	*A New Index of Middle English Verse*, J. Boffey and A.S.G. Edwards (London, 2005)
NLS	National Library of Scotland
ODNB	*The Oxford Dictionary of National Biography*, http://www.oxforddnb.com
OED	*The Oxford English Dictionary*, 2nd edition, http://www.oed.com
Ovid *Met.*	Ovid, *Metamorphoses* [1998, trans. Melville]
Reg. Privy	*Register of the Privy Council of Scotland*, vol. 2,

ABBREVIAITONS

Council (1878)	1569–78 (Edinburgh, 1878)
RPS	Records of the Parliaments of Scotland to 1707, http://www.rps.ac.uk
SND	Scottish National Dictionary, www.dsl.ac.uk
STC	*A Short Title Catalogue of Books Printed in England, Scotland and Ireland ... 1475–1640*, ed. A.W. Pollard and G.R. Redgrave, 2nd edition (London, 1976)
TA	*Accounts of the Lord High Treasurer of Scotland, 1473–1580*, 13 vols, ed. Thomas Dickson, J. Balfour Paul and C.T. McInnes (Edinburgh, 1877–1916)

Introduction

The Maitland Quarto (hereafter MQ) is a paper manuscript held in the collections of the Pepys Library, Magdalene College, Cambridge, where it is MS 1408. It is the companion manuscript of MS 2553, the Maitland Folio Manuscript (hereafter MF), a slightly earlier collection of verse from which a number of MQ's texts seem to have been copied. MQ contains 95 poems in 138 leaves, copied in a mixture of secretary and italic scripts, probably all the work of one hand.[1] All but two of these poems (MQ 60 and MQ 87) appear to be of Scots origin, though several have English or continental sources. The first folio of the manuscript is inscribed twice with the date 1586 and the name of Marie Maitland, indicating that, like MF, it was copied in the circle of the Maitlands of Lethington, a family of lowland lairds who had become increasingly influential in royal administration during the sixteenth century. Marie Maitland was one of four daughters of Sir Richard Maitland of Lethington, a privy counsellor, royal commissioner, Lord of Session and keeper of the great seal of Scotland: she is explicitly addressed in two poems in the manuscript, MQ 69 and MQ 85. The name of her sister Helen appears in MF (Boffey 2001, p. 41), and her brothers William, John and Thomas were all known to have literary interests and talent for composing in Latin and Scots. Some of John Maitland's vernacular poems and those of Richard Maitland are contained in MQ, along with a number of poems attributed to members of what was presumably the wider Maitland circle including Alexander Arbuthnot, Alexander Montgomerie, and Thomas and Robert Hudson. There is also one poem attributed to 'Jacobus Rex' (James VI) and a substantial body of unattributed and often unique verse probably written by family members and associates. Both MQ and MF may have been copied at Lethington, the family seat in East Lothian. However, given that the family estates were confiscated in 1571 and not returned until 1584, this is not a certainty.

---

[1] Although always carefully presented, the appearance of the secretary hand does vary a little throughout the manuscript. To begin with the secretary is large, its letters well proportioned and lines of poetry well spaced; but gradually the secretary hand appears more cramped and fluid. Compare fols 2–10r with fol. 13 onwards. There is no change in the colour of the ink between italic and secretary scripts, to suggest that another scribe has taken over.

MQ has been regarded by scholars as a commemorative manuscript and a fair copy of Richard Maitland's poems (MacDonald 2001, p. 139) prepared either in anticipation of his death, or in light of his great age: he died on 21 March 1586 aged 90, and the manuscript, which is carefully written and organised, is concluded with a series of epitaphs and elegies for him and his wife, Mary or Mariota Cranstoun, who apparently outlived him only by a few days. However, 1586 was a significant year for the family in other ways too, and this 'literary memorial' (MacDonald 2001, p. 139) perhaps evidences family pride more generally, while foregrounding the fundamental role of the head of the family in the good fortunes of his offspring. On 31 May 1586, Richard Maitland's heir, John Maitland of Thirlestane, was made keeper for life of the Great Seal of Scotland and given the title of vice-chancellor to James VI. In August of that year Marie Maitland married Sir Alexander Lauder of Hatton. Several items in the manuscript display connections to the lives of the Maitlands. MQ 94 is a sonnet sequence in praise of John Maitland. MQ 69 may relate to Marie's marriage, while other poems in MQ concern proper conduct in marriage (MQ 13 and MQ 66) or celebrate other recent family marriages (MQ 63 and MQ 64). MQ 43 and MQ 44 are ascribed to John Maitland in MF, and some anonymous poems in MQ may be either by Marie, or addressed to her (this is discussed further below).

The contents of the manuscript span a wide variety of verse forms (over 60 in total) and poetic genres. As well as reflecting the family's literary tastes, its poetry also speaks to a range of family concerns from the political to the amatory, including family identity and history, local and national affairs, and personal relationships and religiosity. Its strong political and moral emphasis makes it, as I have argued elsewhere (Martin 2013a), readable as an advice book for the ruling classes of James VI's reign, of which the Maitland family clearly regarded itself a distinguished part: William 'Secretary' Lethington was particularly prominent in the 1550s and 1560s, and John Maitland rose to the top of royal administration in the 1570s and 1580s. The Quarto's moral and advisory emphasis is not in conflict with its commemorative role; indeed it is Maitland's poetry which introduces the theme of advice-giving to nobles, monarch, children, and the wider community, and which commemorates important national events. The personal, philosophical and religious contents of the Quarto also relate to the family's recent endurance of and triumphs over political adversity in the 1570s in particular, and its renewed confidence as a result of these experiences. The manuscript's compilation at the beginning of the personal rule of

INTRODUCTION

James VI, the start of a new era in Scottish political and cultural life, as well as its combination of verse composed in earlier decades with more contemporary material, suggests that it is not just a nostalgic anthology, but one which has been constructed with concern for its readers' present and future good.

The Evolution of Maitland's Poetry

MQ is significant for containing the earliest complete collection of the poems of Sir Richard Maitland of Lethington: it includes all but one of the poems attributed to Richard Maitland in contemporary sources, forty-three in total, three more than in MF (these are MQ 8, 16 and 17).[2] MQ 2 is only found in its complete state in MQ: MF is missing the first ten stanzas of the poem. The one poem attributed to Maitland outside MF and MQ is in the Bannatyne Manuscript, fols 12–14, and appears here in Appendix 1. MQ's collection of Maitland's verse is significant not only for its completeness, but also for its organisation, which is carefully executed to offer the reader a history of family, local and national events, as well as a commentary on social and religious attitudes and developments in Scotland in the third quarter of the sixteenth century. Indeed, Richard Maitland's poems are considerably earlier than the date of the compilation of MQ, and those that can be dated relate to the period of the Guise regency (1554–59), and thus the years of Mary's minority (1542–53) and absence from Scotland (1548–61), and the years of civil war in Scotland following Mary's deposition (1567–73). His datable corpus thus spans the mid 1550s to the early 1570s.

As these dates suggest, much of Richard Maitland's poetry in MQ was written when he was already of advanced years, much of it when he was a septuagenarian. If he composed poetry earlier in his life, it has not been preserved, with the possible exception of the poem in the Bannatyne Manuscript which is of uncertain authorship (MacDonald 2001, p. 138 and Appendix 1). However, given that his prose history of the Setons dates from the 1550s and his surviving datable poetry from this decade onwards, it is equally possible that his advancing years, despite his blindness, provided him with the first opportunity to spend time on literary interests and activities, his long legal career and experience of

---

[2] More work, however, remains to be done on the many unattributed poems in MF that may have a claim to be included in Maitland's canon.

court life and government supplying much material to draw on. His *Practiques*, a collection of summaries of decisions made by the Court of Session, also covers the period c.1550–c.1577 (Sutherland ed. 2007).

Maitland was primarily a lyric poet: none of his poems is more than 120 lines long, and few contain any extended narrative, though some, such as MQ 23, in which the narrator relates his experiences of avarice at court, contain succinct, exemplary narratives. He commanded a high number of verse forms (around thirty-four different stanzas are showcased in a collection of forty-three poems: MacDonald 1972, pp. 17–18), and lyric voices, thus firmly situating him in the tradition which produced the metrical innovations and variety of Dunbar, Scott and Montgomerie. His subjects are topical, political and moral, and include reflections on his family and on matters of faith and philosophy. He addresses his poems to his social and professional equals (including judges)[3] and his superiors, and to those he regards as in need of moral direction (see for example MQ 2).[4]

Poems 2–8, likely to be among the earliest of Maitland's poems in MQ, offer detailed observations about social practices and changes, and reflections on the administration of government. Although the social commentary of these poems is influenced by earlier poets such as Dunbar and Lyndsay (see below) it nevertheless reflects concerns which were likely to appear very relevant to lairdly administrators such as Maitland. MQ 2, for example, focuses on the sumptuary transgressions of townswomen, which threaten social and moral propriety. The poem is highly class-conscious, and nostalgic, comparing the riotous extravagance of contemporary women (which is observed in rich material detail) with the frugal and sober conduct of 'thair motheris' (l. 63). MQ 5 also complains of the decline in traditional values in Scottish society, examining the conduct of all the estates, and looking back to the better example of 'our foirbearis' (l. 38). The poem begins by lamenting the loss of traditional courtly recreation, hospitality and the maintenance of the noble household, and ends by blaming the nobility for failing to set a wise example through their 'honorabill deidis' (l. 81). Its last thirty lines confront the reader with evidence of social decline, including intimidation of the courts, and the corruption of the justice system which results in the decay of the 'commoun weill' (l. 82) as criminals escape punishment for their crimes.

---

[3] See, for example, MQ 16, ll. 67–68.
[4] See, for example, MQ 2.

Indeed, the 'common weill', and how it should 'induire' (MQ 27, l. 1) in troubled times, is a major preoccupation for Maitland throughout his poetry. This reflects an outlook widely found in the political discourses of the first half of the sixteenth century (Mason 1998, pp. 91–92): for Maitland and his contemporaries, care for the commonweal encompasses the efficient and equitable government of the realm, and social justice, especially the protection of 'our commounis' (MQ 6, l. 61) and the poor. These concerns, and evidence of Maitland's immense legal experience, continue to underpin his poetry, and are reflected in references to specific social abuses and hardships such as rack-renting (MQ 5, l. 34; MQ 16, ll. 13–14; MQ 21, ll. 9–14), lairdly interference with the livings tenants drew from their 'malingis' (MQ 21, ll. 22–24), inflation and tax increases. Such abuses in turn are placed in the context of the mutual dependency of the estates for the benefit of the 'haill commounitie' (MQ 21, l. 36). For example, in MQ 21 Maitland reminds landowners of their responsibility to the commons and to their tenants, on whom they rely for various services, including military support; in MQ 22 he counsels rulers that loyalty from their subjects must be repaid with equitable rule and protection.

Older theories of social order also combined with more contemporary concerns to shape the development of Maitland's poetry. For example, classical and medieval notions of the relationship between the individual's moral world and state of society, the microcosm and the macrocosm, as well as a protestant preoccupation with virtuous living, inflect many of Maitland's moral and penitential poems. Encouraging a sense of collective responsibility for social reform, rather than mutual blame for Scotland's troubles, is therefore a priority in his writing:

> The greit men sayis that thair distres
> Cummis for the peopillis wickednes;
> The peopill sayis the transgressioun
> Of greit men and thair oppressioun,
> Bot nane will thair awin syn confes. (MQ 27, ll. 16–20)

Maitland's social complaint poems draw attention to his advisory lyric voice, a constant element in his poetry. For example, in MQ 2 Maitland's narrator addresses his advice to '3oung wyffis' (l. 66) and then 'generallie / to all wemen' (ll. 81–82), anticipating the parental advice mode that he adopts in MQ 11, a father's advice to his son at court, and MQ 15, a simple and direct distillation of this kind of wisdom, comprising a clear code of personal ethics for any social or political context. The short, playful lyric, MQ 32, a reversible 'grammar' poem, suggest that his self-appointed role as paternal advice giver was sometimes executed with a sense of fun. However, advice-giving is often combined with direct exhortation in Maitland's poems. MQ 5 makes a general appeal to his readers for their moral reform – 'Amend ȝour lyffis ane and all' – and this is paralleled in many of his later poems (compare MQ 10, l. 44 and MQ 19, l. 64). At times these appeals and directives to 'leiff in godlines' (MQ 33, l. 4) are resonant of hortatory devotional writing such as that found in the *Gude and Godlie Ballatis*: 'Sinneris, repent that ȝe haue spent / ȝour tyme in wickednes', is the opening to MQ 33.

The fierceness of these imperatives is moderated in poems which include the narrator's remorse and culpability in their calls for improvement, creating a sense of common endeavour between 'freindis' (MQ 23, l. 42; MQ 31, l. 10): 'Let *ws* at God ask grace' (MQ 31, l. 66, italics mine). Maitland sometimes offers the reader his own poetic persona as exemplary, or as the recipient of advice, in the discussion of ethics and morality. MQ 14 is addressed to Maitland's persona, a 'Blind man' who is the victim of a violent raid on his property, who will yet be blithe again when justice is done, and whose own virtue assures him the joys of heaven: a degree of self-righteousness is not uncommon in Maitland's writing on his family's experiences. In MQ 24 the elderly persona describes his desire to turn from worldly pleasures to the comforts of faith. As in MQ 14, MQ 20 presents the narrator as the victim of injustice, made more poignant by his age (he is 'sa auld', l. 30). But in this poem the sense of indignation, and the protestations of innocence, are combined with the narrator's comic reflections on and remorse for his misspent youth, and satisfaction that, despite his advanced years, he can still anticipate justice for those who 'did me wrang' (l. 55). Thus, both MQ 20 and MQ 24 give more personalised versions of the advice directed at the foolish 'senex amans' of MQ 13, a poem possibly directed at the fifty-year-old John Knox on his marriage of 1564 to Margaret Stewart, aged seventeen. Both MQ 23 and MQ 52, poems on the virtue of 'kyndnes' (loyalty between kin and friends), are voiced by a narrator whose bewilderment at the machinations and misconduct of his contemporaries at court leads him to voice and recommend an ironic detachment from worldly self-interest.

Despite the cultivation of an advising voice, advice-giving poems directed to the monarch are rare in Maitland's oeuvre, with MQ 59 being the only full-length 'advice to princes' poem directed to a sovereign (see Martin 2013a), which tellingly also includes a direct appeal to James's 'counsell' (l. 65). This is a reflection of the times in which

Maitland was writing: between 1542 and 1573/74 Scottish politics were dominated by the minorities and regencies of Mary, who was absent from her realm for over a decade, and her son James, and the sense of a power vacuum is acute in Maitland's works. Maitland's poems to those in power which date from the Guise regency show attempts at optimism and a desire to emphasise his loyalty to royal authority as a 'trew seruand' of the regent and the queen (MQ 9, l. 49). Thus, MQ 6, on Mary's French marriage settlement, MQ 9 on her return to Scotland in 1561, and MQ 10 on the Duke of Guise's recapture of Calais, fulfil the role of public, celebratory verse on major occasions. However, all these poems show signs of strain and sound notes of caution. MQ 6, with its rallying calls for elaborate public festivities, and flattery for Mary's spouse, François, as 'the gretest 3oung prince in Christintie' (l. 7), attempts to celebrate Franco-Scottish unity, but acknowledges that this is artificial:

> Scottis and Frenche now leif in vnitie
> As 3e war brether borne in ane countrie. (ll. 64–65, italics mine)

The poem concludes with an address to the 'noble princes and mother to our Quene', Mary of Guise, which reminds the reader of the precarious position of a realm without an adult monarch, which is dependent on a regent's policies and the involvement of external powers in its affairs for its protection. The problems inherent in the Guise alliance are revisited in a number of other poems by Maitland, including MQ 9 on Mary's homecoming, which cautions the widowed queen to protect the 'libertie' (l. 45) of Scotland if she chooses to marry again. MQ 8, MQ 19 and MQ 25 all remind Scots that the intrusion of French, or for that matter English, politics in Scotland's affairs is never in the interest of the realm, but rather part of the acquisitive foreign policies of a powerful neighbour. MQ 10 marks the capture in January 1558 of Calais from the English by the forces of the Duke of Guise, Henri II's *lieutenant général* from 1557, and Mary of Guise's brother, with attention to the details of the campaign and some flattery of the 'michtie valil3eant campioun' (l. 29). However, Maitland also manages to turn the military triumph of the French into a call for repentance, and an occasion for a lesson on God's omnipotence, on the impermanence of worldly power and the vanity of man's ambition without his favour. Ultimately the military conquest was God's, Maitland reminds us: 'Think that it wes his hand that brak the wall' (l. 15).

Maitland's addresses to James VI are usually, with the exception of MQ 59 (c.1573?), embedded within poems which do not initially or solely seek royal influence and authority, but which express hopes for their restoration. These poems all date either from James's minority, or from early in his personal rule. Thus MQ 16, which draws disturbing parallels between the treachery of Jerusalem at the time of the crucifixion and the cruelty and duplicity of contemporary times, ends with a prayer for the 'kingis maiestie' (l. 113) in hope that peace, justice and liberty may return to the realm. In MQ 19, with its startling disjunction between its pleasant garden setting, echoic of the *chanson d'aventure* tradition, and the narrator's troubled reflections on the civil war, Maitland appeals to the lords of Scotland to settle their differences so that the king, 'quhen he is of aage to ring' (l. 97) still has a country to govern. In MQ 51, a complaint about the inefficient workings of the Court of Session, Maitland alludes to the precariousness of James's position in the aftermath of the civil war, appealing to 'our souuerane lord' (l. 51) to reform the college of justice, because 'It will the helpe for to maintein thy croun' (l. 55).

Maitland's frequent direct appeals for divine help in his poems have the effect of reminding us that the realm lacks an adult monarch. This is particularly evident in his adaptation of the tradition of writing the New Year poem to the monarch or patron, addressing God in lieu of any effective temporal authority, in MQ 4, MQ 7 and MQ 8 (all composed before c.1561). MQ 4 is a prayer for guidance for the queen and queen regent, with pleas to God in eight of the poem's nineteen stanzas. In the rest of the poem Maitland's narrator is forced to appeal to those in positions of temporal authority under the sovereign, the 'Lordis of the sait' (Court of Session).[5] This anticipates Maitland's frequent addresses to the ruling classes of Scotland in poems from the civil war period which exhort the lords to settle their differences for the good of the commonweal. 'Quhat is the caus of all this greit confusioun' he asks, 'Bot the diuisioun of lordis ...?' (MQ 18, ll. 16–17). MQ 19 appeals to 'my lordis' to 'aggrie in haist' (ll. 91, 96); MQ 25 is addressed to 'ȝe nobillis all that sould this countrie guyde', accusing them of pursuing an 'vnkyndlie weir' (l. 15), of negligence in their care for the commonweal, and suspicion of each other which prevents them from being 'knit ... togidder' (l. 79) in the interests of Scotland's liberty and stability. In these poems his sense of a lack of political stability is particularly acute, as he expresses doubt at the very existence of any wise (MQ 5, l.

---

[5] Also compare MQ 18, which asks for God's help in ending the civil war and the disorder associated with it.

79, MQ 25, l. 21) or 'zelous' (MQ 19, l. 28) men within the realm, who will be able to restore peace.

Throughout his poetry Maitland is preoccupied with the subject of unjust acquisitiveness, loss and reparation, and particularly breaches of neighbourliness which involve the wrongful conquest of land. This is not just a concern which coincides with Maitland's own experience of loss during 1570–71, when his barony of Blyth was attacked by Scottish and English troops loyal to the King's Party, and Lethington was confiscated by the regent, events explicitly addressed in MQ 14 and MQ 20 (see headnotes to these poems). Rather it seems to be related to his desire for just government and his own experience of overseeing court cases. Indeed, among his *Practiques* are many summaries of legal cases concerning land transfers, forfeiture and restoration, and 'spuilȝie' or 'wrangous melling with geir' (Sutherland ed. 2007, p. 385). In MQ 7 (dated to 1559) God is asked that justice is done to ensure that all 'trew folk may bruik thair iust possessioun' (l. 61). In MQ 57, an advice poem to those wishing to maintain their noble lineage, Maitland uses legal formulae to suggest the gravity of wrongful acquisition, instructing his reader to 'Intromet not with wrangous geir' (l. 4, compare MQ 19, l. 63). In MQ 58, which is probably datable to 1573, the appeal is the same: 'I pray the leving Lord' (l. 43) that,

> ... sic iustice be done this kinrik throw,
> The quhilk may gar the rasche-bus keip the kow,
> And euerie man bruik his awin land and geir ... (ll. 46–48)

The experience of personal loss, in his own life or in the lives of those close to him, does nevertheless make Maitland's observations on this theme keener. MQ 28, MQ 29 and MQ 30 are all poems on the state of the realm, but foreground the theme of greed, especially in terms of taking another's land and breaching natural bonds of kinship, friendship and neighbourliness. MQ 30 in particular gives us an unsettling insight into the violence of such attacks on personal property, a perspective which is concealed in the self-deprecating humour of MQ 20 or the self-righteousness of MQ 14 (though the scale of the attack on Blyth is indicated in the note which accompanies the text in MF).

> Sum hes thair place brint in ane gleid,
> Thair guddis spuilȝit halallie;
> Thair seruandis slaine, sum brint to deid,
> Thair selfis taine vncourteouslie,
> And hauldin in captiuitie,
> Quha wald haue, for ane missiue bill,

> Obeyit the auctoritie,
> And cummit at my lord Regentis will. (ll. 41–48)

The protests of innocence and injustice here, and the iteration of unquestioning loyalty to authority, surely reflect Maitland's family position, even though the terms of the poem are general. The poem's reference to unlawful imprisonment may refer to William, Secretary Lethington who was imprisoned on charges related to the murder of Darnley in 1569–70.

Maitland's philosophical poems recommend to the reader the consolations of faith as a way of understanding and triumphing over persecution and injustice. Trust in God's mercy, an acceptance of one's lot as God's will, and therefore that hardship is either a punishment for sin, or a trial of faith for the righteous, are themes which recur in such poems. MQ 31 offers a typical summary of these ideas:

> Quhat God plesis to doe,
> Accept it thankfullie;
> Quhat paine he put ws to,
> Receave it patientlie;
> And gif that we wald be
> Relevit of our paine,
> For sin ask God mercie:
> Offend him not againe. (ll. 25–32)

Maitland avoids specific references to doctrine or devotional practice and distils faith to its essentials: dread and love of God, repentance, charity to one's neighbour; and an anticipation of the joys of heaven for the virtuous.

Indeed, Maitland's writing on both the political and religious situation is carefully non-partisan, and thus in contrast to many of the contemporary poems to the lords which circulated in civil war Scotland (many printed by Lekpreuik), which were often explicitly addressed to one side or the other.[6] Maitland's commentary on one of the most significant changes of his lifetime, the Scottish Reformation, focuses not on individual matters of doctrine or right, but on personal virtue and responsibility. Thus in MQ 7, which perhaps dates from the Wars of the Congregation (1559), churchmen are implored to do their 'dewtie' (l. 45): this poem's plea that God free the Scots from all 'heresie' gives no more details on this subject than that people may be led in the 'richt

---

[6] Many of these poems are collected and edited in J. Cranstoun, ed., *Satirical Poems of the Time of the Reformation*, 2 vols, STS, 1st ser., 20, 24 (Edinburgh and London, 1891–93).

INTRODUCTION

way' and not 'begylit' by either side of the religious debate (ll. 49–50, 52). MQ 12 notes with disappointment that despite the rise of Protestantism, '3it as now ma vycis neuer rang' (l. 35); and reserves censure for 'fleschlie gospellaris' (l. 62, those who preach the gospel but are carnally minded). Nevertheless it attacks the conduct of both the Catholic and reformed clergy, articulating impatience with churchmen on both sides whose claims for the superiority of their denomination fail to tally with their deeds, and who disregard the lives of 'faythfull Christianis' (MQ 12, l. 57). MQ 8 laments the trouble caused by the Lords of the Congregation, but also that caused by Guise's French support. If MQ 13 is an attack on Knox, as MacDonald has convincingly suggested (MacDonald 2001, p. 145), then no names are mentioned. When Maitland's poems which refer to the Reformation are more politicised, his aim is simply to draw attention to suffering. Thus MQ 51 articulates concerns about the enrichment, to the detriment of the poor, of secular lords with ecclesiastical revenues after the Reformation (see MQ 51, ll. 61–63).

Similarly, Maitland seldom makes explicit references to influential political events such as Mary's deposition or the assignation or untimely death of a regent. Thus in MQ 22, a poem on treason, Maitland asserts, 'I will not speik in speciall, / Bot pray all in generall, / That wicked vyice to flie' (ll. 16–18). Despite the clear affiliation of his sons with the Queen's Party up until 1573, Maitland declines to make clear his own allegiances in the conflict, and instead addresses his pleas for peace and unity to both factions in the struggle: 'I speik this to the lordis of bayth the syidis' (MQ 18, l. 41).

Writing in the uncertain and violent climate of the third quarter of the sixteenth century, Maitland does not prioritise self-reflexive pondering of the process of writing or the value of literature. MQ 55, however, does offer us something of a literary manifesto. In this poem Maitland writes against his contemporary 'poetis and makeris' (l. 1) who compose and have printed defamatory verses which ruin the reputation of 'monye gud honest man' (l. 8) with their accusations of improbable crimes. Although improper speech such as backbiting and flattery is cautioned against in his advisory poems such as MQ 11 and MQ 59, in MQ 55 Maitland sets out what he considers the duty of the poet to be. Evoking classical theories of the utility of poetry for instruction he counsels:

> ... mak sum mirrie toy to gud purpois,
> That may the herar or reader bayth reioys,
> Or sum fruitfull or gud moralitie,
> Or plesand thingis may stand with cheritie. (ll. 35–38)

Above all, poets are advised to 'Put not in writ that God or man may greif' (l. 34), a good description of Maitland's own endeavours as a writer.

Sources and Influences: Maitland and Sixteenth-Century Literary Culture

Both of the literary manuscripts associated with Richard Maitland and his family suggest that he had an acute sense of and enthusiasm for the Scottish literary tradition and, to a lesser extent, for English writing. This enthusiasm and knowledge emerge strongly in Maitland's poetry. The earlier of the two family manuscripts, MF, appears to function in part as a poet's source book for Maitland, and its rich collection of Scottish and (some) English poems reveals much about his sense of his poetic heritage and his own place within literary tradition (on MF as a verse anthology and household book, see Boffey 2001). The influence can be traced in his works of poems found in MF such as the personification allegory *King Hart*, the advisory and court poems of William Stewart, the pious and philosophical 'Now man behald this warldis vaniteis' (from the *Gude and Godlie Ballatis*), or the sixteenth-century English friendship poem by Thomas Churchyard, 'The thoctis of men dois daylie chynge'. Some of Maitland's poems are eclectic in their responses to earlier texts. MQ 28, one of Maitland's most lively poems on the estates, creates a personification allegory which has echoes of *King Hart*, Douglas's *Palice of Honour* (see Bawcutt, ed. 2003), Lyndsay's *Ane Satyre of the Thrie Estaitis* and several poems by Dunbar.

Indeed, MF's large body of works by Dunbar is particularly significant for understanding the literary background to Maitland's work. MacDonald has demonstrated that Maitland's interest in the poetry of Dunbar extended to shared themes, and stylistic choices, and even to the reworking of individual poems: MQ 11 in particular, Maitland's paternal advice poem addressed to a son who must learn how to negotiate the ways of court, is a reworking of Dunbar's 'To dwell in court, my freind, gife that thow list' (see MacDonald 2001, and headnote to MQ 11).[7] Like Dunbar, Maitland aspired to being regarded and rewarded as a loyal royal servant, and offers advice and comment on public occasions accordingly. For example, MQ 9, Maitland's welcome poem to

---

[7] All references in Dunbar's poetry in this edition are to Bawcutt, ed. 1993.

Queen Mary, consciously looks back to and echoes details of Dunbar's 'Gladethe, thoue queyne of Scottis regioun' (c.1503–7), addressed to James IV's queen, Margaret Tudor, and 'Blyth Aberdeane, thow beriall of all tounis', a celebration of Margaret's entry into Aberdeen in 1511. Maitland's advice poem to the young James VI, MQ 59, echoes the listing techniques and diction of Dunbar's warnings to James IV about the unsuitable individuals who cluster around him at court in 'Schir ȝe haue mony seruitouris'. Maitland's New Year poems also echo those Dunbar addressed to James IV. MQ 4, for example, borrows syntactical structures from Dunbar's 'My prince in God, gif the guid grace', but, as we have seen, poignantly addresses not the king, as Dunbar was able to do, but God. Indeed, the unpredictability and corruption of the court, which is a common subject in Dunbar's poems, is also taken up by Maitland. MQ 23, in which Maitland's narrator approaches a well-connected kinsman at court to ask for assistance with his affairs only to find that financial bribery, rather than the ties of kinship, is the only way to advancement, recalls Dunbar's complaint about the dominance of avarice at court in 'Fredome, honour and nobilnes'. Maitland may also have had in mind when writing this poem and MQ 52 Dunbar's 'Doverrit with dreme, devysing in my slummer' in which legal and material favours at court are procured by kinsmen willing to engage in financial arrangements:

> Sa mony ane sentence retreitit for to win
> Geir or acquentance or kindnes of thair kin,
> Thay think no sin, quhair proffeit cumis betuene. (ll. 51–53)

While Dunbar did not often write on wider political disorder, his poem on the highland rebel Donald Dubh, 'In vice most vicius he excellis', clearly interested Maitland as he wrote about the thieves of Liddesdale in MQ 3 and denounced treasonable conduct in MQ 22. The fast-paced metre and use of the present tense in MQ 3 is directly modelled on Dunbar's work.

Maitland's many pithy poems on morality also draw on Dunbar's lyric poems of a moral and philosophical outlook and the traditions that shaped them. Thus in MQ 26, Maitland's narrator comforts all who have been wronged by friends, neighbours and political aggressors, with the 'contemptus mundi' advice, 'Of this fals warld tak neuer thocht'. Though conventional, this refrain seems to echo parts of Dunbar's 'Full oft I mvse and hes in thocht' with its complaint about 'How this fals warld is ay on flocht' (l. 2) and 'warldlie onkyndnes' (l. 31). Dunbar's 'Quhom to sall I compleine my wo', with its narrator's sense of social isolation and the refrain, 'For in this warld may none assure', is also likely to be an influence on MQ 26. These poems by Dunbar also lie behind MQ 52, 'This warld so fals is and vnstabill'. The blend of nostalgic complaint and personification allegory to describe social corruption in Dunbar's 'Quhome to sall I compleine my wo' also finds an echo in Maitland's 'It is ane mortall paine to heir and sie', MQ 28, with its sadness for the loss of honour, virtue and political unity, and dramatic allegorical conflict between the personifications of greed and kindness.

Dunbar's moral lyrics often advocate contentment and acceptance rather than despair at mutability and disorder. The refrain of 'Full oft I mvse and hes in thocht' is 'For to be blythe me think it best': this may be echoed in Maitland's highly personal poem on the attack on Blyth in 1570, MQ 14, 'Blind man be blyithe thocht that thow be wrangit'; and in MQ 31, Maitland's exhortation to 'My freindis all' (l. 10) that 'to be mirrie is best. / Let ws be blyith and glaid' (ll. 8–9). Dunbar's 'Quho thinkis that he hes sufficence' seems to provide Maitland with material for several of his poems, including MQ 17, in which he weighs the difficulty of personal loss against the need to endure patiently and seek happiness through faith rather than possessions:

> Trowble sumtymes is profitable,
> And gevis men intelligence,
> To ken thair God makis thame able,
> And of thame selff experience. (ll. 5–9)

Although much of the influence from Dunbar comes from his philosophical lyrics and his poems on court life and morality, Maitland also shows knowledge of Dunbar's longer debate poem, the *Tretis*, echoing its portrayal of the first wife and her older husband, in MQ 13, a poem on the folly of old lovers who marry young women. Indeed, where Maitland does write about love, he does so, rather like Dunbar, to highlight the foolishness it can engender. This also informs the ironic and humorous presentation of his poetic personae in a way that can be highly reminiscent of Dunbar's self-mockery. In MQ 20, for example, Maitland complains about the serious business of the confiscation of his family seat, Lethington, in 1571, through the creation of a bewildered elderly persona, who protests his innocence in all matters. The narrator will not, he says, 'flyte lyik ane scauld' because of his age, and instead he cheers himself with thought that all worldly cares are now past, including his dalliance with young lasses which roused his wife's jealousy. This comic persona is revisited in MQ 52, where the narrator reflects on the mercilessness with which old lovers are cast out of Venus's court despite their long service. This particular image looks back to Gower's *Confessio Amantis*, perhaps through Henryson's *Testament of Cresseid*, but the melancholy idea of being outcast and past one's best is also suggestive of knowledge of Dunbar's 'Schir, lat it neuer in toune be tald', where the narrator takes on the identity of a worn-out horse to complain of his misfortunes.

David Lyndsay (c.1486–1555), with whom Maitland shared an interest in and knowledge of Dunbar, was only a decade his senior. Although he is not a lyric poet, Lyndsay is also an important influence on Maitland's poems, especially in the areas of social and religious critique and estates satire. Maitland seems to have been well acquainted with many of Lyndsay's works, from his early poetry (especially *The Complaynt*) to *Ane Satyre of the Thrie Estaitis*: Lyndsay's works are known to have been circulating in print copies by the mid sixteenth century and Maitland may have had access to them in this form, or perhaps in manuscript.[8] It is not always easy to separate the influence of Dunbar and Lyndsay on Maitland. For example, MQ 6, Maitland's poem on the marriage of Mary and the Dauphin, François, son of Henri II of France, in April 1558, naturally looks back to recent poems on public celebrations including Dunbar's 'Blyth Aberdeane, thow beriall of all tounis', and also Lyndsay's more recent, but melancholy poem, on Edinburgh's celebrations planned, but never executed, for James V's queen, *The Deploratioun of the Deith of Quene Magdalene* (1537). However, Lyndsay's influence on Maitland seems particularly strong in his poems on aspects of social and religious reform. In matters of social critique Maitland seems to have appreciated Lyndsay's humorous and sharply satirical attacks on contemporary disorder caused by failings in the estates. MQ 2, Maitland's poem on the extravagant ways of socially ambitious town dwellers, draws on a section of Lyndsay's *Ane Supplication Directit ... to the Kingis Grace, in Contemptioun of Syde Taillis* (c.1539–41) as well as on Maitland's own knowledge of legal matters such as sumptuary law. While Lyndsay's narrator bemoans the wearing of long 'syde taillis' by men, including the clergy, and by women,

---

[8] The earliest surviving print of any of Lyndsay's poems is *The Testament of the Papyngo* in John Byddell's London edition of 1538 (*STC* 15671). *The Tragedie of the Cardinall* also appeared earliest in a London print, in 1548 (*STC* 15683). John Scot's Edinburgh edition of *Ane Dialog betuix Experience and ane Courteour* ... appeared in 1554 (*STC* 15672) and is the earliest Scottish edition of any of Lyndsay's works. References to Lyndsay's works are to Hadley Williams, ed. 2001, and Hamer, ed. 1931–36.

Maitland focuses on the abuse among women, apparently picking up on details from the section of Lyndsay's poem concerning the 'wantoun burges wyiffis' (l. 71) and adding many more of his own about female misconduct in spending, eating and socialising, as well as in fashion. Maitland prefers suggestion rather than explicitness (shortened skirts in his poem reveal petticoats, while in Lyndsay's they reveal unappealingly 'sweitie theis', l. 82), but like Lyndsay he is anxious about the encouragement of sexuality immorality (both poets compare the women to 'giglottis'), and the erosion of boundaries between the estates. MQ 3, Maitland's poem on the raiders of Liddesdale, draws on a contemporary discourse of anxiety about border unrest and Maitland's own experience of border administration as a commissioner for border affairs in 1553 or 1559, but seems to show knowledge of Lyndsay's *Ane Satyre of the Thrie Estaitis* (1554) in which Liddesdale is said to be the home of the characters Thift, Oppressioun and Falset (ll. 3273–90 and 4190–95). Maitland's criticism of the lairds of Liddesdale for protecting the rievers and his desire to see the reassertion of justice in the region, including the severe punishment for wrongdoers, probably shows knowledge of the scene in *Ane Satyre* where 'Thift' is hanged and on the gallows bids farewell to various Border families who are his 'bretheren common theifis' (ll. 3990–4011).

Lyndsay's attacks on the clerical abuses of the pre-reformation Scottish church, especially the clergy's neglect of spiritual and pastoral matters in favour of inappropriate activities and preoccupations (concerns shared by many moderate and humanist reformers), clearly interested Maitland. In particular, Lyndsay's ubiquitous anxiety over the clerical neglect of preaching and teaching – 'That callit ar preistis and can nocht preche, / Nor Christis law to the peple teche' (*Complaynt*, ll. 323–25) – often appears in Maitland's oeuvre. Maitland expresses concern that 'kirkmen keipis na professioun' (MQ 5, l. 55) and that few 'the worde of God syne preichit faythfullie' (MQ 12, l. 30). In MQ 4 Maitland prays for good 'pastouris' (l. 21) to guide the Scots, fearful that churchmen are leading their flock 'arreir' (backwards), in an echo of the estates 'gangand backwart led be thair vyces' in Lyndsay's *Ane Satyre of the Thrie Estaitis* (1554, ll. 3865–73). In MQ 5 Maitland complains about 'kirkmen cled lyik men of weir' (l. 14), articulating a disapproval of ecclesiastical involvement in military service. This may echoes Lyndsay, who in the *Monarche* or *Ane Dialog betuix Experience and ane Courteour* (c.1551–52), ll. 5422–23, and *Ane Satyre* (ll. 4578–79) appears to mention Julius III's campaign against the French in Parma. Lyndsay died in 1555, well before the Reformation Parliament of 1560, but Maitland observed reform in practice. His immediately post-Reformation poem, MQ 12, enumerates the 'vycis' (l. 21) that ruled the unreformed priests in a way that recalls the anticlericalism of Lyndsay's *Satyre* and earlier poems such as the *Testament of the Papyngo*, but he also accuses some of the reformers of hypocrisy and warns them that they too could be punished for their sins. His desire for Christian brotherhood (see MQ 22, l. 48) seems to revisit and update Folie's fears about the lack of 'fraternall charitie' among the warring princes of Christendom in *Ane Satyre* (1554, l. 4582).

Maitland's reference to and reworking of the some aspects of the poetry of Dunbar and Lyndsay locate his own poetry firmly in the literary traditions of pre-Reformation Scotland and to a certain extent shape his lyric voice as conservative and respectful of poetic authority. However, it also transmits the concerns of these earlier poets to new generations of readers in the second half of the sixteenth century. Rather than only being imitative, Maitland's recuperation of earlier sixteenth-century styles and concerns is crucial to his formulation of a lyric voice which is both nostalgic and transformative. His poems urge readers to reclaim the lost values of a more peaceful and united Scotland, to reform society and self, and return a sense of integrity and godliness to personal ambition, and his echoes of Dunbar and Lyndsay, while not transcending the skill or breath of their poetic talents, are important to this project. Nevertheless, it is evident from Maitland's poetry that he was well aware of other aspects of Scottish literary culture, poetry and prose, apart from those works of Dunbar and Lyndsay. He clearly knew early sixteenth-century chronicle literature, including Hector Boece's *Scotorum Historia*, which was translated into Scots prose by John Bellenden in 1531. This is most evident from his *History of the House of Seyton* (c.1559, see Ewan 2004, pp. 14–15; Royan 2008, p. 136), but also from MQ 25. This poem alludes to Boece's account of an episode in which Edward I was alleged to have promised Bruce the throne of Scotland in return for his support, but treacherously decided in favour of Balliol in November 1292.

On the contemporary scene there are analogues to Maitland's topical poetry and political exhortations among the poems which circulated in broadside form in Edinburgh during the late 1560s and early 1570s. These include poems probably by Robert Sempill, whose political sympathies were directly opposed to those of Maitland's sons. Maitland's addresses to the nobility of Scotland in MQ 25 (an appeal for reconciliation between the lords during the civil war) and MQ 58 (a poem on the end of hostilities between the parties of the king and queen in the summer of 1573) are similar in their opening and concerns to a poem circulating in a black letter broadside, printed in Edinburgh in 1567 by Robert Lekpreuik (STC?), which begins 'My Lordis, now, gif ʒe be wyse', written after the defeat of Mary at Carberry Hill. Cranstoun judged this to be by Sempill (Cranstoun ed. 1891–93, II, p. 46). For example, this poem's lesson about acquisitiveness, 'For Godis saik, aboue all thing, / Keip clene ʒour handis fra wrangus geir' (ll. 81–82), mirrors what we have seen to be a major preoccupation of Maitland's. Thus in MQ 58 he warns that those who profit through illegal conquest of lands are a major impediment to the peace process:

> Thair will na bodye be aganis this peace,
> Bot gif it be of men of weir the bandis,
> Quhilk fra all kynd of scafrie can not ceis,
> And thay that bruikis otheris mennis landis,
> Fra wrangous geir that can not keip thair handis. (ll. 8–12)

Although much of the rhetoric of the broadside poem is more inflammatory than is typical of Maitland, there are other parallels to Maitland's political and moral poems. Its reminder that human achievement is simply a manifestation of God's power resembles Maitland's exposition of this theme in his poem on the Duke of Guise's recapture of Calais in MQ 10 (ll. 9–16). It calls for reconciliation between the lords, the reform of the justice system and care for the commonweal, the preservation of social order ('Gif euerie man his awin degre') and obedience to the prince, just as Maitland does in many of his poems. These correspondences suggest that Maitland was acutely aware of contemporary themes in the poetry circulating in Edinburgh.[9]

The satirical works of Sempill and others which are targeted at members of the Queen's Party, were influential for Maitland in a different way. MQ 55, Maitland's complaint against slanderous poets, is certainly a response to poems of propaganda which circulated in broadsides (many printed by Lekprevik) or manuscripts during the civil war. For example, the poem known as 'The Bird in the Cage', printed in 1570 by Lekprevik (STC 3084) and probably by Sempill (Cranstoun ed. 1891–93, poem XXII) is an attack on Secretary Lethington as a flatterer, and 'Machiauellus lair' (8), who has condemned the country to civil war

---

[9] The social and complaint poems of William Lauder, such as *The Lamentatioun of the Pure* (printed in 1568) also invite comparison with Maitland's verses on the theme of the oppression of the poor and disorder of the times. For Lauder's poems, see Hall and Furnivall ed. 1870, pp. 26–29.

through his specious advice; 'A Rhime in Defence of the Queen of Scots against the Earl of Murray, (Cranstoun IX) describes William Maitland as 'Traitor Lethington', and again as a 'False Machivilian' (ll. 111–13).

Maitland favoured subjects and genres such as friendship poetry and court satire which appealed to younger poets such as John Stewart of Baldynneis (c.1545–c.1605) and Alexander Montgomerie (early 1550s–1598), who were closely connected to James VI's court (see Crockett, ed. 1913 and Parkinson, ed. 2000). Although, as already stated, Maitland was not a love poet, he certainly knew the poetry of his near contemporary Alexander Scott (c.1520–1582/83), prebendary of the Chapel Royal in Stirling, even though it did not seem to have a major impact on his own. MF contains just one poem attributed to Scott, '3e blindit luiffaris luke', compared with the thirty-plus poems which are attributed to Scott in the Bannatyne Manuscript. Scott's *Ane New 3eir Gift to the Quene Mary, quhen scho come first hame, 1562*, almost certainly presented to Mary at the home of her supporter and Maitland's kinsman and neighbour, Lord Seton (see van Heijnsbergen 2008), may have been known to Maitland too. Maitland's own welcome poem to Mary on her return to Scotland (MQ 9) is succinct compared to Scott's but is nevertheless similar to it in style (both are written in ballat royal), and both issue conventional 'advice to princes' lessons to Mary (on her obligations to choose good counsel, to cultivate virtue, to rule in peace and to consider her marriage prospects carefully), combined with optimistic expressions of support for her rule. Scott's poem to Mary is distinctive in devoting about half its length to criticism of the conduct of both Catholics and reformers in Mary's realm, and is thus similar to Maitland's poem on the Reformation, MQ 12, with its observations on the hypocrisy of both sides of the religious debate (see Donald, ed. 1902). Thus immediately current verse writing, as well as the writing of his poetic precursors, Dunbar and Lyndsay, seems to have been both accessible to and thought-provoking for Maitland.

MQ's Shaping of Maitland's Corpus

Maitland's poems are divided in MQ into two groups, and occupy folios 1–42v (MQ 2–MQ 34) and fols 80–87v (MQ 50–MQ 59). These groups and their contents have been carefully arranged. The first group of his poems includes some texts on perennial moral themes, such as MQ 15, MQ 32 and MQ 33, but is generally social and political in emphasis. This group indicates the prominence of Maitland's public role at local and national level as a loyal crown servant, as well as his desire to be a voice of exhortation and advice. Most poems in this group relate to the period c.1555 to early 1573, and many are datable and are presented in a rough chronological order (also see Martin and McClune 2009, pp. 250–54). Thus, MQ 3 may reflect Maitland's service as a commissioner for Border affairs up to 1559; MQ 4 and MQ 7 make reference to the Guise regency; and MQ 6, MQ 9 and MQ 10, poems on public occasions discussed above, relate to the period up to 1561. MQ 12, 16, 18, 19, 25, 30 and 34 certainly relate to the civil wars between the parties of Mary and James (1567–73) while other poems (MQ 14, 20, 26) allude to the family's own difficulties in this period, and especially during the years of 1570 and 1571 when the family lands at Blyth were raided and Lethington was confiscated by the Regent Lennox. Not only are Maitland's poems in this group of value to historians for what they tell us about individual events and attitudes to these events, but they also remind us of the cultural significance and impact in this period of the literate laird or gentleman who retained considerable local importance, while also gaining political influence, and using literary culture as a way of expressing and augmenting his roles at court and in the community.

The poems in the second group of Maitland's works (MQ 50–59) are difficult to date, with the exception of MQ 58, which may be related to the end of the civil war in 1573, and includes an address to James VI. MQ 59 addresses the king in his 'tender aage' so it is likely that it comes from James's minority, perhaps c.1573, after the defeat of the Queen's Party (see Martin 2013a). MQ 53 was clearly an earlier composition, and was revised (a reference to the queen replaced with one to the king), perhaps specifically for inclusion in MQ. It seems that in dealing with this second group of Maitland's poems the compiler opted for grouping texts on thematic grounds, and the way in which this is done also recalls the chronological sequence of the first group of his works by bringing the scope of the collection up to James VI's reign. MQ 51, MQ 58 and MQ 59 all make explicit reference to James VI, and MQ 53 and MQ 57 exhort the reader to loyalty to the sovereign, while MQ 56 lists the reasons for the ruin of realms, including civil war. MQ 50 and MQ 51 are complaints about the legal system, clearly informed by Maitland's professional knowledge and experience, and MQ 52, a poem on mutability, also includes reference to 'doubilnes' (l. 3) in public life and the corruption of the Court of Session. MQ 53, MQ 54, MQ 56 and MQ 57 concern moral themes including piety and public duty, distilling many of the themes found throughout Maitland's corpus. Interestingly MQ 55, MQ 57 and MQ 58, as well as being concerned with contemporary politics, all make oblique reference to matters of family difficulty in the early 1570s. It seems that the compiler may also have been guided by metrical as well as thematic characteristics when grouping these poems. As Appendix 2 shows MQ 51 and MQ 52 are metrically close, as are MQ 50, MQ 53 and MQ 54, while MQ 55–MQ 57 are composed in rhyming couplets.

Order in Other MQ Texts

Other groupings of poems in MQ also show evidence of design, indicating the compiler's desire to reveal thematic relationships between them, and to the earlier works by Richard Maitland, and to showcase Scottish poetry from several decades. A general chronological sequence is sustained where possible for the datable works, and attributed poems are usually grouped together (or in near proximity to one another) by author. Poems 35–40 are amatory rather than topical, and also introduce the attributed poems of Alexander Arbuthnot, MQ 35, MQ 36 and MQ 37. MQ 37 is a rejection of worldly love, and the MQ attribution to Arbuthnot is likely to be reliable even though the poem is given to Maitland in MF and 'sumbodie' in R: the MQ text of this poem is also the more reliable and gives several better readings than that in MF. As love poems MQ 35–MQ 40 show many similarities of diction and style, their grouping probably another deliberate editorial move by MQ's compiler, or the reflection of the design of an exemplar. MQ 41 and MQ 42 are also attributed to Arbuthnot and are general complaints on the times, with implicit topical reference to the early 1570s. MQ poems 43 and 44, attributed to John Maitland in MF but not MQ, again belong to c.1571–72: the compiler of MQ, unlike that of MF, has chosen to place these as a pair. Also relating to c.1571–72 are MQ 46 and MQ 47. Focusing on faith, family trials and survival, both poems are highly significant works in the collection. MQ 45 (attributed to Arbuthnot), MQ 48 and MQ 49 concern amatory or literary matters and are difficult to date. The next three poems (MQ 60–MQ 62) belong to c.1572, all concerning the surrender of Thomas Percy, seventh earl of Northumberland, to the English. The marriage poems MQ 63 and MQ 64 belong to c.1582, and are attributed to Montgomerie. Poems 65–89 become harder to date as they are amatory, religious or philosophical in nature. However, at least three have explicit relevance to family members and family events (these are MQ 68, MQ 69 and MQ 85, but MQ 65 should perhaps be read alongside with them even though the terms of its reference are now rather oblique). MQ 66 and MQ 67 are both attributed, the former to the mysterious G.H., and the latter to James VI. The rest are anonymous. Finally, poems MQ 90–MQ 93 and MQ 95, elegiac verses for Richard Maitland and his wife, including two attributed to the Hudson brothers, must be dated to c.1586, and MQ 94, the sonnet sequence in praise of John Maitland is likely to be nearly contemporary with these threnodic compositions. MQ 1 probably also dates from 1586, completing the life cycle of the manuscript, which represents Scottish verse from approximately three decades in around sixty different verse forms.

Alexander Arbuthnot

More should be said here about Alexander Arbuthnot, to whom six poems are attributed in MQ. Indeed, as for Richard Maitland, MQ contains the most complete collection of the poems of Arbuthnot. MF has only two poems attributed to him (which in MQ are MQ 41 and MQ 42). In MQ there are four more attributed to him, only one of which is in MF (MQ 37, where it is ascribed to Richard Maitland). As I argue below, MQ is also likely to contain more unattributed poems by Arbuthnot. While the texts that can be associated with Arbuthnot only run to a small number it nevertheless seems significant that Arbuthnot is the most frequently named author after Richard Maitland in the manuscript, followed by Alexander Montgomerie with two poems, and the Hudson brothers, and James VI, and G.H., with one each.

The name Alexander Arbuthnot is a common one. However, it is likely that the individual named here is identifiable with the Alexander Arbuthnot (1538–1583), who was brother of the laird of Arbuthnot, and trained in civil law at St Mary's College, St Andrews University, where he was licensed to teach by 1556. At St Andrews Arbuthnot may have encountered John Maitland, a law student of St Salvator's College, or Thomas Maitland, who matriculated at St Mary's in 1559. Arbuthnot left to study at Bourges in c.1560 and returned to Scotland in 1566 to become a minister in Aberdeenshire. He contributed to the *Second Book of Discipline* in 1568, and was made Principal of King's College Aberdeen in 1569 (on his career, see Arbuthnot 1920, pp. 42–48, Kirk *ODNB* and Stevenson 1990, pp. 25–30). His poems only survive in Maitland manuscripts, though the historian Archbishop Spottiswood mentions his talents for poetry alongside his gifts in other branches of learning (Stevenson 1990, p. 27). Like Richard Maitland, he also had an interest in family history, and he wrote a prose history of the Arbuthnot family (*Originis et Incrementi Familiae Arbuthnoticae, Descriptio Historica*, now Aberdeen University Library, MS 27643/1/1), apparently with the assistance of his father.[10] He died on 10 October 1583, aged only 45, so the presence of six of his works in MQ may be part of the memorialising tendency of the manuscript.

The poems attributed to Arbuthnot in MQ, love complaints and complaints on the times, certainly suggest an author of some learning and poetic skill, and one who had a degree of familiarity with contemporary fashionable literature. MQ 35 purports to be a defence of women, though it has subtle shades of misogyny typical of its genre. Nevertheless, it is tonally sophisticated and employs biblical and classical references, albeit of a fairly standard kind for poems on the nature of women. MQ 36 is amatory in theme, and HQ 45 contains an interesting meditation on the challenges facing the writer in times of social and moral disorder, and may be compared to Maitland's poem on the duties of poets, MQ 55. It is possible that the amatory complaints MQ 38 and MQ 39, both spoken by melancholic lovers and both containing a degree of self-reflexivity, may be by Arbuthnot too (contrast Newlyn 2004, p. 97) though their use of conventional motifs makes it difficult to arrive at a conclusive judgement. MQ 38 is written in a stanza which is very similar to that of MQ 35 (the rhyme scheme is the same, though line lengths differ slightly) and considers the value of complaint. MQ 39 is an epistolary complaint ('I ȝow papeir now propyne', l. 74) and places considerable emphasis, like MQ 36, on loving virtuously.

Arbuthnot's committed Protestantism is evident in MQ 37, a poem on the importance of self-governance in times of personal difficulty. While in MQ 39 the 'tender hairt' is kept in captivity by the lady, MQ 37 advocates freeing the heart from all worldly cares (also compare MQ 47) so that it can glorify its creator. MQ 41 and MQ 42 should be read as a pair of poems in which the narrator has to learn to put aside his dismay at the degeneracy of his contemporaries, and his own feelings of isolation and coercion in an ungodly society, and find consolation in faith. MQ 42 in particular has some verbal similarities to MQ 37, especially in its presentation of personal trouble as 'chaistning' (l. 57), helping

---

[10] The work was translated into Scots by William Morrison, parson of Benholme, and a continuation was added to it in c.1680. Arbuthnot 1920, p. 43; *Scots Peerage* I, p. 273.

the sufferer to know himself and his God because they are among the chosen:

> Thocht God hes not appointit the
> To bruik honouris amang the laif
>
> 3et hes ordanit that thow be
> Ane quhome his sone Iesus sall saif. (MQ 37, ll. 113–16)
>
> ... he will and hes ordanit that thow be
> Ane quhome his sone the Lord Iesus sall saif.
> (MQ 42, ll. 171–72)

It seems to me that MQ 46 and possibly MQ 65 are also candidates for Arbuthnot's authorship, or at least echo his concerns, and both poems appear to show familiarity with Maitland family affairs and the writer's close relationship to Richard Maitland. MQ 46, a poem addressed to Richard Maitland, shares the consolatory tone and religious perspectives of MQ 37 and MQ 42 in particular, especially in terms of counselling patience in suffering and the value of reposing in the confidence of God's providential plan. Like MQ 37 and MQ 42, MQ 46 alludes to the protestant, especially Calvinist, theology of the elect: though 'lothsum is the lot of the elect / Bot thay at lenth with ioy salbe relevit' (MQ 46, l. 54). Both MQ 42 and MQ 46 make striking use of the imagery of the cleansing fire, drawn from various biblical texts including Revelations 3 (see MQ 42 ll. 122–23, MQ 46 ll. 35–36), to demonstrate that for good men, 'tribulatioun' (MQ 42, l.22) is preparation for salvation and reawakens their commitment to God:

> Bot sic tryall lyik ane clengeing fyire,
> Thame to prepair to thair saluatioun. (MQ 42, ll. 122–23)
>
> Sa in afflixioun, as ane furneis fyire,
> We ar prepared be prove to the impyire
> Quhair God sic schreudis sall from his sanctis dissever.
> (MQ 46, ll. 36–8)

MQ 65, an ambitious and at times ambiguous framed dream vision, concludes with a stylistically adept exposition of the salvation of the elect, and has verbal similarities to both MQ 37 and MQ 42. In particular both MQ 42 and MQ 65 make use of concatenation in their final stanzas, which focus on the rewards of the faithful (compare MQ 42 ll. 175–76, and MQ 65, ll. 160–84). MQ 65 shares a rhyme scheme with MQ 46, and in offering Christian consolation again makes use of a number of phrases and ideas which we have seen in MQ 46 and those poems attributed to Arbuthnot. For example, it positions its reader as 'the Lordis elect' (l. 169), promises the 'hie impyire' of heaven as a 'perfyte rest' (l. 166) for the faithful.

Although Arbuthnot's corpus is small, a close creative relationship between Maitland and Arbuthnot is suggested by their poems. Both writers compose complaints on the times, a genre with a long literary history, and they both use such complaints to encourage the reader, as Maitland puts it, to 'In troubill tak patience' (MQ 54, l. 9), and to learn to receive worldly hardships as a divine gift to be used for the sufferer's moral improvement. Stylistically, they made similar choices of diction and stanza form: both use a form (ababbcbC^5) which was popular in the late medieval period for verse of an instructional or religious nature (compare MQ11 and MQ 41); and the closely related stanza ababbcbc^4 (compare MQ 30 and MQ 37).

Beyond their poetic works, both Maitland and Arbuthnot also showed an interest in the history of the family: Arbuthnot's Latin family history has already been mentioned, and Richard Maitland composed a Scots history of his mother's family, the Setons, in c.1559. The extent of the social and professional connections between the Maitlands and Arbuthnot is difficult to determine. Arbuthnot's birth into a landed, if not aristocratic, family, his university and continental education, and his ability to rise to positions of some prominence, demonstrates like origins and similar aspirations to Maitland and his sons, which would perhaps result in natural sympathies with such a family. As a minister and reformer, Arbuthnot had Protestant views more strongly held than those of Maitland, who, though pious, was notoriously cautious about expressing his religious preferences in his poems. As we have seen, Maitland's devotional poems are doctrinally non-specific and politically cautious. Yet the Maitland family were nevertheless moderate Protestant sympathisers, with links through marriage and professional connections to other local Protestant families such as the Cockburns of Ormiston (Wingfield 2012), and a number of works in MQ besides those by Arbuthnot may suggest their commitment to the reformed faith. For example, the importance of reading the bible (including the shared reading of the bible, mentioned in MQ 24) and the cultivation of a personal relationship between the sinner and God is advocated in MQ 24 (SRM), MQ 73, MQ 77, MQ 81. MQ 84 and MQ 73, in particular, show knowledge of biblical texts including the psalms. Several poems in MQ (including MQ 73 and MQ 81) have analogues to poems in the popular collection of protestantised lyrics, *The Gude and Godlie Ballatis*, which may have been circulating in the Maitland household or intellectual circle (Martin and McClune 2009, pp. 246–47), of which Arbuthnot may well have been a prominent or influential member.

The Anonymous Verse in MQ

Around one third of the poems in MQ are unattributed, and many of these are unique to MQ.[11] In a few cases it is clear that the poems have been copied from corrupt exemplars. Such is certainly the case for MQ 65, which has some problematic readings and obvious scribal errors. For most of the unattributed poems, however, it is generally difficult to be certain of the degree of circulation they had outside MQ. The largest group of anonymous poems are MQ 68–MQ 89. These poems tend to avoid social and political subjects (with the exception of MQ 70) in favour of amatory and religious themes, and most prominently, explorations of the subject of friendship, a theme foregrounded by the use of titles in this part of the MS. Some of these anonymous poems, including MQ 38, lament the separation of lovers, and others, such as MQ 65, are explicitly concerned with the loss of love in death; MQ 89, the last poem in the MS before the epitaphs, calls for 'The building of rememberance' (l. 6) in the face of oblivion, and the dangers of a 'lak of memorie' (l. 7) when lovers are separated by absence. Indeed, the amatory poems, be they on constant or faithless friends and lovers, prepare us for the double epitaphs for Sir Richard and his wife which celebrate their long marriage and proclaim that their enduring love has 'the force of death defyd' (MQ 93). In addition to this, the subject of friendship (see especially MQ 72, MQ 75, MQ 76, MQ 80, MQ 83 and MQ 84) broadly reflects the concerns of Sir Richard's poems on the importance of faithful relationships and returns us to the interest in family evinced throughout the anthology. Several of Maitland's poems on court life (MQ 23, MQ 28 and MQ 52) remind us of the polysemy of the word 'friend' in the early modern period. In Maitland's lexicon words and phrases such as 'Neirnes of bluid', 'kinsman', 'affinitie' (strictly the relationship between persons established by a marriage), 'friend', 'kyndlie friend', and 'nychtbour' overlap and express the relationships he regards as entailing reciprocal obligations of loyalty and mutual assistance – what he calls 'kyndness' (that which is natural because of a relationship through blood). Thus, in the context of this

---

[11] These are MQ 1, 38, 39, 40, 47, 48, 49, 61, 62, 65, 66, 68, 69, 71–86, 88, 89, 94, 95.

collection, the friendship and amatory poems relate to the importance of sustaining networks, such as the household, and kin group, and community, through loyalty and virtuous conduct.

Despite the lack of attribution in this part of MQ, it is almost certain that the authorship of these poems was known to the compiler(s) of MQ. Their inclusion in the collection, given the distinctive identity it derives from the poems of or about Richard Maitland and those by Arbuthnot, is a manner of signing or ascription in itself (see Powell 2009, p. 32), authors' names perhaps being omitted out of deference to the more distinguished individuals (especially Richard Maitland and Arbuthnot) who are named by the scribe. Furthermore, it seems likely that some of the poems in this section share a common authorship. For example, MQ 73 and MQ 81, while being thematically alike by virtue of both being religious poems, also share verbal similarities. The poems on friendship also share many similarities of style and phrasing, and may be the products of the literary leisure time of a small number of closely linked poets. The threnodic compositions MQ 93 and 95 show similarities of phrasing to the dedicatory sonnet, MQ 1. Family authorship, or the authorship of close family friends, seems likely for these works, and for poems such as MQ 68, a poem in praise of Lethington, and MQ 69, a dream vision in which Marie Maitland appears. Indeed, given the strong theme of family pride in the MS, it is striking that MQ was not designed to show off the Maitlands' wider cultural links with writers closely associated to the court of James VI, especially in light of the political prominence of John Maitland by the early 1580s. The two poems by Alexander Montgomerie (MQ 63 and MQ 64) probably ended up in the MS because of their relevance to the family (they concern the marriage of Margaret Montgomerie to Robert Lord Seton, and thus to a relation and neighbour of the Maitlands) rather than because Montgomerie was a fashionable poet. These two lyrics are not known elsewhere. MQ 60, an English invective against Scottish conduct in the Northumberland affair, is also found in London, Society of Antiquaries MQ 87, papers apparently relating to Thomas Randolph,[12] and its presence in MQ may reflect William Maitland's political associations (see headnote to poem). But MQ 67, attributed to James here and in other witnesses, and MQ 90 and 91, by the court poets and musicians Robert and Thomas Hudson, are the only certain emissaries from the royal court. MQ 94, a sonnet sequence in praise of John Maitland, remains a mysterious pres-

---

[12] More work is required on the contents and connections of these papers.

ence in the collection. Sebastiaan Verweij has recently identified two remarkably similar sonnets among the Hawthornden papers.[13] These are attributed to 'Andro K' and to 'A. Cokburn', whose identities are not yet known, but who may in future help to illuminate the exact make-up of the Maitlands' literary circle. However, poems like MQ 40, entitled 'Ane Ballat to be Songe with the Tuine of Luifer Come to Luifeiris Dore', and MQ 48, 'Declair 3e Bankis of Helicon', once attributed to Montgomerie, certainly acknowledge contemporary literary culture in their apparent references to well-known dance tunes. Other poems among the anonymous works contain diction and phrasing that recalls the writings of Scott and Montgomery (see, for example, MQ 47 and MQ 71). Furthermore, friendship was a popular theme for lyric poetry, as the near contemporary poems of John Stewart of Baldynneis suggest. Earlier sixteenth-century poetry also clearly remained of interest to the authors of the anonymous verse in MQ, and quite apart from Richard Maitland's interest in Dunbar's writing, texts such as MQ 35 and MQ 69 also show his influence, and poems such as MQ 95 suggest that Lyndsay's works were still being read within the Maitland circle.

Women and the Culture of MQ

Given the family-focused nature of MQ, the involvement of women in the composition, compilation and copying of its texts is significant. As mentioned above, the name of Marie Maitland appears at the beginning of the manuscript, and several poems in the collection mention her. Newlyn (2004, pp. 89–103) has argued that at least some of the anonymous poems in the MS might be ascribed to her or to other women in the Maitland circle. It is certainly the case that several poems in the manuscript explore women's perspectives on virtue, love and creativity. MQ 66 is a *chanson de mal mariée* spoken by an unhappy wife, who describes with poignancy her husband's ill treatment of her, and her betrayal by her parents who have condemned her to such a doomed match. The poem ends piously with the speaker able to confide in God and learning to accept her hardships as his will, a major theme in MQ texts, especially those by Arbuthnot and Richard Maitland. MQ 66 claims a French source, identified by Bawcutt (2001) and Dunnigan (2005) as a poem by Clément Marot, and it may be the work of a female

---

[13] Personal communication, 2012.

translator. MQ 75 and MQ 79 also suggest distressed female speakers who have been wronged by their lovers. However, there was a long tradition of ventriloquising the female voice in male-authored lyric poetry in the sixteenth century (see Marotti 1995, p. 60; van Heijnsbergen 2002), and it is difficult to make a case for the sex of the author on the grounds of sincerity and poignancy alone, though these poems are certainly characterised by these qualities.

Perhaps the most distinctive poem on female experience in MQ is MQ 49, a lyric in celebration of the constancy of (erotic) love between women, which the speaker longs to formalise. The poem has been discussed by several critics (see headnote to the poem), and Marie's authorship of it has been suggested (Stevenson and Davidson, eds 2001, p. 96). MQ 72, which studiously avoids gender pronouns and leaves the reader uncertain as to the identity of the speaker and the addressed, expresses a similar wish for a formal bond to recognise constant love, perhaps that of women. It should be noted, however, that on the continent in particular there are several near-contemporary examples of tender Sapphic verse written by male poets such as Pierre de Ronsard and Pontus de Tyard, writers who were certainly known to Montgomerie and whose works may have been more generally in vogue in Scotland. Nevertheless MQ 49's place in an anthology so closely associated with a woman may tip the balance in favour of female authorship.

Other poems in MQ certainly have a close link to Marie Maitland. As noted above, MQ 69 names her, and celebrates her virtues. The poem should be read as a pair with MQ 68, a poem in praise of Lethington and Maitland's heirs, and its placing after this work seems a bold assertion of Marie's importance in the family and in the anthology which celebrates it. Although MQ 69 is a commendation of her chastity it is possible that it relates to her betrothal or marriage (see headnote to poem) because it also celebrates her abundance, especially her ability to provide for others in terms of land and sustenance, perhaps a reference to a marriage settlement. MQ 77 is addressed to a pious book owner, probably Marie, and MQ 85 is addressed to Marie in encouragement of her literary gifts, talents which are hinted at more discreetly in MQ 69. Indeed, MQ 85 confirms that Marie had a reputation within her circle as a poet and thus makes the possibility that works in MQ are written by her both tantalising and real. This poem also mentions one 'Olimpia, O Lampe of Latine land' (l. 6), probably the Italian poet, scholar and Protestant convert Olimpia Morata (Dunnigan 1997, pp. 29–31), a reference which lends some weight to the connection between the owner of the bible addressed in MQ 77 and Marie, who might wish to be identified with such a well-known female protestant writer. MQ 86 concerns the completion of a scholarly labour, perhaps the copying of MQ, and therefore may also be connected to Marie if she is indeed the scribe or editor of the collection.

Varieties of Scripts

The eighteenth-century editor of poems from MF and MQ, John Pinkerton, asserted that Marie Maitland was responsible for copying the collection, which is written in a combination of neat secretary and italic scripts (Pinkerton ed. 1786, ii, p. 467). Craigie was more cautious (Craigie ed. 1920, pp. v–6) and attributed the work to 'some expert penman', but subsequent scholars such Priscilla Bawcutt (2005, p. 198), Evelyn Newlyn (2004, p. 93) and Sarah Dunnigan (1997, pp. 29–31) continue to argue both for her role as scribe and as editor of MQ. The prominence and care with which her name is written (twice, in different scripts) on the title page of the manuscript certainly suggests a degree of scribal skill which, given the position and nature of the inscription, is more likely to be her own than that of an employed scribe. More importantly the prominence of her name here suggests that she wished her close connection with the manuscript to be known. It was not uncommon for educated women to be trained in ornamental scripts such as italic (Marotti 1995, pp. 25–26). Examples of italic hands by women, beside secretary hands by men, are sometimes found in family or household papers, as the account book of Elizabeth Lady Cavendish and Sir William Cavendish (c.1548–50) shows (Preston and Yeandle 1992, p. 32). This may be what we have in MQ with its movement between the secretary and italic scripts. However, there is evidence that some women in the early modern period were trained in secretary hands, as well as in italic, and that they mastered mixed hands. Indeed, the skilled protestant calligrapher, Esther Inglis (c.1570–1624), trained by her mother, also an accomplished scribe, mastered various hands including French secretary and chancery script, as well as roman and italic (Zeigler 2000, pp. 23, 27, 30–31; Frye 2002). There is also evidence of women of Marie Maitland's social status acting as an amanuensis within the family (Love 1993, p. 99). The possibility that Marie was the scribe of MQ should therefore not be ruled out.

But what of the distribution of secretary and italic scripts in MQ? Only five of the poems of Richard Maitland, all of which are relatively short moral verses, are copied in italic, and the rest are in secretary.

Italic is used for two of the poems attributed to Arbuthnot; for the poem attributed to G.H., for the two epitaphs by Robert and Thomas Hudson, and the anonymous eulogy for John Maitland (MQ 94). The poem attributed to James VI (MQ 67) is copied in both scripts, as is MQ 95. The italic script is also used for the dedicatory sonnet, and many of the unattributed poems, be they on the subjects of love, faith, loss or personal and family matters. MQ 40 and MQ 48 with their links to contemporary musical traditions are copied in italic. MQ 84–95 is the longest run of copying in italic. In all just under one third of the poems in MQ are copied in italic.

While it is not uncommon to find a combination of scripts in sixteenth- and seventeenth-century literary manuscripts (Dawson and Kennedy-Skipton 1981, pp. 9–10), these scripts are often understood to exist within a discernible hierarchical relationship with each other (see Marotti 1995, pp. 26–27). Sometimes the use of scripts indicates something of the identity of the manuscript's audience or patron (Lucas 1982, pp. 229–30; Love 1993, pp. 108–9). Italic was (and is) relatively easy to read, and was therefore preferred by (and for) those with less experience of secretary hands, and yet was also deemed to be of the elegance required for a presentation volume (Love 1993, p. 108). Nevertheless, the reason for the division of scripts in MQ is not obvious: neither theme nor authorship seem to entirely explain the distribution, and it is not clear that italic is meant to be regarded as the superior script (as was usual) given the rarity of its use for the poems of Richard Maitland which dominate the collection. It should be noted, however, that none of the explicitly political poems are in italic; and yet there are several amatory poems, including friendship poems, which are written in secretary. It is possible that the poems in italic were judged by the scribe to be the most fashionable in subject matter and verse form (see, for example, MQ 35, MQ 38, MQ 40 and MQ 48), and italic is also used for some of the most intimate poems of address in family terms (MQ 1, MQ 31, MQ 57, MQ 68, MQ 84, MQ 85) in MQ. Perhaps the use of secretary and italic was intended as a rough guide for the readers of the manuscript, with the poems in italic thus marked out as being primarily of interest to the collection's female readers, and those in secretary marked as being directed primarily to male readers in the Maitland circle.

The scribe introduces considerable calligraphic complexity and elegance to MQ in the way titles and attributions are written, and particularly in the more elaborate forms of italic used for the epitaphs and eulogies at its conclusion. For poems written in secretary, titles or attributions are usually written in an italic hand,[14] and titles for poems written in italic are in another display script.[15] The verse at the end of the manuscript is laid out with considerable stately care, with poems only being written on the rectos of folios 129–38 in dark ink. In the careful presentation of the manuscript, corrections are added neatly between lines, and the scribe omits many of the informal notes and memoranda of MF. Thus, for example, the long note which accompanies MQ 14 in MF has not been copied into MQ. The scribe of MQ has also omitted or altered some titles which are used in MF (see, for example, titles to MQ 6, MQ 9, MQ 44 and MQ 90). The clarification or formalisation of attribution is another important modification by the MQ scribe of the practice of MF. Some attributions from MF are omitted altogether (for example, those to John Maitland for MQ 43 and MQ 44). Others are altered: MQ 37 is reattributed to Arbuthnot, rather than Richard Maitland. Perhaps most significantly, attributions to Sir Richard undergo a degree of standardisation in MQ compared to MF: 'S.R.M' is the preferred form of attribution, and his full name and title is only used on seven occasions. In a similar way, the attributions to Thomas and Robert Hudson are reduced to initials (as is one of the attributions to Montgomerie, MQ 64), and the name of 'G.H.' (MQ 66) is not given in full, probably because of the intimacy of the audience for which MQ was designed. This may also account for the omission of the attributions to John Maitland.

Textual Relationships

Richard Maitland's poems appear in up to four witnesses: MF, MQ, R (CUL Ll.5.10, a partial copy of MF dated to c.1621–22) and D (EUL De.3.71, a partial copy of MQ, dated to c.1627). Apart from the poem attributed to Maitland in the Bannatyne MS, which, if nothing else, shows that he had a reputation as a poet by c.1568, there is no evidence for the wider circulation of his poems beyond the family and its associates. One poem (MQ 53), however, hints at this broader transmission, because it is given the title 'To be put in ony publict houss' in MF, though not MQ. Textual analysis shows that the texts of Richard Maitland's poems in MF and MQ are generally very close and that

---

[14] See the titles for poems MQ 43 and MQ 44 (fols 64v and 66).
[15] See, for example, the title for MQ 40 on fol. 55v.

INTRODUCTION

the scribe of MQ was using MF as a copy text. However, the scribe clearly had access to a copy or copies of Maitland's poems other than MF, where the texts of MQ 8, MQ 16 and MQ 17, and the first section of MQ 2, were found. The two poems in MQ by John Maitland (MQ 43 and MQ 44, though only attributed in MF) also seem to be copied from MF. Only two poems attributed to Arbuthnot appear in MF, but these again are likely to be the copy texts for MQ 41 and MQ 42. Two other poems in MQ exist in unrelated manuscript sources outside the family collections: MQ 60 [L] and MQ 67 [BL]; while one poem is known to derive ultimately from a printed source, Baldwin's *Mirror for Magistrates*, though may have been copied from a similar excerption in another manuscript source.

Textual differences between MQ and MF can therefore be divided into a small number of categories:

1 Substantive differences in diction which alter meaning. In some cases MQ has better readings than MF and suggests that poems copied from MF were corrected by the scribe of MQ. For example, MQ 11, l. 37 reads 'Set ay fordwart the puire', while MF has the difficult reading 'Set ay fordwarde at powar'. Indeed, the text of this poem in MF shows other corruptions. The first half of l. 71 once read 'Or sawe seditioun' but this was crossed out. The scribe of R simply left this part of the line blank. MQ's reading 'Ay nourisch peace flie...' seems to be a sensible revision and fits the context. In other poems, MF confirms that its witness was not always reliable and that its readers, perhaps including the scribe of MQ, had correcting and revising tendencies. For example, MQ 2, l. 96 reads 'Bot wald greit ladyis tak gud heid'. MF has 'lordis' instead of 'ladyis', and a later hand has corrected the line to tally with MQ's reading. Similarly MQ 21 l. 24 reads 'Thair lairdis' where MF had 'land': a later hand has corrected the MF reading to 'laird'.

2 Substantive changes in diction, reflecting a scribal choice to revise or refine, but without significantly altering meaning. For example, MQ 6, l. 13, reads 'That it may cum vnto 3our luiffis eiris'. Here MF has 'ladeis' for 'luiffis', probably 'eye skip' as the word 'ladeis' is used at l. 15 of the poem. The scribe of MQ has chosen to amend this. Similarly, in MQ 4, l. 60, the scribe of MQ rejects the altered refrain in MF and restores the refrain found in all other stanzas to this line: 'heireftir mony 3eir' becomes 'Now into this new 3eir'. MQ 44 l. 69 has 'covene' where MF has 'conand': both

33

nouns mean 'compact or agreement' but according to the evidence supplied by *DOST*, MQ's choice seems to reflect a more common and well-attested word, though we cannot be sure which was the author's choice.

3 Substantive revisions of diction to suit MQ's context. Some discrepancies between MQ and MF are the result of deliberate revision of poems to fit the new times of MQ's readers. MQ 51 has the emotive phrase 'cruell sait' (1.76) to described the cumbersome and inequitable Court of Session, but MF simply has 'ciwell seit' (civil court), which may be closer to Richard Maitland's own usage. Interestingly, MQ 53 has the reading 'Obey and serue ȝour prince trewlie' (l. 5), while MF's text exhorts it readers to obey and serve 'the quein', suggesting that the poem was composed before c.1568 and revised for inclusion in MQ.

4 Nonsubstantive changes in word order which do not affect sense or metre are common. For example, MQ 3 l. 85, 'thocht now', is 'now thocht' in MF.

5 Nonsubstantive changes in pronouns, articles and adverbs, which nevertheless do not impair or change the sense. Thus MQ 5, l. 79, 'Quha is the wyite quha can schaw ws', in MF reads, 'Quhair is the wyt quha can schaw ws'.

6 The omission or addition of words affecting metre. There are a number of instances where the scribe of MQ omits a word thus impairing the metre. For example, MQ 10, l. 11 reads, 'His michtie power is omnipotent'. MF's reading, 'His michtie powar quha is omnipotent', is clearly better and is used to emend the line in this edition. Emendations of this sort are introduced (in square brackets) on the authority of MF only where metrically necessary. In some cases emendation is not necessary as discrepancies of this sort between the two manuscripts suggest a degree of linguistic flexibility in the pronunciation of unstressed final syllables. In MQ 2, for example, l. 51 reads:

For sumtyme wyffis sa grave hes bein **MQ** *Sum tyme* wyfis sa grave hes bene **MF**.

MF appears to scan better, preserving the octosyllabic metre. However, the MQ reading only fails to scan if one pronounces the inflection on the end of 'wyffis' as a separate syllable. The same is found in l. 56 of this poem:

Thay say *wyffis ar* sa delicat **MQ** Thay say *sum ar* sa delicat **MF**.

Yet in MQ 25 l. 12, 'Amang ȝow lordis the inimitie', the final syllable of 'lordis' presumably was to be pronounced. Here MF has an additional word, so the line reads 'Amang ȝou lordis the grit inemete'.

7 Alterations of line and stanza order. In a few cases (MQ 11, MQ 26) the order of two stanzas has been changed from MF, although the sense of the poem is not altered. The transposition of lines in a few cases does alter or impair the sense as in MQ 25, ll. 75–76, and in this edition it has been necessary to follow MF to restore the meaning of this particular line.

8 Distortion of rhyme. Rhyme is occasionally distorted by orthography in MQ. See for example, MQ 30 ll. 84–85, where the rhyme words are 'king / ȝoung'. In MF they are 'king / ȝing'.

The Drummond and Reidpeth Manuscripts

It is clear that the compiler of MQ was determined to pay tribute to Maitland's public experience and wisdom, and to give his poems a coherence which would make them accessible to a new generation of family readers. The appeal of his works to later readers is suggested by their presence in the Reidpeth MS (CUL Ll.5.10), which was copied in c.1622–23 by John Reidpeth (Mapstone 2005, pp. 181–83), servitour of Thomas Young of Leny. The manuscript seems to have been owned by Christopher Cockburn of Choicelea, and probably came into his hands via family links to the Maitlands: Helen Maitland had married Sir John Cockburn of Clerklington (Bawcutt 1991, pp. 193–94). Of most interest to Reidpeth were the poems by Dunbar in MF (see Boffey 2001, pp. 45–50), but he nonetheless copied other works from MF, including some which also appear in MQ: these are MQ 37, MQ 46 and MQ 47, the Hudsons' epitaphs MQ 91 and MQ 92, and ten poems by Maitland, though two of these (MQ 21 and MQ 59) are incomplete, which is odd if his copying was performed to commission, as Mapstone has argued (2005, pp. 181–83).

More significant for evidence of the importance of Richard Maitland's poems to later readers, however, is the Drummond Manuscript (Edinburgh, University Library, De. 3.71). In the later 1620s (the manuscript includes the date 1627, the year it was given to the University of Edinburgh Library by William Drummond of Hawthornden) the scribe of the Drummond MS compiled from MQ a largely 'single-author' anthology focused on the work of Richard Maitland. It includes all of his poems in MQ, in the same order as they appear in its copy text with the exception of MQ 13, which opens the collection. After the full run of Richard Maitland's poems, D also includes a very small number of poems which are not by him, but by Arbuthnot (MQ 35, MQ 36, MQ 42) and one (MQ 44) which is attributed to John Maitland in MF, and is unattributed in MQ and D. The scribe of D concludes his collection with the very personal consolatory poem addressed to Richard Maitland, MQ 46. It was from the Drummond Manuscript that Joseph Bain's edition of Richard Maitland's poems for the Maitland Club was made.

R and D provide us with useful insights into the transmission and reading of MQ's texts, even if they do not give us additional textual information. In the case of the attribution to MQ 37 R suggests that there was indeed some family controversy about the authorship of the poem: Reidpeth has simply attributed it to 'sumbodie', rather than trusting MF's attribution to Richard Maitland. D generally provides evidence of its scribe's careful treatment of MQ, even when he apparently misreads. For example, when the scribe of D makes word substitutions, they are usually intelligent ones which do not much alter sense, such as 'defend' for 'decyde' at MQ 44, l. 35. In the opening of MQ 18, 'O leving Lord, that maid bayth hevin and hell', the scribe of D writes 'O lowing Lord', a reasonable, if erroneous reading. The refrain of lines 1–84 of MQ 42 was a similar problem for D's scribe, and up until l. 64 MQ's 'leving' is again replaced by 'lowing' in D; the same happens in MQ 51, l. 76. These sorts of changes are interesting and may suggest that he occasionally had difficulty with the secretary hand of MQ, even though he was able to transcribe accurately much of the time. He sometimes also seems to have had trouble with particular terms such as 'blak maill' (MQ 3, l. 31), which he renders as 'great mell'; or 'doutsum' (MQ 11, l. 57), which he replaces with 'counsall'. D's scribe sometimes also corrects his copy to produce better readings. Thus in MQ 7, l. 25 reads, 'Trow ȝe to ly, lurk and doe na mair'. D alone adds another syllable to make the line scan: 'Trow ȝe to ly to lurk and do no mair'. But D's scribe is susceptible to more substantial error too. In MQ 52, the scribe of D omits ll. 16–20, probably due to eye skip – this stanza and the previous one begin 'Thocht ȝe'. Interestingly though, the omitted lines concern past amorous behaviour and their omission may be an indication of censorship.

About this Edition

Richard Maitland's poems and other texts from MF and MQ were first made available in print in the 1786 edition by John Pinkerton. Pinkerton had access to both MF and MQ, which were by that time in the Pepys Library Cambridge, after purchase from Richard Maitland's direct descendant, John, first duke of Lauderdale (1616–1682). John Sibbald's *Chronicle of Scottish Poetry* included some of Maitland's poems, as well as the poems attributed in MF to John Maitland, and two by Arbuthnot (Sibbald, ed. 1802, v. 3).[16] He also consulted MQ and makes some interesting, though usually unreliable estimations of the date and context for some of Maitland's poems. He also attempted to expand the canons of Maitland and John Maitland. Joseph Bain's edition of Richard Maitland's poems for the Maitland Club followed in 1830, and was, as noted, based on the Drummond MS, rather than on MQ and MF, though with heavy punctuation, and non-contemporary titles, and some quite significant (and also not noted) examples of editorial intervention in D's text, which have led to subsequent editorial error.[17] In 1920 the Scottish Text Society published W.A. Craigie's valuable edition of MQ. Craigie's edition is a combination of a diplomatic edition and a facsimile edition, in that it reproduces the text with minimal emendation, and also reproduces the non-textual features of the manuscript. Thus manuscript layout is followed page by page and the blank pages which appear in MQ are also reproduced in the edition. Other typographical attempts are made to reproduce the 'appearance of the original' (p. vi), including the reproduction of catch words, the representation of the italic and secretary scripts used by the scribe, titles and attributions, capital letters, otiose strokes and scribal flourishes. Craigie's transcription is highly accurate: no punctuation is introduced which is not present in the manuscript, scribal errors are ('with a very few exceptions', p. vi) not emended, but

---

[16] Those poems by Maitland included by Sibbald are MQ 2, 5, 55, 4, 10, 6, 7, 8, 9, 3, 23, 11, 13, 12, 20, 51, 21. Sibbald also includes MQ 43, 44, 41, 35 and 94. He also includes a poem from the Bannatyne MS, which he regards as being 'partly altered from a familiar ballad by Richard Maitland', III, p. 319: 'This warld is all bot fenyeit fair'.

[17] See Craigie's edition of MF, where he believes a reading in Maitland's poem to his son (MQ 11, l. 71) to come from 'the Drummond text' when it is actually Bain's invention. Craigie ed. 1919–27, I, p. 23. A selection of Maitland's poems was made from Bain's edition (without notes) for the Akros Pocket Classics Series in 1995. See Glen ed. 1995.

are listed in the notes at the end of the volume. Manuscript spellings are followed, for example 'y' for thorn; and the reproduction of the Scottish letter form 'long s' (see below 'A note on the texts'). The scribe's use of 'z' for yogh is retained. The text is accompanied by brief notes (mainly indicating the relationship between the texts of MQ and MF and pointing out the errors and peculiarities of John Pinkerton's 1786 edition), a limited glossary, and an index of proper names and first lines.

While Craigie's edition allows the reader access to the layout of the manuscript, and gives an accurate transcription of its contents, a fully annotated edition of MQ's texts is required for a literary and historical appreciation of the poems. The present edition makes all of MQ's texts available for the first time in a critical edition with full interpretative apparatus. Texts are punctuated according to modern usage, and a small amount of modernisation is introduced to assist the reader (see 'Note on the Texts'). Each poem is accompanied by on-page textual notes, and each has a headnote and commentary which illuminate aspects of dating, authorship, and bibliographical and literary contexts. The glossary is fuller than Craigie's and is thus intended to be helpful to readers whose experience of reading Older Scots is limited.

A Note on the Texts

The spelling of MQ is preserved (with the exception of obvious errors which are problematic to the reader. See comments on the spelling of 'maiestie' above.). However, the following points should be noted:

- Long 's' is transcribed as 's'.
- The Scottish letter form long 's' attached to a curved loop presents some ambiguities. Where it appears in initial positions, but does not indicate an abbreviation ('ser-'), it is transcribed as 's' (MQ 30, l. 42 'seruandis'). Where it appears in final positions following another 's' it often represents '-is', and is printed thus here ('hoisis' MQ 2, l. 6, plural of 'hois' (hose/stocking)). In final positions it can simply indicate 's' and is transcribed as single 's' (as MQ 2, l. 12, 'veluous').
- Yogh [ȝ] is retained. Initial 'z' for yogh (generally found in the poems copied in an italic script) is replaced with yogh.
- Because thorn and 'y' are difficult to distinguish in the manuscript when used to indicate 'th', they have been modernised to 'th'.
- The manuscript use of <i, j> is retained, except when <J> is used for the first person singular pronoun (principally in texts copied in

italic), where it is chanded to I. Initial J is replaced by I in words such as 'it' ('Jt', MQ 31, l. 16) and 'in'. Such spellings are generally only found in texts copied in italic script.
- The forms <u, v, w> are transcribed as they appear in the manuscript.
- The few abbreviations and suspensions used by the scribe of MQ are silently expanded, except in the case of the abbreviated text of the refrain to MQ 8, which is shown in the edition in italics.
- All capitalisation is editorial. As is common in literary manuscripts of this date, capitalisation is often applied to nouns or key words in the middle of sentences and this is disregarded. I capitalise honorific titles such as Queen, King, Prince or Princess, when a historical figure is intended.
- Punctuation is editorial. Although the scribe of MQ has used some punctuation (chiefly virgules), it is too different from modern conventions, and thus impossible to retain in this edition except where it accords with modern usage. The punctuation of the MS is normally disregarded.[18]
- Word division generally follows that of MQ despite inconsistencies of usage. However, in some cases hyphens have been added to help the reader when consulting the glossary. Some obvious scribal errors of word division are amended, for example, MQ 3, l. 67 'trowit' is corrected to 'trow it'; 'on socht' to 'onsocht' (MQ 29, l. 12, on the authority of MF); MQ and MF 43 'defyit' to 'defy it'.
- Scribal errors are emended, corrected in square brackets and noted in the textual apparatus.
- Poems are numbered consecutively according to their order in MQ. Manuscript titles are used where they appear as well. Variations in the titles used in MF are given in the textual notes.
- The textual notes to this edition record substantive variations in all witnesses. Non substantive differences including spelling variations, and variations of word division (such as MQ 9, l. 51: alsweill v. MF als weill) are not given.
- In only a few cases are readings introduced into the text from MF or D. This is done when it is not possible to explain apparent corruptions in MQ's text as anything other than scribal error

---

[18] The exception to this is that the full stops which appear at the end of titles in the manuscript are retained.

which has produced a poor or ambiguous reading in the poem. MQ's strange spelling of 'maiestie' as 'maiestitie' (found in MQ 9, MQ 16 and MQ 59) is corrected on the authority of MF. Readings are occasionally introduced from MF to restore metre. For example, MQ 4, l. 5 'Now in this new ʒeir' is changed to 'Now in to this new ʒeir' on the authority of MF and because all other refrains in MQ read thus.

- In a few cases I have set poems out according to metre and modern editorial conventions for representing metre, rather than follow the layout of MQ. This affects MQ 3, MQ 8, MQ 35, MQ 48, MQ 68, MQ 77, MQ 93a. In the case of MQ 8 I have expanded the abbreviated refrain. In the case of MQ 35 I have restored the stanza form in the one instance where the scribe runs two lines together.

1. Ane Sonet to the Authour in Commendatioun of his Buik.

3our predicessouris prayse and prowes hie,
Thair hardie hairtis, hawtie, heroicall,
Of dew desert deseruis neuer to die,
Bot to be pennit and placit as principall
And metest mirrour of manheid martiall, 5
Vnto thair lyne and linage to give licht,
Of quhome 3e come, quhose ofspring 3ow to call,
3e merit weill, ressembling thame so richt.
Thocht thay wer manfull men of mekill micht,
Thair douchtie deidis in 3ow hes not decayit. 10
3e, wittie, wyse and val3eant warriour wicht
Hes with the pen the poetis pairt weill playit,
Quhairby 3our lordschip enlairgit hes thair fame,
And to 3our self maid ane immortall name.

2.
Sum wyfes of the borroustoun
Sa wonder vaine ar, and wantoun.
In warlde thay wait not quhat to weir,
On claythis thay wair monye a croun:
All for newfangilnes of geir.   5

Thair bodyis bravelie thay attyire,
Of carnell lust to eik the fyire.
I fairlie quhy thay haue no feir
To gar men deime quhat thay desyire:
And all for newfangilnes of geir.   10

Thair gounis ar coistlie and trimlie traillis,
Barrit with veluous sleif, nek, and taillis,
And thair foirskirt of silkis seir,
Off fynest camreche thair fuk-saillis:
And all for newfangilnes of geir.   15

And of fyne silk thair furrit cloikkis,
With hingand slevis lyik geill-poikkis;
Na preiching will gar thame foirbeir
To weir all thing that sinne provoikis:
And all for newfangilnes of geir.   20

Thair wylie-coittis man weill be hewit,
Broudrit richt braid with pasmentis sewit:
I trow quha wald the maner speir
That thair gudmen had caus to rewit
That euer thair wyfis wair sic geir.   25

Thair wovin hoisis of silk ar schawin,
Burrit aboue with tafteis drawin,
With gartennis of ane new maneir,
To gar thair courtlines be knawin:
And all for newfangilnes of geir.   30

22 sewit] hewit D

Sumtyme thay will beir vp thair goun
To schaw thair wylicot hingand doun,
And sumtyme bayth thay will vp beir
To schaw thair hoisis of blak or broun:
And all for newfangilnes of geir.   35

Thair collarris, carcattis, and hals-beiddis,
With veluot hattis heicht on thair heidis,
Coirdit with gold lyik ane ʒounkeir,
Broudrit about with goldin threiddis:
And all for newfangilnes of geir.   40

Thair schone of velwot, and thair muillis,
In kirk ar not content with stuillis,
The sermon quhen thay sit to heir,
Bot caryis cuschingis lyik vaine fuillis:
And all for newfangilnes of geir.   45

I mein of thame thair honour dreidis,
Quhy sould thay not haue honeist weidis,
To thair estait doand effeir?
I mein of thame thair stait exceidis,
And all for newfangilnes of geir.   50

For sumtyme wyffis sa grave hes bein,
Lyik giglettis cled wald not be sein.
Off burgesis wyffis thocht I speik heir,
Think weill of all women I mein,
On vaniteis that waistis geir.   55

Thay say wyffis ar sa delicat
In feding, feisting, and bancat,
Cannot content thame with sic cheir
As weill may suffice thair estait,
For newfangilnes of cheir and geir.   60

42 with] of D
51 For sumtyme] Sumtyme MF   wyffis] *om.* D
56 wyffis] sum MF

And sum will spend mair, I heir say,
In spyice and droggis on ane day,
Nor wald thair motheris in ane ȝeir,
Quhilk will gar monye pak decay,
Quhen thay sa vainlie waist thair geir.   65

Thairfoir ȝoung wyffis speciallie,
Of all sic faultis hauld ȝow frie,
And moderatlie to leif now leir,
In meit and clayth accordinglie,
And not sa vainlie waist ȝour geir.   70

Vse not to skift athort the gait,
Nor na mumschancis air nor lait.
Be na dainser for this daingeir
Of ȝow be taine ane ill consait
That ȝe ar habill to waist geir.   75

Hant ay in honest companie,
And all suspitious placis flie.
Lat neuer harlot cum ȝow neir,
That wald ȝow leid to leicherie,
In houp to get thairfoir sum geir.   80

My counsell I geve generallie
To all wemen, quhat euer thay be,
This lessoun for to quin perqueir:
Syne keip it weill continuallie
Better nor onye warldlie geir.   85

Leif, burges men, or all be loist,
On ȝour wyffis to mak sic cost
Quhilk may gar all ȝour bairnis bleir;
Scho that may not wante wyne and roist
Is abill for to waist sum geir.   90

61 And sum] Sum MF
65 Quhen] And MF
83 quin] cun MF

Betwene thame and nobillis of bluid,
Na difference bot ane veluous huid.
Thair camreche courches ar als deir,
Thair other claythis ar als gud,
And als coistlie in other geir.   95

Bot wald greit ladyis tak gud heid
To thair honour, and find remeid,
And thoill na burgesis wyfe to weir
Lyik lordis wyffis in ladyis weid,
As dames of honour other geir.   100

I speik for na dispyit, trewlie,
(My self am not of faultis frie)
Bot that ȝe sould not perseueir
Into sic folische vanitie
For na newfangilnes of geir.   105

Off burgesis wyffis thocht I speik plaine,
Sum landwart ladyis ar als vaine,
As be thair clething may appeir,
Werand gayer nor thame may gaine,
On our vaine claythis vaistand geir.   110

Finis quod Richart Maitland of Lehingtoun, Knycht.

---

96 ladyis] Lordis MF (*corrected in a later hand*)
97 and] wald MF
Attribution: Quod Richard maitland off Lethingtoun knycht in MF.

3.
Of Liddisdaill the commoun theiffis
Sa pertlie steillis now and reiffis,
That nane may keip
Hors, nolt, nor scheip,
Nor ȝit dar sleip   5
For thair mischeiffis.

Thay plainlie throw the countrie rydis:
I trow the mekill devil thame gydis.
Quhair thay onset,
Ay in thair gait   10
Thair is na ȝet
Nor dure thame bydis.

Thay leif richt nocht quhair euer thay ga;
Thair can na thing be hid thame fra:
For gif men wald   15
Thair houssis hauld,
Then waxe thay bald
To burne and sla.

Thay haue neir-hand hereit haill
Ettrik Forrest and Lawderdaill.   20
Now ar thay gaine
In Lowthiane,
And spairis nane
That they will waill.

Thay landis ar with stouth sa socht,   25
To extreme povertie ar brocht:
Thay wicked schrowis
Hes laid the plowis,
That nane or few is
That ar left ocht.   30

Be commoun taking of blak maill,
Thay that had flesche, and breid, and aill,
Now ar sa wraikit,
Maid puir and nakit,
Faine to be staikit   35
With walter caill.

Thay thefis that steillis and tursis hame,
Ilk ane of thame hes ane to-name:
Will of the Lawis,
Hab of the Schawis,   40
To mak bair wais
Thay think na schame.

Thay spuilȝie puire men of thair pakis,
Thay leif thame nocht on bed nor bakis:
Bayth hen and cok,   45
With reill and rok,
The lairdis Iok
All with him takis.

Thay leif not spindill, spone, nor speit,
Bed, boster, blanket, sark, nor scheit.   50
Ihone of the Park
Rypis kist and ark,
For all sic wark
He is richt meit.

He is weill kend 'Ihone of the Syide':   55
A gretar theif did neuer ryde.
He neuer tyris
For to brek byris,
Our muire and myris,
Our gud ane gyide.   60

Thair is ane callit 'Clementis Hob':
Fra ilk puire wyfe reiffis thair wob,
And all the laif,
Quhat euer thay haif,

31 Be] MF R Bot MQ D   blak maill] great mell D
32 and breid] gud breid MF R

The deuill ressaif   65
Thairfoir his gob.

To sie sa greit stouth, quha wald [trow it],
Bot gif sum greit man it allowit?
Richt sair I rew,
Thocht it be trew,   70
Thair is sa few
That dar avow it.

Of sum greit men thay haue sic gait,
That redye ar thame to debait,
And will vp-weir   75
Thair stollin geir,
That nane dar steir
Thame air nor lait.

Quhat causis theiffis ws our-gang
Bot want of iustice ws amang?   80
Nane takis cair,
Thocht all forfair:
Na man will spair
Now to doe wrang.

Of stouth, thocht now thay cum gud speid,   85
That nather of men nor God hes dreid,
ʒit, or I die,
Sum sall thame sie
Hing on a trie,
Quhill thay be deid.   90

Finis quod S. R. M. of Lethingtoun, Knicht.

65–66 ressaif / Thairfoir] thairfoir ressaue R
67 trow it] trowit MQ
68 Bot gif] onles MF R
72 avow it] MF avowit MQ
74 to] no D
85 thocht now] now thocht MF R
86 of men nor God] of god nor man MF R
Attribution: Quod Richard maitland in MF R.

4.
O hie eternall God of micht,
Of thy greit grace graunt ws thy licht,
With hairt and mynde sinceir,
To leif efter thy lawis richt,
Now in to this new 3eir.   5

God keip our Quene and grace hir send
This realme to gyde and to defend,
In iustice perseueir,
And of thir weiris mak ane end,
Now into this new 3eir.   10

God send grace to our Quene Regent
Be law to mak sic punischment
To gar limmeris forbeir
For till oppres the innocent,
Now into this new 3eir.   15

Lord, schent all saweris of seditioun;
Remove all rancour and suspitioun
Quhilk may this countrie deir.
Put all perturbers to punitioun,
Now into this new 3eir.   20

God send pastouris of veritie,
By quhome we may instructit be
Our God to serue and feir,
And to set furth his worde trewlie,
Now into this new 3eir.   25

And tak away thir ignorantis
Of kirk-men that vycis hantis
And leidis ws arreir,

5 in to] MF R in MQ
6 hir send] *om*. R
7 to defend] MF R   defend MQ

That bayth gud lyfe and cunning wantis,
Now into this new ȝeir.   30

God give our lordis temporall
Grace to geif ane trew counsell,
This realme to guyde and steir,
To be obedient and loyall,
Now into this new ȝeir.   35

And tak away all greit oppressouris,
Commoun mantenaris of transgressouris,
Moveris of stryfe and weir,
For theiffis and reveris intercessouris,
Now into this new ȝeir.   40

Lordis of the sait, mak expeditioun;
Gar euerilk man mak restitutioun
Of wrangous land and geir,
And we sall eik ȝour contributioun,
Now into this new ȝeir.   45

Men of law, I pray ȝow mend:
Tak na euill querrellis be the end
For proffeit may appeir.
Invent na thing to gar ws spend
Our geir in this new ȝeir.   50

God graunt our ladyis chastetie,
Wisdome, meiknes and grauitie,
And haue na will to weir
Thair clething full of vanitie,
Now into this new ȝeir.   55

Bot for to weir habulȝement,
According to thair stait and rent,
And all thingis forbeir,

52 grauitie] *om.* R

That may thair bairnis gar repent,
Now into this new ȝeir.

And send our burgesis wit and sceill
For to set furth the commoun weill;
With lawtie sell thair geir,
And to vse meit and mesour leill,
Now into this new ȝeir.

And all vaine waistouris tak away,
Regrateris that takis dowbill pay,
And wyne selleris our deir,
Dyuouris that drinkis all the day,
Now into this new ȝeir.

Grace be to the gud burgesis wyffis
That be lesum labour thryvis,
And dois vertew leir,
Thriftie and of honest lyvis,
Now into this new ȝeir.

For sum of thame wald be weill fed,
And lyik the Quenis ladyis cled,
Thocht all thair bairnis sould bleir;
I trow that sa sall mak ane red
Of all thair pakis this ȝeir.

God send the commounis will to wirk,
The ground to labour and not to irk,
To win gud quheit and beir,
And to bring furth baith staig and stirk,
Now into this new ȝeir.

60 Now into this new ȝeir] heireftir mony ȝeir MF R
61 And] God MF R
71 burgesis] burges MF R
79 sa] sic MF R
82 not to] nocht MF R D

And tak away thir ydill lounis,
Crame-craikeris with cloutit gounis,
And soirnaris that ar sweir,
And put thame in the gailȝeounis
Now into this new ȝeir.   90

I pray all staitis and degrie
To pray to God continuallie,
His grace to graunt ws heir,
And send ws peace and vnitie,
Now into this new ȝeir.   95

S. R. M. of Lethingtoun

87 Crame] Cryand MF R
Attribution: Quod Richart Maitland of Ledington Knycht in MF R.

5.
Quhair is the blyithnes that hes beine,
Baith in burgh and landwart sene,
Amang lordis and ladyis schene,
Daunsing, singing, game and play?
Bot now I wait not quhat thay meine: 5
All merines is worne away.

For now I heir na worde of ȝuile
In kirk, on calsay, nor in scuile.
Lordis lattis thair kitchingis cuill,
And drawis thame to the abbay, 10
And scant hes ane to keip thair muile:
All houshaulderis is worne away.

I saw na gysaris all this ȝeir
Bot kirkmen cled lyik men of weir
That neuer cummis in the queir; 15
Lyik ruffiaris is thair array;
To preiche and teiche that will not leir;
The kirk gudis thay waist away.

Kirkmen afoir wer gud of lyfe,
Preichit, teichit, and stainchit stryfe; 20
Thay feirit nather sworde nor knyfe;
For love of God, the suith to say,
All honourit thame, bayth barne and wyff,
Deuotioun wes not away.

Our fatheris wyse wes, and discreit; 25
Thay had bayth honour, men, and meit;
With luiff thay did thair tennentis treit,
And had aneuche in poise to lay;
Thay wantit nather malt nor quheit,
And mirrines wes not away. 30

23 barne] man MF

And we had nather ȝuill nor Pace,
Bot seikis our meit from place to place;
And we haue nather luck nor grace.
We gar our landis doubill pay;
Our tennentis cryis, 'Alace! Alace! 35
That reuthe and pitie is away.'

Now we haue mair, it is weill kend,
Nor our foirbearis had to spend,
Bot far les at the ȝeiris end,
And neuer hes ane mirrie day. 40
God will na ritches to us send
Sa lang as honour is away.

We waist far mair now lyik vaine fuillis,
We and our page to turse our muillis,
Nor thay did than that had greit ȝuillis: 45
Of meit and drink sayid neuer nay;
Thay had lang formis quhair we have stuillis,
And mirrines wes not away.

Of our wanthrift sum wytis playis,
And sum thair wantoun vaine arrayis, 50
Sum the wyte on thair wyffis layis
That in the court wald gang sa gay,
And cairis not quha the merchand payis,
Quhill pairt of land be put away.

The kirkmen keipis na professioun; 55
The temporall men committis oppressioun,
Puttand the puire from thair possessioun:
Na kynd of feir of God haue thay.
Thay cummer bayth the kirk and sessioun,
And chasis Cheritie away. 60

31 had] hald MF
43 mair now] mair D
45 Had] held MF

Quhen ane of thame sustenis wrang
We crye for iustice, heid and hang.
Bot quhen our nichtbour we our-gang
We labour iustice to delay:
Affectioun blindis ws so lang,   65
All equitie is put away.

To mak actis we haue sum feill:
God wait gif that we keip thame weill.
We cum to bar with iak and steill,
As we wald boist the iudge and fray: 70
Of sic iustice I haue na sceill
Quhair reull and ordour is away.

Our lawis ar lichtleit for abusioun
Sumtyme is cloikit with collusioun
Quhilk causis of bluid the greit effusioun,   75
For na man spairis now to slay.
Quhat bringis countreis to confusioun
Bot quhair that iustice is away?

Quha is the wyite quha can schaw ws?
Quhat bot our nobillis that sould knaw ws,   80
And till honorabill deidis draw ws.
Let neuer commoun weill decay,
Or ellis sum mischeif will fa ws,
And nobilnes we put away.

Put our awin lawis to executioun;   85
Vpon transgressouris mak punitioun;
To cruell folk seik na remissioun.
For peace and iustice lat ws pray,
In dreid sum strainge new institutioun
Cum and our custome put away.   90

69 iak and steill] iak of steill MF
72 Quhair] Quhen D
79 Quha] Quhair MF
80 Quhat] quha D

Amend ȝour lyffis ane and all,
And be war of ane suddaine fall,
And pray to God that maid ws all
To send ws ioy that lestis ay,
And lat ws not to sinne be thrall,   95
Bot put all vyice and wrang away.

S. R. M.

95 to] be D
Attribution: S. R. M. Finis in D; Finis quod Richart maitland of ledingtoun knycht in MF.

6.
The greit blyithnes and ioy inestimabill,
For to set furth we Scottis ar not abill,
Nor for to mak conding solemnitie
For the gud newis, and tydingis confortabill,
Of the contract of mariage honorabill 5
Betuixt the Quenis maist nobill maiestitie,
And the gretest ȝoung prince in Christintie,
And allya to ws maist profitabill,
Of France, the Dolphin, first sone of King Henrie.

All lustie wowaris and hardie cheualeiris, 10
Go dres ȝour hors, ȝour harneis, and ȝour geiris,
To rin at listis, to iust, and to tornay,
That it may cum vnto ȝour luiffis eiris
Quha in the feild maist valiantlie him beris.
And ȝe, fair ladyis, put on ȝour best array, 15
Requeist ȝoung men to ryde in ȝour leueray,
That for ȝour saik thay may brek twentie speris,
For luif of ȝow, ȝoung lustie ladyis gay.

All borrowis tounis, euerilk man ȝow prayis
To mak baine-fyris, fercis and clerk playis, 20
And throw ȝour rewis carrous daunce and sing,
And at ȝour croce gar wyne rin sindrie wayis,
As wes the custome in our elderis dayis
Quhen that thai mad triumphe for ony thing;
And all ȝour stairis with tapestrie gar hing; 25
Castellis schut gunnis, schippis and galeyis
Blaw vp ȝour trumpettis and on ȝour drummis ding.

Preistis and clerkis and men of religioun,
With deuot mynd gang in prosessioun
And in ȝour queiris sing with melodie; 30
To the greit God mak intercessioun
To send our Princes gud successioun,
With hir ȝoung spous to our vtilitie,

13 luiffis] ladeis MF R
18 ȝoung] ȝe lustie R

That efter hir may gouerne this countrie,
And ws defend from all oppressioun 35
And it conserue in law and libertie.

3e lordis all and barrounis of renoun,
And all estaitis of this natioun,
Mak greit triumphe, mak banket and gud cheir,
And euerilk man put on his nuptiall goun. 40
Lat it be sene into this borrowstoun
That in 3our cofferris hes lyne this mony 3eir,
Sen that 3our Quene hes chosin hir ane feir,
Ane potent prince for to mantein 3our croun,
And interteney 3ow in peace and weir. 45

Lat all the warld be 3our proceding sie,
That thair is fayth and treuth in 3our countrie,
Luif, lawtie, law, and gud conscience,
Concord concurrand in peace and vnitie,
Obedience to the authoritie, 50
Foirsicht, provisioun, and experience,
Honour, manheid, iustice, and prudence,
Quhilk, gif 3e haue, 3e sall estimit be,
And be ilk man hauldin in reuerence.

O michtie Prince, and spous to our maistres, 55
Ressaue this realme in loue and hairtlines;
Set furth our lawis, mantein our libertie;
Do equale iustice bayth to mair and les;
Reward vertew, and punische wickitnes;
Mak ws to leif in gud tranquillitie; 60
Defend our commounis, treit our nobilitie,
And be thy mein our commoun weill incres,
That we tak plesour to mak policie.

Scottis and Frenche now leif in vnitie
As 3e war brether borne in ane countrie, 65

37 3e lordis all and barrounis] 3e lordis and all barounis MF R
46 be 3our proceding] MF R 3our proceding MQ D

Without all maner of suspitioun,
Ilk ane to other keip trew fraternitie.
Defend ane other bayth be land and sie;
And gif onye of euill conditioun
Betuixt ȝow twa wald mak seditioun, 70
Scottis or Frenche, quhat man that euer he be,
With all rigour put him to punitioun.

O noble Princes, and mother to our Quene,
With all thy hairt to God lift vp thy eine,
And geve him thankis for grace he hes the send, 75
That he hes maid the instrument and mein,
With mariage to couple in ane chein,
Thir twa realmes ather to defend.
Think weill warit the tyme thow hes done spend,
And the travell that thow hes done sustein, 80
Sen it is brocht now to sa gud ane end.

S. R. M.

68 Defend ane other] Defendand vther MF R
Attribution: S. R. M. Finis in D; quod R M of Ledingtoun knycht in MF R.

7. Ane Ballat maid at the [ne]w ȝeirismess in the ȝeir of God 1559 ȝeiris.

Eternall God, tak away thy scurge
From ws Scottis, for thy greit mercie.
Send ws thy help this land to clenge and purge
Of discord and inanimitie
Betuixt the leigis and auctoritie,   5
That we may leif in peax withouttin weir,
In lawtie, law, in luif and libertie,
With merines into this new ȝeir.

Almichtie God, send ws support and grace.
Of mannis help we ar all dispairit,   10
To mak concord, that had sic tyme and space;
And nane as ȝit hes thair labour warit,
As na man war that for this countrie carit;
Bot, and this stryf and troubill perseueir,
He salbe sage that sall eschape vnsarit,   15
And not thoill paine into this new ȝeir.

Think ȝe not schame, that ar Scottis borne,
Lordis, barounis of auctoritie,
That throw ȝour sleuth this realme sould be forlorne,
ȝour ground distroyit and ȝour policie?   20
Sic wraik sall cum vpon ȝow haistallie
That ȝe sall say, 'Alace we wer our sweir,
Quhill we had tyme, that maid na vnitie'.
Amend it ȝit now, into this new ȝeir.

Trow ȝe to ly, lurk and doe na mair,   25
To sie quhilk syid sall haue the victorie,
The quhilk at last sall not help ȝow ane hair.
Ryise vp, concur and thame certifie

6 weir] deir MF
13 this] his D
15 that] and D
25 lurk] to lurk D
27 ȝow] om. D

Quhilk with ressoun will not rewlit be!
3e will with force, withoutin fraud or feir,   30
Mak weir on thame as commoun enemie,
And thame correct, now into this new 3eir.

God graunt his grace to the inferiouris
Of this puir realme, thair querrell to considder,
And till obey to thair superiouris,   35
So that our heid and leigis doe considder
In peace and luif for to remaine togidder:
Syne we wer quyte of all thir men of weir,
That all trew folk from Berwik to Baquhidder
May leif in rest vnreft in this new 3eir.   40

The Quenis grace, gif scho hes offendit,
In hir office lat it reformit be,
And 3e leigis, let 3our faill be mendit,
And with trew hairt serue the auctoritie;
And 3e kirkmen, doe 3our dewtie,   45
And all estaitis syne and vyce forbeir,
The quhilk to doe I pray the Trinite
To 3ow send grace, now into this new 3eir.

God, mak ws quyte of all heresie,
And put ws anis into the richt way,   50
And in thy law we sa instructit be
That we be not begylit euerie day:
Ane sayis this, ane other sayis nay,
That we wait not quhomto we sould adheir.
Christ send to ws ane reull to keip for ay,   55
Without discord, now into this new 3eir.

God send iustice this land to reull and guyde,
And put away thift, reif and oppressioun,

---

38 thir] the MF
41 grace] MF D g MQ
43 faill] falt MF
Attribution: finis S. R. M. in D; quod R m of ledingtoun knycht in MF.

That all trew folk may suirlie gang and ryde,
Without discord had parliament and sessioun,   60
To gar trew folk bruik thair iust possessioun,
And geve ws grace, gud Lord, quhill we ar heir,
To ceis from syn, repentand our transgressioun,
And leif in ioy, now into this new 3eir.

S. R. M.

8.
>   In this new ȝeir, I sie bot weir,
>   Na caus to sing.
>   In this new ȝeir, I sie bot weir,
>   Na caus thair is to sing.

I can not sing for the vexatioun   5
Of Frenchemen and the Congregatioun,
That hes maid trowbill in this natioun,
And monye bair biging.

>   In this new ȝeir, I sie bot weir,
>   Na caus to sing.   10
>   In this new ȝeir, I sie bot weir,
>   Na caus thair is to sing.

I haue na will to sing or dans,
For feir of England and of France:
God send thame sorrow and mischance,   15
Is caus of thair cumming.

>   In this new ȝeir, I sie bot weir,
>   Na caus *to sing.*
>   In this new ȝeir, *I sie bot weir,*
>   *Na caus thair is to sing.*   20

We ar sa rewlit, ritche and puire,
That we wait not quhair to be suire,
The bourdour as the borrowmuire,
Quhair sum, perchance, will hing.

>   In this new ȝeir, *I sie bot weir,*   25
>   *Na caus to sing.*
>   *In this new ȝeir, I sie bot weir,*
>   *Na caus thair is to sing.*

22 As] is D

And ȝit, I think it best that we
Pluck vp our hairt and mirrie be,   30
For thocht we wald ly doun and die,
It will ws helpe na thing.

   In this new ȝeir, *I sie bot weir,*
   Na caus to sing.
   In this new ȝeir, I sie bot weir,   35
   Na caus thair is to sing.

Lat ws pray God to stainche this weir,
That we may leif withouttin feir,
In mirrienes, quhill we ar heir,
And hevin at our ending.   40

   In this new ȝeir, I sie bot weir,
   Na caus to sing.
   In this new ȝeir, I sie bot weir,
   Na caus thair is to sing.

S. R. M.

29 we] ȝe D
30 our] ȝowr D
Attribution: in D only.
MQ and D give the refrain in part after first and final stanza.

9.

Excellent Princes, potent and preclair,
Prudent, perles in bontie and bewtie,
Maist nobill Quene of bluid vnder the air,
With all my hairt and micht I welcum the
Hame to thy native people and countrie,   5
Beseikand God to give the grace to haue
Of thy leigis the hairtis faythfullie,
And thame in luif and fauour to ressaue.

Now sen thow art arryvit in this land,
Our native Princes, and illuster Quene,   10
I traist to God this regioun sall stand
Ane auld frie realme, as it lang tyme hes bene,
Quhairin richt sone thair salbe hard and sein,
Greit ioy, iustice, gud peace and policie,
All cair and cummer baneist, quyte and clein,   15
And ilk man leif in gud tranquillitie.

I am not meit nor abill to furthset
How thow sall vse discreitlie all thing heir,
Nor of ane Princes the dewtie and det,
Quhilk I beleif thy hienes hes parqueir;   20
Bot gif neid be thair is anew can leir
Thy maiestie of thy awin natioun,
And geve the counsale how to reull and steir
With wisdome all belangand to thy croun.

ȝit I exhort the to be circumspect   25
Of thy counsell in the electioun:
Cheis faythfull men of prudence and effect,
Quha will for wrang mak dew correctioun,
And doe iustice without exceptioun,
Men of knawledge, gud lyfe, and conscience,   30
That will not failȝie for affectioun,
Bot of gud fame and lang experience.

14 gud] great D
17 abill to] abill D
22 maiestie] MF maiestitie MQ

Quhilk gif thow doe, I houp that thow sall ring
Lang in this land, in greit felicitie.
Will thow pleis God, he will the send all thing 35
Is neidfull to maintein thy royaltie,
Quha geif the grace to guyde sa prudentlie,
That all thy doing be to his plesour,
And of Scotland to the commoditie,
Quhilk vnder God thow hes now in thy cuire. 40

And gif thy hienes plesit for to marie,
That thow haue hap, I pray the Trinitie,
To cheis and tak ane housband, without tarie,
To thy honour and our vtilitie,
Quha will and may maintein our libertie, 45
Repleit of wisdome and of godlines,
Nobill, and full of constance and lawtie,
With gud successioun to our quyetnes.

Madame, I wes trew seruand to thy mother,
And in hir favour stuid ay thankfullie, 50
Of my estait asweill as onye other,
Prayand thy grace I may ressauit be
In siclyik fauour with thy maiestie,
Inclynand ay to me thy gracious eiris,
And amang otheris servandis think on me: 55
This last requeist I leirnit at the frieris.

And thocht that I to serue be not sa habill
As I wes wont, becaus I may not sie,
3it, in my hairt I salbe firme and stabill
To thy hienes with all fidelitie, 60
Ay prayand God for thy prosperitie,
And that I heir thy peopill with hie voice,
And ioyfull hairt cryand continuallie:
'Viue Marie, trenoble Royne d'Escos!'

S. R. M.

53 maiestie] MF maiestitie MQ
63 hairt cryand] hartis cry MF
Attribution: quod richart maitland of ledingtoun knycht in MF; finis quod Sir Richart Maitland of Lethingtoune Knicht in D.

66

10. Ane Ballat Maid at the Winning of Calice.

Reioyis, Henrie, maist Christiane King of France!
Reiois, all peopill of this regioun,
That hes with manheid and be happie chance,
Be thy lieutenent trew of greit renoun,
The Duik of Guise, recouerit Calice toun,   5
The quhilk hes bene twa hundreth ʒeiris bygaine
Into the handis of Englis natioun,
Quha neuer thocht be force it micht be tane.

Bot we may sie that mennis iudgment
Is all bot vaine quhen God plesis to schaw   10
His michtie power, quha is omnipotent.
For quhen he plesis, he can gar princes knaw
That he it is alane that rewlis all,
And mannis helpe is all bot vanitie.
Think that it wes his hand that brak the wall: 15
Thairfoir, give gloir to him eternallie.

Sa hie ane purpose for to tak in hand,
Quha gef that prince sa greit audacitie
To seige that toun that sa stranglie did stand?
And quha gave him sic substance and supplie,   20
And quha gave him the end and victorie?
Quha bot greit God, the guyder of all thingis,
That quhen he plesis can princes magnifie,
And for thair syne translait realmes and kingis.

That noble King wes greitlie to advance,   25
Quhilk efter that his capitaines of renoun

---

2 this] that MF
3 hes] *om.* MF
3 Be] with D
8 thocht] *om.* D
11 power quha is] MF power is MQ, poweris D
13 That he it is alane] That it is he allane MF
21 the] at MF
26 Quhilk] Quha MF

Had tint ane feild, be hasard and mischance,
3it tint na courage for that misfortoun,
Bot lyik ane michtie vail3eant campioun,
Be his lieutenent and nobill men of weir, 30
Tuik vpon hand to seige that strongest toun,
Into the deidest tyme of all the 3eir.

Thairfoir, 3e all that ar of Scottis bluid,
Be blyith, reioyis for the recovering
Of that stronge toun, and of the fortoun gud 35
Of 3our maist tender frend that nobill king,
Quhilk ay wes kynde in help and supporting
Of 3ow be men and money copious,
And in his hand hes instantlie the thing
To 3ow Scottis that is maist precious. 40

Sen 3e luif God in thingis outwardlie,
In fyris and processioun generall,
So in 3our hairtis luif him inwardlie;
Amend 3our lyiffis, repent 3our sinnis all,
Doe equall ressoun bayth to greit and small, 45
And euerie man doe his vocatioun:
Than God sall graunt 3ow, quhen 3e on him call,
Of 3our fais the dominatioun.

Sen God, in the biginning of this 3eir,
Vnto that King sa gud fortoun hes send, 50
We pray to him sic grace to graunt ws heir,
That we get Berwik our merchis for to mend,
Quhilk, gif we get, our bordouris may defend
Aganis England, with his helpe and supplie.
And then I wald the weiris had ane end, 55
And we to leif in peace and vnitie.

S. R. M.

---

35 that] *om.* D
Attribution: quod R m of Ledingtoun knycht in MF.

11. The Laird of Lethingtounis Counsale to his Sone, Beand in the Court.

My sone, in court gif thow plesis remaine,
This, my counsale, into thy mynd imprent:
In thy speiking luik that thow be not vaine;
Behauld and heir, and to thy tounge tak tent.
Be no lear, els thow ar schent; 5
Found the on treuth, gif thow wald weill betyide.
To gouerne all and reull be not our bent:
He reullis weill that weill in court can guyde.

Be not ane scorner, nor fein3it flatterar,
Nor 3it ane rounder of inuentit taillis. 10
Of it thow heiris, be not ane clatterar;
Fall not in plie for thing that lytill vaillis;
Haue not to doe with other mennis faillis;
Fra wicked men thow draw the far on syde.
Thow art ane fuile gif thow with fuillis deillis: 15
He reullis weill that weill in court can gyde.

Be war quhomto thy counsale thow reveill:
Sum may seme trew, and 3it dissemblit be.
Be of thy promeis and conditioun leill;
Waist not thy gud in prodigalitie, 20
Nor put thy honour into ieopardie;
With folk diffamit nather gang nor ryide;
With wilfull men to argone is folie:
He rewllis weill that weill in court can gyde.

Be no dyissar, nor player at the cairtes, 25
Bot gif it be for pastyme and small thing;
Be not blawin with windis of all airtis;
Constant of gud of wosdome is ane sing;

5 els] or ellis MF R
27 all] sindrie R
28 of] in MF R

Be wyise and tenty in thy gouerning,
And trye thame weill in quhome thow will confeid: 30
Sum fair wordis will gif wald sie the hing.
He reullis weill that weill in court can gyde.

Attour all thing ay to thy prince be trew,
In thocht an deid, in word, in work and sicht,
Fra tressonabill companie eschew. 35
Thy princes honour and proffeit at thy micht,
Set ay fordwart the puire, bayth day and nicht,
And let na thing the commoun weill elyde,
And at all tyme maintein iustice and richt:
He reullis weill that weill in court can gyde. 40

Preis not to be exaltit abone other,
For gif thow doe, thow salbe sair invyit:
Greit perrell is to tak on hand the ruder
Quhill first that thy experience be tryit.
Think at the last thy doing wilbe spyit, 45
Thocht thow with slicht wald cover it and hyide,
And all thy craft sall at the croce be cryit:
He rewlis weill that weill in court can gyde.

Thocht thou in court be with the hiest placit,
In honour, office, or in dignitie, 50
Think that sumtyme thow may be fra it chasit,
As sum hes bene befoir and ȝit may be.
Neidfull it is thairfoir to gang warlie,
That rakleslie thow snapper not nor slyide.
Ken ay thy self best in prosperitie: 55
He rewlis weill that weill in court can gyde.

Bewar in geving of ane hie counsale
In materis greit and doutsum speciallie,

---

31 will gif wald] wald gif wald R
33 thing] thingis D   thy] ȝor R
34 in work] and wark D
36 honour and proffeit] proffitt and honour MF R
37 the puire] at powar MF R   bayth] *om.* MF R
41–56] order of stanzas reversed MF R
58 greit] *om.* R   doutsum] consall D

Quhilk be the working of the warld may faill,
Thocht it seme neuer sa apperantlie. 60
Behauld the warldis instabilitie
That neuer still intill ane stait dois byide,
Bot changeand ay, as dois the mone and sie:
He rewlis weill that weill in court can gyde.

Gif with the people thow wald louit be, 65
Be gentill, lawtie, and meik in thy estait.
For and thow be vncourtius, proud, and hie,
Then all the warld sall the detaist and hait.
Flie fein3ing, flattering, falsat and dissait;
Inuent na thing that may the realme devyide; 70
Ay nourisch peace, flie troubill and debait.
He rewlis weill that weill in court can gyde.

Ground all thy doing vpon suthfastnes,
And hauld the ay gud companie amang;
Gadder na geir with craft and wrachitnes; 75
Preis not to conqueis onye thing with wrang:
Evill gottin guddis lestis neuer lang.
Thocht all wer thyne within this warld sa wyde,
Thow sall fra it, or it fra the sall gang:
He rewlis weill that weill in court can gyde. 80

Aboue all thing, I the exhort and pray,
To pleis thy God set all thy bissie cuire,
And syne thy prince serue, loue weill, and obey;
And as thow may be helpand ay the puire,
Sen erdlie thingis will not ay induire. 85
Thairfoir in hevin ane place for the provyide,
Quhair thair is ioy, rest, gloir, and all plesour,
Vnto the quhilk eternall God ws guyde.

S. R. M.

66 Be gentill, lawtie, and meik] Be gentill meik and lawlie R
67 For and] For gif R
69 Falsat] falsheid MF R
71 Ay nourisch peace, flie] Or sawe seditioun (*erased*) MF, *om*.R.
Attribution: Quod richart maitland of ledingtoun knycht in MF R.

12.
O gratious God, almichtie and eterne,
For Iesus saik, thy sone, we ask at the
Ws to defend, conserve ws, and guberne,
And tak fra ws, Lord, for thy greit mercie,
Thir plagis that apperis presentlie: 5
Pest, povertie, and maist vnkyndlie weir,
Hunger and derthe, that now is lyik to be,
Throw deid of beistis and scant of corn this ȝeir.

Bot Lord, this commis of thy iust iudgment,
For punischment of our iniquitie, 10
That neuer of our sinnis will repent,
Bot perseueir in impietie.
We are sa soppit in sensualitie,
Baith spirituall and temporall estait;
The peopill all misguydit haillalie: 15
Not regnis now bot troubill and debait.

Sum tyme the preistis thocht thay did weill
Quhen that thay maid thair berdis and schuif thair croun,
Vsit round cappis and gounis to thair heill,
And mes and mateinis said of thair fassioun, 20
Thocht that all vycis rang in thair persoun:
Leicharie, gluttonie, vaine gloir, and avarice,
With sworde and fyire, for zeill of religioun,
Of Christiane peopill oft maid sacrifice.

For quhilk God hes thame puneist richt scharplie: 25
Bot had thay left thair auld abusioun,
And turnit tham fra vyice to God trewlie,
And syne forthocht thair wrang intrusioun
Into the kirk be fals elusioun,
The worde of God syne preichit faythfullie, 30
Thay had not cummit to sic confusioun,
Nor tholit had as ȝit sic miserie.

12 Bot] to D
17 thocht thay] thocht that thai MF

Now is Protestanis rissin ws amang
Sayand thay will mak reformatioun:
Bot ʒit as now ma vycis neuer rang,   35
As pryide, inuy, fals dissimulatioun,
Dissait, adulterie, and fornicatioun,
Thift, reif, slauchter, oppressioun of the puire,
Of policie plaine alteratioun,
Of wrangous geir now na man takis cuir.   40

Thay think it weill, and thay the Pape doe call
The Antechrist, and mes idolatrie,
And syne eit flesche vpon the fraydayis all,
That thay serue God richt then accordinglie,
Thocht in all thing thay leif maist wickedlie.   45
Bot God commandit ws his law to keip:
First honour him, and syne haue cheritie
With our nychtbour, and for our sinnis weip.

Think weill that God that puneist the Papistis
Is ʒit on lyfe, and ʒow to puneische abill,   50
As he did thame, that in ʒour sinnis insistis,
As Goddis worde wer hauldin bot ane fabill.
Bot gif ʒour hairt on God be firme and stabill,
Thocht that his worde into ʒour mouth ʒe haue,
Except ʒour lyfe be thairto conformabill   55
In worde and worke, ʒe bot ʒour self dissaue.

I mein not heir of faythfull Christianis,
Nor ministeris of Goddis worde trewlie
That at the samyn steidfastlie remanis,
In worde and work, without hypocresie.   60
Bot I doe mein of thame allanerlie

40 now na] now a D
44 richt then] than richt D
45 thing] thingis D
46 Bot God commandit] Bot commandit D
52 bot] as D
59 That] quha MF
Attribution: Finis quod Richart maitland of lethingtoun knycht 1570 in MF;
Finis quod S. R. M. in D.

That callit ar the 'fleschlie gospellaris',
Quha in thair wordis apperis richt godlie,
Bot ʒit thair workis the plaine contrair declaris.

Bot, thocht of Papistis and Protestantis sum 65
Hes bayth gane wrang, and Goddes law transgressit,
Keip ws, gud Lord, that neuer mair we cum
To sic errour, bot grace to doe the best,
That with all men thy trew fayth be confest,
That Christiane folk may leif in vnitie, 70
Vertew set vp and all vycis supprest,
That all the world, gud Lord, may honour the.

S. R. M.

13.
Amang foleis ane greit folie I find,
Quhen that ane man past fiftie ȝeir of aage,
That in his vaine consait growis so blind
As for to ioyne himself in mariage
With ane ȝoung las, quhais bluid is ȝit in raige,   5
Thinkand that he may serue hir appetit,
Quhilk and he faill than will sche him dispyite.

Agit men sould ioyis in morall taillis
And not in tailis, for folie is to marie
Fra tyme that bayth thair strenth and nature faillis,   10
To tak ane wyf, and bring him self in tarie.
For fresche Maij and cauld Ianuarij
Agreis not vpon ane sang in Iune,
The trebill wantis that sould be songe abone.

Men sould tak voyage at the larkis sang,   15
And not at evin, quhan passed is the day.
Efter midage, the luiffar lyis full lang,
Quhen that his hair is turnit lyart gray;
Ane auld gray berd on ane quhyte mouth to lay
Into ane bed, it is ane piteous sicht: 20
The ane cryis 'Help!', the other hes no micht.

To haue bene merchant, bygaine monye ane ȝeir,
In Handwarpe, Burges, and in the toun of Berrie,
Syn into Deip, for to tyine all his geir,
With vaine consait to puire him self and herrie: 25
Greit perrell is for to pas our the ferrie

1 Amang foleis] Among all folleis D   greit] gren D
3 consait growis] conseat he growes D
5 Is ȝit in] is in ane MF R
7 and] gif MF R
11 him self] thame selfe MF R
19 on] till D
21 hes no] wantis MF R
23 in] *om.* MF R

Into ane lekand bot not naillit fast,
To beir the saill, not havand ane steif mast.

To tak ane melein, that greit labour requyris,
Syn wantis graith for to manuire this land; 30
Quhair seid wantis, then men of teilling tyris;
Then cummis ane, findis it waist lyand,
ȝoikis his pleuche teillis at his awin hand,
Better had bene the first had neuer kend it,
Nor thoill that schame. And so my taill is endit. 35

S. R. M.

30 this] the MF R
31 Quhair] Quhone MF R
34. kend it] MF R D kendit MQ
Attribution: unattributed in D; Finis quod Richard maitland of Lethingtoun in MF R.

14.
Blind man, be blyithe, thocht that thow be wrangit;
Thocht Blyithe be herreit, tak na melancholie:
Thow salbe blyithe quhen that thay salbe hangit
That blythe hes spuilȝit so malitiouslie.
Be blyithe and glaid that nane persaue in the 5
That thy blyithnes consistis into riches,
Bot thow art blyith that thow eternallie
Sall ring with God in eternall blyithnes.

Thocht thay haue spuilȝit Blyith of gud and geir,
ȝit haue thay left lyand still the land, 10
Quhilk to transport wes not in thair power,
Nor ȝit wilbe, thocht no man thame gainestand.
Therfoir, be blyith! The tyme may be at hand
Quhen Blyithe salbe ȝit, with Goddis grace,
Als weill pleneist as euer thay it fand, 15
Quhen sum sall rew the rinning of that race.

Ay to be blyithe, outwartlie appeir,
That be na man it may persauit be,
That thow pansis for tinsell of thy geir;
That thy onfreindis, that ar proud and hie, 20
Be blyith and glaid of thy aduersitie.
Thairfoir, be stout, and lat thame vnderstand
For loise of geir thow takis na sussie,
For ȝit behind thow hes aneuch of land.

Be blyith and glaid ay in thy intent, 25
For lesum blyithnes is ane happie thing.
Be thou not blyithe, quhat vaillit land or rent?

1 thocht that thow] thocht thow D
18 be blyithe] be blyth ay D
22 lat thame] gar thame MF
27 thou] added above the line in MQ as correction, perhaps by another hand
Attribution: finis quod S. R. M. in D; Quod Sir richart maitland of lethingtoun knycht ... in MF.

And thow be blyith is caus of lang leving:
Be thow not blyithe, thocht thow wer ane king,
Thy lyif is not bot cair without blyithnes. 30
Thairfoir be blyith and pray to God ws bring
Till his blyithnes and ioy that is endless.

S. R. M.

15.
Luik that na thing to sine the tyice,
Bot ground the ay vpon iustice;
Ay follow vertew and flie vyce;
Of toung be trew.

Ay hait all kyinde of covatice;   5
Waist not thy guddis at the dyice;
Flie fra all fuillis that ar nyice,
And thame eschew.

Hauld the in honest companie;
Thy persoun gyide ay honestlie;   10
And haunt na kyinde of harlatrie;
Fra syne abstein.

Deill with all folkis faythfullie,
And vse the neuer for to lie;
Conqueis na guddis wrangouslie;   15
Be na fals mein.

To euerie persone doe ressoun;
Keip the fra melling with tressoun,
And tak in thank and gude sessoun
Quhat God will send.   20

Put na man be oppressioun
Furth of thair iust possessioun;
To God mak intercessioun
For ane gud end.

Finis quod S. R. M.

Attribution: unattributed in MF.

16.
The Lord that raise from lyif againe,
That deid for ws on Gud Fryday,
Quhilk sufferit mekill woe and paine,
With Iewis that wer hard of fay,
Wer he amang ws now this day, 5
He wald far mair thoill and sustein:
For now, as I heir all men say,
Is the worst warld that euer wes sein.

Ane Heroid rang into thay ȝeiris,
Ane murtherar of innocentis; 10
Bot now he hes ane thowsand feiris,
Far crueller in thair intentis,
To rug and reif, and tak vp rentis,
The poure peopill oppressand clein:
For the quhilk thing sum fair repentis 15
In this worst warld that euer wes sein.

That tyme thair wes bot ane Pilat:
Now is thair ma nor fiftie scoir,
With als fair wordis of dissait,
As had the other of befoir. 20
Sa fast into this warld thay soir;
To trew men dois mekill tein;
Thair craft ay kyithis moir and moir,
As in this warld it is now sein.

That tyme thair wes bot ane Caiphas, 25
That did accuse our Lord Iesus,
Bot now is mony ma, alace,
The innocentis for to persew.
Thair is bakbyteris now anew,
Bot of gud men thair is our quhein 30
That will and can gif counsell trew,
As in this warld it may be sein.

1 raise from lyif] raisit lyfe D
12 Far crueller] For trewlie D
18 ma nor] mae than D

The tormentaris wer then so scant
Chryist for to scurge, scairis found wer sax;
Now of ane thousand, not ane dois want,   35
Thair wicked number so dois wax,
To spoilʒie pour men of thair pakis;
To reif can na man thame refraine,
Quhill that thay gar ane widdie rax,
In this worst warld that euer wes seine.   40

Thair wes ane Iudas in that tyme,
For syluer did his maister sell;
Bot now is smittit with that cryme
Ane thowsand ma, nor I can tell,
That dois in this countrie dwell,   45
Wald sell thair saullis, as I wein,
For geir, vnto the deuill of hell,
In this worst warld that euer wes sein.

Peter to Annas hous him drest,
Quhair he his maister did deny;   50
Monye with mouth hes now confest
Thay ar of Christis companie,
Bot and ʒe will thair workis espy,
ʒe sall sie thame, befoir ʒour ein,
Denyand Christ alluterlie,   55
As be thair lyffis may be sein.

Pilat let bot ane theif gang,
Quhen he put Iesus Christ to deid;
Bot now fyve hundreth theiffis strang
At anis will thair remissioun speid;   60
And trew folk can get na remeid,
Quhat wrang that euer thay sustein,
Quhilk garris monye beg thair breid,
In this worst warld that euer wes sein.

Fra Pilat fand of deid na caus   65
In Christ, he wald haue lattin him ga:
I wald thay that leidis our lawis,

44 nor] than D

And our iudges, wald now doe sa,
Compell no innocent to pay,
Nor thame convict be subtell mein,   70
Nor in thair [sysis] put not thair fa,
Let na partialitie be sein.

Thairfoir, princes and magistratis,
And 3e in court that office beir,
That for auctoritie debaittis,   75
To hurt the innocent tak feir,
For seid, suspitioun, or for geir;
Fra wrang proceding ay abstein;
In dreid God athar hyne or heir
His vengeance gar on 3ow be sein.   80

As Iewis wer to Christ vnkynd,
For all his werkis and gudnes,
His miraclis put furth of mynd,
Quhen that to deid thay did him dres,
Swa in this warld all thankfulnes   85
And all auld kyndnes that hes bein,
And all gud turnis, mair and les,
Ar clein for3et, and now oursein.

Apperantlie now all men sayis
That all staittis ar in dispair,   90
Thinkand can thay put of thair dayis:
Quhat sall cum efter thay tak no cair.
Thocht all this regioun sould forfair,
Of thair will, will not want ane prein,
Quhilk will mak monye biggingis bair,   95
And ane waist countrie to be sein.

Quhair is the zelous men and wyise
Of kirk, and of the temporall stait,
That in this realme hes bein oft sysis,

71 Sysis] sysisis MQ, syes D
77 seid] leid D
84 thay] he D
94 Of thair will, will not] Of thair will nocht D

That wald tak travell, air and lait, 100
To stainche all trowbill and debait,
And ane greit perrell could prevein?
And now the lordis to gang ane gait
The commoun weill to be forsein.

God mak ws quyte of all blasphemaris, 105
And of all men of euill conditioun;
God mak ws quyte of all mentenaris
Amangis ws of seditioun,
And all raseris of suspitioun;
Send ws gud men to gang betwein 110
The lordis to mak vnioun,
That peace may in this land be sein.

God keip the Kingis maiestie
And gif him graces monyfauld
This land to keip in libertie 115
In peace and iustice to ws hauld
Sa that na persoun ȝoung nor auld
Sall ony caus haue to complein
That iustice now is cost and sauld
As other tymes hes bein sein. 120

S. R. M.

103 ane gait] on gett D
113 maiestie] D maiestitie MQ

17.
Gif trowbill cummis be eventour,
And not throw thy misgouernance,
Then patientlie thow it induire,
Quhill God plesis send bettir chance.

Trowble sumtymes is profitable, 5
And gevis men intelligence,
To ken thair God makis thame able,
And of thame selff experience.

Behauld the instabilitie
Of this fals warld, and how it gais: 10
This day ane man set vp in hie,
To morne set doun amang his fais.

Thow may sie greit vnfaythfulnes
Intill all staitis regnand now;
Amang thame is sic doubilnes, 15
That na man may ane other trew.

For and thy bak be at the wall,
Or sum infortoun happin the,
Then will thy quentance leif the all,
How neir of bluid that euer thay be. 20

And gif thow helping at thame crave,
Thy kinsmen will neuer knaw the,
Nor ȝit mair pitie on the haue,
Nor will the man that neuer saw the.

Quhairfoir my councell is trewlie, 25
How euer the warld ga vp or doun,
Be glaid in hairt ay lesumlie,
And iust in thy vocatioun.

11 vp in] vpoune D
12 To morne] to morrow D
29 now for] thow of D

For thocht now for this miserie
And displesour thy self wald sla, 30
Quhat kynd of gud will that doe the,
Bot greif thy freind and glaid thy fa?

Thairfoir, thank God quhat euer he send,
And to thy nychtbour doe na wrang,
And ay thy iust querrell defend, 35
And neuer by the richt way gang.

Pray thow to God, bayth evin and morrow,
To keip ay clein thy conscience;
Quhat euer cummis, seill or sorrow,
To tak all thing in patience. 40

S. R. M.

Attribution: Finis quod Sir Richart Maitland of Lethingtoune knycht in D.

18.
O leving Lord, that maid bayth hevin and hell,
Fra ws expell this cruell ciuill weir,
That all this 3eir hes done this countrie quell,
That nane can tell how thay sall keip thair geir,
Nor without feir quhair thay sall rest or duell. 5

Alace, this is ane miserabill lyfe
Of sturt and stryfe, that na man can wit how
Keip ox or kow, the theiffis ar so ryfe.
3e, evin to Fyfe, thay ryid the countrie throw;
Rax thay, I trow, thay sall wrak man and wyfe. 10

For thift, nor reif, nor men of euill conditioun
Is na punitioun, nor for na wicked deid:
Bot deidlie feid gif 3e ask restitutioun;
Wrang intromissioun now cummis waill gud speid.
We had greit neid of iustice the fruitioun. 15

Quhat is the caus of all this greit confusioun,
Bot the diuisioun of lordis maist potent
In land and rent, mony wrangous intrusioun,
And greit effusioun now of bluid innocent?
For punischment thair is bot abusioun. 20

Sum mennis land, and melling with kirk geir,
Makis all this weir; discord makis additioun;
Sum sayis ambitioun, that wald haue reull and steir.
Bot 3it, I feir that men full of seditioun
Hes sawin suspitioun that credence is areir. 25

1 leving] lowing D
5 or] and MF R
11 nor] and MF R   euill] ill MF R
14] *om* R
15 We] *om* R
24 that] *om.* D

Inimitie is ane richt wicked seid,
Quhat deidlie feid it workis 3e may sie;
Continuallie 3our lyffis ar in dreid,
Quhairfoir, of neid, 3our geir man wastit be:
Gud vnitie for that is best remeid.   30

God give his grace the lordis till agrie
That we may sie sum iustice in this land,
Quhilk can not stand, and thay diuydit be,
This to supplie gud men put to 3our hand,
Mak ane suir band, syn keip it faythfullie.   35

3e lordis all, at God mercie imploir:
Discord, vaine gloir, is caus of this mischeif;
All thift and reif 3e man anser thair foir,
And it restoir, or hang revar or theif.
God send releif that wrang induire na moir.   40

I speik this to the lordis of bayth the syidis,
And all that rydis the countrie to oppres,
And to purches pour mennis gud thame prydis,
And not confydis that thay sall mak redres,
Or thay posses the ioy that God provydis.   45

S. R. M.

29 of] on MF R
30 is] war MF R
35 syn] and MF R
39 or] and MF R
41 of] on MF R
Attribution: Quod Richard maitland in MF, R; finis S. R. M. in D.

19.

At morning, in ane gardein grein,
I went alone to tak the air,
Quhair mony plesand treis wes sein,
And sindrie kynd of flouris fair.
Quhen I did walk and gang, 5
Thir fair flouris amang,
Into my mynd thair come with cair
Ane thing that maid my hairt full sair,
That lestit hes our lang.

Quhen I think on the greit mischeiff 10
That regnis now in this countrie,
Withouttin houp syne of releif,
Wnles that God of his mercie,
And his divyne power
Stainche this vnkyndlie weir, 15
Without the quhilk, apparandlie,
This haill land will destroyit be
Richt haistalie, I feir.

It is ane pitie to heir tell
How the puire commounis of this land 20
Fra wrang cannot debait thair sell,
Fra reif and spoylȝie of sum band
Of suddartis of sum syde,
That nane dar gang nor ryde,
For trowbling of sum wicked hand: 25
I wait not how this realme sall stand,
And lymmaris wak so wyde.

O Lord, quhair ar thais zelous men
That in this land hes bene oft syis?
That quhen they could persaue or ken 30
Ane trowble in the countrie ryis,

3 wes] war MF
8 full] rycht MF
21 thair] thame MF
28 thais] sa D
30 could] sould D

With wisdome and foirsicht
Thay wald set all thair micht,
Be greit travell, and wordis wyse,
And remedie wald sone devyise, 35
And set all thingis aricht.

Bot now thair is not ane, alace,
That I ken in this regioun,
That ather hes hap, wit, or grace
To mak concord and vnioun. 40
Thairfoir, God send remeid
And helpe ws in our neid.
For mony hes inuentioun,
For to incres dissentioun,
And foster deidlie feid. 45

The gretest caus of this discord
Is for our sinnis punischment:
With mouth we say we loue the Lord,
And far fra him in our intent:
To speik of God delytis, 50
In doing him dispytis,
Reddie to reif ane man his rent,
Not dredand Goddis iudgment,
As fein3it ipocreitis.

I ken nane now, for Goddis love, 55
To doe ane wrang that will forbeir,
Nor 3it will stope for to remove,
His nychtbour baith fra land and geir;
And nothing by thay set it,
How wrangouslie thay get it: 60
For of thair God thay haue no feir,
To gar thair nychtbour leif perqueir,
Fra thay haue intromettit.

35 And] Ane MF
36 thingis] thing MF

England is glaid quhen it is tauld
Of Scottis the diuisioun;   65
And for our folischnes thay hauld
Our doingis in derisioun.
Bot wald we weill considder,
Thay hound ws ay togidder,
Makand thair awin provisioun,   70
For our greit scayth and lesioun,
The grip of thame is slidder.

ȝit the ane part on thame dependis,
The other on France for thair supplie;
Ilkane fra other thame defendis,   75
As fra ane commoun enemie.
I pray God, I heir tell,
We grie amang our sell,
And syne that all this haill countrie
Of France and England bayth wer frie,   80
With thame na mair to mell.

Quhen that the ane the other wraikis,
The quhilk will not be done lichtlie,
Without travell and monye straikis;
Bot quhat sall this worke finallie   85
Bot rais ane deidlie feid
Of quhilk we haue na neid?
In the meintyme greit policie
And gud tounis destroyit be,
And monye man lye deid.   90

Thairfoir, my lordis, hauld vp ȝour handis,
Thocht of ȝour will ȝe want sum thing,
Or be distroyit, men and landis,
Quhilk wilbe hurtfull to the King:
For his weill it is maist   95
That ȝe aggrie in haist;
For quhen he is of aage to ring,

97 For] Or MF

Quhair on to leif sall find na thing,
Bot all the contrie waist.

God give the lordis grace till aggrie 100
And baneische all seditioun,
Syn ay to leif in vnitie,
And quyte of all suspitioun;
And then to mak ane band,
Ay in kyndnes to stand; 105
Ilk man get restitutioun,
And fullie intromissioun ,
Of thair awin geir and land.

I pray to God omnipotent,
To send ws peace quhill we ar heir, 110
Ilk ane may leif vpon thair rent,
Or on thair craft withouttin feir;
And with Sanct Paull I pray,
To tak thame sone awaye
That caus is of this mortall weir, 115
And the first tydingis that I heir,
That thay be laid in clay.

S. R. M.

105 Ay in kyndnes] In kyndnes ay MF
Attribution: quod R. maitland of Lethington in MF; S. R. M. K. in D.

20.
Thocht that this warld be verie strainge,
And theiffis hes done my rowmes range,
And teynd my fauld,
3it I wald leif, and byide ane chainge,
Thocht I be auld.

Now me to spoil3ie sum men not spairis,
To tak my geir na capitane cairis,
Thay ar sa bauld:
3it tyme may cum, may mend my sairis,
Thocht I be auld.

Sum now be force of men of weir
My hous, my landis, and my geir,
Fra me thay hauld:
3it as I may, sall mak gud cheir,
Thocht I be auld.

Sa weill is kend my innocence,
That I will not for non offence,
Flyte lyik ane scauld;
Bot thank God, and tak patience,
For I am auld.

For eild, and my infirmitie,
Warme claythis ar better for me
To keip fra cauld,
Nor in Dame Venus chalmer be,
For I am auld.

Of Venus play past is the heit,
For I may not the misteris beit
Of Meg nor Mald:
For ane 3oung las I am not meit,
I am sa auld.

4 3it I wald] 3it wald I MF R
22 ar better] is better R
25 For I am auld] now being ald MF R

The fairest wenche in all this toun,
Thocht I hir had in hir best goun,
Richt bravelie brald,
With hir I micht not play the loun,
I am so auld.   35

My wyf sum tyme wald taillis trow,
And mony lesingis weill allow,
Wer of me tauld;
Scho will not eindill on me now,
I am so auld.   40

My hors, my harneis, and my speir,
And all other my hoisting geir,
Now may be sauld:
I am not abill for the weir,
I am so auld.   45

Quhen ȝoung men cummis fra the grein,
Playand at the futball had bein,
With brokin spauld,
I thank my God I want my ein:
I am so auld.   50

Thocht I be sweir to ryide or gang,
Thair is sum thing I wantit lang,
Faine haue I wald,
And thame punische that did me wrang,
Thocht I be auld.   55

S. R. M.

40 I am so auld] and I sa ald MF R
47 Playand at the futball had bein] At the futball playing had bene MF R
50 I am so auld] and am so ald MF R
Attribution: quod R maitland of lethingtoun in MF, R; Finis quod Sir Richard Maitland of Lethingtoune Knicht in D.

21.
It is greit pitie for to se
How the commounis of this countrie,
For thift, and reif, and plaine oppressioun,
Can na thing keip in thair possessioun,
Quhairof that thay may mak ane lyfe: 5
3it nane will punische that transgressioun,
Thocht nocht be left to man nor wyfe.

Sum with deir ferme ar herreit haill,
That wont to pay bot pennie maill;
Sum be thair lordis ar opprest, 10
Put fra the land that thay possest;
Sair service hes sum hereit sone;
For cariadge als sum hes no rest,
Thocht thair awin worke sould ly vndone.

Sum commounis that hes bene weill staikit 15
Vnder kirkmen ar now all wraikit,
Sen that the teynd and the kirklandis
Come in greit temporalle mennis handis:
Thay gar the tennentis pay sic sowmes
As thay will ask, or quha gainestandis 20
Thay wilbe put sone fra thair rowmes.

The teynd that tennentis had befoir,
Of thair awin malingis, corne and stoir,
Thair lairdis hes taine it our thair heid,
And garris thame to his 3aird it leid; 25
Bot thair awin stok thay dar not steir,
Thocht all thair bairnis sould want breid,
Quhill thay haue led that teynd ilk 3eir.

5 may] can D
7 be] *om.* D
21 rowmes] landis D
24 lairdis] laird MF
25 his] thair D
28 that] thair D

Sic extortioun and taxatioun
Wes neuer sene into this natioun,   30
Taine of the commounis of this land,
Of quhilk sum left waist lyand,
Becaus few may sic chairgis beir;
Mony hes quhippis now in thair hand,
That wont to haue bayth iak and speir.   35

Quhairthrow the haill commounitie
Is brocht now to sic povertie,
For thay that had gud hors and geir,
Hes scantlie now ane cruikit meir,
And for thair saiddillis thay haue soddis;   40
Thay haue no wappinnis worth for weir,
Bot man deffend with stanis and cloddis.

Thairfoir, my lordis, I 3ow pray,
For the puire commounis find sum gud way
3our land to thame for sic pryice geif,   45
As on thair maling thay may leif
Sufficientlie, to thair estait;
Syne thame defend that nane thame greif,
That may serue 3ow bayth air and lait.

Riche commounis ar richt proffitabill   50
Quhen thay to serve thair lord ar abill,
Thair native countrie to defend
Fra thame that hurt it wald pretend.
For we wilbe our few ane nummer
Gif commounis to the weir not wend: 55
Nobillis may not beir all the cummer.

32 sum left] sum is left MF
33 sum left] sum is left MF R
44 gud] *om*. MF D
49 That may serue] That thai may serue MF
Attribution: quod Richard maitland of lethingtoun MF; unattributed in R; finis quod S. R. M. of Lethingtoune Knicht in D.

95

Help the commounis, bayth lord and laird,
And God thairfoir sall ȝow rewaird;
And gif ȝe will not thame supplie,
God will ȝow plaige thairfoir iustlie,   60
And ȝour successioun efter ȝow,
Gif thay sall haue na mair pitie
On the commounis, nor ȝe haue now.

S. R. M.

22.
Treasone is the maist schamfull thing
That may in onye countrie ring,
And sould be hatit maist:
Bot now, in this vnhappie tyme,
Sa monye ar smittit with that cryme, 5
That few dar other traist.

Thair is sa mony subtill wyile,
Ilkane ane other to begyile,
Fra lawtie so thay leip;
For gredines of geir and land 10
Thair will na kyndnes, bluid, nor band,
Gar sum thair credence keip.

Greit number ar in dyuers landis
That prince and magistrat gainestandis,
Rebelland crewallie: 15
I will not speik in speciall,
Bot I pray all in generall,
That wicked vyice to flie.

The deith of Christ wes confortabill,
To Christiane men maist profitabill, 20
3it foull wes Iudas pairt.
Men sould hald thame abominabill,
Abone all other detestabill,
That studeis in that art.

Lyik as subiectis with trew intent, 25
Sould be leill and obedient
To thair superiouris,
Sua sould na prince, nor magistrat,

5 Sa monye ar smittit] Sa mony smittit MF
8 ane other] vther MF, ane and other D
9 so thay leip] say thai keip D
14 magistrat] magistrattis D
17 Bot I pray] MF Bot pray MQ D
19 Christ] Christianes D
22 hald] MF haue MQ D

Be craftie meinis and dissait,
Hurt thair inferiouris.   30

Quhilk gif thay doe, thame selff thai schame,
And thocht men dar not thame defame,
3it God, that seis all,
May punische thame within schort space,
And fra thair heiche and princlie place,   35
Gif thame ane schamefull fall.

Thairfoir, all subiectis, I 3ow pray,
Love 3our princes and thame obey!
Aganis thame work na tressoun.
Siclyik, princis and magistratis,   40
Wraik not 3our awin with fals consaittis,
Bot doe thame richt and ressoun.

All 3e that sould be Christin men,
3our honour and 3our dewtie ken,
Quhat 3e sould doe to other;   45
And for na proffeit 3e may haue,
3our freind or nychtbour nocht desaue,
Bot luiff 3our Christiane brother.

Sua I exhort 3ow, all estaitis,
Ceis fra dissimulance and dissaitis,   50
And of fals punkis 3ow purge;
And ilkane be to other trew,
Or ellis 3e sall not eschew
Of God the mortall scurge.

S. R. M.

38 Love 3our princes] 3our princis luif MF
46 And for na] MF For na MQ D
52 And ilkane be to other trew] Ilkane to vther syne be trew MF
Attribution: quod R.m. of lethingtoun in MF; Finis quod S. R. M. in D.

23.

Sumtyme to court I did repair,
Thairin sum errandis for to dres,
Thinkand I had sum freindis thair,
To help fordwart my busines;
Bot nocht the les, 5
I fand na thing bot doubilnes:
Auld kyndnes helpis not ane hair.

To ane greit court man I did speir,
That I trowit my freind had bene,
Becaus we war of kin so neir; 10
To him my mater I did mein,
Bot with disdaine
He fled as I had done him tein,
And wald not byide my taill to heir.

I wend that he, in word and deid, 15
For me his kinsman sould haue wrocht,
Bot to my speiche he tuik na heid,
Neirnes of bluid he set at nocht;
Then weill, I thocht,
Quhen I for sibnes to him socht, 20
It wes the wrang way that I ȝeid.

My hand I put into my sleif,
And furth of it ane purs I drew,
And said I brocht it him to geif:
Bayth gold and siluer I him schew. 25
Then he did rew
That he vnkyndlie me misknew,
And hint the purs fast in his neif.

Fra tyme he gat the purs in hand,
He kyndlie 'cousing' callit me, 30

Attribution: Quod R. Maitland of le*thington* in MF. Finis quod Sir Richard Maitland in D.

And bad me gar him vnderstand
My busines all haillalie;
And swore that he
My trew and faythfull freind sould be
In court, as I pleis him command.　　　　　　　　　　35

For quhilk better it is I trow,
Into the court to get supplie,
To haue ane purs of fyne gold fow,
Nor to the hiest of degrie
Of kin to be;　　　　　　　　　　　　　　　　　40
Sa alteris our nobilitie:
Greit kynred helpis lytill now.

Thairfoir, my freindis, gif ȝe will mak
All courtmen ȝouris, as ȝe wald,
Gud gold and syluer with ȝow tak,　　　　　　　　45
Then to get help ȝe may be bald;
For it is tald
Kyndnes of court is cost and sauld:
Neirnes of kin nathing thay rak.

S. R. M.

24.
Pastyme with godlie companie
Now in this warld is left for me,
Sen that I am of sa greit aage,
All displesour for to assuage.
Gud is to luik in Goddis buik 5
Quhair may be found
The perfectioun of religioun,
Of fayth the ground.

All plesour vaine I will refuise,
For my pastyme the byble vse; 10
Thocht I be auld and may not sie,
I sall it gar be red to me;
Quhair I sall leir for to forbeir
All wickednes,
Vyce to refuise, vertew to vse 15
With godlines.

To reid or heir the holie writ,
Trew knawledge sall I get in it,
How I sall haue me, at all houris,
Bayth to my God and nichtbouris; 20
Instructand me to patientlie
My troubill beir,
Syne to repent, with trew intent,
Quhill I am heir.

Sen in this erd I find no rest, 25
Reioyis in God I think it best,
Quha in this lyfe geve me his grace,
Syne bring me to that resting place
Quhair ioy and gloir is euer moir,

1 Pastyme] Pas tyme MF
2 left] best MF
13 for] quhair D
Attribution: quod R. maitland of lethingtoun in MF.

Peace and concord: 30
To that ilk ioy doe me convoy
Iesus, our Lord.

S. R. M.

25.
3e nobillis all that sould this countrie guyde,
It to preserue, quhy doe 3e not provyide?
As of the commoun weill 3e had na cair,
For quhilk this realme is liklie to forfair
Throw 3our greit negligence,   5
That makis na defence
Fra scayth it for to keip,
Bot thoillis it to be spilt,
Throw 3our greit sleuth and gilt,
Quhilk garris mony weip.   10

It is the caus of our calamitie,
Amang 3ow lordis the inimitie,
That ar devydit now in parteis twa,
Persewand other as 3our mortall fa,
With maist vnkyndlie weir.   15
For the quhilk thing I feir,
Without thair be sum dres,
That all this land sall rewit,
And enemeis persew it,
Thay sall it sone oppres.   20

Is thair na wyse and gud men of renoun,
Luifand the commoun weill of this regioun,
That will vpon thame paine and travell tak
Amang the lordis gud vnitie to mak;
And sic ane perfyte peace   25
That may our sorrow ceis,
Ilkane other assist,
Sic quyetnes to stabill,
That we may be mair abill
Our fais to resist?   30

8 it to be] it be MF, it for to be D
11 our] 3our D
12 the inimitie] the grit inimitie MF, of inimitie D
19 persew it] persewit MF

Better it wer the lordis till aggrie
Nor with straingeris to cummer this countrie:
Gif ony cum we sall foirthink it sair
Ws to oppres, for na man thay will spair,
And nathing thay will want,   35
That is quhair that thay hant,
And lytill for it pay;
Thay will not spair to spuilʒie,
Or ellis thay will tuilʒie,
Gif ony thame gainesay.   40

For gif that ʒe that dependis on the King,
For ʒour support the Englismen inbring,
At lenth thairof ʒe sall mak litill ruse.
Think on the wordis King Edward spak to Bruse,
'Haue we not ellis to doe   45
Bot win ane roume ʒow to?',
Quhilk pat the Bruse to paine.
Gif thay cum heir, I trow,
The same sall say to ʒow,
And ʒe ask ocht againe.   50

And gif it chance the Quenis syide to be,
With all straingeris cummand in hir supplie,
With Englismen vanqueist and put away,
Then will thay hauld ʒow for ane facill pray;
And quhat thay get in hand,   55
Castell, toun, or land,
Thay will it not restoir,
Bot keip it to thame sell,
And think thairin to duell,
As thay haue thocht befoir.   60

31 for till aggrie] till aggrie MF
34 thay will spair] will thai spare MF
36 That is quhair that thay hant] That salbe quhair thai hant MF, That is quhair thay hant D; 37 it pay] to pay D
41 that ʒe] ʒe that MF
58 thame sell] thair sell MF

And gif that ȝe that dependis on the Quein,
Frenchmen bring in, hir quarrell to sustein,
Remember how thay pleit ȝow befoir:
Ȝe war richt red thay sould ȝow not restoir
To ȝour auld libertie,   65
Bot thocht that ȝe sould be
Subiect ay thame to;
Gif I sall trewlie wryte,
Or ȝe war of thame quyt,
Ȝe had aneuch to do.   70

Thairfoir, my lordis, into ȝour hairtis imprent,
To bring straingeris the inconvenient;
Thay help ȝow not for loue thay haue to ȝow,
Bot for thair awin greit proffeit and thair prow;
Quhilk greitlie sould ȝow move   75
Ilkane other to love,
And caus ȝou to aggrie,
And ȝour awin weill considder:
Thairfoir knit ȝow togidder
To keip our libertie.   80

And ȝe in hand quhilk hes the gretest strenth,
Quhat it will serve I wait not at the lenth:
It may be wyne, it may be teint be tressoun;
Thairfoir applye ȝou ay to richt and ressoun,
And of peace be content,   85
Thocht sum of ȝour intent
Ȝe want for euer mair;
Ȝe ar not swir I trow,
Quha will cum relief ȝow,
And ȝe be seigit sair.   90

61 And gif that ȝe] And giff ȝe that MF
66 sould] wald D
70 to do] ado MF
75–6 Follows MF – order of lines reversed in MQ and D
77 caus ȝou to] MF caus to MQ D
81 quhilk] that MF

Sum ar dissemblit, ȝit proud in thair consait,
Bot other spyis weill aneuche thair gait;
Nother for Kingis nor Quenis auctoritie
Ȝe stryfe, bot for particularitie
That can not be content 95
Of thair awin land and rent,
As thair fatheris befoir,
Bot gif thay fill thair handis
With other mennis landis,
Geir, vittall, and stoir. 100

Ane other caus thair is of this seditioun:
Amang the lordis the vehement suspitioun
The ane trowis gif that the other be
Abone thame put into auctoritie,
Thay sall haue caus to dreid 105
Forfaltis and auld feid,
That thai sall tak revenge;
Of this wicked consait,
That noureist hes debait,
God all this countrie clenge. 110

I pray to him that is of lordis Lord,
Bring all our lordis to ane perfyte concord,
And with thi grace thair sprits all inspyire;
Amang thame kendill of cheritie the fyire,
All rancour and invy, 115
And faultis passit by,
To be forȝettin clein;
That iustice executioun,
For wickednes punitioun,
May in this land be sein. 120

Sir Richart Maitland of Lethingtoun.

93 Kingis nor] King nor MF
98 Bot gif thay] Onles thai MF
114 of] *om.* D
Attribution: Quod R maitland in MF; S. R. M. Finis in D.

26.
3e that sumtyme hes bene weill staikit,
Thocht of 3our geir sum be inlaikit,
And 3our self into trouble brocht:
Of this fals warld tak neuer thocht.

Of houshald graith sum richt scant war, 5
With other mennis geir now plenisit ar,
Better nor euer thair fatheris bocht:
3it of this fals warld tak no thocht.

To sum thair is bot lytill left,
Bot with greit wrang ar plainlie reft, 10
With diuillis limmis that neuer docht:
3it of this fals warld tak no thocht.

To reve thair nychtbour now few rakis,
For feir of God, bot daylie takis
Fra thame that neuer ocht thame ocht: 15
3it of this fals warld tak no thocht.

Sum to thair freind wes so faythles,
That vnder colour of kyndnes,
Thame to destroy did all thay mocht:
3it of this fals warld tak no thocht. 20

Sum that richt weill pleneist hes bein,
Thair landis now ar waistit clein,
With commoun theiffis that leiffis nocht:
3it of this fals warld tak no thocht.

1 sumtyme hes bene] hes bein somtyme D
8 3it of this fals warld tak no thocht] Off this fals warld tak neuer thocht MF (and throughout, except last stanza)
13 now few] few no MF
15 ocht] nocht D
17 freind] freindis D
19 mocht] micht D

Distroyit is the policie, 25
For the maist pairt of this countrie;
To wraik the rest sair wayis ar socht,
Ʒit of this fals warld tak no thocht.

I houpe the tyme sall cum schortlie,
Sall gar all wicked companie 30
Repent the wrang that thay haue wrocht,
For punisching thay sall tak thocht.

S. R. M.

28 fals] *om.* D
Attribution: Quod richard maitland in MF; Finis quod Sir Richard Maitland of Lethingtoune Knicht in D.

27.
How sould our commoun weill induire?
God to offend we tak no cuir,
And nane preissis thair lyfe to amend,
For na trowbill that God will send,
As plaigis cum be eventuire.   5

Quhen derth cummis, or pestilence,
We say it is be accidence;
And gif weir cummis ony way,
The moveris hes the wyte, we say,
And cummis not be our offence.   10

And gif we move the weir our sell,
We say we haue ane gud querrell,
And will nather persaue nor kna
That God, for syn, will lat ws fa
Into mischeif, and oft perrell.   15

The greit men sayis that thair distres
Cummis for the peopillis wickednes;
The peopill sayis the transgressioun
Of greit men and thair oppressioun,
Bot nane will thair awin syn confes.   20

S. R. M.

9 we] I D
13 will nather] nowder will MF
14 fa] fra D
18 sayis the] sayis for the MF.
Attribution: Quod Richard maitland in MF.

28.

It is ane mortall paine to heir and sie
Of this fals warld the mutabilitie:
Fra weill to wo, fra treuth to doubilnes,
Fra perfyte lyfe to fraud and fikilnes,
Fra godlie lyf to sensualitie.   5

And fra honour to warldlie wretchitnes,
And fra vertew to vyice and wickednes,
Fra all gud ordour to confusioun,
Fra law and iustice to abusioun,
Fra trew mening to colowred craftines.   10

Fra policie to plaine destructioun,
Fra vnitie to greit diuisioun,
Fra cheritie to malice and inuy,
Fra clein leiffing in carnell lust to ly,
All euill is vp and all gudnes is doun.   15

Fra nather honour, fayth, nor conscience,
Nor gratitude done of beneuolence,
Neirnes of bluid, nor ȝit affinitie,
Can in this warld gar kindnes kepit be,
As may be sein be plaine experience.   20

For Gredines now gydis all estaitis,
Instructand thame with covetous consaittis,
Sayand to sum, 'Quhy doe ȝe want this land?
This tak, this steid, that lyis so neir hand,
It for to get I can find twentie gaittis.'   25

Quhen Gredines had found sum wicked way,
Then come Kyndnes that purpose for to stay,
And said to him that Gredines had drest
Be his counsell his nychtbouris to molest,
'Tent to my taill and heir quhat I will say:'   30

1 and sie] or sie D
5 lyf] *om.* D; 30 will] sall D

'Quhy will ȝe now commit so greit offence
Againe all ressoun and gud conscience,
To tyne ȝour nichtbour, ȝour kinsmen, and ȝour freindis,
For gredines of onye land or teyndis
And to the puire to doe sic violence?' 35

Then cummis in Sir Gredines belyiff
With thir wordis, away Kyndnes to dryiff:
'Quhat is scho this can paint so fair a taill,
Sa far aganis ȝour proffeit and ȝour availl?
Get scho credence, scho will stope ȝow to thryif!' 40

'And ȝe hir counsell other doe or heir,
Ȝe will not conqueis mekill land or geir.
Put hir away, and mell with hir na mair.'
With that thay kest Dame Kyndnes over the stair,
And Gredines held hir ay areir. 45

Quhen Dame Kyndnes wes rebuikit sa,
Then Cheritie and Dame Pitie can ga,
And said, 'It is ane verie wicked deid
To tak thy nychtbouris maling over his heid,
And with greit rigour baneische him thairfra.' 50

'And als it is aganis Goddis command
For to desyre ȝour nichtbouris geir or land,
With violence to put ane puir man out:
God will ȝow plaig, thairfoir, withouttin dout;
Except ȝe mend, ȝe sall not chaipe his hand.' 55

Then Gredines said, with ane sturtsum cheir,
'Quha mekill deuill brocht thir twa harlottis heir!'
Furth at the dur he schot thame quyte away,

37 away] ay D
39 and ȝour availl] and availe MF D
42 conqueis mekill] conqueis ather meikill D
50 Him] thaim MF
51 als] *om.* D

And syne he said, 'Gif ȝe wald cheir thair tway,
Ȝe wald not purches mekill land this ȝeir.'   60

Alace! Quhair is the warld that sum hes sein
Sic cheritie in all estaittis hes bein,
That na man wald for steding, tak, nor teyndis,
Displeis thair nichtbouris, na pour man, nor frend,
Dame Kyndnes ay sa travelit thame betwene?   65

Thairfor, I pray to God that is above,
Fra all our hairtis this gredines remove,
That euerie man may, with cheritie,
Of his awin rentis so contentit be,
That we may leif into fraternall love.   70

S. R. M.

59 cheir] heir MF
63 teyndis] teynd MF
64 nor freind] MF nor thair frendis MQ
Attribution: Quod R maitland in MF; Finis quod S.R.M. in D.

29.
Greit paine it is now to behauld and sie
Into this realme the greit cupiditie,
For this fals warld the peopill hes so blindit,
To thair intent thay trow to euer bind it.
All haill thair hairtis to covetice ar growin;   5
Thay seik aneuch, bot thay sall neuer find it,
Quhill that thay cum other to hell or hevin.

With gredines ar infectit all staitis,
For to get land and geir thay seik all gaittis,
And cuiris not to get it wrangouslie,   10
Be fraud or force, or with subtilitie;
To find proffeit thay leif na thing on-socht;
Sumtyme not spair to vse crudelitie
To thair purpose, gif that may help thame ocht.

Sum to get land or geir will nourische stryfe,   15
Sum it to get will be of ane wratchit lyfe,
Sum will not spair, for favour not for feid,
To tak thair nychtbouris rowmes ouer thair heid,
Quhilk thay and thairis hes brukit this lang tyme;
And sum wald haue thair nychtbour put to deid   20
To get thair land for ane inventit cryme.

Sum gadderis geir and hes na grace to spend it,
Sum dois wrang and hes no will to mend it,
Sum leiffis all thair dayis wickedlie;
To reve the puire richt few hes now pitie,   25
And thair is monye ane that lytill cairis

1 it is now to] MF it is to MQ D
4 to euer] evir to MF, euer D
5 growin] gewin MF
8 ar infectit] infeckit ar MF
12 To find proffeit] Proffeit to find MF
16 it to get] to get D   will be of] will tak ane MF, will of D
18 To tak thair nychtbouris rowmes] Thair nychtbouris rowmes to tak thame MF
23 hes no will] na will hes MF

113

To put bayth saul and lyif in ieopardie,
To mak ane mekill conqueis to thair airis.

Syne wait not weill quhat thair airis wilbe,
Nor quhat will cum of thair posteritie;   30
For sum may be greit fuillis naturall;
Sum may be westouris and mak quyte of all;
Sum greit druncardis and spend thair thrift at wyne;
Sum may commit sic deidis criminall,
That may thame gar bayth geir and landis tyne.   35

Thairfoir, I think it is ane greit folie
For to mak onye conqueis wrangouslie;
Syne wait not gif thay [bruik it] lang thame sell,
And quha sall bruik it efter can not tell;
To conqueis lairge sum hes greit wrangis wrocht,   40
And put thame sell in danger of the hell,
And in schort tyme thair conqueis turne to nocht.

I counsell all, thairfoir, to be content
Of iust conqueis with ane sufficient rent:
Quha hes maist land is not the best at eis,   45
Quha mekill hes, the ma thai haue to pleis,
And with monye thair deidis salbe spyit.
It is not best ane heiche estait to cheis:
The gretest ar with monyest invyit.

Sum hes bene greit and fallin fra hie estait: 50
The gretest now may gang the samyn gait,
And thay crab God in thair governament.
Monye ar now that hes aneuch of rent,
3it to get land and geir thay neuer rest,
Thair gridie hairtis can neuer be content   55
Lyike as this warld and thay sould euer lest.

35 gar] *om.* D
38 bruik it] bruikit MQ brouke it MF
39 bruik it] bruikit MQ brouk it MF
45 not the best] not ay best MF
50 fallin] fain MF
56 lest] rest D

Bit I doe not forbid alluterlie
To mak conqueis, sa it be done iustlie,
First for to mak thame self ane honest lyife,
To helpe thair bairnis, freindis, and wyfe; 60
And as thay may the puire to help hes neid,
Syne weill provyide that thair follow na stryif,
For thair conqueis efter that thay be deid.

All ʒe that hes bene gevin to gredines,
Of all ʒour vniust conqueis mak redres, 65
And it restoir to thame it did belang,
And think thair is ane God to puneis wrang,
At quhome of our misdeidis ask mercie,
For sumtyme ʒe fra land and geir sall gang,
In all ʒour workes: remember ʒe man die. 70

S. R. M.
This taill is trew and surer nor the Bass. Malorum radix cupiditas.

58 To mak conqueis] Conqueis to mak MF
60 wyfe] thair wyff MF
68 our] ʒour MF
Attribution: Quod R maitland in MF.

30.
O Lord, our sin hes done the tein,
That plagit thus hes this countrie:
I trow wes neuer harde nor sein
In Scotland greter miserie.
Greit euill into this land we sie, 5
As slauchter, heirschip, thift, and reif,
Destructioun of all policie,
And all maner of maist mischeif.

Now warldlie wisdome is dissait,
And falset hauldin policie; 10
Richt few from gyle can now debait,
Sa greit is the hypocresie.
Sum will speik fair and freindfullie,
For proffeit wald dissaue thair brother:
Sa ryff is infidelitie, 15
Ane kinsman scant may trow ane other.

Amang the lordis syne the greit stryif,
Misreull in all this regioun,
Quhilk hes garrit monye loise thair lyfe,
And troublit burges and barroun; 20
Craftismen and commounis ar put doun
Be thift, reif, and continuall weir;
Neir herreit is our principall toun,
Our merchandis daylie waistand geir.

All this is for our punischment 25
Becaus our God we will not knaw,
Ay brekand his commandement,
Lyik as of him we stuid na aw:
Monye ar Goddis word will schaw
That ar far contrar in thair deidis, 30
And cuiris not agane the law
To tak that onye man posseidis.

11 now debait] thame debait MF
17 Amang the lordis] Amang lordis MF
18 Misreull in] Misreuland MF

Fra sum is taine bayth hous and land
Wrangouslie, as the maner schawis,
Quhome doing wrang thay neuer fand,   35
Bot for all cryme will byide the lawis,
Bayth of thair deidis and thair sawis;
3it ar thay spoil3it of thair rent
Quha hes this done, the greit God knawis,
Quha graunt thame grace for to repent.   40

Sum hes thair place brint in ane gleid,
Thair guddis spuil3it halallie;
Thair seruandis slaine, sum brint to deid,
Thair selfis taine vncourteouslie,
And hauldin in captiuitie,   45
Quha wald haue, for ane missiue bill,
Obeyit the auctoritie,
And cummit at my lord Regentis will.

Alace! It is ane cairfull caice
That our lordis can not aggrie,   50
Quhilk for to doe, gif thay had grace,
Wald stanche this greit iniquitie.
Ane thing thair is that trowbillis me:
Thocht sum wald faine mak gud concord,
3it ay for ane thair is twentie   55
To hound mutine and saw discord.

Bot we sould rather all lament
Thir plages, perturbing ws sa sair,
And of our sinnis ws repent
With firme purpois to syne no mair;   60
Syne pray to God, bayth lait and air,
To tak fra ws this cruell scurge,
And for his mercie stainche our cair,
And of all weir this countrie purge.

80 our court is] 3our courtis ar D
76 bene] cum MF
Attribution: Quod richard maitland of L. in MF.

117

My lordis all, that are diuydit, 65
Could 3e aggrie, it wer the best,
And gar this realme be godlie gydit,
All thing to be with wisdome drest;
Then better micht 3e put to rest
This land, that now is furth of ordour, 70
And thame releif that ar opprest,
The theiffis stainche, and reull the bordour.

Sen 3e ar of ane natioun all,
Ilkane of other haue pitie.
3e wait not 3it quhat may befall, 75
Sic chance hes bene richt haistallie,
May gar 3ow think that vnitie
Sall to 3ow all be profitabill,
And neidfull that 3e freindis be;
3e ken our court is neuer stabill. 80

Quha euer get the vpper hand,
Of thair rewaird thay knaw na thing,
Not 3it how lang that thay sall stand
To haue the reull of Quein or King,
And speciallie quhen thay ar 3oung. 85
Thairfoir 3e sould tak richt gud gaird
Of lestand feid 3e on 3ow bring,
Vncertane syne of 3our rewaird.

O Lord, sic grace send to ws heir,
All Scottismen for to aggrie; 90
Ilkane to bruik thair land and geir,
That thame pertenis richteouslie;
Syne perfyte iustice we may sie
In courtis, consistorie, and sessioun;
Craftismen and commounis may peceablie 95
Thair leving win without oppressioun.

S. R. M.

31.
Quhen I haue done consider
This warldis vanitie,
Sa brukill and sa slidder,
So full of miserie,
Then I remember me 5
That heir thair is no rest:
Thairfoir, apperantlie,
To be mirrie is best.

Let ws be blyithe and glaid
My freindis all, I pray; 10
To be penseif and sad
Na thing it helpe ws may;
Thairfoir, put quyite away
All hevines of thocht:
Thocht we murne nycht and day 15
It will availl ws nocht.

It will not be our sorrow
That will stope Goddis hand
To stryike, bayth evin and morrow,
Bayth on the sie and land; 20
Sen nane may it gainestand,
Let ws all be content
To vnderlye the wand
Of Goddis punishment.

Quhat God plesis to doe, 25
Accept it thankfullie;
Quhat paine he put ws to,
Receave it patientlie;
And gif that we wald be
Relevit of our paine, 30
For sin ask God mercie:
Offend him not againe.

27 paine he] pane to MF
49 ay] lay D

Gif we will mak murning,
Sould be for our offence,
And not that God dois bring   35
On ws for violence,
For ane dyuers pretence;
For sum he will puneis,
To prove thair patience,
And sum for thair greit miss.   40

Sen first the warld bigane
Thair hes bene troubill ay,
For punishment of man,
And sall quhill domisday;
And sen we may not stay,   45
Quhat God pleis doe ws till,
Quhat he will on ws lay
Receave it with gud will.

For God will ay sum scurge,
Quhill that the warld tak end,   50
Fra syne the warld to purge,
Will ay sum plaigis send;
Bot quha will lyife amend,
And preis to sin no mair,
Then God will him defend   55
Fra euerlasting cair.

3it plainlie I conclude,
Intill all wardlines,
Na thing for man sa gude,
As lesum mirrines;   60
For thair is na ritches,
Sa lang his lyife can lenth,
Conserue him fra seiknes
And keip him in his strenthe.

55 Then God will him] Thair God will thame MF
Attribution: Quod richard maitland in MF; Finis quod S. R. M. in D.

Thairfoir, with trew intent, 65
Let ws at God ask grace
Our sinnis to repent,
Quhill we haue tyme and space;
Syne bring ws to that place
Quhair ioy is euermoir, 70
And sie God face to face
In his eternall gloir.

Sir Richart Maitland of Lethingtoun

32.
Loue vertew over all, and all vyces flie;
Wickednes hait; alwayis gudnes imbrace;
Remove rancour, and ay keip cheritie;
Proudnes detest; invy fra the far chaise;
Gredines, neuer let it in the tak place;   5
Be honorable, and weill credence keip;
Besines, not sleuth, havand tyme and space;
Trewlie serue God, and als for sinnis weip.

Thir 8 lynes ȝe may begin at ony nuik ȝe will and reid bakwart or fordwart, and ȝe sall find the lyike sentence and meter.

S. R. M.

1 over all] euer MF
5 neuer let it in] neuer lat in MF, let it neuer in D
Attribution: quod richard maitland in MF.

33.
Sinneris, repent that ȝe haue spent
Ȝour tyme in wickednes;
Bot now be bent, with trew intent,
To leiff in godlines.

Ȝour lyiffis mend and not offend 5
Ȝour gratious God na mair;
Think on the end, and how ȝe man wend
Away, naiked and bair.

Thairfoir, ask grace, quhill ȝe haue space,
At God for ȝour greit mis; 10
Sin fra ȝow chaice, preis to the place
Quhair ay is ioy and blis.

Ȝour God ay feir, folie forbeir,
On vertew follow aye;
Pryidfull nocht be, vse not to lie, 15
Advyis weill quhat ȝe say.

Keip ay kyndnes and faythfulnes
To ȝour freindis ilkane;
Hait gredines and doubilnes;
Vnder trust dissaue nane. 20

Leif modestlie, luif honestie;
Vse not in sin to ly;
Nane in ȝow sie crudelitie
Ir, malice, nor invy.

Love God ay best, all sin detest, 25
And fals ypocresie;
Louf pece and rest, and nane molest,
Bot leif in cheritie.

S. R. M.

11 the] that MF
Attribution: Quod richard maitland in MF.

34.

Mair mischevous and wicked warld
Nor thair is now, saw nane, I trow;
The countrie throw is quyte our-harld,
Now in this trouboulous tyme.

Lowthane, quhair sumtyme hes bene 5
Maist policie, tranquillitie,
Greit suirtie for king and quene,
Befoir this troublous tyme,

Be men of weir is waistit haill,
With thift and reif, weir and mischeif; 10
Gretar releif in Liddisdaill
Now in this troublous tyme.

The toun, quhairin to duell wes best,
Withouttin feir, ritchest of geir,
With men of weir richt sair opprest, 15
Now in this troublous tyme.

Thairfoir, all men be now of gud will,
And fast ȝow preis to mak gud peace,
Think tyme to ceis Scottis bluid to spill,
Now in this troublous tyme. 20

And sen sum abstinence is taine,
Na tyme oursie, bot bissie be
This haill countrie to mak at ane,
And stainche this troublous tyme.

That it be sa, we hairtlie pray 25
To God abuif, for Christis luif,
And to remuif this plaig away,
And this mischevous, troublous tyme.

S. R. M.

3 throw] now D
7 Greit] grittest MF
19 Scottis] Godis D
24 troublous] *om.* MF
Attribution: Finis quod Richart maitland of Lethington knycht in MF.

35. Ane Contrapoysoun to the Ballat Falslie Intitulit the Properteis of Gud Wemen.

Quha dewlie wald decerne
The nature of gud wemen,
Or quha wald wis or ȝairne,
That cumlie clan to ken,
He hes greit neid, I say indeid,　　　　　　　　　　5
Of toungis ma then ten:
That plesant sort ar all confort,
And mirrines to men.

The wysest thing of wit,
That euer nature wrocht,　　　　　　　　　　10
Quha can fra purpose flit,
Bot fikilnes of thocht.
Wald ȝe now wis ane erthlie blis,
Solace gif ȝe haue socht,
Ane marchandice of gretest price,　　　　　　　　　　15
That euer ony bocht?

The brichtest thing bot baill,
That euer creat bein,
The lustiest and leill,
The gayest and best gein;　　　　　　　　　　20
The thing fairest with langest lest,
From all canker maist clein,
The trimmest face with gudlie grace,
That lichlie may be sein.

The blythest thing in bour,　　　　　　　　　　25
The bonyest in bed;
Plesant at euerie hour,
And eithe for to be sted;
Ane innocent, plaine and patent,
With craftines oncled,　　　　　　　　　　30

6 ma then] ma nor D
13 Wald ȝe now wis] wald now wiss D
14 ȝe] *om.* D

Ane simpill thing, sueit and bening,
For deir nocht to be dred.

To man obedient,
Evin lyik ane willie wand;
Bayth faythfull and feruent, 35
Ay reddie at command,
Thay luif maist leill, thocht men doe feill,
And schaikis oft of hand;
Quhair anis thay loue, thay not remoue,
Bot steidfastlie they stand. 40

And richtlie to compair,
Scho is ane turtill trew:
Hir fedderis ar richt fair,
And of ane hevinlie hew;
Ane luifing wicht, bayth fair and bricht, 45
Gud properteis anew;
Freind with delyte, fa but dispyit,
Quha lovis hir sall not rew.

Suppose scho seme offendit,
Quhen men dois hir constraine, 50
That fault is sone amendit,
Hir mynde is so humaine;
Sho is content, gif men repent
Thair fault and turne againe;
Sho hes no guyle, nor subtill vyile - 55
Hir pathis ar ay plaine.

Ane lyife full of delyite,
Gif ȝe ȝour dayis wald drie;
In pastyme maist perfyite,
Gif that ȝe list to be; 60
In gud estait, bayth air and lait,
Gif ȝe wald leif or die:
With wemen deill it is trew I tell,
Ȝeis luik, I sall not lie.

Gif onye fault thair be, 65
Alace, men hes the wyit,

That gevis sa gouketlie.
Sic rewleris onperfyite
Sould haue the blame and beir the schame;
Thocht thay wemen bakbyit, 70
Wer thay wittie wemen wald be
Ane happie hairtis delyit.

The properteis perpend
Of euerie warldlie wicht,
Sa comlie nane ar kend 75
As is a ladye bricht,
Plesand in bed, bowsum and red,
Ane daintie day and nicht;
Ane helsum thing, ane hairtis lyking,
Gif men could reull thame richt. 80

Quhen God maid all of nocht,
He did this weill declair,
The last thing that he wrocht,
It wes ane woman fair.
In workes we sie the last to be 85
Maist plesand and preclair:
Ane help to man God maid hir than,
Quhat will ȝe I say mair?

The papingo in hew
Exceidis birdis all, 90
The turtill is maist trew,
The pawne but peregall;
Ȝit neuertheles, ȝe may confes,
Wemen is worthe thame all:
Fair, sueit, plesand, trew, meik, constant, 95
Without all bitter gall.

Considder and behauld
Ingrat, vnthankfull man;
Repeit the poetis auld,
And reid thame gif thow can: 100

71 Wemen] Wemen wemen D
100 Thow] ȝie D

Thair thou sall find, les thou be blind,
The vertewis of wemen,
With heich ingyne how muses nyne
All science first began.

Minerue ane woman was, 105
Quha wisdome did inuent,
Of Greikis namit Pallas,
And from the hevin wes sent
To leir men wit that wantit it,
And in thair hairtis it prent: 110
To wemen than, say quhat ȝe can,
Sic giftis first wes lent.

The wyise Ceres also
Did first inuent the corne,
And mony thousand mo 115
Wer mortell wemen borne;
ȝit for thair meid, and thair gud deid,
The poetis all hes sworne
To thame to pray as goddis ay,
And worschip thame but scorne. 120

Iesabell wicked was,
Sa was Achab hir king;
Curst wes Herodias,
Dalila did maling.
Will ȝe thairfoir, withouttin moir, 125
All wemennis gloir doun-thring?
Be that same way wemen may say
That men ar worthe na thing.

For suithlie, of man kynd
Ma wicked may be called 130
Then of the wemen stryinde,
And worss ane hundreth fauld,
Quha will tak heid and dewlie reid
The wryte and storeis auld:

127 Be] Bot D

Thocht sum do faill to wyite thame all,　　　　　　135
I think 3e be to bauld.

Quhair 3e can ane me schaw
Of wemen wicked bein,
I ansueir I doe knaw
Of gud wemen fiftein.　　　　　　　　　　　　　　140
Go serche thame out, withouttin dout
3e sall thame find be-dein.
Gif I wald lie, 3our selfis may sie
The sampillis may be sein.

Did not the Virgine myilde,　　　　　　　　　　　145
That blissed bird Marie,
Bring furth to ws ane chylde,
Quha did ws sanctifie?
And Debora rewlit Iuda
With spreit of prophecie,　　　　　　　　　　　　150
Quhen men wes sueir, and durst not steir,
Bot lurkit lidderlie.

The blissed Susanna
Wes flour of womanheid;
The prophites Anna　　　　　　　　　　　　　　155
Knew Christ first, as we reid;
That bousteous bairne, proud Oliphern,
Gud Iudith garrit him bleid:
Ane woman than, but force of man,
Saifit the toun at neid.　　　　　　　　　　　　　160

Hester, that lustie quene,
Saifit the peopill all;
Abigaal, the schene,
Saifit hir man Naball;
Mical his wyife keipt Dauids lyife,　　　　　　　165
Quhen Saul did for him call;

139 knaw] ken D
155 we] he D
165 keipt] saifit D

And monye may, as I heir say,
Hes saifit men fra thrall.

Quhen the Canarianis
In strang prisoun wes set,   170
Inclosit be Spartanis,
And could na succour get,
Then thair sueit wyfis hasart thair lyfis,
And fred thame fra that net,
Chaingit thair weid baid in thair steid,   175
For trewluif hes no let.

Honest Lucretia
Wes flour of chastitie;
And prudent Porcia,
Lamp of fidelitie;   180
Of trew constance, but variance,
Perle wes Penelope;
Of loue maist leill, that neuer did faill,
Exempill wes Thisbe.

The fair Cornelia   185
Wes ieme of eloquence;
Prudent Aspasia
Excellit in sapience:
Socrates wyise thocht na dispryis
To leirn at hir prudence;   190
Quha list to reid micht leir indeid
At Grissell patience.

And thocht for wemennis saik
Greit trouble hes bene sein,
ȝit that dois nawayis maik   195
That wemen wicked bein.

187 ieme] fain ? D
Attribution: Finis quod Magister Alexander Arbuthnat in D.

We sie that kingis, for pretious thingis,
Dois gretest weir sustein,
And ȝit the geir, for quhilk thay weir,
Is not the worse a prein.   200

Realmis and greit impyris
Then sould be worthe na thing,
For cruell bluide and fyris
Ar sein in conquesing.
All pretious geir we sould forbeir,   205
Refuis to be ane king:
Ȝe, Christis word sould be abhord,
For all dois troubillis bring.

Confes, thairfoir, for schame,
For so ȝe must in deid,   210
That it is na defame
To pryss of womanheid.
Suppose that men, for loue of thame,
In battellis oft did bleid,
That settis thame furth to be maist worthe,   215
And so thay ar indeid.

Ȝe wemen vitious,
Gif onye sic be now,
Grow not our glorious,
I spak nothing of ȝow.   220
Thair is anew, bayth traist and trew,
Quhome onlie I allow:
Thocht sum be ruid monye ar gud,
Ilk man cheis him ane dow.

Finis quod M. A. Arbuthnat.

36.
He that luifis lichtliest
Sall not happin on the best.
He that luifis langest
Sall haue rest suirest.
He that lovis all his best 5
Sall chaunce vpon the gudliest.
Quha sa in luif is trew and plaine,
He salbe luifit weill againe.
Men may say quhat euer thay pleis,
In mutuall loue is mekill eis. 10

Arbuthnat

37.
Ceis hairt, and trowbill me no moir,
And lat alaine all pansivnes,
And rander to thy maker gloir,
Ather of plesour or distres.
Content thy self with sobernes,   5
And put thy traist in God alone.
Forʒet this warldis wratchidnes,
And sie for it thou mak no mone.

Sen God, thy souuerane, hes the send
Into this vaile of miserie,   10
Amang the rest thy tyme to spend
Quhill it him pleis to call on the,
Receave his giftis, quhat euer thay be:
Stand still, quhair euer he dois the place;
Worke thy vocatioun steidfastlie,   15
And rander to thy maker grace.

Grudge not aganis his godlie will,
Thocht thou get not thy hairtis desyire;
Accuse him not, bot hauld the still,
Lest thow provoike his michtie yre.   20
Perchaunce the thing thow wald requyire,
And frainis fast grauntit to be,
Wald rather cast the in the myire,
Then from all dainger set the frie.

Thy blindit wit can not considder   25
His worke of wosdome and prudence.
Thy spreit can not controll togidder
His rigour with his pacience,
His yre with his beneuolence,
His mercie and his iudgment richt.   30

16 And rander to thy maker grace] Calling on him to grant the grace MF, Call on him to grant the grace R
21 thing thow] thing quhilk thow MF R
28 *om.* R
30 mercie and his iudgment] iudgement and his mercie R

Feir him, thairfoir, with reuerence,
Sen thou can not conceave his micht.

No warldlie thing sould the effray,
Gif thow till him have conscience clein;
Thocht it be loist, or tint the day   35
Quhilk thow had haill and sound ʒeistrein,
In hairt, therfoir, tak thou na tein,
Bot in thy mynd leif onmolest,
For monye tymes it may be sein
That sic thingis cummis for the best.   40

Thow nocht invy, thocht wicked men
In warldlie welth doe the excell;
And thocht thay that the Lord misken
Into the erthe beir now the bell.
Remember that thair is ane hell,   45
Quhair sinneris all salbe forloir,
And how the ioy, na toung can tell,
Quhilk thow sall have in hevenis gloir.

Think on quhome God dois heir torment,
And chastisis quhome he luiffis best,   50
That thay may not set thair entent
Vpon this warld, nor thairon rest,
Bot rather hait, flie, and detest,
The rout of pryde that thairin ringis,
Eschewand plesour as ane pest,   55
Quhilk drawis ʒou from the king of kingis.

Remember als how sic chaistning
Dois ws alluire our selfis to knaw,
The quhippis of the Lord feling,
Becaus we daylie brak his law: 60
Sic punisching hauldis ws in aw,

38 leif] luif MF R
41 Thow] Haif MF R
47 how] quhen R
55 Quhilk drawis ʒou from] quhilk drawis frome MF

That we stray not over far asclent,
Nor with the wicked in ȝoike draw,
Quhome in his wraith the Lord will schent.

Also, sic tribulatioun 65
Sould the admonische, and mak plaine
That thy chief consolatioun
Into this warld is not certaine,
Bot that in heavin it dois remaine,
Vnto the quhilk thow sall pretend, 70
Without regaird to triffillis vaine,
Lovand the Lord quhat euer he send.

Stoupe then vnder his michtie hand,
And the content of his gud will;
Thocht thow haue nother geir nor land, 75
Think not, therfoir, he luiffis the ill,
Bot rather think he dois fulfill
His promeis, quhen he dois the bring
Be that same trace the heavenis vntill,
By quhilk first enterit Christ our king. 80

Thocht thow be heir in vncouthe land,
And dois the indignatioun beir
Of countrie men quhilk, in ane band,
Conspyris still to doe the deir,
Tak thow, thairfoir, of thame na feir, 85
Sen thay can not annoy thy saull,
For in the scriptour thow may leir
Quhen sumtyme lyik sufferit Sanct Paull.

Gif God vpon thy pairtie stand,
Quhat misteris the for to tak feir? 90
Gif he defend the with his hand,
Thy enemeis can not doe deir.
This reill, this raige, this cruell weir,

68 not certaine] nocht found certane MF R
71 to triffillis] of triffillis MF
79 trace] trane MF R
88 Quhen] Quhou MF

Thocht it a quhyill doe the molest,
3it, as thow may in Scripture leir,   95
All thing sall turne the to the best.

In God, thairfoir, the confort ay,
And quyite this warld, for it is vaine;
Preis to the place can neuer decay,
Seik to the sait that is certaine,   100
For erthlie ioy can not remaine,
And quhair that it is vnperfyte,
With small plesour is mekill paine,
And doubill duill with small delyite.

Sen but all paine plesour perfyt   105
Into this warld can not be found;
Sen doulfull dolour and delyt,
Ilkane with other fast ar bound;
Sen our foirfatheris deidlie wound
Hes privat men of perfyit ioy,   110
Quhow lang that thow lest on this ground,
For warldlie geir tak neuer noy.

Thocht God hes not appointit the
To bruik honouris amang the laif,
3et hes ordainit that thow be   115
Ane quhome his sone Iesus sall saif;
Quhat greater gift than can thow craif,
Than be at ane with sic ane Lord,
And that eternall ioy till haif,
Quhilk he hes promesit be his word?   120

Finis quod Arbuthnatt.

95 3it] 3e MF; 102. that] it MF
109 foirfatheris] first fatheris MF R
111 Quhow] Quhane MF R   lang that thow] *om.* R
112 tak neuer noy] tak 3e na noy MF R
115 3et hes] 3it hee hes MF R
116 sall] MQ R still MF
Attribution: Finis Richard Maitland in MF; Finis quod sumbodie in R.

38.
Sen that eine that workis my weilfair
Dois no moir on me glance,
A thousand sichtis, with suelting sobbis sair,
Dois throw my bowellis lance.
I die ȝairning;   5
I leif pyning;
Woe dois encres;
I wax witles:
O sindring, O wofull doleance!

The day quhen as the fair pairtit me fray,   10
Plesour me left also.
Quhen that from hir I sinderit wes away,
Mischance me hint but ho.
I waxit wan,
the same hour than,   15
Sorrow sensyne
Dois still me pyine.
O, that gudnicht hes causit mekill wo.

Evin as men may the turtill trew persaif,
Once having loist hir feir,   20
On the dry brainche ay faythfull to the graif,
Bewayling perseueir,
So my desyire,
Kindlit in fyire,
Dois soir lament   25
My luif absent.
O God, gif amour be ane paine to beir!

Neuer in somer the haitt canicular day,
So hote with beamis brent,
As dois that fyire quhilk me devoring ay,   30
Hes saull and bodie tint.
And neuer a dairt
So persit my hairt,
As dois the bolt,
Quhilk luif me schot: 35
O god Cupid, gif bitter be thy dint!

As he that suimmis, the moir he ettill fast,
And to the schoire intend,
The moir his febill furie, throw windis blast,
Is backwart maid to wend.   40
So wors be day,
My greif growis ay;
The moir I am hurte,
The moir I sturte:
O cruell love, bot deid, thow hes none end.   45

The faithfull messinger, quhilk is the nicht,
To luiffaris langorous,
Augmentis my woe, and als the dayis licht
Makis me moir dolorous.
The day I dwyine,   50
The nicht I pyine,
Evin eikis my sorrow
Wors then the morrow.
O God in love, gif I be malhourous.

And gif that neid to slumber me constraine,   55
Faint throuch melancolie,
Vnrest dois walkin me againe
To muse my miserie;
Quhat euer chanche
Dois me outtrance,   60
Saif fals thinking
In sueit dreming:
O dreame maist sueit, gif it war not a lie.

In cairfull bed, full oft in myne intent,
To twitche I doe appeir;   65
Now syde, now breist, now sweit mow redolent,
Of that sueit bodye deir;
I stretche my hand,
In vaine ernand:
My luif is far,   70
And not found nar.
O scorne of luifaris, Cupid, blind archeir!

Syne quhen the morning, with hir mantill grein,
Opinis the dayis face
With Phoebus licht, the cairfull thochtis [kein] 75
Renewis thair wofull raice.
My fyrie raige
Dois then aggrage;
My soir torment
Dois moir augment: 80
O, gif absence be paine in luifis caice.

So monye starris ar nocht in nichtis sein,
Nor in drawing colouris,
Nor scipping froggis amid the medow grein,
As I thocht of dolouris: 85
Noy vpon noy
Markis to destroy
My wofull lyfe,
Fechting in stryife.
O, gif vnhap be found in paramouris. 90

The day befoir the suddane nichtis chaice
Dois not so suiftlie go,
Nor hair befoir the ein and grewhoundis face
With speid is careit so,
As I with paine, 95
For luif of ane,
Without remeid,
Rinnis to the deid:
O God, gif deid be end of mekill wo.

O goddis hiche, gif in the hevin be found 100
Sum band of amitie,
I ȝow beseik, be movit with my wound,
And haue sum iust pitie.
My proper lyif
I hait with stryif; 105
I me forsaik

75 kein] dein MQ

For otheris saik:
O, gif luif causis strainge inamitie.

Ha! Now my muse, my soucy, and my cair,
Leif of thy lamenting. 110
Ceis to complaine of mishap ony mair:
End now! I ceis to sing.
He that can plaine
Dois thoill leist paine;
Soir ar the hairtis 115
But plaint that smartis:
Silence to dolour is ane nowrisching.

Finis.

39.
Sen Fortoun hes now randerit me subiect,
And luiffis ȝoik subdewit hes my neck,
I thank my God that to hir am thrall,
Quha neuer wes of onye vyice suspect,
Bot of all vertew choise is and elect,   5
And in all bewtie is but peregall.
Hir presentlie I serue, and euer sall,
And gif scho plesis my seruice not reiect,
For my rewaird I crave no moir at all.

Sumtyme I leifit at libertie at list,   10
And thocht I could to luiffis force resist
Be cunning craft, convoyit with prudence,
Bot hir bewtie caist in my ein sic mist,
Hir greit bontie me trappit, or I wist,
That I vnabill am to mak defence.   15
Then ȝeild I me to hir obedience,
Thinking that ȝit sic seruitude is blist,
To serue ane flour of sic preeminence.

Gif Bewtie has me bound in thrall,
And wer overcum with lustis sensuall,   20
Then micht I, thocht my wisdome faillit me;
Bot sen hir bontie supernaturall
To Bewtie couplit is collaterall,
In heichest staige of excellent degri,
I traist that nane can me accuse trewlie,   25
Gif bewtie, bontye, and the vertewis all,
My tender hairt keip in captiuitie.

For scho, to quhome I servitour am bound,
Is sic as in the erthe can not be found;
Ane perles perle and patroun maist perfyte,   30
The gle, the grace, the gloir of all the ground,
Maist sueit, maist meik, maist saige, maist suire, maist sound,
Royall rubie with all riches repleit,
Roise of renoun, and dasie of delyte:
With sic a lance for to ressaue a wound,   35
Albeit I wis, I wait nane will me wyte.

Ane thing thair is that I doe soir lament,
That for hir saik, thocht I be daylie schent,
To schaw my paine I dar scars interpryis:
Quhen I me anis befoir hir face present, 40
All wit and spreit that euer wes to me lent,
Is me bereft and chainged so my guys,
That quhowsoeuer to other I seme wyis,
To hir my mynd I can not mak patent,
Thocht lyif and deid bayth in hir plesour lyis. 45

Sen tongue can not my troubillis then expres,
And countenance dois failȝie me no les
To get the graice of that sa gudlie wicht,
Wald God, sen scho sic other wosdome hes,
My inward mynd scho could persaue and ges, 50
And all my hairt wer patent in hir sicht;
Then sould scho ken that my luif wer not licht,
Bot of hir honest, courtes gentilnes,
As I deserue scho wald me rander richt.

I knaw otheris hes mair experience 55
In craft of loue, and greater eloquence,
And subtellie thair purpose can persew;
Bot for leill love, and constant permanence,
Inward favour with honest reuerence,
Ane hairt enteir, quhilk bayth is traist and trew, 60
Moir nor in me, thocht all the warld scho vew,
Scho sall not find, I speik with hir licence:
Few ar found leill, thocht loveris be anew.

Then sen I can na other way declair
My troublit hairt to that princes preclair, 65
Bot be my wryte and schedull quhilk I send,
Heir I beseik hir Bewtie singulair,
Have sum respect vnto my daylie cair,
Sen onlie scho my meladie may mend;
And sen I doe bot honestie pretend, 70
Let luif meit luif of hir, I seik na mair,
And be sum signe let this be to me kend.

Hairt and sueit luiff, and onlie maistres myne,

Craib not, thocht I 3ow papeir now propyne,
Ane gift ungenand for 3our excellence: 75
Gif I may knaw that 3our hairt dois inclyne,
Sum better thing sall follow efter syne,
Quhilk may be meit for 3our magnificence,
As for my self, with dew obedience,
My strenth, my wit, my force and haill ingyne, 80
Heir I doe raunder to 3our reuerence.

This poure propyne refuis not, I 3ow pray,
This simpill sute cast it not quyte away.
Tyme will trye furth quha masit trewlie dois mein:
Thir gay gallandis with thair dres and deray, 85
Thair luif tareis bot for ane nicht or tway;
Be that be past thay will for3et it clein.
Thocht I wald lie, the sampillis may be sein,
Maist feruent luiff dois sonest ay decay,
Advyis 3ow now, the flour of feminine. 90

3it howsoeuer heirin 3e counsell tak,
Quhidder 3e prayse my purpose, or 3e lak,
My hairt alwayis to luif 3ow man proceid,
Thocht 3e be daingerous and beir abak,
And of my miserie 3our mirth wald mak. 95
That I 3ow luiff I sall schaw ay indeid:
Sum houpe is 3it that my seruice sall speid,
Without the quhilk I wait I am bot wraik.
With wisdome work now, waill of womanheid.

With licence then, my luif, I tak my leif, 100
Fering with langer purpose 3ow to greif.
For new taking God will send tyme and place;
Tryall of treuth my permanence sall preif.
With reuthfull hairt, gif 3e wald me releif,
Then wer my paine turnit in perfyte peace.
Bot howsoeuer with me chancis the case, 105
A thowsand tymes quhidder I die or leif,
I me commend vnto 3our nobill grace.

Finis.

40. Ane Ballat to be Songe with the Tuine of 'Luifer Come to Luifeiris Dore' etc.

O blissed bird brichtest of all,
O flour of femenein,
O perles perle, but peregall,
O lustie lady schein:
Crab not gif I to mynde doe call   5
The paine that I sustein;
Cast me not quyite away.

Quho so ȝour bewtie wald behauld
Must neidis in ȝow delyit;
Bot I regaird mair monifauld   10
Ȝour properteis perfyit:
Ȝour bontie, quhilk can not be tauld,
Ȝour vertewis ar so gryit;
Have pitie, I ȝow pray.

I am ane prenteis bot in luif,   15
And lak experience;
Bot gif ȝe list my lawtie pruif,
And try my permanence,
My constant hairt sall neuer remuif
From ȝour obedience: 20
Haue pitie, I ȝow pray.

I grant thair is na gift in me,
Ȝour fauour to procuire;
I knaw ȝour greit excellencie
All hairtis dois alluire.   25
Ȝit since I am, be destanie,
Becum ȝour seruituire,
Haue pitie, I ȝow pray.

For quhat in me can not be found,
Throw lak and indigence,   30
That same in ȝow dois moir abound
With richlie opulence.
Let ȝour fulnes my faultis refound,

And faillis recompence.
Haue pitie, I ȝow pray. 35

So nature hes ordanit wyislie
That in all kynde of thing
Perfyite the vnperfyte supplie,
And to perfectioun bring:
Sua maistres, may ȝe doe with me, 40
Gif it be with ȝour lyking.
Have pitie, I you pray.

Ȝour gud behaving to rehers
I can not, thocht I wald;
Ȝour graces greit to put in vers 45
I dar not be so bauld,
For my ingyine can no way pers,
So far a thousand fauld.
Haue pitie, I ȝow pray.

It semis to me quhen ȝe appeir 50
Amang the madinnis all,
Ȝe ar lyik Phoebus in his spheir,
Amid the starnis small,
Quha with his glistering bemis cleir,
Thair brichtnes causis fall. 55
Haue pitie, I ȝow pray.

It semis to me quhen ȝe resort
Amang thir ladyis schein,
Ȝe haue the countenance and port
Of Diana the quein, 60
Quhen with the nymphes scho dois sport,
Amang the leiffis grein.
Haue pitie, I ȝow pray.

It semis to me quhair ȝe repair
Amang thir ladyis quhyte, 65
Ȝe ar as in ane gairdein fair
Ane lillie of delyte,
Ane roise maist plesand and preclair,

Ane ianetflour perfyite.
Have pitie, I 3ow pray. 70

Fra 3e appeir anis in my sicht,
All other forme dois faid,
I think 3ow lyik the golde so bricht,
And all the rest bot leid:
Thay ar bot darknes of the nicht, 75
And 3e the morning reid.
Haue pitie, I 3ow pray.

3our goldin hair lyik Phoebus schein,
Quhair euer 3e go dois glance;
3our gudlie face, 3our colour clein, 80
3our cumlie countenance;
3our plesand twincling cristall ein
Dois cast me in ane trance.
Have pitie, I 3ow pray.

3our smyland, seimlie mouth is sueit, 85
Lyik rosis redolent,
With vermell lippis of balme repleit,
3our tonge most eloquent;
3our teith lyik yuore baine poleit,
Or perle of Orient. 90
Have pitie, I 3ow pray.

Quhat tounge can tell 3our bewteis all,
And properteis preclair,
3our bodye brent, 3our middill small,
3our fingeris quhyte and fair? 95
One thing I wait, in erthe thair sall
None be found 3our compair.
Have pitie, I 3ow pray.

Now sen 3our giftis ar so greit,
That 3e can haue no peir, 100
Bewar 3e stein3ie thame not quyt
With crueltie seueir;
Do not into my duill delyt,

That comptis ȝow so deir.
Haue pitie, I ȝow pray. 105

To knaw the bewteis in ȝou bein,
Can not ane rude ingyine;
Ane lurdane spreit can not attein,
To ȝour graces divyne.
Bewar thairfoir, O ladye schein, 110
Cast not ȝour perle to suyne!
Haue pitie, I ȝow pray.

Beistow ȝour giftis then, I pray,
On sic as can thame sie,
Or at the list on sic as may 115
Esteme thame worthelie.
So sall I houpe that, ȝit sum day,
Ȝour reuthe sall rew on me.
Haue pitie, I ȝow pray.

Not willing longer ȝow molest, 120
I bid ȝow hairt 'Adiew!'
God gif ȝow grace to cheis the best,
Sen monye ȝow persew.
One thing I wait, amang the rest
Ȝe sall me find most trew, 125
Quhill lyife doe in me byide.

Sen ȝe so far haue persit my thocht,
Quhidder ȝe me accept or nocht,
My myinde sall neuer slyide.

Finis.

41.

O wratched waird, O fals fein3it fortoun!
O heiche vnhappie, O cruell destanie!
O clein mistemperit constellatioun!
O evill aspect in my nativitie!
O waird sisteris, quhat ellis 3ow at me   5
That all dois work this contrar my intent,
Quhilk is the caus that I murne and lament.

All thing dois quyte proceid aganis my will,
Bayth hevin and erthe ar contrair me coniurit;
I luif the gud and cummerit am with ill,   10
With wicked bait I daylie am allurit;
To cheis my lyif I can not be assurit,
Now till ane thing, now till ane other bent;
Quhat mervell is, thocht I murne and lament.

My hairt dois love the trew religioun,   15
And the trew God wald trewlie serue but dout;
Bot atheisme and superstitioun,
Hes so me now enuironit about,
That scantlie can I find quhair to get out,
Betuixt thir twa I am so daylie rent;   20
Quhat mervell is, thocht I murne and lament.

Vnder my God I wald obey my prince,
Bot ciuill weir dois so troubill that caise
That scairslie wait I quhome to reuerence,
Quhat till eschew, or quhat for till embrace.   25
Our nobillis now sa fikill ar, alace,
This day thay say the morne thay will repent.
Quhat mervell is, thocht I murne and lament.

Faine wald I leif in concord and in peace,
Without diuisioun, rancour, or debait,   30
Bot now, alace, in euerie land and place,
The fyire of haitred kindlit is so hait,
That cheritie doeth ring in none estait,
Thocht all concur to hurt the innocent;
Quhat mervell is, thocht I murne and lament.   35

I hait thraldome, ȝit man I binge and bek,
And iouk and nod sum patroun for to pleis;
I luif fridome, ȝit man I be subiect;
I am compellit to flatter with my fais,
I me torment sum other for till eis   40
Quha of my travell scantlie is content;
Quhat mervell is, thocht I murne and lament.

I luif nathing bot poure simplicitie,
And to dissembill man my tounge assyile;
The plaine hie path is maist plesand to me,   45
ȝit sumtyme man I arme me with a wyile,
Or doe I not men sall me sone begyile,
First me desave, syne lauch quhen I am schent;
Quhat mervell is, thocht I murne and lament.

I luif larges and liberalitie,   50
ȝit povertie to spend dois mak me spair;
I hait avarice and prodigalitie,
To git sum geir ȝit man I haue sum cair,
In vanitie syne man I it outwair,
Wone be ane wratch and into waistrie spent;   55
Quhat mervell is, thocht I murne and lament.

I luif the vertew honest chastitie,
To bawdische bourdes ȝit man I oft gif eir;
To satisfie ane fleschlie companie
Lyik ruffian I man me sumtyme beir;   60
In Venus scuill I man sum lessoun leir
Gif I wald comptit be courtes and gent;
Quhat mervell is, thocht I murne and lament.

I luif delyite and wrappit am in wo,
I luif plesour and plungit am in paine,   65
I list to rest, ȝit man I ryid and go,
And quhen I list to flie, I man remaine:
With warldlie cair a gentill hairt is slaine,
I feill the smart and dar not mak my plent;
Quhat mervell is, thocht I murne and lament.   70

I hait flatterie and into wordes plaine

And vnaffectit langage I delyit,
3it man I leir to flatter, gloise, and faine,
Quhodder I list to speik or 3it to wryte,
Or ellis men sall not count me worth a myite,   75
I salbe raknit rude or negligent;
Quhat mervell is, thocht I murne and lament.

Scorning I hait, 3it man I smyll and smirke
Quhen I the mokkis of other men behauld;
3ea! oftymes man I lauche, suppose I yrke   80
Quhen bitterlie thair tauntingis thay haue tauld;
And sumtyme als quhidder I nil or wald,
Ane scorne for scorne to gif I man tak tent;
Quhat mervell is, thocht I murne and lament.

I luif modest sober ciuilitie,   85
Mixt with gentill, courtes haimlines,
Bot ather man I vse scurrilitie,
Or ellis sic strainge and vncouth fremmidnes,
That I wait not how to mak mirrines,
Nor be quhat mein with men me to aquent;   90
Quhat mervell is, thocht I murne and lament.

With temperance I wald vse meit and drink,
And hes all surfet banket in dispyit,
And 3it at feist and banket man I wink,
And with thame hant quhair I haue no delyit;   95
I vse the euill and hes not all the wyit,
Thocht bodye bow, 3it dois the hairt dissent;
Quhat mervell is, thocht I murne and lament.

All coistlie claythis I compt not worth ane prein
Quhilk dois bot foster pryide and vanitie,   100
3it dar I not in commoun place be sein
Les I be clothit sumquhat gorgeouslie,
And be I not, then men sall talk of me,
And call me ather 'wratche', or 'indigent';
Quhat mervell is, thocht I murne and lament.   105

95 with] at MF

With hairt and mynd I luif humilitie,
And pauchtie pryde richt sair I doe detest,
Bot with the heiche ȝit man I heichlie be,
Or with that sort I sall not sit in rest.
This warld hes maid the proverb manifest: 110
'Quha is ane scheip, the wolf will sone him hent'.
Quhat mervell is, thocht I murne and lament.

With patience I wald richt faine ourcum,
With other mennis infirmiteis induire,
Bot then am I countit ane betie bum, 115
And all men thinkis a play me to iniure;
My sufferance to vyice dois thame alluire:
The mair I thoill, the mair I me torment;
Quhat mervell is, thocht I murne and lament.

I love silence and taciturnitie, 120
And in few woordes wald my purpois tell;
Ȝit sumtyme man I wordes multiplie,
And mak my toung to ring as dois ane bell;
With wilfull folk I man bayth cry and ȝell,
Or ȝeild to thame and quyte the argument; 125
Quhat mervell is, thocht I murne and lament.

And haittis all schaimles gloriositie,
And me delyt in modest schamfastnes,
Ȝit sall I not be countit worthe ane flie
Without I speik of all mater be ges, 130
Gloir and brag out, and tak ane face of bres,
Na thing misknaw vnder the firmament;
Quhat mervell is, thocht I murne and lament.

To chairge to ask to put ane man to paine,
I wald be courtes, gentill, and discreit; 135
Bot quhill I on ane ganand tyme remaine
I am ay seruit at the latter-meit,
And sum other is placit in my sait,

113 I wald richt faine ourcum] richt ferme I wald ourcum MF
127 And haittis] I hait MF

That thocht nocht schame for to be impudent;
Quhat mervill is, thocht I murne and lament. 140

I luif the vertew callit gratitude,
And lyik for lyik I ȝairne to ȝeild againe,
Ȝit can I not resaue bot ill for gud,
And thay in quhais dainger I remaine
I can not quyte, albeit I wald richt faine; 145
I want all micht, na power is me lent.
Quhat mervell is, thocht I murne and lament.

I luif iustice, and wald that euerie man
Had that quhilk richtlie dois to him pertene,
Ȝit all my kin, allya, or my clan, 150
In richt and wrang alwayis I man manteine;
I man applaud quhen thai thair materis mein,
Thocht conscience doe not thairto consent.
Quhat mervell is, thocht I murne and lament.

Sua thocht I luif the richt and not the wrang, 155
Ȝit gif ane freindis caus sall cum in hand,
It to assist I man bayth ryde and gang,
And as ane scoller leir to vnderstand
That it is not repute vyice in this land
For wrang to rander wrange equiualent; 160
Quhat mervell is, thocht I murne and lament.

Of trew freindis faine wald I haue sum stoir,
With thame the leig of amitie to bind,
Bot thocht I seik amang ane hundreth scoir,
Ane faithful freind now scantlie sall I find 165
That is not licht lyik weddercok in wind:
It is thocht vyice now to be permanent;
Quhat mervell is, thocht I murne and lament.

---

153 doe not thairto] thairto do nocht MF
173 me als burding] me burding als MF

In poetrie I pleis to pas the tyme,
Quhen cairfull thochtis with sorrow sail3eis me, 170
Bot gif I mell with meter or with ryme,
With rascall rymouris I sall reknit be,
Thay sall me als burding with monye lie,
In chairging me with that quhilk neuer I ment.
Quhat mervill is, thocht I murne and lament. 175

I wald travell and ydilnes I hait,
Gif I could find sum gud vocatioun;
Bot all for nocht! In vaine lang may I wait,
Or I get honest occupatioun.
Letteris ar lichtleit in our natioun, 180
For lerning now is nather lyif nor rent;
Quhat mervell is, thocht I murne and lament.

And schortlie now at ane worde to conclude,
I think this warld sa wrappit in mischeif,
That gud is ill, and ill compted is gud: 185
All thing I sie dois bot augment my greif;
I feill the woe and can not sie releif.
The Lordis plaige throwout the warld is went;
Quhat mervell is, thocht I murne and lament.

Finis quod Arbuthnet.

---

185 compted is] is callit MF
Attribution: unattributed in MF.

42.
Religioun now is reknit as ane fabill,
And feir of God is comptit foolischnes;
Thair is no man to leif now iudgit abill,
Bot cairles cativis full of cursednes;
Ane wicked lyif is iudgit welthines: 5
So vyce vertew, and vertew is thocht vyce;
O leving God, this chainge is wonder nyce.

Remors for syne is thocht bot foolisch feir,
And fleschlie loving iudgit libertie;
God is forʒet for gredines of geir; 10
All houpe of hevin is hauldin vanitie,
And hellis paine is comptit poetrie:
Swa vyce vertew, and vertew is thocht vyce;
O leving lord, this chainge is wonder nyce.

Vaine voluptie is thocht welth and weilfair, 15
And fekill ritches thocht felicitie;
Gud exerceis is thocht torment and cair,
And honest labour comptit miserie,
And best estait ay ydill for to be:
Sua vyice vertew, and vertew is thocht vyice; 20
O leving God, this chainge is wounder nyice.

Self luif is thocht a vertew souerane,
And privat proffeit prudent policie;
For commoun weill, travell, labour or paine,
Is comptit bot ane folisch fantasie. 25
Flatterie prevaillis, treuth makis inimitie:
Sua vyce vertew, and vertew is thocht vyce;
O leving Lord, this chainge is wonder nyce.

Treuth is iudgit bairnlie simplicitie,
And doubilnes of wosdome hes the name; 30

3 man to leif now] man now to lewe D
7. leving] lowing D (error of lowing for leving of repeated in each stanza until l. 64 and then again at l. 77)
14 wonder] verray MF

Meiknes is thocht pusillanimitie,
And vtterance is to forʒet all schame,
And merines is all men to defame:
Sua vyice vertew, and vertew is thocht vyce;
O leving Lord, this chainge is wonder nyce.   35

Craft and dissait is callit quick ingyne,
And fals semblance is callit courtesie.
He that can best his nychtbour vndermyne
Is hauldin schairpe, weill workand, and wittie,
And blak falset is namit sutteltie: 40
Sua vyice vertew, and vertew is thocht vyice;
O leving Lord, this chainge is wounder nyce.

Fersnes and yre is callit kein courage,
And patience is countit cowardnes;
Vaine braggis and boist is reknit vassalege,   45
And wode folie is hauldin hardines,
Bot modestie is termit simpilnes:
Swa vyce vertew, and vertew is thocht vyce;
O leving Lord, this chainge is wonder nyce.

Filthie lucre is countit honest schift,   50
And oppressioun is thocht bot princes play;
Maistreis and reif is gyding and gud thrift,
Fraud in iustice is thocht craftie delay;
Ane thing to think ane other ay to say
Is countit now for vertew and na vyce;   55
O leving Lord, this chainge is wonder nyce.

Knawledge of God is curiositie,
And wosdome standis in prophanitie;
Grave countenance is gloriositie;
Dissolute lyfe is thocht humanitie;   60
Gud fellowschip standis in vanitie:
Sua vyce vertew, and vertew is thocht vyce;
O leving Lord, this chainge is wonder nyce.

31 Meiknes] Wisdome D
45 braggis] brag MF   reknit] compte D

Now filthie speich is thocht purpose most meit,
And hourdome hauldin is ane prettie sport;   65
Pudicitie is countit lak of spreit,
And ruffianis now gettis best report;
All grave purpose is trist and but confort:
Swa vyce vertew, and vertew is thocht vyce;
O leving Lord, this chainge is wounder nyce.   70

Waisting is countit liberalitie,
And gredines is thocht ane gudlie gaine;
Honest spending is prodigalitie,
Ay gretest coist is vpon thingis vaine,
And that is socht quhairof thee flesche is faine: 75
Sua vyice vertew, and vertew is thocht vyce;
O leving Lord, this chainge is wonder nyce.

Pryde now is countit magnanimitie,
And lawlines is comptit bas courage;
Trew monissing dois mak inimitie,   80
And fein3it favour takkis vp the wage;
Trew preiching makis the wicked mair to raige,
The mair the[y] heir, the mair thay rin in vyce;
O leving Lord, this chainge is wonder nyce.

Quhen I behauld the warld thus rin areird,   85
And seis how vyce dois all vertew suppres,
Then I accuse my fortoun and my weird,
Throuch passioun and fleschlie febilnes.
Bot quhen I luik the deipis bothumles
Of Goddis secreit, then I clein recant,   90
And cry for mercy, and my crymes grant.

For I sould not my destanie despyte,
As ethnik authouris, full of ignorance,
Nor gif my weird and my wanhap the wyite,

74 coist is vpon] MF coist vpone MQ
79 comptit] iugeit MF
83 the[y]] thai MF
86 suppres] oppres MF
94 and] nor D

156

Nor of my birth warie the influence.   95
I ken richt weill nothing cummis be chance,
For fortoun is nocht bot ane fabill vaine,
Inuentit be philosophouris prophaine.

Bot euerie thing that in this warld dois fall
Dois cum be Goddis michtie Providence,   100
And be that spreit supercelestiall,
Be his divine and supreme sapience;
Thocht it exceid our dull intelligence
Of euerie thing the ressoun till invent,
Ʒit of our part we aucht to stand content.   105

And thocht the warld be holie set on ill,
Ʒit aucht we not to grudge nor to repyne,
Bot on the Lord depend and on his will,
Reposing ws on his power devyne.
Quha is his awin, he will thame neuer tyne,   110
Bot caus all thing to thame work for the best:
On this promeis we sould repose and rest.

For erdlie ioy then sould we not attend:
Erd is no place of our felicitie;
Welth in this warld is not our finall end,   115
Nor troubill heir is not our miserie.
Our trew rewaird nather the ein can sie,
Nor eiris heir, nor to the hairt is knawin,
Quhilk our Lord God prepairis for his awin.

In warld the prince of darknes hes impyire,   120
And gud men thoillis tribulatioun;
Bot sic tryall lyik ane clengeing fyire

103 divine and supreme] supreim divyne D
105 Ʒit] (faded in MF)
107 repyne] reproiwe D
117 the] our D
119 Lord God] gude Lord MF
120 In warld] In the warld MF
122 clengeing] MF chainging MQ

Then to prepair to thair saluatioun,
To walkin thame in thair vocatioun,
And monische thame thair missis to amend, 125
And to remember on the latter end.

For trowbill heir dois testifie our sin,
And dois convict ws of iniquitie;
Trowbill dois schaw the stait that we ar in,
And dois declair our imbecillitie; 130
Of Goddis wraithe it is ane testimonie
Aganis sin and crymes execrabill:
Sua to ws troubill is richt proffitabill.

Our conscience it movis to remoird
Quhen we thairof doe taist the bitternes; 135
It makis ws to cleiff vnto the Lord
Quhen we behauld our folische febilnes;
Throuch it we hait the warldis wretchidnes
Quhen we sie nothing heir that standis stabill:
Sua to ws troubill is richt proffitabill. 140

It garris ws luik vnto the latter end,
Quhen we sie not in erd ws to alluire;
It causis ws on Providence depend,
With patience it drawis till induire;
Of hevinlie ioy our houp it makis suire; 145
It dois conforme ws vnto Christ our heid,
And leirnis ws to muse vpon the deid.

And monye other thowsand proffeittis mo
Dois ay proceid of persecutioun,
For lak of tyme, quhilk I now let ourgo. 150
Bot this I gadder in conclusioun:
Thocht all this warld rin in confusioun,
3it godlie men sould not be drawin bak,
Bot of the present paine ane proffeit mak.

123 Then] Thame MF
124 walkin thame] walk in thame MF D
141 luik] wink D
145 our houp] of houp D

Ceis then my saull, and trowbill me no moir, 155
And let allaine all paynfull penseifnes,
And rander to thy hevinlie maker gloir,
Of paine and plesour, confort, and distres;
Content thy self with simpill sobernes,
And traist into the leving Lord alaine, 160
And for this warldlie troubill mak na maine.

For but all paine ane plesour heir perfyit
Into this warld be no wicht may be found,
Bot dulfull dolour and plesand delyit,
Ilkane with other be the top is bound; 165
And our foirfatheris Adamis deidlie wound,
In erd hes privat ws of perfyte ioy,
Quhy sould we then at troubill ws annoy?

Thocht God haue not in erthe appointit the
To bruik worschip and honour with the laif, 170
3it he will and hes ordanit that thow be
Ane quhome his sone the Lord Iesus sall saif.
Quhat gretar gift, I pray the, can thow craif?
With him he sall the na gud thing refuis:
Desist, thairfoir, thy fortoun till accus. 175

Desist and ceis thy self for to torment
For troubill, or for paine terrestriall;
Of thy estait stand quyet and content
Sen erthlie plesour is bot bestiall;
Bot lippin for the lyife celestiall: 180
Repose thy spreit vpon thys hevinlie ioy
Vnto the quhilk the Lord mot ws convoy.

M. A. Arbuthnot.

160 leving] lowing D
162 For but all paine ane] (half line faded in MF)
163 In] (faded in MF)
169 God] *om.* D
170 worschip and honour] honour and worschip D
181 thys] that MF
Attribution: Finis quod maister Alexander arbothnat In anno 1571. in MF; unattributed in D.

43. Aganis Sclanderous Toungis.

Gif bissie branit bodyis 3ow bakbyit,
And of sum wicked wittis 3e ar invyit,
Quha wald deprave 3our doingis for dispyit
Dispyis thair divelische deming and [defy it].
For fra that tyme and treuth thair tailles haue tryit,   5
The suithe sall schaw it self out to thair schame,
And be thair speiche thair spyit salbe espyit,
And haue na fayth nor force aganis 3our fame.

Misknaw thair craft and kyithe not as 3e kend it,
Thair doingis will thair deillingis sone detect;   10
For gif 3e freit, find fault, or be offendit,
Thair sawis to be suithe sum will suspect;
Bot gif thair leyis 3e lichtlie and neglect,
And lat thame lie, and lak 3ow as thay list,
Fra tyme thay find thair fabillis faill effect,   15
Thay will deny thair deilling and desist.

As furious fluiddis with greter force ay flowis
And starker stewin, quhen stoppit ar the streamis,
And gorgit wateris euer greater growis,
And forcet fyris with greater gleidis out glemis,   20
And ay mair bricht and birning is the bemis
Of Phoebus face, that fastest ar reflexit,
Sa gud renoun, quhilk railleris raige repremis,
Advancis moir, the moir invyaris vexit.

The moir thay speik, the soner ar thay spyit;   25
The moir thay lie, 3our lak wilbe the les;
The moir thay talk, the treuth is soner tryit;
The moir plainlie thair poysoun thay expres,
The les thay caus thair credit to incres;
The moir thay wirk, the les thair work avancis;   30
The moir thay preis 3our prayses to oppres,
The greter of 3our glorie is the glancis.

4 defy it] defyit MQ MF
23 repremis] reprevis MF

Doe quhat 3e dow detractouris ay will deme 3ow,
Quhais craft is to calumpniat but caus;
Bakbyteris ay be brutis will blaspheme 3ow,   35
Althocht the contrar all the countrie knawis,
And wald 3e waird 3ow vp betwene twa wais,
3it so 3e sall not from thair sayingis saue 3ow;
Bot gif thay sie 3e sussie of thair sais,
Blasone thay will, how euer the behaif 3ow.   40

Gif 3e be secreit, sad, and soliter,
Pairtlie thay speik that privelie 3e play;
And gif in publict places 3e repair,
3e seik to sie and to be sene, thay say.
War 3e a sanct, thay sould suspect 3ow ay;   45
Be 3e humaine, our humble thay will hald 3ow;
Gif 3e be strainge thay esteme 3ow our stay,
And trowis it is 3e, or ellis sum hes it tauld 3ow.

Gif 3e be blyithe, 3our lichtnes thay will lak;
Gif 3e be grave, 3our gravitie is geked;   50
Gif 3e lyik musick, mirth, or mirrie mak,
Thay sweir 3e feill ane string and bownis to brek it;
Gif 3e be seik, sum slichtis ar suspectit,
And all 3our sairris callit secreit sun3eis.
Dayis thay dispyte and be 3e daylie dekit: 55
'Persaue', thay say, 'the papingo that pruin3eis'.

Gif 3e be wyis and weill in vertew versit,
Cunning thay call vncumlie for 3our kynd,
And sayis it is bot slichtis 3e haue schersit,
To cloik the craft quhairto 3e are inclynd;   60
Gif 3e be meik, 3it thay mistak 3our mynd,
And sweiris 3e ar far schrewdar nor 3e seme:
Swa doe 3our best, thus sall 3e be defynd,
And all 3our deidis sall detractouris deme.

47 thay esteme 3ow] thai 3ow esteme MF
50 Geked] chekit MF

ȝit thay will leif thair leing at the last, 65
Fra thay advert invy will not availl;
Bakbyteris brutis bydis bot ane blast:
Thay flouris sone, but farder fruit thay faill.
Rek not, therfoir, how rascall raveris raill,
For neuer ȝit wes vertew without invy: 70
Swa promptlie sall ȝour patience prevaill,
Quhen thay perhap sic deming sall deny.

Finis.

70 neuer ȝit wes vertew] never wes vertew ȝit MF
72 sall deny] sall deir by MF
Attribution: Finis quod Iohne maitland commendatar of coldinghame and sone eftir L*ord* thirlstane and chancellor of scotland and died 3 october 1595 in MF.

44. Ane Admonitioun to My Lord of Mar, Regent.

Maist loyall lord, ay for thy lawtie lovit,
Now be not lakit for deloyaltie,
Thocht to the princes place thow be promovit;
Be not abusit be auctoritie,
Bot schaw thy treuth and thyne integritie,   5
Sen we so far our selfis hes submittit,
And king and countrie, lawis, and libertie,
Vnto thy cuire and credit haue committit.

Thy hous hes ay bene trustie and inteir,
Defamed not with fraud or fikilnes,   10
Bot schaw thy self bayth saige, schairpe, and sinceir,
Indewed with vertew, wit, and worthines,
Ingyne, iudgment, iustice, and gentilnes,
Craft, conduct, cair, and knawledge to command,
Heroik hairt, honour, and hardines,   15
Or in this storme thay stait will neuer stand.

We have the chosin to the cheifest chairge
Our tossit galay to gouerne and guyde.
Bewar! with bobbis scho is ane brukill bairge,
And may not bitter blastis weill abyide;   20
Thow may hir tyne in turning of ane tyde.
Cast weill thy cours, thow hes ane kittill cuire,
Of perellis pance, and for sum port provyide,
And anchour siker quhair thow may be suire.

All Boreas bitter blastis ar not blawin: 25
I feir sum boid and bobbis be behind;
Be tyde and tempest thow may be overthrawin,
And monye fairlie fortounis thow may find
As channellis, craiggis, beddis, and bankis blind,

2 Now] *om.* D
3 thow] ȝie D
8 Vnto thy cuire and credit] Vndir thy cuir and cair D
11 sinceir] seweir D
16 storme] storne MF
18 guyde] to gyde MF

Lekis, and wanlukis, quhairby thow may be loist. 30
Bewar, therfoir, with wedder, waw or wind,
With vncouth courses and vnknawin cost!

Thow may put all into apperand perrell,
Gif Englisch forces in this realme repair;
Sic ar not meit for to decyide our querrell: 35
Thocht farland foullis seme to haue fedderis fair,
Cum thay acquent, thay will creip inner-mair,
And wilbe noysum nichtbouris and enorme,
And schortlie will sit to our syidis as sair
As now the rebellis quhome thay sould reforme. 40

That freindschip is ay faithfullest a far,
And langest will induire with littill daill:
I feir be vse and tyme it work to war,
Fra thay aganis our partie anis prevaill.
Quha wait bot sen our selfis thay will assaill? 45
Auld fais ar seindill faithfull freindis found,
First help the half, and syne ourharle the haill,
Wilbe ane wofull weilfair to our wound.

Be thair exempill learne experience,
Ane forrane matche or maister to admit. 50
Reid quhen the Saxonis gat preeminence,
Howsone thay socht as soveranis for to sit;
Reid how thay forcit the Britonis folkis to flit,
And ȝit posseidis that peopillis propertie.
Be war! We may be walterit or we wit, 55
And lyikwyis lois our land and libertie.

Ane thowsand sic examples I could schaw,
And monye nobill natioun I may name
Quho loist at lenth thair libertie and law,

31 or] and MF
33 may] will MF
35 decyide] defend D
40 the] thy MF
43 be] with MF
45 our selfis thay will] thay will our selffis MF

And sufferit hes baith sorrow, scayth, and schame,   60
That for to help thair hairmes and hurt at hame
Fetchit forraine forces into thair support,
Quha fuilȝeit syne thair fredome, force, and fame,
And thame subdewit in the samyn sort.

Fleand Charibde, be war in Scill to fall,   65
And so eschew ciuill dissentioun,
That our estait to straingeris be not thrall.
The canker of our auld contentioun
Will keip no covene nor conventioun,
And gif thow gif thame credit to correct ws,   70
Be craftie wayis, will, and inventioun,
And subteill slichtis, thay will seik to subiec ws.

Scotland come neuer ȝit in servitude
Sen Fergus first, bot euer hes bene frie,
And hes bene alwayis bruiked be a bluid,   75
And king of kingis discendit, grie by grie.
Gif that it be in boundage brocht be the
Then waried war thy weirdis and wanhap!
Thairfoir, thir forraine fais sa foirsie
That catched we be not with thy eistclap.   80

Mark and mint at thy honour, laud, and prays,
The vertew, worschip, word, and vassalledge,
Of sic as hes done douchtellie in theis dayis,
To keip this realme from thraldome and boundage.
Mark als the vyilde vituper and the waige   85
Of vntreuth, tressoun, and of tyrannie,
And how sone honour hes ane heritage,
And lyffis lost, for thair deloyaltie.

63 fuilȝeit syne thair] MF fuilȝit thair MQ D
69 covene] conand MF
71 wayis] way MF
80 eistclap] efte[r]clap MF
81 thy] the MF
87 ane heritage] and heretage

So for thy factis thow be suire to find
The lyik rewaird of vertew or of vyce. 90
Be not, thairfoir, syild as ane bellie-blind,
Nor let thy self be led vpon the yce;
Not to content thy marrowis covatice,
Put not thy self in perrell for to peres,
Nor beir the blame quhair otheris takis the pryce, 95
Nor beit the bus quhair otheris eatis the bereis.

The trone of tryall and theatre trew,
Is for to regne and reull aboue the rest:
Quho hes the wogue him all the warld dois vew,
And magistrat the man dois manifest. 100
Sua sen thow hes the princes place possest,
Luik to be praysit as thow playis thy pairt,
And as thow luiffis so luiffed be and lest,
And alwayis delt with efter thy desert.

Finis.

89 suire] sene MF

45.
Gif it be trew that storeis doe rehers,
That sorrow souppis sinceritie of sens;
Gif it be suithe that poetis put in vers
That langour makis dull intelligens
Of the wryter, gif suire be the sentens, 5
That troublit hairt makis a rurell ryme;
Thocht this, my wryt, be void of eloquens,
Accuse not me bot wyite the wicked tyme.

The simpill wit, and schairpnes of ingyne,
Quhilk quhylome wes, now quyte is taine away; 10
The stering spreit, quhilk poetis call devyne,
Into my febill breist I find decay.
I nather courage haue to sing or say,
Quhen I behauld this warldis wickednes,
And quhen I find I am so far thame fray, 15
Quha wes my onlie confort and glaidnes.

My fais fall and freindis gud succes
Sumtyme my pen wes bessie till endyite;
Of nobill men the valiant prowes
Sumtyme my courage ȝairnit for to wryte; 20
The laud, honour, and the prayses greit
Of thame, sumtyme, I wissed till advance,
Quhome now, of neid, my hairt hes in dispyte,
And quhome I wyit of this vnhappie chance.

Then, maistres, luik na mair for onye fruitt, 25
Or onye worke to cum of my ingyne,
For now I nather cair for fame nor bruit;
I haue sa tint that I na mair can tyne;
Gaine is my huik, and cuttit is my lyne,
Amang thir poetis I will fische na mair. 30
No man regairdis renoun in rowyne:
In miserie I sussie not for gloir.

My hairt fainteth, my fingeris failleth me
To wryte, or dyte, of mirrines to mein,
Finding me far fra that gud cumpanie, 35
Sa willinglie quhair I sumtyme haue bein;

And knawing the sorrow that I than sustein,
Be fein3eit falset and vnthankfulnes,
The moir I think, the moir my woundis grein,
My breist, in baill, boudnes with bitternes.   40

M. Arthbuthnot

TEXTS

46. Ane Consolatore Ballad to Sir Richart Maitland of Lethingtoun Knicht.

Tobie most trew, in monye troubillis tryit,
And Iob most iust, in Goddis iudmentis reioyis;
Of prudence perle, now in 3our paine applyit,
Doe quhat 3e dow all dolour to depois.
Nane can eschew, nor have thair chance as chois,   5
Thairfoir be glaid and gif all gloir to God,
Quhais bontie neuer dois abandoun those
That restis on him, reiosing in his rod.

3our greif is greit, I graunt, in sa greit aage,
Thus to be maid a martyre, but a mis,   10
With los, alace, so lairge of linage,
And childrein wyse and verteous at 3our wis,
Besyide aboundance of all erdlie blis.
Bot weill 3e wait all warldlie welthe is vaine:
Then thank 3our God and tak na thocht of this;   15
Goddis giftis thay wer, glaidlie gif thame againe.

3our wit with vertew in 3our woe declair;
Let no mishap nor miserie 3ow move,
Nor be not drawin be dolour to dispair,
Bot patientlie prays God that dois 3ow prove.   20
Think it not baill, bot blising from above,
And singe maist suir that 3e ar not forsakin;
For ay sic lote is linked to his love,
Quhairof tak this 3our tryell for a takin.

For quha with Christ cravis to communicat,   25
The cairfull croce man carie as thair heid

5 thair] his R
6 Glaid] glair D
10 Thus] This MF R
11 of] MQ of 3our MF R
13 aboudance] all boundance D
14 all] that R
17 with] and MF R; 23. to] with D

169

Be paine, his passioun, and participat,
Suffer ennuy, necessitie, and neid,
Duill and disdaine, distres, dolour, and dreid;
And patientlie pas our this pilgramage 30
Be paine to perfyte plesour to proceid
In hevin, our hairbour, hame, and heritage.

For as the mas, misforme of mudie mold,
Be quelling dois fair qualiteis acquyire,
And grethed in gleid growis glorious, gleting gold; 35
Sa in afflixioun, as ane furneis fyire,
We ar prepared be prove to the impyire
Quhair God sic schreudis sall from his sanctis dissever
That hevin hes heir, and hence none other hyire
In warldlie welth wrapit in woe for euer. 40

Quhair, as the chosin be correctioun,
As in the fyire are fraimed to his feir,
Bot euer, with so fatherlie affectioun,
That in thair paine his pitie dois appeir;
And blist ar thay dois sa thair burding beir, 45
That faintis not, bot faithfull still ar found,
And patientlie in pruif dois perseueir,
For ay the rod dois to thair rest redound.

To mak his micht and mercie manifest,
God his peculiar, proper peopill previt; 50
Bot ay thair trowbillis turnit to the best
That constantlie vntill his cunnand cleved.
Evin so ar now the godlie greitlie greved,
And lothsum is the lot of the elect;
Bot thay at lenth with ioy salbe relevit, 55
That patientlie his plesour dois expect.

The croce of Christ, and eik his cair contempill,
Our aduocat and most assured ayd;
Propone that perfyte patroun for exempill

34 fair] seir MF, feir R
40 in woe] wp to wo MF R
46 faithfull] faithfullie R

For to withstand all woe that can invaid. 60
Gif him all gloir, and in 3our greif be glaid,
Sen 3e haue lerned 3e ar the Lordis elect,
Sa suir seilled vp, sen him self hes said:
'Quhome that I luif, be croce I doe correct'.

I neid no auld exempill to receit, 65
As Tobie, Iephe, Iob, Iacob, or Samson;
3our self may be a patroun mair perfyte
Of patience, and perles paragon:
A thowsand tymes 3e thame excell ilkone.
In frowning Fortoun nane I find so fit 70
As perfyte patroun to 3ow to propone,
As 3e 3our self, gif 3e will vse 3our wit.

3e ar so wittie, verteous, and wyis,
I dar not preis to preitche 3ow patience
With 3our awin wit, bot wis 3ow to advyis, 75
And to continew clein in conscience.
Let prudence, prattick, and experience,
3our weill and woe advyisedlie revolue,
So thocht 3e seme a sessoun in suspence,
3our ressoun ryipe will richtlie 3ow resolue. 80

Wo workis to weill be vyice alternatiue,
And tein and troubill baith ar transitorie;
Quhen syt and sorrow semis superlatiue,
Sagis sould seme leist sussious and sorie:
The greter greif, the greter is the glorie, 85
Quhen is maistred with magnanimit mynd.
Let vertew then and wit haue victorie,
According to the courage of 3our kynd,

63 Sa] Sene MF R
69 Ilkone] aboue D
73 wittie] worthie MF R
77 prattick] practice MF R
82 ar] *om.* D
86 is] it is MF R   Magnanimit] magnanimie MF R

Quhilk wes ay wittie, vail3eant, and wyis,
Magnanime, manfull, and of mirrie muid, 90
Of prudence baith, and prowes had the pryis,
Of modestie, meiknes, and mansuetud.
Greit is the gloir of 3our grandfatheris gud,
That stoutlie stuid in monye stalwart stour;
Bauld and but blot or blemische is 3our bluid, 95
And ay hes bene in honour to this hour.

Sic destanie and derf devoring deid,
Oft hes 3our hous in hazaird put of auld;
Bot 3our foirbearis fraward fortounis feid,
And bitter blastis ay buir with breistis bauld; 100
Luit wanwerdis work and walter as thay wauld,
Thair hardie hairtis hawtie and heroic,
For fortounis feid or force wald neuer fauld,
Bot stormis withstuid with stomak stout and stoic.

Renowned Richard, of 3our raice recoird, 105
Quhais prayis and prowes can not be exprest,
Mair lustie linage neuer had a lord,
For he begat the bauldest bairnis and best,
Maist manfull men, and madinis maist modest,
That euer wes sen Priamis tyme of Troy; 110
Bot piteouslie thay peirles perlis a pest
Bereft him all bot burdalane, a boy.

Him self wes aged, his hous hang be a hair,
Doull and distres almost to deid him drew;
3it burdalaine, his onlie sone and air, 115
As worthie, wyse and vail3eant as the lave,
His hous vpheld, quhilk 3e with honour have;
So nature then the lyik enuy and name,
In kyndlie cair dois kyndlie courage crave
To follow him in fortoun and in fame. 120

89 wittie] worthy MF R
90 of mirrie muid] merie of muid R
91 pryis] prais R

Richard he wes, Richard 3e ar also,
And Maitland als, and magnanime ar 3e,
In als greit age, als wrappit ar in wo.
Sevin sonnis 3e had, micht contravaill his thrie,
Bot burdalane 3e haue behind, as he.   125
The Lord his linnage so enlairge and lyne,
As monye hundreth nepotis, grie be grie,
Sen Richard wes, as hundreth 3eiris ar hyne.

3our cairfull caice to his is so conforme,
Greit caus 3e haue lyik confort to consave.   130
Esteme this sturt as ane vnstabill storme:
Will God, quha him sic grace and glaidnes gave,
Sic hap and honour efter harme to have,
Vphauld his hous so mony hundreth 3eiris.
Let 3our gray hairis, but greif, go to the grave   135
With better hairt, mair bitternes that beiris.

Na na! confide his clemence will not quyte
Sic sobernes with sic seueritie,
Bot send 3ow schortlie secours in 3our syte,
Peace, perfyte plesour, and prosperitie,   140
And propagat so 3our posteritie
From sone to sone, as he did Sarais seid.
Seik him and serue him with sinceritie:
He will deny 3ow nathing in 3our neid.

3our hous is build on him, as he hes biddin,   145
For not availlis warldlie welthis or wit;
Gif sic had seruit, forsuith, it had not sliddin.
God is the ground: be him it man grow greit,
Not be 3our brain, bot be his benefeit.

122 ar 3e] than 3e ar MF, 3e ar R
126 and] in D
128 ar] *om.* R
131 as] *om.* D
134 Vphauld] Wpheld MF
137 his] this D
145 is] hes R   he hes] 3e haue R
149 his] 3our D

So now I houp his help and halie hand 150
Sall found and fix it faster on ane fit,
Nor quhen it semed be stranger stouppis to stand.

Iob wes deiected and iudgit lang vniust,
Puire with reproche he did his paine deploir,
Be miserie almost moved to mistrust, 155
Sa greitlie God him greifed to his gloir;
Syne rest, renoun, and ritches did restoir,
And for his sonnis, that suddanlie wer slaine,
By doubling of all blis he had befoir,
Encressed his seid with sonis sevin againe. 160

And quhen Tobias for his sone tuik thocht,
Baith blind and boun almost to beg his breid,
He send him sicht and saif his sone hame brocht,
And with aboundance blist him to the deid,
And luit him sie his sonis sonis seid. 165
Sa to his awin his ayd is alwayis ane:
He will confort ȝow, constantlie confeid,
Bring ȝow from baill and blis ȝour burdalane.

Ȝour hous of auld oft had no hair but ane,
Ȝea, worne away oftymis the warld it wenit; 170
Quhen it was waik, and without vther waine,
Oftymis his micht and mercie did maintein it;
And laitlie onlie on the Lord it lenit,
Was demed doun and to the dust deiectit,
Quha send ȝour self to saue it and [susten it], 175
And in renoun and ritches to [erect it].

152 Nor] *om.* MF R
155 mistrust] distrust R
156 greifed] moved R
163 He] And D
171 waik] *om.* D
173 onlie] *om.* D
174 doun] *om.* D
175 susten it] sustenit MQ MF R
176 erect it] erectit MQ MF R

And gif 3e mark his merceis moniefauld,
Forsuith sensyne he hes not bene a sleip,
Bot did 3our baill most bonteouslie behauld.
3our onlie sone, quha semed a slauchter scheip,   180
With als greit cair he did conserue and keip,
As Noe, Lothe, or Susan, monye wayis;
And in sic stormis as may gar straingeris steip,
Sustenis 3our self and gevis 3ow monye dayis.

Think not sic pitie is but providence,   185
Or he hes wrocht sa wonderouslie in vaine,
Or that his micht and mercie maist immens,
In thair distres his darlingis will disdaine.
No pitie is a perfyte presage plaine
He will 3our hous in honour 3it vphauld,   190
A monument of mercie to remaine,
From hence furth ay, as it hes bene of auld.

Thairfoir reioyis in him and tak 3our rest;
As 3e wald wische, 3our wo away sall wend;
Be mirrie for his mercie manifest.   195
Promptlie a perfyte plesour dois portend,
And he 3our hous, 3our self, and sone will send
Mair solace schortlie nor 3e can consave,
Helthe, ioy in hairt, honour, and in the end
3our gray heid sall with glaidnes go to grave.   200

Finis.

183 in] *om.* R
187 immens] *om.* R
196 portend] pretend MF R
198 consave] contein D
Attribution] Finis quod in MF.

47.
Vp hairt! Thow art the pairt
Of man most souuerane;
Let seruile memberis smart
And bound alaine remaine;
For gif thow doe not staine   5
Thy treuth and honestie,
How can thow be in paine?
No, suirlie thow art frie.

The boundage of the hairt
With schame is for to serue,   10
And from his honest pairt
And vertew for to suerue.
Gif thow doe not deserue,
That blot of infamie,
Thocht captive flesche do sterue,   15
ȝit suirlie thow art frie.

Thocht fortoun, fraud, or force
Detein the in suspence,
Gif thow haue no remorce
In mynde, nor conscience,   20
And hes done none offence,
Thocht in captiuitie
Thow suffer violence,
ȝit suirlie thow art frie.

Bot gif thow micht be taxit,   25
Or falset with the found,
The corps micht be relaxit,
Bot schame sould the confound;
And gif the suche a wound
Sould lest perpetuallie,   30

10 serue] serue MF R *altered to* suarue
13 doe] *om.* R
17 suspence] dispence MF R
Attribution] finis Huius in MF, R.

And mak the sclaue so bound
That thow couldest neuer be frie.

Bot sen it is no so,
Reioyis and tak the rest;
Thocht Fortoun be thy fo 35
Hir frowning sall not lest,
Bot cummis for the best,
Thy treuth to testifie;
So thocht thow be opprest
3it suirlie thow art frie. 40

Then, hairt, heild not ane hair,
Nor in thy prisoun ply;
Thy vertew now declair,
And fortounis feid defy;
For tyme thy treuth sall try, 45
And gif the victorie
Of fortoun and invy,
And thow for euer be frie.

Finis.

48.
Declair, ȝe bankis of Helicon,
Pernassus hillis and daillis ilkon,
And fontaine Caballein,
Gif onye of ȝour muses all
Or nymphes may be peregall, 5
Vnto my ladye schein;
Or of the ladyis that did lave
Thair bodyis by ȝour brim,
So seimlie war, or sa suave,
So bewtifull or trim. 10
Contempill, exempill
Tak be hir proper port,
Gif onye so bonye,
Amang ȝow did resort.

No no, forsuith wes neuer none, 15
That with this perfyte paragon
In beawtie micht compair;
The muses wald haue gevin the grie
To hir, as to the aperse,
And peirles perle preclair, 20
Thinking with admiratioun,
Hir persone so perfyite;
Nature, in hir creatioun,
To forme hir tuik delyite.
Confes then, expres then, 25
Ȝour nymphes and all thair trace,
For Bewtie, of dewtie,
Sould ȝeild and give hir place.

Apelles, quha did sa decoir
Dame Venus face and breist befoir 30
With colouris exqueseit,
That nane micht be compared thairtill;
Nor ȝit na painter had the skill,
The bodye to compleit;
War he this lyvelie goddes grace 35
And bewtie to behauld,
He wald confes his craft and face
Surpast a thousand fauld:

Not abill in tabill,
With colouris competent, 40
So quiklie, or liklie,
A forme to represent.

Or had my ladie bene alyve
Quhen the thrie goddessis did stryve,
And Paris wes maid iudge, 45
Fals Helene, Menelaus maik,
Had neuer caused King Priamus wraik
In Troy, nor had refudge;
For ather scho the pryiss had wone
As weill of womanheid, 50
Or ellis with Paris, Priamus sone,
Had gone in Helenis steid,
Estemed and demed,
Of colour twyis so cleir,
Far suetar and metar, 55
To haue bein Paris feir.

As Phoebus tress, hir hair and breeis
With angell hew and cristall eeis,
And toung most eloquent;
Hir teithe as perle in curall set, 60
Hir lippis and cheikis pumice fret,
As rose maist redolent;
With yvoire nek and pomellis round,
And comlie intervall;
Hir lillie lyire so soft and sound, 65
And proper memberis all;
Bayth brichter and tichter,
Then marbre poleist clein,
Perfyter and quhyter,
Then Venus, luiffis quein. 70

Hir angell voice, in melodie,
Dois pas the hevinlie harmonie,
And Sirens songe most sueit.
For to behauld hir countenance,
Hir gudlie grace and governance, 75
It is a ioy compleit.
Sa wittie, verteous, and wyis,

And prudent but compair,
Without all wickednes and vyce,
Maist douce and debonair;   80
In vesture and gesture
Maist seimlie and modest,
With wourdis and bourdis,
To solace the opprest.

Na thing thair is in hir at all   85
That is not supernaturall,
Maist proper and perfyte,
So fresche, so fragrant, and so fair
As dees, and Dame Bewteis air,
And dochter of delyte;   90
With qualeteis and forme devine,
Be nature so decoird,
As goddes of all feminine,
Of men to be adoird;
Sa blissed, that wissed,   95
Scho is in all mennis thocht,
As rarest and fairest,
That euer nature wrocht.

Hir luikis as Titan radiant,
Wald pers ane hairt of adamant,   100
And it to love alluire;
Hir birning beawtie dois embrayis
My breist, and all my mynd amayis,
And bodye haill combuire.
I haue na schift bot to resing   105
All power in hir handis,
And willinglie my hairt to bring,
To bind it in hir bandis:
To langwiss in angwiss,
Soir woundit and opprest;   110
Forleit it or treit it,
As scho sall think it best.

I houp sa peirles pulchritud
Will not be voyide of mansuetud,
Nor cruellie be bent;   115
Sa ladye, for thy courtesie,

Have pitie of my miserie,
And lat me not be schent.
Quhat prayis haue 3e to be seueir,
Or cruellie to kill   120
3our wofull, woundit prisoneir,
All 3ouldin in 3our will,
Ay preissing but ceissing,
Maist humlie for to serue:
Then pruif me and luif me,   125
As deidis sall deserue.

And gif 3e find dissait in me,
Or ony quent consait in me,
3our bontie till abuse,
My dowbill deling be disdaine   130
Acquyt, and pay me hame againe,
And flatlie me refuise.
Bot sen I mein sinceritie,
And trew luif from my hairt,
To quyite me with austeritie,   135
Forsuith, war not 3our pairt;
Or trap me, or wrap me,
Maist wrangfullie in wo,
Foirsaking and wraiking,
3our seruand as 3our fo.   140

Alace! let not trew amitie
Be quyite with so greit crueltie,
Nor seruice be disdaine;
Bot rather, hairt, be reuthfull,
And 3e sall find me treuthfull,   145
Constant, secreit, and plaine.
In sorrow lat me not consome,
Nor langer dolour drie,
Bot suddanlie pronunce the dome
Gif I sall leif or die;   150
That having my craving,
Mirthfull I may remaine,
Or speid sone the deid sone,
And put me out of paine.

Finis.

49.
As Phoebus, in his spheris hicht
Precellis the kaip Crepusculein,
And Phoebe all the starris licht,
3our splendour so, madame, I wein,
Dois onlie pas all feminine,   5
In sapience superlative,
Indewit with vertewis sa devine,
As leirned Pallas rediviue.

And as be hid vertew vnknawin,
The adamant drawis yron thairtill,   10
3our courtes nature so hes drawin
My hairt, 3ouris to continew still;
Sa greit ioy dois my spreit fulfill,
Contempling 3our perfectioun;
3e weild me holie at 3our will   15
And ravis my affectioun.

3our perles vertew dois provoike,
And loving kyndnes so dois move
My mynd to freindschip reciproc,
That treuth sall try, sa far above,   20
The auntient heroicis love,
As salbe thocht prodigious,
And plaine experience sall prove
Mair holie and religious.

In amitie Perithous   25
To Theseus wes not so traist;
Nor, till Achilles, Patroclus;
Nor Pilades to trew Orest;
Not 3it Achates luif to lest
To gud Aenee; nor sic freindschip   30
Dauid to Ionathan profest;
Nor Titus trew to kynd Iosip.

Nor 3it Penelope, I wis,
So luiffed Vlisses in hir dayis;
Nor Ruth, the kynd Moabitis,   35
Nohemie, as the scripture sayis;

Nor Portia, quhais worthie prayisis
In Romaine historeis we reid,
Quha did devoir the fyrie brayisis,
To follow Brutus to the deid. 40

Wald michtie Ioue grant me the hap
With 3ow to haue 3our Brutus pairt,
And metamorphosing our schap,
My sex intill his vaill convert.
No Brutus then sould caus ws smart, 45
As we doe now, vnhappie wemen!
Then sould we bayth, with ioyful hairt,
Honour and blis the band of Hymen.

3ea, certainlie we sould efface
Pollux and Castoris memorie, 50
And gif that thay deseruit place
Amang the starris, for loyaltie,
Then our mair perfyte amitie,
Mair worthie recompence sould merit
In hevin, eternall deitie 55
Amang the goddis till inherit.

And as we ar, thocht till our wo,
Nature and fortoun doe coniure,
And Hymen also be our fo;
3it luif of vertew dois procuire 60
Freindschip, and amitie sa suire,
With sa greit feruencie and force,
Sa constantlie, quhilk sall induire,
That not bot deid sall ws divorce.

And thocht aduersitie ws vex, 65
3it, be our freindschip salbe sein,
Thair is mair constancie in our sex
Then euer amang men hes bein:
No troubill, torment, greif, or tein,
Nor erthlie thing sall ws disseuer; 70
Sic constancie sall ws mantein
In perfyte amitie, for euer.

Finis.

50.
Lord God, how lang will this law lest,
Be quhilk sum trew men ar opprest,
Of [hous] and landis dispossest,
Without ane caus?
Sum sair ar drest,   5
Sum sair molest,
Be new found lawis.

For lak of iustice sum gettis wrang,
And sum be tratouris tyrannis strang;
Sum in the sessioun lyis our lang,   10
And hulie speidis.
Sair is the sang
Poure folkis amang,
That iustice neidis.

Be mein of court sum gettis land,   15
Thinking that conqueis ay sall stand,
Thocht courtis ay hes bene chaingeand
As dois the mone,
That sum hafand
Ane work in hand,   20
And leif it sone.

Think 3e, that ar sa proud oppressouris,
Thocht 3e in court haue intercessouris,
That God will thoill sa greit transgressouris
Vnpunischit be: 25
Fra God digressouris,

1 this] sic MF R
3 Hous] housis MQ MF R
5 sair ar drest] ar sair drest MF R
9 tratouris tyrannis strang] tretit tirranttis strang MF R
13 folkis] folk MF R
17 ay] *om.* D
20 Ane work] aneuche MF R
21 leif] lost MF
26 God] MF R Goddis MQ D

And wrang possessouris,
Repent sall ȝe.

In haist, I counsell ȝow, thairfoir,
All gottin wrangouslie restoir, 30
Or ȝe sall not cum to the gloir
Of hevinis impyire,
Bot euer moir,
Tormentit soir,
In hellis fyire. 35

Lord, punische thame that ay pretendit
For to doe wrang, or it defendit;
In haist lat thame be apprehendit
And thoill the law,
Or gar thame mend it
Quhome thay offendit 40
In deid or saw.

And ȝe that hes the law to leid,
Without favour, friendschip, or feid,
Ay forder iustice to proceid 45
Indifferentlie.
Ȝour proces speid,
Help thame hes neid,
Quhat euer thay be.

S. R. M.

29 In haist] MQ R In Christ MF
39 mend it] MF D mendit MQ
Attribution: Quod richart maitland of lethingtoune knycht in MF.

51.
Sair is the recent murmour and regrait
Amang the leigis, rissin of the lait,
Throw all the countrie bayth of riche and puire,
Plenand vpon the Lordis of the Sait,
That thair lang proces may na man induire. 5

The barounis sayis that thay haue far mair spendit
Vpon the law, or thair mater wes endit,
Nor it wes worth; thairfoir richt sair thay rew
To found ane plie that euer thay pretendit,
Bot left it to thair airis to persew. 10

The puire folk sayis that thay, for falt of spending,
Man leif the law, it is sa lang in ending;
Lang proces thame to povertie hes brocht,
For of thair scayth be law can get na mending,
That thay ar faine to grie for thing of nocht. 15

Sum gevis the wyit that thair is on the sessioun
Sum not sa cunning, nor of sa gud discretioun
As thay befoir into that rowme hes bein,
Quhilk doing iustice keipit thair professioun,
Of quhome thair wes na caus for to complein. 20

Now, ʒe that ar not of this sait content,
Pas to the prince to him ʒour caus lament,
And him exhort, and pray effectiouslie,
That in that sait he wald na man present
In tyme to cum, bot thay that ar worthie. 25

Gud cunning men, that ar wyis and discreit,
Practiciens gud, and for that senat meit,

8 wes] *om.* D
16 Sum gevis the wyit] Thai giff sum wyt MF
18 As thay] As thair MF
19 Doing] to do MF
22 caus] caice MF
24 in that] to that MF
27 for that] to that MF

Men of gud conscience, honestie, and fame,
That can, with wit and treuth, all materis treit,
And hes be prudence purchast ane gud name. 30

And syne gar call the Colledge of Iustice,
All thair dependeris, and vtheris that ar wyis,
And trye the caus of law the langsumnes,
And gar thame sone sum gud ordour devyis,
To furder iustice, and schortin the lang proces. 35

Bot gif this mater vnmendit be oursein,
The leigis can na greter sckayth sustein,
For na man sall be suir of land or geir,
The trew and poure salbe oppressed clein,
And this colledge sall not lang perseueir. 40

And gif this sait of senatouris gang doun
The spunk of iustice in this regioun,
I wait not how this realme sall rewlit be;
Better it wer gud reformatioun,
Nor let it perische so imprudentlie. 45

For gif this sait of iustice sall not stand,
Then euerie wicked man, at his awin hand,
Sall him revenge as he sall think it best;
Ilk bangeister and limmer of this land
With frie brydill sall doe quhat pleis thame best. 50

Our souuerane lord, to this mater haue ee,
For it pertenis to thy maiestie
This colledge to vphauld, or lat it doun;
Bot will thow it vphauld, as it sould be,
It will the helpe for to maintein thy croun. 55

41 And gif] Bot giff MF
42 in this] off this MF
43 not] *om.* D
45 to imprudentlie] sa vnprudentle MF D
47 euerie] ilk ane MF
50 quhat pleis thame best] quhilk thing thame lest MF, quhat pleis him best D

Caus ilk day so faist dois multiplie,
That with this sait can not over takin be,
Bot wald thy hienes thairof eik the nummer
Of senatouris men, cunning and godlie,
Wald monie matter end that makis cummer.   60

Sir, at thy gift is monye abeceis,
Personagis, provestreis, and prebendareis;
Now sen doun is the auld religioun,
To eik sum lordis gif sum benefeis,
And sum to help the auld fundatioun.   65

Becaus the lordis hes our litill feis,
Bot of vncertaine casualiteis,
Of quhilk thay neuer get payment compleit;
And now sic derth is rissin, all men seyis,
That coist ane pound befoir now coistis thrie.   70

Sir, thow may gar vnhurt thy propertie,
The sait of iustice weill advancit be,
Quhilk, being done, thair sall daylie incres
Into this land gud peace and policie,
And thow be brocht to honour and riches.   75

O leving Lord, support this cruell sait,
And give thame grace to gang the narest gait
Iustice to doe with expeditioun,
And bring all thing againe in gud estait,
Following the first gud institutioun.   80

S. R. M.

68 compleit] compleitlie MF
76 leving] loweing D; cruell] ciwell MF
Attribution] Quod Richard maitland of Lethingtoune in MF; Finis S. R. M. in D.

52.
This warld so fals is and vnstabill,
Of gredines vnsatiabill;
In all estaitis sic doubilnes,
To find trew freindis few ar abill,
For keipit is na auld kyndnes.					5

Thocht ȝe doe plesour to greit men,
Thairfoir thay will ȝow scantlie ken;
Gif ȝe haue ocht with thame to dres,
Ȝe ar not abill to get ben,
For kepit is na auld kyndnes.					10

Thocht ȝe haue servit monye ane ȝeir
Ane lord, on ȝour awin cost and geir,
And ȝe be fallin in distres,
Ȝow to releif he wilbe sueir,
And count nathing ȝour auld kyndnes.				15

Thocht ȝe haue ladyis seruit lang,
And previt ȝour pith hes thame amang,
And ȝe of Venus game decres,
Out of thair court then man ȝe gang,
Not regairding ȝour auld kyndnes.				20

Sum to thair nychtbouris hes bene kynd
That now thairof hes neuer mynd,
Bot notit with newfangilnes
Of ingraitnes it hes ane stryind
That can not keip na auld kyndnes.				25

Sum to communiteis hes done
That ingraitlie forȝeit it sone,
Sua full thay ar of fikilnes,

1 so fals is] is sa fals D
3 In] Of D
16–20] *om.* D
17 And previt ȝour pith hes] And hes ȝour pithe prewit MF

Changing as oft as dois the mone,
And cuiris not for auld kyndnes. 30

Sum did for thame in court and sessioun,
That now falslie, without discretioun,
In tyme of troubill and busines,
Melled with thair land, geir, and possessioun,
That schew to thame sa greit kyndnes. 35

Thair is that sum men did reset,
With meit and claythis hes him bet,
That efter in court gat entres,
And wald not ken him quhen thay met,
Of quhom he gat sa greit kyndnes. 40

Thocht 3e with courteouris hes bein
Acquentit lang, be onye mein,
And 3e thame chairge with busines,
Ar abill to misknaw 3ow clein,
And will for3et auld kyndnes. 45

Sen in this warld, in na degrie,
Is kyndnes nor fidelitie,
Lat ws pray God, of his gudnes,
To bring ws to the hevinis so hie,
Quhairin thair is perfyte kyndnes. 50

S. R. M.

29 Changing] Thai chenge MF
34 land, geir] geir land D
39 And] That MF
41 Thocht 3e] 3e that MF
45 And will for3et auld kyndnes] bot 3e be buddis by thair kyndnes MF
Attribution] Quod richart maitland of lethingtoun knycht in MF; finis quod S.R.M. in D.

53.
Dreid God and luif him faythfullie,
Have fayth in Chryist ay constantlie,
And with thy nychtbour cheritie;
For grace on God ay call.
Obey and serue ȝour prince trewlie, 5
Keip iustice, peace, and vnitie,
Fra all sort of seditioun flie,
And doe ressoun to all.

Hait pryide, invy, and lecherie,
All yre, sueirnes, and gluttonie, 10
Avarice and idolatrie,
All treasoun and debaittis.
Love vertew, richt, and honestie,
In cheritabill deidis exerced be,
All lesume promeis keip iustlie 15
To all maner of staittis.

Keip ȝow fra prodigalitie,
Oppressioun, wrang, and crueltie,
And fra all vyce and vanitie,
And ground ȝow vpon treuth. 20
Hant gud, and honest cumpanie,
Vse wyse counsale and gravitie,
Do all ȝour thingis discreitlie,
And of the puire haue reuth.

S. R. M.

5 ȝour prince] the quein MF
Attribution] Quod R. m. of Ledingtoun knycht in MF.

54.

Ground the ay on gudnes,
Rewll the with richteousnes,
In tyme doe thy busines,
And cheis ay the best.
Preis the not to oppres, 5
Help ay the fatherles,
Have na pryide nor proudnes:
This warld will not lest.

In troubill tak patience,
Keip clein thy conscience, 10
To God doe reuerence,
Be to thy prince trew.
Keip ay weill thy credence,
Tyne nocht throw negligence,
Proceid ay with prudence, 15
Ydilnes eschew.

Exceid not thy degrie,
Doe all thingis iustlie,
Haue God befoir thy e
Quhair euer thow gang. 20
Guyde thy self honestlie,
Hant in gud companie,
Of the puire haue pitie,
And doe nane wrang.

At experience leir, 25
Folisch speking forbeir,
With mesour spend thy geir,
Na gud turne delay.
Vse na ryatous cheir,
Doe thy nichtbour na deir, 30
Goddis worde glaidlie heir,
And syne it obey.

S. R. M.

12–13] order of lines reversed in D
24 doe nane wrang] do to nane wrang MF
Attribution: Quod Richard maitland in MF.

55.
Sum of the poetis and makeris that ar now,
Of greit dispyite and malice ar sa fow,
Sa that all lesingis that can be inventit,
Thay put in writ and garris thame be prentit,
To gar the peopill euill opinioun tak 5
Of thame quhome of that thay thair balladis mak.
With sclanderous wordes thay doe all thing thay can
For to defame monye gud honest man,
In setting furth thair buikis and thair rymis,
Accusand sum of improbabill crymis; 10
And thocht that sum thair libellis dois allow,
3it few that will thair awin workes avow,
And thocht that thay bakbyteris and blasphemeris,
Now at this tyme hes monye thair mantenaris.
The day will cum that thay sall forthink it 15
That thai haue put sic lesingis into writ:
To steill ane mannis fame is greter sin
Nor onye geir that is this warld within.
Therfoir repent, 3e railleris, and restoir
To thame thair fame quhom 3e sclanderit befoir; 20
To that effect 3our word apply and deidis,
Euill bruite to tak out of the peopillis heidis.
Cry toung! I leid throw all this natioun,
Mak buikis and rymes of recantatioun;
Sic alteratioun may cum in this land, 25
May gar ane tak ane other be the hand,
And say, 'Think on 3e maid of me ane ballat,
For 3our rewaird now I sall brek 3our pallat!'
Men sould be war quhat thing thay said or did,
For it may cum to licht lang hes bene hid. 30
Therfoir, na man mak ballatis, nor indyte,
Of detractatioun, ill sclander, nor dispyte.

6 quhome of] of quhone D
8 gud] ane D
15 day] tyme D
21 3our word apply] apply 3our worde MF
22 out] furthe MF
25 in this] in to this MF
29 thing] *om.* D D

Put not in writ that God or man may greif:
All vertew luif and all vycis repreif;
Or mak sum mirrie toy to gud purpois,   35
That may the herar or reader bayth reioys,
Or sum fruitfull or gud moralitie,
Or plesand thingis may stand with cheritie.
Dispyitfull poetis sould not tholit be
In commoun weillis, or gud companie,   40
That sort ar ay to saw seditioun,
And put gud men into suspitioun.

S. R. M.

35 Or] And MF
40 gud] godlie MF
Attribution: Finis quod Sir richart maitland of lethingtoun knycht in MF.

56.
Of God the misknawlege,
Of sin the greit vsage,
Na punishment for vyce,
The wanting of iustice,
Invy and gredines,	5
Debait and vnkyndnes,
Oppressioun of the puire,
Of common weill na cuire,
Pryide and weir intestine,
Bringis realmis to ruine.	10

S. R. M.

6 Debait] Desait MF
Attribution: Finis quod richart maitland in MF.

57.
Gif thow desyire thy hous lang stand,
And thy successioun bruik thy land,
Above all thing love God and feir;
Intromet not with wrangous geir,
Nor conqueis na thing wrangouslie;   5
With thy nichtbour keip cheritie.
Obey dewlie thy magistrat,
Exceid in na thing thyne estait;
Oppres not, bot support the puire,
To helpe the commoun weill tak cuire.   10
Vse na dissait, nor mell with treasoun,
And to all men doe richt and reasoun;
Baith into word and deid be trew,
All kynde of wickednes eschew.
Slay na man, nor thairto consent,   15
Be not cruell, bot patient.
Allya ay in sum gud place,
With noble, honest, godlie race.
Hait hurdome, and all vycis flie,
Be humbill, hant gud companie,   20
Help thy freindis and doe na wrang,
And God sall gar thy hous lest lang.

S. R. M.

1 stand] lestand D
2 thy] *om.* D
11 nor mell] mell not MF
16 bot] nor D
Attribution: Finis quod Sir richart maitland of lethingtoun in MF.

58.
My lordis all, sen abstinence is taine,
In the meintyme, that concord may be drest,
Now tyne na tyme, as 3e haue done bygaine,
Since 3e may haue conferring as 3e list;
Doe 3our power this realme to put to rest,   5
Let neuer weir againe amang 3ow ryis,
Then all the warld will 3our proceding pryis.

Thair will na bodye be aganis this peace,
Bot gif it be of men of weir the bandis,
Quhilk fra all kynd of scafrie can not ceis,   10
And thay that bruikis otheris mennis landis,
Fra wrangous geir that can not keip thair handis:
This sort of men wald haue na quyetnes,
For feir thay want sumthing that thay posses.

Bot at that sort 3e sould na counsall tak,   15
That hes na feir of God, nor conscience;
To vse all thing impediment may mak
To 3our concord, and 3e gif thame credence;
How thay proceid thair is experience,
For it is said that sum man sair may rew   20
That in this land sa monye capitaines grew.

For onye plesour of thir gredie men,
This commoun weill put not in ieopardie;
At 3our conventioun gar the countrie ken
That 3e travell to mak tranquillitie,   25
And that 3e ar content for till aggrie,
All fail3eis past to be for3et for euer:
I trow 3e ken bot few that faultit neuer.

Greit is the scayth that cummis of this weir,
Of slauchter, heirschip, oppressioun, and mischeif;   30
It is pitie the commounis for to heir,
How thay ar drest with thift and opin reif,
Syne seis nane apperance of releif:
Thir cruell crymis thay feir vnpunischit be,
Sa lang as lestis this inanimitie.   35

3it of all weir peace is the finell end;
Thairfoir aggrie, my lordis, or it be war:
Thair is na thing bot peace that may this mend,
And that 3e wald this commoun weill prefer
To all causis that ar particular,   40
And for na privat proffeit that may be,
Stop not to mak ane perfyte vnitie.

The quhilk to do I pray the leving Lord
To gif 3ow grace in sic aboundance now,
That neuer mair be distance nor discord,   45
And sic iustice be done this kinrik throw,
The quhilk may gar the rasche-bus keip the kow,
And euerie man bruik his awin land and geir,
All trew leigis to leif withouttin weir.

S. R. M.

37 aggrie my lordis] my lordis aggre MF
49 weir] feir MF
Attribution: Finis quod R maitland in MF; Finis quod S. R. M. in D.

59.
Our souuerane lord, into thy tender aage,
Lerne to serue God, him luif aboue all thing.
Thy counsell cheis of gud men, iust and sage,
That ar expert, maist abill and conding,
To geve ane faithfull counsell to ane king,   5
How he sould rewll his realme in peace and rest,
Vertew to luif, and all vycis doun-thring,
Thame to releif that lang hes bene opprest.

Syne be thy counsell gar it be provydit
How thow sall leif to thy royall estait,   10
And how thy nobill persoun salbe gydit
In tyme to cum, quha sall on the wait,
To be thy gairde, and serue the air and lait,
And quhat barrounis sall in thy court remaine,
Thair tyme about it to decoir all gait,   15
Of thy affaires to tak sum thocht and paine.

Thy propertie and casualiteis,
That thay be put to thy vtilitie,
Will hauld thy hous and pay thy seruandis feis,
And find all thing that neidfull is to the,   20
Gif thow will vse na prodigalitie,
And vainlie waist the rentis of thy croun:
Now in thy ȝouth experience haue we,
Thy leving haill brocht to confusioun.

Wes neuer king nor prince in this countrie,   25
To leif vpon that had sa greit ane rent,
To thy proffeit gif it weill guydit be,
And not in vaine consumit and mispent.
Thairfoir, be ressoun, thow sould be content

3 Thy counsell cheis] Cheis thi counsell MF R
7 Vertew to luif] to luif wertue MF R
8 that lang hes bene] that hes bene lang MF R
16 to tak sum thocht and paine] for to tak swm paine MF R
18 That] And MF R
24 brocht] neir broght MF R

To leif on it that to thy croun pertenis, 30
That on thy leigis taxatioun nor stent
Be neuer rasit, be vnlauchfull menis.

Sir, at thy barrounis, thrie thingis requyre,
Quhilk be ressoun can not denyit be:
First to brek iustice that nane the desyire; 35
The secound is that thow may vse trewlie
Thy awin leving, that it may be frelie
Put to sic proffeittis as gudlie it may be;
Thridlie that thay the help and fortifie,
Iustice to doe at all tymes, nicht and day. 40

Sir, give na eiris to vaine flatteraris
Quha at the lenth will bot the plaine desave,
Na credence give to commoun clatteraris,
Nor in thy court na bakbyteris resave,
That will of thame at quhome thay malice have 45
To thy hienes monye loud lesing mak,
And gar thy grace ane hatred consave
Aganis trew men, fra the to hauld abak.

Micht sclaunderit men of the get audience,
Or wer present quhen evill taillis wer tauld, 50
Thay sould sa weill defend thair innocence,
Thair honestie sa iustifie thay wald:
Gar thame think schame to lie, that wes so bauld,
And caus thy grace so ken the veritie

31 thy] this R
35 nane] nane sall MF R
36 trewlie] frillie MF
37 frelie] trewlie MF R
37 that] so that MF
38 proffeittis] proffeit MF   may be] may MF
43 Na credence give] gif na credens MF
47 ane hatred] in heitrent MF
50 wer] ar D
54 caus] gar MF   so] to D

That thow sould for honest men thame hauld, 55
And tratling toungis had our lang leif to lie.

O royall roy, thy realme ay rewll be richt,
And be wyse counsell guyde thy maiestie;
About thy persoun haue, bayth day and nicht,
Godlie gud men of fame and honestie, 60
And doe na thing in thy minoritie,
Be persuasioun of euill tailles not trew,
That quhen thow comis to maioritie,
Experience will geve the caus to rew.

ȝoung nobill king and thy counsell, I pray, 65
This commoun weill keip in tranquillitie,
Sua set it furth it may incres ilk day;
To thy leigis doe iustice equallie,
Without respect to persone or pairtie;
In this land na tuilȝie be, nor sturt, 70
And in sum caice thy grace to schaw mercie,
And speciallie quhair na pairtie is hurt.

I pray to God, the gyder of all thing,
Our souuerane save fra dolour and decay,
And give him grace to be the noblest king, 75
That in this regioun rang this monye day,
That he may tak our lang dolour away,
In his nonage that we have done sustein,
Falset and wrang be now baneist for ay,
That gud iustice amang ws may be sein. 80

Finis quod Sir Richard Maitland of Lethingtoun, Knycht.

55 sould] sould thane MF
57 ay] *om*. D
58 maiestie] MF maiestitie MQ
67 may] will D
70 na tuilȝie be] be na tuilȝe MF
Attribution: Finis quod R. maitland in MF; Finis quod S. R. M. of Lethingtoune knicht in D.

60. Ane Exclamatioun Maid In England Vpon The Delyuerance Of The Erle Of Northumberland Furth Of Lochlevin, Quho Immediatlie Thairefter Wes Execute In ʒorke.

Quho list to mark the Scottisch gyse,
Or knaw the customes of thair kyndis,
Sall weill persave thair craftie wyse,
And fals, dissaitfull, doubill myndis:
For quhair as thay gud will profes, 5
The treuthe apperis thay mein no les.

Gif travell, be occasioun, try
Of forraine landis the inclinatioun,
Be pruif richt weill, I doe espy
The Scottisch tred and nauchtie fassioun 10
To be so bad, that from the rest
Thair lyfis and guydingis ar detest.

Thair fassioun I abhor in deid;
Thair conuersatiounis is defylit;
Fair speich prevaillis thame selfis to speid; 15
Quho to thame trustis ar clein begylit;
For thay richt simplie will declair
Of quhome the iust aucht to be war.

The fairer speich, the falser hairtis;
The suirest bandis, the sonest brokin; 20
The greater lordis, the falser partis,
Gif this worde may againe be spokin:
For lordis and lairdis ar nather iust,
Nor ʒit the commounis to be trust.

In falset thay excell in kynd; 25
In wordes thay maist of all exceid;
In treasoun none lyik doe I find;

2 Or knaw the customes of thair kyndis] And custome of there kindes L
4 dissaitfull, doubill myndis] deceytfull mindes L
8 the] there L
25 falset] falsehode L

In treuth thay neuer obserue the creid:
For say and promeis quhat thay can,
Thair wordes and deidis will neuer pan. 30

Gif Iudus pairt wes tressonabill,
Or Pylatis iudgmentis comptit bad,
Quhy sould I think thame ressonabill?
For honest trust thay neuer had;
Experience be thame selfis appeiris 35
Of thair greit tressoun in few ȝeiris.

And now, of lait, the gretest wrang
That euer nobill man possest,
Ane baneist lord wes thame amang,
Quho fled for feir to be opprest: 40
Northumberland hecht this lord to name,
Sumtyme of honour and greit fame.

Quho, for releif in tyme of wo,
Did helples wander in thair land,
As baneist wichtis wer wont to go, 45
Till efter grace thay better fand.
Murray, Mortoun, and Ruthvenis caice,
For slauchter in thair princis place,

With thowsandis mo of lordis and lounis,
Of that vngratious natioun bred, 50
Quho fand releif in all our tounis,
As custome and gud fassioun led.
Thocht vnder colour thay pretendit,
Ȝit baneist wichtis wer ay defendit.

31 pairt wes] partes were L
35 Experience] examples L
44 Did helples wander] And helpless wanderinge L
45 wer wont to go] had wonte to doe L
46 Till efter grace thay better fand] And better grace they after fande
49 lounis] lardes L
50 Of] With L
52 custome] constant L

Gif trespas be so greit ane sin   55
As disobedience dois deserue,
Gif no refudge ane man may win,
The penitent for helpe may sterue.
In Scotland had not bene sic tuill
Gif this had bene the commoun reull.   60

Fy on the Scotland and thy seid!
Aboue all realmis woe the befall!
Thy lordis hes done so schamfull a deid
That traitouris ay men will 3ow call:
3ow ar so gredie on Englisch gold   65
That all 3our credit now is sould.

And gif that you had borne in mynd
The auncient leig, as trewis requyrit,
Nocht heirtofoir 3ow sall on find
That to thair deith hes bene delyuerit,   70
Muche moir ane nobill baneist lord:
Quhy sould 3e sell him to the cord?

This cryme of 3ouris is so manifest
Aboue all subtill treasounis greit;
The gold 3e gat for suche ane gaist   75
Will neuer by 3our childring meit.
It will decay, and 3it 3our fame
Continew sall with cruell blame.

Gif France had bene of 3our accord,
Or Flaunderis gevin thame selfis to gaine,   80
Thair is remaning 3it one lord
That had possest this wofull paine;

58 The penitent for helpe may sterue] Of forren landes man may serue
62 realmis] naciones L
66 gif that] yet yif L
66 borne] L bene MQ

Bot ȝit these lordis sall honour haue
Quhen ȝe with schame sall go to graue.

And thocht I wryte aganis ȝour act, 85
Ȝit am I glaid we have the man:
God may be gude, and ȝit ȝour fact
Ȝour childeris childrein may it ban.
God is gratious quhen we repent,
And our Quene mercifull in iudgment. 90

Finis.

83 lordis] landes L
88 it ban] have ban L
89 God] For God L

61. The Answeir to the Englisch Ballad.

3ow that doe wryte aganis the Scottis,
Thair actioun for to deprave,
Thame taxing with so schamfull blottis,
Sould haue alledgit ressounis grave:
I 3ow advyise, call in 3our scroll;   5
3ow wait not quho will it controll.

Thocht sum have playit Iudas pairt
In selling gud Northumberland,
Quhy sould the hoill, for thair desert,
That faine wald haue that fact withstand,   10
Or 3it the countrey beir the blame?
Let thame that sauld him haue the schame.

Mar and the divelische Douglassis,
And namelie Mortoun and Lochlevin,
Mackgill and Orknay, Scottish assis,   15
And Cleisch, quhomto the gold wes gevin,
Dumfermling that the py prepaird,
And lowse Lindsay, quho wes his gaird.

These onlie wer the Iudassis;
These onlie gave thairto advyise;   20
And onlie these twa Douglassis
Participatit of his pryce.
So lat his bluid be on thair heidis,
On thair posteritie and seidis.

3our Quene had pruif that Mortounis race   25
To covatice wes hoill inclynde;
And so, to prosecute this caice,
Addrest hir onlie to that kynd,
And not to all, bot Mortoun rather,
Be money that corrupt his father.   30

Quho tuik King Hareis money so,
Our cardinall to keip in hauld,
And syne for money luit him go,
And for fyve hundreth crounis him sauld?

Of kynd so Mortoun hes it then,   35
To chope and chainge and to sell men.

3ow sould not preis disestimatioun
To suche as thairin no lak had;
Thocht thair be also of our natioun,
As of all otheris, gud and bad,   40
3it blame not all for one or two
That meinis no treuth to freind nor fo.

Sen France producit ane Gan3elon,
And England monye tratouris bred,
Quhat fairlie then, thocht we haue on?   45
3it it is not ane Scottische tred,
For Scotland ay of auld and new,
To baneist wichtis wes euer trew.

Henrie the sext wes heir exylde,
For quhome we micht haue had greit gaine;   50
As for his Quene and onlye chyild,
3it wer thay nather sauld nor slaine.
3our storeis schawis, wer thay [perversit],
Greit stoir, bot nane that wes euill vsit.

This lordis wyfe socht to Lord Home,   55
As Leonard Dakeris and monye mo,
Quhome all the gold in Christindome
Wald not have movit to sell thame so:
3e knaw quhat hairme he hes susteind,
For that he trewlie thame mainteind.   60

The Erle of Sussix can recoird,
Quhen he desyrit thame of his hand,
The generous anser of that lord,
That he maid to his schairpe demand:
Said he wald rather give his heid   65
Or he sould doe so vyild ane deid.

53 perversit] pervsit MQ

For deid wald lest bot for ane sessoun,
And pas sone with celeritie;
The vyile and filthie blot of tressoun
Wald staine his haill posteritie: 70
Wer it to doe, he wald ressaue thame,
And he nor nane sould neuer have thame.

So tressoun is no Scottische gyse:
To terme it so, ʒe haue no ground,
Sen heir afflictit wichtis alwyse 75
Hes euer ayd and favour found.
Althocht sum tratouris be amang ws,
In blaming all, forsuith, ʒe wrang ws.

ʒe sould not all the realme detract,
Nor impute falset to our kynd, 80
Sen monye with that filthie fact
Ar soir offendit in thair mynd,
And to avenge it wald be glaid:
Will ʒe concur, ʒe sall have ayd.

ʒour Quene abhorris thame in hir hairt, 85
Mislyking far thair filthie naturis;
And wald be glaid to sie thame smart,
Lyking the treasoun, bot not the tratouris,
Scho knawis thay did it not for love:
It wes hir gold that did thame move. 90

Wald ʒe doe for ʒour countrie man,
As for our honouris caus we wald.
We sall avenge it on that clan,
ʒour freind that to the scambillis sauld:
So pruif and deid sall testifie 95
ʒour kyndnes, and our honestie.

Finis.

62. Ane Schort Inveccyde Maid Aganis the Delyuerance of the Erle of Northumberland.

Quhat faithfull hairt dois not for sorrow burst
To heir thair realme blasonit and blasphemit,
And of all other countreis comptit as accurst,
Discreditit, disdainit, and disestimit,
And men thairof as doubill tratouris demit,   5
And taxit with so monye schamfull blot,
So poyntit out and from all faithfull flemit,
Saying 'Avoyde the fals dissaitfull Scot'?

'Avoide', thay bid, 'Thay fals and filthie tratouris':
So generallie we ar of straingeris stylit,   10
And repute of sa fals, mischevous naturis,
As na man may beleif ws vnbegylit.
God wait how we ar ralit on and revylit,
And blamit for monye tressounis moniefauld,
And quhat inveccyde ballatis ar compylit,   15
Sen the gud erle Northumberland wes sauld.

Alace! quhy sould not wit and worthines,
Honestie, honour, and humilitie,
Assuagit sumquhat have sic gredines?
That paragon of trew nobilitie,   20
And perfyte patroun of civilitie,
So courtes, stout, trew, liberall, and kynd,
Sould have bene quyte with moir fidelitie,
And have with mercye movit ȝour mynd.

That loving lord, sa voyde of all dispyte,   25
Of vertewis having sic pluralitie,
In honest pastyme takand his delyte,
With monye rair and princlie qualitie,
So nobill port and liberalitie,
Sic hardines and hairt heroicall,   30
Deseruit rather immortalitie
Then to haue had ane end so tragicall.

Alace! that euer Scotland sould haue bred
Sic to thy awin dishonour, schame, and greif,

That quhen ane nobill man wes thairto fled, 35
At neid to seik sum succour and releif,
Sould have bene coulpit twyise; first be ane theif,
Then be Lochlevin, quho did thrie ȝeir him keip,
That gat greit gaine to saue him from mischeif,
Syne sauld him to the skambillis lyik ane scheip. 40

Our antecessouris, and fatheris honorabill,
Could not be movit be favour, force, nor feir,
To doe ane deid so vyle and detestabill,
And mekill les for gredines of geir,
As be our storeis plainlie dois appeir; 45
Bot oft incurrit monye doutfull daingeris,
And oft tymes baid the hasard of the weir,
For the resset and succouring of straingeris.

Greit lordis and erlis, the dyuers duikis and kingis,
For quhome this realme hes sufferit mekill paine, 50
Exylit from thair countreis and thair ringis,
In Scotland saiflie lang tyme did remaine,
As Richard and Henrie the sext makis plaine,
And monye ma exampillis may be gevin,
Of quhome thay micht haue gottin gretar gaine, 55
Quhose luk wes gud thay come not in Lochlevin.

Fy on the Mar that euer thow consentit
Ane nobill man sa falslie to dissave!
Thow may weill leif quhill thow at lairge repent it,
And thou trowit Mcgill, that drunking knaif, 60
Or Dumfermling, that the sic counsall gave,
Or had to doe with Mortounis fellowschip:
Lowse Lyndsay ȝit did better with the laif,
That tuik thair geir, and luit thame selfis slip.

Fals mischeant Mortoun, febill and vnkynd, 65
Thy wretchit hairt could neuer schame eschew!
How could so small ane sowme haue movit ȝour mynd
Be this vyild act auld tressounis to renew?
Thow neuer wes vpricht, trustie, nor trew
To freind, to fo, nor to na other man: 70
On sic vyild tresoun vengeance man ensew

On the, and all thy fals degenerat clan.

Lochlevin, that wes ay faithles to thy brother,
To quhome thow wes so bound be benefeit,
How could thow keip thy credit to ane other, 75
That schamefullie aganis his will and wit
The air of Buchane, quhom he did commit
To thy keping, put in thy brotheris bed;
And sen his deith, him to dishonour ȝit,
Hes rasit ane schamefull summoundis to heir red? 80

Thow left him falslie in aduersitie,
And all his freindschip vtterlie refusit,
And work buir witnes of thy loyaltie,
Quhen that the Quene wes in the Louche inclusit;
Baith hir and him thow tratourouslie abusit, 85
And gave gud tryell of thy lytill treuth:
Quhen scho escapit, how could thow be excusit,
Bot thair wes slicht, or ellis ane wilfull sleuth?

ȝit tratour, this vnhonest, bludie blok
Surpassis far thy tressounis all of auld; 90
Quhair euer thow gangis, thow art ane gasing-stok
For all the peopill cryis, 'cum and behauld
The tratour that the gud lord Persie sauld!',
Wissing his bluid to be vpon thy heid.
From age to age thy treasoun wilbe tauld, 95
And be ane schame for euer to thy seid.

Iudas, that sauld our saluiour to be slaine,
Ane vyler draucht nor thow did neuer draw;
Nor Ganȝelon aganis Charles the Maine;
Nor Andro Bell, that wicked vyld outlaw; 100
Nor ȝit the tratour, Eckie of the Hairlaw,
That sayis he sauld him to redeme his pledge:
ȝour deid is war, as all the warld dois knaw,
ȝe can nothing bot covatice alledge.

ȝit sen the act wes so inordinat, 105
And it behuiffit be cheif tratouris to be,
I wait ȝe wer thairto preordinat,

Not be ane chance, bot fatall destanie,
That nane it could have execute bot 3e;
For quha 3our nature cleirlie vnderstandis   110
Will think ane act of so greit villanie
Behovit of force to fall into 3our handis.

As metest merchand for ane maister-steik,
Baith fals of kynd, and in the craft expert,
And thairby garris 3our kitchingis daylie reik;   115
Na other men could haue found in thair hairt
To sell the saikles as ane slauchter-mairt;
Had Christ him self bene in Perseyis rowme,
I wait 3e wald haue playit Iudas pairt,
Gif Cayphas had offerit 3ow the sowme.   120

3it, for 3our mischeant and mischevous deid,
The countrey aucht not for to beir the blame,
Bot onlie that fals and degenerat seid
Of Douglassis, fals, wratchit, and infame;
And cheiflie Mortoun and Lochlevin be name,   125
And of his bluide resavit the pygrall pryce:
So with the siluer sall 3e haue the schame,
And sic 3our freindis as gave thairto advyise.

O cruell, fals, dissaitful, bludie beistis!
To faythfull men how dar 3e hauld vp face?   130
How could sic tressoun breid into 3our breistis?
Quhy leit 3e not pitie rather haue place
Sen 3e 3our selfis wes in the samyn caice,
And wait not quhen thairto 3e sall returne?
His bluide salbe on 3ow and all 3our race,   135
And 3e and 3ouris sall for that murther murne.

Had 3e him gevin but pryce gratuitlie,
Be benefeit 3ow thinkand thairto bound,
Or to declair 3our luif and amitie,
So that no proffeit sould to 3ow redound,   140
3our crueltie had not bene so euill found;
Bot 3e ressauit the pryce and it procurit:
Euill gottin gaine is ane vngratious ground
Quhairon to found ane welth and weill assurit.

The Iewis wald not put in thair commoun purs 145
The pryice of Christ, quhilk Iudas kaist againe:
The pryice of bluid bringis ay with it ane curs,
Quhilk on thy race for euer sall remaine.
Sum day, be suire, thocht thow sic dome disdaine,
Deir of his bluid the bargane wilbe bocht: 150
Vengeane will wirk, and will not licht in vaine,
Bot the, thy hous, and name, sall bring to nocht.

Out of thy hand his bluid salbe requyrit,
Thow sall not chaip mischeif, doe quhat thow can;
Nor thay that in that blok with the conspyrit, 155
Cheiflie the bucheris of thy bludie clan,
Quha vantis be bluid thay all thair worschip wan,
And ȝit be bluid mair proudlie dois pretend:
Be bluide thay leifit, be bluide thay first began,
And so for bluide sall haue ane bludie end. 160

Finis.

63.
ȝe hevinis abone, with heavinlie ornamentis,
Extend ȝour courtingis of the cristall air;
To asuir colour turne ȝour elementis,
And soft this seasoun, quhilk hes bene schairp and sair;
Command the cluddis that thay dissolue na mair,   5
Nor ws molest with mistie vapouris weit.
For now scho cummis, the fairest of all fair,
The mundane mirrour of maikles, Margareit.

The myildest may, the mekest and modest;
The fairest flour, the freschest flourisching;   10
The lamp of licht, of ȝouth the lustiest;
The blythest bird of bewtie maist bening,
Groundit with grace and godlie governing,
As A per C, aboue all elevat,
To quhome comparit is na erthlie thing,   15
Nor with the goddis so heichlie estimat.

The goddes Diana, in hir hevinlie throne,
Evin at the full of all hir maiestie,
Quhen scho belevit that daingar wes thair none,
Bot in hir sphere ascending vp maist hie,   20
Vpon this nymph fra that scho caist hir ei,
Blusching for schame, out of hir schyire scho slippis,
Thinking scho had bene Phoebus verelie,
At quhose depart scho fell into the eclips.

The asteres cleir, and torchis of the nicht,   25
Quhilk in the sterrie firmament wer fixit,
Fra thay persavit Dame Phoebus lost hir licht,
Lyik diamontis, with cristall perlis mixit,
They did discend to schyne this nymph annixit
Vpon hir schoulderis, twinkling euerie on,   30
Quhilk to depaint it wald be ouer prolixit,
How thay in ordour glisteris on hir goun.

Gif scho had bene into the dayis auld,
Quhen Iupiter the schap of bull did tak
Befoir Europe, quhen he his feit did fauld   35
Quhill scho throw courage clam vpon his bak,

Sum greater magik, I wait, he had gart mak,
Hir to haue stollin be his slichtis quent,
For to haue past aboue the Zodiak,
As quein and goddes of the firmament.	40

With goldin schouris, as he did Clemene,
He wald this virgine furteouslie desave;
Bot I houp in the goddes Hemene,
Quhilk to hir brother so happie fortoun gave,
That scho salbe exaltit by the laif,	45
Baith for hir bewtie and hir nobill bluid,
And of my self ane seruand scho sall have,
Vnto I die; and so I doe conclud.

Finis quod A. Montgomerie

64.
Luiffaris, leif of to loif so hie
3our ladyes, and thame styill no mair
But peir, the erthlie E per sie,
And flour of feminine maist fair;
Sen thair is ane, without compair, 5
Sic tytillis in 3our sanges deleit,
And prays the pereles [perle] preclair
Montgomerie, maikles Margareit;

Quhose port and pereles pulchritud,
Fair forme and face angelicall, 10
Sua meik and full of mansuetud,
With vertew supernaturall,
Makdome, and proper memberis all,
Sa perfyte, and with ioy repleit,
Pruiffis hir but peir or peregall, 15
Of maidis the maikles Margareit.

Sa wyse in 3outh and verteous,
Sic ressounis for to reull the rest,
As in greit age wer marvelous;
Sua manerlie, myld, and modest, 20
Sa grave, sa gratious, and digest,
And in all doingis sa discreit,
The maist bening and boniest,
Mirrour of madinis, Margareit.

Pigmalion, that ane portratour 25
Be painting craft did so decoir,
Him self thairwith in paramour
Fell suddanlie, and smert thairfoir;
Wer he alyve he wald deploir
His folie, and his love forleit, 30
This fairer patrone to adoir,
Of maidis the maikles Margareit.

7 pereles [perle] preclair] pereles preclair MQ

216

Or had this nymphe bene in these dayis
Quhen Paris iudgit in Helicon,
Venus had not obtenit sic prayis, 35
Scho, and the goddessis ilkone,
Wald haue preferrit this paragon,
As marrowit, but matche most meit,
The goldin ball to bruik alone,
Merveling in this Margareit; 40

Quhose nobill birth and royall bluid
Hir better nature dois exceid;
Hir native giftes and graces gud,
Sua bonteouslie declairis indeid
As waill and wit of womanheid, 45
That sa with vertew dois ouerfleit:
Happie is hie that sall posseid
In mariage this Margareit.

Helpe, and graunt hap, gud Hemene;
Lat not thy pairt in hir inlaik; 50
Nor lat not doulful destanie,
Mishap, or fortoun, worke hir wraik;
Graunt lyik vnto hir self ane maik
That will hir honour, luif, and treit,
And I sall serve him for hir saik: 55
Fairweill, my Maistres Margareit.

A. M.

65.
With siching sad and surging sorrow soir,
My cairfull corps richt peteouslie opprest
And wrappit in wo, desyring no thing moir
Then dolent deith the samyn sould haue in haist,
By cours of nature, luiking for sum rest;   5
Quhen fair Venus, the bewtie of the nicht,
Had set hir face direct into the west,
I prostrat law, and thus closit my sicht.

Into my swuning slumring, as I lay,
Most feirfull formes did soir assault my thocht;   10
The roring of the raiging seyis gray,
Quhilk Boreas blast from bank to bray had brocht;
The thundring doun of cannounis, warlie wrocht,
As did appeir maid hevin and erthe to schaik:
For to expande my dreame all meinis I socht   15
Quhen I awouk, with monye a cruell crak.

Sumtyme the scripturis in my hand I volue,
Gif happelie I could find suche a caice;
Sumtyme vaine wryteris red I to resolue
Me of my folische fantasie, allace.   20
Sumtyme I call the michtie God for grace,
That I micht have the spreit for to persaue
Quhat misterie apperit in that place,
Or gif my wittis waik did me dissave.

Voluing this way into my maucles mynd,   25
Perhaps I hard ane cative full of cair,
To weping prone, to murning soir inclynd,
From blyithnes baneist, drawin to dispair;
Creusa kynd to hir wes na compair,
Nor Phaetusa, nor murning Phaeton,   30
Quhose tyrit visage sumtyme wes preclair,
My feirfull dreame did perfytlie expone.

Hir trimbling teiris did represent the iawis
Of Neptunis raige, quhilk rasit bene by raine;
Hir siching braith the budding blast that blawis   35
Quhen Boreas list to prove his power plaine;

Hir voice so rauk with reuthfull roir againe,
Most lyik the thundring thuddis of cannoun din,
Affrayit me, ȝit wald I not refraine,
Bot kepit me close my cabinat within.   40

This piteous wicht, werid and woe begon,
Teare all hir hair, that sorrow wes to sie,
And as the drope of water weris the stone,
So dentit wer hir cheikis cruellie
By trimbling teiris, distilling ithinglie   45
Out from hir eis lyik flowing stremis of raine:
For to behauld hir dolour outwardlie
Wes to my hairt ane inwart heavie paine.

Hir bodye small wes widderit and [brent]
As is the staik quhilk someris drouth opprest;   50
Hir visage pale declarit hir to be schent,
In sichis and sobbis reposit wes hir rest;
Hir febill handis togidder oft scho prest
With reuthfull roir that echoit in the sky.
In doulfull duill this cairfull cative west,   55
Ȝeit furth hir plaint with monye ane cruell cry.

Thus, hering hir bewailing all hir wo,
In studie still ane lytill quhyle I stuid,
Bot quhen I saw hir deidlie duill wes so,
And scho of ioy and confort wes denude,   60
To speik to hir a lytill thocht me gude,
Gif my word micht solace to hir mak,
Or gif I micht hir cair sum part seclude;
With doulfull voice this way to hir I spak:

['Vnwrape] tha woes, quhat wicht that euer ȝe be,   65
And stint, in tyme, to spill thy self but plaint;
Till quhat thow art, from quhence, for suir, I sie,
Thow may not duire with sorrow thus attent'.
And with that word hir face with teiris besprent

49 brent] berent MQ
65 Vnwrape] In wrape MQ

Scho liftit vp, and prostrat quhair scho lay, 70
With heavie hairt, with monye a piteous plaint,
And wofull stound scho thus begane to say:

'Alace! I, wretche, quhom thus thow heiris bewaill,
Am bot a mortall murning my mischance,
Quhome duill and dolour daylie dois assaill, 75
Intoxicat with sorrowis poysonit lance,
All tyme and houris I mak obedience
Vnto that wofull maistres of mischeif.
Is no remeid, saif onlie patience
And houp the health and haist of my releif. 80

And I am cum my drerie destanie
And lukles lot for to bemone with those
Quhome Fortoun, in this nest of miserie,
To be the mirrour of mishap hath chose.
Vpon the onlie God we aucht repose, 85
For all thingis feidis that we doe think most suir:
The bad abydis, the best ay sonest gois,
Then men may sie no erthlie thing can duir.

Then quhat ar we to trust into our strenth,
Our wisdome, wit, or staittis variabill, 90
Quhilk tyme will chainge, and als devoir at lenth?
Thocht by Fortoun it wes not chaingabill,
This warld is bot ane vaill most miserabill,
To dolent deith subdew with bitter schouris,
Quhilk makis me weip ane freind, with murning vaill, 95
Amang the Muses nurischit with thair flouris;

Quhose vertewis rair Pallas may soir lament
All thocht I pas thame ouer with secreit thocht,
The wit, the wisdome als, that involent
Scho may deploir, gif that avaleth ocht; 100
Iustice, thy sword befoir thy face is brocht,
Quhilk he did clein, ay keip with kyndlie cair,

83 Quhome Fortoun, in this nest of miserie] the line is repeated in an erroneous form after l. 84; 148. balefull] betfull MQ

And Faith, thow wantis ane piller, suirlie wrocht,
To beir thy throne triumphand euerie quhair.

And thocht this heavinlie wichtis healthe cause to weip   105
The lose of him, that wes to thame so deir,
Thair woundis, quhilk ar bayth voyd and deip,
In me alone maist plainlie may appeir;
For I haue lost his vertewis all sinceir,
Ane piller als, ane freind I want also,   110
Quho wes ane reddye scheild and feirfull speir,
The sword I want for to resist my fo.

Quhat, sall I murne my nauchtie frivoll stait,
Or sall I spurne with Fortounis quhirling quheill?
Sum, I suppose, ar borne infortunat,   115
Or ellis gud labouris could not prosper ill;
Sum men hes wrocht baith werlie and with skill,
And ȝit thair labour all hes bene in vaine,
And vtheris hes the warld waild at will,
Quho hes not taine such travell for suche paine.   120

Of the first number I compt me not the last,
To all mishap, I mein, predestinat,
For I in cruell bandis of cair am chaist,
In prisoun strang, with sorrow carcerat,
Quhair still I duill of plesour deprivat,   125
Ane mirrour maid, quhairin all men may find
Quha stryvis with nature is in the estait
Of him that stryvis againe the streme and wind.

Thus, to my lot is chanced the mishap
Quhilk in my lyfe I neuer moir did serve;   130
For I wes suirlie trappit in the trap
Befoir I could the bad or gud discryve:
So may I not my self from woe prescryve
Sen I wes borne evin from my motheris wombe,
In flitting dolour day and nicht to stryve,   135
Quhairin I knaw Fortoun hes maid my tombe.'

Hir wofull voice no soner had out bred
Thais wofull wordes, quhairwith scho sorrowed so,

Bot scho, alace, soir sicht and neuer stayed,
Syne fell doun flat vpon the ground for wo,   140
Quhose soir regret did so my strenth over go,
That I not wist quhair that I did remaine,
Brocht fra my wittis, all wer rest me fro,
Quhilk, as I micht, I gadderit sone againe.

Then siching, sad I to that wofull wicht,   145
'Sen to thy lot by nature doeth pertene
The seid of sorrow, sonkin day and nicht
Into thy [balefull] forrest, ay to remaine,
I, as ane man with surging sorrow slaine,
Into dispair most duilfullie to die,   150
Doe seik to confort the, alace, in paine
Quhomto I find no helpe nor remedie.'

With painfull paine thir wordes skairs birst out,
Quhen I wes forcit to turne my face away
From hering of the wofull, werye schout   155
That scho all tyme and houris did bewray;
Bot as I past this, siching, could I say,
'All men sall die that euer draweth braith;
Then set thy thocht on God, the onlie stay;
Thy best clething salbe the scheild of deith.   160

Sen deith is onlie the rewaird of sin,
And syn convoyit all erthlie wit to grave,
To grave we go, from grave we doe begin;
Quhen we begin in sorrow, rest we crave;
It that we crave we most of death resave;   165
Resaving deith we find a perfyte rest,
And perfyte rest ane thing is best to have,
Ane blissit thing then deith most be confest.

Imbrasing deith we ar the Lordis elect,
Gif we elect ane lyf efter his will;   170
His will is trew, and then will thame elect
That doeth elect thair hairt with treuth him till,
Him till obey and all his lawis fulfill,
He sall fulfill thair hairtis haill desyre:
Lat thy desyire than', said I, 'cative still,   175

Ay still obey that princelie princes impyre;

Quhose hie impyire, and restfull richt renowne,
Mot plesour bring vnto all painfull wicht;
All painfull wicht mot think on thy ransoun,
Quhilk ransoun brocht from darknes all our licht: 180
O lat that licht destroy that drerie nicht,
Quhilk nicht suche sorrowis suddanlie me send,
And gif ws grace to sie that plesand sicht,
Quhilk sicht sall bring our cairfull cairis to end.'

Finis.

66. Ane Elagie Translatit Out of Frenche in English Meter. G.H.

Is thair in erthe, or hes thair euer bene,
That greater sorrow nor I doe sustene?
Is thair woman, so full of woe and mone
As I am now? I trow thair be not one,
Or sall thair be in onye tyme or place,   5
That may so richteouslie lament thair cace.
Vnder the sone, quhilk all thing makis cleir,
The phoenix bird hes nather maik nor peir:
So lyke to me I trow can not be found,
Quhome dolent duill with dolour so dois wound.   10
I am phoenix of ladyis disolat,
And, but all caus, the most infortunat
That is, or was, or ȝit perchance salbe.
I am exampill of all miserie,
And he that to me cause of all this duill is   15
Quhat sall I call bot the phoenix of [fuillis]?
Alace I pleinȝie not as Dido Quein,
Schot in the hairt with Cupids arrowis kein,
Nor ony sic: mair painfull is my pairt,
Quhome blind Cupid hes persit with his dairt.   20
Ȝe sall not heir my lamentatioun
Of my luifar mak narratioun;
Ȝe sall not heir me for ane lemmand wo,
As did Sapho and monye otheris mo,
Bot for ane husband, quhilk is greater paine,   25
For luiffaris with thair luifis to remane
Ar not compellit, bot quhat soeuer betyide,
The husband to the deathe man euer abyide,
Gud or bad, quhat sort euer he be.
This is the caus of my melancolie: 30
Not that I doe him to the deid desyire,
Bot rather pray that God wald him inspyire
Me to intreit as sould ane trew husband,
And as he aucht, and I serve at his hand.
For him to serue and honour I am bent,   35
Becaus I knaw it is convenient,

16 fuillis] foullis MQ

Becaus I knaw it is ane semelie thing,
Thocht he thairof schaw him self inding
And vnworthie of me, and all that I can:
As I am wyise, wald God that he war man.   40
Quhat euer bewtie Nature dois to me grant
I pas it over and will not of it vant.
One thing, I wait, may weill be vnderstand,
Our gude it is to be at his command;
To haue sic plesour he is vnworthie,   45
Or to ly in that bed of chastetie
Of hir to him that ay faythfull hes bene,
Or haue the cheirfull blenking of hir eine,
Or that ane mouth, so modest and plesand,
Sould smyll on him, or call on him husband.   50
Bot sen the Lord and his eternall law
Hes chairgit me in sic ane ȝoike to draw,
I not refuis at bidding for to be,
Sua of frie will he hes all this of me.
ȝit notwithstanding, his ingratitude   55
Randeris for plesour paine, and ill for gude;
He randers calf for my gud solid graine;
For sueit meiknes, nothing bot bitter paine;
For faithfull treuth and for ane honest pairt,
I get dissait and doubilnes of hairt;   60
For my chaist love and cheirfull countenance,
I get againe bot anger and greifance.
His stonie hart to fauld can not be brocht,
Quhome I with all humilitie haue socht.
The ferce lyoun will not his pat erect   65
Aganis the beist that will the self subiect.
Quhen Rome wes vanqueist, with ane Attyla baild
ȝeildit the self, his cruell hairt did fauld.
The blak Pluto, thocht he war neuer so schairpe,
[Orpheus] mouit with sueitnes of his hairpe.   70
The hardest hairt, be it assailȝit oft
With sueit meiknes, it may be makin soft,
And namelie be the dulcour feminine,
Quhilk at all tyme the maist motive hes bene

70 Orpheus] Morpheus MQ

225

To gentill hairtis of onye thing alyfe, 75
To move thair myndis maist insensative.
Bot all this in his hairt can tak na place,
Sua he dois seme mair cruell in this caice
Then fers lyounis, or tyran barbarous,
Or Pluto, prince of the infernall hous. 80
Quhen I think on with quhat paine I am pynd,
The fouleris malice cummis into my mynd,
Quha sueitlie tonis his instrument and sang;
Thairefter then he beginnis to chaunge his not,
And ather cruellie dois cut thair throt, 85
Or in ane cadge, inventit be ingyne,
The sillie bird full painfullie dois pyne.
Evin so it is become now of me,
Taine in the snair of fals subtilitie,
And thocht the sillie bird into hir caidge 90
Wareis hir taker in hir awin langage,
3it my nature sufferis me not to wis
Vengeance to him that it the caus of this.
Quhat sall I doe then? Quhair sall I me addres?
To quhome sall I my painfull wo expres? 95
To him that is the caus of my mischeif
That wald him glaid, and wald augment my greif.
Quhat sall I than? Sall I ane lemmand tak,
Ane servitour that will me service mak,
And in all purpois preis me for to pleis, 100
And be pertaker of my woe and eis?
Thocht sum may think I war not far to blame,
The contrair forbiddis my gud honour and fame:
Rather let the erthe opin and swallow me,
Then I for3et my God and honestie. 105
Rather lat dolour dryve me to the deid
Or I offend my God and womanheid.
Thairfoir, all 3e that into lyfe delyte,
Go hence, for me I have 3ow in despyite!
Of love balladis I bid not for to reid, 110
Go seik otheris gif that 3e think to speid:
I will nather haue seruitour nor luif.
Quhat I haue promesit sall na thing me remuif;
Quhair I haue promesit I sall faithfull be,
And keip my treuth evin to myne enemie. 115

Quhair sall I then pour out my bitter plaint?
Quhomto sall I my cruell paine lament?
To plein3ie to my parentis is bot vaine,
That quhilk is done can not be brocht againe.
Quhen that the mater wes not past remeid,   120
O God, give then thay had taine better heid.
Alace! quhair then wes thair experience?
I prayis thair mynd, bot curs thair negligence!
Quhy wald thay not at leist seik my consent?
To freindis counsall quhy tuik thay nocht gud tent? 125
Sua thair rememberance dois augment my wo.
To mak my plaint then quhomto sould I go?
I knaw not ane bot the eternall Lord,
Quha of my bitter paine can beir record.
To the only I doe my plaint out pour,   130
And the I thank bayth of the sueit and sour.
Thow creat me and formit hes of nocht,
Thow hes me als to that perfectioun brocht
Quhairin I am. All iustice is with the.
Thocht men be blind, 3it thow dois cleirlie sie, 135
The iust ressoun is patent in thy sicht.
Quhy thow me thoillis to be a wofull wicht?
Quhen thow thinkis gud, thow will redres my paine,
And gif thow will that I this still remaine,
In paine and wo, arme me with patience.   140
And gif it pleis thy godlie providence
To send remeid, send it in sicker sort
That efter paine I may resaue confort
With honestie, without my fyne or schame.
Grant this, O Lord, in Iesus Christis name.   145

G.H.

67. The Subiect.

Sen thocht is frie, think quhat thow lykis,
And play thy self with thy awin consait;
Let aboundance brek out, bot ȝit in temperance,
Preferring wisdome to will. Mak vertew
Of neid, sen necessitie hes no law, ȝit 5
Not doubting, bot patience in end
Salbe victorious.

Sen thocht is frie, think quhat thow will,
O troublit hairt, to eis thy paine.
Thocht vnrevelit can doe na ill,
Bot wordes past out cummis not againe:
Be cairfull ay for to invent 5
The way to get thy awin intent.

To play thy self with thy awin consait,
And lat nane knaw quhat thow dois mene;
Houp ay at last, thocht it be lait,
To thyne intent for to attene; 10
Lat quhyllis it brek furth in effect,
Bot ay let wit thy will correct.

Sen fuilhaist cummis not greatest speid,
I wald thow souldest learne to knaw
How to mak vertew of thy neid, 15
Sen that necessitie hes no law,
With patience then thow attend,
And houp to vanqueis in the end.

Iacobus Rex

1–7 Om. BL
1 lykis] will BL
3 ill] euill BL
7 play] pleis BL (*corrected from* 'playe')   awin] *om.* BL
11 Lat] Thoght BL
12 Bot] Yet BL
14 to knaw] for to knaw BL
15 thy] a BL
17 then thow] then see thou BL

68.
Virgil his village Mantua
Did prayse aboue the rest,
And Lucane thocht that Corduba
Amang all wes the best.
Catullus Verone did commend   5
As his native countrie,
And Ouid to that samyn end
Did Sulmon magnifie.

Sua euerie poet hes sum place
To prayse and to commend   10
For sum excellent gift and grace
That God hes to it send,
Quhilk makis thair immortall fame
Out throuch the warld be knawin,
Thair heich renoun, honour, and name,   15
Throw all countreis be blawin.

Quha dois misken the praysis greit
Of nobill Gretia?
Quha dois not knaw quhat poetis wryte
Of auld Sicilia?   20
Of Pernassus, the doubill toppis,
Ar nane bot hes harde tell.
Quha dois not knaw the siluer droppis
Of Hypocrene the well?

Of Permessis, the water cleir,   25
Ar nane that can misknaw;
Nor of the birdis, bruit and beir
Is maid in Tempe schwa;
And ʒit thir places can not be
Sa plesand and preclair   30
That in our tyme, nor ʒit countrie,
Nane may be thair compair.

Bot prudent poetis, with thair pen,
Hes so thair name extold,
That euerie wicht thair vertew ken,   35
And praysis monyefauld.

Then quhy sould we the praysis greit
With dark silence put doun,
Quhilk micht be magnifeit be writ,
Of monye tour and toun?   40

Quhilk micht, perchance, all thir exceid
In all magnificence,
Gif thay wer celebrat in deid
With als greit eloquence?
As for my self, without I wald   45
Ingrat be and vnkynd;
I can na mair my silence hauld,
Bot man put furth my mynd

To speik of the, O Lethingtoun,
Quhilk standis fair on Tyne,   50
Quhais worthie praysis and renoun,
Transcendis my ingyne.
Thow meritis Homer or Virgill
Thy worschip till advance,
And put thy name, digne and nobill,   55
In dew rememberance.

Thy tour, and fortres, lairge and lang,
Thy nychtbouris dois excell,
And for thy wallis, thik and strang,
Thow iustlie beiris the bell.   60
Thy groundis deip, and toppis hie
Vprysing in the air,
Thy voltis plesand ar to sie,
Thay ar so greit and fair.

Thy work to luik on is delyite,   65
So clein, so sound, so evin;
Thy alryne is a mervall greit,
Vpreiching to the hevin.
O quhat plesour is to be thair,
As Phoebus dois vpryise,   70
To sie the wod and feildis fair,
Quhilk round about the lyis.

O quhat plesour may thair be sene,
As the dayis lamp dois lout,
To sie thy medowis fair and grene, 75
Quhilk lyis the about.
O quhat plesour is to be thair,
Quhen as the sone is doun,
To heir the [bumming] of the air,
And plesand evenis soune. 80

O quhat plesour is thair and ioy,
Quhen day hes lost his licht,
To sie the tyme sa calme and coy,
And silence of the nicht.
Lang tyme sould I thair remaine, 85
Or that I wereit grew,
And sone sall I desyire againe,
Quhen I bid thee 'Adiev!'.

Greit was the work to houke the ground,
And thy fundatioun cast; 90
Bot greater it was the to found
And end the at the last.
I mervell that he did not feir,
Quha rasit the on hicht,
That na fundatioun sould the beir, 95
Bot thow sould sink for wecht;

Or ellis the air sould not haue tholit,
So heich for to be persit,
Nor ȝit the erd for to be holit,
And so deip doun be sersit. 100
Then michtie wes that man in deid,
That first the tuik in hand,
And in his worke did so proceid,
That he the maid vpstand.

Bot the to plenische and fulfill, 105
And mak thy worke compleit,

79 bumming] bŭning MQ

Quho so it richt considder will,
Wes worke of no les spreit.
Thy beddis soft and tapeis fair,
Thy treitting and gud cheir, 110
Gif I the treuth wald now declair,
I wait thow hes no peir.

The deid it self will schaw it ay,
It misteris not my pen,
And thay that travellis be the way, 115
Thay may full weill it ken.
Bot sic and other profeitis mo
I pas and leif behind,
And only I rehers the ioy
That I did in the find. 120

Thy arbour and thy orchard grene
I can not pas it by,
A thing maist semelie to be sene
Vnder thy wall dois ly;
Maist plesand place to mak repair, 125
Thairin to sit or gang,
Thy knottis and thy alleis fair,
Quhilk ar bayth braid and lang.

Thy buttis biggit neir thame by,
Sa suire but sone or wind, 130
Maist plesand place of archerie
That euer I ȝit could find.
Thow hes a thousand plesouris ma
That my tounge can not tell.
O happie war he that micht ay 135
But troubill in the duell.

And happie art thow sic a place
That few thy maik ar sene;
Bot ȝit, mair happie for that race
To quhome thow dois pertene. 140
Quha dois not knaw the Maitland [bluid],
The best in all this land,
In quhilk sumtyme the honour stuid,

And worship of Scotland?

Of auld Sir Richard of that name 145
We haue hard sing and say
Of his triumphant nobill fame,
And of his auld baird gray;
And of his nobill sonnis thrie,
Quhilk that tyme had no maik, 150
Quhilk maid Scotland renoumit be,
And all England to quaik;

Quhais luiffing praysis maid trewlie,
Efter that simpill tyme,
Ar soung in monye far countrie, 155
Albeit in rurall ryme.
And gif I dar the treuth declair,
And nane me fleitschour call,
I can to him find a compair
And till his bairnis all. 160

Finis.

141 bluid] bliud MQ

69.

Intill ane morning, mirthfullest of May,
Or Phoebus bemis did gleit aganis the west,
I rais and saw the feildis fair and gay,
Syne to ane riuer syde anone me drest,
Quhair as the merle, and maveis mirriest,   5
And lark thair nottis maist curiouslie did sing:
Thay birdis blyithe with angell voice possest
Maid all the hevinis abone me for to ring.

Depaintit wer the feildis with all kynd hewis
By Dame Nature, that lustie ladye schene;   10
The syluer droppis of dew hang on the bewis
Lyik orient perle in gold quhilk set hathe bene;
The holsome air, the firmament serene,
And blisfull blenkis of Phoebus beamis bricht
Bad me go sleip on Florais mantill grene,   15
Quhome to resist I no wayis could nor micht.

Heirfoir I vewit the feildis, baith daill and schaw,
Quhair I ane place maist plesand micht espy,
And so perhaps ane grene medow I saw,
Quhair all wes blyith that sprang vp neir hand by.   20
Furthward I went, and thidder come in hy,
Amang thay smelling flouris me to repose,
Quhair Morpheus his mantill suddanlie
Did on me spred, syne did my eeis close.

Into my dreame behauld, quhairas I lay,   25
First did appeir, within ane lytill space,
Two lustie hairtis, the lyik befoir that day
I neuer saw, into no land nor place,
With hornis greit, and plesand weill maid face;
Syne thame betuixt ane lyoun woundit sair   30
Thay buire, crying with voces rauk and hace,
'Keip reull in haist and leif thir feildis fair'.

Thay me demandit gif I wald assent
With thame to go thair lasoris for to sie;
With aureit termis, and style most eloquent,   35
Thay maid me sone to thair assent aggrie,
So vp I rays and furth the wayis went we.

Thay me convoyit into ane gardene grein,
Quhair euerie plant and wod micht callit be
That spred vpon thay branchis micht be sein.   40

Marie, I thocht, in this wod did appeir,
Mait, land, and gold scho gave aboundantlie;
Syne in hir hand ane flourishit trie did beir,
Quhairin wes writtin, with letteris properlie,
'This is in sing of trew virginitie,   45
Quhilk I haue socht and luiffit best of all;
Heirfoir I sall, with cair most diligentlie,
Sustein the same that it ressaue no fall.'

This plesant plant, pereles but paragone,
Stuid on ane ruit of semelie sickernes,   50
The bark thairof wes fair proportion,
The bodye haill wes luifsum lawlines,
The hairt, but dreid, wes maid of faythfulnes,
The blomes quhyte and reid wes bewtie bricht,
The braunche and leifis wer all of propernes,   55
Weill wrocht for till alluire all erdlie wicht.

In quhose crope ane plesand sicht thair wes
Of ladyis fair as Phoebus in mid day,
For thair wes Venus, Iuno, and Pallas,
Minerua, Cleo, and Tersiphone,   60
Proserpina, and Diana the may,
Dame Beawtie bricht, and als Dame Chastitie,
For to impyire abone the rest for ay,
And Laulines lay law vnder the trie.

Thir ladyis bricht on lenthe quhair as thay sat,   65
Begouthe ane sang to glaiddin all the spray,
Out of my dreame quhilk did me excitat;
Then did I luik about me quhair I lay,
Quhen I persauit that thay wer all away,
And all wes fantasie that I had sene,   70
With wofull hairt then did I seik the bray
Abone the water brok, quhair I had bene.

Finis.

70.
To ȝow, my lordis of renoun,
The haill peopill of Rugling toun,
Burgesis, merchandis, and indwellaris,
Craftismen, officeris, and meit selleris,
Riche men, puire anis, and gud ȝemen, 5
Widowis, madines, and hyire-wemen,
Honest matronis, and gud wyffis,
Ȝoung men, and ȝounkouris that sindill stryffis,
Magistratis, and men of degrie,
Seruandis, and sic as leiffis on sie, 10
Schortlie of the toun the haill meinȝie,
Maist humblie to ȝow dois pleinȝie,
That our traffique dois clein decay,
Our schift and gaine is quyte away.
We haue no change within our burgh, 15
The grein gers growis our streittis throuch,
Our baxteris of breid hes no saill,
The browsteris hes no chainge for aill,
The fleschouris skambillis ar gaine dry,
The heilland men bringis in na ky, 20
The merchaundis hes no chainge of wair,
The hostleris gettis no repair,
The craftismen ar not regairdit,
The prenteisboyis ar not rewairdit,
The stabilleris gettis na stabill feis, 25
The hyire-wemen gettis na babeis,
The hors boyis ar hurt of thair wage,
Thair is na proffeit for a page.
Schortlie, thair is na thing within,
The court of straingeris is sa thin, 30
And all this sorrow and mischeif
Is nather cum of huire nor theif,
Nor be the force of enemeis,
Nor be privat conspiraceis,

1 ȝow] MF *om.* MQ
10 leiffis] luifis MF
12 to ȝow dois] to ȝow now dois MF
16 streittis] streithis MF
29 thing] change MF

Bot becaus men hes lattin doun 35
The fair and mercat of our toun.
I mein the mercat of our hors,
Quhilk nather cummis to port nor cors,
Nor to the croft our toun besyde,
Quhair monye ane wes wount to ryde, 40
At gud Sanct Lukis noble fair,
Quhair monye nobill did repair,
And for the werie winter tyide
For riddin hors did thame provyide,
For thame and all thair cumpanie, 45
That it wes plesour thame to sie.
Bot now the nobillis takis na fors,
And cairis not for riddin hors;
On hors thay will no monye spend,
Bot spairis it till ane other end. 50
Sua neuer is sein intill our toun
Lord, laird, burges, or barroun,
And quhair that mony gay gelding
Befoir did in our mercat ling,
Now scantlie in it may be sene 55
Twelf gait glydis deir of a prein.
This cummis not, as we considder,
That men to travell now ar slidder,
For monye now so bissie ar,
Quidder 3e trauell neir or far, 60
Go befoir, or byid behind,
3e sall thame ay in 3our gait find,
Thocht na thing to thame thair pertene,
3it thay will ay be bissie seine;
Nor 3it tak thay this cair and paine 65
On fute traveland on the plaine,
Bot rydis richt softlie on a meir,
Weill mountit in thair ryding geir.
The richt ressoun then till espy,

38 port] pors MF
40 Quhair] For
41 Gud] guit MF
46 Thame] thane MF
65 tak] MF *om*.MQ

237

Quhy riddin hors men will not by, 70
Is that thay get ane meir onbocht,
And sua thay think thay ryde for nocht,
And thinkis it wer ane foolish act
On riddin hors to spend thair pak,
Havand ane ȝad at thair command 75
To ryde on, baith in burgh and land.
This wicked meir sa weill thame staikis,
And amblis with thame in the glaikis,
That quha to hir dois anis him hant,
Thairefter he can not hir want, 80
For scho so gloriouslie dois ryde,
That scho thame puffis vp with pryde.
Be thay anis mountit on hir bak
Thay think in thame thair is no lak:
Thair meit doublet dois thame reioyis, 85
Thay spred abrod thair buffit hois,
Thay tak delyte in nedill wark,
Thay gloir into thair ruffit sark.
Thair lytill bonet, or braid hat,
Sumtyme heiche, and sumtyme plat, 90
Waittis not how on thair heid to stand.
Thair gluiffis perfumit in thair hand
Helpis meikill thair countenance,
Et toute est a la mode de France.
Thair dry scarpenis, baith trim and meit, 95
Thair muillis glitterand on thair feit,
Thair gartenis knottit with a rois,
Puttis all the lassis in thair chois.
Thay snyte, thoght thair na mister be,
That ȝe may thair trim naipkin se; 100
And gif ȝe richtlie it considder,
The goldin knappis sall hing togidder.
Quhen as thay talk of onye thing
All tendis to thair awin loving:
Wald ȝe esteme thame, be thair crakis, 105

82 scho] *om.* MF
88 Thay gloir into thair ruffit sark] Thay gloir in thair weill ruffit sark MF
102 hing togidder] hing the gidder MF

Thay wer Caesar in weirlie actis.
For lordlie liberalitie
Thay gaine bot kingis for to be;
Thair riches, as thame selfis dois count,
King Cresus thresour will surmount. 110
Vnto thair taillis, quha list attend,
Thay knaw all to the warldlis end;
Gif 3e will trow all that thay tell,
In euerie thing thay doe excell.
Thir ar the fassiounis, as I leir, 115
Of men that ryidis on the meir.
The wemen als, that on hir ryidis,
Thay man be buskit vp lyik bryidis,
Thair heidis heisit with silkin saillis,
With clairtie silk about thair taillis, 120
Thair gounis schent to schaw thair skin,
Suppois it be richt oft full dun.
To mak thame small thair weist is bound,
A buist to mak thair bellie round,
Thair buttokis bousterit vp behind, 125
A fartigard to gadder wind;
Thair hois mad of sum wantoun hew,
And quhen thay gang as thay not knew,
Thay lift thair goun abone thair schank;
Syne lyik ane bryidlit cat thai brank, 130
Sum taunting wordes thay haue parqueir,
That seruis thame in all mateir.

106 Thay wer Caesar in weirlie actis] Thay wald be Cesaris in thair actis MF
109 thame] thair MF
110 will] may MF
115 fassiounis] sasonis MF
127 sum] *om.* MF
Explicit: Finis MF only

71.
My ladyis pulchritud
Hes me so plonged in paine
That, mard in mynd and muid,
Mirthles I man remaine,
Vnles that fluid 5
Of graces gud,
be mansuetud,
My rest restoir againe.

Blind boy, thou dois so beir
My fortoun in ballance. 10
I flow from houp to feir,
From feir till esperance:
Now thair, now heir,
Now peace, now weir,
Chainging my cheir 15
As chaingis ay my chance.

As in the wind I wie,
Ay wauering with the wechtis,
Feir wald force fayth to flie,
And faith with Fortune fechtis; 20
And this 3e se
Is my degrie:
Now low, now hie,
As houp gud hap me hectis.

3it houp hingis be ane hair, 25
Houping aganis al houp;
Albeit from cair to cair,
Thou catche my hairt in coup;
3it mair and mair
I lyik thy lair, 30
And for no sair
Nor sorrow can I soup.

[Ane] hap I apprehend,
Be houp, I wait not how,

33 Ane] And MQ

And pertlie I pretend, 35
And preis aganis the prow;
And ay intend
That way to wend,
And in the end
For to attein I trow. 40

Finis.

72.
Gif faithfulnes 3e find,
And that 3our mynd content,
Ane band heirby I bind
Of firme fayth and feruent;
And to be permanent, 5
For ocht that may befall,
My hairt heir I present
In pledge perpetuall.

Quhilk simplie I resing
As hostage in 3our hand, 10
And willinglie it bring
To bind it in sic band
As plesis 3ow command,
To lest till I may leif,
Quhilk is the gadge and pand, 15
Maist suir that I can geif.

Resaue it then, and treit it,
As treuth sall try my part;
Gif I be fals, forleit it,
And let me suffer smert; 20
Deill efter my desert,
Than dreid I no disdaine,
Bot houpis to haue ane hairt
In recompence againe.

Gif loyaltie may love 25
Ane recompance procuire;
Or honest mening move
3our favour to induire;
Gif lawtie 3ow alluire,
Or constance mak 3ow kynd, 30
Firme faith sall me assuire,
And treuth content 3our mynd.

Finis.

17 treit] intreit MQ
22 dreid I] I dreid I MQ

73. Ane Prayer.

O Lord in heavin above, that rewlis all,
Quhose merceis greit induiris for euermoir;
O God of hostes, to the I call therfoir,
Whose blissit name I prais, and euer sall,
Becaus thow set me frie quhen I wes thrall; 5
To the Iehoua great, and Lord most hie,
To the my God for succour I doe flie;
Graunt me, O Lord, grant me, in mynd and spreit,
To doe thy will,
And so fulfill 10
Thy lawis, my God, with humble hairt contreit.

Befoir the glansing day doeth schaw his face,
My saull doeth stay and watche for the, O Lord,
And all the nicht on the I doe record,
Befoir the morning bricht I ask for grace, 15
Deploring all my wofull sinnes, alace!
Heir me, my Lord, heir me, my God and king!
Thow art of mercie great, thow art bening;
Thair is no strenth nor help but only thow,
For firme and suire 20
Thow dois induire
To sinneris all that willinglie dois bow.

Cum sinneris now, the Lord doeth on ws call.
Cum all with me, cum pray with one consent,
Cum, cum in tyme, and doe our sinnis repent; 25
Cum now with humble hairtis, ȝe wretchis all,
Befoir our God for mercie lat ws fall,
He is the God that heiris the penitent,
He is of nature slaw to punishment,
He will ws save and in his merceis tak; 30
Throuch Christ his sonne,
Who sittis abonne,
He will ws saue, ȝea for his onlie saik.

With heavie hairt, thairfoir, to God alone,
To the, O Lord, I mak my plaint and cry, 35
With humble hairt lo prostrat I doe ly,

To the I call, to the I mak my mone,
With sobs and sighs, with bitter tearis I grone.
Heir me, thairfoir, heir me, O Lord, I say,
To the I flie, to the I rin and pray, 40
Graunt me at last, graunt me, a sinner puir,
That all the mas
Of my trespas
Thow will forʒet and maik me euer suir.

What mortall man is he, O Lord, that can 45
Thy merceis comprehend, so monyfauld;
What sinfull wratche is he that dar be bauld
Thy secreittis, Lord, for to vnfauld and skan.
O simple saul, O wretche, O wicked man!
Thy awin consait lat be thy fond pretence, 50
Submit thy self with all dew reuerence,
And graunt the Lord, ʒea, all that is his richt:
In mynd him beir,
Sie thow him feir,
And vnto him maik haist with all thy micht. 55

O that I could set fourth thy prais aricht,
And thame in mynd to beir for euermoir.
O happie thryis that thame can keip in stoir;
O happie most if that with all our micht
We meditat thairin, boith day and nicht. 60
Graunt Lord, therfoir, graunt Father deir to me,
Quhen lyfe is past thy endles gloir to sie,
For heir, O lord, thair is no thing can stand,
Vnles thow plaice
With ws thy graice, 65
And ws defend with force of thy richt hand.

My God is onlie he quhom on I stay;
All warldlie thingis as vaine I will reiect:
Thay ar but licht and thingis of nane effect,
Quhairfoir on the my hoill repois I lay. 70
Refuis me not: thow art my God for ay,
And ay salbe, whill braith and lyf dois lest.
My mynd sall neuer suerve, I doe protest,
Vnto the Lord, my God, now will I sing

For euer moir, 75
Be prais and gloir,
To the, O Lord, that sittis in heavin as king.

Finis.

74. In Prais of ane Gentle Woman.

To prais that perfyte is, the labour wer but vain;
To seik to pas the painters art, but lytill wer my gain;
3it if I could performe that dewtie bindis as dew,
In simple style, as best I micht, this worthie work persew,
Then wald I taik in hand that now dois pas my skill,　　　5
To prais the passing bewtie brave; quhilk now aganis my will,
Perforce, I man be dum, and so contentit be,
And onlye leif by luiking on, till farther happin me.
But Love dois so me move, and Houp sayis, 'Doe thy best:
Behauld 3one faice that thow dois sie, in it salbe thy rest,　　　10
Say on, thairfoir, be bauld and lytill as thow can
Set furth hir praysis worthelie, and vow thy self hir man.'
3e heavinlie goddis above, 3e most celestiall,
Vnto my muse 3our earis doe bend, and for 3our help I call:
Give me Pernassus styll, and als Mont Edees smell,　　　15
With water Helicon to drink, or els Pegasus well.
3e loveris then, that boist to serve with loyaltyie
3our ladyis fair, as 3e suppon, now list a whyll to me:
My ladie, I dar vow, in bewtie all doeth pas,
And for hir cumlie, courtlie graice, may be 3our luiking glas.　　　20
Dame Vertew in hir hairt with Pitie taikis thair place,
And whosoeuer on hir luikis, dois prais hir noble grace.
Remors and Temperance dois hir accumpanie,
And from hir staitlie presence dois all filthie vycis flie.
No virtew sho dois want, sho is both trew and kynd,　　　25
In constancie, no matche alyfe, and faythfulnes of mynd.
And now
I am hir awin: quhat than? It is the onlye thing I crave.
Scho will me not refuis, I knaw. Quhat farther wauld I have?

Finis.

75. Of Ane Vnthankfull Freind.

Vnto a freind I proferd once gud will,
Thinking thairby to play a freind him till:
But now to lait thairof I me repent,
Since he for doing so hes maid me schent,
Quhairfoir the proverb auld I put in vre, 5
'Quhen stead is stollin, then steik the stable dure';
Quhilk causis me full oft to call and cry,
What fuill, what beast, what simple saull wes I!
Is not a trustie freind by tryell bocht,
And moir account then ten obteynd for nocht? 10
3it, I am lyik the blind that blamis the licht,
As thocht in him thair wer no want of sicht;
For I the samyn freind have tryid full oft,
And found his honestie; but euer nocht,
For so wes love by blind effectioun cast, 15
That seing wauld not sie, till at the last
Bewar of, had I wist, I did record,
And then to lait my love I did remord.
For I wes lyik the hen that skrepis the knyfe
3it ignorant it sould bereve hir lyfe. 20
But he dois weill thairin him self declair,
And als the fayth and treuth to me he bair,
And schawis him lyik the cur that bytis the man
Quhen he hes fed and done him all he can.
Quhairfoir, with wit now coft, I doe protest, 25
I vow, I sweir in hairt, that it sall rest.

Finis.

76. To His Freind.

O michtie Iove that rewlis all,
O king that ringis in skyis above,
Graunt me sum rest, a wretch and thrall,
If the to pitie I may move:
Quhat mortall wicht alyfe abydis 5
As I so monye turning tydis?

O happie is that mortall wicht!
O happie thryis, ȝea, him I call,
In love that all succeidis aricht,
And neuer teastis of Fortounis thrall. 10
Ȝea, moir then hap it that he may
My haples haps avoyd for ay.

But I, alace, to tell you moir,
A double dolour I induir,
And nane but ane dois cair, thairfoir. 15
Now death is nixt, I you assuir,
Ȝit ladye leif, O ladye myne,
Not thou, but I, deseruis the pyne.

Tak on, thairfoir, thy doulfull weid;
Cast of thy proud and staitlie hewis; 20
Tak blak, it best becumis thy heid,
But cullouris mo sie thou refuis,
For Fortun now hes chaingit hir face,
And thou abydis in wo, alace.

My awin mishap I nothing deime, 25
O dear to me, and dear againe.
It's the, my hairt, that I esteime,
As for my self I cair no paine.
O godis, on me your yre than cast
And leive my ladye at the last. 30

O ladye, moir then lyfe to me,
Thou art the onlye foode I taist.
O Tisbe trew for the I die.
Onles that thow remaine at rest,

Thou art the caus of all my fall, 35
And ȝit to the I am a thrall.

Thow hes no blame, my faythfull hairt,
It's my ill luk that troublis the.
Our great and wechtie is the pairt
That thou alone sould die for me, 40
Aganis my will, I the assuir,
For all of richt I sould induir.

Finis.

77. In Prais of ane Gilt Bybill.

Who takis in hand by pen
To prais a wark with fame,
Advysedlie sould luik, then loup,
For hazard of his name.

This buik all prais deseruis, 5
My prais it wer but vain;
3it, gentle reader, mark, I say,
And thyne salbe the gain.

A cot bedect with gold
and syluer streamis it weiris, 10
As iust rewaird the maistres gave,
For love to it scho beiris.

But opin vp the same,
And luik with single ei,
Bayth glistering gemmis, and pearlis of pryce 15
Thair schyning sall thou sie.

Finis.

78. Ane Freindlye Letter to his Freind

The piteous plaint of heavie hairt,
Complaning but releif,
The cruell pain of wofull smairt,
Deploring great mischeif,
Declairis thair is no rest,   5
But mynd full soir opprest.

Whan most of all to rest I wish,
And greatest eis I crave,
When most securitie I wish,
And greatest ioy wald have,   10
Then draweth on my paine,
And sighe it dois constraine.

Wherfoir, O God omnipotent,
My prayer graunt to me,
And of thy wraith, I pray, relent,   15
With favour thyne to sie,
That I obtene I may
The thing quhairon I stay.

For, whill that braith and lyfe dois lest,
I promeis and avow   20
That nane in hairt with me sall rest,
Nor thair to duell allow,
But onlye thow for ay
Sall thair remain and stay.

It sall not be the cruell spyt   25
Of thame that workis vneis,
Nor ȝit, in thame that takis delyt,
To hinder with thair leis;
But fayth and promeis suir
Sall euer moir induir.   30

Persuaid thy self, my faythfull hairt,
I will for the abyd,
In perrells all to play my pairt,
And dainger set asyd,

Refusing not for the 35
The pain, how great it be.

Fairweill, thairfoir, my hairt, adew.
Fairweill, and haue gudnicht;
God graunt that we doe neuer rew,
Bot to have chosin richt. 40

Finis.

79. To Ane Angrie Freinde.

The lyon for hir tender whelpis dois roir,
And quhy? Becaus in thame scho set hir stoir;
The turtill for the lose of maik, thay say,
Doeth neuer rest, bot workis hir awin decay;
And euerie thing that Nature furth hes brought,   5
Or ȝit to licht with schap and lyfe hes wroght,
Dois seik to keip the thing it loves best,
And so with it to leif in ioy and rest.
But Fortoun, cruell and malitious,
In rest doeth schaw hir most pernitious,   10
And quhen with countenance sho smylis maist,
Then sould scho have of all but credit leist.
For quhy the turtill trew, bereft of ioy,
Doeth now to lait complaine for great annoy.
Fy on the fickill stait of warldlie thingis!   15
Fy on plesour schort that murning bringis!
Sall fayth and treuth, sall promeis firme and suir,
Be now cast of, no langer to induir?
Na, God forbid, the saying meanis not so;
Thay never thocht in hairt me to forgo,   20
And now the hand, that wounded me so soir,
Sall end the lyfe, or ellis againe restoir.

Finis.

80. To His Freind.

The beatin bark with bloistrous blastis,
And dunge with wavering wind,
Into the port hir self sho castis,
Thair lyfe or death to find.

The pilgrim, wereid with tormoill, 5
And transing monye a land,
At lenth vnto his native soill,
He doeth mak haist in hand.

The painfull pangs of passing pain,
Tormenting birthfull wombe, 10
ȝit ioyfull, mirrie, glaid and fain,
The ȝouth anis sene at home.

Thair, doutfull daingers all foirpast,
And mirth for murning set,
Now onlye to reioyis thay cast, 15
And sorrowis all forȝet.

But I, alace, bewrapt with wo,
In laberinth I ly,
And I my self remanis my fo,
Houping that will not be. 20

ȝit, who can tell the goddis remord,
And me in favour taik,
And thay among them selfis accord,
On me thair yre to slaik.

And I obtain my faythfull hairt, 25
My onlye ioy and grace,
Remaining constant for my pairt,
With houp for to embrace.

Then I, with humble hairt contreit,
The goddes sall adoir, 30
On bended kneis and handis vpset,
And prais them euer moir.

Lo! heir a toy and licht conset,
And loveris new devyce,
Both for the auld and sage vnfet, 35
And also for the wyse.

But onlye for ane treuth and prove
To ladye maistres myne,
For otheris all, howbeit it move,
I cair it not a pryne. 40

Finis.

81. Ane Prayer.

With weippin eis and face defigurat,
My hairt to the, O God, I elevat,
But mynd and bodye humblie doe prostrat,
And als thy glorious name I invocat.

Acknawledging my sinnes so monyfauld 5
That scarce for grace to call I dar be bauld,
Vnles that thow, with merceis monyfauld,
A wretche and sinner pour thow doe vphauld.

O God eternall and omnipotent,
My sinnes forgeve and let me not be schent; 10
Thair is no cours of 3outhfulnes 3it spent,
But with thy help, in tyme, I may relent.

Thow sekest not, O Father dear, I knaw,
To deill with ws by rigour of the law,
But rather mercie vnto ws to schaw, 15
And so thairby to keip ws in thy aw.

Give me, thairfoir, ane pour and humble spreit,
Give me, my God, ane mynd not counterfeit,
That wordes and thochtis, and all in one, may meit,
So I to the may call with hairt contreit. 20

My hairt and mynd to the sall euer bend,
And to thy lawis and statutis eik attend,
That I vnto thy seit divine may send
My sobs, my sighis, my lyfe, for till amend.

Thairfoir, O God, I cry behauld and lo! 25
Thy holie bluid is not 3it waistit so
But that it may help me with sinners mo,
Howbeit to the I am a wretch and fo.

Iehoua greit and Lord maist hie,
To futestule thyne for succour I doe flie, 30
Grant me, O Lord, thy endles gloir to sie,
And so with angellis bricht to cumpanie.

Finis.

82.
To michtie Ioue above that ringis
In heavenis so hie, quhair angels singis;
To Christ his onlie sone, our Lord,
Who shed his bluid for euerie sinner;
To Holie Ghost, the confort bringer, 5
We rander thankis with one accord.

Finis.

83. To Ane Vnthankfull Freind.

Ane new fairweill, a strainge gudnicht,
Of the, periurd and ladye fals,
I now will tak, quho wes thy knicht,
Thy faythfull freind, and lover als;
But now from the my hairt is rent, 5
For fayth ne treuth wes by the ment.

Thy pryde, thy hicht, thy arrogance,
Thy wylie woordes sall the deiect,
And not as thow dois trow advance,
But filthie lyfe and deidis detect, 10
Whairwith, abone all womankynd,
I dar avow, thow beiris in mynd.

I loved the ance, I doe confes;
My hairt wes thyne, I did protest.
Thow said thow loved me, nathing les, 15
But me preferd above the rest:
But so the end did weill declair
The faith and treuth to me thow bair.

Fy on the, filthie, faithles dame!
Fy on thy cruell tygirs hairt! 20
For I am not the onlye man
To quhom thow playis ane whoris pairt,
But hard it is to chainge thy mynd:
Thow boght it not, thou hest of kynd.

Baith treuth and promeis did thow geif 25
To me by fayth and aithe coniurd,
And suair that, as the Lord did leif,
With me to rest and die assuird.
Quhat other secreit thingis thair was
Thow knawest thy self, I let thame pas. 30

3it, sum will say I wes bot blunt
Till wow a wedow in sic wys,
And namelie ane wha had bene brunt,
And myndit not to hazard twys;

Gif farther wes not done in deid 35
Thow knawis thairof thow had na neid.

But, for my pairt, into that game,
I of my self will bauldlie say,
With wyfe or maid to play the man
In honestie, bayth nicht and day; 40
But for to satefie ane whore
Fiftene sies I can not induire.

Thow thinkis thow hes obteind a pray
In that a pecok thow hes taine,
And me perhaps, as thow will say, 45
Left as a simple saull alaine.
A, pray thow gat a prys of wourth:
Fairweill, the deuill of hell go with!

He is of noble bluid, I knaw,
By the no honour he can get, 50
But as a dastard did him schaw,
And dewtie lyik a theif forʒet,
He tuik the onlye for thy gear,
And thow chust him for lance and speir.

And now, fairweill, as I begoude, 55
Gudnicht, as thow deseruis best;
And so I end and will conclud
That lust and avarice takis no rest;
But when that all is gone he sought,
Than think his lance wes deirlie bought. 60

I ... sendis
This ragment, lytill wourth,
Not caring for amendis,
My mynd but to schaw fourth,

And wissis everie man 65
To iudge of me aright,
For thair is nane that can
Eschew ane whoris slicht.

The schame is hirs, I sueir,
The los not myne, ȝe knaw, 70
Of nane sho standis na feir,
Nor of reproche ne aw.

Finis.

84. In Prais of ane Buik Send to his Freind.

This buik, who taikis in hand to reid,
Let thame the same peruse
With diligence and taking heid,
Or ellis the same refuse;
And efter reading twyis, 5
Laith not to read it thryis.

For thingis of great and high affairs
In simple style he schawis,
And als the end of worldlie cairs
In shape of beastis he drawis. 10
Assuir thy self, thairfoir,
In it of tresour stoir.

For wysest workis of all we sie
In colours to be drawin,
And so set furth by misterie, 15
And thairin to be schawin;
The wordes I doe not mein,
But sentence to attein.

Finis.

85. To Your Self.

If Sapho saige, for saphic songe so sueit,
Did pleid for prais and place amangs the nyne;
If trustie talk and taillis so trew do meit,
Amids the gods dois duell that dame devyne.

And now, of lait, that lustie ladie rair, 5
Olimpia, O lampe of Latine land,
So doeth thy workes vnto this day declair,
For lyflie art who list thy vers to scand.

A thrid, O Maistres Marie, maik I pray,
And put in vre ʒour worthie vertewis all, 10
For famous is your fleing fame, I say,
Hyd not so haut a hairt in slugish thrall.

This buik then bear and beat your branis therin:
A plesant poet perfyte sall ye be
And, lytill labour lost, the laurell win, 15
Adorn'd with cumlie croun of poesie.

And than:
For sicophant, for simple saull, for sott,
Maik weill, mar not, for Momus cair ʒe not.

Finis.

86.
Ʒe heauinlie goddis and goddessis,
Ʒe most celestiall,
Vnto my muse ʒour helpis doe bend,
And for ʒour aydis I call.

And thow Diana, ladye bricht, 5
With nymphes of chastetie,
Graunt me your favours, I requeist,
To end this worthelie.

Finis.

87.
Quhen houp and hap, and weill and health bene hiest,
Then wo and wrack, diseis and neid bene niest.

Be war to ryiss in serving princelie lust;
Suirlie to stand is one meane rysing iust.

1 and weill and health] whan helth and welth BALDWIN
3 ryiss in] ryse by BALDWIN
4 Is one meane] one meane is BALDWIN

88. The Reid in the Loch Sayis.

Thocht raging stormes movis ws to schaik,
And wind makis waters ws overflow,
We ȝeild thairto, bot dois not brek,
And in the calme bent vp we grow.

So baneist men, thocht princes raige, 5
And prisoners, be not disparit,
Abyde the calme, quhill that it suaige,
For tyme sic caussis hes reparit.

Finis.

89.
As absence is the greatest fo
That Cupids clientis dois suspect,
Lang out of sicht engendris so
To presence the contrair effect.
And as obliuioun dois deiect 5
The building of rememberance,
So lak of memorie neglect
The deidis deserving recompance.

Of absence langour dois proceid,
And langour breidis melancolie; 10
Melancolie procuiris the deid
Be sindrie kyndis of meladie.
Thus may I gatther easalie
That absence is ane homiceid,
To martyre men maist cruellie, 15
Except thair be found out remeid.

Now thocht, the causer of thir thre,
Langour, melancolie, and deid,
This present tyme dois threattin me
To pour thir plages on my heid. 20
Laking that grace my caus to pleid,
At Bewteis bar to seik refuge,
3it in 3our iustice I confeid,
Absence my richt sall not preiudge.

Thocht other loveris doe alledge 25
For to defend thair libertie,
Sum other caussis to repledge
Thame selfis from absence tyrannie;
3it, into that securitie
With thame I put na confidence, 30
Suppose in love my constancie
Deservis als great recompance.

To find ane trew Penelope
Quhair other sum hes wrocht in vaine,
3it I beleif to find 3ow sa, 35
And constanter for to remaine

In easing thus ȝour loveris paine,
As scho wes to be registrat;
And sua thocht absence me disdaine   40
I sall induire the last combat.

Thocht absence be
The meladie
Tormenting me
With daylie greif,   45

ȝour constancie
May remedie.
Gif not, I die
Without releif.

Finis.

90. Epitaph of Sir Richard Maitland Knight.

The slyding tyme so slylie slippes away,
It reaves from vs remembrance of our state;
And whill we doe the cair of tyme delay,
We tyne the tyde and doe lament to late.
Then to eschew such daingerous debate 5
Prepone for patren manly Maitland knight:
Learne by his lyfe to live in semble rate,
With love to God, religion, law and right;
For as he wes of vertew lucent light,
Of antient bloode, of noble spreit and name, 10
Beloued of God, and euerye gratious wight,
So deit he olde, deseruing worthy fame,
A rare example set for ws to see
What we haue bene, now ar, and ought to be.

T. H.

11 wight] *om.* R
12 he] *om.* R
13 for ws to see] sett for to sie R
Attribution: Quod Thomas hudsone in MF, R.

91. Ane Other.

Thy surname Maitland shewes thyne antient race,
Thy martiall acts the cronicles display,
And speake thou Iustice, whilst he had thy place,
Yf iustlye he thy ballance did not sway.
He wes ay prest Gods treuth to plant alway,   5
Who gave him long yeares and a faithfull wyfe;
His childrens children flourishit day by day,
In wealth he lived, with honour left this lyfe.
Then thou who hears his birthe, his lyfe, and end,
May say his soule to lasting lyfe is send.   10
Thus, may ȝe sie none may from deathe refraine,
But lives to die and deis to live againe.
We that him wantis may waill his death, alace,
Wer not his worthye imps suppleis his place.

R. H.

3 he] thow R
5 ay] *om.* R
9 hears] knawis MF R
11 ȝe] we MF R   none may] may nane R
R.H.] Quod Robert Hudson MF; Finis R.H. R

92. Epitaphe vpon the Death of the Right Honorable Sir Richard Metland, Knight, Lord of Leidingtoun.

This hallow grave within her bounds dois close
An worthy knight, baith valiant, grave, and wyse,
And in the same his breathles banes repose,
Quhase lyflye spreit did warldlye things despyse.
Within this place the maist vnspotted lyese   5
And blamles iudge that iustice did maintene.
ȝit from his tombe (thought he be deid) doith ryse
The glorious praise, to verteuous dois pertene,
For in his breist, quhilk wisdome did contene,
Lay steidfast treuth and vncorrupted fayth.   10
His honest hands from brybing did abstene,
His fautles feit did [marche] in honours paith,
His feit, hands, breist lye buried in this grave,
Bot this, his saule, the heavens dois receave.

12 marche] marthle MQ

93a. A Luid Of Him Self and His Ladyie Quho Dyed On His Burial Day.

Loe heir tuo wights inburied be,
Off noble birth and bloud,
Quha by thair death hes naturs course
By naturs lyne conclud.

In mariage-band they liued long,   5
thrie scoir of ȝeirs and foure;
In honour maist contentedlye
Thair lyfe they did dryue ouer.

Bot now hes Death thair aged dayes
Defaced by his dairt,   10
And hes thair brethles weryit corps
Conuoyed to this pairt.

Bot ȝit, quhat Death hes preast to doe
thair loue for to devyde,
Loue hes againe, surmounting Death,   15
the force of Death defyd.

93b. A Luid To The Passer By.

Looke to thy self by vs:
Suche wer we ons as thow;
And thow by tyme sall be consemud
To dust, as we ar now.

94.

In Commendation of the Right Honorable Syr Iohne Maitland of Thirlstaine Knight, Secretair to the King, his Maiestie.

1. The First Visiovn.
Before my face this nyght to me appeird
My silent muse, in sorrou all confound,
And half dismayd, this questioun at me speird:
'Quhy doe we not his glorious praise resound?
Quhase goodnes we beyond our hope hes found,   5
Quhase fauour hes surmounted our desert,
And as he dois in pouer maist [abound],
So to our ayd the same he dois conuert.'
'O muse', quod I, 'euen with a willing hairt
I sall fulfill this chairge with bent desyre,   10
So that to me your furye ȝe impart;
And thir my verse, with lerned skill, inspyre,
For sen I suld the maist renoumd commend,
Ȝe lykwyse ought ȝour ayde and help extend.'

2. Visiovn.
Thus, as I spak, I saw the muses nyne,
With harpes in hand, about me sone repair,
Sa that thair hymns, and voces maist devyne,
By sympathie resonded in the air:
'Sing! lett vs sing, and by our sangs declair   5
His worthye stock, baith valiant, stout and wyse,
From quhilk hes sprung of muses all the cair,
Ȝea, off the gods, from quhome all grace dois ryse.
His father deir, quha neir his buriall lyess,
Ane Homer auld of euerlaisting fame,   10
A iudge maist iust, and lord, quha hes the pryse
For conscience pure, of ane vnspotted name,
Off prences loued, in honour lang he liuis,
Quhase memorie his learned sones reuiuis.'

3. Visioun.
And heir they stayd, till they had drawen thair breath.
Than they began with schiller toons of joy:
[Euterpe] sang, 'His fame suruiueth death!'
And Clio sayd, 'No force sal him destroy!'

Thalia spak, 'Lat vs our sangs employ 5
To blaise his praise, and eternise his glore!'
Polhymina sayde, 'I will and sall conuoy
His consell, witt, quhilk he hess in greate store,
Through all the warld, and will him sa decore,
That as he now surpassis, with his prence, 10
In grace and loue all vthers, so before
He sall thame pass in creddit, but offence.
Lang sal he liue in ioy, in bliss, and helth,
And on his bak sall leane this coumoun welth.'

4. Visioun.

As they did end, than Ouide from [exyle]
Of Pontus cam, quhair he til death remaind,
Induiring cauld and hounger all that quhyle,
Conseumd with woe that August him disdaind.
'Alas!', sayd he, 'in vaine have I complaind 5
For to assvuage Augustus yre and wreath,
And thought that thou in presoun was detaind,
3ie happy thou, quho fauourd is of death.
Thy monarch, and thy great Augustus, heth
Extend his grace, att thy good lords requeist, 10
Quhose honour thou, til waisted be thy breath,
Sall keip in mynde within thy thankfull breist:
Thou sall his glore with his desairts proclame,
And celebrat within the kirk of fame.

Musis sine tempore tempus.

94.1.7 abound] abbund MQ
94.3.3 Euterpe] A uterpe MQ
94.4.1 exyle] exyde MQ

95.
O Deith, allace! with dairt so dolours,
Quhy art thow so iniust withowt respect
To ȝouth and eild, and mid age odious?
Obscuir and noble, quhy haldis thow of ane fect?
Quhat is the cause nane may thair nek [withdraw] 5
From thy tyrannical and inamiable ȝok?
Quhy art thow so vnequal to neglect
Thair vertew that discendis of noble stok?

Did thow not knaw the maist excellente graces
Vnto our knycht, Sir Richard Maitland, geuin, 10
Quhom of the fame is planted in all places,
And reaches vp vnto the hichest hevin?
Reioyse now, Deid, and hald thy heid full evin!
Luik with thy piteous eine throuch all this land,
Sen thow that perle hes cruellie from vs reuin: 15
Vpon the lyk thow sall not lay thy hand.

Of noble bluid he hes be lyne [descended],
Wantand na gift ane mortall wycht could craif;
Against all vyce with vertew weill defended,
As justice, temperance, and pacience by the laif; 20
Of all maist constant that did Christis word ressaif,
With equitie and faythfulnes possest,
As be his deuoit death all may persaif,
And godlie liuing, sa lang as lyfe did lest.

O cruell Deith! thow wes nocht ȝit content 25
To cutt this noble lord with thy scharp huik,
Except his verteous lady excellent
Thow cleik also, and in thy bosome bruik,
Quhom of he in his lyif sik plesour tuik,
So joyfullie that nane could leif in eird. 30
Quhy wald thow nocht vpon their vertew luik,
Sine for to straik thame wes nocht soir effeird?

5 withdraw] *om.* MQ
17 descended] defended MQ

Quhat hes thow win? Thy triumph is bot small.
Vnto the nobles done is masit iniure,
Quha spoyled ar of sick ane speciall   35
That lyk a lanterne schynit to thame suir,
Nixt to thair bairnes, kinsfolk, and the puir,
And to thair faithfull seruandis, deu elk eane.
Thair saules ar entred in att heuins duir,
And for thy vglie dairtis makis na mane.   40

3e gentil men, excuise my ruid indyit,
Quha with 3our presence ornis this funerall.
It is of zeil that I with Deith doe flyit,
And mouit with ane dolour principall:
For lak of cunning my verse will seim rurall.   45
Couer my ignorance and tak it in guid pairt:
My will is guid, my lerning is bot small,
My strenth is nocht, I haue ane willing hairt.

Wer Ihone Bocace callit again to lyif,
And syne had not for3et his former style,   50
In painted termes and rethorik flouris ryif,
And quikned with sum mater for a quhyle,
Suffice he mycht in meter to compyle
The praises of thir blissed saules tway:
3it, gentil men, houbeid my ryme be vyle,   55
[...]

---

56 The folio has been cropped and the final line of the stanza is no longer legible.

Explanatary Notes

1. Ane Sonet to the Authour in Commendatioun of his Buik

This dedicatory sonnet is likely to date from the time of the completion of the compilation of MQ, perhaps 1586, the date inscribed twice at the beginning of the manuscript. It is not clear from the poem whether it anticipates or follows Sir Richard Maitland's death in March 1586, although the reference to Maitland's immortal fame (l. 14) might suggest that it is posthumous. Certainly its concern with Maitland's family history, and his exemplary status, anticipates the commemorative poems at the end of the manuscript, MQ 90–95. Maitland's poetry (l. 12) is said here to augment the family fame, and is thus a fitting counterpart to the valiant deeds of his ancestors. While his prose *History of the House of Seyton* (c.1559, Fullerton ed. 1829) may certainly have achieved this end, few of Maitland's surviving poems concern the history of his surname. Nevertheless, literary pursuits were regarded as fitting pastimes for the gentleman. The poem is likely to be by a member of the Maitland family (perhaps one of Maitland's 'ofspring', l. 7, possibly Marie Maitland) or immediate circle of friends and close associates.

Stanza: sonnet ababbcbccdcdee[5].
Text: unnumbered folio at beginning of MQ.
Authorship: unattributed.
Date: c.1586.

Commentary

1 *Your predicessouris prayse and prowes hie.* Maitland's most distinguished predecessors were Setons, to whom he was related through his mother, Margaret Seton, and about whom he composed a prose history (see headnote). The Setons' reputation for prowess, especially during the Siege of Berwick, was well known (see *Scots Peerage* VIII, pp. 559–606 (563–69)). Compare MQ 90, l. 10, MQ 91, ll. 1–2, MQ 94.2, ll. 6–7.

6 *Vnto thair lyne and linage to give licht.* Compare MQ 95, l. 36.

7 *quhose ofspring.* Other descendants of the predecessors mentioned in l. 1, including Maitland's own children.

11 *3e, wittie, wyse and val3eant warriour wicht.* Maitland is presented here as an educated statesman and as militarily active. On this renaissance ideal, see Brown 2000, p. 199. He had a reputation for sagacity in diplomatic circles, Sir Ralph Sadler commenting on the wisdom he showed as one of Elizabeth's commissioners for border affairs in 1559. There are no records of Maitland's military activity, though the exact nature of his youthful service at James V's court is not known. See Spiller *ODNB*.

12 *the poetis pairt weill playit.* Most of Maitland's surviving poems seem to have been composed between the 1550s and early 1570s, by which time he was well established in his legal and administrative career.

2. Sum wyfes of the borroustoun

This poem is a satirical complaint at townswomen's love of novelty ('newfangilnes'), especially in fashions and personal possessions ('geir'). Pinkerton entitled it 'Satire on the toun ladyes' in his 1786 edition (p. 326). The women's love of fine attire is linked to their 'carnell lust' (l. 7) and desire to provoke sinful conduct in others (l. 19). Complaints on the infringement of sumptuary laws are common in medieval literature, especially in didactic works such as *The Ship of Fools* (see Jamieson ed. 1889, pp. 35–8), and the *sermones ad status* tradition, and often target the wives of town dwellers, especially merchants and the wealthy urban elite (see Owst 1966, pp. 390–411; Scattergood 1996, pp. 240–57).

Much of Maitland's poem is concerned with the details of women's clothing. As a judge and Lord of Session, Maitland may have been familiar with the sumptuary legislation of the Scottish Parliament, which was designed to defend the rights and distinctiveness of the estates and protect the livelihoods of those who depended on the domestic cloth industry. Sumptuary legislation was motivated by the importation of fine fabrics, which was widely blamed for impoverishing the realm by denying employment to local cloth workers. Such legislation forbade the inhabitants of the burghs to wear costly silks and furs, imported and expensively dyed fabrics, trains or elaborate head gear, except on holidays. Legislation of 1458 exhorts merchants to 'make their wives and daughters be dressed in like manner, suitable and corresponding to their estate' (see *RPS* 1458/3/2; also see 1471/5/7). An act of 1581, partly designed to protect the Scottish cloth industry, sought to curtail the 'great abuse standing among [the king's] subjects of the mean estate, presuming to copy his highness and his nobility in the use and wearing of costly clothing and silks of all sorts, linen and cambric, fringing and trimmings of gold, silver and silk, and woollen cloth ... as it is not able to be longer sustained without great hurt and inconvenience of the commonwealth' (*RPS* 1581/10/37; also see Shaw 1979). Cambric and elaborate golden and silver trimmings on clothing are mentioned in Maitland's poem (ll. 14 and 22). The moral, economic and social debates behind sumptuary laws are alluded to in a number of late fifteenth- and sixteenth-century Scottish poems including *The Prestis of Peblis*, ll. 201–12; and Dunbar's 'Doverrit with dreme, devysing in my slummer' (with which Maitland's poem shares a rhyme scheme), ll. 71–80. Also see *The Thewis off Gud Women*, ll. 29–36. They are a major concern in Lyndsay's *Ane Supplicatioun Directit ... to the Kingis Grace, in Contemptioun of Syde Taillis* (c.1539–41). See especially lines 71–100 on the 'wantoun burges wyiffis'. This poem is discussed in Harker 2005.

Lines 1–65 of Maitland's poem form the complaint about the love of extravagance among the wives of the 'borroustoun' (the burgh). The last forty-five lines of the poem are advisory. The narrator directs his advice to young wives (l. 66), in a passage that recalls the parental advice genre (see MQ 11 and 15), and then more generally to all women (ll. 81–2). Lines 96–100 are addressed to noble women, whom the narrator regards as having the responsibility of setting a good example to other women (ll. 96–100), and may also have something to learn from his counsel (see Brown 2000, pp. 83–4).

The evils of extravagant clothing are also mentioned in MQ 4, ll. 51–60 and 76–80. For related poems, see MQ 5, 33, 52, 53.

Stanza: aabaB[4]. The refrain puns on the word 'geir' in its multiple senses (see note to l. 5). The stanza is also used in MQ 4 and 52 (both by Maitland). It was used earlier by Dunbar for moral and comic verses, and by William Stewart (see Bawcutt ed. 1998, pp. 318–18). Both poets were known to Maitland.

Text: MQ fols 1–3v; MF pp. 265–66. MF lacks lines 1–50. D fols 1v–3v.

Authorship: attributed to Sir Richard Maitland of Lethington in MF, MQ and D.

Date: uncertain.

Commentary

1 *Sum wyfes of the borroustoun.* 'Wyf' is probably used here in the specific sense of 'married woman' (*DOST*, *Wyf*, n. sense 2): burgesses and their wives occupied a high station in society. The narrator purports to be discriminating in his comments rather than to be accusing all town wives of the same faults. (MQ 3 includes a prayer for grace for the 'gud burgess wyffis' who live 'Thriftie and ... honest lyvis' (ll. 71–4)). The criticism of the female inhabitants of the 'borroustoun' (the burgh, a town with special trading privileges) is briefly extended to all wasteful women (ll. 54–5) and to 'landwart' women (l. 107). The comparison or opposition of the moral conduct of town and country dwellers is conventional. See Henryson, *Morall Fabillis*, ll. 164–5; MQ 6, l. 2.

1–3 The wives' love of novelty leaves them with a dilemma about what to wear. Vanity (a species of pride), and wantonness or lust (l. 7), are cited as common faults of women in the misogynistic tradition. See Blamires 1992, pp. 70–1, 122–4, 192–3. 'Vaine' (l. 2) has the sense of 'devoid of wisdom, foolish, idle, and silly', as well as of being excessively concerned with one's appearance and qualities. See *DOST, Vain(e)*, adj. 2.

4 *croun*. The women spend (*wair*, see *DOST, War(e), wair*, v. 2) lots of gold coins (*DOST, Croun*, n. 5) on clothing.

5 *geir*. Personal possessions, including clothing or apparel, but also 'wealth, money' (see l. 65 for this sense) and 'equipment'. See *DOST, Gere*, n. 1b, 2.

6 *Thair bodyis bravelie thay attyire*. 'They attire their bodies splendidly'.

8 *I fairlie*. 'I marvel'. The narrator is an incredulous observer up to line 66 when he then takes on the role of counsellor.

11–12 *Thair gounis ar coistlie and trimlie traillis, / Barrit with veluous sleif, nek, and taillis*. 'Their gowns are expensive and trail smartly [along the ground], ornamented with velvet sleeve, collar and trains'. Long clothes that trail on the ground are often the target of sumptuary complaints. Compare ll. 17–18, where preaching against long sleeves is mentioned. Compare Chaucer's *Parson's Tale* on 'superfluitee of clothynge', ll. 416–20; and Dunbar's 'Doverrit with dreme, devysing in my slummer', l. 73; also see Scattergood 1996, pp. 244, 250.

13 *foirskirt*. The front skirt of a dress, here made of a combination of different silks.

14 *camreche*. A fine white cloth or linen named after its place of manufacture, Cambray in Flanders (Flemish *Kameryk*). *Fuk-saillis*. 'Foresails': here used metaphorically of a woman's billowing skirt, and with possible crude word play, as in Dunbar's 'Doverrit with dreme, devysing in my slummer', l. 74 ('Sic fillokis with fuk salis'). See Bawcutt ed. 1998, p. 315. Also see the play on 'fukscheit' in Sempill's *The Flemyng*

Bark (l. 30), a satirical ballad on Margaret Fleming contained in the Bannatyne MS (Cranstoun ed. 1891–93, I, pp. 391–93).

17 *geill-poikkis*. A 'poik' is a small bag (*DOST, Poke*, n., 3a, 3c). The word was used metaphorically to refer to the bulbous or puffed out part of a sleeve. It was also used of a hood or an appendage to a hat. A 'geill-pock' is a jelly bag (*OED, Geill*, n.). The sleeves on the women's cloaks are therefore imagined as hanging like jelly bags, ridiculous, rather than elegant, in appearance.

21 *wylie-coittis*. A warm undergarment or a woman's petticoat. See *DOST, Wylecot*, n. Later in the poem the women are imagined as provocatively pulling up their dresses to show off their petticoats, and then their petticoats to show off their stockings (ll. 32–4).

22 *Broudrit richt braid with pasmentis sewit*. The petticoats are embroidered amply with strips of gold or silver lace. 'Passment' refers to strips of gold or silver lace or braid used as decorative trimming on garments. See *SND1, Passment*, n.

24 *gudmen*. Husbands. Perhaps Maitland has in mind the husband of the widow in Dunbar's *Tretis of the Twa Mariit Wemen and the Wedo*, ll. 365–76. He provided her with expensive silks and jewels, which she delighted in being able to use to gratify other men after his death.

27–28 *Burrit aboue with tafteis drawin*. The silken hose worn by the women are 'furnished with padded rolls' (*DOST, Burrit*, ppl.a), in this case of taffeta. For the sense of 'drawin', see *DOST, Draw*, v., h: 'To ornament or band (a garment) by applying a different material'. In this sense, the word is frequently used of the banding of hose or sleeves. The hose are then held up with garters ('gartennis').

29 *To gar thair courtlines be knawin*. The town wives have aspirations above their status and courtly pretensions. Also see note to ll. 38 and 46–9. Sumptuary complaints and legislation frequently express a fear of social disorder caused by individuals behaving in a way inappropriate to their estate or class.

36 *carcattis*. Along with fancy collars and beads the women are said to favour the 'carcanet', an elaborate, jewel-encrusted necklace or ornamental collar.

38 *3ounkeir*. The women's ornate accessories are those suited to young nobles, rather than towndwellers. See *OED, Younker*, n.

41 *schone ... muillis*. Now that the narrator has described every item of the wives' apparel he concludes his comments on their appearance by observing their dainty shoes. Inappropriate conduct while in church, such as seeking comfort, or attending to the appearance of oneself or others, is often singled out for rebuke in misogynistic and satirical literature. See Dunbar's *Tretis*, ll. 422–31.

44 *vaine fuillis*. Formulaic for Maitland. See MQ 5, l. 43.

46 *I mein of thame*. There is a perhaps an error in the scribe's use of 'of' in this line. It appears that the narrator does *not* concern himself with those who are concerned about their honour, but those who do not care about respectability.

46–49 Maitland arrives explicitly at his main point in the complaint – the danger of exceeding one's estate and not conducting oneself in an honest and honourable manner. Compare MQ 54, l. 17, and MQ 57, l. 8. 'I mein of thame' – 'I speak of them ...'.

51 *Sumtyme*. In the past: nostalgia is typical of such complaints on the times. Compare ll. 63–64 and MQ 5.

52 *giglettis*. Wanton women or girls. Cf. Robert Henryson, *Testament of Cresseid*, l. 83 ('Sa giglotlike'). Also compare Lyndsay's *Ane Supplicatioun*, l. 86: 'I think sic giglottis ar bot glaikit'.

56 *delicat*. Refined or dainty, but often, as here, used in a derogatory sense to mean fastidious or over-fond of fine things or luxury (therefore connected to the sin of gluttony). See *DOST, Delicat(e)*, a. Also see Chaucer's *Parson's Tale*, ll. 825–30; and *The Thewis off Gud Women* (l. 21, 'Nocht nyss, proud na our-deligat').

62 *droggis*. Spices used to make sweatmeats. See *DOST, Drog*, n. sense 2.

64 *pak*. One's fortune or wealth. See *DOST, Pak*, n., 2b.

66–68 *3oung wyffis ... moderatlie to leif now leir*. This is reminiscent of parental advice literature, in which moderation in all aspects of conduct was highly prized. See *Ratis Raving*, ll. 425–31.

71 *Vse not to skift athort the gait*. 'Do not make the habit of skipping about the town'.

72 *mumschancis*. A 'mumchance' (*OED, Mumchance*, n.) is either a masquerade, or a game of cards or dice (according to *OED* the usage is rare before the 1600s). *DOST* records the verb 'mum(s)chance' ('we mumchance'). The sense is, 'Do not skip about town or take part in mummings'. In terms of theme, pastimes such as mumming or dicing were often frowned upon for women. In Dunbar's *Tretis*, the first wife shockingly expresses her wish to be seen, finely clad, at 'fairis', 'playis ... preichingis and pilgrimages' (ll. 70–71). Also see the advice given in *The Thewis*, ll. 109–20.

73–74 The specific danger here is to the young wife's reputation. An 'ill consait' is a 'bad opinion of one'.

76–81 For similar warnings, see MQ 15, ll. 9–11.

78 *harlot*. This word has the general meaning of someone who is dishonest or disreputable. The added sense of 'unchaste person, a prostitute or fornicator', especially when applied to women, seems to have been common in Scots by the sixteenth century. See *DOST*, *Harlot*, n. 1b, 2.

83 *quin perqueir*. Word for word ('learn this lesson off by heart').

86–90 Here Maitland urges husbands not too spend too much on their wives. The sense here seems to be that she who has been overindulged is prone to be wasteful.

88 *bleir*. To weep, *DOST*, *Bleir*, v. Compare MQ 78, where some burgess's wives are said to dress like the queen's ladies even though their children weep (in poverty and hunger).

91 Maitland's narrator moves on to complain that the infringement of sumptuary laws by the burgesses diminishes the dignity of the 'nobillis of bluid'.

93 *camreche courches*. Kerchiefs or caps worn over the hair by women, and here made of fine Cambray linen. See note to l. 14.

95 *other geir*. Presumably 'geir' is here used with the sense 'possessions' or 'accoutrements'.

107 *landwart ladyis*. Women in the countryside as opposed to those of the town.

3. Of Liddisdaill the commoun theiffis

This poem is a complaint against the notorious lawbreakers of Liddesdale in the Middle March, and their contribution to the disorder of the Scottish Borders. The thieves, also known as reivers, were led by members of the Armstrong and Elliot families, some of whom may be indicated in the nicknames mentioned in the poem between lines 40 and 65. That Liddesdale came to typify the worst sort of cruelty and dishonesty is suggested by Lyndsay's association of the place with the characters Thift, Oppressioun and Falset, in *Ane Satyre of the Thrie Estaitis* (1554), ll. 3273–3290 and 4190–4195. In a 1563 text (*To the Caluiniane Precheouris*), Ninian Winzet also uses the 'theif in Liddisdale' as a byword for 'barber ruidnes' (Hewison ed. 1887–88, I, p. 108, l. 7). The Liddesdale men were known for their treachery as well as their violence and thieving: after the battle of Solway Moss (1542) they robbed and killed Scots soldiers and turned some of their leaders over to the English (see Donaldson 1965, p. 60).

Attempts were made throughout the century by the Scottish parliament to curb their abuses, and the thieves of Liddesdale are frequently mentioned the official records. An act of 1524 (*RPS* 1524/11/15) concerns 'the staunching of theft throughout all the realm and especially in Liddesdale and upon the borders' and decreed that 'the lords and headmen ... be bound for their men ... for the keeping of good rule'. This use of the 'general band' was designed to ensure that landlords who signed it were responsible for the crimes of their tenants and were obliged to hand them over promptly to the justice ayre or expel them from their lands (see Goodare 1999, pp. 258–60).

Richard Maitland was appointed commissioner to settle disputes in the Borders in 1552 and 1559 and so would have had personal knowledge of the problems of the region. In 1554, Mary of Guise made a royal progress to the Border, and her efforts to enforce order in the region continued through 1555 and 1556 (see Ritchie 2002, pp. 145–57). Morton's regency refocused attention on lawlessness in the area, and he led nine raids on the Border between 1573 and 1580 (Goodare 1999, p. 262). An act of 1587, for the 'quieting and keeping in obedience of the disordered subjects, inhabitants of the borders, highlands and isles', which post-dates the compilation of the Quarto, makes clear the longevity of the problem: the act seeks to control those 'delighting in all mischiefs and unnaturally and cruelly wasting, slaying, harrying, and destroying their own neighbours and native country people' (*RPS* 1587/7/70). Specific mention is made in this act of the thieves of Liddesdale. The poem may date from the years around or between Maitland's commissions, although James Sibbald dated it to 'summer 1561' on the grounds the Border unrest worsened after the end of Mary of Guise's regency (Sibbald ed. 1802, III, p. 104).

Maitland's poem attacks the indiscriminate acquisitiveness and brutality of the raiders, especially when they meet resistance (ll. 14–19), and he notes how their attacks impoverish the countryside. The poem also voices criticism of the 'want of iustice' (l. 80) in the realm, and, as in so many of his poems, Maitland expresses particular concern for the poor who suffer as a result. On this theme, see MQ 5, 18, 19, 21, 26, 30. The problems of Liddesdale are alluded to in MQ 34, and those of the Borders in MQ 8 and 30. Maitland's own experience of his lands at Blyth being raided is described in MQ 14.

The poem owes much in tone and form to Dunbar's 'In vice most vicius he excellis', a poem against Donald Owyr, who is often associated with the highland rebel Donald Dubh (c.1490–1545). See MacDonald 2001, p. 142.

Pinkerton entitled the poem *Aganis the thieves of Liddisdail* (1786, p. 331). The text of the poem is printed in Reed 1973, pp. 53–56.

Stanza: aa⁴bbba². This is used in Dunbar's 'In vice most vicius he excellis' but is not a common form (Bawcutt ed. 1998, p. 349). The poem is set out in quatrains in MF. On the literary effect of the metre, see MacDonald 1972, p. 15.

Text: MQ fols 3v–5; MF pp. 266–67; R fols 23–24; D fols 3v–5.

Authorship: attributed to Sir Richard Maitland of Lethington in MF, MQ and D.

Date: c.1552–63?

Commentary

1 *Liddisdaill ... commoun theiffis*. The valley of Liddel Water in Roxburghshire, in the far south of the Scottish Borders. It was one of many troubled areas in the region. See Lyndsay's *Testament of the Papyngo*, l. 495. *Commoun theiffis* is a standard collocation: compare Lyndsay *Complaynt*, l. 363. The term 'thief' was specifically used of the Border and Highland reivers. See *DOST*, *Thef*, n.

4 *Hors, nolt, nor scheip*. Compare *TA* 9, p. 477: 'Item, to ane pure wife fra quhom the Liddisdail men had tane an ox, xl s'.

6 *mischeiffis*. Misfortune, distress, or hardship (arising from the theft). See *DOST*, *Mischef(e)*, n.

7 *plainlie throw the countrie rydis*. The thieves ride without any attempt at concealment, with blatant disregard for the law.

10 *Ay in thair gait*. With possessive pronouns, 'gait' means 'The way one goes or takes'. See *DOST*, *Gate*, *Gait*, n. especially sense 4. The sense here is that 'wherever they attack, there is no door or gate in their path that can withstand them'.

20–22 *Ettrik Forrest ... Lawderdaill ... Lowthiane*. Maitland imagines the raiders moving due north from Liddesdale to Lothian. Compare MQ 18, ll. 8–9. The Maitland home of Lethington (now Lennoxlove, near Haddington) is situated in East Lothian and is the subject of MQ 68. Maitland also had lands in Blyth, and Thirlestane in Lauderdale. Compare Dunbar's *Flyting*, 'Fra Etrike Forest furthward to Drumfrese', l. 425.

27–28 Translate 'Those wicked scoundrels have put the ploughs out of action so that there are none or few [people] who are left anything'. A 'schrow' is a contemptuous person or villain. See *DOST, S(c)hrew*, n. On the use of 'laid', see *DOST, Lay*, v., sense 3.

31 *Be ... blak maill*. *OED* defines this as a 'tribute formerly exacted from farmers and small owners in the border counties of England and Scotland, and along the highland border, by freebooting chiefs, in return for protection or immunity from plunder'. See *OED, Blackmail*, n., apparently rare in usage before the 1560s. An act of 1567 decrees that persons paying blackmail were liable to be punished by death and confiscation of goods. See *RPS* A/1567/12/26.

35–36 *Faine to be staikit / With walter caill*. Translate 'Grateful to be provided for with cold water' – an ironic comment on the gratitude of those made destitute by the raids to receive even the most meagre of refreshment.

37 *tursis hame*. Carry off booty. See *DOST, Turs*, v.

38 *To-name*. A nickname or alias. See *DOST, To-name*, n. Pinkerton writes, 'The to-names, or nicknames ... were the usual badges of these banditti. Mr Pennant from a book on the Clans, 1603, gives several cant names of moss troopers, or thieves on the borders, such as Tom Trotter of the Hill – The Land's Jok – Wanton Sym – Will of Pouderloupat – Arthur fire of the braes – Willie of Gratna hill – The griefs and cuts of Harlaw, &C' (Pinkerton ed. 1786, p. 431).

39 *Will of the Lawis*. 'Will of the hills'. A 'law' is a hill. See *DOST, Law*, n. A place called Lawshill is marked on Blaeu's map of Liddesdale. See http://maps.nls.uk/atlas/blaeu/view/?id=106.

40 *Hab of the Schawis*. A 'schaw' is a small copse or wooded grove, see *DOST, S(c)haw*, n. A place called Schawes is marked on Blaeu's map of Liddesdale. See http://maps.nls.uk/atlas/blaeu/view/?id=106. Hab is presumably a shortened form of a personal name, perhaps Herbert. This individual may also relate to the ballad hero, 'Hobbie Noble'. See Robson 1971, p. 11.

41–42 *To mak bair wais / Thay think na schame*. Here 'wais' probably means 'side wall or aspect of a building' rather than 'road / highway': 'They see no shame in destroying buildings'. See *DOST, Wal*, n.

44 *on bed*. People used to hang up their possessions, wrapped in cloths, on bedposts.

46 *reill and rok*. Bobbin (see *DOST, Rele*, n.) and spindill (*DOST, Rock*, n.). Compare l. 49 ('spindill'). This section of the poem sharply delineates the nature of the rural economy in the Borders, based on cottage industry and hill farming.

47 *lairdis Iok*. Jock is a personal name (a hypocoristic form of John), but also a general term for a man. See *DOST, Jok*, n. The use of 'lairdis' here may suggest 'son of the laird'. Child identifies 'the Laird's Jock' as 'John the son of the laird of Mangerton' [of the Armstrong family]. See Child ed. 1861, vol. 6, p. 67.

51 *Ihone of the Park*. The Park is identifiable with an area which is now modern Newcastleton.

55 *Ihone of the Syide*. John Armstrong of the Syde is mentioned in two bonds dated 1562 and 1563, printed in R.B. Armstrong 1833, pp. lxv–lxvi (also see Reed 1973, p. 57). A place called Syid is marked on Blaeu's map on Liddesdale (Reed 1973, p. 57; http://www.nls.uk/maps/atlas/blaeu/view/?id=106). Several versions of the ballad Jock o' the Side are printed by Child. See Child ed. 1861, vol. 6, pp. 80–88. Maitland indicates here that this figure is the most dangerous individual among the thieves ('a gretar theif did neuer ryide', l. 56).

59 *muire and myris*. Formulaic. Compare Henryson's *Two Mice*, l. 184, 'mosse and mure'. The rest of the line is formulaic: John of the Syde is a good guide – he knows the lie of the land all too well.

68 *sum greit man*. Maitland suggests here and in ll. 61–65 that the lairds of Liddesdale are failing in their duty to control and punish wrongdoers, and even go as far as protecting them. Compare Lyndsay, *Ane Satyre of the Thrie Estaitis* (1554), ll. 3817–24.

73 *gait*. Here meaning manner, way of behaving or habit. See *DOST, Gait*, n.

74–75 *debait ... vp-weir*. Protect and defend, see *DOST, Debate*, v.; *Vpweir*, n. The great lords would rather aid the thieves and allow them to keep their stolen good than bring them to justice.

85 *cum gud speid*. To have successfully achieved their aim.

89 *Hing on a trie*. In early modern Scotland, capital crimes included theft and fire-raising, as well as murder and treason, and hanging was the most common form of execution (Bland 1984, p. 11). Maitland may be echoing Lyndsay's *Complaynt* here, where 'Oppressioun and his fallowis' who persecute 'the Heland and the Bordour' are, through the king's justice, 'hangit heych apon the gallous' (ll. 384–86). Also in Maitland's mind might be *Ane Satyre of The Thrie Estaitis* (1554), where 'Thift' is hanged and on the gallows bids farewell to various Border families who are his 'bretheren common theifis' (ll. 3990–4011). For the thieves of Liddesdale, other punishments were also meted out. The Treasurer's Accounts for 1553 record the purchase of 'ane byrnyng irne to byrn the thevis of Lyddisdale on the cheik' (*TA*, X, p. 208).

4. O hie eternall God of micht

This poem is written in the tradition of the New Year poem to a monarch or patron, though for Maitland the addressee is God rather than any temporal authority. It combines prayer and a 'sermon to the estates', addressing churchmen, lords, women, burgesses and common people to remind them of their social and moral responsibilities. Lines 61–90 comprise a vivid picture of urban life. Maitland's influences include the two New Year poems associated with Dunbar ('My prince in God, gif the guid grace' and 'This hinder nycht, halff sleiping as I lay'). Maitland's habit of beginning several stanzas of his poem with the formulae 'God keip', 'God send', God give', 'God graunt' is particularly indebted to the practice of Dunbar's 'My prince in God, gif the guid grace'. There are also several later sixteenth-century examples of the genre that are found in MF. These are William Stewart's 'Lerges of this new ʒeirday' (MF pp. 220–21) and 'Schir sen of men ar dyuerss sortis' (MF pp. 218–20), and the unattributed poem, 'Excelland michtie prince and king' (MF pp. 183–85), which is addressed to the monarch in 'this new 3eir'. Later examples include Alexander Scott's *New 3eir Gift to the Quene Mary*, which was delivered at Seton Palace in 1562 (see van Heijnsbergen 2009, pp. 118–20); John Stewart's 'To his Maiestie the first of Ianvar. 1582 and 'To his Maiestie the first of Ianvar vith presentation of ane lawrell trie formit of gould. 1583', and Sir Robert Ayton's *To Queen Anne upone New-year's-day 1604*. New Year poems addressed to monarchs are often thinly disguised pleas for timely changes to royal conduct and usually focus on the administration of justice and distribution of fair reward to royal servants. They often combine deference, flattery and didacticism, though sometimes also satire, as in the case of Stewart's 'Schir sen of men ar dyuerss sortis' (see MacDonald 2001,

p. 141; Bawcutt ed. 1998, p. 367, van Heijnsbergen 2001, pp. 109, 115).
For Maitland's other New Year poems, see MQ 7 and 8.
Stanza: aa⁴b³a⁴ B³.
Text: MQ fols 5v–7v; MF pp. 21–23; R fols 15v–17, and D fols 5–7.
Authorship: attributed to Sir Richard Maitland in MQ, R and D. The attribution in MF is in a seventeenth-century hand.
Date: c.1557–early 1558? Given the prayer for the queen regent, the poem cannot have been written before 1554 and must pre-date June 1560. No mention is made in the poem of Mary's marriage to the Dauphin, which took place in April 1558, and is the subject of MQ 6. Pinkerton dates the poem to 'perhaps 1557' (1786 p. 279).

Commentary

5 *Now in to this new ʒeir*. A refrain emphasising the seasonal association of the poem is common in other examples of the genre, including those by Dunbar, Stewart and Scott (see headnote).

6 *our Quene*. Mary Queen of Scots (1542–87). The queen was sent to France in 1548 and did not return to Scotland until August 1561 (an event marked by Maitland in MQ 9). The present poem was thus written during Mary's absence.

9 *thir weiris*. This may refer to the European context (the Habsburg–Valois wars had resumed in 1552), but in 1557 Scotland had become part of the wider conflict, declaring war on England, in support of France. In the autumn of that year an army of French and Scots marched on the Border but refused to engage with the English (see Donaldson 1960, p. 88; Wormald 1988, pp. 86–87).

11 *our Quene Regent*. Mary of Guise (d.1560), regent from 1554. She is also addressed in MQ 6, ll. 73–81, where her role in arranging the marriage between her daughter and the dauphin is mentioned.

12 *Be law*. The exhortation that the ruler administers justice effectively is a staple of the New Year poem. See Dunbar's 'My prince in God, gif the guid grace', ll. 13–15; Scott's *New ʒeir Gift*, l. 29.

13 *gar limmeris forbeir*. A 'limmer' here is a scoundrel, but also a thief. The term was often applied to Border and Highland raiders, the subject of MQ 3. See *DOST*, *Limmar*, n, especially 1.b. The complaints here about freebooters oppressing the poor resonate with those of MQ 3, especially ll. 79–80. Several acts of the 1555 parliament held in Edinburgh addressed general aspects of law and order, including curbing the making of leagues against the crown through bonds of manrent and maintenance, and the problems of poaching and begging. See Ritchie 2002, pp. 130–33, 140–44.

16 *saweris of seditioun*. Formulaic phrasing – 'sewers of sedition'. See *DOST, Sawar -er(e)*, n. In 1555 parliament passed an act 'concerning the speaking ill of the queen's grace or of Frenchmen' which aimed to suppress rumours and sedition against the queen regent and Henri II. See *RPS* A1555/6/40. It also passed an act condemning all who bear false witness to having their tongues pierced and possessions forfeited. See *RPS* A1555/5/23.

21–29 Compare Lyndsay, *Ane Satyre of the Thrie Estaitis* (1554), ll. 3865–73. Maitland's sense that churchmen are leading their flock 'arreir' (l. 28, backwards), may echo the estates 'gangand backwart led be thair vyces' in Lyndsay's play. Maitland's prayer for good 'pastouris' (l. 21) to instruct the people and for the eradication of clerical vice should be seen in the context of the appetite for internal reform of the Catholic church in Scotland at this time, as well as in light of the increasing political strength of the Protestant faction during the Guise regency. In 1555 and 1556 Pope Paul IV had received petitions from Scotland seeking support for the reform of the clergy (see Ritchie 2002, pp. 198–204). MQ 12 relates more securely to the activities of Scottish Protestants in 1558–59. Scott's *Ane New ȝeir Gift* also addresses religious change, criticising the vice of the Catholic clergy and expressing concerns about the rapacity of the new Protestant order, ll. 19–22, 57–95, 113–52.

31 *lordis temporall*. Those who have jurisdiction over human affairs and secular matters.

39 *For theiffis and reveris intercessouris*. A complaint against those who intercede on the behalf of thieves in court proceedings, and so perpetuate the oppression of the poor. An echo of MQ 3, ll. 67–78.

41 *Lordis of the sait, mak expeditioun*. 'The Lords of the Seat' is the 'Court of Session', Scotland's supreme civil court. Maitland became an extraordinary Lord of Session in 1553 and an Ordinary Lord of Session in 1561. Compare MQ 50 and 51. To 'mak expeditioun' here means to engage promptly with a task. See *DOST, Expeditioun*, n.

44 *eik ȝour contributioun*. Maitland seems to suggest that the Lords of Session should receive additional pay for efficient administration of justice, though in the next stanza he cautions them against profiteering. See *DOST, Contributioun*, n. The Lords of Session were a professionalised judicature by the mid sixteenth century.

47–48 *euill querrellis ... / For proffeit.* Translate, 'Do not take on malicious law-suits in hope of gain'.

49 *Invent na thing to gar ws spend.* In 1560, Mary of Guise's opponents criticised her for high taxation. Her administration had inherited a financial deficit and raised taxes in 1555–56 to assist with the defence of the Border, and in 1557 to fund negotiations for the marriage of her daughter. The tax assessment scheme of 1556, designed to recalculate levels of tax and increase the efficiency of collection, was particularly unpopular and was rejected by parliament (see Ritchie 2002, pp. 136–39).

51–52 Conventional feminine virtues, described in many poems, for example Henryson's 'The Garmont of Gud Ladeis' and several of the poems among the Bannatyne Manuscript's 'ballattis of the prayiss of wemen' (fols 269–80). Also see MQ 35, MQ 63, MQ 64, MQ 69. Here 'ladyis' are women of some social standing, in contrast to the burgesses' wives whose virtues are mentioned at ll. 73–4. See *DOST, Lady,* n. sense 3.

53–60 On the conventions of sumptuary complaint, see headnote to MQ 2. The complaint about women's deviance in fashion is continued at l. 76.

60 *Now into this new ȝeir.* Craigie suggests that, given the anticipatory nature of this stanza, that line should read 'hierefter mony ȝeir' (Craigie ed. 1920, p. 283).

61 *And send.* 'God' is to be understood here.

62 *commoun weill.* The health of the community and realm as a whole, a central concept in late medieval ethical and political theory, ultimately derived from Aristotelian thought (see Edington 1994, p. 117). In the early sixteenth century the term 'commonweal' replaced that of 'common profit' and, according to Mason, 'acquired powerful and decidedly patriotic resonances for contemporary Scots' (Mason 1998, p. 91). The shared responsibility of all members of society for their community is a major preoccupation of Maitland's poems, and this term recurs frequently. Compare MQ 57, l. 10.

64 *to vse meit and mesour leill.* A 'meit' is a unit of measurement. The collocation 'meit and mesour' is commonplace. See *DOST, Met,* n. and *DSL-SND1, Mett,* n. Complaints against merchants using false measures and weights were common in sermon literature. See Owst 1966, pp. 353, 356–57. Successive Scots parliaments attempted to deal with the problem, and the parliament of 1555 renewed earlier acts to this end. See *RPS* A1555/6/21.

66 *waistouris.* A waster (a spendthrift, good for nothing) is a familiar figure from late medieval literature. He is a protagonist of the late fourteenth-century alliterative debate poem *Wynnere and Wastoure*, and also features in *Piers Plowman*. Also see Dunbar's 'Doverrit with dreme, devysing in my slummer', l. 17: 'So mony westouris to God and all his werkis'; and MQ 29, l. 32.

67–68 *Regrateris that takis dowbill pay / And wyne selleris our deir.* A 'regrater' is one who buys to resell for profit and the word has negative connotations (*DOST*, *Regratar*, n.). There is also a character of this name in *Piers Plowman*. *DOST* records citations in legal and documentary, but not literary, texts, other than Maitland's poem. On the dubious practices of merchants, see note to l. 64. Also compare Dunbar's complaints in 'Quhy will ȝe, merchantis of renoun' about the tendency of merchants to over-price goods and to pursue their 'Singular proffeit' (ll. 64–72). In Lyndsay's *Ane Satyre of the Thrie Estaitis* (1554) (ll. 4106–89), Falset catalogues all such malpractices of merchants and craftsmen.

69 *Dyuouris that drinkis all the day.* See *DOST*, *Dyuour*, n. debtors or bankrupts. Also see MQ 29, l. 33. The second husband of the widow in Dunbar's *Tretis* was a merchant, but with her love of finery she reduces him to a 'dyuor', l. 410.

77 *lyik the Quenis ladyis cled.* Compare Lyndsay, *Ane Supplication Directit ... to the Kingis Grace, in Contemptioun of Syde Taillis* (c.1539–41), ll. 65–66: 'Kittock, that clekkit wes ȝistrene, / The morne wyll counterfute the Quene'.

79–80 *I trow that sa sall mak ane red / Of all thair pakis this ȝeir.* To make a 'red' means 'to set in order' or 'make a clearance'. See *DOST*, *Red*, n. sense 1. The latter seems to be intended here, and the lines translate 'It is my beleif that such [views] will result in the loss of all their wealth within the year'.

82 *not to irk.* See *DOST*, *Irk*, v., 'to grow weary or tired; to become bored or irritated ...'. The commons are to earn their food through agricultural labour and not to be idle. An act to curb begging was renewed in the 1555 parliament. See *RPS* A1555/6/39.

84 *bring furth baith staig and stirk.* Rear young horses and cattle. See *DSL-SND1*, *Staig*, n. and *DOST*, *Stirk*, *Styrk*, n.

86 *ydill lounis*. The word 'loun' (ruffian, wastrel) carries strong moral disapproval or censure, as in Lyndsay's *Complaynt*, ll. 405–6 'sleuthfull idyll lownis, / Sall fetterit be in the gailyeownis', which Maitland seems to echo in this stanza. See *DOST, Loun, Lown,* n. See note to l. 82.

87 *Crame-craikeris*. Translate 'market-stall criers' (see *DOST, Crame,* n.). The Folio reading is 'Cryand crakkaris' and echoes Dunbar's 'Schir, ȝe haue mony seruitouris', l. 40: 'Cryaris, craikaris and clatteraris'.

88 *soirnaris that ar sweir*. A 'soirnar' is one who 'extracts free quarters and provisions by threats or force, as a means of livelihood' (*DOST, Sornar,* n.). Maitland regards this as another form of idleness. See notes to ll. 82 and 86.

89 *the gailȝeounis*. Compare Lyndsay's *Complaynt*, l. 406 and see note to l. 86. Galleons were sailing vessels used as warships or for trade, but Maitland has in mind here the oar-propelled galleys of the French navy, which were rowed by forced labour. The suggestion is that those who will not work honestly should be compelled to labour in arduous or dangerous conditions. The French galleys have been described as 'the labour camps of the sixteenth century' and a life sentence in them 'the heaviest punishment after the capital punishment' (Ridley 1968, pp. 67–68). John Knox spent time on them as a prisoner following the murder of Cardinal Beaton and surrender of St Andrews castle in 1547.

5. Quhair is the blyithnes that hes beine

This poem begins as a lament for the absence of traditional festivity in contemporary Scotland: 'blyithnes' here encompasses merriness and good spirits (*DOST, Blithnes, Blythnes* n.). Maitland also criticises the loss of other traditional values in all estates of society ('ane and all', l. 91), but especially among the first two estates, the landowners and churchmen. These values include hospitality, honour, compassion, charity, piety and especially justice. His concern in the poem is with reform and with the commonweal. Lines 61–78 and 85–90 are particularly concerned with the efficient and equitable administration of justice: claims of disdain for the law, scheming to pervert the course of justice, and the intimidation of the courts reflect Maitland's professional concerns as an extraordinary Lord of Session (a role he assumed in 1554). The poem ends with a pious exhortation to readers to mend their ways.

The poem has been dated to the immediate post-reformation period

by MacDonald. See MacDonald 1972, pp. 14–15; MacDonald 2001, p. 148. It may be earlier. The phrase 'kirkmen afoir' probably relates to a perceived golden age before the onset of clerical corruption and to the movement for the reform of the Church in Scotland from within during the 1550s. See notes to MQ 4, ll. 21–29. Maitland is usually explicit about religious difference between Catholics and Protestants in MQ 12, but here the criticism of the clergy surrounds their inability to preach and teach and failure to resolve conflict, as well as their extravagance, and their involvement in military service, all of which were concerns for reformers from within the established church.
Stanza: aaabaB[4].
Text: MQ fols 8–10; MF pp. 32–35; D fols 7–9.
Authorship: attributed to Maitland in MQ, MF and D. The ascription to Maitland in MF is in a later hand.
Date: c.1558–60?

Commentary

4 *game and play*. Maitland's poem may be echoed in the 1567 poem, 'Adew all glaidnes, sport and play!' (*The Complaynt of Scotland*). See Cranstoun ed. 1891–93, I, pp. 95–99.

7 *now I heir na worde of ʒuile*. The festival of Yule extended from Christmas day to New Year. As well as being associated with seasonal celebrations, it was the time at which courtiers received livery, as was Whitsuntide, and Maitland later complains about how neither 'ʒuill nor pace' are properly celebrated (l. 31). Compare Dunbar's 'Schir, lat it neuer in toune be tald', l. 6: 'I wald at ʒoull be housit and stald'.

8 *on calsay*. Translate 'in the street'. The 'calsay' is the paved part of the street. See *DOST*, *Calsay*, *Calsy*, n.

9–12 Compare Dunbar, 'Fredome, honour and nobilnes', ll. 13–15: 'Honorable houshaldis ar all laid doun. / Ane laird hes with him bot a loun'. Maitland's criticism relates both to a lack of hospitality and a decline in the maintenance of the noble household, which allowed for the support and employment of tenants and the effective administration of rural estates, as nobles began to favour keeping urban homes. See Brown 2000, p. 212.

13 *gysaris*. Maitland alludes to 'mumming' or masquerading, a type of secular theatre that often took place within the noble or royal household (often involving members of that household or touring players), and frequently in connection with seasonal festivity. See *DOST*, *Gysar*, -ard, -art, n. See McGavin 2007, p. 89.

14 *kirkmen cled lyik men of weir*. In the absence of festive mummers, the churchmen are masquerading as something they are not. See Cowan 1982, p. 79. Statutes of 1549 and 1559 banned members of the clergy from wearing clothing inappropriate to their estate and which did not distinguish them from laymen. However, a parliamentary act of 1547 makes provision for the benefices of kirkmen slain in the army in the war with England. See Bain ed. 1830, p. 159; *RPS* A1547/9/3. Distaste at ecclesiastical involvement in military service was common among moderate reformers and humanists. Compare Lyndsay's *Dreme*, 'Lordis of religioun thay go lyke seculeris' (l. 983); and *Monarche* (c.1551–52), ll. 5422–23, 'Paip Iulius manfullye / Passe to the feild', in reference to Julius III's campaign against the French in Parma (echoed in *Ane Satyre*, 1554, ll. 4578–79).

16 *ruffiaris*. A ruffiar is a violent and immoral person, and sometimes one particularly associated with sexual immorality (*DOST*, *Ruffian*, n.). *DOST* suggests that the word may be used to indicate a professional killer or bully.

28 *aneuche in poise to lay*. Translate 'enough (money) to put aside'. See *DOST*, *Pose*, *Pois*, n.

31 *we had*. We obersve (the verb is in present tense). See *DOST*, *Hald*, v.

34 *We gar our landis doubill pay*. This reference is to the increasingly common practice of rack-renting by landlords, or rent increases whereby old tenants were replaced by wealthier individuals. Maitland's concern for the hardship this caused was shared by many of his contemporaries. See Brown 2000, pp. 42–44. Compare MQ 21, ll. 22–28.

36 *reuth and pitie*. A conventional collocation of virtues to be cultivated by those in power. Compare, *The Buik of Alexander*, l. 2116: 'Thairfoir shir ... Haif of thir folk reuth and pitie'.

43 *lyik vaine fuillis*. A favourite formula of Maitland's. Compare MQ 2, l. 44.

50–54 The complaint that family lands are sold off to pay merchant's bills for extravagant clothing recalls the complaint in *The Thre Prestis of Peblis* that lords are forced to provide finances through selling their heirs in marriage to wealthy but low-born individuals: 'And quhen 3our

Lords ar puir, this to conclude, / Thay sel thair Sonnes and aires for gold & gude' (ll. 307–8).

55 *The kirkmen keipis na professioun.* In this context, 'professioun' is 'The solemn undertaking, declaration or vow made by one entering a religious order or some other dedicated mode of life'. See *DOST*, *Professio(u)n*, n. The clerical 'professioun' according to Lyndsay is a commitment to preaching (see *Complaynt*, ll. 323–25: 'That callit ar preistis and can nocht preche, / Nor Christis law to the peple teche').

62 *heid and hang.* A popular phrase used to describe capital punishment (beheading and hanging). Compare *King Hart*, l. 528.

69 *We cum to bar with iak and steill.* Armed intimidation of the courts by the retinues of powerful individuals engaged in litigation was not uncommon. See Donaldson 1965, p. 222.

82 *commoun weill.* See MQ 4, note to l. 62.

89 *Sum strainge new institutioun.* Here 'institutioun' has the meaning of 'An established law, custom or usage in a community'. See *DOST*, *Institutio(u)n*, n., sense 4. Maitland alludes to the prospect of foreign intervention in Scottish affairs, a concern perhaps linked to the close relationship with France in the mid to late 1550s. One of the aims of the Lords of the Congregation in 1559 was to oppose the intervention of strangers in Scottish affairs.

6. The greit blyithnes and ioy inestimabill

Rubric: Off the Quenis Maryage with the Dolphin of France MF R. Not in MQ or D.

This poem celebrates the 'contract of mariage' (l. 5) between Mary and the Dauphin, François, son of Henri II of France. The wedding took place in France on 24 April 1558, and a contemporary record of this event, written by a Scottish student in Paris, survives in a fragmentary print (now in Lambeth Palace Library, *STC* 1800:03). See Hamer 1932. The contemporary *Discours du Grand et Magnifique Triomphe facit du Mariage* also describes the occasion and gives an account of the masques, pageants and jousts that followed the marriage (see Bentham ed. 1818).

Maitland's poem exhorts Scottish audiences at home to greet the news of the union with traditional festivities. There are similarities to Lyndsay's account of the celebrations planned, but never implemented, for James V's first queen, Madeleine, in *The Deploratioun of the Deith of Quene Magdalene* (1537): 'Sic banketing, sic aufull tornamentis, / On hors and fute' (ll. 169–70). Dunbar's 'Blyth Aberdeane, thow beriall of all tounis', an account of the entry of James IV's queen, Margaret, into Aberdeen in 1511, is another likely influence on Maitland's poem.

The formal proclamation of the marriage of Mary and the Dauphin was made to the Estates on 26 June 1558, and in the same month Mary of Guise ordered the lighting of 'fyris and processioun(s) generall for the completing and solemnizing of the mariage betuix our Soverane Ladie and the Dolphine of France' to take place throughout Scotland (See *TA*, X, pp. 364–66, and Ritchie 2002, p. 195); Maitland's poem may well emerge from precisely this context (see l. 20) rather from the time of the marriage a few months earlier. Records show that several dramatic elements were devised to mark the occasion in Edinburgh in 1558, including 'The Triumphe and play at the Marriage of the Quenis Grace' (see Mill 1927, pp. 183–88). Maitland also takes the opportunity in the poem to offer advice to François and to Mary of Guise, the regent. He also exhorts all subjects, Scottish and French, to affirm the union, which has brought them into such close alliance.

Stanza: aabaabbab[5].

Text: MQ fols 10–12; also in MF pp. 24–26, R fols 17–18, and D fols 9–10v.

Authorship: attributed to Sir Richard Maitland in MQ, MF and D.

Date: 1558.

Commentary

9 *Of France, the Dolphin, first sone of King Henrie*. The title 'dauphin' was accorded to the eldest son of the king of France. The eldest son of Henri II (d.1559) of France was François, subsequently François II of France (d.1560).

10–13 An evocation of literary convention but also perhaps of the tournaments held at James IV's court that Maitland may have witnessed in his youth, and which are recalled in David Lyndsay's *The Testament of the Papyngo*, ll. 500–6. In the late fifteenth-century Scots romance, *Lancelot of the Laik*, Lancelot fights to win Guinevere's attention, while also winning that of the lady of Melyhault. See I, ll. 1091–1104; 1225–74. Also see Gavin Douglas, *The Palice of Honour* (1501), where the dreamer is shown jousting fields where knights undertake 'deidis of armis for thair Ladyis saikis' (l. 1449). Also see Dunbar's 'In May as that Aurora did vpspring': 'Luve makis knychtis hardy at assey' (l. 83).

12 *at listis, to iust, and to tornay.* Lists are the fenced or palisaded area in which jousts took place. Jousts and tournaments remained important to chivalric training in the sixteenth century and such games provided spectacles associated with public celebration (for example, of royal marriage or royal entry) as well as the practical education of the knight. Maitland may recall here the jousting at the festivities marking Mary of Guise's coronation in 1540. See Stevenson 2006, pp. 63–102.

16 *Requeist ȝoung men to ryde in ȝour leueray.* Livery was a set of distinctive garments, bestowed on servants. Here a courtly ideal is evoked, where ladies give liveries to the suitors who serve them in love, so their affiliation may be recognised during the tournament.

20 *To mak baine-fyris, fercis and clerk playis.* The lighting of bonfires and playing of dramatic performances were traditional forms of celebration associated with royal entry and important state occasions, including the marking of the marriage of Mary and the Dauphin. 'The triumphe and play at the Marriage of the Quenis Grace' at Edinburgh in 1558 (see headnote) included a play. Farces originated as a popular form of short comic play in France, and became influential in the British Isles in the sixteenth century. See Lyndsay's *The Testament of the Papyngo*, l. 41: 'farses and ... plesand playis'. Clerk-plays were religious dramas performed by the clergy or scholars.

21 *carrous daunce and sing.* Carols were sung verses, often accompanied by instrumental music and ring-dancing. They were not necessarily seasonal in nature. See *OED, Carol*, n; *Clariodus* ll. 1562–63.

22 *And at ȝour croce gar wyne rin sindrie wayis.* Maitland imagines fountains flowing with wine at the market or boundary cross of the town, a popular spectacle at public celebrations of this sort. John Yonge's account of the 1503 entry of Margaret Tudor into Edinburgh refers to the Mercat Cross flowing with wine. See Gray 1998, pp. 13, 18. Compare Dunbar, 'Blyth Aberdeane', l. 58: 'at thair croce aboundantlie rane wyne'; and Lyndsay's *The Deploratioun*: 'fontanis, flowing watter cleir and wyne', l. 109.

25 *And all ȝour stairis with tapestrie gar hing.* Compare Dunbar's 'Blyth Aberdeane', 'The streittis war all hung with tapestrie' (l. 49).

26 *Castellis schut gunnis.* Mons Meg was fired from Edinburgh Castle on the day of Mary's wedding.

39 *Mak greit triumphe.* 'Make a great celebration / spectacle'. Compare

Edinburgh Burgh Records, which refer to 'The tryumphe maid at our souerane ladyis mariage' (see Mill 1927, pp. 183–88).

40 *euerilk man put on his nuptiall goun.* Maitland imagines each man wearing finery appropriate to such an occasion or perhaps his own carefully preserved wedding garments. Compare Lyndsay's comment that Madeleine should have been greeted by her subjects, all wearing their finery (*The Deploratioun*, ll. 113–25).

43 *ʒour Quene hes chosin hir ane feir.* Intense negotiations for Mary's marriage to François had been ongoing since early in 1557, but the union had been planned since the Treaty of Haddington in 1548. However, this line echoes courtly poetry in which ladies are free to choose their beloved, for example, Chaucer's *Parliament of Fowls*, l. 416. There is word play on 'feir' meaning 'equal' and 'spouse' / 'companion'. See *DOST*, *Fere*, *Feir*, n.; and MQ 38, l. 19.

44 *Ane potent prince.* Formulaic phrasing. Despite his promise of political power, François was in fact a sickly and deformed child, who was to die prematurely two years after the wedding.

70 *Betuixt ʒow twa wald mak seditioun.* Compare MQ 4, note to l. 16.

73 *O noble Princes, and mother to our Quene.* Mary of Guise, regent (d.1560).

7. Ane Ballat maid at the [ne]w ʒeirismess in the ʒeir of God 1559 ʒeiris

Rubric: the [ne]w] thew MQ; Off the Assemblie of the Congregatioun MF. (Untitled in D.)

Like MQ 4 and 8, this poem is written is in the tradition of the New Year poem (see headnote to MQ 4). Also like MQ 4 it is a prayer for divine, rather than royal, assistance as Scotland finds itself in the midst of political and religious division. Five of the eight stanzas begin with a supplication: the poem opens on a note of penance and develops into a request for God's 'support and grace' (l. 9). A likely influence on the poem is Lyndsay's *Ane Dialog Betwix Experience and Ane Courteour* (1553) (also known as *The Monarche*), which suggests that God 'Hes scurgit this pure realme of Scotland' (l. 49) with war and instability because of its people's sins.

Maitland's poem relates to the 'Wars of the Congregation' (as the title given to the poem in MF, though not MQ, 'Off the Assemblie of the Congregatioun', suggests). The 'Wars of the Congregation' was the name given to the iconoclastic struggle between the Protestant 'Lords of the Congregation of Christ' and Mary of Guise's administration. The rebellion began in May 1559 and lasted until the summer of 1560. It was led by dissident nobles, including some Catholics as well as Protestants, and gained English military support in early 1560. Stanzas 3 and 4 address the nobility of Scotland, exhorting them to settle their differences, and urging those who prefer not to take sides until the outcome is certain, to be more active in bringing about peace. Although the poem is highly topical, it also contains general references to the lack of justice in the realm, especially for the poor. The poem is dated to 1559 in MQ, though not MF. A.A. MacDonald (private communication) suggests that 'the ʒeir of God 1559 ʒeiris' in the title in MQ refers to the traditional year starting on the Feast of the Annunciation (25 March). The New Year mass in that year would take place on 1 January 1560.

Stanza: ababbcbC[5]. On this popular stanza form, used by Henryson and Dunbar, especially for moral or panegyric verse, see Bawcutt ed. 1998, pp. 301–2.

Text: MQ fols 12–13; also MF pp. 28–30; and D fols 10v–11.

Authorship: attributed to Richard Maitland in MQ, MF and D.

Date: January 1560.

Commentary

1 *thy scurge*. For Maitland's sense that Scotland's troubles are inflicted on its people by God as a punishment for its sins, see MQ 30, l. 62. Also compare Lyndsay's *Ane Dialog Betwix Experience and Ane Courteour*, ll. 49, 89.

4–5 *Of discord and inanimitie / Betuixt the leigis and auctoritie*. The discord referred to here is the opposition between the Lords of the Congregation and the authority of the established Scottish Church and the regent, Mary of Guise.

7 *libertie*. The rhetoric of freedom was much employed by the Lords of the Congregation, who regarded Guise's dynastic politics as jeopardising Scotland's liberty. See Ritchie 2002, p. 233, quoting Knox: 'the interprysed destructioun of thair said commoun-weall, and overthrow of the libertie of thair native cuntree' (Laing ed. 1846–64, I, p. 499). Scotland's autonomy is a repeated concern of Maitland's poems from this period. See MQ 6, l. 36 and MQ 9, l. 12.

18 *Lordis, barounis of auctoritie*. Maitland's address is to the all Scottish nobles, but especially the leaders of the Congregation. What Maitland refers to as 'vnitie' was not achieved until the Treaty of Edinburgh was signed in the summer of 1560, following the death of Mary of Guise in June of that year.

39 *Berwik to Baquhidder.* Berwick, on the Scottish Border, and Balquhidder in central Scotland (now Stirlingshire). Both places had strategic importance for the Scottish crown against the English and Highland rebels respectively.

41 *The Quenis grace, gif scho hes offendit.* Particularly unpalatable to the Lords of the Congregation was the arrival of French troops in Scotland in August to September of 1559, authorised by François II and the Guise family. The lords accused Mary of Guise of violating the terms of the Leith Agreement of July 1559 (see Ritchie 2002, pp. 224–30). The Congregation's 'Act of Suspension' of 21 October 1559 attempted to depose Guise from office.

45 *3e kirkmen, doe 3our dewtie.* Compare MQ 4, ll. 21–9 and MQ 5, ll. 14–24, where Maitland outlines what he regards these duties to be, resolution of conflict being one. No doubt, however, Maitland had in mind the involvement of churchmen, including Knox, in the 1559 rebellion. One of the leaders of the Lords of the Congregation was the prior of St Andrews, Lord James, Mary Queen of Scots' half-brother.

49 *heresie.* Though rather vague, this may suggest Maitland's lack of sympathy with the Protestant cause. In his *History of the Reformation in Scotland*, Knox described the laird as 'not persuaded in religion' (Dickinson ed. 1949, I, p. 67), though referring to an event of 1546.

60 *Without discord had parliament and sessioun.* Compare Maitland's condemnation of the violent disruption of legal procedures in MQ 5, ll. 69–70.

8. In this new 3eir, I sie bot weir

This poem, composed in the form of a carol, in uniform stanzas with a free-standing burden, belongs to the tradition of the New Year poem, like MQ 4 and 7. Though it is unattributed in MQ, its place in this part of the manuscripts suggests Maitland's authorship. It is a topical complaint on the times, which ends with an exhortation to prayer. Its concluding advice to be merry and to hope for better things in heaven may be compared to the sentiments of MQ 31.

It is clear from line 6 that the narrator refers to the Wars of the

Congregation, also the subject of MQ 7 (see headnote). French troops had arrived in Scotland in the autumn of 1559, and English military support for the Congregation's cause was secured by January 1560 and ratified under the Treaty of Berwick on 27 February. Thus the threat of 'weir', which troubles the narrator, is an immediate one. The narrator refrains from taking sides and claims to be equally afraid of 'England and of France' (l. 10).

The poem also dwells on one of Maitland's perennial themes, the lack of justice in the realm. The narrator's sadness that contemporary troubles curtail any kind of seasonal recreation (l. 9) recalls MQ 5.

Tonally, the poem shows the influence of a number of poems by Dunbar that counsel countering uncertainty or trouble with philosophical contentment. See, for example, Dunbar's 'Be mery, man, and tak nocht fer in mynd' and 'Full oft I mvse and hes in thocht'.

For a similar employment of the carol form for a new year poem, see Dunbar's 'Schir, lat it neuer in toune be tald' and Stewart's 'Larges, lerges, lerges ay' (Bannatyne MS fols 95v–96). On the metrical form of this poem, which was particularly favoured for carols, see Bawcutt ed. 1998, p. 368.

The scribe of MQ abbreviates the burden after its initial appearance at the head of the poem. The abbreviated sections are shown in the edition in italics.

Stanza: $a^4b^2a^4b^3$ / aaa^5b^3.

Text: MQ fols 13v–14 and D fols 12–12v. Not in MF.

Authorship: unattributed in MQ, but attributed to 'S.R.M.' in D.

Date: c.1560? Pinkerton offers the date 'March 25, 1560' (1786, p. 293) without explanation.

Commentary

6 *Of Frenchemen and the Congregatioun*. In August and September 1559, almost 2,000 French troops were sent to Scotland to support Mary of Guise against the rebellion of Lords of the Congregation, which had begun in May 1559.

8 *monye bair biging*. Perhaps a reference to the widespread destruction of religious buildings during the iconoclasm of the Wars of the Congregation. See Cowan 1982, pp. 189–91

14 *For feir of England*. The English fleet under Admiral Winter entered the Firth of Forth in January 1560 and English troops arrived to support the Congregation in March 1560.

23-4 *bourdour ... hing.* A reference to the problems of bringing Border rebels to justice. Compare MQ 3, ll. 79-90.

37-40 For these sentiments, compare Dunbar 'Fredome, honour and nobilnes', ll. 41-44: 'Man, pleis thy makar and be mirry /.../ Wirk for the place of paradyce'.

9. Excellent Princes, potent and preclair

Rubric: Off the Quenis arrivale in Scotland. MF not in MQ or D.

This poem welcomes Mary Queen of Scots on her return to Scotland from France, where she had lived since 1548. Mary arrived in Scotland on 16 August 1561, and reached Edinburgh on 19 August. The poem expresses hope for a peaceful future and well-governed realm, independent of any foreign influences. While praising the nineteen-year-old Queen for her virtues, Maitland also makes discreet reference to her inexperience and need for guidance (ll. 21-24). The poem draws on the tradition of 'advice to princes' literature, especially in its recommendation that the queen seek the counsel of prudent and loyal men who will ensure the equitable administration of justice (ll. 25-32). See Martin 2013a.

Another welcome poem for Mary was composed by Alexander Scott. His 'New 3eir Gift' was probably presented at Seton Palace in the new year of 1562 and is composed in the same stanza form (ballat royal) as Maitland's. Mary's official welcome to Edinburgh included didactic pageants and tableau, though with strong overtones of anti-Catholic and anti-French feeling. On these, see Mill 1927, pp. 188-91; MacDonald 1991b; Davidson 1995; MacDonald, A.R. 1997; Gray 1998, pp. 26-28. For an earlier welcome poem to a Scottish Queen, see Dunbar's 'Blyth Aberdeane, thow beriall of all tounis' (1511), which probably influenced Maitland.

Stanza: ababbcbc^5.
Text: MQ fols 14-15v; also in MF pp. 30-31; D fols 12v-13v.
Authorship: attributed to Richard Maitland in MQ, MF and D.
Date: 1561.

Commentary

1 *Excellent Princes, potent and preclair*. This is formulaic, and possibly also echoic of Dunbar's 'Blyth Aberdeane, thow beriall of all tounis', l. 65: 'O potent princes, pleasant and preclair'.

12 *Ane auld frie realme.* An allusion to the anxieties surrounding the Franco-Scottish alliance of the Guise regency, following the Treaty of Haddington, 1548, and also the Congregation's reliance on English intervention. See headnote to MQ 7.

15 *All cair and cummer baneist.* See MQ 7 and 8. The end of the Guise regency had been overshadowed by the Wars of the Congregation. Mary returned as a Catholic monarch to a country that had a powerful Protestant political faction. Scotland had been without a ruling monarch for nineteen years, and without any kind of legally constituted government for fourteen months. See Wormald 2001, p. 103.

25–32 A traditional theme of advice to princes literature. Compare MQ 59, ll. 9–16 and ll. 33–35.

39 *of Scotland to the commoditie.* Translate 'To the advantage of Scotland'. See *DOST, Commodite*, n., sense 2.

41 *gif thy hienes plesit for to marie.* Mary's first husband, François II, had died in December 1560. She did not remarry until 1565.

48 *gud successioun.* Maitland here alludes to the duty of the monarch to produce an heir. Compare Dunbar 'Gladethe, thoue queyne of Scottis regioun' (ll. 29–30): 'Gret Gode ws graunt that we haue lang desirit / A plaunt to spring of thi successioun'.

49 *I wes trew seruand to thy mother.* Maitland became an extraordinary Lord of Session in 1554. He served as a commissioner for border affairs in 1559.

55 *amang otheris servandis think on me.* This request apparently did not fall on deaf ears. Maitland became an ordinary Lord of Session in 1561. Mary made him Keeper of the Great Seal of Scotland for life in 1562.

56 *This last requeist I leirnit at the frieris.* Compare Henryson, *Morall Fabillis*, l. 2971: 'I left the laif vnto the freiris'. Friars were well known for their teaching through didactic sermon exempla. Maitland may also be humorously suggesting the self-interested tendencies friars were often accused of: he is using his didactic poem to also secure his interests.

58 *becaus I may not sie.* Maitland went blind in 1561 (Spiller, *ODNB*). His blindness is also alluded to in MQ 14 and MQ 46.

10. Ane Ballat Maid at the Winning of Calice

Rubric: Ane Ballat maid at the winning of Calice MQ D; Off the wynning of Calice MF.

This poem celebrates the capture in January 1558 of Calais from the English by the forces of the Duke of Guise, Henri II's *lieutenant général* from 1557, and Mary of Guise's brother. Calais was the last territory held by the English on the Continent. The poem is addressed to Henri II of France, protector of Scotland under the terms of the Treaty of Haddington (1548).

Maitland records that the French victory took place 'Into the deidest tyme of all the ʒeir' (l. 32): the mid-winter attack was unusual but was timely because of recent English retreats. The freezing conditions also made it easier for the French troops to cross the marshes around Calais. See Potter 1983.

As well as celebrating the French victory, Maitland also uses the poem to urge his countrymen to piety, emphasising that Henri's victory over the English has been decided by divine will rather than human judgement or strength, and thus it is to God, not to the French, that Scotland should look for help to resolve its troubles, including its defence of its border with England and the recovery of Berwick. In this the poem may be compared to George Buchanan's poem to Henri II. See Ford 1982, pp. 133–38.

Stanza: ababbcbc⁵.
Text: MQ fols 15v–16v; MF pp. 26–28; D fols 14–15.
Authorship: attributed to Richard Maitland in MQ, MF and D.
Date: 1558.

Commentary

1 *maist Christiane King of France*. The title of *roi troi très chrétien* or *rex christianissimus* was given to Christian Roman emperors and to Charlemagne, and later became used for the kings of France only.

5 *The Duik of Guise*. Françios de Lorraine, Prince of Joinville, duke of Guise and Aumale (1519–1563).

6–7 *twa hundreth ʒeiris bygaine / Into the handis of Englis natioun*. Calais had been in English hands since its capture by Edward III in 1347. See Rose 2008.

9–11 Also see l. 22. For this sentiment compare 'My lordis, now, gif ʒe be wyse' (1567), ll. 11–14:

> Think well that nouther men nor hors
> Off sic ane act sould get the gloir:
> Bot he that ringis euer moir
> Hes luikit on ȝoure quarrell rycht
> (Cranstoun ed. 1891–93, I, pp. 46–51)

19 *that toun that sa stranglie did stand*. Maitland overstates the difficulty of the siege for the French. Also see l. 35. The fortress of Calais was in poor repair, and badly defended, and so little able to withstand the attack. See Grummitt 2008, pp. 168–86.

24 *translait realmes and kingis*. A conventional allusion to the 'de casibus' tradition. Compare *The Kingis Quair* (c.1424), ll. 55–56: 'how that eche estate, / As Fortune lykith thame will oft translate'.

36 *ȝour maist tender frend that nobill king*. Under the terms of the Treaty of Haddington (1548) Henri II of France offered protection to the Scots against the English.

38 *be men and money copious*. French financial and military support for Scotland in the immediate aftermath of the Treaty of Haddington was substantial, although tailed off during the course of the next decade. In 1549–50, 'almost a tenth of the revenue of the French crown was devoted to the Scottish campaign' (Lynch 2001, p. 249).

52 *That we get Berwik our merchis for to mend*. Berwick, on the Scottish Border ('merch'), an important strategic town and long-standing object of Anglo-Scottish rivalry, was taken by the English in 1482 and never regained by Scotland. With Calais it was a symbol of English ambition and conquest. Dunbar writes of 'all Yngland, frome Berwick to Kalice' ('This nycht befoir the dawing cleir', l. 34). Berwick is also mentioned in MQ 7, l. 39. In both poems, as in Dunbar's, it is a way of indicating extent.

11. The Laird of Lethingtounis Counsale to his Sone, Beand in the Court

Rubric: MQ and D. Part of the MF rubric has been lost, leaving '[…] beand in the court'. The Laird of Ledingtounes counsall to his [*sic*] being in court, R.

This poem belongs to the popular 'parental advice' genre, which can be traced back to Cato's *Disticha*. Several earlier examples of such poems survive in Older Scots, such as the fifteenth-century verse in

Cambridge, University Library MS Kk.1.5 (Ratis Raving, *The Thewis of Gudwemen*, *The Foly of Fulys and the Thewis of Wysmen*, and *The Consail and Teiching at the Vys Man Gaif his Sone*), and an anonymous work in the Maitland Folio, 'My sone gif thow to the court will ga' (pp. 148–52). For other poems by Maitland with an affiliation to the genre, see MQ 15 and MQ 32. Maitland's main source, however, is Dunbar's 'To dwell in court, my freind, gife that thow list' (See Bawcutt 1992, pp. 141–42; MacDonald 2001, pp. 139–41, Lyall 2005, pp. 200–1). The refrain to Maitland's poem echoes that to Dunbar's: 'He rewlis weill that weill him self can gyd'. Maitland also follows Dunbar in advising his son to be cautious in offering advice, to avoid vain ambition, flattery and gossip, and to keep only the company of honourable men. Indeed, like Dunbar's poem, Maitland's has much in common with poems on the instability of court life, a topic popular in the sixteenth century in poems such as William Stewart's 'Rolling in my Remembrance' (MF pp. 311–12, Bannatyne MS, fol. 94), and Maitland's own 'Sumtyme to court I did repair' (MQ 23). For discussion of the 'anti-aulic' satire, see Lyall 2005, pp. 195–226. In addition, Maitland advises his young reader to be a good public servant, to safeguard the commonweal and to maintain justice. He reminds the reader of the precariousness of public office (ll. 49–51), something Maitland's son William discovered to his own cost when the Queen's Party were defeated in 1573.

References to 'thy prince' (l. 33, compare l. 36) need not suggest a date of composition before 1542, during the reign of James V, or after 1567, during that of James VI. 'Prince' here refers to a monarch or sovereign and may be applied to a female monarch (see *DOST*, *Prince*, n.), although Bain suggests that Henry Stewart is being referred to (Bain ed. 1830, p. 159). Moreover, the poem need not be connected precisely to the lives of any of Maitland's own sons: 'sone' here may merely indicate a younger man, addressed by a more experienced figure, and is characteristic of the mode of address of such poems. See *DOST*, *Son*, n. sense 3.b. However, both Pinkerton and Bain supposed the addressee to be William Maitland, the eldest son of Sir Richard. Pinkerton rewrites the Quarto title thus: 'Counsale to his sone [William] Beand in the Court. Written about the yeir 1555' (1786, p. 275). The date of William's birth is uncertain, but is estimated to have been between 1525 and 1530. He went to St Leonard's College, St Andrews in 1540 and to the University of Paris in 1542 and his ascendency at court did not begin until the 1550s. Maitland's other surviving sons were John (later Chancellor of Scotland), born c.1543, and Thomas, born c.1548. Both served Mary of Guise and Mary Queen of Scots, as well as James VI.

Stanza: ababbcbC[5].
Text: MQ 16v–18v, MF pp. 19–21, R fols 14v–15v, D fols 15–17.
Authorship: attributed to Richard Maitland in MQ, MF, R and D.
Date: uncertain.

Commentary

4 *to thy tounge tak tent*. Compare Dunbar's 'To dwell in court', l. 3: 'lat thy tung tak rest'.

7 *To gouerne all and reull be not our bent*. Compare Dunbar 'To dwell in court', ll. 6–7: 'Als trubill nevir thy self, sone, be no tyd, / Vthiris to reiwll that will not rewlit be'.

8 *He reullis weill*. The refrain, which ultimately relates to Boethian ideals, refers to the connection between self-governance and successful integration at court. See Bawcutt, 1992, p. 140.

9–10 *Be not ane scorner, nor fein3it flatterar, / Nor 3it ane rounder of inuentit taillis*. Compare Dunbar's 'To dwell in court', ll. 33–35: 'be thow not ane roundar in the nwke /... / Be nocht in countenance ane skornar nor by luke'. Lyndsay also condemns the actions of 'schir Flattre', and 'Roundand and rowkand', at the court of the young James V, in *The Complaynt*, ll. 184–85.

14 *Fra wicked men thow draw the far on syide*. Compare Dunbar's 'To dwell in court', l. 14: 'And fra vyle folkis draw the far on syd'.

15 *Thow art ane fuile gif thow with fuillis deillis*. Proverbial: 'He is not the foole that the foole is, but he that with the foole deals' (see *Fergusson's Scottish Proverbs*, Beveridge ed. 1924, p. 41). The source is ultimately biblical: 'Answer not a fool according to his foolishnes, lest thou also be like him' (Proverbs 26.4, Geneva Bible 1560). Compare MQ 15, l. 7: 'Flie fra all fuillis that ar nyce'.

17 *Be war quhomto thy counsale thow reveill*. Compare Dunbar's 'To dwell in court', l. 9: 'Be war quhome to thy counsale thow discure'.

19 *Be of thy promeis and conditioun leill*. On the importance of being true, compare 'My sone gif þow to the court will ga', ll. 43–46.

20 *Waist not thy gud in prodigalitie*. Compare MQ 59 (addressed to the young James VI), l. 21: 'vse na prodigalitie'.

22 *With folk diffamit nather gang nor ryide*. Compare Dunbar, 'To dwell in court', l. 25: 'Fle frome the fallowschip of sic as ar defamit'.

23 *With wilful men to argone is folie*. Compare Dunbar's 'To dwell in court', l. 30: 'With wilful men, son, argown thow no tyd'.

EXPLANATORY NOTES

25 *Be no dyissar, nor player at the cairtes*. Dicing and card games are often identified in didactic literature with moral degeneracy. See *Ratis Raving*, l. 1248; Owst, 1966, pp. 371–72, 418, 430. Compare Lyndsay's condemnation of such pastimes at the court of the young James V in *The Complaynt*: 'Thare was no play bot cartis and dyce', l. 183, echoing Dunbar's condemnation of avarice in 'Fredome, honour and nobilnes', l. 11. Also Dunbar's 'Doverrit with dreme, devysing in my slummer', l. 56: 'Sic knavis and crakkaris to play at cartis and dyce'; and compare Maitland's MQ 15, esp. l. 6.

27 *Be not blawin with windis of all airtis*. An 'art' is a quarter or point of the compass. See *DOST*, *Art*, *Ayrt*, n. Compare Shaw's 'Suppois the courte ȝow cheir and tretis' (MF, pp. 320–21), where life at court is likened to a voyage through stormy seas; and John Stewart of Baldynneis, *To his familiar friend in cowrt*, ll. 3–6. Also see note to l. 43 below.

29 *Be wyise and tenty*. Compare John Stewart, 'Ane New sort of rymand rym', l. 31: 'Tentie, Sir, be, And grant not all thair asking' (Crockett ed. 1913, p. 150).

43 *Greit perrell is to tak on hand the ruder*. The metaphor of the state as a ship, which requires expert navigation, is conventional. Compare MQ 44, 'Ane Admonitioun to my lord of Mar, Regent', ll. 17–32, and Shaw, 'Suppois the court ȝow cheir and tretis', ll. 28–29: 'knaw courtis and wynd hes oft syss vareit / keip weill to ȝour cours and rewle ȝour rudir'.

47 *And all thy craft sall at the croce be cryit*. A reference to the making of public proclamations and announcements at the mercat cross of the burgh. The mercat cross was also the site for public events (including executions) and gatherings, and where criminals were brought to make public penance. See Scott's 'Ane New ȝeir Gift', l. 49, 'Att croce gar cry, be oppin proclamatioun'.

49–54 This is conventional advice from the fall of princes tradition. Compare 'The Bird in the Cadge', l. 46: 'Quha heichest clymmis the soner may thay slyde' (Cranstoun ed. 1891–93, I, p. 161).

71 *Ay nourisch peace, flie....* The MF text shows evidence of revision at this point. The words 'Or sawe seditioun' are crossed out but the marginal correction has been lost due to the cropping of the manuscript. Compare Dunbar, 'Be mery, man, an tak nocht fer in mynd': 'Follow pece, flie trubill and debait' (l. 17).

71 *flie troubill and debait*. Compare 'My sone gif þow to the court will ga', ll. 69–82, where the reader is advised to avoid quarrels and boasting, which will lead to strife or violence.

78 *Thocht all wer thyne within this warld sa wyde.* An echo of Dunbar's 'To dwell in court', l. 22: 'Thocht all war thyne this warld within so wyd'.

82 *To pleis thy God set all thy bissie cuire.* A pious convention of the parental advice genre. Compare 'My sone gif þow to the court will ga', ll. 5–15.

12. O gratious God, almichtie and eterne

This poem is both a penitential supplication and a complaint on the times, in which the failings of both the secular and religious estates are detailed. The poem is dated to 1570 in MF, but it makes no direct mention of the significant event with which this year began, the murder of the Regent Moray, Lord James Stewart, in January 1570.

The first two stanzas request God's merciful deliverance from plague and famine caused by drought and failure of the harvest. Such afflictions were indeed common in Scotland in the second half of the sixteenth century. Maitland interprets them as instances of divine punishment, and they are reminiscent of those meted out in the Old Testament (see Genesis 14, Exodus 7–12, Ezekiel 5:16, Deuteronomy 28:48 and 28:21). The comparison of such events to biblical ones was a common literary trope: the author of *The Complaynt of Scotland* (printed in Paris in 1550) wrote:

> Ve maye persaue for certan, that ve haue bene scurgit vitht al the plagis, that ar befor rehersit in the xxviii cheptour of deuteronome, that is to say vitht pestelens, vitht the sourde, vitht brakkyng doune of our duelling housis, vitht spulʒe of our cornis ande cattel.
> (Stewart ed. 1979, pp. 22–23)

Stanzas three and four of Maitland's poem comprise a complaint on the corruption of the pre-Reformation Church, culminating in criticism of the clergy's failure to preach the word of God faithfully (l. 30), a major preoccupation of the Reformers. However, the narrator moves on to criticise the Protestants' claims to reform, which have been undermined by their own sins, and to caution them that God may yet punish them as he did the 'Papists' (l. 49). This emphasis on the equal hypocrisy of the religious factions may be compared to Scott's 'New ʒeir

Gift', ll. 57–96 and 113–60. Poetic attacks on the vices of the Protestant clergy, such as *A Lewd Ballet* (c.1571, see Cranstoun ed. 1891–93, I, pp. 201–3), were also in circulation by the early 1570s.
Stanza: ababbcbc[5].
Text: MQ fols 18v–19v; MF pp. 35–7; D fols 17–18v.
Authorship: attributed to Richard Maitland in MQ, MF and D.
Date: 1570.

Commentary
6 *vnkyndlie weir*. This refers to the struggle for power between the King's Party and the Queen's Party between 1567 and 1573. The war is 'vnkyndlie' because its perpetrators are lacking in brotherly feeling for each other.

5 *plagis*. There were several outbreaks of bubonic plague in sixteenth-century Scotland. Haddington had witnessed a severe episode in 1548, and Edinburgh in 1564 and 1568–69. Plague was still prevalent in the lowlands of Scotland in1570. See Shrewsbury 1970, repr. 2005, pp. 208–9. Maitland regards such events as divine punishment. Compare MQ 42 (attributed to Arbuthnot), l. 188: 'The Lordis plaige throwout the warld is went'.

7 *Hunger and derthe*. The late sixteenth century witnessed serious food shortages caused by failure of the harvest, population growth and inflation. See Wormald 1981, repr. 2001, p. 51, p. 167: 'Between 1550 and 1600 there are 24 years of scarcity (local or national) mentioned in the sources, where people starved to death.' The 1560s opened and closed with dearth. See Lythe 1960, p. 17.

18–19 *Quhen that thay maid thair berdis and schuif thair croun, / Vsit round cappis and gounis to thair heill*. The criticism is that churchmen invested too much effort in outward things – shaped beards, tonsures and long gowns – and neglected spiritual matters. Compare Lyndsay's *The Testament of the Papyngo*, ll. 676–77:

> The Payngo said, 'Father, be the rude,
> Howbeit your rayment be religious lyke,
> Your conscience, I suspect, be nocht gude'.

Also *Ane Satyre of the Thrie Estaitis* (1554) where the Vices disguise themselves in 'Clarkis cleathing' to give themselves 'graue countenance' (ll. 722–73).

24 *Of Christiane peopill oft maid sacrifice*. The reference to 'fyire' in line 23 suggests that Maitland has in mind the persecution and execution as heretics of those holding reformist views. The last Protestant martyr to be executed in Scotland was William Milne, in 1558. Relatively few Scots had suffered this fate since 1528, when Patrick Hamilton was put to death in St Andrews.

33 *Now is Protestanis rissin ws amang*. The Reformation Parliament of 1560 gave authority to a Protestant Confession of Faith and removed the jurisdiction of the Pope; but it was not until after the deposition of Queen Mary in 1567 that the prospect of a Catholic revival declined.

41–42 *doe call ... mes idolatrie*. *The First Book of Discipline* (1560), chapter 3, names the Mass as a form of idolatry, along with the adoration of images and invocation of saints. Knox had delivered his *Vindication of the Doctrine that the Sacrifice of the Mass is Idolatry* in Newcastle in 1550.

43 *eit flesche vpon the fraydayis all*. Protestants permitted the consumption of meat on Fridays, a practice forbidden by the established Church in memory of the Crucifixion. See *The First Book of Discipline*, chapter 1 on the abolition of such non-Scriptural doctrines. Compare Scott's 'An New ȝeir Gift', l. 74, 'And quha eit flesche on Frydayis was fyrefangit' (executed as a heretic by burning).

62 *the 'fleschlie gospellaris'*. An ironic oxymoron: the carnally minded preachers of the gospel. See *DOST, Fleschly*, a.; *Gospellar*, n.

13. Amang foleis ane greit folie I find

A.A. MacDonald has suggested that this poem may be connected with the marriage of the fifty-year-old John Knox to the seventeen-year-old daughter of Andrew Stewart, second Lord Ochiltree, Margret, in March 1564. See MacDonald 1972, pp. 9–10 and 2001, p. 145. If so, the poem emerges from the context of the strained relationship between Knox and the Maitland family. Knox was critical of Richard Maitland's lack of support for Protestantism, and William Maitland's hostility to the cause, in his *History of the Reformation* (see Dickinson ed. 1949, I, p. 167, II, p. 104 etc.).

Whatever the topical nature of the poem, its witty denunciation of the age-disparate marriage belongs to a long literary tradition. In particular, Maitland draws on the literary presentation of the foolish *senex amans*, especially that of Chaucer's 'The Merchant's Tale', and possibly Gower's *Confessio Amantis*, where the narrator, Amans, has to learn the

harsh lesson that 'loves lust and lockes hore / In chambre acorden neveremore' (VIII, ll. 2403–4). Other analogues known to Maitland include Dunbar's *Tretis of the Tua Mariit Wemen and the Wedo* (particularly its account of the first wife's unhappy marriage to an older man) and *King Hart*, both of which are included in MF. Like these poems, Maitland's has links to the misogynistic tradition in its portrayal of women as sexually insatiable (ll. 5–6; see Blamires 1992, pp. 68, 100, 169; Newlyn 1999, pp. 60–62), although the principal butt of its jokes is the foolish old lover who believes he can please a young bride. The style is characterised by word play and double entendre (note especially ll. 28 and 33), and employs both seasonal and temporal metaphors, as well those of life as a journey, the body as a vessel, and sex as ploughing. See MacDonald 1972, pp. 9–11. For a contrasting portrayal of a pious and virtuous old age, see MQ 20 and MQ 24, and Dunbar's 'Now cumis aige quhair ȝewth hes bene'. MacDonald has suggested that an additional source for the poem is Alexander Barclay's English version of Sebastian Brant's *Narrenschiff*. See MacDonald 2001, p. 146.
Stanza: ababbcc⁵.
Text: MQ fols 20–20v; MF pp. 54–55, R fols 18–18v, and D fols 1–1v.
Authorship: attributed to Richard Maitland in MQ and MF.
Date: c.1564?

Commentary

1 *Amang foleis*. As MacDonald points out, the opening of the poem recalls phrasing from Barlcay's *Ship of Fools*, such as 'Amang our folys delytynge them in vyces …'. See Jamieson 1889, pp. 41–43; MacDonald 2001, p. 146.

2 *ane man past fiftie ȝeir of aage*. According to *Ratis Raving*, during the fifth and sixth ages of man's life, spanning the years of 50 to 70, one should love 'ernyst mar than play' (l. 1663). Yet age is also attended by other vices, including 'lichery' (l. 1449), idleness and avarice: 'This eild that passis fyfty ȝer / Is stabile, couatus and swere' (ll. 1636–37).

9 *not in tailis*. Here 'tailis' has several meanings. It suggests the fashionable 'sidetails', or trains on gowns (see MQ 2, note to ll. 11–12), and so is used as a metonymy for young women. It also indicates the genitalia of men or women. See *DOST*, *Tail*, n. especially sense 5. The wordplay on 'taillis' and 'tailis' therefore juxtapositions worthy moral (literary) and immoral pursuits (fornication).

12–13 *fresche Maij and cauld Ianuarij*. A reference to the protagonists of Chaucer's 'Merchant's Tale'. May is frequently referred to as 'fresshe

May' (*Canterbury Tales*, IV, ll. 1782, 1822); January takes 'spices hoote t'encreessen his corage' (IV, l. 1808). The seasonal associations for the different parts of man's lifecycle are commonplace. See *Confessio Amantis*, 'I made a liknesse of miselve / Unto the sondri monthes twelve' (VIII, ll. 2837–38). The reference to coldness in Maitland's poem, as well as having seasonal associations, is related to the medieval physiological belief in the humours: coldness is equated with melancholy and impotence. Compare *Confessio Amantis*, VII, ll. 401–20. Also see MQ 20: 'Of Venus play past is the heit' (l. 26).

13 *Agreis not*. The disagreements of youth and age are conventional and often the topic of debate poems, such as Henryson's 'Quhen fair Flora, the godes of the flouris'. Compare *Fergusson's Scottish Proverbs:* 'Youth and age will never agree' (Beveridge ed. 1924, p. 112).

14 *The trebill wantis that sould be songe abone*. A reference to the singing of a part song, where the 'treble' is the highest or second highest part in the composition. The lack of the treble part perhaps indicates a lack of youth in one of the singers. In the 'Merchant's Tale', January sings after the consummation of his marriage: 'And after that he sang ful loude and cleere', IV l. 1845. Maitland is also referring here to Dunbar's 'This hindir nycht in Dumfermeling', ll. 18–19, 'The silly lame wes all to small / To sic ane tribbill to hald ane bace'.

19 *Ane auld gray berd on ane quhyte mouth to lay*. Compare Dunbar's *Tretis*, l. 106: 'He schowis on me his schewill mouth and schendis my lippis'.

21 *The ane cryis 'Help!', the other hes no micht*. Contrast the plight of the first wife in Dunbar's *Tretis*: 'I schrenk for the scharp stound, bot schout dar I nought' (l. 109).

22 *haue bene merchant*. Perhaps a reference to the narrator of Chaucer's 'Merchant's Tale', or to the widow's second husband in Dunbar's *Tretis*: 'Syne maryt I a merchand' (l. 296).

23–24 *Handwarpe, Burges, and in the toun of Berrie, / Syn into Deip*. All major centres of trade for Scottish merchants in the fifteenth and early sixteenth centuries, though both Antwerp and Bruges were in decline by the 1550s. Dieppe was one of the most lucrative markets of northern France. 'Berrie' is Bury St Edmunds in Suffolk, an important centre of the English wool trade. To France, the main exports were wool, cloth and salt fish; to the towns of the Low Countries, hides, sheep skins, coal, salt. Guicciardini's account of Scottish commerce in

Antwerp in c.1560 records that Scotland also exported fine pelts and pearls. See Lythe 1960, pp. 236–37.

28 *To beir the saill.* Compare MQ 2, l. 14: 'fuk saillis'. The 'saill' here indicates a woman's skirts, and ultimately the woman herself.

28 *not havand ane steif mast.* Another reference to the old husband's lack of sexual potency. Compare Dunbar's *Tretis*, 'He may weill to the syn assent, bot sakles is his deidis' (l. 95).

29 *ane melein.* A tenant farm. See *DOST, Mailing,* n.

30 *graith.* Another likely pun. Here 'graith' means tools or equipment, and the traditional association of farming implements and the penis is suggested. See *DOST, Graith,* n. Compare the use of 'pleuch' at l. 33. Also see Venus's advice to Amans in *Confessio Amantis* 'Bot mor behoveth to the plowh, / Wherof thee lacketh, as I trowe' (VIII, ll. 2426–27).

31 *Quhair seid wantis, then men of teilling tyris.* A further punning reference to the lack of sexual potency. See *DOST, Seid,* n. sense 5.

32–33 *Then cummis ane, findis it waist lyand, / ʒoikis his pleuche teillis at his awin hand.* It is suggested that the young and sexually dissatisfied wife of an older husband is easily seduced by other suitors. Again this recalls the 'Merchant's Tale' and Damyan's wooing of May, and the complaint of the first wife in the *Tretis* that her jealous old husband imagines that 'he sall tak me with a trawe at trist of ane othir' (l. 124). The 'pleuche teillis' are the lower part of the plough (here signifying the penis). For the association of farm tools and the penis, see note to l. 30.

35 *that schame.* The shame of being cuckolded.

14. Blind man, be blyithe, thocht that thow be wrangit

The poem concerns the attack by the troops of the King's Party and English forces, led by Rowland Forster, Captain of Wark in Northumbria, in May 1570, on Blythe, Richard Maitland's barony in Lauderdale (now in Peebleshire) in the Scottish Borders, which he acquired in 1537. The rights of Maitland and his heirs to Blythe and Thirlestane were formally ratified by Mary in 1567 in recognition of Maitland's faithful service (RPS *1567*/4/8). The attack was provoked by the political allegiance with the Queen's Party of his son William Maitland, Secretary

Lethington. In MF the poem concludes with the following note (copied in the same hand as that responsible for the poem) which describes the assault:

> Quod Sir Richart Maitland of Lethingtoun knycht, quhane his landis of the bararonie of Blyth in Lawderdaill was heriet be Rollent Foster, Inglisman, kapitane of Wark, with his cumpanye to þe nomber of thre hunder men; quha spulȝeit fra the said Sir Richard, and fra his eldest sone, thair serwandis, and tennentis furthe of the said baronie, fowr thowand scheip, ȝoungar and elder, twa hundrithe nowlt, threttie horsis and meiris, and insycht furthe of his howsis of Blythe, wourthe ane hundrithe pund, and the haill tennentis insycht of the haill baronrie that was tursabill. This spulȝe was committit the Xvj day of Maij, þe ȝeir of M D. LXX ȝeiris. And the said Sir Richart was thre scoir and xiiij ȝeiris of age, and growin blind in tyme of peice, quhane nane of that cuntra lippint for sic thing. (MF, p. 38)

The poem is based on an extended play on words, drawing together the name of Maitland's barony and the virtue of being blithe in adverse circumstances in hope of seeing justice done and receiving eternal reward for such stoicism. The poem is full of pride in the Maitland family's status, history and long-standing connection to the locality. The narrator remarks on the irony of the raiders being unable to take away the most valuable asset of all – the land itself. His counsel to be happy in the face of personal loss, and to find contentment in patience and faith rather than riches, has its basis in philosophical and biblical traditions (see Bawcutt 1992, pp. 142–43). Maitland is strongly influenced in his handling of this theme by Dunbar, in poems such as 'Be mery, man, and tak nocht fer in mynd' and 'Quho thinkis that he hes sufficence'. Dunbar's 'Full oft I mvse and hes in thocht', with its refrain, 'For to be blythe me think it best', has also influenced Maitland's poem. The exhortation to be blithe and rejoice in the comfort of Christ is similar to that in 'Be blyith, all Christin men and sing', in *The Gude and Godlie Ballatis* (Mitchell ed. 1896–97, pp. 46–47). Also compare MQ 15 and MQ 17.

Though attributed to Richard Maitland in MF, MQ and D, the poem casts him (the 'Blind man' of the opening line) as its addressee. Compare MQ 24 (by Maitland) and the anonymous poem MQ 46, 'Ane Consolatore Ballad to Sir Richart Maitland of Lethingtoun knicht'. The loss of family lands (this time the confiscation of Lethington in 1571) is alluded to in MQ 20.

Stanza: ababbcbc[5].

Text: MQ 20v–21; MF pp. 37–38; D fols 18v–20.

EXPLANATORY NOTES

Authorship: Attributed to Richard Maitland in MQ, MF and D.
Date: 1570.

Commentary

1 *Blind man*. On Maitland's blindness, see MQ 9, l. 58 and headnote.

2 *Blyithe*. Blythe in Lauderdale (now Peebleshire), which had been in Maitland's possession since 1537. The family's right to the barony was ratified in the parliament of 1567. See headnote.

3 *Thow salbe blyithe quhen that thay salbe hangit*. The hope is that the perpetrators are to be treated as common thieves. Compare MQ 3, l. 75.

5–6 *Be blyithe and gaid that nane persaue in the / That thy blyithnes consistis into riches*. Compare Dunbar's 'Quho thinkis that he hes sufficence', ll. 3–5: 'Thocht he haue nowder land nor rent /... / He hes anewch that is content'.

14–15 *Quhen Blyithe salbe ȝit, with Goddis grace, / Als weill pleneist as euer thay it fand*. For a similar conviction of Maitland righteousness, see MQ 46: 'he ȝour hous, ȝour self, and sone will send / Mair solace' (ll. 197–98).

20 *thy onfreindis*. Probably the political enemies of William Maitland, Secretary Lethington, and therefore by association, of the Maitland family. In September 1569 Maitland had been arrested and imprisoned on charges relating to Darnley's murder, and was regarded with particular suspicion by the Regent Moray. However, Maitland had considerable support and by 1570 emerged as the clear leader of the Queen's Party, and principal adversary of the King's Party. After Moray's assassination he was acquitted of all charges, and returned to the Privy Council. See Loughlin, *ODNB*.

21 *Be blyith and glaid of thy aduersitie*. Compare Dunbar, 'Be mery, man, and tak nocht fer in mynd', l. 9: 'Mak gud cheir of it God the sendis'.

24 *thow hes aneuch of land*. Maitland also possessed lands at Lethington, near Haddington (acquired by royal charter in 1345), and Thirlestane in Lauderdale.

28 *And thow be blyith is caus of lang leving*. Compare Dunbar, 'Be mery, man, and tak nocht fer in mynd', l. 14: 'Thy lyfe in dolour ma nocht lang indure'.

29–30 *Be thow not blyithe, thocht thow wer ane king, / Thy lyif is not* *bot cair without blyithnes*. Compare Dunbar, 'Full oft I mvse and hes in thocht', ll. 16–19:

> Quha with this warld dois warsill and stryfe
> And dois his dayis in dolour dryfe,
> Thocht he in lordschip be possest,
> He levis bot ane wrechit lyfe.

15. Luik that na thing to sine the tyice

This moral and admonitory poem is reminiscent of the parental advice tradition: its simple and direct counsel is paralleled in MQ 32 and 33 (also by Maitland). As well as addressing the theme of self-governance (stanzas 1 and 2), the poem offers advice on the proper regulation of the self in public (stanza 3), including the right sort of ('honest') company one should keep. The warning about avoiding treasonable conduct in l. 18 suggests that like MQ 11, to which it shows several similarities in phrasing and theme, it is concerned with the conduct of its imagined reader in a political or court context. It revisits many of Maitland's favourite themes such as the importance of truth, loyalty and justice, and the protection of the poor. The poem may have been composed around the same time as MQ 11, but it is not possible to date it with any certainty. Like MQ 14 and MQ 17, its concern with the importance of the pious acceptance of one's circumstances has probably been influenced by Dunbar's poems, including 'Be mery, man, and tak nocht fer in mynd' and 'Quho thinkis that he hes sufficence'.
Stanza: aaa^{4}b^2.
Text: MQ fols 21–21v; MF p. 38; D fol. 19v.
Authorship: attributed to Richard Maitland in MQ and D, but not MF.
Date: uncertain.

Commentary

6 *Waist not thy guddis at the dyice*. Compare MQ 11, l. 25 and note.

7 *Flie fra all fuillis that ar nyice*. Compare MQ 11, l. 15 and note.

9 *honest companie*. Compare MQ 11, l. 74.

11 *harlatrie*. In this context meaning both any kind of moral laxity or lack of chastity. See *DOST, Harlotry*, n.

15 *Conqueis na guddis wrangouslie*. Compare MQ 4, ll. 41–43.

19–20 *And tak in thank and gude sessoun / Quhat God will send*.

Compare Dunbar's 'Be mery, man, and tak nocht fer in mynd': 'Mak gude cheir of it God the sendis' (l. 9). Also see Dunbar's 'Quho thinkis that he hes sufficence': 'Thank God of it is to the sent, / And of it glaidlie mak gud cheir' (ll. 13–14). Also see MQ 17, l. 33.

16. The Lord that raise from lyif againe

In this poem, Maitland compares the cruelty and injustice of the events leading up to Christ's Passion to what he regards as the even greater moral degeneracy and treachery of his own society. The refrain to stanzas 1–6 and 8 ('In this worst warld that wes sein') suggests an almost apocalyptic perspective, and later in the poem all estates are said to be in 'dispair' (l. 90), the people of Scotland having turned their backs on all goodness, just as the Jews forgot Christ's miracles at his crucifixion. Although Maitland would have been familiar with passion lyrics such as Dunbar's 'Amang thir freiris within ane cloister' or Kennedy's 'Þe passioun of Crist', this poem has little in common with the meditations on the sufferings of Christ found in such pre-Reformation poems. Instead, Maitland develops a series of observations on the faults of the main figures of the Gospel narratives of the Crucifixion (Herod, Pilate, Caiaphas and Annas, Judas and Peter) into a complaint on the times which focuses the reader's attention on the oppression of the poor, the perversion of the judicial system, and on the lack of spiritual and temporal authority in contemporary Scotland. Many of these themes are reminiscent of MQ 3, 4, 5 and 7. The terms of reference in the poem are broad rather than specific, although in the light of MQ 14 Maitland may regard himself and his family as among those who have suffered at the hands of 'backbyteris' (l. 29) and thieves.

The poem was apparently composed during the Civil War period of 1567–73 (see ll. 110–11). It ends with a prayer for King James VI (b. 1566) and his just and peaceful reign of Scotland. The poem is not in the Maitland Folio.

Stanza: ababbcbc[4].
Text: MQ fols 21v–24; D fols 20–22.
Authorship: attributed to Richard Maitland in MQ and D.
Date: c.1567–73.

Commentary

4 *hard of fay*. Perhaps 'ignorant of the true faith', a reference to the

Jews' refusal to accept Christ's divinity. Here 'hard' has the sense of 'insensitive' or 'dull'. See *DOST, Hard*, a. sense 2b.

9–10 *Ane Heroid ... / Ane murtherar of innocentis.* Herod, king of Jerusalem, ordered the massacre of the infants of Bethlehem after the birth of Jesus. Matt 2: 16–17.

13 *tak vp rentis.* Compare MQ 5, l. 34 and note.

17 *Pilat.* Pontius Pilate, procurator of Judea and chief justice. Finding no fault in Jesus, he nevertheless handed him over to the Jews to be crucified.

25 *Caiphas.* Caiaphas, the high priest in Jerusalem who presided over the trial of Christ, and is portrayed in Matthew and John as the one who gives counsel to the Jews that Jesus should be killed (Matt 26: 3–4; John 18: 14). Compare MQ 62, l. 120. The rhyme scheme is irregular in this stanza.

33 *The tormentaris.* The gospels do not mention the precise number of Christ's tormentors. In Matthew he is handed over to a group of soldiers (Matt 27: 27).

37 *To spoilʒie pour men of thair pakis.* Compare MQ 3, l. 43.

39 *Quhill that thay gar ane widdie rax.* 'Until they cause the hangman's rope to stretch'. A reference to execution by hanging as the appropriate punishment for those who steal from the poor. A 'widdie' is a noose. See *DOST, Widdy,* n.

41 *Iudas.* Judas Iscariot, one of the twelve disciples, and betrayer of Jesus. The chief priests gave him thirty pieces of silver in exchange for delivering Christ to them (Matt 26: 14–16).

49 *Peter to Annas hous him drest.* Annas, father in law to Caiaphas, was a high priest in Jerusalem and presided over a preliminary trial of Jesus before sending him to Caiaphas. Peter's betrayal at the house of Annas is recounted in John 18: 16–17.

57 *Pilat let bot ane theif gang.* The Jews requested that Pilate release Barabbas, a robber, rather than Jesus, in accordance with their Passover custom to free a prisoner (John 18: 39–40).

65–66 *Fra Pilat fand of deid na caus / In Christ....* According to Matt 27: 24, Pilate washed his hands before the crowd to demonstrate his innocence in the death of Jesus, in whom he could find no fault. The presentation of Pilate in medieval literary and dramatic tradition is complex. He is sometimes partially exonerated for his role in the Crucifixion because of his attempt to release Jesus (John 19: 12), while the Jews instead bear most blame for their implacable hatred and desire for his death. See Kolve, 1966, pp. 231–34.

71 *Nor in thair [sysis] put not thair fa.* Translate 'nor subject their enemy to judicial review'. Lines 67–72 are a plea for the eradication of corruption in the legal system. Here Maitland is apparently requesting that individuals do not seek to settle personal scores through the courts without proper cause.

72 *partialitie.* Reminiscent of legal usage, and meaning bias or unfairness. See *DOST, Part-, Parcialitié,* n.

86–88 *all auld kyndnes ... clein forʒet.* Compare MQ 23, l. 7: 'auld kyndnes helpis not ane hair'.

93–96 A second personal pronoun is suppressed in line 94, making the sense awkward. Translate, 'Although this entire region be brought to ruin, through their own will, they will not be able to do anything, and this will make buildings / settlements destitute and a devastated country to be seen'.

110–11 *Send ws gud men to gang betwein / The lordis to mak vnioun.* A reference to the difficulties of addressing the division between the King's Party and Queen's Party in the years 1567 to 1573. Maitland's poems often call for assistance (divine or human) in bringing unity to Scotland's lords. Compare MQ 5, l. 79, MQ 25, l. 21, MQ 18, l. 31, MQ 19, l. 28.

113 *God keip the Kingis maiestie.* James VI (b.1566). Mary abdicated in favour of her son in 1567.

17. Gif trowbill cummis be eventour

This philosophical poem on the virtue of patience and the value of suffering in developing understanding ('intelligence', l. 6), self-knowledge and knowledge of God, is Boethian in character. Like MQ 14 and MQ 15 it shows the influence of Dunbar, especially poems such as 'Be mery, man, and tak nocht fer in mynd' and 'Quho thinkis that he hes sufficence': it advises that in adversity faith, a glad heart and an acceptance of one's duty ('vocatioun', l. 28) are essential. It is likely that the poem was composed during the civil war given its reference to the present 'vnfaythfulnes' of all the estates in ll. 13–16. The mention of the importance of defending a just quarrel suggests that Maitland may

have had some particular family or personal grievance in mind. See note to l. 35. Stanzas 5 and 6 explore a theme dealt with at greater length in MQ 23, the unreliability of kin and acquaintance. The poem is found only in MQ and D.
Stanza: abab[4].
Text: MQ fols 24–24v; D fols 22v–23.
Authorship: attributed to Richard Maitland in MQ and D.
Date: c.1567–73, perhaps c.1569–70.

Commentary

2 *not throw thy misgouernance*. Misfortune caused by one's own intemperance is, by inference, just punishment, whereas that which comes through adventure or chance ('eventour', l. 1) must be patiently endured. Compare David Lyndsay's *The Testament of the Papyngo*, l. 513: 'be his awin wylfull mysgovernance'.

8 *experience*. Experience seems here to be equivalent to self-knowledge, and is closely linked to the quality of 'intelligence' (l. 6). Compare MQ 11, l. 44. Experience is personified in Lyndsay's *Ane Dialogue Between Experience and ane Courteour* (1555). On the treatment of experience in sixteenth-century Scottish texts, see McClune 2010.

9–10 *the instabilitie / Of this fals warld*. Reminiscent of Dunbar's 'Full oft I mvse and hes in thocht', ll. 2–3: 'this fals warld is ay on flocht / Quhair no thing ferme is nor degest'.

11–12 *This day ane man set vp in hie, / To morne set doun* .... This recalls popular images, visual and literary, of Fortune turning her wheel, onto which cling individuals, their position on the wheel indicating the state of their fortune. Compare *The Kingis Quair*, ll. 1135–55; MQ 22, ll. 35–36.

17 *For and thy bak be at the wall*. An idiom used to indicate a desperate situation. The *OED*'s first citation of this is from William Stewart, *The buik of the cronicilis of Scotland*, 1535: 'That we may haif thair bakis at the wall, Without defend that ar oure commoun fa' (Turnball ed. 1858, II, 73). See *OED*, *Bak*, n., sense 25.

19–20 *Then will thy quentance leif the all, / How neir of bluid that euer thay be*. On the untrustworthiness of kin and friends, compare MQ 23, l. 18.

28 *iust in thy vocatioun*. On the importance of knowing and being true to one's estate, compare MQ 2, ll. 48–49. See *DOST*, *Vocatioun*, n., especially sense 3.

30 *thy self wald sla.* Compare MQ 8, ll. 31–32.

33 *Thairfoir, thank God quhat euer he send.* Compare MQ 14, l. 21 and note; and MQ 15, ll. 19–20.

35 *thy iust querrell defend.* Maitland may have in mind the political dealings of his son William, Secretary Lethington, and his opposition to Moray, which resulted in the latter's imprisonment at the end of 1569 and trial on charges relating to Darnley's murder in 1570. For other family troubles at this time, see MQ 14 and headnote.

36 *neuer by the richt way gang.* Perhaps 'never deviate from the right course of action'.

18. O leving Lord, that maid bayth hevin and hell

The poem refers to the 'ciuill weir' following Mary's forced abdication and thus dates from the period 1567–73. It is not possible to be certain which year Maitland refers to in l. 3 ('this ȝeir'), but the phrasing here suggests that the conflict is still relatively new. Given the rough chronological order of Maitland's poems in the Quarto, it may pre-date 1571, a year to which MQ 20 relates. However, and perhaps ironically, some of the fears voiced in this poem, concerning threats to lands and possessions, anticipate the concerns of MQ 20.

Like Maitland's poems MQ 4, MQ 7 and MQ 12, this poem begins as a petition for divine help with Scotland's afflictions of war and violent disorder. It develops into an exhortation to the divided lords of Scotland to ask for mercy for their sins, and to put their political differences aside in favour of unity. In particular, Maitland urges them to administer justice fairly, especially by punishing those who oppress the poor. Maitland complains that hostile reprisals, 'deidlie feid' (l. 13), rather than justice, are presently the result of pleas for restitution for those who have been wronged.

Maitland declines to make his own allegiances in this conflict clear and instead addresses the poem to those on both sides of the struggle: 'I speik this to the lordis of bayth the syidis' (l. 41).

Stanza: ababa[5].
Text: MQ fols 24v–25v; MF pp. 267–68; R fols 24–24v, D fols 23v–24.
Authorship: attributed to Richard Maitland in MQ, MF, R and D.
Date: c.1567–73, perhaps before 1571.

Commentary

2 *this cruell ciuill weir*. The struggle for authority between the King's Party and the Queen's Party. See headnote and compare l. 17 and l. 41.

8 *the theiffis ar so ryfe*. Compare MQ 3. These 'theiffis' are probably the raiders or reivers that afflicted the border regions such as Liddesdale.

9 *evin to Fyfe*. Again compare MQ 3, ll. 20–22. Maitland appears to imagine the sort of raiding that characterises border life spreading up through Scotland as far as Fife, on the north side of the Firth of Forth.

19 *greit effusioun now of bluid innocent*. Small-scale conflict, rather than pitched battles, characterised the civil war years, leading to bloodshed and localised destruction. However, there was substantial loss of life during the Battle of Langside in 1568 and the siege of Edinburgh Castle between 1571 and 1573. Blood feud between families and the pursuit of personal vendettas also cost many lives, and some episodes from the period, such as the burning of the towerhouse of Forbes at Towie, with women and children inside, by the troops of the Gordon clan, were particularly notorious. See Dawson 2007, pp. 264–82, esp. p. 276.

21 *melling with kirk geir*. The First Book of Discipline stipulated that church revenues be redirected towards poor relief and education, but in reality such reallocation of these funds was limited. The gradual lay annexation of church lands had been a feature of pre-Reformation Scotland (Wormald 1991, p. 125), and after 1560 'the beneficiaries from the dispersal of church property [were] ... the landed classes' (Goodare 1999, p. 109).

23 *Sum sayis ambitioun, that wald haue reull and steir*. Compare MQ 11, l. 43, where Maitland warns his son against ambition to govern others without first having the necessary experience.

35 *Mak ane suir band*. Bands, or bonds, were documents, written in the vernacular, 'describing a one-sided obligation whereby a man bound himself to another in matters of money or land'. See Wormald 1985, p. 14.

19. At morning, in ane gardein grein

The poem begins with the narrator walking, in the style of the *chanson d'aventure*, in a pleasant garden, perhaps that of Lethington (see MQ 68, ll. 121–32; and Brown 2000, p. 209 on Scottish nobles and the 'fashionable idea of neo-Stoic rusticity'). However, this idyllic garden makes him think, by contrast, of the sufferings endured by the people of Scotland, and especially of the poverty of the 'commounis of this land' (l. 20). The reference to 'vnkyndlie weir' (l. 15) refers to the civil war of 1567–73 (compare MQ 18), although the poem may date from c.1569–70 (see notes to ll. 73–74 below). The poem is nostalgic for a time when Scotland was guided by 'zelous men' (l. 28), and penitential, regarding Scotland's problems as a result of the sinfulness of its people, and urging readers to reform and pray for mercy. As well as describing political division (according to Maitland, perpetrated by the self-interest of the factions, ll. 43–44), feuding, lawlessness and oppression, Maitland's narrator longs for a time when the realm can be free of both English and French intervention. Lines 64 to 81 remark on the allegiance between the King's Party and England, which had been fostered by Moray during 1568 and 1569, and the Queen's Party and France, pointing out that the relationship with England is particularly harmful to Scotland, for the English exploit it for their 'awin provisioun' (l. 70). The young King James VI (b.1566) is mentioned at l. 94 and the lords are exhorted to preserve the realm so that he has a kingdom to rule when he comes of age.

Stanza: abab⁴cc³bb⁴c³.

Text: MQ fols 25v–26v; MF pp. 268–71; D fols 24v–26v.

Authorship: attributed to Richard Maitland in MQ, MF and D.

Date: c.1569–70?

Commentary

22–23 *sum band / Of suddartis of sum syde*. The suggestion here is that the poor suffer as the result of the raids of troops belonging to individual feuding factions. Lords on both sides of the political divide employed large bands of armed retainers. See Dawson 2007, p. 272.

38 *in this regioun*. Maitland uses 'regioun' to refer to Scotland ('in this country / part of the world'). See *DOST*, *Region*, n., sense 1.

64 *England is glaid*. The main motivation for English involvement in Scotland was its own succession crisis and national security.

73–74 *3it the ane part on thame dependis, / The other on France for thair supplie*. Lord James Stewart, earl of Moray and regent, had secured a subsidy from Elizabeth in 1569 as well as some military help to resolve border conflict; in 1570 his successor, Lennox, arrived in Scotland with 1,000 English soldiers (Dawson 2007, pp. 265, 272). The Queen's Party looked to France for support, but received little practical help.

89 *gud tounis destroyit be*. Localised skirmishes throughout Scotland resulted in much destruction, for which few were brought to justice. In the Spring of 1570, the Earl of Sussex carried out raids on the Scottish Border to punish those who had assisted the Northern Rebels of November 1569. In the summer of 1570, English artillery was particularly destructive in Clydesdale. Dawson 2007, p. 264.

94 *the King*. The child James VI, crowned in Stirling on 29 July 1567. James assumed personal rule in c.1584–85. Compare MQ 16, l. 113.

104–5 *to mak ane band, / Ay in kyndnes to stand*. This refers to the making of a bond of unity, or to ratifying neighbourly or friendly feeling. Compare MQ 18, l. 35 and note.

113 *Sanct Paull*. The apostle Paul.

20. Thocht that this warld be verie strainge

This poem relates to the confiscation of Lethington in 1571: the Maitlands were forfeited by a parliament of the King's Party held in the Canongate of Edinburgh in May 1571. For some time afterwards Richard Maitland was resident at Dundas near Edinburgh (Bain ed. 1830, p. 1, note). Meanwhile, Lethington was occupied by David Hume of Fishwick (see *RPS* 1578/7/31, 1579/10/63; *Reg. Privy Council* 2, pp. 80–81), and despite Maitland's efforts, including an appeal to Elizabeth, his lands were not returned for over a decade. The poem briefly notes the benefits of cultivating patience and faith in the face of adversity (compare MQ 14 and 26), but is not overtly moralistic.

On Maitland's skilful and ironic creation of 'a persona of bewildered simplicity' in this poem, see MacDonald 2001, p. 144; also see van Heijnsbergen 2005, pp. 339–44. The poem begins with the narrator lamenting the unjust confiscation of his home and possessions as a result of the activities of 'men of weir' (l. 11). However, the tone of the poem shifts at line 21 and Maitland creates a witty far-fetched sketch of his narrator's younger self as a one-time womaniser who provoked his wife's jealousy. The depiction of the faded lover who now embraces the comforts of old age because he cannot satisfy the needs of the town's wenches ultimately draws on a long literary tradition: for example, the old man reflecting on the passing of his desire to indulge in 'Venus play' recalls the presentation of Henryson's narrator in *The Testament of Cresseid* (ll. 22–35). On this tradition, see the headnote to MQ 13, to which this poem should be compared.

EXPLANATORY NOTES

    The poem also provides touching insights into family life, albeit ones shaped by humour and literary convention. For example, there is reference to the support of the narrator's wife for her defamed husband, and of his thankfulness that his blindness means that he cannot see the broken bones of the young men who have been playing football on the green.

    The poem closes with the narrator's wish to see his enemies punished. However, his protestations of innocence and his lack of appetite for conflict are typical of Maitland's insistence on detachment from factionalism in his poems of the civil war.

Stanza: aa⁴ b²a⁴B².
Text: MQ fols 26v–27v; MF pp. 285–86; R fols 26–26v; D fols 26v–27v.
Authorship: attributed to Maitland in MQ, MF and D.
Date: c.1571. Pinkerton estimates that this poem was 'Written about his [Maitland's] Eightieth year' [1576] (1786, p. 318).

Commentary

2 *theiffis hes done my rowmes range.* Compare MQ 3 and MQ 14. The noun 'rowm' has the meaning of landed estate or possessions, as well as the more narrow sense of 'room or chamber'. See *DOST*, *Roum*, n., especially sense 6b. Maitland may be playing on both of these senses here as the verb 'range' has the meaning of 'to search through'. See *DOST*, *Rang*, v.

3 *teynd my fauld.* Compare the note following MQ 14 in MF (p. 38), where the loss of livestock from Blythe is detailed.

5 *Thocht I be auld.* Maitland was probably in his mid 70s at the time of the composition of this poem.

7 *na capitane cairis.* Probably Captain David Hume, who seized and then resided at Lethington. See Bain ed. 1830, p. liii.

12–13 *My hous, my landis, and my geir / Fra me thay hauld.* Lethington was not restored to the family until 1584.

16 *Sa weill is kend my innocence.* Lethington was confiscated from the family not because of Richard Maitland's activities, but because of the adherence of Maitland's sons to the Queen's Party, of which William Secretary Lethington was leader by 1570.

18 *Flyte lyik ane scauld.* Kennedy accuses Dunbar of being a 'scald' – a libellous person – in *The Flyting*, l. 322. Maitland's persona declines to scold or chide in this way.

21 *my infirmitie*. Probably a reference to Maitland's blindness, apparently an affliction since the early 1560s. Compare MQ 9 and MQ 14.

24 *Dame Venus chalmer*. A euphemism for the female genitalia. The first wife of Dunbar's *Tretis* complains that her feeble (young) husband was not 'val3eand in Venus chalmer' (l. 183). The wedo now seeks a young man who can please her in this domain (l. 431). Also see Chaucer's 'The Wife of Bath's Prologue' (*Canterbury Tales*, III, ll. 617–18).

28 *Meg nor Mald*. 'Meg' is a conventional name for a country girl. Compare David Lyndsay, *In Contemptioun of Syde Taillis*, l. 67. *DOST*, *Meg*, n. Mald is probably another common name used, with derogatory connotations, to refer to the lower-class girl or woman of dubious morals and may be linked to Maud or Moll. See *OED*, *Maud*, n. and *Moll*, n. Also compare the use of 'Malkin' and 'Marioun' in Lyndsay's *Syde Taillis* (ll. 91, 101). The narrator's apparent former liking for such girls perhaps partly recalls the scenarios of poems such as Dunbar's 'In secreit place this hinder nycht' and other poems in the tradition of *pastourelle*, in which a girl is wooed by her social superior. Bawcutt draws attention to examples of the genre in the Bannatyne Manuscript. See Bawcutt ed. 1998, p. 343.

33 *brald*. 'Decked out'. This is the only recorded instance of the word in *DOST*.

34 *play the loun*. Perhaps 'be a lecher' (or whoremonger). See *DOST*, *Loun*, n. sense 1d.

36 *My wyf*. Maitland married, in c.1521, Mary or Mariota, daughter of Sir Thomas Cranstoun of Corsbie. Also see MQ 93 and MQ 95.

41–42 *My hors, my harneis, and my speir, / And all other my hoisting geir*. Because of his age, the narrator no longer needs his campaigning gear. However, the association of riding and sexual intercourse was well established by this time and perhaps colours these lines, suggesting the old man's impotence. In *King Hart*, the aged protagonist leaves in his testament 'To fayr dame Plesance, ay quhen sche list ryde, / My prowde palfray, Vnsteidfastnes …' (ll. 897–98). Hart also leaves his unmistakably phallic 'brokin speir' (959) to Danger. See Bawcutt, ed. 2003.

44 *I am not abill for the weir*. Because of his old age, Maitland excuses himself of any part in the civil war afflicting Scotland. This is another instance of his notable refusal in his poetry of this period to state where his political affiliations lie.

47 *Playand at the futball*. Compare the anonymous quatrain in MF

'Brissit brawnis and brokin banis' (MF p. 215), and in *King Hart* the protagonist leaves his 'brokin schyn', a legacy of playing 'at the ball', to Deliuerance in his testament.

21. It is greit pitie for to se

This poem revisits one of Maitland's main concerns, the oppression of the commons, and especially the plight of the rural dispossessed. The narrator draws attention to the injustice of rack-renting in the post-Reformation period, which forced tenants off the land from which they had made a living. He also notes that some are ruined by their masters compelling them to burdensome work ('sair service', l. 12) in return for land, so that they are unable to produce their own food or tend their livestock. Maitland places their predicament in the context of the declining fortunes of the 'haill commounitie' (l. 36) of Scotland. He appeals to the lords and lairds (the non-magnatial landowners) to improve the situation, and also appeals to their self-interest, reminding them that they are dependent on the service of their tenants, particularly for military services, a burden which the nobles cannot bear alone. The poem ends with a warning that failure to help the common man will have long-lasting consequences for future generations.

The poem clearly belongs to the period after 1560, but it is not possible to date it precisely.
Stanza: aabbcbc^4.
Text: MQ fols 27v–28v; MF pp. 286–87; R fol. 37 (lines 1–24, 33–6 only); D fols 27v–29.
Authorship: attributed to Richard Maitland in MQ, MF and D.
Date: after 1560.

Commentary

8–9 *Sum with deir ferme ar herreit haill, / That wont to pay bot pennie maill*. Those who were accustomed to pay only a modest monetary rent ('pennie maill') now have to pay a larger sum. See *DOST, Penny-Male*, n. and *Ferme*, n.

12 *Sair service*. Presumably, hard physical work demanded by a landlord. Compare Lyndsay's collocation, 'Sore laubouryng', *Ane Dialogu betuix Experience and ane Courteour*, l. 1089.

13 *For cariadge als sum hes no rest*. See *DOST, Average*, n. Here Maitland refers to an uncertain form of feudal service, perhaps involving the carrying of goods, or work with heavy horses or cattle.

14 *thair awin worke*. The small-scale tenant farming from which families used to make their living and pay their rent. See l. 23.

16–18 Maitland observes that tenants fared better when land was in the hands of churchmen. Although the Church was a major landowner before the Reformation, it often released land under the system of feuing, to laymen, as a way of raising money to meet large tax demands during the reign of James V (Cameron 1998, pp. 259–62). These lands stayed in the hands of those who had rented them for life after the Reformation Settlement. When these new landlords died, such former ecclesiastical property was used by the crown to bestow favour, and so there was little stability of landownership, and tenants indeed faced many changes in their conditions. See Lythe 1960, p. 26. Also see Brown 2000, pp. 43–44.

17 *teynd*. A tenth-part of land or produce, or tithe, owed to the ecclesiastical landowner before the Reformation.

19 *Thay gar the tennentis pay sic sowmes*. A comment on the practice of rack-renting. Compare MQ 5, l. 34 and note.

23 *awin malingis, corne and stoir*. From their leased land ('maling') tenants could produce their own grain and foodstuffs, including from livestock.

26–28 Translate, 'They do not dare to do anything to help themseleves, even though their own children lack bread, until they have paid their tithe each year'.

29 *extortioun and taxatioun*. Compare MQ 4, l. 49 and MQ 59, l. 31. This is a conventional complaint, and Maitland may have had in mind an enactment such as that of the parliament of 10 October 1570 which legislated for £12,000 to be raised in taxes for the sending of a delegation to England 'for [the] treating of sic materis as sall tend alsweill to the advancement and furtherance of the kingis grace auctoritie' (*RPS*, 1570/10/1).

34–35 *Mony hes quhippis now in thair hand, / That wont to haue bayth iak and speir*. Bain suggests that this refers to a lack of military employment, which reduces men to more menial roles including animal husbandry (Bain ed. 1830, p. 163).

40 *for thair saiddillis thay haue soddis*. See *DSL-DOST*, *Soddis*, n. pl. This refers to the forming of a saddle from a cloth bag stuffed with straw.

EXPLANATORY NOTES

41 *Thay haue no wappinnis worth for weir.* The appearance of ill-equipped tenants at 'weaponshowings', which from 1540 were to be held twice a year, was not uncommon. See Wormald 1985, pp. 44, 91–2. A government commission of 1567 was concerned that poverty and evictions from the land reduced the number of tenants able to fight in 'the kingis weiris' (Goodare 1999, p. 137).

52 *Thair native countrie to defend.* Scottish military arrangements remained less organised and less well financed than those of England and France, and the raising of the common army depended on lairds being able to bring out their tenants, armed, when summoned to do so by a magnate (see, for example, *RPS* 1545/9/28/38). See note to l. 41 above; Goodare 1999, p. 140.

22. Treasone is the maist schamfull thing

Maitland declines to link this poem to the contemporary situation ('I will not speik in speciall', l. 16) yet its complaint against treason is clearly intended to resonate with a contemporary audience. This 'vnhappie tyme' (l. 4) is likely to be to the civil war period, 1567–73. It is possible that ll. 34–36 may relate to the assignation of the Regent Moray (see note to ll. 35–36), although this is not explicitly stated. It is thus not possible to date the poem precisely. The poem's clear topical reference and use of the present tense, as well as its complaint against the crime of treason, recalls Dunbar's 'In vice most vicius he excellis'.

The poem addresses Scottish subjects of 'all estaitis' (l. 49) and urges them to create a unified Christian brotherhood. The mode of address is advisory, and the poem echoes some of the lessons given in MQ 11 in exhorting it readers to be obedient to their prince. It also offers advice to princes and nobles, reminding those in power of their obligation to their inferiors (ll. 28–30).

This poem may be compared to MQ 23 in its regret for the failure among Scots to honour ties of amity and blood, and those ratified by bonds.
Stanza: aa^{4}b^{3}cc^{4}b^3.
Text: MQ fols 29–30; MF pp. 287–88; D fols 29–30.
Authorship: attributed to Richard Maitland in MQ, MF and D.
Date: uncertain, but c.1570.

Commentary
1 *Treasone.* Both the crime of treason (against the monarch and state),

and the act of being disloyal to or betraying the trust of one's peers. See Goodare 1999, p. 48.

11 *na kyndnes, bluid, nor band.* Compare MQ 23; MQ 19, ll. 104–5. In this context 'kyndnes' has the sense of kinship, as well as amity, and neighbourliness. See *DOST, Kind, Kyndnes,* n. On the making of bonds see MQ 18, l. 35 and note.

13–14 *Greit number ar in dyuers landis, / That prince, and magistrat gainestandis.* Perhaps a reference to the Northern Rising against Elizabeth I England in 1569. See MQ 60–62.

19–21 The paradoxical notion that Christ's death was a source of strength and comfort to Christian men, yet still the result of a heinous betrayal, is a theological commonplace. See 2 Cor 1: 3–5, Kennedy, *Þe Passion of Crist,* ll. 1003–4 ('thy passioun to murne ... / My wofull mynd It wald to confort bring'), and 'Help, God, the formar of all thing', in *The Gude and Godlie Ballatis* (Mitchell ed. 1896–97, pp. 42–46).

21 *foull wes Iudas pairt.* Compare MQ 16, ll. 41–48; MQ 62, ll. 97, 119, 146.

25–27 For Maitland's views on the importance of loyal service to the monarch, compare MQ 9, ll. 49–55; MQ 11, l. 33.

33–35 For Maitland's confidence in divine punishment awaiting those who abuse the poor, compare MQ 21, ll. 59–61.

35–36 *... fra thair heiche and princlie place, / Gif thame ane schamefull fall.* This conventional reference to the *de casibus* tradition (for example, see Lyndsay's *The Testament of the Papyngo,* ll. 434–36; MQ 17, ll. 11, 12 and note) may be connected to recent events in Scotland. The regent Moray (Lord James Stewart), an adversary of Secretary, was assassinated in Linlithgow in January 1569/1570.

51 *fals punkis.* Translate 'false ideas'. Not glossed by Bain or Craigie, but see *DOST, Punk,* n. and *Punct,* n.

23. Sumtyme to court I did repair

Rubric: Of ane freind being in court, in D only.

This poem belongs to the tradition of anti-court satire, which enjoyed considerable popularity in the sixteenth century in England and Scotland (see, for example, Montgomerie, 'The court and Concience wallis not weill'). It is also related to the popular genre of friendship poetry. (D alone gives the poem the title 'of ane freind being in court', fol. 30).

Poems such as Dunbar's 'Quhom to sall I compleine my wo' may have influenced Maitland, and maxims from parental advisory literature (for example the advice, 'To thi frendis kep thi kyndnes' in *The Consail and Teiching at the Vys Man Gaif his Sone*, l. 130), were probably also in his mind. Poems on the nature of true friendship survive in the oeuvres of near-contemporary poets such as John Stewart of Baldynneis, and there are many examples in MQ (see MQ 52 and MQ 75), and MF (for example, 'The thochtis of men dois daylie chynge', MF pp. 258–59, a version of Thomas Churchyard's 'Of the Fickle Faith of Men', 1580).

Maitland's poem explores the theme of loyalty and especially the obligations that exist between those connected by blood. It provides a commentary on the importance of patronage and clientage at court, reminding us of the role of powerful courtier-nobles (the great court man described in l. 8) who represented networks of clients and could advise the monarch on the distribution of administrative offices and rewards. Like MQ 5 it also laments the changing values of the poet's world, and particularly the decline in certain aspects of noble conduct (ll. 41–42), which are replaced by duplicity and greed.

The poem consists of a short narrative, describing how the narrator approaches a powerful kinsman at court to ask for assistance with his affairs. Sibbald identified this kinsman as George, firth Lord Seton, Mary's Master of the Royal Household, and Lord of the Privy Seal, but there is no evidence to support this (Sibbald ed. 1802, III, p. 108). The kinsman is unreceptive to the natural ties of family, and only responds to the narrator's request with the inducement of money. In this the poem resembles Dunbar's complaint about the dominance of avarice at court in 'Fredome, honour and nobilnes' with its refrain, 'And all for caus of cuvetice'. Maitland may also have in mind a stanza in Dunbar's 'Doverrit with dreme, devysing in my slummer' in which legal and material favours at court are procured by kinsmen willing to engage in financial arrangements:

> Sa mony ane sentence retreitit for to win
> Geir or acquentance or kindnes of thair kin,
> Thay think no sin, quhair proffeit cumis betuene. (ll. 51–53)

Maitland exploits the different meanings of 'kyndnes', which include consideration towards another, noble conduct (including generosity and courtesy), and natural inclinations, including those generated by close relationships, especially within a kin group. See *DOST*, *Kind-*, *Kyndnes*, n. The near synonymous terms and phrases used in the poem such as 'kinship', 'Neirnes of bluid' and 'sibnes', also describe family bonds. In

this context 'friendship' refers to connections between kin, as well as to amity and close acquaintance (see ll. 9–10). The poem is discussed in MacDonald 1972, pp. 12–14.
Stanza: abab⁴b²ba⁴.
Text: MQ fols 30–30v; MF pp. 288–89; D fols 30–31.
Authorship: attributed to Richard Maitland in MQ, MF and D.
Date: uncertain.

Commentary
2 *errandis*. These errands are described as 'busines', ll. 4, 32 but their exact nature is not specified. The narrator's quest may be for some kind of preferment that he believes he is due.

3–4 *sum freindis thair, / To help fordwart my busines*. Contrast the position of Montgomerie's narrator in 'The court and Concience wallis not weill', ll. 19–22:

> Syn evirie minioun thou man mak
> To gar thame think that thou art thairs
> Houbeit thou be behind thair bak
> No furtherer of thair effairs ...

7 *Auld kyndnes*. This suggests long-standing acquaintance and established ties of family. The quality of 'kyndnes' may also be related to 'nobilitie' (l. 41). Compare the contextualisation of this virtue in the Bannatyne MS version of Henryson's 'The Want of Wyse Men': 'Lawty, luve with kyndnes and liberalitie' (Smith ed. 1908, III, p. 173, l. 26). Also compare MQ 19, ll. 104–5 and the personification of 'Dame Kyndnes' in MQ 28 (l. 46).

15–16 *I wend that he, in word and deid, / For me his kinsman sould haue wrocht*. Compare MF's copy of 'The thochtis of men dois daylie chynge', ll. 19–20: 'A friend in wordis quhair deidis be deid / Is lyke ane spring þat watir wantis'.

18 *Neirnes of bluid he set at nocht*. Compare MQ 28: 'Neirnes of bluid, nor ȝit affinitie, / Can in this warld gar kindnes kepit be' (ll. 18–20).

30 *He kyndlie 'cousing' callit me*. A 'cousing' is a general term for a kinsman and an appropriate form of address for a relative.

41 *Sa alteris our nobilitie*. Compare Dunbar, 'Quhom to sall I compleine my wo', ll. 26—27: 'All gentrice and nobiliti / Ar passit out of hie degre'.

24. Pastyme with godlie companie

This is a pious reworking of a poem that occurs in three English manuscripts, and which is in one version attributed to Henry VIII (MacDonald 2001, p. 145; Stevens 1961, pp. 344–45, 388–89; *IMEV* 2737.5). Maitland borrows the first line of the English poem, its basic stanza form, and a little of its phrasing. The poem also shows the influence of Dunbar (see note to l. 26).

The poem's theme is aging, and especially growing old with sobriety, and this is dealt with in some personal detail: Maitland's blindness, which apparently afflicted him from the early 1560s, is mentioned at l. 11 (compare MQ 14, MQ 46). Although this theme is shared with MQ 13 and MQ 20, also by Maitland, it lacks the humour of these poems. As in MQ 17 the narrator considers the importance of patience and faith in response to his afflictions. The emphasis on the individual's engagement with the bible through personal study and shared reading suggests a Protestant perspective. The Geneva Bible (1560) was in circulation in Scotland and may be the version that a lairdly family like the Maitlands had access to. The ownership of a copy of the bible is the subject of MQ 77.

Stanza: aabbc^{4}d^{2}e^{4}d^2.
Text: MQ fols 30–30v; MF p. 289; D fols 31–31v.
Authorship: attributed to Richard Maitland in MQ, MF and D.
Date: uncertain, after 1560.

Commentary

1 *Pastyme with godlie companie.* MF has the construction verb + noun: 'Pas tyme'. Both readings are valid so I have not amended MQ's use of the noun here, which is echoed at l. 10. D follows MQ. The English poem describes the narrator's ideal company as 'good', rather than 'godlie', and unfolds into a defence of courtly pleasures. See Stevens 1961, pp. 344–45.

9 *All plesour vaine I will refuise.* See, for example, MQ 13's warning against improper pleasures for an old man, ll. 8–9.

15 *Vyce to refuise, vertew to vse.* The phrasing is formulaic, but perhaps a borrowing from the English poem. See Stevens 1961, p. 345, ll. 39–9: 'Vertu to use / Vyce to reffuse'.

26 *Reioyis in God I think it best.* Compare the refrain to Dunbar's 'Full oft I mvse and hes in thocht': 'For to be blythe me think it best'.

25. 3e nobillis all that sould this countrie guyde

This hortatory poem relates to the civil war of 1567–73. It may be compared to a number of poems on this subject by Maitland, including MQ 18 and 19. It is a rebuke to the divided lords of Scotland, split between the King's Party and that of the deposed Queen, for their disregard for the 'commoun weill' (ll. 3, 22), as they pursue their own self-interest. Maitland's narrator at first presents the realm as pursued by unnamed 'enemeis' (l. 19) and 'straingeris' (l. 32), who are waiting for the opportunity to oppress the Scots and deprive the realm of its 'auld libertie' (l. 65). His political observations then become more focused, identifying the twin evils of the King's Party's pro-English policy (l. 42) and the Queen's Party's dependence on the French. The poem may therefore date from c.1569–70 when both sides were courting external support. See MQ 19 note to ll. 73–74. The narrator offers a historical perspective on each position, reminding the reader of the treacherous treatment of Bruce by Edward I, and of the more recent events of the Guise regency, when large numbers of French troops were garrisoned in Scotland in the late 1550s (see Ritchie 2002, pp. 181–87, 225–26). The poem ends with a prayer for peace and unity.

Stanza: aabb[5]ccdeed[3].
Text: MQ 31v–33v, MF pp. 271–73, D fols 32–34.
Authorship: attributed to Richard Maitland.
Date: c.1569–70?

Commentary

3 *the commoun weill*. Compare MQ 27, l. 1. A concern for the community and national interest is common in Maitland's poems. The phrase was highly resonant in sixteenth-century Scotland. See Mason 1998, pp. 91–92; Goodare 1999, p. 73.

12–13 *Amang 3ow lordis the inimitie, / That ar devydit now in parteis twa*. A reference to the division of the political community between the opposed parties of the child king and deposed Queen Mary.

15 *vnkyndlie weir*. 'Civil war'. Compare MQ 12, l. 6 and MQ 19 l. 15.

21 *Is thair na wyse and gud men of renoun*. Compare MQ. 19, ll. 28–37.

41–42 *3e that dependis on the King, / For 3our support the Englismen inbring*. On English military and financial support for the King's Party, see note to MQ 19, ll. 73–74. For another warning of English speciousness, see MQ 44, ll. 33–40 (a poem attributed to John Maitland).

EXPLANATORY NOTES

44 *Think on the wordis King Edward spak to Bruse*. Edward I was alleged to have promised Bruce the throne of Scotland in return for his support, but Edward decided in favour of Balliol in November 1292. Maitland probably has in mind Bellenden's claim, in his translation of Boece's *Chronicles of Scotland*, that 'King Edward was reconseld with Robert Bruce, in sic familiaritie, that he promittit to mak him King of Scottis', but that there turned out to be only 'dissait and treason under the wordis of King Edward' (book 14, chapters 2–3). On being reminded of his promise, Edward is reported to have asked Bruce, 'Belevis yow, that we haif na other besines ado bot to conques realmes and kingdomes to the?' See Bellenden 1821, II, pp. 365–67.

55–57 On fears surrounding earlier French military intervention in Scotland, see note to l. 63 below.

63 *Remember how thay pleit ʒow befoir*. Maitland suggests that earlier French promises of assistance were not beneficial to Scotland. The belief that Mary of Guise was abetting Henri II in his plans to invade Scotland and advance his claims to the English succession was widely held by the end of her regency, particularly among the Lords of the Congregation. On the nature of the Franco-Scottish alliance during the Guise regency, see Ritchie 2002, pp. 226–28. Thus the French have 'pleit' or 'got the better of' the Scots. See *DOST*, *Pley*, v, sense 5b.

65 *auld libertie*. Compare l. 80. A resonant concept for Maitland (see MQ 6, l. 57, MQ 9, l. 45, and MQ 44, l. 59), and a significant one in the political discourse of mid sixteenth-century Scotland, often used in conjunction with that of the 'commonweal'. See Mason 1998, p. 91.

91 *Sum ar dissemblit, ʒit proud in thair consait*. On the dangers of pride and deceitfulness for those in high office, compare MQ 11, ll. 65–72.

97 *As thair fatheris befoir*. For other comparisons with the more frugal and honourable conduct of earlier generations, see MQ 5, ll. 25–42.

98–100 The loss of 'Geir, vittall, and stoir' to an aggressor was a personal experience for Maitland by 1570. See headnotes to MQ 14 and MQ 20.

103–4 *The ane trowis gif that the other be / Abone thame put into auctoritie*. For a similar warning against the envy of power and authority, see MQ 11, ll. 41–56.

26. 3e that sumtyme hes bene weill staikit

This consolatory poem relates to Maitland's loss of property and possessions and the tribulations of his family, including, perhaps, ill treatment by a kinsman or associate (see ll. 17–19). It is likely that the principal 'trouble' that the poem refers to is the confiscation of Lethington in 1571. Lines 21–24 perhaps also allude to the destructive raid on Blythe in 1570. See MQ 14 (headnote) and MQ 20 (headnote). The narrator's complaint about those who themselves possess insignificant inheritance or fortune (l. 7) and now benefit from the misfortunes of another, no doubt refers to those who profited from the Maitland family's losses, including possibly the dependant of the Regent Morton, David Hume, who inhabited Lethington during the period of the forfeiture. Breaches of neighbourliness, friendship, and kindness concern the narrator here, as in MQ 23.

The narrator's philosophical advice about the importance of cultivating detachment from the values of a false world is similar to that offered in MQ 31. The tone of the poem and its refrain is perhaps influenced by that to Dunbar's 'Quhom to sall I compleine my wo ('For in this warld may none assure'), and it is likely that Dunbar's 'Full oft I mvse and hes in thocht' and 'This waverand warldis wretchidnes' also influenced Maitland.

Stanza: aabB[4].

Text: MQ fols 34–34v; MF pp. 39–40; D fols 34–34v. The order of stanzas two and three is reversed in MF.

Authorship: attributed to Richard Maitland in MQ, MF and D.

Date: c.1571?

Commentary

5 *houshald graith*. Furnishings and other domestic possessions. See *DOST*, *Graith*, n. sense 5.

11 *diuillis limmis*. A figurative expression for wicked individuals, those who do the work of the devil. See *OED*, *Limb*, n., sense 3b. Compare, Rolland's *Sevin Seages of Rome*, l. 2695: 'Quha can excuse this dowbill Deuillis lim?' (Black, ed. 1932)

18 *vnder colour of kyndnes*. Compare MQ 28, l. 10, 'colowred craftines'. Here 'colour' refers figuratively to an outward appearance that is deliberately deceptive. See *DOST*, *Colour*, n. sense 3. Compare Dunbar's complaints about speciousness in 'This waverand warldis wretchidnes', l. 10: 'The figurit speiche with faceis tua'. Also see MQ 23 and headnote for significance of 'kyndnes'.

EXPLANATORY NOTES

23 *commoun theiffis*. The epithet used by Maitland for lawless individuals such as border raiders. Compare MQ 20, l. 2.

27. How sould our commoun weill induire?

This poem inveighs against the lack of collective responsibility shown by Scots for the welfare of the nation, as each troubled group, rich and poor, seeks to blame others for their predicament. Its references to plague, pestilence and dearth, well-documented events in Maitland's world, as signs of God's anger, recall MQ 12 (see headnote). Maitland accuses his contemporaries of refusing to recognise their afflictions as evidence of their sinfulness rather than random acts of fortune.
Stanza: aabba^4.
Text: MQ fols 34b–35; MF p. 40; D fol. 35.
Authorship: attributed to Richard Maitland in MQ, MF and D.
Date: uncertain, but c.1567–73.

Commentary
1 *commoun weill*. Compare MQ 25, l. 3 and note.
6 *Quhen derth cummis, or pestilence*. Compare MQ 12, ll. 5–7 and note. Lowland Scotland had suffered several outbreaks of plague and harvest failure during the 1560s.
9 *The moveris hes the wyte*. The 'moveris' here are those who instigate conflict. On Maitland's views on Scotland's responsibility for inviting the aggression of its enemies, see MQ 19, ll. 64–72.
11 *the weir*. The Scottish civil war of 1567–73.

28. It is ane mortall paine to heir and sie

This poem is a complaint on the world's mutability and the failings of each of the estates. It ends nostalgically by lamenting the loss of an earlier society based on the values of charity and loyalty, and with a prayer for the readers' moral reform. The central section of the poem develops an allegorical narrative featuring the characters Gredines (Greed), and Kyndnes, who offer contradictory advice to the estates. Also featured are the characters Charitie and Pitie who attempt to support Kyndnes when she is assaulted by Gredines. Personification allegory was a popular mode in many genres, and allegories depicting the conflict between good and evil tendencies in man derive ultimately from the *Psychomachia* of Prudentius (348–410). Maitland would

339

have encountered personification allegory in the works of Dunbar (for example, 'This hinder nycht, halff sleiping as I lay', and 'Quhom to sall I compleine my wo') and Lyndsay (especially *Ane Satyre of the Thrie Estaitis*), two poets that he read carefully. The inset allegory in Gavin Douglas's *The Palice of Honour* (ll. 1789–1827), and the anonymous *King Hart* (which survives uniquely in MF), may also have influenced him.

The allegorical section of the poem is full of vigorous action and dialogue. The figure of Dame Kyndnes represents moral kindness, charity, generosity or consideration, but also the proper feelings of affinity and loyalty to one's friends, neighbours and countrymen – what is described at the end of the poem as brotherly love. Characteristically, the personification allegory is concerned with the conflict between virtues and vice within the individual, but the social and political consequences of this conflict, including the oppression of the poor, are foremost in the poet's mind.

The poem is difficult to date, but the references in it to the wrongful loss of land and possessions may relate to the Maitland's family's loss of Lethington, and so suggest a date of 1571 or later. Lord Seton, Maitland's kinsman and neighbour, also had his property seized in the same period (*CPS Scotland*, 3, p. 392). It is closely linked in theme to MQ 29.

Stanza: aabba[5].
Text: MQ fols 35–36v; MF pp. 275–76; D fols 35v–36v.
Authorship: attributed to Richard Maitland in MQ, MF and D.
Date: c.1571?

Commentary

3 *Fra weill to wo, fra treuth to doubilnes*. Formulaic phrasing, compare *Troilus and Criseyde*, 1. 4. This also recalls Dunbar's 'Off Lentren in the first mornyng', ll. 25–35. See especially l. 30: 'trewth returnis in dowbilnes'.

7 *And fra vertew to vyice*. Compare Dunbar, 'Off Lentren in the first mornyng': 'Vertew returnis in to vyce' (l. 33).

10 *colowred craftines*. Compare MQ 26, l. 18.

18 *Neirnes of bluid*. Close kinship. Compare MQ 23, l. 18.

21 *For Gredines now gydis all estaitis*. Also see MQ 29, l. 8. Compare Dunbar, 'This hinder nycht, halff sleiping as I lay', l. 99: 'With gredines I sie this world ourgane'. Gluttony is one of the seven deadly sins, and

EXPLANATORY NOTES

is often dramatised in personification allegory. See, for example, *Piers Plowman*, passus 5. 'Full of Glutony' is also attendant to the young King Hart (*King Hart*, l. 31). See Bawcutt, ed. 2003.

27 *Then come Kyndnes*. Kyndnes appears as a personification in King Hart's youthful entourage (*King Hart*, l. 118), representing friendliness in a courtly and amorous context. While 'Kyndnes' retains this meaning here, the personification also encompasses consideration, courtesy, love, charity, generosity and the loyalty engendered by close relations. See headnote and compare MQ 23.

32 *ressoun and gud conscience*. Although not allegorised here, these qualities are frequently dramatised in personification allegories, such as that in *The Buik of King Alexander the Conquerour* (ll. 9740, 9750), and *King Hart* (ll. 521, 578 etc.), as important mechanisms of self-restraint.

36 *Then cummis in*. The allegorical action now seems to be taking place in a building. The use of architectural metaphors (particularly the castle) for the human body in such personification allegories is common. See Cowling 1998; Whitehead 2003.

44 *thay kest Dame Kyndnes over the stair*. In allegorical narratives, vigorous and violent action is commonplace, and stairs are particularly dangerous places. Compare *King Hart*, l. 362, 'And Pietie doun the stare full sone is past'; l. 759: 'Than Ielosie come strekand vp the stair'.

47 *Cheritie and Dame Pitie*. Common figures in personification allegory and psychomachia. Cheritie is 'Maister houshald' (l. 1795) and 'Pietie is the Kingis Almoseir' (l. 1821) in Douglas's *Palice of Honour*. Also see MQ 41, l. 33.

57 *thir twa harlottis*. The use of abusive terms for figures of virtue in personification allegory is common. In Lyndsay's *Ane Satyre of the Thrie Estaitis* (1554), Dame Chastitie is addressed with the term 'duddron' ('slut', l. 1338) and chased away by the wives of the Tailor and Souter before being placed in the stocks. The term 'harlot' is more appropriately used of Sensualitie in Lyndsay's play (l. 1720).

58 *at the dur*. Another dangerous and contested space in the allegorical narrative. Compare Dunbar, 'Quhom to sall I compleine my wo': 'Trewthe standis barrit at the dure', l. 38.

64 *nor frend*. The reading is introduced from MF, MQ's reading ('nor thair frendis') being metrically defective.

70 *fraternall love*. Compare Lyndsay, *Ane Satyre* (1554), l. 4582, where

Folie questions the existence of 'fraternall charitie' among the warring princes of Christendom. Also compare MQ 22, l. 48.

29. Greit paine it is now to behauld and sie

This poem recalls MQ 28 in opening and theme, particularly in its complaint against the pervasiveness of avarice in Scottish society. Trespasses against one's neighbour, particularly the wrongful acquisition of land, preoccupy the narrator, and perhaps relate to Maitland's experiences in 1571 following the confiscation of Lethington (subsequently inhabited by David Hume of Fishwick in the Scottish Borders), and the similar experiences of his neighbours such as the Setons (see headnote to MQ 20 and MQ 28; on the theme of the confiscation of land, also see MQ 19, ll. 55–58, and MQ 26, ll. 21–24). Lines 21 and 50 probably refer to contemporary events. See notes to these lines. The poem also includes warnings on the perils of holding and falling from high political office. Its morality is simple and directly expressed: one should live an 'honest lyife' (l. 59), caring for the needs of family and friends, looking after the poor, and not aspiring to more than one is entitled to. Though stylistically less vibrant than MQ 28, the poem nonetheless makes effective use of rhetorical devices, especially anaphora. The Latin quotation that follows the poem alludes to 1 Timothy 6: 10. The proverbial phrase 'surer nor the Bass' probably refers to the security of the Bass Rock, with its defensive fortifications and prison, in the Firth of Forth.

Stanza: aabbcbc^5.
Text: MQ fols 36v–37v, MF pp. 274–75 and D fols 37–38v.
Authorship: attributed to Richard Maitland in MQ, MF and D.
Date: uncertain, but probably c.1571.

Commentary
18 *To tak thair nychtbouris rowmes ouer thair heid.* See headnote for the prevalence of this theme in Maitland's poems and its possible connection to Lennox's confiscation of Lethington in 1571.

21 *To get thair land for ane inventit cryme.* Maitland may have in mind the forfeiture of his sons in 1571 for their support for the Queen's Party. William Maitland was also charged by Moray with the 'invented crime' of involvement in Darnley's murder, and was arrested in September 1569.

29 *Syne wait not weill quhat thair airis wilbe.* The narrator's anxiety concerns the potentially wasteful heir, who will jeopardise the lineage so carefully built up by his forebears. Compare the *History of the House of Seytoun*, c.1559 (Fullarton ed. 1829, p. 10), where Maitland stresses that family histories can teach 'thair posteritie to be vertuous, and na waistouris'. Also see Brown 2000, pp. 33–34.

34–35 *Sum may commit sic deidis criminall, / That may thame gar bayth geir and landis tyne.* Forfeiture of lands was the punishment for serious state crimes including treason.

48 *It is not best ane heiche estait to cheis.* On the dangers involved in holding high office, compare MQ 11, ll. 41–43; MQ 44, especially ll. 17–24.

50 *Sum hes bene greit and fallin fra hie estait.* For a similar *de casibus* warning, see MQ 22, ll. 34–36 and note. It is possible that events such as the murder of the regent Moray in January 1570, and the death of his successor, Lennox, in Stirling in September 1571, were in Maitland's mind.

30. O Lord, our sin hes done the tein

This penitential complaint on the times dates from the civil war between the parties of the Mary and James VI. The reference to the harrying of 'our principall toun', mentioned in l. 23 presumably dates the poem to the period between 1570 and 1573 when the hostilities focused on Edinburgh, or perhaps more precisely to that of 1571–72, when the struggle was most intense, with the King's Party established at Leith and that of the Queen in Edinburgh Castle (Dawson 2007, pp. 264, 277–79). The poem begins with a generalised lament for the disorder of the country and oppression of the poor. It then focuses on hypocrisy and faithlessness in political circles and the failure of bonds of kinship and friendship (compare MQ 23). The narrator criticises some for deliberately prolonging the conflict, and suggests that all estates, not just the ruling class, have exacerbated Scotland's troubles. For its penitential tone compare MQ 7, MQ 12 and MQ 31; and for its plea for political fraternity, see MQ 18, ll. 41–45, and MQ 19, ll. 91–108.

Maitland family troubles are also mentioned here, though discreetly, as in MQ 29. The references to the violent deprivation of 'hous and land' (l. 33) probably refer to the confiscation of Lethington in 1571; or perhaps the raid on Blythe in 1570, a prose account of which is given in MF. (See headnote to MQ 14.) Other contemporary accounts describe

the extent of the family's loses on these occasions in a way that suggests the poem's basis in their experience (*CPS Scotland*, 3, 1569–71, pp. 239, 392, 436, 468). It is possible that the allusion to wrongful imprisonment in ll. 44–45 refers to the plight of William, Secretary Lethington who was imprisoned on charges related to the murder of Darnley in 1569–70. John Maitland also suffered imprisonment after the fall of Edinburgh Castle (1573–78).
Stanza: ababcbcbc^4.
Text: MQ fols 38–39v; MF pp. 277–78; D fols 38v–40v.
Authorship: attributed to Richard Maitland in MQ, MF and D.
Date: c.1571–2.

Commentary

10 *And falset hauldin policie.* Falset (Falsehood) appears as a character in Dunbar's 'Quhom to sall I compleine my wo' ('Oft Falsatt rydis with a rowtt', l. 11); in *King Hart* ('Out at ane dore ran Falset and Invy', l. 548); and in David Lyndsay's *Ane Satyre of the Thrie Estaitis*.

13 *Sum will speik fair and freindfullie.* On such insincere kindness, compare MQ 23, l. 30.

16 *Ane kinsman scant may trow ane other.* Compare MQ 23, l. 18.

17 *Amang the lordis syne the greit stryif.* The civil war between the supporters of Mary and James VI. See headnote.

23 *our principall toun.* Edinburgh. See headnote. Also compare *Ane Ballat of the Captane of the Castell*, on the fate of 'Edinburch toun' (ll. 113–20) where the narrator imagines that 'fyre may thair buildings sacke, / Or bullat beat thaim downe' (Cranstoun ed. 1891–93, I, p. 178).

24 *Our merchandis daylie waistand geir.* Anti-mercantile complaints usually focused on deception (using false weights and measures), greed and social aspirations, rather than wastefulness. See Owst 1966, pp. 352–61. See Dunbar, 'Quhy will ʒe, merchantis of renoun', in which merchants are accused of greed, self-interest and lack of care for the common profit.

33–34 *Fra sum is taine bayth hous and land / Wrangouslie.* Maitland's insistence here on the political innocence of his family and its loyalty to authority should be compared to MQ 14, MQ 20, ll. 16–17, and MQ 29, l. 21.

46 *ane missiue bill.* An official or formal document, issued by an authority and with legal status. See *DOST*, *Missive*, a. (see especially sense 4).

48 *my lord Regentis will*. The earl of Lennox (regent from July 1570 to September 1571) ordered the confiscation of Lethington, forfeiting William, John and Thomas Maitland at the 'Creeping Parliament' of 1571.

56 *mutine*. According to *DOST*, this noun is not widely attested in Scots; and according to *OED* is not attested in English until 1560. See *DOST*, *Mutine*, n; *OED*, *Mutine*, n. and adj.

72 *The theiffis*. Border raiders. See headnote to MQ 3 on the ongoing problem of border unrest in the second half of the sixteenth century.

85 *speciallie quhen thay ar ȝoung*. A reference to the political uncertainty of minority government in the light of James VI's youth. Compare MQ 19, ll. 94–97 (and note to l. 94), and MQ 59.

31. Quhen I haue done consider

This poem's philosophical and pious advice for addressing personal misery and worldly instability make it a worthy companion piece for MQ 30. The last line of stanza one recalls the refrain of Dunbar's 'Full oft I mvse and hes in thocht' – 'For to be blythe me think it best'. However, despite the opening and closing injunctions to be happy in adversity, the main thrust of the poem is penitential, and the observation that God punishes some to prove their patience is reminiscent of the teachings of the Book of Job. Also compare MQ 14 and MQ 17, and 'Now man behald this warldis vaniteis' in the Maitland Folio (p. 326), also found in some editions of *The Gude and Godlie Ballatis* (see Martin and McClune 2009, pp. 246–47).

The poem is copied in an italic script.
Stanza: ababbcbc^3.
Text: MQ fols 39v–41, MF pp. 278–80, D fols 40v–42.
Authorship: attributed to Richard Maitland in MQ, MF and D.
Date: uncertain.

Commentary

23–24 *the wand / Of Goddis punishment*. See *DOST*, *Wand*, n. sense 5. Compare David Lyndsay, *The Monarch* or *Ane Dialogu betuix Experience and ane Courteour*: 'Gret God, in to His handis, To dant the warld, hes diuers wandis' (l. 417).

57–64 Compare Dunbar 'He that hes gold and grit riches', ll. 1–5:

> He that hes gold and grit riches
> And may be into mirrynes,
> And dois glaidnes fra him expell
> And levis in to wretchitnes,
> He wirkis sorrow to him sell.

71 *sie God face to face*. Biblical, see Genesis 32: 30: 'I haue sene God face to face' (Geneva Bible 1560).

32. Loue vertew over all, and all vyces flie

Rubric: Thir 8 lynes] Thir last aucht lines MF; or fordwart] *om.* D

As the note following the poem states, each line is reversible and can be read from right to left as well as conventionally, with the sense retained. Its advice is of a general moral nature, and it has much in common with the poems of fatherly advice in Maitland's repertoire. Faith, honour, industry and charity are to be cultivated, and hatred, pride, envy, greed and laziness avoided. Compare MQ 15, MQ 33, MQ 53 and MQ 54.
Stanza: ababcbc^5.
Text: MQ 41–41v; MF p. 40; D 42–42v.
Authorship: attributed to Richard Maitland in MQ, MF and D.
Date: uncertain.

33. Sinneris, repent that ȝe haue spent

This vigorous hortatory poem, written in quatrains with emphatic internal rhyme (compare MQ 34) in the tetrameter lines, urges penance and moral reform in its reader. Like MQ 31 and 32, its tone is paternalistic. Although its advice is perennial, its closing sentiments probably have relevance to the troubled civil war years of 1567–73.
Stanza: a^{4}b^{3}a^{4}b^3.
Text: MQ fols 41v–42, MF p. 39, D fols 42v–43.
Authorship: attributed to Richard Maitland in MQ, MF and D.
Date: uncertain.

Commentary

1 *Sinneris, repent*. For a similarly hortatory opening see 'Sinneris, vnto my sang aduert' in *The Gude and Godlie Ballatis* (Mitchell ed. 1896–97, pp. 34–39).

16 *Advyis weill quhat ȝe say*. Circumspect speech, a commonplace in parental advice literature, is also counselled by Maitland in MQ 11, ll. 4, 9–11.

17 *Keip ay kyndnes*. On the significance of 'kyndnes' compare MQ 23 (headnote) and MQ 28.

34. Mair mischevous and wicked warld

The 'troublous tyme' of the refrain is the early 1570s during which period southern Scotland was the focus of much violence. Local unrest is also the focus on MQ 14, which relates to the attack on Maitland's lands at Blyth in Lauderdale in 1570, by troops of the King's Party and English forces, and MQ 20, on the loss of Lethington. A fierce conflict to control Edinburgh dominated 1571–72, the burgh besieged for a period by the King's Party (see Dawson 2007, pp. 277–79). Edinburgh Castle, held by the Queen's Party, fell in May 1573.

The poem contrasts the past tranquillity and order ('policie', l. 6) of Lothian, not known, unlike other troubled areas of Scotland, for rebellion against the monarch, with its present turmoil. It laments the oppression of the town (Edinburgh), once a place of safety and prosperity, by military force. Maitland avoids any alignment of his poetic voice with one or other of the factions, but pleads for peace. The reference to 'abstinence' in l. 21 may suggest that an agreement between the two parties has been reached: a truce was agreed in February 1573 but hostilities continued into the spring. See note to l. 21 below, and compare MQ 58.
Stanza: aba^{4}B^3.
Text: MQ fols 42–42v, MF p. 281, D fols 43–43v.
Authorship: attributed to Maitland in MQ, in MF in a different hand, and in D.
Date: c.1572–73.

Commentary

1–2 The implication that the world has never been as wicked and disaster-prone as it is at the time of writing is a commonplace of complaints on the times. See Loughlin 1994, p. 238 (on 'The Dialogue of the Twa Wyfeis').

5 *Lowthane*. Lothian, in the south east of Scotland, and the area in which the Maitland family seat of Lethington (now Lennoxlove) is located.

11 *Liddisdaill*. On the association of Liddesdale, in the Middle March of the Scottish Borders, with extreme lawlessness, see MQ 3 and headnote.

13 *The toun.* Maitland was in Edinburgh when Lethington was raided (*CPS Scotland*, 3, p. 468). However, it is suggested here that the town no longer represents a place of refuge and it is likely that the violent struggle for Edinburgh of 1571–72 is referred to in this stanza.

21 *And sen sum abstinence is taine.* The use of 'sen' here is important for the dating of the poem. The context of ll. 21–23 suggests it is used as a conjunction, 'since / because', rather than a preposition, 'after'. See *DOST*, *Sen*, prep. and conj.

24 *stainche.* Wordplay, referring back to line 19. See *DOST*, *Stanche*, v., meaning both to put a stop to an event, and specifically to stop the flow of blood.

35. Ane Contrapoysoun to the Ballat Falslie Intitulit the Properteis of Gud Wemen

This unique poem is attributed to Master A. Arbuthnot, who is likely to have been the lawyer, churchman, Protestant convert and writer of that name (1538–1583). See MacDonald 1998, p. 84; Stevenson 1990, pp. 25–30. He was the author of a Latin history of the Arbuthnot family (see Kirk, *ODNB*), and contributed to *The Second Book of Discipline*. His poems are known only here, in MF and in D.

This poem takes as its subject the popular theme of the nature of women, and purports to be a defence of their virtues. The manuscript title describes it as a 'contrapoysoun' (a French word meaning 'counterpoison' or an antidote) to another poem misleadingly entitled 'the properteis of gud wemen'. It is not possible to identify the poem which this text answers. However, there are many near contemporary examples of misogynistic poetry, including those found amongst the 'Remeidis of Luve' in the Bannatyne Manuscript, which would be good candidates. The third section of the 'luvaris ballattis' in the Bannatyne Manuscript also contains poems that defend women against the complaints of male detractors: 'ballatis in the prayiss of wemen and to þe reproche of vicious men' (see. for example, 'All tho þat list of wemen evill to speik', or 'Now of wemen this I say for me', items 362 and 366 in Fox and Ringler 1980; Ritchie ed. 1928–34, IV, pp. 64–70, 75–76).

Arbuthnot's poem is playful and tonally complex. Its praise of women is packed with superlatives, and it criticises women's detractors as ungrateful and spiteful. It also makes the point that all men may be easily condemned on the strength of a few infamous individuals, just as women usually are (ll. 125–36). However, it also deploys some of the characteristic strategies of satirical writing on women, which subtly undermine claims to praise them. Compare Hoccleve's translation of Christine de Pisan's *Letter of Cupid*, which is found in the Bannatyne Manuscript (fols 269–74). Readers may find, for example, the description of the obedient woman as a 'willie wand' (l. 34) to be problematic, as is the narrator's admission that women need to be ruled properly by men (l. 80). Moreover, the tendency of defenders of women to take on the accusations made against them, point by point and in the same diction, has the unfortunate (or deliberate) effect of reiterating misogynistic accusations (Blamires ed. 1992, p. 14). The list of virtuous women made known by 'poetis auld' (l. 99, all typical examples adduced in writing on the nature of women from the Church fathers onwards) only consists of two examples, before the narrator recalls some infamous and wicked women, delaying his catalogue of good women. Recourse to hyperbole, repetition, and formulaic diction and imagery used to describe women ('blythest thing in bour / the bonyest in bed', ll. 25–26) generates humour rather than encourages reverence. The poem's concluding instruction that every man choose himself a 'dow' (a dove) may respond to the question posed to readers of Dunbar's The *Tretis of the Tua Mariit Wemen and the Wedo* (see note to l. 224). On images of women in sixteenth-century Scottish manuscripts, see Newlyn 1999.

The stanza form is intricate, with line lengths varying between trimetre and tetrametre, and internal rhyme in the fifth and seventh lines. The poem is copied in an italic script.

Stanza: abab^{3}c^{4}b^3 d^{4}b^3.

Text: MQ fols 43–48, D fols 54–59v.

Authorship: attributed to Master Alexander Arbuthnot.

Date: uncertain.

Commentary

34 *willie wand.* See *DOST*, *Will(i)e*, n. a weak or pliable person.

38 *schaikis oft of hand.* Desert, cast off an obligation. See *DOST*, *Shaik*, v. sense 15.

83 *The last thing that he wrocht.* God's shaping of Eve from Adam's rib on the last day of Creation. Genesis 2: 21–22.

89 *papingo.* The parrot was often associated with pride or luxury. See Whiting 1941–51, Papingo. Also see Holland's *Buke of the Howlat*, l. 125: 'the proper papejaye, proude in his apparale'. This is not, therefore, necessarily a flattering point of comparison.

91 *turtill.* The turtledove's reputation for fidelity is traditional. Compare Chaucer, *Parliament of Fowls*, ll. 355, 582–88; and Alanus, *De planctu naturae*, 2. 164–65. Also see MQ 38, ll. 18–21.

92 *pawne.* Another troubling point of comparison, as the peacock is frequently a symbol of vanity and pride. See Lyndsay's *Testament of the Papyngo*, l. 207 ('prude pacoke') and Dunbar's *Tretis*, l. 379 ('pako, proudest of fedderis').

103 *muses nyne.* The daughters of Zeus and Mnēmosynē, or Jupiter and Memoria, who preside over learning and the arts.

105 *Minerue.* The Roman goddess of wisdom, known to the Greeks, as the narrator notes here, as Pallas (l. 107).

113 *Ceres.* Known for her chastity. See Juvenal, *Satire* VI, ch. 2 (Blamires ed. 1992, p. 26).

121–22 *Iesabell ... Achab.* Jezebel, wife of Ahab, King of Israel. Both were seen as exemplifying wickedness because of their cruel treatment of the people of Israel. 3 Kings 21: 7.

123 *Herodias.* Mother of Salome, and accused of incest with Herod Antipas. Matt 14: 1–11.

124 *Dalila.* Delilah, who betrayed the warrior Samson, her lover, to the Philistines. See Judges 15–16. Compare 'Devyce proves and eik humilitie' (*NIMEV* 679): 'Sampsone ... throw the distroyit was' (ll. 22–23).

146 *blissed bird Marie.* Invoking the example of the Virgin Mary was often used as a conclusive way of settling the argument in the defence of women in *querrelle des femmes* writing. Compare 'For to declair the he magnificens' (Bannatyne Manuscript, fols 277–78v, Ritchie, IV, pp. 71–73, Fox and Ringler, item 364) with its account of 'Mary myld þe maid' (l. 41) as upholding the fame of women.

149 *Debora.* Deborah, widow and wise ruler of the Jews. Judges 4.

153 *Susanna.* The Biblical woman who resisted the lusts of the Elders, and became an exemplum of chastity. Daniel 13: 10–14.

155 *Anna.* Anna the prophetess, mentioned in Luke 2: 36.

157–58 *Oliphern ... Iudith.* The widow Judith freed the Bethulians by seducing and decapitating the Roman general Holofernes. Judith 12–15. Though celebrated for her bravery, such violent and manipulative actions in a woman troubled some commentators.

161 *Hester.* Esther, the Jewish queen of the biblical Book of Esther, usually a model of humility and beauty, who was also famed for giving good counsel to her husband Ahasuerus in order to save her people. See Chaucer's 'Tale of Melibee' (*Canterbury Tales*, VII, l. 1101).

163–64 *Abigaal ... Naball.* Known for her wise counsel to King David, and thus for saving her husband Nabal. I Kings 25. She is mentioned, with Esther in Chaucer's 'Merchant's Tale' (*Canterbury Tales*, IV, ll. 1369–74).

165 *Mical.* The daughter of Saul, who loved King David, and saved him from her father's plot to murder him. I Samuel 18: 20–27.

169–71 *the Canarianis ... Spartanis.* A reference to the Spartan attack on the Canaries during the Peloponnesian Wars.

177 *Lucretia.* A Roman woman who, after being raped by Tarquinus, took her own life in order to avoid shame, despite the reassurances of her family and community. Her actions resulted in the exile of King Tarquin and his son, and the formation of Rome as a republic. She was often adduced as a model of fidelity, though was sometimes criticised for pride. Ovid, *Fasti* II. 685ff; Livy, *History*, I, 57–59; contrast Augustine, *City of God*, I. 19. She has a tale in Chaucer's *Legend of Good Women*.

179 *Porcia.* Wife of Brutus, who refused to remarry after his death. She was often used as a symbol of fidelity, for example, in Chaucer's 'Franklin's Tale' (*Canterbury Tales*, V, ll. 1448–49).

182 *Penelope.* Known for chastity and fidelity (see Chaucer, 'Franklin's Tale', *Canterbury Tales*, V, ll. 1443–44). Left at home while her husband Ulysses fought at Troy, Penelope remained faithful to him for the ten years of his absence (Ovid, *Heroides* I).

184 *Thisbe.* Ovid *Met.* 4.55–166. She is given a legend in Chaucer's *Legend of Good Women* and a tale in Gower's *Confessio Amantis*, III, ll. 1331–1494. In these vernacular versions her hasty folly, rather than her fidelity and the purity of her love, is stressed. A more sympathetic mention of her made in Lydgate's *Temple of Glass*, ll. 80–82.

185 *Cornelia.* Probably the daughter of Scipio Africanus. After the death of her husband she refused to remarry, and devoted herself to educating her children. The narrator here specifically mentions her eloquence rather than her chastity.

187 *Aspasia.* The mistress of the Athenian statesman, Pericles, reputed for her wisdom and skill in rhetoric, and for her intellectual disputation with Socrates. She is mentioned in the works of a number of ancient writers including Plato.

192 *Grissell*. Griselda, an exemplum of patience and fidelity, and the heroine of Chaucer's 'Clerk's Tale' (*Canterbury Tales*, IV), which is based on the concluding story of Boccaccio's *Decameron*. Compare Alexander Scott, 'That evir I luvit, allace þairfoir!': 'Grissall wes nevir so pacient / As I am for my lady gent' (ll. 7–8).

213–14 *men for loue of thame / In battellis oft did bleid*. A very common point made in the defence of love. See Dunbar's 'In May as that Aurora did vp spring': 'Luve makis knychtis hardy at assey', l. 83.

224 *Ilk man cheis hime ane dow*. Compare the Wedo's advice in Dunbar's *Tretis*, l. 263: 'Be dragonis baitht and dowis ay in double form', and the narrator's closing question as to which of the three women in the poem the reader would choose to wed: 'Quhilk wald ȝe waill to ȝour wif, gif ȝe suld wed one?' (l. 530).

36. He that luifis lichtliest

This poem is a succinct account of the rewards of loving virtuously. Faithful and devoted love will be rewarded by love of the same quality, and such 'mutuall loue' is a great comfort. The poem is unique. It is copied in an italic script.
Stanza: $aa^4aa^3aabbcc^4$.
Text: MQ fols 48–48v, D fol. 59v.
Authorship: attributed to Alexander Arbuthnot.
Date: uncertain.

Commentary
10 *mutuall loue*. Compare MQ 39, l. 71, and MQ 93.

37. Ceis hairt, and trowbill me no moir

This poem is attributed to Alexander Arbuthnot (d.1583, see headnote to MQ 35) in MQ but to Richard Maitland in MF (where the text is divided between the disordered pages at the beginning and end of the manuscript). The scribe of R did not trust the MF attribution, ascribing his copy to 'sumbodie'. Given the care with which the Quarto has been compiled and presented, it seems unlikely that its attribution is incorrect. It should be noted that the first stanza of the poem is identical, apart from metre, to MQ 42 ll. 155–61, a poem also attributed to Arbuthnot in MQ and MF. Lines 113–20 are also very similar to MQ 42, ll. 169–75.

They contain reference to the theology of the salvation of the elect based on Biblical texts such as Matthew 24: 24.

The poem seems to be addressed (see, for example, l. 75) to Maitland in the manner of the consolatory poem, MQ 46 (unattributed). It has thematic similarities to other works by Maitland on sufferance and faith (compare MQ 32) and may suggest a close creative relationship between Maitland and Arbuthnot.

Poetic orations to the heart are often amatory in nature, in the manner of Alexander Scott's 'Hence, hairt with hir that most departe', or 'Haif hairt in hairt, ʒe hairt of hairtis haill'. However, this poem is a farewell to worldly love and all other temporal desires and aspirations, especially the material and political. It is more akin to 'Go, hart, vnto the lampe of lycht' in the *Gude and Godlie Ballatis* (Mitchell ed. 1907, pp. 162–63) and has an analogue in MQ 47, 'Vp hairt thow art the pairt', which celebrates the heart as the seat of reason and virtue. The poem develops into a pious advisory piece on acceptance, embracing duty and the glad anticipation of heaven's rewards. Self-knowledge is regarded here as one of the valuable consequences of meekly bowing to God's will, however unjust it seems: what appears to be punishment is divinely ordained to make the virtuous man hate the world and hasten to the next. The poem's consolatory tone, and suggestion of recent material loss and political trouble, suggests a date in the early 1570s.

Stanza: ababbcbc[4].
Text: MQ fols 48v–50v, MF p. 2, pp. 361–63, R fols 53–54v.
Authorship: Richard Maitland or Alexander Arbuthnot.
Date: 1571–72?

Commentary

1 *Ceis hairt*. This opening stanza should be compared to MQ 42, ll. 155–61. Also compare the opening address of Scott's 'Hence hairt, wt hir þat most departe', in which the narrator bids his heart accompany his beloved who is leaving him. See ll. 5–6: 'Thairfoir go ... / And lat me leif thus vnmolest'. For a sustained devotional use of the address to the heart see 'Go, hart, vnto the lampe of lycht' in *The Gude and Godlie Ballatis* (Mitchell ed. 1896–97, pp. 162–63). On the personification of the heart in Older Scots literature, see Martin 2008, pp. 137–38.

10 *vaile of miserie*. Compare Dunbar's 'O wreche be war, this warld will wend the fro', l. 7: 'this vaill of trubbill'.

43 *thocht thay the Lord misken*. Compare 'Till trew in hart God of Israell is sweit' in *The Gude and Godlie Ballatis* (a version of Psalm

73, see Mitchell ed. 1896–97, pp. 101–3): 'wickit men / Prosper alway, thocht thay did God misken' (ll. 3–4).

44 *Into the erthe beir now the bell.* The phrase to 'bere the bell' means to be distinguished above others. See *DOST, Bell*, n. sense 2; *Fergusson's Scottish Proverbs* (Beveridge ed. 1924, p. 60). Also see MQ 68, l. 60.

50 *chastisis quhome he luiffis best.* Compare MQ 31, ll. 38–39.

72 *Lovand the Lord quhat euer he send.* Compare MQ 15, ll. 19–20.

75 *Thocht thow haue nother geir nor land.* Probably a reference to the confiscation of Lethington in 1571. See headnote to MQ 20.

81 *Thocht thow be heir in vncouthe land.* The 'vncouthe land' may either be a reference to the world as a place of exile for the righteous (compare the 'desert' in Dunbar's 'O wreche, be war, this warld will wend the fro', l. 10), or a more literal reference to the displacement of the Maitland family on the confiscation of the family seat at Lethington. Maitland was in Edinburgh at the time of the raid by Lennox's troops. See MQ 34, note to l. 13.

83–84 *countrie men quhilk, in ane band, / Conspyris still to doe the deir.* A reference to the King's Party (a 'band' here meaning troop or company). Maitland's sons were at this point aligned with the party supporting the deposed Queen Mary.

88 *lyik sufferit Sanct Paull.* A reference to Paul and the troubles of his mission, which included opposition to his ideology, shipwreck, imprisonment and trial, described in Acts 9–28.

90 *Quhat misteris the.* 'What need is there for you...?'

93 *this cruell weir.* The civil war between the parties of James and Mary, 1567–73.

95–96 *as thow may in Scripture leir, / All thing sall turne the to the best.* Perhaps a reference to Romans 8: 28: 'Also we knowe that all thing worke together for the best vnto them that loue God' (Geneva Bible, 1560).

109 *our foirfatheris deidlie wound.* Original sin. See Genesis 3: 17, Romans 5: 12–21, Corinthians 15: 22. See MQ 42, l. 166.

115–16 *ʒet hes ordainit that thow be / Ane quhome his sone Iesus sall saif.* Compare Matthew 20: 23: 'to sit at my right hand, and at my left hand is not mine to giue: but it shalbe giuen to them for whome it is prepared of my Father' (Geneva Bible, 1560).

EXPLANATORY NOTES

38. Sen that eine that workis my weilfair

This unique poem is the complaint of an abandoned lover. The motif of the departing lady is a popular one in contemporary verse. See, for example, Alexander Scott's 'Hence hairt, wt hir þat most departe', or 'Departe, departe, departe', and Montgomerie's 'Now since the day of our depairt apperis'. The narrator of this poem has had to bid farewell after a final night with his beloved, and is suffering from the traditional afflictions of love sickness – melancholy, swooning, sleeplessness, madness (l. 8) and yearning, to which he sees the only remedy as being death. The poem ends with an acknowledgement that complaint can lessen pain while silence merely nourishes sorrow. The style is characterised by the hyperbole, paradoxes, and apostrophe of courtly love poetry. The poet makes frequent use of personification (see ll. 45, 46–49, 73–74) and lively comparisons (see ll. 37–40, 82–95), and the stanza shows metrical ingenuity with four rhymes and four different line lengths. Discussed in Newlyn 2004, pp. 96–100. Newlyn suggests that the poem forms a pair with MQ 39 and is perhaps written by a female poet (p. 97). Pinkerton attributed it to James I (p. xiv, pp. 425–26).

The poem is unique. It is copied in an italic script.
Stanza: $a^5b^3a^5b^3cc^2dd^2b^4$.
Text: MQ fols 51–53.
Authorship: the poem is unattributed.
Date: uncertain.

Commentary

4 *my bowellis lance*. Compare Montgomerie 'Now since the day of our depairt appeirs', l. 7: 'That Absence els does all my bouells byt'.

9 *O sindring*. 'O parting'. See *DOST, Sind(e)ring*, vbl. n. It is not clear at this point, what has caused the parting (or forced separation) of the narrator and his beloved, though compare l. 12.

12 *sinderit*. This may suggest some other agency has been involved in separating the lovers (*DOST, Sinder*, v.).

19 *the turtill trew*. The faithful turtledove. See MQ 35, note to l. 91.

24 *Kindlit in fyire*. The use of the verb 'kindill' with erotic connotations has precedence in Older Scots poetry. See Henryson, *Orpheus and Eurydice*, l. 87: 'kendill and encres'; Scott 'Lo! quhat it is to lufe': 'Lufe is ane fervent fyre, / Kendillit without desyre'.

28 *the haitt canicular day*. Here 'canicular' refers to Sirius, the 'dog-

355

star', the brightest star in its constellation. The implication is that the hottest day in summer is not as hot as the fire of love experienced by the narrator. See *DOST, Caniculare*, a.

34 *the bolt.* Cupid's arrow, conventional. Compare Montgomerie, 'In throu the windoes of myn ees': 'Cupid hurt my hevy hairt /.../ Throu poyson of his deidly dairt' (ll. 3–5).

46 *faithfull messinger, quhilk is the nicht.* The night is personified as the messenger of lovers. Later in the poem the night is imagined as their pursuer (see l. 91).

48–49 *als the dayis licht / Makis me moir dolorous.* Reminiscent of an *aubade*. Compare Chaucer's *Troilus and Criseyde*, III, ll. 1450–51: 'O cruel day, accusour of the joie / That nyght and love han stole and faste iwryen'; and Montgomerie's 'Hay nou the day dauis', ll. 5–8: 'The thissell-cok cryis / On Louers vha lyis /... / The nicht is neir gone'.

57 *Vnrest dois walkin me againe.* Sleeplessness through anxiety is typical of the unhappy lover. It is personified as 'Vnrest' in *King Hart*, l. 31, and personification is hinted at here too.

72 *scorne of luifaris, Cupid.* For negative portrayals of Cupid as love's enemy, see Montgomerie's 'Blind brutall Boy that with thy bou abuses' and John Stewart's *Vpone the Portrait of Cvpid*.

73 *the morning, with hir mantill grein.* The idea of the morning or season clad in a garment is common. Compare Dunbar 'Ryght as the stern of day begouth to schyne' (*The Goldyn Targe*): 'On Florais mantill I slepit', l. 48.

75 *thochtis [kein].* The MS reads 'thochtis dein'. As Craigie suggests, 'dein' is likely to be a scribal error and the emendation to 'kein' (fierce, violent) is his suggestion (Craigie ed. 1920, p. 287).

101 *band of amitie.* Compare MQ 41, l. 163 Also see Dunbar, 'Sen that I am a presoneir': 'band of freindschip', l. 103. A band or bond was a formal agreement or contract, and a band of friendship was contracted between those of equal status. See Donaldson 1965, p. 14; 1970, pp. 140–43.

109 *my muse.* Perhaps the sorrowful heart, or the poem itself as a complaint, rather than the lady.

39. Sen Fortoun hes now randerit me subiect

The narrator of this epistolary love complaint presents himself conventionally as the obedient 'servitour' (l. 28) of his lady. In the manner of the courtly love tradition to which the poem belongs, the lady is described as peerless, matching beauty with her 'bonte' (goodness) and wisdom. However, the idea that she derives some amusement from the narrator's love-sick misery (l. 95) is less flattering. The poem makes use of several conventional poetic devices and motifs, including the emphasis on Fortune's role in the love affair, the personification of the lady's beauty, the idea of the lover's heart being held in captivity by the lady, and the comparisons made between the narrator's inexpert but sincere advances, and those of eloquent and flamboyant suitors whose affections are transitory (compare MQ 40 ll. 15–16). Its symbolic imagery and diction, particularly that used to describe the lady's physical beauty, has many analogues in contemporary poetry, such as that of Alexander Montgomerie. The first part of the complaint reveals the unrequited nature of the narrator's love, and the section from l. 64 onwards is addressed directly to the lady: thus the poem is the narrator's 'wryte and schedull' (l. 66) to her. This, he insists, is the only way he can communicate his feelings, having failed to impress his beloved on their meetings.

The poem has thematic links to MQ 36 with its emphasis on loving virtuously, and to MQ 39 and MQ 40 for its presentation of the lovesick narrator and depictions of the lady. On the epistolary form in sixteenth-century Scottish lyrics, see van Heijnsbergen 2005, pp. 314–45.

Stanza: aabaabbab^5.
Text: MQ fols 53v–55.
Authorship: the poem is unattributed.
Date: uncertain.

Commentary

1 *Sen Fortoun hes now randerit me subiect.* The interference of Fortune in the lover's fate is traditionally noted in love complaints. See Douglas, *The Palice of Honour*, l. 166: 'Cruell Fortoun, quhy hes thow me betraisit?'

2 *luiffis ʒoik.* Formulaic. Compare *The Kingis Quair*, l. 1346: 'In lufis yok that esy is and sure'.

10–11 *Sumtyme I leifit at libertie at list / And thocht I could to luiffis force resist.* The lover's reminiscence of a time when he regarded himself as strong enough to resist love is conventional. Compare *Troilus* *and Criseyde* I, ll. 507–8: "'O fool, now artow in the snare, / That whilom japedest at loves peyne'". The conventional idea of love as warfare or siege is also implied here. Compare Dunbar's *Goldyn Targe* (ll. 137–207), and *King Hart* (ll. 137–255) (Bawcutt, ed. 2003, also see Hebron 1997, pp. 136–65).

13 *Bot hir bewtie caist in my ein sic mist.* In Dunbar's *The Goldyn Targe*, which may be in the poet's mind here, Beauty leads the assault on the narrator: 'first of all with bow in hand ybent / Come dame Beautee, rycht as scho wald me schent' (ll. 145–46). In Dunbar's poem it is Presence who 'kest a pulder' (l. 203) in the narrator's eye.

27 *My tender hairt keip in captiuitie.* For the lady's imprisonment of the lover or lover's heart, a motif which derives ultimately from *Le Roman de la Rose*, compare *King Hart*: 'Richt þair king Hairt he wes in handis tane' (l. 233); also Dunbar 'Sen that I am a presoneir', ll. 1–4:

> Sen that I am a presoneir
> Till hir that farest is and best,
> I me commend fra ȝeir till ȝeir
> In till hir bandoun for to rest.

28 *servitour*. The lover as obedient and willing servant of the beloved is a staple of the tradition of courtly love writing. Compare MQ 40 l. 27, and Scott 'Haif hairt in hairt, ȝe hairt of hairtis haill', l. 17: 'Gif my hairt be ȝour hairtis seruiture'.

30 *Ane perles perle*. Formulaic. Compare MQ 40, l.3. The language of the lapidary is conventional in love lyrics.

33 *Royall rubie*. See note to l. 30. Pearls and rubies, precious stones of particular value, are traditionally symbolic of womanly perfection in secular and devotional lyrics. See Montgomerie's 'Thoght peirlis give pryce and Diamonds be deir', l. 2: 'Of royall rubies countit rich and rare'.

34 *Roise of renoun, and dasie of delyte*. The rose and daisy are traditional images of perfect femininity both in secular and religious lyrics. Compare l. 90 and MQ 40, ll. 67–68. Also see Scott, 'Ane New ȝeir Gift': 'oure rubent roiss' (l. 4) and Montgomerie, 'Adeu O Desie of delyt' (l. 1).

35 *lance*. Cupid's arrow. Compare MQ 38, ll. 1–4, 32–36.

56 *craft of loue*. Formulaic, but reminiscent of Chaucer, *Parliament of Fowls*, ll. 1–4: 'the craft so long to lerne /... /Al this mene I by Love'.

65 *princes preclair*. Formulaic. Compare MQ 9, l. 1; Dunbar, 'Blyth

EXPLANATORY NOTES

Aberdeane, thow beriall of all tounis', l. 65: 'O potent princes, pleasant and preclair'.

66 *wryte and schedull.* That the poem is a 'bill' addressed to the lady is a typical claim made in love complaints. The use of 'schedull' here has legal overtones. See *DOST, Sedule,* n. Compare Scott 'Luve preysis but comparesone', l. 33: 'Suld I presome this sedull schaw'.

71 *Let luif meit luif of hir.* See MQ 36 for the ideal of 'mutuall love'.

90 *the flour of feminine.* Formulaic. Compare MQ 40, l. 2, and MQ 64, l. 3 (Montgomerie).

94 *Thocht ȝe be daingerous and beir abak.* The lady's 'danger' or aloofness towards her lover is conventional and derives ultimately from *Le Roman de la Rose* where 'Dangier' guards the Rose. Compare Dunbar's *Tretis,* l. 132: 'Than am I dangerus'.

40. Ane ballat to be Songe with the Tuine of 'Luifer Come to Luifeiris Dore' etc.

Like MQ 38 and 39 this is a love complaint addressed to a lady, praising her many physical attributes and virtues, which the narrator hopes will have an improving effect on him. He nevertheless insists on his worthiness above her many other admirers. Its apostrophes, hyperbole, superlatives, and symbolic imagery of light, flowers, gems and material luxuries, are rather formulaic. For a similar, if more skilled, deployment of such conventions, compare Montgomerie's description of the beloved's body in 'Quhy bene ȝe Musis all so long', where the lady's lips are rosy, her teeth are likened to 'pearle of Orient', and white breast to ivory. The refrain (found in all but the first and last stanzas) is an appeal for the lady's mercy that is typical of the courtly love lament.

Though highly conventional, the imagery and diction (the lady being described as a pearl and rose, for example) shared with MQ 39 may suggest a common authorship for MQ 39 and MQ 40. The poems also have many thematic similarities, albeit conventional ones, especially in the way in which the lover-narrator presents his suit.

The poem is unique. The manuscript title suggests it was to be sung to the tune of 'luifer come to luifeiris dore', though this title seems to have been truncated. I have not been able to find an exact reference to this tune elsewhere. There are records, however, of songs and ballads on the night visit, including the popular 'Undo your dore'. This title is used by William Copland for his c.1560 print of *The Squire of Low Degree* in which the squire appeals to his beloved with a version of this song (*ESTC* S95321, *STC* 23112; on de Worde's print of 'Undo thy dore', and a 1586 reference to the ballad, see Baskerville 1922, pp. 571–72). It may also be noted that although MQ 40 is a secular poem, the form of its title has some similarities to the echoes of Song of Songs 5: 2 and Revelation 3: 20 in religious lyrics such as the Grimestone Lyric, 'Undo þi dore, my spuse dere'. The devotional version of the secular song 'Quho is at my windo, quho, quho?' (see Frankis 1955, pp. 301–2) in the *Gude and Godlie Ballatis* also contains an allusion to this imagery in Christ's address to welcome the sinner, which establishes the main refrain for the poem:

> Nay, I call the nocht fra my dure, I wis,
> Lyke ane stranger that vnknawin is,
> Thow art my brother, and my will it is,
> In at my dure that thow go. (Mitchell ed. 1896–97, pp. 132–36)

MQ 40 is copied in an italic script; the title is in a combination of a display script and italic. The refrain, which appears from the second stanza until the last two verses, is abbreviated at ll.77, 98, 105.
Stanza: $a^4b^3a^4b^3a^4b^3C^3$.
Text: MQ 55v–58v.
Authorship: the poem is unattributed.
Date: uncertain.

Commentary

2–3 *O flour of femenein, / O perles perle.* Highly formulaic epithets for the lady. Compare MQ 39, ll. 30, 90.

15 *I am ane prenteis bot in luif.* Compare MQ 39, l. 55.

22–23 *I grant thair is na gift in me / 3our fauour to procuire.* Compare MQ 39, ll. 74–77.

26–27 *3it since I am, be destanie, / Becum 3our seruituire.* Compare MQ 39, ll. 1, 28.

52 *Phoebus in his spheir.* Phoebus or Apollo, the sun. Compare l. 78.

60 *Diana the quein.* Diana, accustomed to bathe in a secluded woodland pool with her nymphs, was often associated with chastity. See Ovid *Met.* 3. Compare MQ 63, ll. 17–24.

62 *Amang the leiffis grein.* Formulaic, but compare MF poem 130, 'Still vndir the levis grene' (pp. 302–5).

EXPLANATORY NOTES

67–68 *Ane lillie of delyte, / Ane roise maist plesand.* Compare MQ 39, l. 34.

69 *Ane ianetflour perfyite.* The 'Janet-flower' is a white and yellow flower, possibly a water lily, and is used elsewhere as a comparison to feminine beauty. Compare *Kingis Quair* l. 326; and Montgomerie, 'Quhy bene ȝe Musis all so long', l. 39.

111 *Cast not ȝour perle to suyne!* Biblical. Matt 7: 6.

120 *Not willing longer ȝow molest.* See note to l. 121. Also compare MQ 39, l. 101.

121 *I bid ȝow hairt 'Adiew!'* For the farewell to the heart, see headnote to MQ 37, and compare Scott 'Hence, hairt with hir þat most departe', ll. 1–6:

> Hence, hairt, with hir þat most departe,
> And hald the with thy souerane
> For I had lever want ane harte
> Nor haif the hairt þat dois me pane;
> Thairfoir go, with thy lufe remane,
> And lat me leif thus vnmolest.

41. O wratched waird, O fals feinȝit fortoun!

This complaint on Fortune and the times is attributed to Alexander Arbuthnot (d.1583) in MQ, but is unattributed in MF (on Arbuthnot, see headnote to MQ 35). It depicts society as morally impoverished and politically unstable. The narrator makes particular mention of the civil war (1567–73) and of political fickleness among the nobility during this period (ll. 23, 26). He presents his own values as at odds with those of contemporary society, yet complains that he is compelled to participate in practices he disapproves of. He considers the difficulty of finding true allies at court, a theme found in poems by Richard Maitland in MQ (see MQ 11 and 23). Like Maitland's poems on court life, Arbuthnot's poem is preoccupied with the misuse of language (including flattery, deceit, and taunting), and culminates in an attack on the misreading of poetry (compare MQ 55, by Maitland) and false representation of poets. Similarities of theme and phrasing (detailed in the notes) with poems by Richard Maitland suggest a close creative relationship between the two poets.

The poem's refrain suggests the futility of complaining, and its

opening apostrophes against the cruelty of fortune are never replaced by a mood of philosophical acceptance. Contrast MQ 42.
Stanza: ababbcC⁵.
Text: MQ fols 58v–62, MF pp. 41–45.
Authorship: attributed to Arbuthnot.
Date: c.1567–73, probably c.1570°71 (see headnote to MQ 42).

Commentary

1 *O wratched waird, O fals feinʒit fortoun!* The terms of the narrator's complaint against fortune are conventional, and reminiscent of many such complaints in earlier Scots verse. See, for example, that of Cresseid, in Henryson's *Testament of Cresseid*, l. 412: 'Fell is thy fortoun, wickit is thy weird'; and Montgomerie's *An invectione against Fortun*, l. 6: 'fals and feinʒed fortun'.

3–4 *mistemperit constellatioun! / O evill aspect in my nativitie!* The narrator regards the stellar influences at the time of his birth to have been malignant.

5 *O waird sisteris*. The Fates, regarded in Greek mythology as having the power to determine the future.

15 *the trew religioun*. A general reference to formal Christian worship, though perhaps with some Protestant connotations. See note to l. 17.

17 *atheisme and superstitioun*. According to *DOST* the word 'atheism' is rare in Scots before the 1570s. See *DOST Atheisme*, n. and *Atheist*, n. Also see *OED*, *Atheism*, n. After 1560 'superstitioun' usually refers to the teachings of the Pre-reformed church. See *DOST*, *Superstitio(u)n*, n.

22 *obey my prince*. The sovereign generally, rather than an explicit indication of the writer's adherence to the King's Party.

23 *ciuill weir*. The conflict between the parties of Mary Queen of Scots and James, 1567–73.

33 *cheritie doeth ring in none estait*. Personification allegory is gestured towards here, but not sustained, so I have chosen not to treat 'cheritie' as a proper noun. On the importance of charity as a governing virtue, see Douglas, *Palice of Honour*, ll. 1795–96: 'For Cheritie, of gudlines the flour, / Is Maister houshold'. Also see MQ 28, l. 47.

34 *Thocht all concur to hurt the innocent*. A repeated concern in Maitland's poems. Compare MQ 4, l. 14, MQ 16, ll. 27–28, and MQ 18, l. 19.

39 *I am compellit to flatter*. Contrast the advice given in poems by Maitland, such as MQ 11, l. 9 and MQ 59, l. 41.

61 *In Venus scuill I man sum lessoun leir*. The narrator is a reluctant lover. Compare MQ 20, ll. 24–26.

78 *Scorning I hait*. Compare MQ 11, l. 9: 'Be not ane scorner'.

99 *coistlie claythis*. A gesture towards sumptuary complaint. Compare Maitland's poems, MQ 2 and MQ 4, ll. 76–77.

111 *'Quha is ane scheip, the wolf will sone him hent'*. Proverbial, see Whiting 1941–51, Sheep, and Biblical. See John 10: 12: 'an hierling ... seeth the wolfe coming and he leaueth the shepe, and fleeth, and the wolfe catcheth them' (Geneva Bible, 1560).

115 *ane betie bum*. A feckless person. See *DOST*, *Batie bum*, n.

116 *all men thinkis a play me to iniure*. Translate 'everyone thinks it is a joke to wrong me'.

127 *And haittis*. The first person pronoun is omitted for metrical reasons.

131 *tak ane face of bres*. Put on an arrogant expression, assume infallibility. Proverbial. Compare Dunbar, 'Memento, homo, quod cinis es', l. 7: 'thocht thy bodye ware of bras' and Job 6: 11–12. See Bawcutt ed. 1998, p. 360.

163 *the leig of amitie*. Compare MQ 38, l. 101, and note.

166 *not licht lyik weddercok in wind*. A 'weddercok' is an unreliable person. Proverbial, see Whiting 1941–51, Weathercock. Compare Lyndsay, *Testament of the Papyngo*, l. 368: 'Cheangyng als oft as woddercok in wynd'; Montgomerie, 'ʒong tender plante in spring tym of ʒour ʒeirs', l. 56: 'Bot wavers lyk the widdircok in wind'.

172 *rascall rymouris*. Poor or troublesome poets. Compare Maitland's complaint against slanderous poets in MQ 55.

188 *The Lordis plaige throwout the warld is went*. Biblical. A comparison of Scotland's current troubles with God's punishment of the Egyptians with ten plagues in Exodus, 5–11. Compare Maitland's poems, MQ 12, l. 5 and MQ 31, l. 52.

42. Religioun now is reknit as ane fabill

The first 84 lines of this poem are a complaint against fortune and the tendency to vice and impiety in the narrator's world. From line

85 onwards the narrator attempts to reconcile himself to the workings of God's will. With the change in perspective the two-line refrain is dropped. The influence of Calvinist theology is evident in the narrator's comments on the salvation of the elect (ll. 169–72), and these echo MQ 37, ll. 113–16, a poem attributed in MQ, though not MF, to Alexander Arbuthnot (d.1583, see headnote to MQ 35). They are also similar both in style and substance to MQ 65, ll. 160–84. That this poem, with its extensive similarities to MQ 37 (see notes below), is attributed to Arbuthnot in both MQ and MF, provides further support for his authorship of MQ 37. However, the themes of acceptance, and of the value of suffering, may also be compared to poems by Maitland. See, for example, MQ 31, ll. 25–48.

A note in MF, which does not appear in MQ, dates the poem to 1571, and it is possible therefore that the poem's advice on the value of suffering is specific to the Maitland family's recent troubles, as well as perennial in nature. Compare MQ 20 (and headnote) and MQ 46.
Stanza: ababbCC^5 (ll. 1–84), ababbcc^5 (ll. 85–182).
Text: MQ fols 62–64v, MF pp. 45–50, D fols 60–64.
Authorship: attributed to Alexander Arbuthnot.
Date: 1571.

Commentary

87–90 *Then I accuse my fortoun and my weird ... I clein recant.* The narrator's self-realisation, and movement away from blaming fortune, is comparable to that of Cresseid in Henryson's *Testament of Cresseid*, l. 575: 'Nane but my self as now I will accuse'. It may also be compared to that of the narrator of Montgomerie's *A Ladyis Lamentatione*, whose narrator begins blaming her 'wicked weard' and ends requesting God's mercy for her error.

90 *Goddis secreit.* Divine mysteries which pass human understanding, linked to Providence, which is explained at ll. 100–5. On the place of Providence in Calvinist thought, see Mullan 2010, pp. 287–95.

93 *ethnik authouris.* Pre-Christian writers.

120 *In warld the prince of darknes hes impryire.* Satan, worldly evil. Compare Ephesians 6: 12: 'we wrestle ... against the princes of darkenes of this worlde' (Geneva Bible, 1560).

122 *clengeing fyire.* The reading 'clengeing' is from MF, where MQ has 'chainging fyire' (transforming fire). The idea of a cleansing fire perhaps better echoes the biblical idea of the purifying fire, or trial by fire to prove integrity. See Zech 13: 9 ('I wil bring that third parte thorow the fyre, and wil fine them as the siluer is fined, and wil trye them as golde is tryed', Geneva Bible, 1560); 1 Corinthians 3: 13–15 ('the fyre shal trye euerie mans worke', Geneva Bible, 1560). Thus the text has been emended from MF. Compare MQ 46, ll. 36–39.

136 *cleiff vnto the Lord.* Biblical, see Acts 11: 23, also Joshua 23: 8.

146 *Christ our heid.* Biblical, see 1 Corinthians 11: 3, 'Christ is the head of euerie man' (Geneva Bible, 1560).

155–61 *Ceis then my saull and trowbill me no moir ... And for this warldlie troubill mak na maine.* This stanza is very close to MQ 37, ll. 1–8.

166 *our foirfatheris Adamis deidlie wound.* Original sin, the fall. See Genesis 3: 17, Romans 5: 12–21, Corinthians 15: 22 and compare MQ 37, l. 109.

171–72 *and hes ordanit that thow be / Ane quhome his sone the Lord Iesus sall saif.* A reference to the Calvinist theology of election, based on texts such as Matthew 20: 23 and 24: 24. See MQ 37, ll. 113–16.

175–76 The verbal linking of the two stanzas (*vers enchaînée* / anadiplosis) may be compared to the use of the device in MQ 65 from l. 160 onwards.

43. Aganis Sclanderous Toungis.

This alliterative poem is ascribed to John Maitland (1543–95) in MF, and there given the title 'Aganis sklandrous toungis in anno 1572', though by a hand later than that which copied the text (c.1590?). It is unattributed and undated in MQ. The later attributor in MF adds an explicit to the poem stating that it was composed when John Maitland was 'commendatar of coldinghame', an office he assumed in 1567 and held until his forfeiture in 1571 (Coldingham was never restored to him). The MF attributer also takes the opportunity to note that John Maitland was 'eftir L[ord] thirlstance and chancellor': he was elevated in 17 May 1590 (*Scots Peerage* V, p. 299).

Like some of the other poems in this part of MQ (especially MQ 37, MQ 42 and MQ 46), this poem offers consolation and counsels patience in the face of suffering. It is concerned with the abuses of language in political life, and especially the hardships caused by defamation, something suffered by William Maitland in particular, as a result of satirical ballads that circulated in Edinburgh in the early 1570s. Compare the themes of MQ 55 and see Lyall 2005, p. 200; Louglin 1994.

The MF text is found in Cranstoun ed. 1891–93, I, pp. 254–56 (poem XXXVII), II, pp. 169–71.

Stanza: aaaaabab[5].
Text: MQ fols 64v–66, MF pp. 257–58.
Authorship: Attributed to John Maitland in MF.
Date: 1572.

Commentary

1 *bissie branit*. 'Diligent'.

18 *And starker stewin*. 'And a more powerful din' (literally, 'roar of the water'). See *DOST*, *Stevin*, n.

19 *gorgit wateris*. Waters impeded by some barrier or dam. See *DOST*, *Gorgit*, ppl.a.

41–64 For a similar exploration of the impossibility of pleasing those less virtuous than oneself, see MQ 41 (by Arbuthnot), especially ll. 36–182.

42 *privelie ȝe play*. Perhaps the accusation is 'you are unsociable' (literally, you amuse yourself in private).

47–48 *Gif ȝe be strainge thay esteme ȝow our stay, / And trowis it is ȝe, or ellis sum hes it tauld ȝow*. See Cranstoun ed. 1891–93, II, p. 170: 'If you keep your distance they think you haughty, and that you think yourself a somebody, or that someone has told you that you are'.

55 *Dayis thay dispyte and be ȝe daylie dekit*. The sense of this line is difficult. 'Dayis' means 'slatterns' or 'slovenly persons'. See *DOST*, *Daw*, *Da*, n. Thus 'They despise slovens, and you are well dressed everyday'. See Cranstoun ed. 1891–93, II, p. 170.

56 *'the papingo that pruinȝeis'*. The parrot, here preening itself, is a symbol of pride. See MQ 35, l. 89 and note.

67 *Bakbyteris brutis bydis bot ane blast*. The sense is, 'rumours of backbiters last only a short time'.

68 *Thay flouris sone, but farder fruit thay faill*. Proverbial: 'They flower quickly, but fail to produce further fruit'. Compare Montgomerie, 'ȝong tender plante in spring tym of ȝour ȝeiris', l. 26: 'Als trees may floorish and bring furth feu fruit'.

69 *rascall raveris*. Compare MQ 41, l. 172 ('rascall rymouris').

EXPLANATORY NOTES

44. Ane Admonitioun to My Lord of Mar Regent.

Title: Ane admonitioun to my Lord Regent Maid be I.M.P. off C. MF

This poem is addressed to John Erskine, earl of Mar, and regent of Scotland from 3 September 1571 to 28 October 1572. It is a mixture of praise for Erskine's personal qualities and pedigree, and cautionary advice about his policies, warning him of the consequences for his position and Scotland's future if he fails to govern sagaciously. It recalls the advice Maitland gave to his son in MQ 11 that 'greit perrell is to tak on hand the ruder' (l. 42). In particular the narrator urges Erskine to ensure Scotland's independence from other realms, especially England: in the autumn of 1571 the Regent and King's Party were urging Elizabeth to send military support for their cause. The expression of fear about Scotland's loss of autonomy recalls Richard Maitland's anxious observations about the Marian Franco-Scottish alliance (see, for example, MQ 5, ll. 89–90, MQ 6, l. 36, MQ 9, ll. 41–48, MQ 19 ll. 64–81).

The poem shows some stylistic skill. The narrator imagines Scotland as a ship tossed on the sea of fortune, in need of a skilled pilot, and Erskine's role as regent as a performance for public scrutiny (l. 97). Much of the advice is couched in vigorous proverbial terms.

MF attributes the poem to John Maitland, when he was Prior of Coldingham. See headnote to MQ 43. It is unattributed in MQ and D. The poem is discussed by Lee 1954, p. 34, and Martin 2013a. Previously edited by Cranstoun from MF (Cranstoun, ed. 1891–93, I, pp. 186–92 and II, pp. 125–29). For near contemporary poems addressing Scottish regents, see Cranstoun ed. 1891–93, poems VI (Moray) and VIII (Mar).
Stanza: ababbcbc[5].
Text: MQ fols 66v–68, MF pp. 357–59, D fols 64v–67.
Authorship: attributed to John Maitland in MF.
Date: 1571–72.

Commentary

1 *Maist loyall lord.* John Erskine, earl of Mar and regent of Scotland.

3 *the princes place.* Mar was the third regent of the minority of James VI, his regency following those of Moray and Lennox.

9 *Thy hous.* The Erskine family had a long history of loyalty to the Stewart dynasty, and of royal service, in the military and in administration, dating back to the mid fourteenth century. See Boardman 1996. Mar's father was John fifth Lord Erskine (d.1555), who had been a prominent figure in the minorities of James V and his heir, Mary. Mar had also been central to the care of the infant James VI during Lennox's regency.

16 *in this storme*. The struggle for power between the parties of Mary and James, 1567–73, which was particularly violent in the early 1570s when the poem was composed. See Dawson 2007, pp. 272–82.

18 *Our tossit galay*. The metaphor of the ship of state, tossed on the sea of fortune or the world, is commonplace in medieval and early modern political philosophy. It can be traced back to Horace's *Odes* (I. 14) and Plato's *Republic*, and was developed explicitly in Thomas Aquinas' influential *De Regimine Principum* (1265–67). Also see Sobecki 2008, pp. 20, 34–41 on the idea of the steerless boat and the dangers represented by the sea. The image of the ship of state is used to represent the perilous position of Scotland in 'The Poysonit Schot' ll. 9–17 (Cranstoun ed. 1891–93, I, pp. 132–38, poem XVII), printed in 1570; also see 'The Bischoppis lyfe and testament' where the world is 'Lyke to ane Schip that saillis on the seis, / Tost with windis ...' (Cranstoun ed. 1891–93, I, p. 193, poem XXVIII). The important association of the navigation of the sea and kingship underlies Montgomerie's educational poetic narrative of a sea voyage, composed for James VI, *The Navigatioun*.

25 *Boreas*. The north wind.

34 *Englisch forces*. Mar made repeated requests to Elizabeth, whose approval as regent he had won, for both financial and military support for the King's Party. Some monetary help was forthcoming in 1571 and again after surrendering the Earl of Northumberland in 1572 (see MQ 60–62), but he did not receive the guns and infantry he requested. See Summerson, *ODNB*.

36 *farland foullis seme to haue fedderis fair*. Proverbial, with the sense, 'Exotic birds seem to have beautiful feathers'. See Montgomerie, 'ʒong tender plante in spring tym of ʒour ʒeiris', l. 38: 'Far foullis hes ay fair fethers'.

40 *the rebellis*. It is probable that 'rebellis' is simply being used in the general sense of those who oppose established authority and order, rather than in a partisan sense. The Maitland brothers were of course associated with the Queen's Party, and Mar with that of the King.

50 *Ane forrane matche or maister to admit*. It is likely that the poet has in mind the marriage of Mary Tudor to Phillip II of Spain in 1554. However, Scotland had experience of problematic foreign matches, that of Mary Queen of Scots to the Dauphin being one such example. Compare MQ 6 and MQ 9 and headnotes.

51–53 *the Saxonis ... Britonis folkis*. The narrator summarises an account of how the Germanic invaders of southern Britain caused the Britons to flee, and then claimed their land. See Bellenden's translation of Boece's *Chronicles of Scotland* ([1829], Book 9).

57–64 According to Cranstoun ed, 1891–93, II, p. 127, this is a reference to the Siege of Leith in 1559–60.

65 *Fleand Charibde, be war in Scill*. Charybdis, the whirlpool at the entrance of the Strait of Messina, and Scylla, the rock facing it (see Ovid *Met.* 13–14). Compare Montgomerie, 'Displesur with his deadly dairt', l. 61: 'For from Carybdis vhill I flie'.

68 *our auld contentioun*. The historical enmity with England.

74 *Fergus first*. Fergus I, the mythical king of Scotland, who was said to have died c.305 BC, mentioned in Fordun and by later Scottish historians. See Boece's *Chronicles of Scotland*, book I, chapters 6–9. For Bellenden's translation, see Chambers and Batho 1936, vol. 1, pp. 35–49. Also see Cranstoun ed. 1891–93, poems V, l. 105 and XI, l. 28.

91 *ane bellie-blind*. A blindfolded person. See *DOST*, Belly-blind, n; Montgomerie, *An invectione against Fortun contening ane Admonitione to his freinds at Court*, l. 43: 'that buskit belly blind'.

93 *thy marrowis covatice*. 'Your neighbour's avarice'. See *DOST*, Marrow, n. The greedy neighbour, especially one who lays wrongful claim to land, appears frequently in Maitland's poems. Compare MQ 19, ll. 55–63 and MQ 29, l. 5.

96 *Nor beit the bus quhair otheris eatis the bereis*. Proverbial. See Whiting 1941–51, Bush, and Scott, *A Luvaris Complaint*, 'How suld my febill body fure', ll. 47–9:

> Sa bissely to busk I boun,
> And vþir eitis the berry doun
> That suld be myn.

45. Gif it be trew that storeis doe rehers

This poem, attributed to Alexander Arbuthnot (d.1583), is a complaint on the times and a lament for the poet-narrator's removal from the company that he craves. Its subject is writer's block, a theme explored in poems such as Dunbar's 'My heid did ȝak ȝester nicht', and the anonymous 'Fane wald I with all diligence' (MF pp. 210–11), which playfully deploy the paradox of writing about being unable to write (see Bawcutt 1992, pp. 115–17). In this case, the narrator's poetic inspiration has been lost as a result of a separation from a loved one (see ll. 15–16, 35–5), addressed as his 'maistres' (l. 25), and the degeneracy of the times (l. 8). Not wishing to write of misery, he chooses to give up composing poetry. Although there is no way of conclusively dating the poem at present, it is likely that it belongs to the same period as the datable poems in MQ attributed to Arbuthnot, such as MQ 41 and MQ 42, and its bitterness about the wicked ways of the world may be linked, like the content of these, to Scotland's civil war and the early 1570s in particular. On Arbuthnot, see headnote to MQ 35.

Stanza: ababbcbc[5].
Text: MQ fols 68v–69, D fols 67–68.
Authorship: attributed to Arbuthnot.
Date: uncertain, c.1570s.

Commentary

7 *Thocht this, my wryt, be void of eloquens*. The modesty topos is conventional. Compare MQ 39, ll. 55–56.

28 *I haue sa tint that I na mair can tyne*. 'I have lost so much that I am unable to lose any more'.

39 *my woundis grein*. 'My wounds yearn'. See *DSL*, *Green*, v. This invokes the language of love complaint but a degree of ambiguity remains as to whether the wounds are caused by the loss of love, or the narrator's dissatisfaction with contemporary society. Contrast Craigie ed. 1920 (p. 288), who suggests emending to 'wound is grein'.

46. Ane Consolatore Ballad to Sir Richart Maitland of Lethingtoun Knicht

This poem offers consolation to Richard Maitland on his family's troubles. It seems to have been composed when Richard Maitland had only one living son: it must therefore post-date the death of William Maitland, Secretary Lethington, in 1573 after the fall of Edinburgh Castle to the King's Party. Thomas Maitland had died in 1572, while travelling to Rome, and thus by 1573, Maitland's son John Maitland, was his heir. The poem suggests that Maitland had previously lost four other sons, perhaps in infancy (though see *Scots Peerage* V, p. 293). None of the deceased sons are named and there is no eulogy here for William or

Thomas. The fact that Maitland's lineage is so reduced is placed in the context of other afflictions including Maitland's age and grief (see note to l. 9, l. 123).

The first part of the poem praises Maitland's personal qualities. After l. 88 the narrator turns to Maitland's family history, holding up his ancestors, alongside Old Testament figures, as examples of those who have triumphed in adversity. Equally important to the poem's attempt to console Maitland is its invocation of the theology of election (compare MQ 37, l. 115 and MQ 42, ll. 172–73), and references to and quotation from the Bible, especially from the Old Testament and the Book of Revelation. The reference to the safe return of Tobit's son, Tobias, at ll. 161–65, is particularly pertinent to Maitland's situation. Thematic similarities to Arbuthnot's poems contained in MQ, as well as similarities of diction (some rather legalistic) and imagery, suggest that this poem may be by his pen, though it is unattributed in all witnesses, an attribution in MF having been deleted. The poem also bears some similarities of diction to MQ 47, which is unattributed.
Stanza: ababbcbc^5.
Text: MQ fols 69–73, MF pp. 343–48, R fols 46v–49v, D fols 68–73.
Authorship: unattributed but possibly by Arbuthnot.
Date: c.1573.

Commentary

1 *Tobie*. Tobit, of the Old Testament (or Apocryphal) Book of Tobit, who was persecuted for his religious faith. Tobit is also mentioned at ll. 66 and 161–65.

2 *Iob*. Job, of the Old Testament Book of Job, whose loyalty to God appeared to be met with the infliction of suffering, including the loss of his children and property. Job's friends advise him to endure his suffering without complaint. Job is also mentioned later in this poem at ll. 66, 153.

9 *sa greit aage*. Maitland would have been in his late seventies on the composition of this poem. Maitland's advanced age is mentioned in his own poems: see MQ 20, l. 5 etc., MQ 22, l. 3.

11–12 *With los, alace, so lairge of linage, / And childrein*. Thomas Maitland died in 1572, and William in 1573. The narrator states that Richard Maitland had seven sons in total, and that only one remains at the time of writing (ll. 124–25).

27 *and participat*. Translate 'sharing'. See *DOST*, *Participat*, a. Those who wish to find communion with Christ are those sharing in his sorrows, identifying with the torments of his passion.

30 *this pilgramage*. The metaphor of life as a pilgrimage to heaven is commonplace. See Dunbar, 'O wreche, be war, this warld will wend the fro', ll. 9–10: 'Walk furth, pilgrame, quhill thow hes dayis licht, / Dres fra desert, draw to thy duelling place'.

36 *Sa in afflixioun, as ane furneis fyire*. Revelation 3: 'I counsel thee to bie of golde tryed by the fyre' (Geneva Bible, 1560); also Zech 13: 9. Compare MQ 42, l. 122 and note.

41 *the chosin be correctioun*. A reference to the Calvinist theology of election, which is based on Matt 20: 23 and Romans 8: 38–30. Compare MQ 37, l. 115, and note, and MQ 42, ll. 172–73.

50 *peculiar, proper peopill*. God's distinguished or chosen people, again a reference to the salvation of the elect. See l. 41 and note.

54 *the elect*. See line 41 and note.

58 *Our aduocat*. Legalistic, compare the use of 'propone' at ll. 59, 71. Perhaps also echoic of John 14: 16: 'And I wil pray the Father, and he shal giue you another Conforter, that he may abide with you for euer' (Geneva Bible, 1560).

64 *'Quhome that I luif, be croce I doe correct'*. Biblical, see Revelations 3: 19: 'As manie as I loue, I rebuke and chasten' (Geneva Bible, 1560).

66 *Iephe, ... Iacob or Samson*. More examples of God's chosen people. Iephe is Jephthah from the Old Testament (Judges 11: 30–40) who sacrificed his daughter to God. The Old Testament figure Jacob, whose story is told in Genesis, is adduced as an example of true faith in Acts 7: 8 and Hebrews 11: 9. Samson the Nazirite was captured and blinded by the Philistines (Judges 16: 4–31).

70 *frowning Fortoun*. Fortune is apparently imagined as the goddess here. Compare MQ 47, ll. 35–36.

79 *... thocht ʒe seme a sessoun in suspence*. The sense here is, 'though you seem to be for a time in uncertainty'. Compare MQ 47, l. 18.

81 *Wo workis to weill be vyice alternatiue*. The phrase 'be vyice alternatiue' means 'by alternation'. Thus, 'Sorrow becomes happiness by alternation'. See *DOST, Alternative*, a.

93 *ʒour grandfatheris*. The Maitlands descended from Thomas de Matalan or Mautalent, and had become established in the lowlands in the twelfth century. See Barrow 1980, pp. 81–82, 185; *Scots Peerage* V,

p. 275. For a similar appeal to family history, compare MQ 68, l. 141, and see note to line 105 below.

101 *Luit wanwerdis work and walter.* Figurative, imagining fortune as a sea. 'Let misfortunes roll to and fro'. See *DOST, Weltir,* v.

104 *stoic.* For a discussion on the place on stoicism in protestant thinking, see Mullan 2010, pp. 288–89.

105 *Renowned Richard.* Maitland's ancestor, active in the first half of the thirteenth century, who established the Maitlands of Thirlestane (see Barrow 1980, p. 185, *Scots Peerage* V, pp. 278–79). He is mentioned in Douglas's *The Palice of Honour*, l. 1717. Compare MQ 68, ll. 141–60. See MacDonald 1998, pp. 85–86.

110 *Priamis tyme of Troy.* Priam, king of Troy at the time of its siege and destruction by the Greeks.

111–12 *Bot piteouslie thay peirles perlis a pest / Bereft him.* 'But sadly an infection bereft him of those peerless pearls'. The metaphor of the beloved as a pearl is commonplace in amatory contexts (see MQ 40, l. 3). However, here the figure of the pearl for the lost child more closely recalls the extended similitude of the Middle English alliterative poem, *Pearl*.

112 *burdalane.* See *DOST, Birdalane, Burdalane*, n. an only child.

122 *Maitland als, and magnanime ar 3e.* The narrator believes the name 'Maitland' to derive from the Latin 'magnanimus' (generous, noble spirited), though its French origin is 'mal talent' which translates as 'evil genius' (Barrow 1980, p. 82). See MQ 69, l. 24, where Marie's family name is the occasion for a pun: 'Mait, land and gold scho gave aboundantlie'.

125 *Bot burdalane 3e haue behind, as he.* This line dates the poem to after the death of William Maitland in 1573.

136 *With better hairt mair bitternes that beiris.* The sense here seems to be that a heart made stronger through faith can endure more difficulty.

137 *Na na! confide his clemence will not quyte.* See *DOST, Na*, adv. 3. 'Na na' is chiefly used in answering a rhetorical question.

142 *Sarais seid.* Sarah, wife of Abraham, to whom Isaac was born in her old age (Genesis 17: 16–19).

158 *his sonnis, that suddanlie wer slaine.* The sudden deaths of Job's seven sons and daughters in a natural disaster is recounted in Job 1:

18–19. God later rewards Job with the restoration of his property and seven more sons and three beautiful daughters (Job 42: 12–13).

161 *quhen Tobias for his sone tuik thocht*. Tobit worries when his son Tobias fails to return from his journey with Raphael and marriage to Sara, but has faith that he is not dead. See Tobit 10 and 11.

162 *blind*. Richard Maitland shared Tobias's affliction in losing his sight. His blindness is mentioned at the outset of MQ 14 (by Maitland): 'Blind man be blyithe'.

178 *not bene a sleip*. For the fear that God is sleeping, see Psalm 44: 23: 'why slepest thou, O Lord' (Geneva Bible, 1560). Also see Henryson's *Morall Fabillis*, l. 1296, where this psalm verse is quoted ('The Sheep and the Dog').

180 *ȝour onlie sone, quha semed a slauchter scheip*. John Maitland, who was arrested by Drury and imprisoned by the Regent Morton, on the fall of Edinburgh Castle and collapse of the Queen's Party in May 1573. After being held in Edinburgh and Tantallon, in 1574 he was placed in the care of his cousin, Lord Somerville, at Cowtally. He was not freed until 1578. See Lee 1959, pp. 36–38. Also see MQ 94.4, l. 7.

182 *As Noe, Lothe, or Susan*. All figures who were chosen by God to be saved when others were destroyed for their sins. God's salvation of Noah and his family is told in Genesis 6–9; of Lot and his family during the destruction of Sodom and Gomorrah in Genesis (Genesis 19: 1–19); and of Susan, who is saved from execution by divine intervention, her persecutors being killed instead, in the Book of Susannah.

47. Vp hairt! thow art the pairt

Like MQ 37, this poem is an address to the personified heart, advising it to dedicate itself to reason and sobriety. It explores the notion that true liberty is gained through the pursuit of virtue, which even the captivity of the body cannot threaten, ideas that may be ultimately traced back to Boethius's *Consolation of Philosophy*, and which are explored in earlier Scottish texts such *The Kingis Quair* (Summers 2004, pp. 60–89) and contemporary prison writing (Strauss 1995).

The poem is, like MQ 46 (which it seems to echo on a few occasions), consolatory in tone and may also speak to the Maitland family's troubles. Its themes of freedom and imprisonment may relate to, or have been seen by the compiler to relate to, the political misfortunes of Maitland's surviving son, John (see MQ 46 and headnote), between 1573 and

1578. William Maitland had also been imprisoned on charges related to the murder of Darnley in 1570. The poem's references to the captivity of the flesh (l. 15, compare l. 42), but the freedom of the heart nonetheless, suggests such a context. In MF the poem is preceded by a short Latin poem on the same theme, 'Ille idem in carcere Carmen' (p. 348). MF gives it the witty but unhelpful attribution 'Finis Huius'.

Like MQ 37, the poem comforts the reader with the thought that misfortune passes, and, like MQ 43 (l. 6), promises that truth always reveals itself. The poem has similarities of phrasing to works by Alexander Scott and Montgomerie. See notes to ll. 15 and 45. Its opening may be compared to Scott's 'Vp helsum hairt Thy rutis rais and lowp' (Bannatyne MS, fols 242v–243). The poem is copied in italic.

Stanza: ababbcbc³.
Text: MQ fols 73–74, MF pp. 349–50, R 49v–50.
Authorship: unattributed.
Date: uncertain, but c.1573–78?

Commentary

1 *Vp hairt!* For the address to the heart, see MQ 37, and headnote. Compare Scott's amatory poem 'Vp, helsum Hairt'.

2 *souuerane.* For the allegory of the heart as a ruler of man's inner kingdom see, *The Buik of King Alexander the Conquerour* (ll. 9659–822) and *King Hart*. Discussed in Martin 2008, pp. 70–71, 137–38.

15 *Thocht captive flesche do sterue.* Compare Scott, 'Hence, hairt, with hir that most departe', ll. 17–19:

> Thocht this belappit body heir
> Be bound to sheruitude and thrall,
> My fathfull hairt is fre inteir.

18 *Detein the in suspence.* Compare MQ 46, l. 79: 'So thocht ȝe seme a sessioun in suspence'.

35–36 *Thocht Fortune be thy fo / hir frowning sall not lest.* Fortune appears to be personified here, though not at l. 47. Also compare MQ 46, l. 70: 'In frowning Fortoun nane I find to fit'.

45 *for tyme thy treuth sall try.* Compare Montgomerie, 'Evin dead, behold I breath', l. 37: 'ȝit tyme sall try my Treuth'; and his 'If faithfulnes suld friendship find', l. 8: 'Sen tym hes tryde my treuth'. Also see MQ 72, l. 18.

48. Declair ȝe bankis of Helicon

Where MQ 47 focused on the freedom of the heart, the narrator of this love complaint voluntarily surrenders his heart to the captivity of his peerless beloved as her 'wofull woundit prisoneir' (l. 121, compare MQ 39, l. 3). The style of the poem is characterised by hyperbole and formulaic diction. The descriptive imagery used of the lady's beauty, especially that of precious stones, expensive materials and flowers, and the classical allusions, strongly recall MQ 38, MQ 39 and MQ 40. This sophisticated stanza form (14 lines with end and internal rhyme in two of these) is also used in a poem in the Bannatyne Manuscript, 'Ane ballat of the creatioun of the warld man, his fall, and redemptioun maid to the tone of the bankis of helecon' (fols 12–14v) which is attributed there to Richard Maitland, but which does not appear in MQ or MF (see Appendix 1 for text and commentary and for discussion, MacDonald 2001, p. 138, Shire 1969, pp. 34–7 and pp. 165–73). The text is set out here in line with conventional treatments of the Helicon stanza, and thus slightly amending the manscript layout, which does not preserve the internal rhyme in the eleventh and thirteenth lines.

Like MQ 40, this text was designed for a musical setting. The text is unique though the song and its associated stanza form seem to have been well known in England and Scotland. The music is attributed to Andro Blackhall. See Elliott and Shire 1957, pp. 170–71, 214. The stanza form was used for varied subject matters, including political poems such as *Ane Ballat of the Captane of the Castell*, c.1571 (see Cranstoun ed. 1891–93, I, pp. 174–79) and love poems such as Montgomerie's *The Cherrie and the Slae*. MQ 40 is thus included in Montgomerie's canon by Cranstoun ed. 1887, I, pp. 274–78.

The poem is copied in an italic script.
Stanza: aa^{4}b^{3}cc^{4}b^{3}dede^{4}fghg^3.
Text: MQ fols 74v–78.
Authorship: uncertain.
Date: uncertain.

Commentary

1 *Helicon*. Mount Helicon, in Boeotia, the location of the sanctuary of the muses, and so associated with poetic skill and inspiration. See, for example, Ovid *Met.* 5, ll. 233–352.

2 *Pernassus hillis*. Parnassus, a sacred mountain. Ovid *Met.* 2, l. 221.

3 *fontaine Caballein*. Hippocrene, the spring on Helicon which was struck by Pegasus from the hillside, and which became an inspiration for poets. Compare MQ 68, ll. 21–24.

4 *muses*. The daughters of Jupiter and Memoria or Zeus and Mnēmosynē, who presided over the arts and learning. See Henryson, *Orpheus and Eurydice*, ll. 29–63.

19 *the aperse*. The paragon. Compare Henryson, *Testament of Cresseid*, ll. 78–79: 'O fair Creisseid, the flour and A per se / Of Troy'.

20 *peirles perle*. Formulaic, compare MQ 40, l. 3.

29 *Apelles*. The painter (who lived in Colophon in the 4th century BC), who painted Aphrodite, among other subjects.

44–45 *Quhen the thrie goddessis did stryve, / And Paris wes maid iudge*. Paris is asked to judge which one of the three goddesses, Hera (Juno), Athena (Minerva) and Aphrodite (Venus), is the most beautiful. Aphrodite promises him Helen and so he chooses her above the others. Ovid, *Heroides* 16.

46–47 *Fals Helene, Menelaus maik, / Had neuer caused King Priamus wraik*. Helen was wife of Menelaus, brother of Agamemnon. The kidnapping of Helen by Paris began the Trojan war. See Ovid *Met.*12, and *Heroides* 16 and 17.

51 *Paris, Priamus sone*. Paris was the son of Priam king of Troy.

57 *Phoebus*. The sun.

61 *Hir lippis and cheikis pumice fret*. The sense is that her lips and cheeks shine as if rubbed with pumice.

73 *Sirens songe*. The song of sea songstresses who lure sailors to their death with their beautiful music.

89 *As dees, and Dame Bewteis air*. 'As goddess and heir of Dame Beauty'. For the personification of beauty, compare Dunbar's *The Goldyn Targe*, l. 146; 'Sen that I am a presoneir', l. 104.

99 *Titan*. The sun.

108 *To bind it in hir bandis*. The heart is to be bound in the lady's chains, or authority. Compare Dunbar, 'Sen that I am a presoneir', ll. 3–4: 'I me commend … / In till hir bandoun for to rest'.

121 *wofull woundit prisoneir*. The scenario is conventional but compare Dunbar, 'Sen that I am a presoneir', l. 32: 'Wo is a wofull presoneir'.

131 *pay me hame againe.* See *DOST, Pay,* v. Sense 2 'beat me home again', 'punish me'.

141 *trew amitie.* Compare MQ 38, l. 101, and MQ 49, l. 72.

49. As Phoebus in his spheris hicht

This poignant poem begins in the mode of a conventional love poem (see MQ 38, 40, 48) with the praise of a peerless lady. It is, however, the address of one woman to another. The speaker's sex is explicitly identified at ll. 41–44. The poem celebrates female friendship, which it regards as a 'perfyt amitie' (l. 72) for its basis in virtue and its constancy. Classical and biblical examples of devoted friends, companions and helpmeets, including husbands and wives and siblings, are adduced by the narrator (that of Ruth and Naomi being the only female pair), but she insists that the relationship between her and the lady addressed has the potential to transcend even these famous relationships in quality and endurance. Indeed, this is more than a friendship poem, for the speaker desires the ability to legitimise her love, wishing for a physical metamorphosis into a man, the union of marriage, and reward in heaven for fidelity. Some of the language used has erotic overtones. See Farnsworth 1996, pp. 62–64. Although the narrator concedes that nature and fortune stand in the way of her happiness with her beloved, the conclusion of the poem shows her resolve to persist in their exemplary love.

Examples of poems on idealised friendship are common, and Scottish analogues may be found in the poems of John Stewart of Baldynneis (for example, 'To his Rucht Inteirlie Belowit Freind'). Those between female friends are rarer, though near-contemporary examples can be found (see Stevenson and Davidson, eds 2001, pp. 4–5). Some of these examples are authored by women, such as the sonnets of Laudomia Forteguerii (1515–1555?), but some are definitely by men. Both Pierre de Ronsard and Pontus de Tyard, whose works were certainly known to Montgomerie, composed love elegies addressed by one woman to another (see Dunnigan 1997, p. 30; Dunnigan 2005, pp. 447–49; Lyall 2005, p. 90; Borris ed. 2003, pp. 322–24; also discussed by Mueller 1992, p. 111). It is thus not impossible that MQ 49 was composed by a male poet and ventriloquises the female voice. However, the poem is unattributed in MQ: that it may be addressed to or even composed by Marie Maitland is considered by Farnsworth 1996, p. 58. Also see Stevenson and Davidson ed. 2001, pp. 96–98; Borris ed. 2003, pp. 295–97; and compare MQ 85 and MQ 68. On expressions of lesbian

EXPLANATORY NOTES

desire in early modern British writing, see Andreadis 2001, and on MQ 49 in particular, see pp. 62–63.
Stanza: ababbcbc⁴.
Text: MQ 78v–79v.
Authorship: uncertain.
Date: uncertain.

Commentary
1 *Phoebus*. The sun

2 *the kaip Crepusculein*. 'The cloak of twilight'. See *DOST*, *Crepusculine*, n.

3 *Phoebe*. The moon.

4 *madame*. This respectful term of address may suggest that the narrator's beloved is of high rank, but not necessarily that she is married. See *DOST*, *Madam(e)*, n. Contrast Farnsworth 1996, p. 60.

8 *Pallas*. The Greek name for Minerva, who was associated with wisdom and creative skills. See MQ 35, l. 107 and note, and MQ 69, l. 59 (a poem addressed to Marie Maitland). Farnsworth suggests this line 'contains a reference, in the choice of the name 'pallas' rather than Athena, to the goddess's childhood friendship with the maiden, Pallas' (1996, p. 60).

25–26 *Perithous / To Theseus*. Pirithous the Lapith, son of Zeus and Dia, and close friend of Theseus. Theseus helped him fight the Centaurs in his quest to win Persephone. See Ovid *Met.* 12.

27 *Nor, till Achilles, Patroclus*. Patroclus, the personal attendant and friend, and in some sources lover, of Achilles. See Hammond and Scullard 1970, pp. 4–5.

28 *Pilades to trew Orest*. Pylades was the friend and helper of Orestes, son of Agamemnon. Hammond and Scullard 1970, p. 755. The example of this friendship is adduced in Ronsard's *Elegy* (1565). See Borris ed. 2003, p. 333.

29–30 *Not 3it Achates luif to lest / To gud Aenee*. Achates was the faithful friend of Aeneas, mentioned often in Virgil's *Aeneid*. This example of friendship is used in de Tyard's *Elegy for One Woman Enamored with Another* (1573). See Borris ed. 2003, p. 330.

31 *Dauid to Ionathan profest*. Jonathan was son of Saul and protector and faithful friend of king David of the Old Testament (1 Samuel 19: 1–7). For David's lament for Jonathan, see 2 Samuel 1: 25–27.

32 *Titus trew to kynd Iosip.* The emperor Titus, AD 79–81. Iosip is Josephus, priest and Pharisee and commander of Galilee. He was captured in the siege of Jotapata, and when released became a friend of Titus and was made a citizen of Rome. Hammond and Scullard, p. 565.

33–34 *Nor ȝit Penelope, I wis, / So luiffed Vlisses.* Penelope was faithful to Ulysses during his long absence at Troy. See MQ 35, l. 182; Ovid, *Heroides* 1.

35–6 *Ruth, the kynd Moabitis, / Nohemie.* Ruth, the Moabitess, of the Old Testament Book of Ruth, who cared for Naomi, her widowed mother-in-law.

37–40 *Portia ... Brutus.* Portia was wife of Brutus. She took her life, following Brutus's exile from Rome and death at the battle of Actium, by inhaling fumes from a brazier.

41 *michtie Ioue.* God (the highest deity in Roman mythology).

42 *Brutus pairt.* Farnsworth 1996, p. 64, argues that 'pairt' may be glossed as 'penis' as well as 'role', though I do not find this convincing. See *DOST, Part,* n. especially senses 2b and 7a.

43 *metamorphosing our schap.* Farnsworth convincingly suggests that this may be a reference to the Ovidian myth of Iphis and Ianthe (Ovid *Met.* 9, ll. 666–797). Farnsworth 1996, pp. 58, 64–5.

48 *the band of Hymen.* Hymen or Hymenaeus is the deity associated with marriage, invoked at Greek weddings.

50 *Pollux and Castoris.* Twin sons of Zeus, renowned for bravery and loyalty to each other. On the death of Castor, Pollux asked to be allowed to die and Zeus granted that the brothers were united, spending alternate days in Heaven and in Hades. They became the constellation Gemini.

50. Lord God, how lang will this law lest

This poem returns to themes explored by Maitland throughout his poetic career, such as the iniquity of the oppression of the poor, the wrongful acquisition of land and failures of the justice system to protect those in need. Like many of Maitland's poems it is confident in the ultimate triumph of God's justice. The poem is also connected to Maitland's family troubles, principally the confiscation of Lethington in 1571 by a parliament of the King's Party (compare MQ 20 and MQ 26), and it contains a plea for the return of unjustly seized lands, warning that the

transgressors cannot escape God's punishment. It is closely related in theme to MQ 51.
Stanza: aaa⁴baab².
Text: MQ fols 80–81, MF pp. 350–51, R fols 50–50v; D fols 43v–45v.
Authorship: attributed to Richard Maitland.
Date: c.1571?

Commentary

1 *this law.* The 'body of statutory or customary law of a state or community' (*DOST*), rather than one particular law or act.

3 *Of [hous] and landis dispossest.* Though general, this reference may also pertain to the loss of Lethington in 1571.

10 *Sum in the sessioun lyis our lang.* The Court of Session, the supreme civil court. See MQ 51 (and headnote) on the delays in getting cases heard in the court.

15 *Be mein of court sum gettis land.* Perhaps a reference to the parliament of the King's Party, presided over by Lennox, held in the Canongate of Edinburgh in May 1571, at which Maitland's sons were forfeited. Lethington was handed over to one of the Regent Morton's supporters, David Hume of Fishwick.

51. Sair is the recent murmour and regrait

This poem represents the complaint of the whole community against the state of the Court of Session, the wealthy resenting the cost of pursuing a case, and the poor lamenting the fact that the law does not alleviate their suffering. The overburdening of the court, and consequently the length of time taken to bring cases to their conclusion, is of particular concern to the narrator. He urges the reader to appeal to the king to appoint worthy judges to the Court of Session and to petition the 'College of Justice' (the body of judges who sit on the Court of Session) to ensure that justice is furthered without delay. The narrator also appeals to the king's self-interest, reminding him of the need to have an effective system of justice if he is to keep his crown, and requesting an increase in the number of qualified judges. Maitland's own experience of the justice system, as a Court of Session judge from 1553 to 1584, is surely reflected in the poem. Other themes, including the protection of the poor, and of personal property and land, are typical of Maitland's poems.

The poem is difficult to date precisely, though given its address to James VI at l. 51 it is likely to date from after the defeat of the Queen's Party in 1573. The narrator seems to regard James's kingship as still precarious (he did not reach minority until c.1584/5; compare MQ 30, l. 85 and MQ 59, l. 13). Complaints against the inefficient or unjust workings of the Court of Session among parliamentary records suggest that problems such as those enumerated in Maitland's poem were widely recognised. See *RPS* 1579/10/54 and *RPS* 1579/10/55. With its direct addresses to the king as 'Sir' at ll. 61 and 71, the poem shows the influence of Dunbar's addresses to James IV. See note to ll. 61–62.

The poem is discussed by Martin 2013a, p. 70.

Stanza: aabab[5].
Text: MQ fols 81–82v, MF pp. 351–54, D fols 45v–47v.
Authorship: attributed to Richard Maitland.
Date. after 1573, c.1579?

Commentary

4 *the Lordis of the Sait*. The Court of Session or College of Justice, established by James V in 1531–32, dealt with all civil cases. It consisted of fifteen senators appointed by the king, as well as four additional 'extraordinary' lords of Session (a position held by Maitland from 1561). See Lee 1959, pp. 8–9; Donaldson 1965, pp. 46–48; Goodare 2004, pp. 160–63.

16–17 *Sum gevis the wyit that thair is on the sessioun / Sum not sa cunning, nor of sa gud discretioun*. Compare ll. 58–60 and note. Complaints about quality of the judges appointed to the Court of Session, both in terms of their moral worth and appropriate training, were made elsewhere. See, for example, *RPS* 1579/10/55.

22 *the prince*. James VI.

27 *that senat*. The College of Justice. See note to ll. 4 and 31 and *DOST*, *Senat(e)*, sense 1d.

31 *Colledge of Iustice*. The judges who make up the Session, Scotland's highest civil court. See note to l. 4 and headnote.

51 *Our souuerane lord*. Compare Maitland's opening address to James in MQ 59.

59 *Of senatouris men, cunning and godlie*. Compare *RPS* 1579/10/55: 'our said soverane lord sall presentt and nominat ... ane man that feiris God, of gude literature, undirstanding of the lawes, of gude fame...'.

61–62 *Sir, at thy gift is monye abeceis, / Personagis, provestreis, and prebendareis*. The phrasing and alliterative listing in this line is reminiscent of Dunbar's technique in 'Schir, ȝe haue mony seruitouris'. Crown patronage had extended to certain valuable church appointments since 1487, and this arrangement increased in 1560. Maitland recommends that this is controlled so that the Church, 'the auld fundatioun' (l. 65), also can maintain some revenue. The 1561 *First Book of Discipline* also complained about the avarice of lords and lairds who took over ecclesiastical estates and incomes and the impact this had on the care of the poor (Brown 2000, p. 44; Donaldson, 1970, pp. 131–32; also see Donaldson 1965, p. 4; Wormald 1981, p. 127).

63 *auld religioun*. The unreformed faith of pre-1560.

66–67 *Becaus the lordis hes our litill feis,/ Bot of vncertaine casualiteis*. The narrator comments on the pressures experienced by the nobility in maintaining their income. A 'fe' is a remuneration of some sort, and a 'casualite' is defined by *DOST* as a 'casual or incidental item of income or revenue', especially 'a payment due from a tenant or vassal in certain contingencies'. See *DOST*, *Fe*, n., and *Causalite*, n.; Brown 2000, pp. 41–46.

69 *sic derth*. Harvest failure and food shortages were a common feature of contemporary Scotland. See MQ 12, l. 7 and note.

70 *That coist ane pound befoir now coistis thrie*. The crown experienced grave financial problems as a result of the civil war and from c.1570 onwards Scotland's currency suffered debasement, and inflation was high. See Lee 1959, p. 131; Stewart 1955, pp. 91–104; Goodare 2004, p. 268.

77 *to gang the narest gait*. Idiomatic. The sense is 'to take the most direct way [to justice]'. See *DOST*, *Gate*, n. sense 4.

52. This warld so fals is, and vnstabill

This poem rehearses a popular theme in MQ and in early modern British poetry more generally – the nature of friendship, especially in court contexts. Maitland considers bonds of 'kyndnes' (kinship or amity) with one's social superiors, neighbours and (humorously) even with lovers, and demonstrates the perceived importance of personal relationships and connections for security of standing and possessions (Wormald 1981, p. 154). Compare MQ 17 (ll. 14–24), MQ 23 and MQ 28 (all attributed to Maitland), and the headnotes to these poems, as well as a later series of friendship poems in the MS, MQ 75–80.

The ending is characteristic of Maitland's poems, turning the reader away from troublesome worldly affairs to faith, and in this case God's 'perfyte kyndnes'. The poem is difficult to date, but lines 31–35 suggest that it was written in the context of Maitland family grievances, perhaps in the early 1570s.

Stanza: aabab[4].
Text: MQ fols 82v–83v, MF pp. 354–56, D fols 47v–48v.
Authorship: attributed to Richard Maitland.
Date: uncertain, possibly early 1570s.

Commentary

1 *This warld so fals is, and vnstabill.* Compare the opening of MQ 34, which draws attention to worldly mutability in similar terms. Also compare Dunbar's 'I seik aboute this warld onstable'.

3–4 *In all estaitis sic doubilnes / To find trew freindis few ar abill.* Compare MQ 17, ll. 15–16.

5 *auld kyndnes.* See headnote to MQ 23. The concept of 'kyndnes' embraces conduct based on gentility and consideration for others, as well as ties of kinship and friendship. See *DOST*, *Kind-*, *Kyndes*, n. sense 3.

6 *Thocht ȝe doe plesour to greit men.* The complaint turns to the abuses of clientage at court. Compare l. 41 and MQ 23 ll. 8–35.

7 *thay will ȝow scantlie ken.* Compare MQ 17, l. 22; MQ 23, ll. 12–21, 27.

16–20 This stanza is omitted in D.

18–19 *Venus game ... gang.* The idea of the lover being turned out of Venus's court, despite long service, recalls Gower's *Confessio Amantis*, VIII, ll. 2398–439. Scottish sources, including *The Spectacle of Luf*, may have mediated this image to Maitland. See Martin 2009, pp. 561–77. For similar self-deprecating comments in Maitland's verse concerning his persona's inadequacy at Venus's court, compare MQ 20, l. 24.

31 *court and sessioun.* The royal court and highest civil court. On the Court of Session see headnote to MQ 51.

53. Dreid God and luif him faythfullie

In MF, though not in MQ, this poem is given the title 'To be put in ony publict houss', suggesting an intended circulation beyond the Maitland household and circle. The MF version of the poem mentions 'the quein' (l. 5), so the poem probably predates 1568 and was revised for copying into MQ.

The moral advice given here is paternalistic and very characteristic of other short aphoristic works by Maitland (see MQ 15, MQ 32, MQ 33, MQ 54 etc.). Indeed, in the context of MQ many of the poem's lines appear highly formulaic in phrasing and can be paralleled in other poems by Maitland. The poem encourages in the reader a steadfast faith, self-governance, and attendance to public duties including care for the poor and peacemaking.

The poem is copied in an italic script.
Stanza: aaa^{4}b^{3}aaa^{4}b^3.
Text: MQ fols 83v–84, MF p. 32, D fols 48v–49.
Authorship: attributed to Richard Maitland.
Date: pre-1568, and later revised for inclusion in MQ.

Commentary
5 *ȝour prince*. The sovereign generally. However MF's reading 'quein', suggests revision to indicate James VI specifically. Compare MQ 54, l. 12.

17 *Keip ȝow fra prodigalitie*. Compare MQ 11, l. 20 and MQ 59, l. 21.

21 *Hant gud, and honest cumpanie*. Compare MQ 2, l. 76, MQ 15, l. 9, MQ 54, l. 22.

54. Ground the ay on gudnes

Like MQ 53, this poem is a series of moral aphorisms on self-rule and public duty. Its advice is underpinned by a reminder of the world's impermanence and the importance of faith. It refers to 'thy prince' at l. 12, and to the necessity of enduring troubles with patience (a common theme in Maitland's poetry), but is nonetheless difficult to date precisely. For theme and mode, compare MQ 15, MQ 17, MQ 32, MQ 33, MQ 53 etc.

This poem is copied in an italic script.
Stanza: aaa^{3}b$^{2?}$aaa^{3}b$^{2?}$.
Text: MQ fols 84v–85, MF p. 280, D fols 49–49v.
Authorship: attributed to Richard Maitland.
Date: uncertain.

Commentary

9 *In troubill tak patience.* Compare MQ 17, especially ll. 1–4.

12 *thy prince.* The sovereign generally, but probably James VI. See MQ 53 and note to l. 5.

55. Sum of the poetis and makeris that ar now

The misuse of language is a common theme in Maitland's poems (compare, for example, MQ 16, ll. 105–9). The poem is also close in theme to MQ 43, attributed to John Maitland. However, like Dunbar's 'Schir, I complane off iniuris', this poem is specifically a poet's complaint against the literary misconduct of other poets. In Maitland's poem the damage done by the 'makeris' (l. 1) and their slanderous texts is not to intellectual or creative property, as it is in Dunbar's complaint, but to reputation, especially that for honest and lawful conduct.

Maitland's objections are to the circulation of libellous 'balladis' (l. 6) in print: he may have had in mind Sempill's ballads, which were printed in Edinburgh by Robert Leprevik. Nevertheless, plenty of slanderous texts also circulated in manuscript, sometimes as a result of direct intervention to stop their print circulation (see Loughlin 1994, especially p. 235). The Maitlands suffered from the prevalence and virulence of civil war propaganda in both media (Loughlin 1994; Lyall 2005, p. 200; Dawson 2007, p. 279; Cranstoun ed. 1891–93, especially poem IX and XXII). William Maitland was a particular target because of his prominence in the Queen's Party, but his brothers and the Maitland family as a whole were often implicated in the charges made against him. For a list of poems from the civil war period and before which specifically ridicule William Maitland, see Loughlin 1994, p. 233. Despite this context, Maitland's poem is difficult to date, but invective directed at the Secretary was most plentiful in the early 1570s, and texts such as 'The Bird in the Cage' and 'The Cruikit Liedis the Blinde' date from the summer of 1570. For an earlier suggested date of composition (the 1550s), see Bain ed. 1830, p. 167.

Maitland's complaint against literary slander is concluded with an appeal for recantation and for different kinds of writing: he suggests that poetry should be morally edifying, even if it amuses or pleases the reader at the same time (a 'mirrie toy to gud purpoiss', l. 35). The poem is discussed in MacDonald 1972, p. 16; Loughlin 1994, pp. 236–37; Martin 2013a.

Stanza: pentameter rhyming couplets (aa^5).

EXPLANATORY NOTES

Text: MQ fols 85–85v, MF pp. 281–2, D fols 50–50v.
Authorship: attributed to Richard Maitland.
Date: early 1570s?

Commentary
7 *sclanderous wordes*. Compare Dunbar, 'Schir, I complane off iniuris', ll. 12, 17: 'crewall sclander seruis ded', 'Quhairin baithe sclander is and tressoun'.

10 *Accusand sum of improbabill crymis*. Defamatory writing aimed at William Maitland chiefly focuses on his political cunning (often said to be based on his knowledge of Machiavelli), changeability, and underhand tactics. He is also widely implicated in such texts in the murder of Darnley. See Loughlin 1994, p. 241; for poems satirising Maitland, see Cranstoun ed. 1891–93, I, pp. 128–64.

13 *bakbyteris and blasphemeris*. For complaints and warnings about backbiting in contemporary Scotland, see MQ 16, l. 29, MQ 59, l. 44.

19 *ʒe railleris*. Compare MQ 43, l. 23.

30 *it may cum to licht lang hes bene hid*. On the impossibility of hiding truth, despite the efforts of those who slander others, compare MQ 43, ll. 26–32.

34 *All vertew luif and all vycis repreif*. Formulaic, compare MQ 24, l. 15.

56. Of God the misknawlege

This short poem probably dates from the civil war of 1567–73 (see note to l. 9). Although its moral observations recall poems such as MQ 53 and MQ 54, it is more politicised than these poems and it catalogues the troubles and failings that bring about the downfall of nations. The poem is copied in an italic script
Stanza: six-syllable lines, rhyming couplets (aa³).
Text: MQ fol. 86, MF p. 282, D fols 50v–51.
Authorship: attributed to Richard Maitland.
Date: c.1567–73.

Commentary
9 *weir intestine*. Domestic conflict or civil war.

57. Gif thow desyire thy hous lang stand

This poem offers advice on ensuring the longevity of one's family line. It recommends piety, neighbourliness, and loyalty to the crown as ways of securing divine favour for one's progeny. The poem also emphasises the benefits for a family's stability and prosperity of its identification with a particular location across the generations. Pride in family and lineage is also expressed in MQ 46 and MQ 68. The poem is discussed in Martin 2013a.
Stanza: octasyllabic rhyming couplets (aa⁴).
Text: MQ fols 86–86v, MF pp. 282–83, D fols 51–51v.
Authorship: attributed to Richard Maitland.
Date: uncertain.

Commentary

2 *bruik thy land*. The idea of being able to enjoy the possession of one's lands was perhaps particularly poignant for Richard Maitland between 1571 and 1584 when Lethington was confiscated and inhabited by David Hume of Fishwick. See headnote to MQ 20. The enduring connection of a family and its lands is a major concern in his *History of the House of Seytoun*: 'his forbearis had brukit the said lands' (1829, p. 16).

4 *Intromet*. A legal term. See Maitland's *Practiques* in Sutherland ed. 2007, p. 28 (item 11); *DOST, Intromit*, v.

7 *Obey dewlie thy magistrat*. The sovereign or secular ruler (including the regent). Compare MQ 11, l. 33. In his *History of the House of Seytoun* (1559), Maitland stresses the obligations of families who received their lands from the monarch, especially that 'thair posteritie to be trew and thankfull servandis to thair superiouris' (1829, p. 10).

17 *Allya ay in sum gud place*. The Maitlands had been associated with their lands in Lethington, East Lothian, since the fourteenth century. The important connections between place and family identity are stressed by Maitland in his *History of the House of Seyton* (1829, pp. 15–16).

58. My lordis all, sen abstinence is taine

This poem is a cautious response to the end of hostilities between the parties of Mary and James in 1573, which came about as the result of the Pacification of Perth (February) and fall of Edinburgh Castle (May). The narrator exhorts the lords to put the needs of the commonwealth above their private concerns. For other addresses by Maitland to the nobility

during the civil war, reminding them of their duty and the consequences of their actions, see MQ 19, ll. 91–99; MQ 21, ll. 43–63; MQ 25; MQ 30, ll. 65–80. On the possibility of peace being established between the warring factions, see MQ 34, l. 21. The mode of address in this poem may also be compared to 'My lordis, now, gif 3e be wyse' (1567). See Cranstoun ed. 1891–93, I, pp. 46–51.
Stanza: ababbcc⁵.
Text: MQ fols 86v–87v, MF pp. 283–84, D fols 51v–52v.
Authorship: attributed to Richard Maitland.
Date: c.1573.

Commentary
1 *abstinence*. The truce between the factions of the civil war. See headnote. Also compare MQ 34, l. 21.

6 *Let neuer weir againe amang 3ow ryis*. A reference to the civil wars of 1567–73, which divided the nobility between the parties of James and Mary.

9 *men of weir the bandis*. Compare MQ 34, l. 9. Bands of troops, Scots sometimes with English support, roamed the countryside during this period and Maitland's own lands fell victim to their violence. See MQ 14 and headnote.

11 *thay that bruikis otheris mennis landis*. Perhaps a reference with personal resonance. Maitland's home of Lethington was inhabited by David Hume of Fishwick after its confiscation in 1571. See headnote to MQ 20. Also compare 'My lordis, now, gif 3e be wyse' (1567), ll. 81–82: 'For Godis saik, aboue all thing, / Keip clene 3our handis fra wrangus geir'.

21 *sa monye capitaines grew*. A 'capitaine' is a military leader (see *DOST*, *Capitane*, n.), but Maitland may have in mind the four regents of the civil war, Moray, Lennox, Mar and Morton.

47 *rasche-bus keip the kow*. A proverb on the cessation of cattle stealing (literally, 'the clump of rushes keep the cow'). Compare *Ane Tragedie in forme of ane Diallog betwix Honour, Gude Fame, and the Authour heirof in a Trance*: 'Than mycht the rasche bus keip ky on the Bordour' (l. 312) (Cranstoun ed. 1891–93, I, p. 91 (l. 312) and II, p. 72); Lyndsay *Complaynt*, ll. 407–8: 'Johne Upeland bene full blyith, I trow / Because the rysche bus kepis his kow' (see Hadley Williams ed. 2000, p. 54 and especially p. 236).

59. Our souuerane lord, into thy tender aage

This poem belongs to an established tradition of 'advice to princes' literature, and to a tradition of such writing in Scotland stretching from Walter Bower to David Lyndsay and John Bellenden that specifically addressed the subject of the king's self-governance during his minority. Several poems on kingship and minority are contained in MF, including the longest witness of *De Regimine Principum*.

In this poem Maitland regards the king's 'nonage' (l. 78) or minority as a dangerous time (compare MQ 51, l. 55). The main concerns of his address to James are with the king's need for wise counsel from expert counsellors, his obligation to live within his means, and to rule in peace. He also returns to themes which occur in many of his poems, including the administration of justice and protection of the poor. The rhyme scheme (ballat royal) adopted by Maitland is the same as that used in his celebration of Mary Queen of Scots' homecoming. Although the poem is conventional in style and content, some of Maitland's observations, especially those on James's finances, show an awareness of contemporary realities. Lines 47–54 may also refer discreetly to Maitland family difficulties. The poem and its literary background are discussed in Martin 2013a.

This is the only poem in MQ to be addressed in its entirety to James VI, though MQ 51 contains an appeal to James for the reform of the Court of Session and so shares this poem's concern with the crown's responsibility to ensure the efficient administration of justice. It is not possible to date the poem precisely, and like MQ 53 it may have been written earlier in Maitland's career for another monarch and revised for new circumstances. For other addresses to monarchs in MQ, see MQ 9 and MQ 10.

Stanza: ababbcbc[5].
Text: MQ fols 87v–89, MF pp. 363–65, R fols 54v–55 (lines 1–37 only), D fols 52v–54.
Authorship: attributed to Richard Maitland.
Date: c.1573.

Commentary

1 *tender aage*. A conventional phrase drawing attention to the vulnerability of the young. It was often used of the youth of monarchs. See *DOST*, *Tendir*, adj. David Lyndsay describes James V as a 'chylde of tender aige' (l. 140) in *The Complaynt*. Bellenden's The *Proheme apon the Cosmographe* (c.1531) describes the narrator's service to 'his grace in yeiris tenderest'. See Watson ed. 1943, pp. 3–31. Also see Stewart's 'Precelland prince haueand prerogative', l. 9: 'And sen thou standis in till so tendir age' (in MF pp. 328–9).

2 *Lerne to serue God, him luif aboue all thing.* Compare *De Regimine Principum* (MF pp. 96–105), l. 125: 'luif weill thy god and serve him'; and Stewart's 'Precelland prince haueand prerogative', l. 4: 'luif thi god aboue all eirdlie thing'.

3 *Thy counsell cheis of gud men, iust and sage.* Compare *De Regimine Principum*, l. 51: 'Thow suld gar cheis the counsale þat war wyse' (MF text).

4 *expert.* It is essential for the king in his minority that his counsellors are 'expert', skilled and experienced (*DOST, Expert,* a.). The adult king may ideally be expected to exercise his own wisdom and experience in governance, as well as listening to the counsel of others. See 'Excelland michtie prince and king' in MF (pp. 183–5), l. 57: 'Quhairfoir sen thow art so expert'.

7 *Vertew to luif.* Compare *De Regimine Principum*, l. 138: 'Hald vertew in thy hart gif thow be wyss'.

21 *vse na prodigalitie.* Conventional, compare MQ 11, l. 20

23–26 *Now in thy ȝouth ... sa greit ane rent.* James inherited grave financial problems as a result of the fiscal mismanagement of Mary's reign and the civil war. According to Gordon Donaldson the crown had a debt of £37,000 in 1574, and an Act of Parliament of 1575 pronounced it 'unable on the present rents thereof to sustain even now the estate of our sovereign lord and public charges of the realm, much less to bear out his majesty's estate and expenses at his more mature and perfect age' (Donaldson 1965, p. 169; *RPS* A1575/3/8).

31 *taxatioun nor stent.* 'Stent' is defined in *DOST* either as an assessment for the purposes of taxation or as a monetary 'exaction imposed by an authority'; an '*ad hoc* tax imposed by the burgh or craft upon those liable for payment'. See *DOST, Stent,* n. sense 3. There were some large taxes demanded during the minority period (see *RPS*, 1570/10/1), although James's major increases in taxation took place in the 1580s and 1590s. On James's education in a king's financial responsibilities, see Cramsie 2002, pp. 13–21. For Maitland's pleas against high taxation, see MQ 4, l. 49, and MQ 21, ll. 29–30.

41–43 *vaine flatteraris ... commoun clatteraris.* Compare Dunbar, 'Schir, ȝe haue mony seruitouris', ll. 39–40: 'Fenȝeouris, fleichouris and flatteraris, / Cryaris, craikaris and clatteraris'. Also Lyndsay, *Testament of the Papyngo*, l. 'fenyeit fulis and flatteraris /... / 'Pandaris, pykthankis, custronis, and clatteraris' (ll. 388–90, part of the Papyngo's Epistyl to 'hir Brether of Courte'). A 'clatterar' is an idle gossiper. See *DOST*, l. *Clatterar, Clattirer*, n. 390. See MQ 11, ll. 11, 69, for Maitland's advice to his son not to be a 'fein3it flatterar' or 'clatterar' at court.

44 *backbyteris.* Compare Dunbar's 'Off Februar the fyiftene nycht', ll. 43–54. On this subject also see MQ 16, MQ 43, l. 35 and MQ 55, l. 13.

49–56 *sclaunderit men ... to lie.* On the dangers of slander compare MQ 43 and MQ 55, ll. 7–8. See headnotes to these poems.

56 *tratling.* Idle prattle or gossip. See *DOST, Tratling -yng*, vbl. n. Compare Lyndsay's *Ane Satyre*, where Diligence begs Folie to 'let allane thy trattilling' (l. 4427).

63 *quhen thow comis to maioritie.* Compare MQ 19, in which Maitland worries that there will be little left of Scotland after the civil wars to sustain the adult James when he enters his majority (ll. 91–99).

60. Ane Exclamatioun Maid In England Vpon The Delyuerance Of The Erle Of Northumberland Furth Of Lochlevin, Quho Immediatlie Thairefter Wes Execute In 3orke

Rubric] not in L.

This is the first of three poems in MQ on the subject of the Scottish surrender of the exiled rebel Thomas Percy, seventh earl of Northumberland (1528–72) to the English in 1572. Percy had sought refuge in Scotland following the Northern Rising of November 1569 against Elizabeth. He found short-lived protection with the Armstrongs of Liddesdale (see headnote to MQ 3), before being betrayed by them, and was arrested by the Regent Moray in December 1569. He was then imprisoned at Lochleven, and used as a negotiating tool in Anglo-Scottish relations by Mar, who was dependent on English support for his regency. Percy was 'sold' to the English on 6 June 1572 and executed in August 1572.

The poem denounces Scottish duplicity and greed, while MQ 61 and 62 answer these charges by laying blame on individual Scots only, members of the King's Party, rather than on the whole nation (see ll. 23–24 of this poem). The poem is indeed of English origin, as the manuscript title claims, and appears in English orthography in Society of Antiquaries of London, MS 87, 'Papers concerning Thomas Randolph', notary and diplomat (see Willets 2000, p. 41). The poem may have been composed between the surrender and execution of Northumberland. See note to l. 87. It is likely that the author was not so much sympathetic to Percy's rebellion (see l. 85), as pleased with the fact that it provided an opportunity to write against the Scots.

For another English invective, see Henry Singleton's *Copie of a Ryme* (c.1572), which also denounces the Scots (including Douglas and Lochleven) for their betrayal of Percy in return for 'Englishe golde', and characterises the nation as a whole as untrustworthy. According to the manuscript note, Singleton, a Lancashire man, was a recusant prisoner. The poem is in London, BL, Cotton Caligula, B. iv, fols 247–247v. See Wright ed. 1838, I, pp. 432–34.

The manner of the transmission of the poem from England to Scotland is not clear. However, the English version's apparent association with Randolph, may provide a partial explanation. Randolph had a long involvement in Scottish affairs, and dealings with William Maitland. See Martin and McClune 2009, p. 249; Martin 2012; Blakeway 2014. However, more research is needed into the provenance Society of Antiquaries of London, MS 87. The text is previously edited by Cranstoun ed. 1891–93, I pp. 240–43, II, pp. 162–66. On English writing in response to the Northern Rising and the Scottish treatment of Percy, see Lowers 1953, especially pp. 147–49.

Stanza: ababcc⁴.

Text: MQ fols 89v–91; Society of Antiquaries of London, MS 87, fols 47v–48 [L].

Authorship: unattributed.

Date: June to August 1572.

Commentary

31 *Iudus pairt*. The archetypal betrayer, Judas Iscariot, one of the twelve disciples. Judas 'sold' Christ for thirty pieces of silver (Matt 26: 14–16). Compare MQ 16, ll. 41–42, and MQ 62, l. 97.

32 *Pylatis iudgmentis*. Pontius Pilate, procurator of Judea and chief justice. His bad judgement was his decision to hand Christ to the Jews, even though he found no fault with him. Compare MQ 16, ll. 17, 65–66.

39 *Ane baneist lord*. Percy.

47 *Murray, Mortoun, and Ruthvenis caice*. James Stewart, earl of Moray, was given English sanctuary in October 1565, after opposing Mary's marriage to Darnley, and returned to Scotland in March 1566 just after David Riccio, Mary's secretary, was murdered. James Douglas, earl of

Morton, and Patrick third lord Ruthven were given refuge in England following Riccio's murder.

48 *For slauchter in thair princis place.* This refers to the implication of Moray, Morton and Ruthven in the murder of David Riccio at Holyroodhouse on 9 March 1566.

53 *vnder colour thay pretendit.* 'Under false pretences'.

55–60 The sense is 'if an error is so great a sin as to deserve the same punishment as disobedience; if no refuge can be found, the penitent will die for want of help'. Also glossed by Cranstoun ed. 1891–93, II, p. 163.

65 *ȝow ar so gredie on Englisch gold.* Moray had depended on English help during his regency and secured a subsidy of £5,000 in 1569. His arrest of Northumberland was unavoidable given his and the King's Party's need for English assistance.

75 *The gold ȝe gat.* Elizabeth paid around £2,000 for securing the return of Northumberland from the Scots. Locke *ODNB*.

81 *one lord.* The reference is to the Charles Neville, sixth earl of Westmorland, who first took refuge with Sir Thomas Ker, laird of Ferniehirst, Roxburghshire, and then fled to the Netherlands, and so escaped punishment for his part in the Northern Rising.

86 *am I glaid we have the man.* This suggests that the poem predates Northumberland's execution on 23 August 1572.

90 *our Quene.* Elizabeth I, against whom Northumberland had rebelled, with the earls of Norfolk (Thomas Howard) and of Westmorland (Leonard Dacre), and Richard Norton and Thomas Markenfield.

61. The Answeir to the Englisch Ballad.

'The Answeir to the Englisch Ballad' is a careful response to MQ 60. It uses the same stanza form and provides a comprehensive rebuttal of the charges laid out there, reminding us that Northumberland's extradition was unpopular among many Scots, partly on the grounds that there was a widely held belief that political exiles should be afforded proper protection in their chosen place of sanctuary (see Lee 1953, p. 270). The poem is also a contribution to the large body of propaganda written by both factions in the civil war. It is strongly condemnatory of prominent members of the King's Party and their conduct in the Northumberland affair. The narrator insists that only those directly implicated in the political bargaining over Northumberland should bear the blame for his fate, and that the Scots nation cannot be accused of the crimes outlined in the English invective. The poem is previously edited in Cranstoun ed. 1891–93, I, pp. 244–47, II, pp. 164–66. See Blakeway 2014.

The poem is unattributed in MQ, but verbal similarites with MQ 62 may suggest a common authorship. MQ 62 is sometimes attributed to John Maitland. See headnotes to MQ 62.

Stanza: ababcc⁴.
Text: MQ fols 91v–93.
Authorship: unattributed.
Date: c.1572.
Commentary

7 *playit Iudas pairt*. An echo of MQ 60, l. 31.

8 *selling gud Northumberland*. Thomas Percy was 'sold' to the English on 6 June 1572.

13 *Mar*. John Erskine, earl of Mar, and regent of Scotland from 3 September 1571 to 28 October 1572. Mar is addressed in MQ 44.

14 *Mortoun and Lochlevin*. William Douglas of Lochleven was Percy's gaoler, and the main financial beneficiary of Northumberland's return to the English. His cousin James Douglas earl of Morton seems to have actually opposed the surrender of Percy (see Lee 1953, pp. 270–71; Locke *ODNB*).

15 *Mackgill and Orknay*. Sir James Mackgill (d.1579), of Nether Rankeillour, Lord Clerk Register, and Adam Bothwell (1529–93), bishop of Orkney, both prominent members of the king's party. In 1571 Mackgill had been to England with Morton to ensure Mary's ongoing detention.

16 *Cleisch*. Robert Colville, Laird of Cleish.

17 *Dumfermling that the py prepaird*. Robert Pitcairn, Commendator of Dunfermline, Secretary and member of the King's Party. In 1571 he was involved in negotiations with and missions to England aimed at gaining English military support. The idiomatic phrase 'the py [pie] prepaird', 'made the plans', suggests plotting or underhand machinations. See *DOST*, *Py*, n. sense 2.

18 *lowse Lindsay*. Patrick Lord Lindsay of the Byres (d.1589) had fled to England following his involvement in the murder of Riccio. He was a prominent member of the King's Party and took an active military role in the civil war (Sharon Adams *ODNB*). On his reputation for an unprincipled nature, see Cranstoun ed. 1891–93, II, p. 164.

21 *these twa Douglassis.* See note to l. 14.

31–32 *King Hareis money ... / Our cardinall to keip in hauld.* George Douglas of Pittenreich, father of Morton, was involved in the arrest of Cardinall Beaton, archbishop of St Andrews, in January 1543. An anglophile and Protestant, he had been in exile in England between 1529 and 1543, and was a supporter of Henry VIII's plans for an Anglo-Scottish alliance. See Donaldson, 1965, pp. 64–65.

43 *Ganȝelon.* Ganelon, betrayer of Charlemagne in 'matter of France' texts. He is mentioned in Rolland's *Court of Venus* (Book II, ll. 273–81) and in 'The Bird in the Cage', l. 21 (Cranstoun, ed. 1891–93), I, p. 161.

46 *tred.* The poet picks up the vocabulary of MQ 60, l. 10.

49 *Henrie the sext.* Following the Battle of Towton in 1461, Henry VI and his queen, Margaret, and their son, Prince Edward, fled to Scotland and were given refuge by Mary of Guelders. They remained in Scotland until 1463. See Wolffe 1981/2001, pp. 333–37.

55 *This lordis wyfe ... Lord Home.* Northumberland's wife had been left in the care of the Armstrongs, but after Percy's arrest was given refuge by Thomas Kerr of Ferniehurst and then by Alexander Hume. She attempted to secure her husband's release with money raised from Pope Pius and Philip of Spain.

56 *Leonard Dakeris.* Leonard Dacre was involved in the Northern Rising of 1569 and fled to the protection of Alexander Hume in Scotland.

61 *Erle of Sussix.* Thomas Radcliffe, third earl of Sussex, and Elizabeth's lieutenant in the north from 1568, and thus during the Northern Rising. He led raids into Scotland in the spring and summer of 1570 to pacify the Border; he was involved in negotiations with both the parties of the civil war, and exchanged letters with William Maitland. See MacCaffrey *ODNB*.

81 *fact.* The poet echoes the vocabulary of MQ 60, l. 87.

94 *to the scambillis sauld.* The sense is 'to betray', 'to lead to execution'. See *DOST*, *Scamel*, n. especially sense 5b. A 'scamel' is a meat or fish market. The phrase is also used in Henry Singleton's *Copie of a Ryme* (c.1572). See Wright ed. 1838, I, pp. 432–34: 'How they for money sold their gest / Unto the shambles like a beast'.

EXPLANATORY NOTES

62. Ane Schort Inveccyde Maid Aganis the Delyuerance of the Erle of Northumberland

This poem focuses on the role played by members of the Douglas family in the surrender of Thomas Percy, 7th earl of Northumberland. Like MQ 61, it also names other culpable members of the King's Party, including the Regent Mar, but it reserves much of its opprobrium for James Douglas, earl of Morton, and William Douglas of Lochleven. It also alludes to problematic episodes in the recent history of the Douglases and the tensions within the family. Blakeway (2014) has suggested that the poem may have been 'the work of a King's man seeking to distance himself and his closest political allies or patrons from a dishonourable decision' (p. 248), and may not be by the same author as MQ 61. However, there are some clear verbal similarities to MQ 61: see notes to lines 40, 63 and 99. Furthermore, both MQ 61 and MQ 62 invoke Douglas family history, drawing attention to the reputation of its members for greed. The poem is attributed to John Maitland by Bain (1830, pp. 173–74).

As well as attacking the conduct of the Douglases in the 'sale' of Northumberland, the poem praises Percy for his virtue and nobility (ll. 20–32). Stylistically, it is rhetorical, hyperbolic and characterised by emotive analogies: Percy is imaged as an ox prepared for slaughter (l. 117) and Lochleven as a dishonest merchant. It characterises the Douglases as a 'bludie clan' (l. 156) of butchers whose descendants will be ever cursed by their involvement in Percy's sale to the English. For another denouncement of the Douglas treatment of Percy, see the popular ballad, *Northumberland Betrayd by Dowglas* (Child no. 176, vol. 3, 1957, pp. 408–16).

The poem must have been written after August 1572, as it refers to Percy's 'murther' (l. 136). As well as being thematically linked to MQ 60 and MQ 61, its concern with family and inherited reputation may be compared to MQ 44, MQ 46 and MQ 57. It is included in Cranstoun ed. 1891–93, I, pp. 248–53.
Stanza: ababbcbc[5].
Text: MQ fols 93v–96v.
Authorship: the poem is unattributed. See headnote.
Date: after August 1572.

Commentary
9 '*Avoide', thay bid, 'Thay fals and filthie tratouris'*. Compare MQ 60, l. 64.

15 *inveccyde ballatis*. Poems such as MQ 60 or Henry Singleton's

Copie of a Ryme in Wright ed. 1838, I, pp. 432–34, or 'Northumberland Betrayed by Douglas' (Child no. 176). See Lowers 1953, p. 47.

24 *And have with mercye movit 3our mynd.* This line is defective metrically. Cranstoun amends it to 'And have with mercye movit [muche] 30ʳ mynd'.

30 *Sic hardines and hairt heroicall.* Formulaic epithets, but compare MQ 1, l. 2.

37 *first be ane theif.* Percy and his wife first sought refuge with John Armstrong, the notorious 'Jock of the Syde' (see MQ 3, l. 55). The earl then moved on to the household of Hector Armstrong of Harlaw. Both Armstrongs were Border rebels, who would have been referred to by contemporaries as 'thieves'. See headnote to MQ 3; Locke *ODNB*.

38 *Lochlevin.* William Douglas of Lochleven. See MQ 61, l. 14 and note.

40 *sauld him to the skambillis.* 'Sold him to the slaughter house'. Compare l. 117. Also see MQ 61 and note to l. 94.

47 *baid the hasard of the weir.* The sense is, 'Endured the hazards of the war'.

53 *Richard and Henrie the sext.* Wyntoun tells the story of the rumour of Richard II's escape to the 'Out Ilis of Scotlande' following his deposition and imprisonment in Pontefract Castle in 1399 (Book IX, chapter 18; see Armours ed. 1914, IV, pp. 390–91). One impersonator of the king, Thomas Ward of Trumpington, was paid by the Scottish court. See Saul 1997, p. 427; McNiven 1994, pp. 93–117; Strohm 1996, pp. 93–96. On Henry VI's exile in Scotland, see MQ 61, ll. 49–54 and note to l. 49.

56 *in Lochlevin.* Lochleven Castle, Fife, where Percy was incarcerated. Also see l. 84.

57 *Mar.* John Erskine, earl of Mar and Regent of Scotland. See MQ 61, l. 13 and note.

60 *McGill.* Sir James Mackgill (d.1579), of Nether Rankeillour. See MQ 61, l. 15 and note.

61 *Dumfermling.* Robert Pitcairn, Commendator of Dunfermline, Secretary and member of the king's party. See MQ 61, l. 17 and note.

63 *Lowse Lyndsay.* Patrick Lord Lindsay of the Byres (d.1589). See MQ 61, l. 18, where the same epithet is used for Lindsay.

73 *Lochlevin, that wes ay faithles to thy brother.* This suggests that William Douglas of Lochleven was faithless to Morton's brother. Morton was son of Sir George Douglas of Pittendriech, Master of Angus. He had an elder brother David, 7th earl of Angus, d.1557 (*Scots Peerage*, I, p. 193). According to Hume, he also had a natural brother, George Douglas of Parkhead (Reid ed. 2005, I, p. 129). Like earlier editors I have not been able to shed any light on this reference. See Cranstoun ed. 1891–93, II, p. 168; Pinkerton ed. 1786, p. 427.

77 *The air of Buchane.* Cranstoun identifies him as Robert Douglas, second brother to William Douglas of Lochleven, who married Christina, heiress of Buchan. William Douglas of Lochleven had the 'ward and marriage of the children of his brother, Robert, Earl of Buchan, in 1580' (*Scots Peerage*, 2, p. 268, and 3, p. 371).

84 *Quhen that the Quene wes in the Louche inclusit.* Mary Queen of Scots was imprisoned at Lochleven Castle from 15 June 1567 to 3 May 1568 when she escaped with the help of George Douglas, brother of the laird of Lochleven (see Wormald 1988, rev. 2001, p. 175).

91 *ane gasing-stok.* A 'gazing stock' or spectacle. *DOST* records this poem as the only instance of the compound. See *DOST, Gasing-stok*, n.

97 *Iudas, that sauld our saluiour to be slaine.* Judas Iscariot, who 'sold' Christ for thirty pieces of silver (Matt 26: 14–16). See MQ 60, l. 31 and note. See ll. 145–46 and note.

99 *Ganʒelon aganis Charles the Maine.* Ganelon, betrayer of Charlemagne. See MQ 61, l. 43 and note.

100 *Andro Bell, that wicked vyld outlaw.* Probably the legendary outlaw Adam Bell (see Cranstoun, ed. 1891–93, II, p. 169; Bawcutt, ed. 1998, p. 371), who is mentioned by Dunbar (as Allan Bell) in 'Now lythis off ane gentill knycht' (l. 29).

101 *the tratour, Eckie of the Hairlaw.* Hector Armstrong of Harlaw who helped Moray's men to capture Northumberland in December 1569 (see Locke *ODNB*).

113 *As metest merchand for ane maister-steik.* 'As the most fitting merchant for a master-work'. A 'maister-steik' is the work or 'masterpiece' made by a craftsman to demonstrate that he can become a master of his craft. See *DOST, Maister-, Master-stick* (etc.), n. Morton is a master of falsity: anti-mercantile satire often depicted merchants as dishonest. See Owst 1933, repr.1966, pp. 352–61. Also see Cranstoun ed. 1891–93, II, p. 129.

118–19 *Had Christ him self bene in Perseyis rowme / I wait ʒe wald haue playit Iudas pairt.* Compare MQ 16, which also compares the troubles of contemporary Scotland to the treacherous events surrounding the crucifixion.

120 *Cayphas*. Caiaphas, high priest, who presided over the trial of Christ (Matt 26: 3–4; John 18: 14). See MQ 16, l. 25 and note.

133 *Sen ȝe ȝour selfis wes in the samyn caice*. On the exile to England of Morton and Lochleven, see MQ 60, ll. 47–52, and note.

145–46 *The Iewis wald not put in thair commoun purs / The pryice of Christ*. See Matt 27: 6: 'And the chief Priests toke the siluer pieces, and said, It is not lawful for vs to put them into the treasure, because it is the price of blood' (Geneva Bible, 1560).

156 *thy bludie clan*. MQ 61, ll. 25–36, associates the Douglas family with avarice, rather than violence.

63. Ȝe hevinis abone with heavinlie ornamentis

This unique poem is attributed by the scribe of MQ to A[lexander] Montgomerie, poet and courtier (d.1598). For a critical biography, see Lyall 2005. The poem forms a pair with MQ 64. The subject of both is Montgomerie's kinswoman, Margaret (named in this poem at l. 8, and in MQ 64 at l. 8), the eldest daughter of Hugh Montgomerie, third earl Eglinton (d.1585). MQ 64 was written to celebrate her marriage to Robert Lord Seton (contracted 10 May 1582), a kinsman of Richard Maitland on his mother's side, so it is likely that MQ 63 is related to the same event, making both 'marriage poems' or *epithalamia*, a popular genre in the sixteenth and seventeenth centuries, and practised, for example, by James VI ('An epithalamion vpon the Marques of Huntlies mariage'). The narrator praises Margaret in terms familiar from contemporary love poems, using analogies of flowers, birds, light and precious stones, to describe her peerless beauty and virtue (see especially ll. 9–16 and compare MQ 39 and MQ 40). The classical analogies used give the poem erotic resonance. The poem ends with the narrator pledging Margaret his service in the manner of the courtly love complaint (ll. 47–48).

The anthologising of MQ 63 and 64 in MQ may be the result of the family connections between the Seton (and therefore Maitland) and Montgomerie families (see note to l. 46, and *Scots Peerage*, 3, pp. 438–40). In 1563 Eglinton received a commission of justiciary with the assistance of Maitland of Lethington (Simmons *ODNB*). He was loyal

EXPLANATORY NOTES

to Mary during the civil war, and his family and its concerns may have been known to the Maitlands as a result.

The poem is discussed by Lyall 2005, pp. 93–94 and Dunnigan 1999 pp. 65–67. It is previously edited in Cranstoun ed. 1887, pp. 216–17, and Parkinson ed. 2000, pp. 277–78 (poem 102).
Stanza: ababcbcbc^5.
Text: MQ 96v–97v.
Authorship: attributed to Alexander Montgomerie.
Date: c.1582.

Commentary

8 *The mundane mirrour of maikles, Margareit.* 'The earthly mirror of perfection, Margaret'. Compare MQ 64, l. 8, where the subject is named fully as Margaret Montgomerie.

14 *As A per C aboue all elevat.* Compare MQ 64, l. 3.

17–22 *Diana ... slippis.* The goddess Diana was often associated with chastity, and the poet appears here to be alluding to her reputation for bathing with her nymphs, away from prying eyes, in a woodland pool (Ovid *Met.* 3). Compare MQ 40, ll. 57–62 and note. Also see Douglas, *Palice of Honour*, ll. 319–36.

25 *The asteres.* The stars.

27 *Dame Phoebus.* The sun, here gendered female (see Parkinson, ed. 2000, II, p. 45). Compare MQ 40, ll. 50–55, and MQ 48, l. 57.

32 *hir goun.* Perhaps Margaret's bejewelled wedding gown. See Dunnigan 1999, p. 66. On the size of Margaret's dowry and the financial problems that followed the marriage when her father was unable to pay it, see Brown 2000, p. 146.

34–35 *Quhen Iupiter the schap of bull did tak / Befoir Europe.* Ovid *Met.* 2, ll. 833–75. Jupiter transforms himself into a gentle young bull so that he can kiss the hands of Europe, daughter of Agenor, when she feeds him, and be stroked by her. He abducts her when she becomes brave enough to ride on his back.

35 *his feit did fauld.* 'When he knelt down' or 'When he fell to his knees'. See *DOST*, *Fauld*, v. sense 1b.

41 *With goldin schouris, as he did Clemene.* Clymene was desired by Apollo, and bore a son, Phaethon, by him. Ovid *Met.* 1, ll. 765–72. There seems to be some confusion in the poet's mind between Clymene and Danae, who was visited in a shower of gold by Jupiter and impregnated (Ovid *Met.* 4, ll. 611, 6.113). See Parkinson ed. 2000, II, p. 168.

43–44 *the goddes Hemene / Quhilk to hir brother so happie fortoun gave.* Hymen is the god of marriage. The poet here may intend Hebe, daughter of Juno and wife of Hercules, who restored her brother's youth (see Parkinson, ed. 2000, II, p. 168). Ovid *Met.* 9, ll. 397–401.

46 *nobill bluid.* The earls of Eglinton were a powerful family in south-west Scotland. Margaret's mother was Margaret Drummond (c.1535–1590), daughter of Sir John Drummond of Innerpeffrey, and her paternal grandmother was Marion Seton. See headnote and compare MQ 64, l. 41.

47 *And of my self ane seruand scho sall have.* Compare MQ 64, l. 55.

64. Luiffaris, leif of to loif so hie

The poem, attributed by MQ's scribe to 'A.M' (Alexander Montgomerie, to whom MQ 63 is ascribed), begins by calling on lovers to cease describing their ladies as peerless, and to praise the only one who deserves that epithet, Margaret Montgomerie (named at l. 8). Margaret's marriage (to Robert Seton) is mentioned explicitly at ll. 47–48. In the manner of MQ 63, Margaret is praised for her noble blood and royal connections, but her good character is said to surpass all other gifts that she has. The narrator offers to serve Margaret's husband for her sake (contrast MQ 63, l. 47), on the condition that he proves himself to be a worthy match for her. He bids her farewell, wishing her good fortune in her married life. On the poem's genre, see headnote to MQ 63.

This poem may also be likened to MQ 39, MQ 40, and especially MQ 48, with which it has many verbal similarities in its depiction of idealised femininity.

The poem is discussed by Lyall 2005, pp. 93–94 and Dunnigan 1999, pp. 65–67. It is previously edited in Cranstoun ed. 1887, I, pp. 214–15, and Parkinson ed. 2000, I, pp. 278–80 (poem 103). Like MQ 63, the poem is not attested elsewhere.

Stanza: ababbcbc^4.
Text: MQ 97v–98v.
Authorship: attributed to Alexander Montgomerie.
Date: 1582.

Commentary

7 The line is metrically defective in MQ and 'perle' should presumably follow 'pereles'. See Craigie ed. 1920, p. 290. Compare MQ 48, l. 20: 'peirles perle preclair'. Also see MQ 39, l. 30; MQ 40, l. 3.

EXPLANATORY NOTES

9 *pereles pulchritud.* Compare MQ 48, l. 113.

10 *face angelicall.* Compare MQ 48, l. 71.

25 *Pigmalion.* Pygmalion is described here as a painter rather than a sculptor, which is how he appears in Ovid *Met.* 10, ll. 243–97. He falls in love with the ivory statue he has created of a beautiful girl, free from the imperfections of real women. The gods bring the statue to life in answer to his prayers. Compare MQ 48, ll. 29–42 and the example of Apelles.

31 *This fairer patrone.* Margaret is the pattern or exemplar of womanhood. Compare MQ 39, l. 30.

34 *Quhen Paris iudgit in Helicon.* The judgment of Paris, when he awards the golden apple to Venus, is usually located to Ida. See Parkinson ed. 2000, II, p. 169. Compare MQ 48 ll. 43–56.

36 *the goddessis.* Hera and Athena or Juno and Minerva. See MQ 48, ll. 44–45.

39 *goldin ball.* The golden apple awarded to Venus. See note to l. 34.

41 *Quhose nobill birth and royall bluid.* Compare MQ 63, l. 46 and see note. Margaret was the eldest daughter of Hugh, third earl Eglinton (head of an influential family in south-west Scotland), and his second wife, Agnes, daughter of Margaret Stewart and John Drummond of Innerpeffray. The royal connections came from Margaret Stewart, an illegitimate daughter of James IV (see *Scots Peerage*, 3, p. 441).

45 *As waill and wit of womanheid.* Compare MQ 39, l. 99.

49 *gud Hemene.* See MQ 63, l. 43 and note. Also see Montgomerie, 'Quhy bene ȝe Musis all so long' (ll. 67–68): 'Diana keeps this Margarit / Bot Hymen heghts to match hir meit' (on the marriage of Margaret Douglas to Robert Montgomerie of Skelmorlie in 1593).

65. With siching sad and surging sorrow soir

This poem is a dream vision with inset complaint. The vision is enigmatic and the narrator struggles to interpret it, but the disturbing content reflects his sorrow, the cause of which is not disclosed. Falling asleep in a state of distress, he sees a woman, apparently stricken by grief for a lost friend (see note to l. 110), and unable to come to terms with what she sees as her misfortunes. The figure describes her lost friend as wise and virtuous, and she associates him with justice and faith in particular (ll. 101–2), yet her grief for him is portrayed as excessive and that of the narrator more moderate and well governed. The narrator's attempts to counsel her fail. It is not clear whether the woman of the vision, her lost companion, or the narrator, are to be identified with any historical figures, though the association of the mourned friend with justice and faith is intriguing and may suggest that such an identification was intended. Pinkerton regarded the poem as having been written on the death of Richard Maitland. See Pinkerton ed. 1786, p. 428.

The distraught female complainant offering herself as a mirror or example of misfortune and misery, and also of self-reform, has an analogue in Henryson's *Testament of Cresseid*, ll. 452–69, *The Laste Epistle of Creseyd to Troyalus* (sometimes attributed to William Fowler) and Montgomerie's *A Ladyis Lamentatione*. Also see note to l. 6. For the narrator's attempts to counsel the lady, compare John Stewart of Baldynneis, 'To ane Honorabill and Distressit Ladie' (Crockett ed. 1913, pp. 110–12).

The poem's device of a supernatural encounter, in which a troubled figure offers herself or himself as an exemplum, may recall a legend associated with Gregory the Great's *The Trental of Saint Gregory* in which the Pope's mother returns from the dead to her son in a vision to confess to a terrible crime. The best-known example is The *Awntyrs off Arthure at the Terne Wathelyn* in which a hideous apparition of Guinevere's dead mother comes from purgatory to counsel her daughter (see Hanna, ed. 1974, pp. 24–32; Klausner, 1972, pp. 307–25). In the Scottish poem it is not clear that the woman is returning from the dead (see note to l. 51), there is no mention of purgatory or hell (probably indicating the poem's Post-Reformation origins), and the exact circumstances that produced the woman's grief are not clearly described. Nevertheless she regards herself as predestined (l. 122) to sorrow. The last stanzas of the poem make clear its Protestant context: the discussion of the 'elect' here may be compared to that in MQ 37, ll. 115–16, MQ 42, ll. 171–72 (both attributed to Alexander Arbuthnot in MQ), and MQ 46, l. 62 (with which the poem also shares a rhyme scheme). Stylistically these stanzas are the most distinctive and tightly organised part of the poem, with the last word of each line echoed in the next (*vers enchaînée / anadiplosis*). This section may be compared to MQ 42 ll. 175–76. On stylistic and thematic grounds Arbuthnot's authorship of the poem is possible (see Introduction).

Although the poem is unique, it shows several scribal errors (emendations are included in the textual notes, and significant errors are discussed below), including a number of imperfect rhymes. It is clear

therefore that it is copied into MQ from another source, and it is possible that this source was either corrupt or difficult to read.
Stanza: ababbcbc[5].
Text: MQ fols 98v–102.
Authorship: unattributed, but possibly by Alexander Arbuthnot?
Date: uncertain.

Commentary

6 *fair Venus, the bewtie of the nicht*. The planet Venus. Compare Henryson, *Testament of Cresseid*, l. 11: 'fair Venus, the bewtie of the nicht'.

11 *the raiging seyis gray*. The wild seascape of the vision is reminiscent of the waking seascape of the Prologue to Lyndsay's *Dreme*, especially ll. 113–45.

12 *Boreas*. The north wind. Compare MQ 44, l. 25.

13–16 *The thundring doun of cannounis ... monye a cruell crak*. Loud noises, such as that of cannon-fire, often wake dreamers from slumber in dream vision poems. Compare Dunbar's *The Goldyn Targe*, ll. 238–43 ('Thai fyrit gunnis ...', l. 238), and Lyndsay's *Dreme*, l. 1023–28: 'All hir cannounis sche leit craik of at anis ... haistalie I stert out of my dreme'.

19 *vaine wryteris*. Perhaps Pagan authorities. Compare MQ 42, l. 93.

29–30 *Creusa kynd to hir wes na compair, / Nor Phaetusa, nor murning Phaeton*. Creusa's ghost appeared in a dream to tell the grieving Aeneas of his future (*Aeneid* 2, ll. 770–84; compare Douglas *Eneados*, II, ch. 12, ll. 23–56); Phaeton, son of Helios and Clymene, was killed by Zeus and mourned by his sisters, the eldest of whom was Phaetusa (Ovid *Met*. 2, ll. 1–413). The mention here of Phaeton's mourning, though rather awkward, may be a reference to his remorse and panic when he realises his inability to control his father's chariot, which he so desired to drive.

40 *my cabinat*. The dreamer seems to sleep indoors in a private chamber or apartment. Contrast the situation of the dreamer in MQ 69. Lyndsay's dreamer sleeps in a cave (*Dreme*, l. 117).

47 *For to behauld hir dolour outwardlie*. The sense is presumably 'To see her outward appearance of sorrow'. See *DOST*, *Outwartly*, adv.

49 *brent*. MQ has 'berent' here, but 'brent' ('burnt up') seems to be a desirable emendation given the nature of the simile that follows. See Craigie, ed. 1920, p. 290.

51 *Hir visage pale declarit hir to be schent.* The sense of this line is ambiguous. The meaning of 'schent' is either 'ruined' or 'distressed', or perhaps 'damned' (the verb is used in this sense in MQ 37, l. 64). See *DOST, Schent*, v.

65 *Vnwrape.* MQ has 'In wrape' here. I follow Craigie in the emendation. See Craigie ed. 1920, p. 290.

78 *that wofull maistres of mischeif.* The lady regards herself as subject to Fortune.

84 *To be the mirrour of mishap.* Compare l. 126 and *Awntyrs off Arthur*, l. 167: 'Muse on my mirror'. Also see MQ 66, l. 14.

93 *This warld is bot ane vaill most miserabill.* Compare MQ 37, l. 10 and note.

96 *the Muses.* The daughters of Zeus and Mnēmosynē, or Jupiter and Memoria, who presided over the arts and learning. Compare MQ 48, ll. 4, 18.

97 *Pallas.* Minerva, associated with wisdom and skill, and with fearlessness. See MQ 35, l. 107 and note, and MQ 49, l. 8 and note, and MQ 69, l. 59.

101 *Iustice, thy sword.* A commonplace. See *DOST, Swerd*, n., especially sense 4.

110 *ane freind.* This may suggest a relation or simply a person one feels affection for. See *DOST, Frend*, n. Sometimes a lover is suggested. See MQ 75, in which the narrator's 'freind' is clearly a faithless lover.

121 *Of the first number I compt me not the last.* This line refers back to l. 115. The 'first number' are those who are born into misfortune.

123 *For I in cruell bandis of cair am chaist.* Craigie (1920, p. 290) suggests amending 'chaist' to 'cast'. I have preserved the manuscript reading on the grounds that 'chaist' makes sense as the past tense of 'chas' – to chase, impel, force. See *DOST, Chas*, v. sense 2b.

128 *Of him that stryvis againe the streme and wind.* Proverbial, 'to strive in vane'. See *DOST, Strem(e)*, n. sense 2b.

148 *[balefull] forrest.* MQ has 'betfull', probably a scribal error for 'baleful'. The use of 'forrest' here is ambiguous. Pinkerton emends it to 'breist' (Pinkerton ed. 1786, p. 251; also see Craigie ed. 1920, p. 290).

160 *the scheild of deith.* The image of God as a shield is biblical. See, for example, Psalm 3:3, Psalm 28: 7, Proverbs 30: 5 etc.

169 *we ar the Lordis elect.* A reference to the Calvinist theology of the election, based on Matt 20: 23. Compare MQ 37, ll. 115–16 and MQ 42, ll. 171–72, MQ 46, l. 62.

171–72 *elect.* Craigie (1920, p. 290) suggests emendation to 'erect'. This edition preserves the manuscript reading.

179 *thy ransoun.* The idea that Christ's death was the payment of a ransom to the devil for freedom of mankind is biblical. See 1 Timothy 2: 5–6 and compare 'Christ thow art the lycht, bot and the day' in *The Gude and Godlie Ballatis*, 1567 edition: 'Thy seruandis gouerne in the steid / For quhais ransoun thow did sair bleid' (Mitchell ed. 1896–97, p. 145).

66. Ane Elagie Translatit Out of Frenche in English Meter

This poem consists of the complaint of an unhappy wife in the tradition of the French *chanson de mal mariée*. Many similar examples of the genre in French survive from the sixteenth century. See Smith 1934, pp. 36–42. On the poem's use of its likely source (Clément Marot's *Suite de l'Adolescence Clementine*, 1533), see Bawcutt 2001, pp. 127–28; Dunnigan 2005, pp. 443–44. Examples of complaints by the unhappily married are found in earlier Scots literature, including *The Quare of Jelusy* (ll. 59–92) and Dunbar's *Tretis of the Tua Mariit Wemen and the Wedow*. MF also contains a pair of anti-marital complaints, one voiced by a wife, 'In bowdoun on blak monunday' (pp. 215–17), which is attributed to Clapperton, and the other by a husband, 'Vnder ane birkin bank me by' (pp. 217–20).

The speaker of this poem distinguishes herself from the great lovers of history (Dido and Sapho in particular) because of her experience of the greater tragedy of complaining an unworthy husband, rather than a false lover: she is bound to a husband until death and emphasises her fidelity to the sacrament of matrimony. She tells the reader that despite her loyalty, meekness, honesty and cheerfulness, her husband repays her with cruelty, anger and duplicity. The complaint derives poignancy from her account of parental negligence in failing to seek her 'consent' for the marriage, her acceptance of her fate as God's bidding (a familiar theme in MQ texts), and her realisation that only God can bear 'record' of her pain.

The manuscript title describes the poem as being composed in 'English meter', perhaps a description of its iambic pentameter couplets. Its style is distinguished by a number of proverbs, and some striking compari-

sons that illuminate the speaker's sense of entrapment (see especially ll. 81–93). The poem is copied in italic script. It is attributed to one 'G.H.' whose identity is not known. MQ 90 and MQ 91 are attributed to 'T.H' and 'R.H', and 'G.H.' may possibly be related to these poets, who are identified in MF as Thomas and Robert Husdon, English musicians and writers associated with the court of James VI. The poem may well have been written by a woman, but on the tradition of male-authored female-voiced lyrics in Older Scots literature, see van Heijnsbergen 2002. Other poems in the MS written from a woman's perspective include MQ 49 and MQ 75.
Stanza: pentameter, rhyming couplets (aa⁵).
Text: MQ fols 102v–105.
Authorship: attributed to G.H.
Date: uncertain.

Commentary
8 *The phoenix bird.* The speaker compares herself to the solitariness of the legendary Phoenix, a bird that lived to a great age and then consumed itself in flames before rising again from its ashes. Only one phoenix was in existence at any one time. Ovid *Met.* 15. Compare l. 11.

10 *Quhome dolent duill with dolour so dois wound:* Translate 'whom sorrowful distress wounds with suffering'. 'Dolour' has the meaning 'Physical pain or suffering; a pain or painful affliction' as well as 'mental pain or suffering' (*DOST*, *Dolour*, *n.*).

17 *Dido Quein.* The daughter of Belus, King of Tyre and legendary founder and queen of Carthage. The poet is doubtless referring to Dido's complaint on her abandonment by Aeneas, which was known from Ovid, *Heroides* XIV, and Virgil's *Aeneid*, Book IV.

18–20 *Cupids arrowis kein ... dairt.* The wounding potential of the god of love's arrows is a commonplace of courtly love poetry. Compare MQ 38, ll. 32–36 and MQ 39, l. 35.

23 *lemmand.* By the third quarter of the sixteent century the term 'lemmand' seems to have specifically denoted a gallant or mistress, and an unlawful lover (*DOST*, *Lemman*, *Leman*, n.).

24 *Sapho and monye otheris mo.* The reference is to Ovid's *Heroides* XV, where Sappho (the lyric poet, born in Lesbos in c.612 BC) complains about her abandonment by her lover Phaon. In MQ 85, ll. 1–4, Sappho is evoked as a model of literary skill.

57 *He randers calf for my gud solid graine.* Proverbial. See *DOST, Caf,*

n. The metaphor sums up the bareness and lack of mutuality that characterises the marriage of the complainant. Her husband gives valueless chaff (the empty husk, which has been separated from the grain during thrashing) in return for her providing him with grain. Compare Gower, *Confessio Amantis*, Prol., l. 844, 'The chaf is take for the corn'.

61 *chaist love*. The speaker insists on the purity of her love. See *DOST*, *Chaste*, a.

63 *His stonie hart to fauld can not be brocht*. The husband's heart is imagined as too hard to yield to affection. For the image of the stony heart, see *King Hart*, l. 109: 'Wald mak ane hart of flint to fald and fle'. Also see *DOST*, *Fald*, *Fauld*, v.

65–66 *The ferce lyoun will not his pat erect / Aganis the beist that will the self subiect*. 'The fierce lion will not raise his paw against the beast that will place itself in subjection to him'. Compare Henryson's 'The Lion and the Mouse', where the Mouse's plea for mercy is respected by the lion (see ll. 1503–7). Also compare Dunbar's 'Quhen Merche wes with variand windis past', l. 119 ('Quhois noble yre is *parcere prostratis*'), which alludes to a Latin distich on the Lion's willingness to spare those who prostrate themselves before him. See Bawcutt, ed. 1998, p. 398; Bawcutt, 1986.

67 *Attyla baild*. Attila (d.453) was king of the Huns and invader of Gaul and Italy. Some sources tell that Pope Leo I, with the authority of St Peter, persuaded him to spare Rome, and ll. 67–68 seem to allude to this legend (see Kelly 2008, pp. 206–7).

69 *blak Pluto*. Pluto, mentioned also at l. 80, was king of the underworld. He raped Persephone (Proserpina) while she was gathering spring flowers and compelled her to live in the underworld with him. See Ovid *Met*. 5, ll. 384–578. Also see *The Quare of Jelusy*, ll. 71–76, where Pluto is described as king of 'the derk regioun'.

70 *[Orpheus]* corrected from the MA reading 'Morpheus'. The harpist of Thrace, who uses music to subdue the underworld in his quest to rescue his wife. Ovid *Met*. 10, ll. 1–128, Virgil, *Georgics*, IV, and Boethius' *De consolatione Philosophiae* Book III, metrum 12. Also see Henryson's version of the fable, *Orpheus and Eurydice*, ll. 366–72.

76 *insensative*. 'Unfeeling'. *DOST* and *OED* indicate that this word not well attested before the early seventeenth century.

79 *tyran barbarous*. The jealous husband is likened to a tyrant in *The Quare of Jelusy* (l. 278).

82–87 *the fouleris malice ... pyne*: Compare the fouler 'Richt cautelous and full off subteltie' and his butchery of the birds in Henryson's *Morall Fabillis*, 'The Preaching of the Swallow', ll. 1811–31, 1841–80.

83–84 *Quha sueitlie tonis his instrument and sang; / Thairefter then he beginnis to chaunge his not.* Compare James I, *Kingis Quair* (ll. 939–42):

> For as the fouler quhislith in his throte
> …
> And feynis mony a swete and strange note …
> Diversely, to counterfete the brid,
> Till sche be fast lokin his net amyd

104 *Rather let the erthe opin and swallow me.* Biblical. See Numbers 16: 32, Deuteronomy 11: 6 and Psalm 106: 17.

124 *Quhy wald thay not at leist seik my consent?* Marital choice in late sixteenth-century Scotland was a matter of parental guidance, though not of coercion. See Brown 2000, pp. 120–21.

128–30 On the emotional efficacy of complaint, compare MQ 38, ll. 113–17.

130 *To the only I doe my plaint out pour.* Compare MQ 73, ll. 34–35.

135 *Thocht men be blind, 3it thow dois cleirlie sie.* Compare MQ 37, l. 25.

67. The Subiect.

This poem is attributed to 'Iacobus Rex' (King James) in MQ. In another witness, BL Additional MS 24195 (where the poem appears in Anglicised spelling), it is given the title 'Song. the first verses that euer the King made'. A further attributed manuscript witness of the poem (NAS RH 13/38) has been identified by Sally Mapstone (unpublished research) among papers probably belonging to the lawyer Thomas Hamilton (1563–1637). This copy asserts that the poem was 'maid in anno 1583, at ye duik of obiynnie his puttingout of Scotland', thus linking it to James's separation from Esmé Stewart. See Lyall 2000, p. 60; Lyall 2005, p. 98. Whether or not this date can be accepted, the poem must pre-date 1586, the date inscribed in MQ. Rickard dates it to 1582. See Rickard 2007, pp. 1–3. For further discussion, see Martin 2013a, p. 80. James's earliest printed collections of verse date from 1584 (*Essayes of a Prentise in the Divine Art of Poesie*, *ESTC* S109018, *STC* 14373)

EXPLANATORY NOTES

and 1591 (*His Maiesties Poeticall Exercises at Vacant Houres*, ESTC S108288, *STC* 14379).

It seems likely, however, that even if James can reliably be associated with the poem that appears in MQ, he based his work on a more widely known and earlier verse beginning 'Sen trew vertew encresses dignytee'. A two-stanza version of this poem survives in CUL Kk.1.5 (part 6), without attribution (see IMEV and NIMEV 3151, DIMEV 4914; Girvan ed. 1939, p. 176). A three-stanza version survives in the Bannatyne MS (Draft, p.32 and Main MS fols 58v–59), and in the 1578 edition of the *The Gude and Godlie Balladis*, where it is attributed to James I (see Fox and Ringler 1980, p. xix; Mitchell ed. 1896–97, pp. 238–39; Skeat ed. 1884, repr. 1911, pp. 51–54).

MQ 67 poem is thematically consonant with many of the poems of MQ: it is concerned with self-restraint, especially in matters of speech (compare Maitland's advisory poems, MQ 11 and MQ 59), the relationship of 'will' and 'wit' (l. 12), and the patient endurance of troubles (compare MQ 37 among others). The first seven lines of the MQ version function as a prologue and summarise the content of the next three verses (drawing especially on ll. 1, 7, 12 and 15–18). They appear only in MQ, where they are copied in an italic script, while the rest of the poem is in a secretary script. They are metrically distinct from the rest of the poem, which consists of three six-line stanzas in octasyllabic lines. The manuscript title 'The Subiect' should perhaps be interpreted simply as 'The poem'. The MQ and BL texts of the poem are included in Craigie, ed. 1955–58, II, pp. 132–33.

Stanza: ababcc^4.

Text: MQ fols 105v–106; BL MS 24195 fols 51–51v; NAS RH 13/38 [not consulted for this edition].

Authorship: attributed to James VI.

Date: c.1583.

Commentary

3 *Let aboundance brek out, bot ȝit in temperance.* Compare l. 11. The sense is, 'Let abundance be had with temperance' or 'Exercise temperance in all things'.

2 *O troublit hairt.* Compare MQ 37, l. 1.

3 *Thocht vnrevelit can doe na ill.* Compare MQ 11, l. 17.

5–6 *Be cairfull ay for to invent / The way to get thy awin intent.* The warning here is against getting one's own way by contrivance or deceit. See *DOST*, *Invent*, v. Compare the advice given in MQ 11, ll. 75–76.

7 *play thy self with thy awin consait.* 'Amuse yourself with your own ideas'.

15 *How to mak vertew of thy neid.* A commonplace. See Chaucer's 'Knight's Tale', I, l. 3042: 'To maken vertu of necessitee'; Henryson, *Testament of Cresseid*, l. 478: 'mak vertew of ane neid'.

68. Virgil his village Mantua

This poem praises the Maitland family seat of Lethington, a fortified tower house, near Haddington, East Lothian (given to the family by royal charter in 1345). While eulogising Lethington, the poet also praises its owners, several generations of Maitlands. The poem is thus characteristic of 'the country house poem' and is perhaps one of the earliest British examples of the genre. The country house poem flourished in the seventeenth century, both in the British Isles and on the Continent, and commonly included praise of the setting, architecture and owners of an important house, often in a bid for patronage. The poem is discussed by A.A. MacDonald 1991a, pp. 24–25, and 1997, pp. 85–86 and Martin 2013b. On the country house poem in Scotland, see Spiller 1974; on country house poems more generally, see McClung 1977; Fowler ed. 1994; McBride 1991. The poem's closest analogue is Thomas Maitland's Latin poem in praise of his father's house, *Domus Ledintona*, which was printed in *Delitiae Poetarum Scotorum* (1637), and which reflects the taste for neo-Latin poems on country estates that developed on the Continent (especially in the Netherlands and Italy) from the 1560s. Thomas Maitland's poem is printed in Bain ed. 1830, pp. 144–48.

Lethington was confiscated from the Maitland family by the Regent Lennox in 1571 because of the support of Sir Richard's sons for the Queen's Party: Maitland wrote about the confiscation of his home in MQ 20. Maitland appealed to Elizabeth on 24 August 1574 requesting her help in securing its return (*CPS Scotland*, V, pp. 46–47). Lethington was not restored to the family until 1584. For part of this time at least, Maitland and his wife were resident at Dundas near Edinburgh (Bain ed. 1830, p. 1 (note). It is therefore likely that the poem was composed either before 1571, or between 1584 and the compilation of the manuscript in c.1586.

The authorship of the poem is not known, though it has sometimes been attributed to Richard Maitland (anon, *The History and Treasures of Lennoxlove House* 1960, p. 14). Maitland includes praise of Seton

Palace in his prose history of the family (see Martin 2013b), but he does not write about the country house elsewhere. The opening lines of MQ 68 mention poets who have written of their place of birth, suggesting that the author may have been born at Lethington (though on the narrator's denial of skill as a poet, see note to l. 9, and l. 52). The narrator expresses fond memories of the place, indicates the cultured and virtuous attributes of the family, and notes how fortunate those are who can count themselves part of the Maitland family. Its closing lines stress the pre-eminence of Maitland descendants. It may have been written by a family member or one on intimate terms with the family.

The poem contains some precise architectural terms and an appealing evocation of Lethington's gardens and recreational spaces, and the topography of its surroundings. It is copied in an italic script.

Stanza: $a^4b^3a^4b^3c^4d^3c^4d^3$ (the text is not set out in stanzas in MQ).
Text: MQ fols 106v–109v.
Authorship: unattributed.
Date: uncertain.

Commentary

1 *Virgil ... Mantua*. Virgil mentions Mantua in the *Georgics* 2, ll. 198–200 and 3, ll. 12–15.

3 *Lucane ... Corduba*. The philosopher and poet Lucius Seneca wrote an epigram addressed to Cordova, Spain, when he was in exile in Corsica. Seneca was uncle to the historian and epic poet Lucan (AD 39–65), who was also born at Cordova.

5 *Catallus*. Catullus's commendation of Sirmio, Lake Garda, in poem XXXI. He was born in Verona.

7–8 *Ouid ... Sulmon*. Ovid's praise of his birthplace, Sulmo, in *Fasti* 4 and *Amores* 2: 16. Also see note to l. 3. Compare the dedicatory sonnet, 'E.D. in prayse of Mr W Foular her freind', in Fowler's *Trivmphs of Petrarke*, ll. 4–5: 'Sulmo thinks her Ouid dois adorne; / The Spanzoll laughs (sawe Lucan) all to scorne' (Meikle ed. 1914).

9 *Sua euerie poet hes sum place*. Perhaps an implicit comparison between these classical writers and Richard Maitland, poet and owner of Lethington, who is compared to Homer in MQ 94. 2, l. 10. The poet/ narrator of MQ 68 later claims that the ability to praise Lethington in fitting terms 'Transcendis my ingyne' (l. 52).

21 *Pernassus*. Mount Parnassus, the mountain sacred to Apollo and the

Muses. Compare MQ 48 and notes to ll. 1–3, and MQ 74, l. 15. Also see Douglas, *Palice of Honour*, l. 1102: 'The twa toppit Famous Pernasus'.

24 *Hypocrene*. The sacred fountain on Helicon. See MQ 48 and note to l. 3.

25 *Permessis*. Permessus, a river on Mount Helicon, sacred to Apollo and the Muses.

28 *Tempe schaw*. The Vale of Tempe in Greece, favoured by Apollo and the Muses (see Ovid *Met*. 1, l. 568).

50 *Tyne*. The River Tyne rises in the Moorfoot Hills in Midlothian and runs through Haddington on its way to the Tyne Estuary.

53 *Thow meritis Homer or Virgill*. A conventional expression of poetic modesty. See Dunbar, *Goldyn Targe*, where the narrator and classical poets are presented as equally unable to accurately describe a scene of natural beauty:

> 'Noucht thou, Omer, als fair as thou coud wryte,
> ...
> Nor yit thou, Tullius, quhois lippis suete
> Off rethorike did in to termes flete.' (ll. 67–70)

57 *tour, and fortres*. The poet evokes the tower house design of Lethington. It was built during the fifteenth century, in an L-shape formation, four stories high, a style that reflected the strategic important of its location in the defence of the Scottish Border. See Small 1833, II, 'Lennoxlove'; *History and Treasures of Lennoxlove House* 1960, pp. 12–13.

58 *Thy nychtbouris dois excell*. On the many other fortified towers in the vicinity (including Hailes Castle and Craigmillar Castle), see Small 1833.

59 *thy wallis, thik and strang*. The walls of Lethington tower are 11 feet thick in places. See *History and Treasures of Lennoxlove House* 1960, pp. 12–13.

60 *beiris the bell*. See MQ 37, l. 44 and note.

63 *voltis*. Arches, or vaulted constructions, in the architecture of the building.

67 *alryne*. A stone walkway behind the battlements of a castle. See *DOST*, *Allouring*, n. A parapet walk survives on Lethington Tower, which is now part of Lennoxlove House.

70 *Phoebus*. The sun.

101–2 *Then michtie wes that man in deid, / That first the tuik in hand.* Robert Maitland of Thirlestane received Lethington from Hugh of Yester (confirmed by royal charter). He was killed in 1346 at the Battle of Neville's Cross, and the tower was probably built by his son or grandson. Compare *Domus Ledintona*, ll. 25–27:

> O quantos animos generoso pectore clausos
> Ille aluit, primus tantae fundamina molis
> Qui posuit. (Bain, ed. 1830, p. 145)

109–10 *Thy beddis soft and tapeis fair, / Thy treitting and gud cheir.* On the house's decoration and the welcome it gives to guests, compare *Domus Ledintona*, ll. 92–115 (Bain ed. 1830, p. 147).

115 *thay that travellis be the way.* Compare the account of Robert Lord Seton's welcoming improvements to his family home in the 'Metrical Chronicle of the House or Setoun': 'the palice was decoird ... To treit strangers quhen they war cum fra far' (Kamington [1839], p. 48). On Robert Seton, also see headnote to MQ 63.

121 *arbour.* A garden, evocative of the garden of courtly love poetry, the *locus amoensus* tradition. Compare Dunbar, *Tretis*, 'grein arbour' (l. 17).

127 *knottis and thy alleis.* The poet is evoking the formal gardens of the house (see Maitland's *History of the House of Seyton*, p. 35: 'the knottis of the flouris') and bowling alley or green. On the increasing interest in gardening and cultivating landscape in sixteenth-century Scotland, see Brown 2000, pp. 208–10.

129 *buttis.* Probably a ground prepared for practicing archery. *DOST, But, Bute,* n. Archery remained an important part of the noble education and a popular pastime. See Brown 2000, pp. 215–16.

130 *Sa suire but sone or wind.* 'So safe from the elements'. Compare *Domus Ledintona*, l. 36: 'Cum tu illaesa fores, saevisque impervia flabris' (Bain ed. 1830, p. 145).

141 *the Maitland [bluid].* Compare MQ 46, l. 95.

145 *auld Sir Richard of that name.* Richard Maitland's legendary ancestor. See MQ 46, l. 105, and note.

149 *his nobill sonnis thrie.* See MQ 46, l. 124.

152 *England to quaik.* The tower house was strategically important in the defence of lowland Scotland and often at the forefront of Anglo-Scottish conflicts. Lethington suffered damage from an English attack during the

Siege of Haddington in 1549: this event is recorded in *Domus Ledintona*, ll. 73–80 (Bain ed. 1830, p. 146) and the *Diurnal of Occurents*.

159 *a compair*. Richard Maitland, the equal of 'auld Sir Richard' (l. 145).

69. Intill ane morning, mirthfullest of May

This dream vision contains many of the conventional elements of its genre, with the narrator falling asleep in a beautiful May landscape and having a vision from which he or she is woken abruptly. It shows the influence of several of Dunbar's poems, especially *The Goldyn Targe*, in its self-conscious use of aureate diction to describe the spring setting, and the description of the classical and allegorical figures in the dream. This poem, like Dunbar's, also shows a concern with matters of literary creativity as well as with feminine virtue.

The poem is one of significance to the Maitlands and contains some intriguing and subtle symbolism. It is probably a dedicatory work to Marie Maitland. In the dream, the narrator is lead by two harts, carrying between them a wounded lion, to 'Marie' and her company of ladies, who are residing in a beautiful garden. The significance of the lion and the harts is difficult to determine, but as in MQ 65, it is likely MQ's readers and compilers made connections now lost to us. Lines 41–42 contain a pun on Marie Maitland's name. Marie is associated with virginity and with writing (see notes to ll. 43–44), and the women in her company signify wisdom, creativity and virtue. Marie carries a branch, which bears a written pledge to 'sustein' virginity, presumably her own, and perhaps also that of others through the influence of her example or writing. She is also invested with a degree of authority, and financial autonomy or abundance in the poem (l. 42). The poem may anticipate her forthcoming marriage in on 9 August 1586 to Alexander Lauder (see note to l. 42), her purity (on chaste married love, see MQ 66, l. 61), her wealth and her creativity being important in this context. The narrator's sorrow at the end of the vision perhaps marks his or her parting from Marie.

The poem is discussed in Newlyn 2004, pp. 97–98, who suggests a female authorship, and Dunnigan 2003, p. 314. Dunnigan points out that it is significant that this poem should follow MQ 68 with its celebration of the Maitland Family and Richard Maitland's 'bairnis' (l. 160).
Stanza: ababbcbc[5].
Text: MQ fols 110–11.
Authorship: unattributed.

EXPLANATORY NOTES

Date: uncertain.

Commentary

1 *Intill ane morning, mirthfullest of May.* Compare Dunbar's *Goldyn Targe*, l. 9: 'In May intill a morow myrthfullest'. Also see the opening of a lyric in *The Gude and Godlie Ballatis*:

> In till ane myrthfull Maij morning
> Quhen Phebus did vp spring
> Walkand I lay, in ane garding gay.
> (Mitchell ed. 1896–97, p. 137)

For a later version of this ballad, see Shire 1969, pp. 30–31.

2 *Phoebus.* The sun, also mentioned at ll. 11 and 14. Compare *Goldyn Targe*, l. 246.

4 *ane riuer syde.* A conventional element in spring landscapes described in dream vision poems. See *Goldyn Targe*, l. 28: 'Doun throu the ryce a ryuir ran'.

8 *Maid all the hevinis abone me for to ring.* Conventional, see Dunbar's *Goldyn Targe*, l. 25: 'The skyes rang for schoutyng of the larkis'; Lydgate, *Complaint of the Black Knight*, l. 45: 'So loude songe that al the wode ronge'.

9 *Depaintit wer the feildis.* Compare Dunbar's *Goldyn Targe*,

> Discriue I wald, bot quho coud wele endyte
> How all the feldis wyth thai lilies quhite
> Depaynt ar brycht ... (ll. 64–66)

10 *Dame Nature.* A conventional figure in medieval dream visions, and important in Dunbar's love visions. See 'Quhen Merche wes with variand windis past', l. 3; *Goldyn Targe*, l. 146.

11–12 *The syluer droppis of dew hang on the bewis / Lyik orient perle.* Compare Dunbar's *Goldyn Targe*, l. 13: 'The perly droppis schuke in silvir schouris'; Henryson, *The Ressoning betuix Aige and Yowth*, l. 3: 'Perly droppis of the balmy schowris'.

13 *The holsome air.* 'Health-giving', pure. Conventional, compare Dunbar's *Goldyn Targe*, l. 248: 'Halesum the vale depaynt wyth flouris ying'.

15 *Florais mantill grene.* Compare *Goldyn Targe*, 'On Florais mantill I slepit as I lay' (l. 48).

17 *feildis, baith daill and schaw.* Perhaps the meadows, dales and woods are evocative of the landscape around Lethington. Compare the landscape described in MQ 68, ll. 71–76.

23 *Morpheus*. The god of sleep, who had the power of metamorphosis. See Ovid *Met*. 11, ll. 61–754.

27 *Two lustie hairtis*. The hart is a common heraldic emblem of nobility. However, Diana, who is frequently associated with chastity, and who appears in Marie's company at l. 61, turned Acteon into a Hart for spying on her and her nymphs. Ovid *Met*. 3, ll. 131–265.

30 *ane lyoun woundit sair*. The significance of the lion is difficult to determine. The most powerful of beasts wounded and carried by animals that would normally be its quarry, the harts, perhaps suggests the subjection of strength to gentleness. Pinkerton suggested that the lion was William Maitland, and the two harts, his siblings. See Pinkerton 1786, pp. 428–29.

31 *rauk and hace*. 'raucous and hoarse'. Compare MQ 65, l. 37. These adjectives suggest a certain amount of distress, but why the harts carry the lion, and why it is wounded, is not explained.

32 *'Keip reull in haist and leif thir feildis fair'*. The harts' command perhaps alludes to the importance of self-governance ('reull'), for example, in chastity, and a rejection of the frivolous pleasures ('feildis fair') of life.

35 *With aureit termis, and style most eloquent*. An allusion to the highly ornamented and rhetorical literary style practised by fifteenth- and early sixteenth-century Scots and English poets. Compare *Goldyn Targe*, l. 71: 'aureate tongis'.

38 *Thay me convoyit into ane gardene grein*. It is common in dream visions for the narrator to be guided by an animal. Compare the 'whelp' in Chaucer's *Book of the Duchess*, ll. 389–99, and lion in Machaut's *Dit dou Lyon*, ll. 325–31. On the garden, a *hortus conclusus*, compare Maitland's evocation of the peaceful estate, removed from contemporary troubles in MQ 29, l. 1.

39–40 *Quhair euerie plant and wod micht callit be, / That spred vpon thay branchis, micht be sein*. The sense is 'Where every plant and tree, possible to name, which spread branches, could be seen'.

41 *in this wod*. See note to l. 17, but perhaps also evocative of the woodland clearing in which Diana, the goddess of chastity, bathes with her nymphs. Ovid *Met*.3, ll. 131–98. See note to l. 61.

42 *Mait, land, and gold scho gave aboundantlie.* 'Food, land and gold she gave in plenty'. 'Mait' may also have the meaning here of 'companionship'. See *DOST, Mate, Mait*, n. Marie's dispensing of hospitality, land and wealth gives her an air of authority. It is possible that the poem marks her betrothal, an occasion that would necessitate the celebration of virginity and her family line, but also her ability to bestow property on another in the form of a tocher (dowry). See Brown 2000, p. 72. For another pun on the family name see MQ 46, l. 122 and note. For another poem, probably connected to marriage, and containing a pun on the names of the dedicatees, see the final stanza of John Stewart of Baldynneis' *In Commendation of Tvo Constant Lvifers* (Crockett ed. 1913, pp. 143–44): 'Behold Rosmarie Spring and lustie greine, / Bebatht vith vapor of the morning Gray'.

43–44 *in hir hand ane flourishit trie did beir / Quhairin wes writtin....* This blossoming branch, with its text, is said to be a symbol of chastity at l. 45. The verb 'flourish' indicates the bearing of fruit or flowers (*DOST, Flourish,* v.). For a similar image, see James I's *Kingis Quair*, ll. 1240–45, where a bird carries a 'bill' 'Of red jorofflis with thair stalkis grene / A fair branche, quhair was written with gold ... a plane sentence'. Here the spray of gillyflowers may represent virtuous love or marriage. See Boffey ed. 2003, p. 151. The inscribed 'trie' carried by Marie may have similar connotations, and may also indicate her fruitfulness in terms of creativity, though the laurel is a more common symbol of literary achievement. See MQ 85 and note to l. 15, and Douglas *Eneados*, prologue to book 12, l. 87: 'On his hed of lawrer tre a crown'.

45 *in sing of trew virginitie*. For a similar attempt to represent the rare virtue of chastity, see John Stewart of Baldynneis, *Of Chastitie. Sonnet*, ll. 9–12 (Crockett ed. 1913, p. 179):

> For as the Rois of flouris all the chois
> Maist semlie sproutith from the scharpest thorne,
> So thow (I dout not) dois vith paine Inclois
> All sort of thois be quhom thy blis is borne

49 *plesant plant*. This refers to the 'trie' (l. 43), but also allusively to Marie, celebrating her beauty. The noun 'plant' often refers figuratively to a young person of distinction. See Dunbar 'Gladethe, thoue queyne of Scottis regioun', where Margaret is described as 'a ȝing tendir plaunt of plesand pulcritude' (l. 2); and Montgomerie, 'Ʒong tender plante in spring tym of ȝour ȝeirs'. See *DOST, Plant*, n. Compare Dunnigan, who reads the stanza as a '*signe* of the chaste and beautiful female body' and remarks that the plant alluded to may signify the lily. Dunnigan 2004, p. 314.

50 *Stuid on ane ruit of semelie sickernes.* A pun on 'ruit' – the root or base of a plant and the ancestry of a person – is likely here. The poem thus celebrates the stability of Marie's family line.

54 *The blomes quhyte and reid.* The red and white blossoms suggest idealised youthful beauty. Compare Dunbar, 'Gladethe, thou queyne of Scottis regioun', l. 25: 'Rois red and quhit, resplendent of colour'; Dunbar, 'Sweit rois of vertew and of gentilnes', ll. 6–9:

> In to ʒour garthe this day I did persew.
> Thair saw I flowris that fresche wer of hew,
> Baith quhyte and rid, moist lusty wer to seyne,
> And halsum herbis vpone stalkis grene.

59–62 All the proper nouns in this list are written in italic script.

59 *Venus, Iuno, and Pallas.* Venus, Juno and Pallas appear in close proximity with each other in *Goldyn Targe*, ll. 73–78. Juno is one of the chief goddesses, associated with childbirth and women; Pallas is the name given by the Greeks to Minerva (see MQ 35, ll. 105–7). Also see MQ 49, l. 8, and MQ 65, l. 97.

60 *Minerua, Cleo, and Tersiphone.* Compare *Goldyn Targe*, ll. 77–78: 'My lady Cleo, that helpe of makaris bene, / Thetes, Pallas and prudent Minerua'. Minerva is the goddess of wisdom, and Cleo (Clio) is the muse of history. See Douglas, *Palice of Honour*, ll. 854–55: 'Lady Cleo, quhilk craftelie dois set / Historyis auld'. Tersiphone is Terpsichore, the muse of dancing and music. See Douglas, *Palice of Honour*, ll. 862–63:'Terpsichore the fyft, with humbill soun / Makis on Psalteris modulatioun'.

61 *Proserpine, and Diana the may.* Compare *Goldyn Targe*, ll. 75–76: 'Proserpyna, / Dyane, the goddesse chaste of woddis grene'. Proserpyna was raped by Pluto while gathering flowers (Ovid *Met.* 5, ll. 384–578, see note to MQ 66, l. 69). Diana is frequently presented as a goddess of chastity, and her bathing pool was situated in a woodland clearing. See John Stewart, *In Commendatione of His Luifing Freind*:

> And chast Diana cled in greine
> Quha causit Acteon to die,
> Because he haid hir nakit seine
> At bathing with hir virginis scheine. (Crocket ed. 1913, p. 140)

Also compare MQ 86, ll. 5–6, where Diana is associated with creativity.

EXPLANATORY NOTES

62 *Dame Beawtie bricht, and als Dame Chastitie.* Dame Beautee appears as an alluring and dangerous presence among the ladies in Dunbar's *Goldyn Targe*, l. 146. Chastity features in many moral personification allegories, for example, Lyndsay's *Ane Satyre of the Thrie Estaitis* (act I).

64 *And Laulines lay law vnder the trie.* 'Lawlynes' or Humility appears among the company of 'Suete Womanhede' in the *Goldyn Targe*, l. 163. The quality is contrasted with pride in MQ 42, l. 79.

70. To ȝow, my lordis of renown

This is a comic and satirical complaint on the decline of good horsemanship. It is also in part a sumptuary complaint, and ends with an antifeminist invective.

The poem begins by listing various hardships suffered by individual traders and townspeople as the result of the decline in the horse market of Rugling (modern day Rutherglen) (ll. 35–37). On the challenges facing Scots nobles in maintaining their horses in the early modern period, see Brown 2000, pp. 214–15. The poem explains this decline as the result of nobles preferring the riding of mares rather than fine geldings, in a bid to save money to spend on extravagancies such as their fashionable clothes. The male riders are foppish, boastful and vain with their perfumed gloves and fancy handkerchiefs; and the women reveal too much flesh as they prance about on horseback. The poem plays on the traditional association of riding and sexual activity, and suggests that the preference for saddling ambling mares is a sign of both the amorous excesses and the emasculation of the male rider. The notion of riding, and by extension, copulating with a mare, is used as an insult in Dunbar's *Flyting* l. 246: 'ȝadswyvar'. The compound 'ȝaldsones' (meaning 'whoresons') appears in *The Alliterative Morte d'Arthure* (Turville-Petre, forthcoming).

The poem shows the influence of various poems by Dunbar and Lyndsay. The extravagantly attired riders are reminiscent of the vain and flirtatious husband of the second wife in the *Tretis of the Tua Mariit Wemen and the Wedow* who is 'curtly of his clething', and wears a 'bonet on syde' (ll. 182, 180). Elements of the sumptuary complaint recall Lyndsay's *Ane Supplication Directit ... to the Kingis Grace, in Contemptioun of Syde Taillis* (c.1539–41). The listing techniques used in the poem recall the style of Dunbar's 'Schir, ȝe haue mony seruitouris'.

The poem may be compared to Maitland's complaints about the decline in noble customs, such as house-holding in MQ 5. It also shows verbal similarities to his sumptuary complaints, especially to MQ 2, but also to MQ 4, ll. 51–60 and 76–80.

The poem ends abruptly in an unfinished state in both witnesses (it is followed by two blank leaves in MQ). With a few exceptions, MQ's text is generally superior to that in MF, which contains some erroneous readings suggesting the scribe's lack of understanding of some parts of the poem.

Stanza: octosyllabic couplets (aa^4).
Text: MQ fols 111v–13v, MF pp. 359–60, pp. 1–2.
Authorship: unattributed.
Date: uncertain.

Commentary

1 *my lordis of renoun*. Compare the opening address to the lords in MQ 25, and also 'My lordis, now, gif 3e be wyse' (c.1567, probably by Sempill, in Cranstoun ed. 1891–93, I, p. 46).

2 *Rugling toun*. Rutherglen in Lanarkshire, a royal burgh.

5 *3emen*. Those holding a small amount of land, but not gentlemen. *OED*, *Yeoman*, n.

13 *our traffique*. 'Our ability to trade'. See *DOST*, *Traffic(que*, n.

14 *Our schift and gaine is quyte away*. 'Our way of making our living and our profit has been lost'.

22 *The hostleris gettis no repair*. 'The innkeepers get no opportunity for visitors'.

27 *hors boyis*. Perhaps grooms, as opposed to the 'stabilleris' (those who run livery stables) mentioned at l. 25.

36 *fair and mercat*. The poet seems to use 'fair' and 'market' as synonyms, though distinctions were often made between the two types of trading events in the early modern period, with fairs attracting business from further afield and markets being smaller-scale and more frequent local events. See Edwards 1988, p. 60.

38 *cors*. The market cross of the town.

39 *croft*. The land adjoining the town.

41 *At gud Sanct Lukis noble fair*. Horse fairs in England and Scotland traditionally took place several times a year (often on feast days), and one was usually held on the feast day of St Luke, 18 October. See further Edwards 1988, pp. 60–70. On Rutherglen's St Luke's fair, which lasted for a week, and attracted traders from England and Scotland, see Cormack 1983, pp. 1, 3; Wilson, 1936, I, p. 4. Wilson describes it as a type of Beltane festival.

56 *Twelf gait glydis deir of a prein.* 'Twelve galled (blistered) old horses of little value'. See *OED*, *Gall*, n., sense 3. Compare Cranstoun ed. 1891–93, I, poem 26 ('Lustie lords and barrounis yat bene hauld'), l. 167: 'Tuiche anis the gaw and yan the hors wil fling'.

67 *a meir.* According to *DOST*, a female horse. See *DOST*, *Mere*, *Meir*, n. In Middle English 'mere' is a riding horse of either sex. *OED*, *Mare*, n.

71 *ane meir onbocht.* Horses that they have not paid a fee for. See *DOST*, *Onbocht*, ppl. adj.

75 *ane ʒad.* A worn-out mare, See *DSL*, *SND1*, 3ad, n. Compare Dunbar, 'Schir, lat it neuer in toune be tald', where the narrator presents himself as an old horse: 'ane ald ʒald auer'.

77 *This wicked meir sa weill thame staikis.* 'This ill-tempered mare suits them so well'. The sense of 'wicked' is presumably weakened here. See *DOST*, *Wikit*, adj.

94 *Et toute est a la mode de France.* 'And all is according to the French fashion'.

95 *scarpenis.* Pumps, apparently following an Italian fashion. *DOST*, *Scarpen*, n., *OED Scarpine*, n.

96 *muillis.* For complaints about fancy footwear, compare MQ 2, l. 41.

97 *gartenis knottit with a rois.* Compare MQ 2, ll. 27–28 and note.

99 *Thay snyte, thoght thair na mister be.* 'They wipe the nose when there is no need'. See *DOST*, *Snyte*, v. An affectation to show off their elegant pocket handkerchiefs bearing tassels ('knappis').

106 *Thay wer Caesar in weirlie actis.* Most Roman emperors of the first to third centuries AD bore the name Caesar. This is probably a metonymy for king. Compare Chaucer, *Legend of Good Women*, F Prol. l. 360.

110 *King Cresus.* King Croesus (c.560–546 BC) of Lydia, who was famed for his treasures.

119 *siklin saillis.* For the use of 'saill' to describe women's clothing, compare MQ 2, l. 14 and note.

120 *clairtie silk*. The silk is presumably filthy from trailing on the ground: over-length garments, such as the trains to women's dresses described here, often attracted the censure of moralists. See MQ 2, l. 13 and headnote. Compare Lyndsay's *Ane Supplication Directit ... to the Kingis Grace, in Contemptioun of Syde Taillis* (c.1539–41), especially ll. 14, 163–64.

124 *A buist to mak thair bellie round*. A pad placed under the dress to accentuate the figure. *DOST, Buist, Bust(e)*, n. A rounded stomach is often regarded as beautiful in medieval literature and art. See Brewer 1955, p. 258.

126 *A fartigard to gadder wind*. A 'fartigard' is a hooped petticoat, with an obvious play on the idea of the garment catching and containing farts.

130 *lyik ane bryidlit cat thai brank*. 'They prance like bridled cats'. Perhaps an echo of Wantonness in Lyndsay's *Ane Satyre of the Thrie Estaitis*, l. 468: 'Hay! As ane brydlit cat I brank'. Also compare the husband of the second wife in Dunbar's *Tretis*, l. 180: 'he is als brankand'. Both 'bryidlit' and 'brank' continue the equine associations. See Douglas, *Aeneid* xi.xii.6: 'The stampand stedis ... Apon thar strait born brydills brankand fast'.

71. My ladyis pulchritud

This love complaint recalls MQ 38, MQ 40 and MQ 48 in its account of the narrator's suffering, conflicted emotions and endangered hope, and in its portrayal of the lady's idealised beauty and conduct. Despite the narrator's protestations of trepidation and subjection to Fortune, the poem ends with a promise of perseverance in hope of good fortune and the reward of the lady's love.

There are some affinities of phrasing with MQ 48. The poem also has thematic similarities with many near contemporary amatory complaints, especially those by Alexander Montgomerie, such as his 'O Cleir / Most deir'.

The poem's style is simple, with some alliteration and also some interesting and ambiguous metaphors. The poem has been attributed to Montgomerie but is not assigned in MQ. It is included in Cranstoun ed. 1887, pp. 278–79.

The poem is copied in italic.
Stanza: abab^{3}aaa^{2}b^3.

Text: MQ fols 115–115v.
Authorship: unattributed.
Date: uncertain.

Commentary

1 *pulchritud*. Compare MQ 48, l. 113, MQ 64, l. 9.

4 *Mirthles I man remaine*. Compare MQ 48, l. 152.

7 *be mansuetud*. Compare MQ 48, l. 114.

9–10 *Blind boy, thou dois so beir / My fortoun in ballance!* The association of fortune and the love deities is conventional. Compare Montgomerie, 'On Love and fortun I complene' (l. 1).

17–18 *As in the wind I wie, / Ay wauering with the wechtis*. 'As if in the wind, I put it in the balance, always vacillating with the weights'. See *DOST*, *We*, v.

24 *As houp gud hap me hectis*. 'As hope promises me good fortune'. Compare, 'The Cherrie and the Slae', l. 512: 'For Hope gud hap hes hect'.

25 *hingis be ane hair*. Formulaic. Compare MQ 46, l. 113.

28 *Thou catche my hairt in coup*. The image here may be of the heart as a leaping salmon caught in a basket. See *DOST*, *Coup*, n., sense, 2. This perhaps relates back to the use of the verb 'flow' at l. 11. However, *DOST* also gives this citation from the poem as an illustration of *(Cowp)*, *Coup*, n., which it describes as of obscure meaning.

30 *I lyik thy lair*. Referring back to l. 9. The 'lair' is Cupid's lore or teaching. See *DOST*, *Lare, lair*, n. See Montgomerie, 'A Counsell aganst Dispair In Love', l. 4: 'It wes no moues to mell with Loves lair'. However, there may be a pun intended here, as 'lair' can also have the sense of resting place or bed and is used in amorous contexts. See *DOST*, *Lair*, n.

35 *And pertlie I pretend*. 'Boldly I put myself forwards'.

72. Gif faithfulnes ȝe find

The speaker of this poem offers perseverance and loyalty in return for the beloved's heart 'in recompense' (reward or payment) for his/her own. There is no clear indication of the speaker's gender, or that of the beloved. He or she proposes that if the addressee finds faithfulness in him/her that they make a band or pledge of permanence, which suggests a formal bond or friendship or even betrothal. For other poems in MQ that are connected to marriage, see MQ 63, MQ 64 and MQ 69; bonds of friendship and love are mentioned in other MQ poems, including in MQ 38 and MQ 49. The diction of the poem contains legalistic and monetary elements, which may suggest its connection to the formal contract of marriage (see note to l. 15), but the poem also contains lexis familiar from the courtly love tradition. Poems on constant love or faithful friendship, which do not necessarily suggest a marital context, were popular in the period. See, for example, John Stewart of Baldynneis 'In Commendatione Of Tvo Constant Lvifers'.

The poem has some verbal similarities to poems by Montgomerie and conventional similarities to poems by Scott, which are mentioned in the notes. The close of the final stanza with the narrator's hope for the mutual comforts of faith and truth echoes the opening of the first, also enacting the idea of the 'band' (both formal contract and material means of securing or fastening something) to be formalised between the narrator and the poem's recipient.

For examples of love complaints in MQ with similar subject matter and style, see MQ 38, MQ 39, MQ 40, MQ 48 and MQ 71. For the suggestion that the poem is by Marie Maitland, see Stevenson and Davidson eds 2001, p. 96.

Stanza: ababbcbc[3].
Text: MQ 116–116v.
Authorship: unattributed.
Date: uncertain.

Commentary

1 *Gif faithfulnes 3e find.* Compare Montgomerie's 'If faithfulnes suld friendship find', l. 1.

3 *Ane band heirby I bind.* A 'band' (or bond) is a formal contract (often documentary). On bonds of friendship in Scotland, see Wormald 1985, especially pp. 34–51; Donaldson 1970, pp. 140–43. Compare the 'band of amitie' mentioned in MQ 38, l. 99 or 'band of hymen' (marriage) in MQ 49, l. 48. Note also Montgomerie, 'If faithfulnes suld friendship find', l. 3: 'If Resone love with bands micht bind'; and Scott's '3e blindit luvaris, luke', ll. 57–61:

> 3it thair is lesum lufe
> That law*t*fully suld lest;
> He is no*t* to reprufe
> That is w*t* ane possest;
> That band I hald it best.

EXPLANATORY NOTES

7 *My hairt heir I present.* The notion of the heart voluntarily offered to the beloved as a pledge or guarantee is found elsewhere in sixteenth-century Scots poetry. See, for example, Scott, 'Hence hairt, wt hir þat most departe', ll. 11–12: 'thow sall gang / And beir thy lady cumpany'; and 'Haif hairt, in hairt, 3e hairt of hairtis haill', l. 2: 'Trewly, sweit hairt, 3our hairt my hairt sal haif'.

10 *As hostage in 3our hand.* The narrator has already offered the heart as a pledge, and extends this image to that of the heart as a hostage taken by the lover in return for constancy. This recalls the common image of the heart as a prisoner, captured by or yielded to the beloved, which is found widely in the poems of Scott and Montgomerie. See Scott, *The Anschir to Hairtis*: 'It is ane hairt bayth air & lait, / That is 3or hairtis presoneir'. For the heart's escape from such bondage, see MQ 47 and headnote.

15 *gadge and pand.* 'The pledge and surety'. A 'pand' is also 'a security payable by betrothed persons, returnable on orderly completion of the marriage'. See *DOST, Pand,* n.

17 *Resaue it then, and treit it.* This recalls the idea of the heart as a gift at l. 7. Compare Scott, *The Anschir to Hairtis*, l. 11: 'This woundit hairt, sweit hairt, ressaif'.

18 *treuth sall try my part.* Perhaps a gesture towards personification allegory. The phrasing is similar to Montgomerie, 'Evin dead, behold I breath', l. 37: '3it tyme sall try my Treuth'; and his 'If faithfulnes suld friendship find', l. 9: 'Sen tym hes tryde my treuth'.

21 *Deill efter my desert.* As a sign of his/her commitment the speaker promises to suffer any punishment due in the unlikely event that s/he should be unfaithful. Knowing that this will not happen s/he remains hopeful. Compare MQ 48, ll. 145–50.

22 *Disdaine.* The lady's contempt is much feared in courtly literature. See *King Hart*, l. 746: 'For hir disdane he culd nocht gudlie beir'.

24 *recompence.* Compare Montgomerie, 'If faithfulnes suld friendship find', ll. 6–7: 'If loving hir allane / Suld Recompense resave'.

73. Ane Prayer.

This is a penitential prayer and evangelical appeal to fellow sinners, which draws heavily on a number of biblical texts, especially the Psalms, including Psalm 51 (one of the Seven Penitential Psalms), a popular choice for poetic reworking (Fein 1989; Hamlin 2004). Although this poem is an eclectic tissue of different biblical allusions it should be related to the tradition of psalm translation, paraphrase and response, which was popular in the sixteenth century in England and Scotland. Thomas Wyatt made a poetic paraphrase of all the penitential psalms, and there is a version of Psalm 51 in the *Gude and Godlie Ballatis* ('Have mercy on me, God of micht'; see Mitchell ed. 1896–97, pp. 120–29), as well as twenty further psalm paraphrases in the collection. Alexander Scott's 'The Fyifty Pshalme' ('Lord God, deliuer me, allace') is a version of Psalm 51. Montgomerie, Fowler and James VI also composed poetic psalm paraphrases, and a collection of psalm paraphrases known as *The Mindes Melodie* was printed in 1605 and 1606 by Robert Charteris (*ESTC* S110024, S94208, *STC* 18051, 18051.3).[1]

The style of the poem approaches the ecstatic with its anaphora, repeated apostrophes to God (appealed to in his many names) and internal rhymes. The spelling is heavily anglicised. Compare MQ 81, with which the poem has similarities of phrasing and theme.

Stanza: abbaaccd^5 ee^{2}d^5.
Text: MQ fols 117–118.
Authorship: unattributed.
Date: uncertain.

Commentary

3 *O God of hostes.* Compare 'Lord of Hosts', a common Old Testament title for God as leader of the Israelite armies. See Psalm 46: 7: 'The Lord of hostes is with vs' (Geneva Bible, 1560).

5 *thow set me frie quhen I wes thrall.* Compare Psalm 142: 7: 'Bring my soule out of prison that I maie praise thy Name'; Psalm 4: 1: 'thou hast set me at libertie when I was in distres' (Geneva Bible, 1560).

6 *Iehoua.* Jehovah, from the Hebrew YHWH / Adonai. Compare MQ 81, l. 29.

11 *with humble hairt contreit.* Compare Psalm 51: 17: 'The sacrifices of God are a contrite spirit: a contrite and broken heart O God thou wilt not despise' (Geneva Bible, 1560); Scott, *The Fyifty Pshalme*, l. 70: 'In humill hairt, contreit alwyiss'.

13 *My saull doeth stay and watche for the, O Lord.* See Psalm 130: 5–6:

---

[1] With thanks to Dr Nicola Royan for sharing her unpublished work on Scottish Psalmody.

'I haue waited on the Lord: my Soule has waited and I haue trusted in his worde. My soule waiteth on the Lord more then the morning watche watcheth for the morning' (Geneva Bible, 1560).

23 *Cum sinneris now, the Lord doeth on ws call.* See Matthew 9: 13: 'I am not come to call the righteous, but the sinners to repentance' (Geneva Bible, 1560).

26 *Cum now with humble hairtis, 3e wretchis all.* Note Psalm 51: 13: 'Then shal I teache thy waies vnto the wicked' (Geneva Bible, 1560); Scott, *The Fyifty Pshalme*, l. 53: 'I sall to synnaris mak narratioun'.

29 *He is of nature slaw to punishment.* Compare Numbers 14: 18: 'The Lord is slowe to angre, and of great mercie'; Psalm 103: 8: 'The Lord is ful of compassion and mercie, slowe to angre and of great kindnes' (Geneva Bible, 1560).

36–37 *With humble hairt lo prostrat I doe ly, / To the I call, to the I mak my mone.* See Psalm 142: 2: 'I powred out my meditacion before him, and declared mine affliction in his presence' (Geneva Bible, 1560).

58 *O happie thryis that thame can keip in stoir.* Perhaps 'Those are three times as happy who can keep [their praise of God] stored in abundance'? 'Thame' seems to refer to l. 56.

68 *All warldlie thingis as vaine I will reiect.* Compare Psalm 119: 37: 'Turne awaie mine eyes from regarding vanitie'.

71 *Refuis me not: thow art my God for ay.* Compare Psalm 51:11: 'Cast me not awaie from thy presence' (Geneva Bible, 1560); and its echo in 'Sore I complaine of Sin' (*Gude and Godlie Ballatis*, Mitchell ed. 1896–97, pp. 21–23): 'O cast me not away / For my grit sinne' (p. 22).

74 *Vnto the Lord, my God, now will I sing.* Psalm 51: 11,: 'Open thou my lippes; O Lord, and my mouth shal shewe forthe thy praise' (Geneva Bible, 1560).

74. In Prais of ane Gentle Woman.

In this poem the narrator struggles with the difficulty of writing about his lady's virtues in a manner that befits her perfection and thus allows him to declare himself her man (ll. 12, 28). It employs the familiar poetic paradox of writing about being unable to write (compare MQ 45). Its insistence on the lady's peerless qualities (some of which are presented in a personification allegory in ll. 21–23) and the narrator's sincerity are conventional but may also be compared to MQ 40 and MQ

48. The lady's elegance, nobility and dignity are fitting for the 'Gentle Woman' of the poem's title.
Stanza: rhyming couplets (aa[6]).
Text: MQ fols 118v–119.
Authorship: unattributed.
Date: uncertain.

Commentary
1–8 The sense of these lines is that it is impossible to offer fitting praise for that which is perfect. It passes the narrator's abilities to do so, despite his wishes, and he must be content to merely look upon the lady as he cannot do her justice in words.

2 *To seik to pas the painters art*. The painter here may be Nature, or God, who has created the narrator's beloved. For a similar statement of the impossibility of representing the lady's peerless beauty, compare MQ 48, ll. 29–42; also see MQ 40, ll. 92–93.

3 *performe that dewtie bindis as dew*. 'Perform that which duty dictates as due'.

9 *Houp sayis*. The encouraging presence of Hope is conventional in love allegories. See *Kingis Quair*, l. 1106: 'Gude Hope my gyde'; Dunbar 'Sen that I am a presoneir', l. 41: 'Gud Houp rownit in my eir'. On the precariousness of a lover's hope, see MQ 71, ll. 24–32.

13 *3e heavinlie goddis above, 3e most celestiall*. Echoic of MQ 63, l. 1.

15–16 *Give me Pernassus styll, and als Mont Edees smell, / With water Helicon to drink, or els Pegasus well*. The narrator asks for poetic skill. Parnassus is the sacred mountain, associated with Orpheus. Mount Edees is Mount Ida, near Troy, the location of the Judgement of Paris. Helicon is sanctuary to the Muses, and home to the fountain, Hippocrene, created when Pegasus' hoof struck the ground. Compare MQ 48, ll. 1–3 and notes.

19 *My ladie, I dar vow, in bewtie all doeth pas*. Compare MQ 64, ll. 1–8.

21 *Dame Vertew in hir hairt with Pitie taikis thair place*. The single personification of 'virtue' itself is not as common as the personification of single good characteristics or virtues (such as the Cardinal Virtues). The lady's pity for the lover, however, is commonly personified. See Dunbar 'Sen that I am a presoneir', ll. 49–56; and in *King Hart*, the presence of 'Rueth' and 'puire Pietie' in the company of Dame Plesance (ll. 116, 120).

23 *Remors and Temperance dois hir accumpanie.* These personifications not among the common figures from the courtly lady's retinue of virtues in love allegories. 'Remors' is related to pity or compassion. See *DOST, Remors,* n. Compare Scott, 'Only to 3ow in Erd that I luve best (l. 38) where the narrator asks his lady to 'Remord and rew and pondir weill my parte'. Temperance (moderation) appears in Dunbar's 'This hinder nycht, halff sleiping as I lay', l. 101, in the company of Nobilnes.

75. Of Ane Vnthankfull Freind.

This complaint is in a woman's voice (for other female voiced complaints, see MQ 49 and MQ 66 and the inset complaint in MQ 65), and is a remorseful lament for misplaced affections, characterised by a proverbial style. Here 'freind' is a synonym for lover or the beloved. The poem is one of a number of lyrics in this part of MQ that examine the theme of friendship (though also see MQ 23 by Maitland), a popular subject matter with near contemporary Scottish writers such as John Stewart of Baldynneis (see McClune 2006, pp. 179–201).
Stanza: pentameter rhyming couplets (aa^5).
Text: MQ fols 119–119v.
Authorship: unattributed.
Date: uncertain.

Commentary

1 *a freind.* One individual well disposed to another person, and sometimes used of kinsmen. See *DOST, Frend,* n. See MQ 65, l. 110. Here, however, an amatory connection between the narrator and this friend is suggested (see l. 18).

2 *to play a freind.* This probably has the sense 'to behave in the manner of' rather than to 'act', 'perform' or participate in a game. See *DOST, Play,* v.

4 *hes maid me schent.* Perhaps 'has brought me low', or 'humiliated me'. See *DOST, S(c)hent,* v.

6 *'Quhen stead is stollin, then steik the stable dure'.* Proverbial. See *King Hart,* l. 613: 'The steid is stollin steik the dure'. Also see 'The Bird in the Cage', ll. 27–28: 'Ouir late it is the stabill dure to steik, / Quhen sturdie steid is stollin' (Cranstoun ed. 1891–93, I, poem XXII).

9 *Is not a trustie freind by tryell bocht.* Proverbial, see Maxwell's Commonplace Book, Proverb no. 219: 'Tryall maketh trust' (cited in

DOST, *Trial*, n. sense 2); also Churchyard's 'The Thochtis of men dois daylie chynge' (MF version), ll. 25–27:

> The sureast way that I can find
> Is first to prufe and syne to trust
> So sall affectioun not be blind.

Also see John Stewart of Baldynneis, *To his Rycht Inteirlie Belowit Freind*, l. 17: 'Thair is no freind except ane freind in neid' (Crockett ed. 1913, p. 113).

11 *I am lyik the blind that blamis the licht*. Proverbial, see Whiting 1941–51, Blind; and Chaucer's *Troilus and Criseyde*, 2, ll. 862–64:

> What is the sonne wers, of kynde right,
> Though that a man, for fieblesse of his yen,
> May nought endure on it to see for bright?

12 *no want of sicht*. 'No lack of evidence'.

14 *but euer nocht*. 'But all was worth nothing'. See *DOST*, *Nocht*, n. especially sense 2a.

19–20 *I wes lyik the hen that skrepis the knyfe / 3it ignorant it sould bereve hir lyfe*. Proverbial, see Whiting 1941–51, Hen: Whiting cites a 1623 translation of Mateo Alemán's *The Rogue*, which has the proverb 'Scraping like the hen to her owne hurt'. Elsewhere, the hen is often a symbol of vulnerability. Compare 'The Bischoppis Lyfe and Testament', l. 112: 'Lyke till ane flok of hennis befoir ane Tod' (Cranstoun ed. 1891–93, poem XXVIII).

23–24 *lyik the cur that bytis the man / Quhen he hes fed and done him all he can*. Proverbial, 'the dog that bites the hand that feeds him'. Compare Montgomerie, *From London to William Murray*, l. 8: 'Vncourtessie comes aluayis of a Cur'.

25 *with wit now coft I doe protest*. 'With wisdom now purchased, I declare'.

76. To His Freind.

This is a complaint against Fortune and an appeal for mercy, both for the narrator and his lady, of the sort that is found widely in late sixteenth-century love poetry (see, for example, Scott's *Adew, Luvaris, Adew*, Montgomerie's 'On Love and fortune I complene' and James VI's *A Dier at the Majesties desyre*). The narrator regards himself as more unfortunate than others in love (compare the narrator of Montgomerie's

'Quha wareis all the wicked weirds bot I?'), but exonerates his lady from any blame. He suggests that his ill luck alone prevents him and his beloved from being together. The friend addressed in the title clearly indicates a beloved, the lady, first addressed at l. 17. See headnote to MQ 75.

The poem is copied in italic script.
Stanza: ababcc^4.
Text: MQ fols 119v–120v.
Authorship: unattributed.
Date: uncertain.

Commentary

1 *michtie Iove*. Jove or Jupiter is the most important of the Roman Gods, and sometimes used to indicate the Christian God. Compare MQ 82.

6 *so monye turning tydis*. A metaphor for the narrator's changing fortunes, linked to the comparison of worldly variance and the changing or unpredictable tides at sea. Compare Sempill, *The Flemyng Bark*, l. 56: 'This tripand tyddis may tyne ws aw' (Cranstoun ed. 1891–93, I, poem XLVI). Also see MQ 44, l. 21.

10 *Fortounis thrall*. The lover's depiction of himself as thrall to fortune in love is conventional. See MQ 39, ll. 1–3, and Montgomerie, 'If faithfulnes suld friendship find', ll. 11–12: 'Quhat neids thou, Cupid all thir dairts / Me to ou'rthrou that els am cum thy thrall?'

14 *A double dolour*. The nature of this double affliction seems to be the narrator's lack of success in love, and yet his continuing thraldom to his lady. For the phrasing compare Chaucer's *Troilus and Criseyde*, I, l. 'The double sorwe of Troilus to tellen'.

21 *Tak blak, it best becumis thy heid*. The narrator instructs his beloved to take the clothes of mourning. Compare *King Hart*, ll. 473–76.

> For saik of the I will no colour reid
> Nor lusty quhyt vpone my bodie beir,
> Bot blak and gray alway quhill I be deid.
> I will none vther wantoun wedis weir.

33 *Tisbe trew*. Thisbe, who killed herself when she believed her lover Priamus to be dead. See Ovid *Met.* 4, ll. 55–166. Her story is recalled again at ll. 39–42.

77. In Praise of ane Gilt Bybill.

This poem, in hymnal stanza, describes an elaborate book cover given as gift to a copy of the Bible by its loving 'mistress' (l. 11). The poem's emphasis on the mistress's affection for her Bible perhaps suggests that it may have been written for the pious and virtuous dedicatee of MQ 69, Marie Maitland, whose name is also inscribed at the beginning of MQ. The poem's enthusiasm for the reading of the Bible recalls MQ 24, ll. 5–30.

The praise of a fine book binding, and comparison of its opulence and artistry to the even greater spiritual value of the text within, is a conceit found elsewhere, and as early as the Old English Riddles of the Exeter Book. Within MQ the poem may be compared to MQ 84, which is also a poem in praise of a book.

The book binding described in MQ 77 has its basis in material reality as well as in literary tradition. Decorative book bindings made for copies of the Bible and for Psalters were prestige items. Examples of fine Scottish work from the sixteenth and seventeenth centuries survive in the collections of the NLS. Some examples of embroidered soft-cover bindings survive from the early seventeenth century (see *Book Bindings, Historical and Decorative*, 1927). It is not clear whether the binding described here as a 'cot' (coat) was embroidered, or a leather binding on boards, intricately tooled (gold or silver was often used in the process), inlaid or onlaid. On Scottish book bindings of the sixteenth-century, see Mitchell 1955, pp. 27–70, and plates 17–27.

Stanza: ab³c⁴b³ (not set out in stanzas in the MS).
Text: MQ fol. 120v.
Authorship: uncertain.
Date: uncertain.

Commentary

3 *luik, then loup*. Proverbial, 'Luke or ȝe loup'. Pause before you take the risk of endangering your reputation (by not being able to adequately describe the book). See *DOST*, *Lowp*, v, sense 2b.

9 *A cot*. A coat, a metaphor for the book binding of the Bible. Compare the idea of the clothed book in poems such as the 'Greneacres Stanza' ('Blak be thy bandis and thy wede also') found in manuscripts of Lydgate's *Fall of Princes* and after Chaucer's *Troilus and Criseyde* in Bodleian Library Arch. Selden B. 24 (fol. 118v) and elsewhere. See *IMEV* 524.

10 *syluer streamis*. Lines or fine streaks of silver. For a silver-tooled bible binding, see NLS Bdg.s.60.

11 *As iust rewaird the maistres gave*. The owner's relationship to the book is described in courtly terms suggesting a lady granting a reward to her suitor. The term 'maistres' suggests a woman of some status or authority.

14 *with single ei*. Perhaps with a 'sincere eye', or 'with concentration' (with one eye, as if taking aim on a target). See *DOST*, *Singil*, adj.

15 *pearlis of pryce*. An echo of Matthew 13: 46, 'a perle of great price' (Geneva Bible, 1560).

78. Ane Freindlye Letter to his Freind.

Described as a letter to a friend, this poem contributes to the exploration of the theme of faithful affinity explored in MQ 72, MQ 75, MQ 76, MQ 80, MQ 83 and MQ 84. Its disconsolate narrator pledges loyalty to his beloved ('my faythfull hairt, l. 31) and appeals to God for support for his love suit. On the epistolary form in sixteenth-century Scottish lyrics see van Heijnsbergen 2005, pp. 314–45. On the possibility of female authorship for the poem, see Newlyn 2004, p. 96.
Stanza: $a^4b^3a^4$ b^3cc^3 (final stanza $a^4b^3a^4$ b^3).
Text: MQ fols 121–121v [title on 120v].
Authorship: unattributed.
Date: uncertain.

Commentary

29 *fayth and promeis suir*. Compare MQ 79, l. 17, also MQ 72, ll. 1, 31–32.

37 *Fairweill, thairfoir, my hairt, adew*. For this conventional leave taking compare Scott, *Adew, Luvaris, Adew*, ll. 32–33: 'Addew, addew, my weill and eik my wo, / Fairweill for now for euirmoir I go'. Also see MQ 40, l. 121, and MQ 83, l. 1.

79. To ane Angrie Freinde

The nature of the proverbial statements with which the poem begins perhaps suggests a female narrator for this complaint against Fortune, although the speaker's gender is never stated. Whatever the case, this is a lament for the loss of, or separation from, a loved one. The poem

has verbal and thematic similarities to other poems in this part of MQ, including MQ 66, MQ 75, MQ 76 and MQ 80.
Stanza: octosyllabic rhyming couplets (aa⁴).
Text: MQ fol. 122 [title on fol. 121v].
Authorship: uncertain.
Date: uncertain.

Commentary
1 *The lyon for hir tender whelpis dois roir*. Proverbial, see Whiting 1941–51, Lioness, and compare *Legends of the Saints*, I, ll. 453, 436–38:

> out of wyt for wa scho ferd
> As a lyones come ful thra,
> Þat men had tane þe quhelpis fra

3–4 *turtill for the lofe of maik, thay say, / Doeth neuer rest, bot workis hir awin decay*. The turtle dove is a symbol of faithful love and preparedness to love unto the death. See Whiting 1941–51, Turtle, and Chaucer, *Parliament of Fowls*, ll. 582–85:

> 'Nay, God forbede a lovere shulde chaunge!'
> The turtle seyde, and wex for shame al red,
> 'Though that his lady everemore be straunge,
> Yit lat hym serve hire ever, til he be ded.'

10 *In rest doeth schaw hir most pernitious*. A conventional account of Fortune's ways, but also compare MQ 76, l. 23 and the couplet from William Baldwin's *A Myrroure for Magistrates* (1559) that comprises MQ 87.

16 *Fy on plesour schort that murning bringis!* Proverbial. Compare Henryson, *Orpheus and Eurydice*, ll. 98–91:

> Off warldlie ioye, allace, quhat sall we say?
> Lyke till a flour that plesandly with spring,
> Quhilk fadis sone, and endis with murnyng.

17 *Sall fayth and treuth, sall promeis firme and suir*. Compare MQ 78, l. 29.

80. To his Freind.

This is a rather conventional love complaint addressed to a 'ladye'. Despite its use of formulaic quasi-religious diction and the familiar theme of the hopeless love suit, the poem contains some arresting imagery as the narrator contrasts himself with those for whom relief

follows sorrow – the storm-assailed ship that finds a harbour, a pilgrim who can return home, and a mother for whom joy follows pain.
Stanza: $a^4b^3a^4b^3$ (set out in octrains in MS).
Text: MQ fols 122–123.
Authorship: uncertain.
Date: uncertain.

Commentary
1 *The beatin bark with bloistrous blastis.* While the boat can find a harbour the narrator is unable to find any such haven in the midst of his troubles. The metaphor of fortune as a sea on which the individual is tossed, is commonplace. For the imperilled boat as an image of the self, see *Kingis Quair*, l. 114: 'My feble bote ... to stere and rowe'; Dunbar, 'O wreche, be war, this warld will wend the fro', l. 13: 'Bend vp thy saill and win thy port of grace'. Also see note to MQ 44, l. 18. A similar image occurs in Pierre de Ronsard, *Les Amours diverses* XI, ll. 5–8:

> Or' je pardonne à la mer inhumaine,
> Aux flots, aux vents, mon naufrage et mes maux,
> Puis que par tant et par tant de travaux
> Une main douce à si doux port me meine.
>
> (I pardon now the sea's fell ebbs and flows, Though tempest-tossed, shipwrecked again, again, Since now a soft and gentle hand would fain Lead me to such a port and end my woes.) See Shapiro ed. and trans. 2002, pp. 304–5.

17 *bewrapt with wo.* Formulaic, but compare Henryson, *Testament of Cresseid*, l. 543, 'Wrappit in wo, ane wretch full will of wane!'; also compare MQ 65, l. 65.

18 *In laberinth I ly.* 'I am in a state of confusion'.

29 *with humble hairt contreit.* This recalls biblical phrasing, such as Psalm 51: 17. See note to MQ 73, l. 11, and compare MQ 81, l. 20.

33–34 *heir a toy and licht conset, / And loveris new devyce.* The narrator admits that his hopes of ll. 21–32 are merely a fancy ('a toy') – an unrealistic plan ('devyce') typical of lovers.

81. Ane Prayer.

This penitential work may be compared to MQ 73, to which it has some verbal similarities, perhaps dictated by the poem's theme, and perhaps by common authorship. The narrator, like that of MQ 73, presents

himself as a sinner begging for forgiveness from a merciful God. Other analogues may be found among the penitential poems included in *The Gude and Godlie Ballatis*: see, for example, 'With heuie hart full of distres, / Lamenting my greit sinfulnes' (Mitchell ed. 1896–97, pp. 170–71). Further near-contemporary analogues include John Stewart of Baldynneis, 'In golfe of greif I grone' (Crockett ed. 1913, pp. 104–6), and Montgomerie, *A godly Prayer*.
Stanza: aaaa⁵.
Text: MQ fols 123–123v.
Authorship: uncertain.
Date: uncertain.

Commentary

1 *With weippin eis*. On the value of sorrowful expressions of penance, see Psalm 126: 5: 'Thei that sowe in teares, shal reape in ioye' (Geneva Bible, 1560).

8 *A wretche and sinner pour*. Compare MQ 73, l. 41. Also compare *Gude and Godlie 'Ballatis*, 'We wretchit sinners pure' (Mitchell ed. 1896–97, pp. 24–25).

13 *O Father dear*. Compare MQ 73, l. 61.

14 *rigour of the law*. The strict interpretation of the law. Compare MQ 37 on God's combined 'rigour' and 'pacience' (l. 28).

23 *seit divine*. The throne of heaven, see Matt 5: 34.

24 *My sobs, my sighis*. Compare MQ 73, l. 38.

26–27 *Thy holie bluid is not ʒit waistit so / But that it may help me with sinners mo*. See Mark 14: 24.

29–30 *Iehoua greit and Lord maist hie /... for succour I doe flie*. These lines are close in phrasing to MQ 73, ll. 6–7.

30 *To futestule thyne*. This is a slightly unexpected use of Matt 5: 34: 'the erthe for it is his fote stole' (Geneva Bible, 1560; compare Montgomerie, *A godly Prayer*, l. 29: 'The erthe thy futstule'). The narrator's wishes to flee not to God's throne (in heaven) but to seek refuge at his 'futestule', perhaps underlining his feelings of unworthiness.

82. To michtie Ioue above that ringis

A doxology, addressed to the Trinity. Compare Montgomerie, *A godly Prayer*, ll. 65–69:

> To grit Jehovah let all glore be gevin
> Vha shupe my saull to his similitude
> And to his sone vhom he sent doun from hevin
> Vhen I wes lost to buy me with his blude
> And to the holy Ghost my gyder gude

The poem is copied in an italic script.
Stanza: aabccb⁴.
Text: MQ fol. 123v.
Authorship: unattributed.
Date: uncertain.

Commentary

1 *Ioue*. Jupiter, God.

4 *Who shed his bluid for euerie sinner.* Mark 14: 24. Compare MQ 81, ll. 26–27 and note.

5 *Holie Ghost, the confort bringer.* A description of the third person of the Trinity based on Biblical texts such as Acts 9: 31: 'the comfort of the holie Gost' (Geneva Bible, 1560).

83. To Ane Vnthankfull Freind.

This poem is described in the metrical coda that follows it as a 'ragment' (see note to l. 63), which is intended to allow the narrator to unburden himself and to warn his readers of the ways of the false woman he once served. The woman of his complaint is revealed to be a rich widow. In early modern Scotland, widows often held important positions in the family, and had considerable financial independence; wealthy widows could expect to have several suitors (Brown 2000, pp. 73, 118).

The literary traditions surrounding widowhood offered contrasting perspectives on the conduct of widows. Patristic and sermon literature recommended that widowhood should be a period of chastity and seclusion (Owst 1966, p. 119). However, another rich literary tradition existed of the lustful and dissimulating widow, evinced for example in Chaucer's 'The Wife of Bath's Tale', Dunbar's *Tretis of the Tua Mariit Wemen and the Wedow* (see Bawcutt 1992, pp. 335–44), *The Spectacle of Luf*, chapter 6 (c.1492, Craigie ed. 1923–25, I, pp. 288–93), and John Rolland's *Sevin Seages*, ll. 7591–7950 (Black ed. 1932). MQ 83 draws on this tradition. Its speaker often employs bitter invective against the behaviour of the widow who has wronged him. However, the poem also offers the reader a lesson against lust and avarice: the widow is castigated for her sexual appetites, and her new lover is presented as a gold digger who is likely to spend all she has.

Stanza: ababcc^4; abab^3 (the 'ragment' is not set out in stanzas in the manuscript).
Text: MQ fols 124–125.
Authorship: unattributed.
Date: uncertain.

Commentary

3 *quho wes thy knicht*. Evocative of the ideals of service in the courtly love tradition, but also reminiscent of the descriptions of Troylus as Cresseid's 'trew knicht' in Henryson's *Testament of Cresseid* (ll. 546, 553, 560).

10 *filthie lyfe*. This charge is repeated at l. 19. Compare Henryson, *Testament of Cresseid*, ll. 80–83:

> ... how was thow fortunait
> To change in filth all thy feminitie,
> ...
> Sa giglotlike takand thy foull plesance.

20 *thy cruell tygirs hairt*. In Dunbar's *Tretis*, the widow advises the wives, 'Thought ȝe as tygris be terne, be tretable in luf' (l. 261). Also compare *Clariodus*, II, ll. 275–76: 'This Lady, birning in hir crueltie / With tygir mynd'.

22 *ane whoris pairt*. 'a harlot's role'. At this date 'hure' has the sense of 'unchaste woman', but also the stronger meaning of 'prostitute' (see *DOST*, Hure, Huir, n).

33 *ane wha had bene brunt*. The sense here seems to be 'one who has been injured'. The implication may be that the lady's previous experiences make her more dangerous and willing to take risks with the affections of others.

44 *a pecok*. The peacock is a symbol of pride and excess. See MQ 35, ll. 89–90 and note.

53 *thy gear*. The widow's wealth may have come from a previous marriage, as is the case for Dunbar's widow in the *Tretis*, whose second husband was a merchant (ll. 296–409), giving her ample funds to make herself attractive to other men: 'I wald me prunȝa plesandly in precius wedis, / That luffaris myght apon me luke and ȝing lusty gallandis' (ll. 374–75).

54 *thow chust him for lance and speir*. Here 'lance and speir' have phallic connotations suggesting the widow's lecherousness. Compare *King Hart* ll. 959–60: 'This brokin speir, sum tyme wes stiff and stout, / To hir I leif'. Also see MQ 21, l. 40 and note.

61 *I ... sendis*. This line is incomplete, a blank space left in the MS, perhaps for the insertion of a name (see Craigie ed. 1920, p. 292).

62 *ragment*. A composition or discourse, often emotional and rambling rather than formally structured or reasoned. See Dunbar *Tretis*, l. 162, 'I sall a ragment reveil fra rute of my hert'.

84. In Prais of ane Buik Send to his Freind.

It is possible that the 'buik' that this poem concerns is MQ. In this case, the author of texts on 'thingis of great and high affairs' (l. 7) may be Richard Maitland: the second and third stanzas of the poem comprise a defence of literary or poetic style and the value of reading, which is appropriate to such a context. The poem's praise of the book as a store of treasure, and its invitation to the reader (the 'freind' of the title) to value it as such, echo MQ 77. Another possibility, therefore, is that the book with which the poem is concerned is, as in MQ 77, the Bible. See note to l. 10 and l. 15.
Stanza: $a^4 \, b^3 a^4 \, bcc^3$.
Text: MQ fol. 125v.
Authorship: unattributed.
Date: uncertain.

Commentary

10 *In shape of beastis he drawis*. Ambiguous, perhaps suggesting the use of allegory, or metaphor. Also suggestive of the beasts of the Book of Revelation.

12 *of tresour stoir*. Compare MQ 77, ll. 13–16.

14 *In colours*. In a literary style, in rhetorical or poetic language.

15 *misterie*. Suggesting something enigmatic, or difficult to understand, such as doctrinal truth.

85. To Your Self.

This poem provides evidence for Marie Maitland's writing of 'vers' (l. 8). Its narrator urges her to fulfil her potential as a poet and complete

a triumvirate of female poets alongside the classical writer Sappho and the sixteenth-century Italian scholar Olympia Fulvia Morata. The narrator encourages Marie to aim for the prestigious laurel crown as a mark of poetic distinction, something claimed by, or awarded to, several male poets of her generation. The poem ends with a couplet urging her not to take heed of flattery or ridicule on her path to literary success. See note to l. 15. The poem is copied in italic script. See Dunnigan 1997, pp. 29–31.
Stanza: abab[5].
Text: MQ fol. 126.
Authorship: unattributed.
Date: c.1586?

Commentary

1 *Sapho*. The poet Sappho of Lesbos, born c.612 BC.

2 *the nyne*. The nine muses.

6 *Olimpia, O lampe of Latine land*. This is probably the Italian poet, classical and biblical scholar, and Calvinist convert, Olympia Fulvia Morata (1526/27–1555). She composed in both Latin and Greek. See further Parker ed. 2003, pp. 1–57; Stevenson 2005, pp. 285–88.

9 *Maistres Marie*. Marie Maitland, daughter of Richard Maitland and signatory of MQ. She is named in MQ 69 and perhaps also addressed in MQ 77.

11 *fleing fame*. The sense here is that Marie's fame is 'flying', or fast increasing.

12 *Hyd not so haut a hairt in slugish thrall*. 'Do not conceal so distinguished a heart in drudgery'. Dunnigan suggests that 'slugish thrall' is a reference to Marie's transcription of MQ. Dunnigan 1997, p. 29, though see note to l. 13.

13 *This buik then bear and beat your branis therin*. The book is perhaps MQ. The injunction to 'beat your branis' means to 'improve your mind'. See *DOST*, *Bete, Beit*, v. Marie's work on 'this buik' is therefore a way of strengthening her own work.

15 *the laurell win*. The laurel is a symbol of poetic achievement. Compare Montgomerie's poem to Marie Maitland's brother, *In Praise of Maister John Maitland chancellor*, ll. 13–14: 'Then lyk his Name the Gods for Armis him gives / Suord, Pen and wingis in croun of laurel leives'. Montgomerie also refers to himself as one of those 'vhose heads weirs laurel plaits' (*Ezechiel Montgomerie's Ansueir to Ladyland*, l. 13), and John Stewart of Baldynneis writes two poems in praise of James VI's crowning with laurel (see Crockett ed. 1913, pp. 128, 130).

19 *Momus*. The Greek god of ridicule.

86. 3e heauinlie goddis and goddessis

This is an invocation to the gods for help in finishing a work, and it has been suggested that it relates to the copying of MQ (Pinkerton ed. 1786, p. 467). The poem certainly seems to mark the ending of a major section of verse in MQ and is followed only by the epigrammatic works on fol. 127, before a poem on absence, and a sequence of epitaphs and eulogies. See Newlyn 2004, p. 94. The poem has been tentatively assigned to Marie Maitland on the grounds of its reference to Diana, which also links it to MQ 69, a poem addressed to Marie and celebrating her virtues, including her chastity. See Dunnigan 1997, pp. 29–30. Pinkerton also thought it to be by Marie (Pinkerton ed. 1786, p. 467), but Craigie was more cautious (Craigie ed. 1920, p. 292).
Stanza: a⁴ b³c⁴b³.
Text: MQ fol. 126v.
Authorship: unattributed.
Date. c.1586.

Commentary

1 *3e heauinlie goddis and goddessis*. Compare the invocation that begins MQ 63 (attributed to Montgomerie).

3 *my muse*. The narrator's inspiration, perhaps the muse of poetry?

5 *Diana, ladye bricht*. Diana, the goddess of chastity and hunting. Compare MQ 69, l. 49 and note.

6 *nymphes of chastetie*. Diana and her nymphs bathe in seclusion, away from the eyes of men. Ovid *Met*.3, ll. 131–98. Compare MQ 69, l. 61 and note, and MQ 40, ll. 60–61.

87. Quhen houp and hap, and weill and health bene hiest

Both couplets are extracted from William Baldwin's *A Myrroure for Magistrates*, which appeared in a number of editions printed in London between 1559 and 1587 (*ESTC* S104522, *STC* 1247–52.5, 1559–78; for an edition, see Campbell ed. 1938). The practice of including short extracts from this work, and others like it, in manuscript anthologies was very popular in the sixteenth century: the Bannatyne Manuscript, for example, contains several texts extracted from Baldwin's *A Treatise of morall philosophye* (1567), and John Maxwell's Commonplace Book contains proverbs, some taken from collections such as George Pettie's *A Petite Pallace of Pettie his Pleasure* (1576) (see Bawcutt 1990, pp. 61–62).

The first couplet is part of the poem 'How Thomas Montague the earle of Salysbury in the middes of his glory, was chaunceably slayne with a piece of ordinaunce' (Campbell ed. 1938, p. 152: 'Whan hope and hap, whan helth and welth is hyest, / Than wo and wracke, desease, and nede be nyest'). It was a popular couplet for excerption and also appears in London, British Library, Additional MS Add 61822, fol. 81v; Harley 6910, fol. 139; and Oxford, Bodleian Library Rawlinson, Poet. 148, fol. 7. (See Martin and McClune 2009, pp. 249–50.)

The second couplet is taken from the poem 'Howe the Lord Hastinges was betrayed by trustyng to much to his evyl counsayler Catesby, and vilanously murdered in the tower of London by Richarde Duke of Glocestre' (Campbell ed. 1938, p. 271: 'Beware to ryse by serving princely lust. / Surely to stand, one meane is rysyng iust'). This tragedy first appeared in the 1563 edition of the *Myrroure*, suggesting that MQ's compiler had access to this or one of the editions of the *Myrroure* to appear in the 1570s.

The couplets are copied in italic script.
Stanza: pentametre rhyming couplets (aa^5).
Text: MQ fol. 127; BALDWIN *Myrroure for Magistrates*.
Authorship: William Baldwin (unattributed in MQ).
Date: c.1559–63.

Commentary
1–2 For this presentation of Fortune compare MQ 76, l. 23 and MQ 79, l. 10.

88. The Reid in the Loch Sayis

This consolatory poem answers the pessimism of MQ 87 by urging its reader to endure hardships (particularly those of a political nature) in the knowledge that calm follows a storm, and suffering can be beneficial. Its appeal to exiles and prisoners (ll. 5–6) may have been seen as of particular relevance to the experiences of members of the Maitland

family, banished from their estates during the period 1571–84. Both William and John Maitland also experienced periods of imprisonment as a result of their political activities. See MQ 46, and note to l. 180 and headnote, and headnote to MQ 30. The poem is copied in an italic script.
Stanza: abab⁴.
Text: MQ fol. 127.
Authorship: unattributed.
Date: uncertain.

Commentary

1 *raging stormes*. A metaphor for personal or political disturbance. Compare the imagery of MQ 44, ll. 17–32 (especially note to l. 18), and MQ 80, ll. 1–3 (note to l. 1).

3 *We ȝeild thairto*. The narrator imagines himself and his intended readers as reeds in stormy water, in an allusion to the poem's proverbial title. Compare Chaucer, *Troilus and Criseyde*, II, ll. 1387–88, 'And reed that boweth down for every blast, / Ful lightly, cesse wynd, it wol aryse' (Whiting 1968 R 71). Also see *Troilus and Criseye*, I, ll. 257–7: 'The yerde is bet that bowen wole and wynde, / Than that that brest' (Whiting 1968 B484); for similar Latin proverbs, see Walther ed. 1963–69, proverbs 3343, 27292, 27336.

4 *bent vp*. Determined, strong.

89. As Absence is the greatest fo

In this poem, the lover complains of his (?) separation from his lady, whom he hopes will be faithful and just towards him, despite his unexplained absence. Absence is a common theme in contemporary lyric poetry. Compare, for example, Montgomerie, 'The cruell pane and grevous smart', ll. 5–6: 'With pansing sair I am opprest / In absence of hir I love best'.

Metaphors of death and illness, typical of the courtly love tradition, personification, and legalistic diction, characterise the poem's style. Like MQ 83, it is concluded with a short coda in a different stanza form from the rest of the poem. It is copied in italic script.
Stanza: ababbcbc⁴; aaab².
Text: MQ fols 127v–128.
Authorship: unattributed.
Date: uncertain.

Commentary

22 *Bewteis bar.* Beauty is imagined presiding at the bar in a court of justice. For a similar allegorical court of love in which the lover has to plead his suit, see Montgomerie, 'Hir brouis, tuo bouis of Ebane ever bent', l. 7: 'My Patience pleidis my proces at the bar'.

27 *Sum other caussis to repledge.* The diction is legalistic. The meaning of 'repledge' is to take back or redeem something, and also to withdraw someone from the jurisdiction of another court to that of one's own. See *DOST, Repledge,* v. See Montgomerie, 'Bright Amorous Ee vhare Love in ambush lyes', ll. 10–11: 'To be repledg't ȝe plainly will appeill / To Love'.

33 *ane trew Penelope.* A common example of fidelity, Penelope was wife of Odysseus, and remained faithful to him during his long absence, despite the many offers of marriage she received during this time (see Ovid, *Heroides,* I). She is also alluded to in MQ 35, l. 182 and MQ 49, l. 33.

90. Epitaph of Sir Richard Maitland Knight

This is the first of four epitaphs for Richard Maitland (who died on 20 March 1586; MQ 93 is a double epitaph for Maitland and his wife). The practice of placing epitaphs at the end of manuscript collections of verse was common in this period (see Hobbs 1992, pp. 35–36).

The name of the author of this poem, Thomas Hudson (d. c.1605), is given in full in MF and in an abbreviated form here. Thomas Hudson was one of a family of English musicians and poets at the court of James VI. He was made master of the Chapel Royal in June 1586. In addition to writing poetry, he was also a translator, *The historie of Judith in forme of a poeme, penned in French by the noble poet, G. Salust, lord of Bartas* (1584), being his most important work.

Thomas Hudson's epitaph for Maitland is in sonnet form, a popular way of structuring commemorative verse in the period, giving such poems a brevity of expression, which encouraged the notion that they were intended to be inscribed on a tomb. Hudson opens the poem with a meditation on the nature of time, and develops this to celebrate Maitland's personal virtues and distinguished public standing, as well as his pedigree. The poem is copied in an italic script.

In MF (and R) the epitaph has a fuller title: 'Epitaph of Schir Richard Maitland of Lethingtoun Knycht, Quho Died of the Aage of Four Scoir and Tene ȝeiris in the ȝeir of God 1585 Die Mensis 20 Martii'.

Stanza: sonnet, ababbcbccdcdee[5].
Text: MQ fol. 129; MF p. 366, R fol. 53.
Authorship: Thomas Hudson.
Date: c.1586.

Commentary

1 *slyding tyme so slylie slippes away*. The adjective 'slyding' in often used of the swift passage of time, fortune or happiness. Compare Dunbar 'This waverand warldis wretchidnes', l. 5: 'The slydand ioy'; 'Quhat is this lyfe bot ane straucht way to deid', l. 3: 'A slyding quheill'. For a similar account of time, see Montgomerie, *A Description of Tyme* ('Tak tyme in tym or tym will not be tane'), especially ll. 1–8.

1–2 *slylie ... reaves*. Time is imagined now as a stealthy thief.

3 *we doe the cair of tyme delay*. 'We put off the anxieties brought by passing time'.

4 *We tyne the tyde*. Proverbial, with 'tyde' used as a metaphor for the passing time. Compare Montgomerie, 'ʒong tender plante in spring tym of ʒour ʒeirs', ll. 45–46: 'Thoght ʒe be ʒong ʒit once ʒe may be ald. / Tyd will not tarie'.

7 *in semble rate*. 'In a similar manner'.

8 *With love to God, religion, law and right*. This line celebrates Maitland's role as a judge (he was an extraordinary Lord of Session from 1554, and became an ordinary Lord of Session in 1561), and while stressing his piety, may also indicate his adherence to the reformed religion. See *DOST, Religion*, sense 4b. Maitland's own works are far from clear in expressing his doctrinal sympathies. See, for example, MQ 12, ll. 33–72.

10 *Of antient bloode*. The family could trace its origins to the twelfth century. See MQ 46 and note to ll. 93–96. Also compare MQ 68, ll. 141–46.

12 *So deit he olde*. Maitland died in 1586 at the age of 90.

91. Ane Other

Rubric] Ane vther Epitaph of the Said Sir Richard MF R

This sonnet is attributed in full in MF (though not in R) to Robert Hudson (d.1596), brother of Thomas Hudson (author of MQ 90), also a poet and musician at James VI's court. His extant poems, and poems addressed to

him, suggest that he was closely associated with King James, William Fowler and Alexander Montgomerie: Montgomerie dedicates a poem to him, which begins, 'My best belouit brother of the band'. Like MQ 90, Robert Hudson's epitaph draws attention to Maitland's lineage, public achievement as a high court judge, and his exemplary virtue and piety. The narrator reminds us of the consolation provided by the survival of Maitland's children, despite the sadness of his death. On the popularity of the sonnet for funerary epitaphs, see headnote to MQ 90. The poem is copied in italic script.
Stanza: sonnet, ababbcbccdcdee[5].
Text: MQ fol. 130, MF p. 366, R fol. 53.
Authorship: Robert Hudson.
Date: c.1586.

Commentary

1 *Thy surname ... thyne antient race.* Compare Maitland's concern with the importance of knowing and celebrating the family name and its history in his *History of the House of Seyton*, 'The Prolog': 'It war veray gude, honorable, plesand, and profitable, that everie grit nobill and gentillmen of heritage ... put in remembrance and maid cronicle of thair housis and surname' (Fullerton ed. 1829, p. xi). Also see MQ 90, l. 10, MQ 46 and note to ll. 93–96, and MQ 68, ll. 141–46.

2 *Thy martiall acts the cronicles display.* There is no surviving history of the Maitland family. Few accounts of the deeds of Maitlands are recorded in fifteenth- and sixteenth-century Scottish chronicles. However, the acts of Maitland's ancestors on his mother's side, the Setons, are recorded with many examples of martial prowess. On the appearance of Seton women in chronicles, see Ewan 2004 and Royan 2008, pp. 134–39.

3 *speake thou Iustice.* Here Justice is personified and asked to give account of Maitland's service as a judge. See note to MQ 90, l. 8.

5 *prest Gods treuth to plant alway.* Compare MQ 90, l. 10.

6 *a faithfull wyfe.* Maitland married Mary/Mariota, daughter of Sir Thomas Cranstoun of Corsbie, in c.1521. MQ 93, a double epitaph, reports that she died on the day of his burial, and MQ 95 also commemorates her.

12 *lives to die and deis to live againe.* This is echoic of various biblical texts on eternal life. Compare 2 Timothy 2: 11: 'For, if we be dead with him, we also shal liue with him' (Geneva Bible, 1560). For a similar use of paradox, see Montgomerie's sonnet *Epitaph of Jhone and Patrik Shaues*, l. 14: 'Deid shawis ȝe live, suppose ȝour lyfis be lost'.

14 *his worthye imps*. 'His worthy offspring'. Maitland's children are imagined as shoots or young plants. See *DOST, Imp*, n. He was survived by his son John Maitland, and his daughters Helen and Marie. The dates of the deaths of his other daughters, Margaret and Isabel, are not recorded.

92. Epitaphe vpon the Death of the Right Honorable Sir Richard Metland, Knight, Lord of Leidingtoun

This epitaph for Richard Maitland, in sonnet form, draws attention to the association of the funerary epitaph with the tomb, and the corpse therein, more directly than either MQ 90 or MQ 91. Unlike these poems it makes no particular mention of Maitland's family line, but is more concerned with the contrast between the dead body and living spirit. However, like the Hudson epitaphs, its praise of Maitland focuses on his faith, and virtue, and his role as a judge. The poem is copied in italic script and concluded with penwork flourishes.
Stanza: sonnet, ababbcbccdcdee^5.
Text: MQ fol. 131.
Authorship: unattributed.
Date: c.1586.

Commentary

4 *Quhase lyflye spreit did warldlye things despyse*. A rejection of the impermanent and untrustworthy things of the world is indeed a theme of Maitland's moral verses. Compare MQ 31, MQ 52, MQ 53 etc.

6 *blamles iudge*. On Maitland's role as Lord of Session, see MQ 90, note to l. 10.

7–8 *ȝit from his tombe (thoght he be deid) doith ryse / The glorious praise*. The reference here is to the poem itself, which is to be imagined as inscribed on Maitland's tomb, and from there broadcasting his fame.

9 *wisdome*. An attribute not mentioned in MQ 90 and MQ 91.

93a. A Luid Of Him Self and His Ladyie Quho Dyed On His Burial Day

This epitaph, in hymnal stanza, is for Richard Maitland and his wife, Mariota or Mary, daughter of Sir Thomas Cranstoun of Corsbie, whom he had married in c.1521, and who, according to the manuscript title for this poem, outlived him by only a few days. MQ 95 also commemorates her. This poem celebrates their long and contented marriage, and sees their almost simultaneous demise as evidence of love's ability to triumph over death. While it is most usual to find epitaphs commissioned for or composed by one spouse for another (see, for example, Stevenson and Davidson, eds 2001, p. 95), there are also some comparable examples of near-contemporary double epitaphs for man and wife, such as the well-known early seventeenth-century poem by Richard Crashaw, 'An Epitaph Upon Husband and Wife who died and were buried together'.

Like MQ 92, this poem evokes the grave, purporting to have been inscribed there. A 'Luid', used in the title for MQ 93a and MQ 93b, is a 'form of speech' and is not otherwise attested before the nineteenth century (see *DOST, Luid,* n.). MQ 93a is copied in a formal version of secretary (compare MQ 95).

Stanza: a^4b^3 a^4b^3 (not set out in stanzas in the MS).
Text: MQ fol. 132.
Authorship: unattributed.
Date: c.1586.

Commentary

4 *naturs lyne.* Nature's practice or usual behaviour. See *DOST, Line, Lyne,* sense 8a.

6 *thrie scoir of 3eirs and foure.* The poet attributes 64 years of marriage to Richard Maitland and his wife.

9–10 *Bot now hes Death thair aged dayes / Defaced by his dairt.* Death's personification here is rather conventional. Compare Montgomerie, 'Evin dead, behold I breath', l. 40: 'Death with deidly dairt'; also John Stewart of Baldynneis, *Of Deth. Sonnet,* l. 10: 'O verray deir thy deidlie dart sould bie'.

93b. A Luid To The Passer By.

This short epitaph is a *memento mori,* which may or may not have originally been connected to Richard Maitland and his wife. Verses such as this, which draw attention to the cadaver in the grave, and remind the readers or onlookers of the certainty of their own deaths, were popular throughout the middle ages and early modern period, and the theme is ubiquitous in funerary art. The poem is copied in an italic script and concluded with decorative penwork flourishes.

Stanza: ab³c⁴b³.
Text: MQ fol. 132.
Authorship: unattributed.
Date: uncertain.

Commentary

2 *Suche wer we ons as thow*. Compare Henryson, *The Thre Deid Pollis*, l. 5: 'As ʒe ar now, in to this warld we wair'.

4 *to dust*. Compare Genesis 3: 19; Ecclesiastes 3: 20.

94. In Commendation of the Right Honourable Syr Iohne Maitland of Thirlstaine Knight, Secretair to the King, his Maiestie

This sonnet sequence contains four poems in praise of John Maitland, chancellor to James VI, and by 1586, the only surviving son of Richard Maitland of Lethington. See MQ 46 and headnote. The first sonnet is an exchange between the narrator and his (or her) muse, the second and third sonnets describe the songs of the muses on John Maitland and his family, and in the fourth sonnet Ovid appears to address Maitland and remark upon his political importance and close relationship with his monarch. The first, third and fourth sonnets clearly celebrate John Maitland at a particularly important point in his career, when his place in the king's favour was confirmed. After the difficulties of the civil war, and the restrictions on his freedom in the 1570s, Maitland's political career was finally in ascendency from c.1580. On 31 May 1586, he was made keeper of the great seal for life and given the title of vice-chancellor. He became chancellor in 1587. He remained the king's most powerful minister until 1592. He died in 1595. For a biography, see Lee 1959.

The sonnet sequence also augments the commemoration of Richard Maitland in this closing section of MQ by stressing John Maitland's noble lineage and moral inheritance. The second sonnet makes particular mention of Richard Maitland whose burial day is said to be near at hand (this sonnet, at least, seems to have been composed shortly after Richard Maitland's death in March 1586), and praises him in terms familiar from the elegies in MQ, especially MQ 91 and MQ 92.

The sonnets are unattributed. Sibbald described them as 'in the manner of James VI' (Sibbald, ed. 1802, III, p. 321). However, the second and third in the sequence show similarities of style and subject matter to two sonnets recently discovered by Sebastiaan Verweij in the Hawthornden papers (Vol. XIII; NLS MS 2065, fols 8r–9r). These sonnets comprise the songs of the muses Euterpe, Clio and Thalia to the king, advancing the fame of an unnamed individual, and appear as a pair, though with different attributions: one is assigned to 'Andro K'; and the other to 'A. Cokburn'.

John Maitland is also eulogised in a sonnet by Montgomerie, *In Praise of Maister John Maitland chanceller* (c.1590), and in a sonnet by James VI, *A Sonnet to Chanceller Maitlane*, which praises Maitland for the translations he made of James's poems into Latin (discussed by Lyall 2005, p. 155). James also composed an epitaph on Maitland's death.

The sonnets are copied in a large italic script. They are followed by a proverb, 'Musis sine tempore tempus'.

Stanza: ababbcbcdedeff[5], ababbcbccdcdee[5], ababbcbccdcdee[5], ababbcbccdcdee[5].
Text: MQ fols 131–136 (rectos only).
Authorship: unattributed.
Date: 1586.

Commentary
94.1
2 *My silent muse.* The poet's genius. The narrator-poet has apparently been experiencing a lack of creative inspiration.

4 *his glorious praise.* Presumably that of John Maitland. The narrator and his muse wish to celebrate Maitland's use of his power to their benefit.

94.2
1 *I saw the muses nyne.* The nine muses, daughters of Zeus and Mnēmosynē, or Jupiter and Memoria, associated with Olympus or Parnassus, and the sources of inspiration for different branches of the arts and knowledge. Compare MQ 35, ll. 103–4.

6 *His worthye stock, baith valiant, stout and wyse.* The Maitland family line is also praised in MQ 91 and MQ 93, also MQ 46 and 68, ll. 141–56. Montgomerie's sonnet to Maitland also associates him with Mars and courage in battle. See Lyall 2005, p. 155. The poems to John Maitland by Mongtomerie and James (see headnote) both associate Maitland with Minerva and thus with wisdom.

9 *His father deir, quha neir his buriall lyess.* Richard Maitland died on 20 March 1586. This line suggests that this sonnet at least was written soon after Maitland's death.

10 *Ane Homer auld.* Maitland is hyperbolically compared to the classical poet Homer. Compare the dedicatory sonnet, 'E.D. in prayse of Mr W Foular her freind', in Fowler's *Trivmphs of Petrarke*, where Homer and Virgil, and contemporary vernacular poets including Ronsard and Surrey, are said to 'yield' before Fowler's art (Meikle ed. 1914). There are implicit comparisons between Richard Maitland of Lethington and other classical poets in MQ 68, ll. 1–8. Also see MQ 68, l. 52. The subtitle to James's 'A Sonnet to Chanceller Maitlane' refers to John Maitland as 'Vigiliae nostrae'.

11 *A iudge maist iust.* Maitland became an extraordinary Lord of Session in 1554, an ordinary Lord of Session in 1561, and continued to serve as a judge until 1584. Compare MQ 90, l. 8 and MQ 91, l. 3.

13 *Off prences loued.* Maitland's career spanned the reigns of James V, Mary of Guise, Mary Queen of Scots and James VI. During the 1550s, he was a councillor to Regent Moray, a commissioner to settle Border disputes, and commissioner to Elizabeth in Border affairs. He became Mary's keeper of the great seal in 1562.

14 *his learned sones.* William, John and Thomas Maitland were all educated in law at St Andrews and in Paris, and had a reputation for embracing humanist learning. See Mason 1998, p. 117; Lee 1959, p. 28.

94.3

3 *[Euterpe].* Euterpe, the muse associated with pleasure. See Douglas, *Palice of Honour*, ll. 857–58: 'Euterpe eik, quhilk daylie dois hir det / In dulce blastis of Pypis sweit but let'.

4 *Clio.* The muse of history. See Douglas, *Palice of Honour*, ll. 854–55: 'Lady Cleo, quhilk craftelie dois set / Historyis auld'. Compare MQ 69, l. 60 and note.

5 *Thalia.* This muse is usually associated with comedy, but sometimes also with other genres. See Henryson, *Orpheus and Eurydice*, ll. 54–56: 'Thelya ... quhilk can oure saulis bring / To profund wit and grete agilitee / To vnderstand'; Douglas, *Palice of Honour*, ll. 858–59: 'The thrid sister, Thalia diligent, / In wantoun writ and Chronikill dois Imprent'.

6 *eternise.* 'To make perpetual'. A rare usage, attested in English texts from 1578 to 1594. See *OED*, *Eternish*, v.

7 *Polhymina.* Polyhymnia is often the muse of hymns (see Henryson, *Orpheus and Eurydice*, ll. 52–53: 'fair Pollymyo, / Quhilk coud a thousand sangis suetly sing'), though is also associated by Douglas with fame. See Douglas, *Palice of Honour*, l. 866: 'Polymnia, the seuint Muse of Renoun'.

10 *his prence.* James VI.

14 *And on his bak sall leane this coumoun welth.* Maitland is presented as upholding the common good. Compare 94.1, ll. 5–8.

94.4

1–2 *Ouide from [exyle] / Of Pontus.* Ovid was expelled from Rome by the emperor Augustus to Tomis on the Black Sea, and died in exile. Ovid's *Epistulae ex Ponto* describes the miseries of his banishment.

4 *August.* The emperor Caesar Octavius Augustus (63 BC –AD 14).

7 *thought that thou in presoun was detaind.* Presumably a reference to John Maitland's imprisonment following the fall of Edinburgh Castle in 1573. See note to MQ 46, l. 180. However, Pinkerton regarded this as a reference to the poet's imprisonment and release at the request of John Maitland (Pinkerton ed. 1786, p. 432).

8 *ȝie happy thou, quho fauourd is of death.* Compare l. 7. Again, perhaps a reference to Maitland's survival following the fall of the Queen's Party in 1573 and death of his brother, William Maitland.

9 *Thy monarch, and thy great Augustus.* James is compared to Augustus, who, despite his banishment of Ovid, took an interest in contemporary literature, especially the works of Horace, Virgil and Livy, and philosophy. (*Oxford Classical Dictionary*, 9th ed., pp. 150–51).

10 *att thy good lords requeist.* The phrase is ambiguous, but the 'good lord' here may refer to one of John Maitland's political supporters, given that Ovid's address seems to be directed to him.

11–12 *Quhose honour thou, til waisted be thy breath, / Sall keip in mynde, within thy thankfull breist.* The honour is presumably James's and the gratitude is felt by Maitland. The sense of *til waisted be thy breath* is 'until you are dead'.

95. O deith, allace! with dairt so dolours

This elegiac complaint against the indiscriminate nature of death commemorates both Richard Maitland and his wife (compare MQ 93). Most of all, however, Richard Maitland's virtues and exemplary status are stressed. He is described as a pearl (l. 15), and as a lantern (l. 36) for his family and household and the rest of the noble community, and

his commitment to justice and piety is particularly mentioned. The poem is imagined as part of the formal mourning for Maitland at his funeral and may well have been intended for and delivered at this occasion (see ll. 41–42): it is addressed to the 'gentil men' who dignify Maitland's burial with their presence. It is likely to have been written by a family member or an intimate of the Maitland circle. The poem is incomplete, though probably only one line at the end of the last stanza is missing, made illegible by cropping to the manuscript. It is copied in a formal script with cursive features up to l. 24 (compare MQ 93 on fol. 132) and in a small, neat italic script thereafter.
Stanza: ababbcbc[5].
Text: MQ fols 137r, 138r.
Authorship: unattributed.
Date: March 1586.

Commentary

1 *O Deith, allace! with dairt so dolours.* The personification of death is expressed in conventional terms and paralleled in MQ 93, ll. 9–10 (and see note).

4 *quhy haldis thow of ane fect?* 'Why do you regard everyone to be of the same value?' See *DOST*, *Fect*, n. The common *memento mori* idea that all are equal before death does not seem to appeal to the poet.

17 *Of noble bluid he hes be lyne [descended].* Compare the praise of the family in the other commemorative poems, MQ 91 and MQ 93, and in MQ 94.2.6. Also see MQ 46 and 68, ll. 141–56. It is possible that the poet wishes the reader to recognise Maitland's descent from the prominent noble family of Seton as well as from those bearing his surname. MQ has the erroneous reading 'defended', which has been amended here.

20 *justice, temperance.* Justice and temperance are two of the four cardinal virtues.

23 *be his deuoit death.* An allusion to the *Ars moriendi* tradition, which recommended making a pious death, and offered advice on how to achieve one. See, for example, Montgomerie, *A lesone hou to leirne to die*.

27 *his verteous lady excellent.* Maitland had married Mariota or Mary, daughter of Sir Thomas Cranstoun of Corsbie, in c.1521. See headnote to MQ 93.

36 *lyk a lanterne.* Compare MQ 1, l. 6.

41 *excuise my ruid indyit.* A conventional modesty topos. Compare *Quare of Jelusy,* l. 185: 'my rude endite'; Douglas, *Palice of Honour,* l. 126: 'in rurall termes rude'. Also see note to l. 45.

42 *Quha with ȝour presence ornis this funerall.* No other records remain of Maitland's funeral. On funerary practices in post-Reformation Scotland, see Brown 2000, pp. 260–64. Calvinism dictated that the funerals of even distinguished individuals should be conducted without pomp, but the burials of members of the noble class remained important occasions and 'a demonstration of the community's hierarchy and of its bonds' (Brown 2000, p. 262).

45 *my verse will seim rurall.* Conventional terms for a modesty topos. Also see note to l. 41. Compare MQ 45 (attributed to Arbuthnot), l. 6, 'rurell ryme'; also MQ 68, l. 156.

49 *Wer Ihone Bocace callit again to lyif.* Perhaps an echo of David Lyndsay, *The Tragedie of the Cardinall,* ll. 27–28: 'Rycht sure I am, war Jhone Bochas on lyve, / My tragedie at lenth he wald discryve'. Also see *Ane Complaint Vpon Fortune,* l. 9: 'The worthie Bocas in his morall buke' (c.1581, Cranstoun ed. 1891–93, I, pp. 325–32). The *De Casibus Virorum* of Giovanni Boccaccio (1313–75) was adapted by John Lydgate (via Laurence de Premierfait's French translation of 1409) in his widely disseminated *Fall of Princes,* a poem that had some circulation in Scotland (Edwards 2010, pp. 189–90).

51 *In painted termes.* Rhetorical or literary language. Compare MQ 69, l. 35 ('aureit termis'), and MQ 84, l. 14.

Appendix 1

Ane Ballat of the Creatioun of the Warld, Man, his Fall, and Redemptioun, maid to the tone of 'The Bankis of Helecon'

God be his word his work began
To forme the erth and hevin for man,
The sie and watter deip,
The sone, the mone, the starris bricht,
The day divydit frome the nicht, 5
Thair coursis for to keip;
The beistis that on the grund do mvfe,
And fische in to the se,
Fowlis in the air to fle abvfe,
Off ilk kynd creat hee: 10
Sum creiping, sum fleiting,
Sum fleing in the air,
So heichtly, so lichtly,
In moving heir and thair.

Thir workis of grit magnificence, 15
Perfytit be his providence,
According to his will;
Nixt maid he man to gif him gloir,
Did with his ymage him decoir,
Gaif parradice him till; 20
Into that garding, hevinly wrocht,
With plesowris mony one,
The beistis of every kynd war brocht,
Thair names he sowld expone:
Thame nemmyng, and kennyng, 25
As he list for to call,
For pleising and eising
Off man, subdewit thame all.

In hevinly ioy man so possest
To be allone God thocht not best, 30
Maid Eve to be his maik;

Bad thame incres and mvltiplie,
And eit of every fruct and trie,
Thair plesour thay sowld taik,
Except the trie of gud and ill,   35
That in the middis dois stand,
Forbad that thay sowld cum it till,
Or twiche it with thair hand:
Leist plucking or lucking
Baith thay and als thair seid   40
Seveirly, awsteirly,
Sowld dye withowt remeid.

Now Adame and his lusty wyfe
In parradyce, leidand thair lyfe
With plesowris infineit,   45
Wanting na thing sowld do thame eis,
Ilk beist obeying thame to pleis,
As thay cowld wis in spreit,
Behald the serpent, subtilly
Invyand manis estait,   50
With wickit craft and subtilty
Eve temptit with dissait:
Nocht feiring, bott speiring
Quhy scho tuke not hir till
In vsing and chusing   55
The fruct of gud and ill.

'Commandit ws', scho said, 'the Lord,
Nowayis thairto we sowld accord
Vnder eternall pane,
Bot grantit ws full libertie   60
To eit of every fruct and trie
Except that tre in plane.'
'No no, not so', the serpent said,
'Thow art dissauit thairin.
Eit ȝe thairof ȝe sall be maid   65
In knawlege lyk to him,
In semying and demyng
Off every thing arricht
Als dewly, als trewly
As ȝe war goddis of micht.'   70

Eve, with thir fals wordis thus allurit,
Eit of the fruct and syne procuirt
Adame the same to play.
'Behald', said scho, 'how pretious,
So dilicat and delitious,   75
Besyd knawlege for ay.'
Adame puft vp in warldly gloir,
Ambitioun and of pryd,
Eit of the fruct, allace, thairfoir,
And swa thay baith did slyd: 80
Neglecting, forȝetting,
The eternall Goddis command,
Quha scurgit and purgit
Thame quyt owt of that land.

Quhen thay had eitin of that frute   85
Off ioy than war thay destitute,
And saw thair bodyis bair.
Annone thay past, with all thair speid,
Off leivis to mak thame selvis a weid,
To cleith thame was thair cair.   90
During the tyme of innocence
No syn nor schame thay knew;
Fra tyme thay gat experience
Vnto ane bus thay drew,
Abyding and hyding,   95
As God sowld nocht thame see,
Quha spyit and cryit,
'Adame, quhy hyddis thow thee?'

'I being naikit Lord, throw feir,
For schame I durst nocht to compeir,   100
And so I did refuse.'
'Had thow nocht eitin of that tre
That knawlege had nocht bene in the,
Nor ȝit no sic excuse.'
'This helper, Lord, thow gaif to me   105
Hes cawsit me transgres.'
Sayd scho, 'The serpent subtilly
Perswadit me no less,
Intreitting, be eitting,

That we sowld be perfyte,
Me sylit, begylit,
In him lyis all the wyte.'

The Lord that evir iugeit richt,
Bringand his iustice to the licht,
The serpent first did iuge:
'Becaus the woman thow begylit,
For evir thow sall be exylit,'
Said he, 'withowt reffuge.
Betuix hir seid and thy ofspring
Na peax nor rest salbe,
And hir seid sall thy heid doun-thring,
For all thy subtilty;
Abhorrit, deformit,
Thow on thy breist sall gang
In feiding and leiding
Thy lyfe the beistis amang.'

The woman nixt, for hir offence,
Did of the Lord ressaif sentence:
Hir sowrrow sowld incres,
With wo and pane hir childrene beir,
Subdewit to man vndir his feir,
No liberty posses.
For Adamis falt he curst the erth,
That barane it sowld be,
Withowt labour sowld 3eild na birth
Off coirnis, erb, nor tre;
Bot wirking and irking
For evir sowld remane,
And being in deing
In erth returne agane.

O crewall serpent vennemus,
Dispytfull and seditious,
The grund of all our cair,
Thow fals bound slave vnto the divill,
Thow first inventar of the evill
Off blis quhilk maid ws bair.
O diuillis slaive did thow beleif,

Or how had thow sic grace,
Thairby for evir thow micht leif
Aboif in to that place? 150
Thy grudgeing gat scrudgeing
And swa God lute the sie
A dissavar no cravar
Off his reward sowld be.

O dilicat dame with eiris bent 155
That harknit to that fals serpent,
Thy banis we may sair ban!
Without excuse thow art to blame,
Thow iustly hes obtenit that name,
'The verray wo of man'. 160
With teiris we may bewaill and greit
That wickit tyme and tyd,
Quhen Adame was caussit to sleip
And thow tane of his syd.
No sleiping, bot weiping 165
Thy seid hes fund sensyne,
Thy eitting and sweitting
Is turnd to wo and pyne.

Adame, thy pairt quha can excuse?
With knawlege thow that did abuse 170
Thy awin felicitie;
The serpentis fals inventing,
The womanis sone consenting,
Was nocht sa wickitlie.
God did prefer the to this day, 175
And thame subdewid to the,
So all that thay cowld mene or say,
Sowld not haif movit the
To brecking, abiecking
That heich command of lyfe, 180
Quhilk gydit, provydit,
The ay to leif but stryfe.

Behald the stait that man was in,
And als how it he tynt throw syn,
And loist the same for ay; 185

APPENDIX 1

Ȝit God his promeis dois performe,
Send his sone of the Virgyn borne,
Oure ransone for to pay.
To that gret God lat ws gif gloir,
To ws hes bene so gude,   190
Quha be his deith did ws restoir
Quhairof we war denude,
Nocht karing, nor sparing
His body to be rent,
Redemyng, releiving   195
Ws quhen we war all schent.

Finis quod Ser Richart Maitland of Lethingtoun, Knycht.

APPENDIX 1

Ane Ballat of the Creatioun of the Warld, Man, his Fall and Redemptioun, maid to the tone of 'The Bankis of Helecon'

BM fols 12–14.
This poem is only found in the Bannatyne MS (NLS Adv. MS. 1.1.6), where it is placed among the 'ballatis of theoligie'. Shire describes it as a '"moralisation", a harnessing of the dance-tune measure to godly usage' (Shire 1969, p. 35). It gives a sober account of the fall of man (Genesis 1–3). In so doing it also echoes short passages from the first book of David Lyndsay's *The Monarche* (1553), ll. 685–1122 and ll. 434–73, a text that was in print by 1554 in an edition by John Scot (*STC* 15672). On the relationship of this poem to Lyndsay's, see Hamer ed. 1931–36, IV, pp. 290–93. Hamer sometimes overstates the correspondences between lines in this poem and in the *Monarche*, and only close parallels are given here in the commentary.

The poem is attributed by Bannatyne to Richard Maitland of Lethington. Given that it is the only extant text attributed to Maitland that does not appear in MF or MQ, Bannatyne's attribution is problematic. There are no solid stylistic or thematic grounds for Maitland's authorship: Maitland's poems, with the exception of MQ 16, rarely engage in detail with a biblical narrative. However, some of his attributed poems in MF and MQ show the influence of Lyndsay's writing (see Introduction, pp. 15–17).

Lines 141–82 of the poem are not paralleled anywhere in Lydnsay's work. These include an apostrophe to the serpent, who is first blamed for his part in man's expulsion from paradise, and to Eve, and an address to Adam. Although the narrator indulges in a misogynistic attack on Eve (ll. 155–68), the most severe reprimand is saved for Adam who is presented as morally weak, and accused of a catastrophic failure of authority and betrayal of God's favour (ll. 169–82). The use of legalistic phrasing in God's speeches, and in the narrator's presentation of his judgement (ll. 113–40), is not found in Lyndsay's poem and may strengthen the case for Maitland's authorship.

On the stanza form, which had considerable currency in sixteenth-century Scotland and England, see headnote to MQ 48. For earlier editions of the Bannatyne poem, see Bain, ed. 1830, pp. 65–72; Hamer ed. 1931–36, IV, pp. 293–97.
Stanza: the 'Helicon stanza', aa^{4}b^{3}cc^{4}b^{3}dede^{4}fghg^3.

APPENDIX 1

Text: Bannatyne MS fols 12–14.
Authorship: attributed to Richard Maitland
Date: before 1568.

Commentary

12 *Sum fleing in the air*. See *Monarche* l. 702: 'sum fleying in the air'.

21 *Into that garding, hevinly wrocht*. Compare *Monarche* l. 739: 'In to that gardyng of plesance'.

32 *Bad thame incres and mvltiplie*. Biblical phrasing (Genesis 1: 38), but also see *Monarche* ll. 778, 840: 'Sayand incres and multyplie', 'to multyplie and tyll incres'.

38 *Or twiche it with thair hand*. Compare *Monarche* l. 750: 'The tre to twyche nocht with his hand'.

40 *awsteirly*. The adverb is not well attested in Older Scots. See *DOST*, *Austerely*, adv. However the adjective is frequently associated with judgement in Older Scots. See *DOST*, *Austere*, a.

49 *Behald the serpent, subtilly*. Compare *Monarche* l. 893: 'The Serpent wes the subtellest'.

60–61 *Bot grantit ws full libertie / To eit of every fruct and trie*. Compare *Monarche* ll. 913–14: 'The quhilk hes geuin ws lybertie / tyll eait of euery fruct and tre'.

74–76 Eve's direct speech to Adam is not paralleled in Lyndsay's poem.

77–78 *Adame puft vp in warldly gloir, / Ambitioun and of pryd*. This condemnatory description of Adam is not in Lyndsay's poem at this point in the narrative, but compare *Monarche* ll. 438–39: 'Be quhose most wylfull arrogance / wes Mankynd brocht to this myschance'.

85–86 *Quhen thay had eitin of that frute / Off ioy than war thay destitute*. Compare *Monarche* ll. 981–82: 'Quhen thay had eaitin of the frute / Of ioye than wer thay destitute'.

91 *tyme of innocence*. Compare *Monarche* l. 987: 'Bot in the stait of Innocence'.

94 *Vnto ane bus thay drew*. Compare *Monarche* l. 991: 'And in ane busk thay hid thame cloce'. In Genesis 3:8 Adam and Eve hide among 'the trees of the garden' (Geneva Bible 1560).

98 *'Adame quhy hyddis thow thee?'* God does not ask this question in Lyndsay's poem. But see Genesis 3: 9: 'Where art thow?' (Geneva Bible 1560).

100 *to compeir.* This is a legal formula with the sense 'to appear before an authority or court'. See *DOST, Compere*, v. It is not used in Lyndsay's poem.

105 *This helper.* The description of Eve as a helpmeet (Genesis 2: 20) comes earlier in the narrative in Lyndsay's poem. See *Monarche* l. 760: 'ane helpare'; and contrast l. 1001: 'This woman that thow gaif to me'.

106 *Hes cawsit me transgres.* This admission of guilt is not paralleled in Lyndsay's poem.

107–12 Eve's speech is more extensive than her response in Lyndsay's poem: 'the Serpent me abusit' (l. 1004).

113–14 *The Lord that evir iugeit richt, / Bringand his iustice to the licht.* This description of God's justice is not in Lyndsay's poem.

116–17 *'Becaus the woman thow begylit, / For evir thow sall be exylit.* Compare *Monarche* ll. 1007–8: 'Because the woman thow begylit / Frome thyne furth sall thow be exylit'.

127 *The woman nixt, for hir offence.* Compare *Monarche* ll. 1051–52: 'Than to the woman, for hir offence / God did pronounce this sore sentence'.

128 *ressaif sentence.* Perhaps reminiscent of legal formulae. See *DOST, Resav*, v. sense 35.

130 *With wo and pane hir childrene beir.* Compare *Monarche* ll. 1057–58: 'all thy bairnis sall thow bair / With dolour and continuall cair'.

133–34 *For Adamis falt he curst the erth, / That barane it sowld be.* Compare *Monarche* l. 1083: 'Curste and baren the erthe salbe'.

135–36 *Withowt labour sowld ȝeild na birth / Off coirnis, erb, nor tre.* Compare *Monarche* l. 1085: 'But labour, it sall beir no corne'.

140 *In erth returne agane.* Compare *Monarche* l. 1092: 'And thow in erthe sall turne agane'.

155 *O dilicat dame.* The adjective 'dilicat' is sometimes used with negative connotations. See MQ 2, ll. 56–57 and note to l. 56. Compare Eve's own usage at l. 75.

188 *Oure ransone for to pay.* The idea of the crucifixion as the payment of a ransom to Satan for mankind's redemption is an ancient one and is often alluded to in passion poems. Compare Dunbar, 'Done is a battell on the dragon blak', l. 7: 'Chryst with his blud our ransonis dois indoce'; and in the *Gude and Godlie Ballatis*, 'Christ thow art the lycht, bot and the day', 'Thy seruandis ... / For quhais rausoun thow did sair bleid' (Mitchell ed. 1896–97, p. 145).

194 *His body to be rent*. Reminiscent of the detail of passion lyrics such as Dunbar's 'Amang thir freiris within ane cloister', ll. 33–96.

Appendix 2

Stanza forms in MQ

Abbreviations
AA – Alexander Arbuthnot
AM – Alexander Montgomerie
B – Baldwin
GH (unidentified)
JM – John Maitland
JR – James VI
RH – Robert Hudson
SRM – Richard Maitland
TH – Thomas Hudson

	Stanza form	Poem
1	aa^3	MQ 56 (SRM)
2	aa^4	MQ 57 (SRM), MQ 70
3	aa^5	MQ 55 (SRM), MQ 66 (GH), MQ 75, MQ 79, MQ 87 (B)
4	aa^6	MQ 74
5	$aaaa^5$	MQ 81
6	aaa^4b^2	MQ 15 (SRM)
7	$aaa^3b^{2?}aaa^3b^{2?}$	MQ 54 (SRM)
8	$aaaaabab^5$	MQ 43 (JM)
9	$aaa^4b^3aaa^4b^3$	MQ 53 (SRM)
10	aaa^4baab^2	MQ 50 (SRM)
11	$aaabaB^4$	MQ 5 (SRM)
12	$aabaabbab^5$	MQ 6 (SRM), MQ 39
13	$aabab^4$	MQ 52 (SRM)
14	$aabaB^4$	MQ 2 (SRM)
15	$aabab^5$	MQ 51 (SRM)
16	$aa^4\ b^2a^4b^2$	MQ 20 (SRM)
17	$aa^4b^3a^4\ B^3$	MQ 4 (SRM)
18	$aabB^4$	MQ 26 (SRM)
19	$aabba^4$	MQ 27 (SRM)

APPENDIX 2

20	aabba^5	MQ 28 (SRM)
21	aa^{4}bbba^2	MQ 3 (SRM)
22	aabbcbc^4	MQ 21 (SRM)
23	aabbcbc^5	MQ 29 (SRM)
24	aabb^{5}ccdeed^3	MQ 25 (SRM)
	aabbc^{4}d^{2}e^{4}d^2	MQ 24 (SRM)
25	aa^{4}b^{3}cc^{4}b^3	MQ 22 (SRM)
26	aabccb^4	MQ 82
27	aa^{4}b^{3}cc^{4}b^{3}dede^{4}fghg^3	MQ 48
28	abab^4	MQ 17 (SRM), MQ 88
29	aba^{4}B^3	MQ 34 (SRM)
30	a^{4}b^{3}a^{4}b^3	MQ 33 (SRM), MQ 80, MQ 93a
31	abab^5	MQ 85
32	ababa^5	MQ 18 (SRM)
33	abab^{3}aaa^{2}b^3	MQ 71
34	a^{4}b^{2}a^{4}b^3 / aaa^{5}b^3	MQ 8 (SRM)
35	a^{4}b^{3}a^{4}b^{3}a^{4}b^{3}C^3	MQ 40
36	abab^{4}b^{2}ba^4	MQ 23 (SRM)
37	ababbcbc^3	MQ 47, MQ 72
38	ababbcbc^4; aaab^2.	MQ 89
39	ababbcbc^4	MQ 16 (SRM), MQ 30 (SRM), MQ 37 (AA), MQ 49, MQ 64 (AM)
40	ababbcbc^5	MQ 9 (SRM), MQ 10 (SRM), MQ 12 (SRM), MQ 14 (SRM), MQ 32 (SRM), MQ 44 (JM), MQ 45 (AA), MQ 46, MQ 59 (SRM), MQ 62, MQ 63 (AM), MQ 65, MQ 69, MQ 95
41	ababbcbC^5	MQ 7 (SRM), MQ 11 (SRM)
42	ababbcc^5	MQ 13 (SRM), MQ 58 (SRM)
43	ababbcC^5	MQ 41 (AA)
44	ababbCC^5 + ababbcc^5	MQ 42 (AA)
45	abab^{3}c^{4}b^3 d^{4}b^3	MQ 35 AA
46	a^4 b^{3}a^4 bcc^3	MQ 84
47	a^{4}b^{3}a^4 b^{3}cc^3 + a^{4}b^{3}a^4 b^3)	MQ 78
48	ababcc^4	MQ 60, MQ 61, MQ 67 (JR), MQ 76
49	ababcc^4 + abab^3	MQ 83
50	abab^{4}cc^{3}bb^{4}c^3	MQ 19 (SRM)

51	$a^5b^3a^5b^3cc^2dd^2b^4$	MQ 38
52	$a^4b^3a^4b^3c^4d^3c^4d^3$	MQ 68
53	$abbaaccd^5\ ee^2d^5$	MQ 73
54	$ab^3c^4b^3$	MQ 77, MQ 93b
55	$a^4\ b^3c^4b^3$	MQ 86

Sonnet forms	**Poems**
56	$ababbcbccdcdee^5$	MQ 1, MQ 90 (TH), MQ 91 (RH), MQ 92, MQ 94.2, MQ 94.3, MQ 94.4
57	$ababbcbcdedeff^5$	MQ 94.1

Glossary

The glossary contains words that are no longer current in Present Day English, or words that are used in senses that are now obsolete. Some surviving words with spellings that might prove problematic to the reader are also included. In a few cases words are not glossed here but explained in the explanatory notes. No more than three illustrative line references are given for words that occur frequently.

It should be noted that the vowels *y* and *i* are used interchangeably: both spellings appear in the alphabetical position of *i*. Instances of initial *i* as vowel are separated from initial *i* as consonant. The same is the case for vowel and consonantal uses of initial *v*. yogh, representing the semi-vowel *y* when used initially, is placed after *w*.

Citations give the poem's manuscript location (Maitland Quarto [MQ] or Bannatyne MS [BM]) and number (for Maitland Quarto poems) followed by the line number, in the format (MQ 1 12). Words placed in square brackets in the glossary are those that are editorial emendations to the manuscript.

Abbreviations

adj(ective), *adv*(erb), *comp*(arative), *conj*(unction), *fig*(urative), *n*(oun), *num*(eral), *p*(articiple), *pa*(st), *pa. p.* = past participle, *phr*(ase), *pl*(ural), *ppl.* = participal, *poss*(essive), *pr*(esent), *pr. p.* = present participle, *prep*(osition), *pron*(oun), *refl*(exive), *sg.* = singular, *superl*(ative), *t*(ense), *v*(erb), *vbl.* = verbal.

A

Abeceis *n. pl.* abbacies (MQ 51 61)
Abiecking *vbl. n.* disregarding (BM 179)
Abone, Abonne *prep.* above (MQ 11 41, MQ 63 1, MQ 73 32)
Aboundance *n.* plenty, abundance (MQ 67 3)
Abstinence *n.* truce (MQ 34 21, MQ 58 1)
Abusioun *n.* misconduct, wrongdoing, deceit (MQ 5 73, MQ 12 26, MQ 18 20)
Accidence *n.* accidental occurrence (MQ 27 7)
Acquent *pa. p.* acquainted (MQ 44 37)
Adamant *n.* diamond (MQ 48 100, MQ 49 10)
Additioun *n.* the action of adding something (MQ 18 22)
Advert *v.* pay attention to, observe (MQ 43 66)
Afflixioun *n.* distress (MQ 46 36)

GLOSSARY

Afoir *adv.* at an earlier time (MQ 5 19)
Aggrage *v.* aggravate, increase (MQ 38 76)
Aill *n.* ale (MQ 3 32)
Air *adv.* early (MQ 59 13)
Airis *n. pl.* heirs (MQ 29 28, MQ 51 10)
Airtis *n. pl.* points on the compass (MQ 11 27)
Aithe *n.* oath (MQ 83 26)
Allanerlie *adj. and adv.* solely, only (MQ 12 61)
Alleis *n. pl.* bowling greens (MQ 68 127)
Allya *n.* ally (MQ 6 8)
Allya *v.* to associate oneself (MQ 57 17)
Alluire *v.* entice (MQ 37 58)
Alluterlie *adv.* completely (MQ 16 55, MQ 29 57)
Alryne *n.* walkway behind a battlement (MQ 68 68)
Alwyse *adv.* always (MQ 61 75)
Amayis *v.* bewilder, astound (MQ 48 103)
Ance *adv.* once (MQ 83 13)
And *conj.* and, supposing that, even though (MQ 7 14)
Aneuche *n.* enough (MQ 5 28, MQ 14 24)
Anew *adj.* enough, aplenty (MQ 16 29, MQ 39 63)
Angwiss *n.* anguish (MQ 48 109)
Annixit *prep.* next to (MQ 63 29)
Annoy *n.* vexation (MQ 79 14)
Aperse *n.* paragon (MQ 48 19)
Apparandlie, Apperantlie *adv.* apparently, evidently (MQ 16 89, MQ 19 16)
Apperand *adj.* visible, apparent (MQ 44 33)
Arbour *n.* enclosed garden (MQ 68 121)
Areir *adv.* behind (MQ 18 25, MQ 28 45)
Areird *adv.* backward (MQ 42 85)
Argone *v.* argue, discuss (MQ 11 23)
Ark *n.* a large chest for holding grain (MQ 3 52)
Arreir *adv.* backwards (MQ 4 28); in the background (MQ 18 25)
Asclent *adv.* astray (MQ 37 62)
Assent *n.* sanction (MQ 69 36)
Assent *v.* agree (MQ 69 33)
Assyile *v.* polish, adapt (MQ 41 44)
Assuage *v.* alleviate (MQ 24 4). **Assuagit** *pa. p.* (MQ 62 19)
Asteres *n. pl.* stars (MQ 63 25)
Asuir *adj.* azure (MQ 63 3)
Athar *pron.* either (MQ 16 79)
Atheisme *n.* atheism (MQ 41 17)
Ather *adj.* each one (MQ 66 85),
Ather *pron.* either (MQ 48 49)
Athort *prep.* across (MQ 2 71)

GLOSSARY

Attein, *v.* attain (MQ 40 108, MQ 71 39)
Attent *pa. p.* assailed (MQ 65 68)
Attour *prep.* above (MQ 11 33)
Aucht *v.* ought (to) (MQ 66 34)
Audacitie *n.* confidence, daring (MQ 10 18)
Auntient *adj.* ancient, belonging to those of antiquity (MQ 49 21)
Avow *v.* declair, affirm, acknowledge (MQ 3 72, MQ 55 12)

B

Babeis *n. pl.* money (MQ 70 26)
Baild, Bald, Bauld *adj.* bold, courageous (MQ 3 17, MQ 46 95, MQ 66 67)
Baill *n.* misery (MQ 35 17, MQ 45 40)
Baine-fyris *n.pl.* bonfires (MQ 6 20)
Bair *adj.* desolate, bare (MQ 8 8)
Bairnes *n. pl.* offspring (MQ 95 37)
Bairne, Barne *n.* youth, man (MQ 5 23, MQ 35 157)
Bairnlie *adj.* childish (MQ 42 29)
Bakbyteris *n. pl.* detractors, backbiters (MQ 16 29)
Bald *see* **Baild**
Ban *v.* curse (MQ 60 88)
Band *n.* a bond of obligation or unity, a contract (MQ 19 104, MQ 38 101); a band used to fasten something (MQ 72 3)
Band *n.* a company of soldiers (MQ 19 22)
Baneist *ppl. adj.* exiled, banished (MQ 9 15, MQ 60 39, MQ 61 48)
Bangeister *n.* bully (MQ 51 49)
Banket *n.* feast, banquet (MQ 6 39)
Bar *n.* the bar in a court of law (MQ 5 69)
Bark *n.* a small ship, a barque (MQ 80 1)
Barne *see* **Bairne**
Bas *adj.* low, base (MQ 42 79)
Bauld *see* **Baild**
Bawdische *adj.* obscene (MQ 41 58)
Baxteris *n. pl.* bakers (MQ 70 17)
Beddis *n. pl.* banks in the sea, the sea bed (MQ 44 29), beds (MQ 68 109)
Be-dein *adv.* straight away (MQ 35 142)
Begoude, Begouthe *pa. t.* began (MQ 83 55, MQ 69 66)
Beir *n.* beer (MQ 4 83)
Beir *n.* clamour (MQ 68 27)
Beir *v.* hold up, carry, bear (MQ 2 31, MQ 24 22, MQ 46 136)
Beit *v.* relieve, supply (MQ 20 27)
Bek *v.* make a gesture of respect, bow (MQ 41 36)
Belyiff *adv.* quickly, at once (MQ 28 36)
Bellie-blind *n.* a blindfolded person (MQ 44 91)
Ben *adv.* to the inner part of the house (MQ 52 9)

Benefeit *n*. kindness (MQ 46 149)
Bening *adj*. gracious, benign (MQ 35 31, MQ 63 12, MQ 73 18)
Bent *ppl. adj*. determined, fixed (MQ 88 4, MQ 94.1 10)
Bereve *v*. take away with violence (MQ 75 20)
Besprent *pa. t*. besprinkled (MQ 65 69)
Bessie *see* **Bissie**
Bet *pa. p*. helped (MQ 52 37)
Betie bum *n*. a helpless person (MQ 41 115)
Betyide *v*. to succeed (MQ 11 6)
Bewis *n. pl*. boughs (MQ 69 11)
Byd *v*. delay, force to wait (MQ 3 12)
Bygaine *adj*. in the past (MQ 10 6, MQ 13 22, MQ 58 3)
Biging, Bigging *n*. building (MQ 8 8, MQ 16 95)
Byide *v*. wait for (MQ 20 4)
Binge *v*. bow in a servile manner (MQ 41 36)
Bird *n*. maiden (MQ 35 146, MQ 40 1, MQ 63 12)
Byris *n. pl*. cattle sheds (MQ 3 49)
Birthfull *adj*. fertile (MQ 80 10)
Bissie, Bessie *adj*. active, diligent (MQ 11 82, MQ 44 1); busy (MQ 45 18)
Blaise *v*. proclaim (MQ 94.3 6)
Blak *adj*. shameful, dark (MQ 42 40)
Blasone *v*. defame (MQ 43 40). **Blasonit** *pa. t*. (MQ 62 2)
Blast *n*.[1] blast of wind (MQ 38 39, MQ 44 20)
Blast *n*.[2] a short space of time (MQ 43 67)
Bleir *v*. weep (MQ 2 88, MQ 4 78)
Blenking *vbl.n*. glancing (MQ 66 48)
Blenkis *n. pl*. flickering beams of light (MQ 69 14)
Blyithnes *n*. happiness (MQ 5 1)
Bloistrous *adj*. blustery (MQ 80 1)
Blok *n*. plot (MQ 62 89)
Blot(t) *n*. ink blot or scribble, stain (of infamy) (MQ 61 3, MQ 61 69)
Bluid, Bloud *n*. family, lineage (MQ 9 3, MQ 44 75, MQ 93 2)
Blunt *adj*. stupid (MQ 83 31)
Bobbis *n. pl*. gusts of wind (MQ 44 19, 26)
Boid *n*. gale (MQ 44 26)
Boist *v*. threaten (MQ 5 70)
Bontie *n*. goodness, excellence (MQ 9 2, MQ 40 12)
Borroustoun *n*. burgh (MQ 2 1)
Borrowmuire *n*. the moor near the town (MQ 8 23)
Boster *n*. bolster (MQ 3 50)
Bothumles *adj*. bottomless (MQ 42 89)
Boudnes *pr. t*. swells (MQ 45 40)
Boun *adj*. ready (MQ 46 162)
Boundage *n*. bondage, captivity (MQ 44 77)

Bour *n.* private apartment, chamber (MQ 35 25)
Bourdes *n.* joke (MQ 41 58)
Bousteous *adj.* violent (MQ 35 157)
Bousterit, *pa. t.* puffed up (MQ 70 125)
Bowsum *adj.* obedient (MQ 35 77)
Bray *n.* shore (MQ 65 12, MQ 69 71); bank (MQ 65 12, MQ 69 71)
Braid *adj. and adv.* broad or wide, broadly (MQ 2 22)
Brayisis *n. pl.* hot charcoals (MQ 49 39)
Brald *adj.* decked out (MQ 20 33)
Branit *adj.* well muscled (MQ 43 1)
Brank *v.* prance (MQ 70 130)
Bravelie *adv.* splendidly (MQ 2 6)
Breeis *n. pl.* brows (MQ 48 57)
Bred *pa. p.* cast (MQ 65 137)
Brek *v.* spring forth (MQ 67 11); bring to light? (MQ 59 35)
[Brent] *adj.* burnt up? (MQ 65 49)
Bres *n.* brass (MQ 41 131)
Brim *n.* brook or stream (MQ 48 8)
Brok *n.* brook (MQ 69 72)
Broudrit *pa. t.* embroidered (MQ 2 22)
Browsteris *n. pl.* brewers (MQ 70 18)
Bruik *v.* enjoy, have possession of (MQ 7 61, MQ 57 2, MQ 95 28)
Bruit *n.* report (MQ 45 27, MQ 68 27)
Brukill *adj.* fragile (MQ 44 19)
Brunt *pa. p.* burnt (MQ 83 33)
Brutis *n. pl.* reports, rumours (MQ 43 67)
Budding *adj.* squalling? (MQ 65 35)
Buffit *ppl. adj.* puffed (MQ 70 86)
Buik *n.* book, written or printed work (MQ 24 5, MQ 55 9)
Buist *n.* padding in a garment (MQ 70 124)
[Bumming] *vbl. n.* humming (MQ 68 79)
Burdalaine, Burdalane *n.* only child (MQ 46 112)
Burding *v.* load (MQ 41 173)
Burgess *n.* citizen, town dweller (MQ 2 53, 86). **Burgesis** *gen. pl.* (MQ 2 98, 106)
Burrit *ppl. adj.* furnished with padded rolls (MQ 2 27)
Bus *n.* bush (BM 94)
Buskit *pa. t.* arrayed, dressed (MQ 70 118)
Buttis *n. pl.* spaces prepared for practising archery (MQ 68 129)

C

Cabinat *n.* chamber, apartment (MQ 65 40)
Cadge, Caidge *n.* cage (MQ 66 86, 90)
Caice *n.* state of affairs (MQ 30 49)

GLOSSARY

Caill *adj.* cold (MQ 3 36)
Cairfull *adj.* unhappy, troubled (MQ 30 49)
Cairtes *n. pl.* playing cards (MQ 11 25)
Calf *n.* chaff (MQ 66 57)
Calsay *n.* the paved part of the street (MQ 5 8)
Calumpniat *v.* to use calumny (MQ 43 34)
Campioun *n.* champion (MQ 10 29)
Camreche *n.* cambric silk (MQ 2 14)
Canicular *adj.* relating to the day star (MQ 38 28)
Canker *n.* sore, ulcer (MQ 35 22, MQ 44 68)
Carcattis *n. pl.* necklaces, collars (MQ 2 36)
Carcerat *pa. p.* imprisoned (MQ 65 124)
Cariadge *n.* the action of carrying goods (as a service) (MQ 21 13)
Carrous *n. pl.* circular dances (MQ 6 21)
Casualitie *n.* source of income, payment due from a tenant (MQ 51 67, MQ 59 17)
Celeritie *n.* swiftness (MQ 61 68)
Certifie *v.* assure by giving a warning (MQ 7 28)
Chaip(e) *v.* escape (MQ 28 55, MQ 62 154)
Chairge *n.* duty of care (MQ 44 17)
Chaist *pa. t.* forced, driven (MQ 65 123)
Chalmer *n.* chamber (MQ 20 24)
Chance *v.* to happen by chance (MQ 39 106)
Chanche *n.* a fortuitous event (MQ 38 58)
Cheifest *superl.* most important (MQ 44 17)
Chein *n.* chain (MQ 6 77)
Cheir *n.* behaviour, display of feeling, including joyful feeling (MQ 2 58, MQ 54 29)
Cheualeiris *n. pl.* horsemen, knights (MQ 6 10)
Chope *v.* chop (MQ 61 36)
Chust *pa. t.* chose (MQ 83 55)
Ciuilitie *n.* good breeding, refined habits (MQ 41 85, MQ 62 21)
Clairtie *adj.* dirty (MQ 70 120)
Clayth *n.* clothing (MQ 2 69)
Claythis *n. pl.* clothes (MQ 20 22)
Clatterar *n.* an idle chatterer or tale teller (MQ 11 11, MQ 59 43)
Cleik *v.* snatch (MQ 95 28)
Clemence *n.* clemency (MQ 46 137)
Clenge *v.* to cleanse, purify (MQ 7 3)
Clengeing *adj.* cleansing (MQ 42 122)
Cloik *v.* cloak, conceal (MQ 5 74, MQ 43 60)
Cloikkis *n. pl.* cloaks (MQ 2 16)
Cloutit *ppl. adj.* patched (MQ 4 87)
Cluddis *n. pl.* clouds (MQ 63 5)

GLOSSARY

Cofferris *n. pl.* chests for the safe keeping of valuables (MQ 6 42)
Coft *pa. p. and ppl. adj.* bought (MQ 16 119, MQ 75 25)
Coy *adj.* quiet (MQ 68 83)
Collarris *n. pl.* ornamental collars on a garment (MQ 2 36)
Collaterall *adj.* by association (MQ 39 23)
Collusioun *n.* scheming (MQ 5 74)
Combuire *v.* burn up (MQ 48 104)
Communicat *v.* partake, be a partaker of (MQ 46 25)
Compair *n.* an equal (MQ 68 159)
Compeir *v.* to appear, as a formal act before authority (BM 100)
Compt *v.* consider, judge (MQ 42 2, MQ 60 32, MQ 66 121)
Conceave *v.* understand (MQ 37 32)
Conclud *pa. p.* concluded (MQ 93 4)
Concur *v.* to unite, act as one (MQ 7 28)
Conding, Condign *adj.* fitting, appropriate (MQ 6 3, MQ 59 4)
Conditioun *n.* bargain, agreement (MQ 11 19)
Conferring *vbl. n.* conference (MQ 58 4)
Confide, Confeid *v.* trust, place confidence in (MQ 46 137, MQ 89 23)
Conform(e) *v.* bring into harmony with (MQ 42 146, MQ 46 129)
Conformabill *adj.* able to conform with, be in keeping with (MQ 12 55)
Confortabill *adj.* comforting, giving of strength (MQ 22 19)
Coniure *v.* conspire (MQ 48 58). **Coniurit, Conuird** *pa. t.* (MQ 41 9, MQ 83 26)
Conqueis *n.* acquisition (MQ 29 42, MQ 50 16)
Conqueis *v.* acquire (MQ 29 40)
Consait(t), Conset *n.* idea, fancy (MQ 13 3, MQ 67 7, MQ 80 33); an opinion of one (MQ 2 74)
Consave *v.* understand (MQ 46 130, 198); conceive (MQ 59 47)
Conserue *v.* to maintain, protect, and maintain in a state of prosperity (MQ 6 36)
Conset *see* **Consait(t)**
Consistorie *n.* a council or court (MQ 30 94)
Consome *v.* waste away (MQ 48 147)
Constance *n.* steadfastness (MQ 9 47)
Contempill *v.* contemplate (MQ 46 57, MQ 48 11). **Contempling** *pr. p.* (MQ 49 14)
Contravaill *v.* to equal in value (MQ 46 124)
Contreit *adj.* contrite (MQ 73 11, MQ 80 29)
Conventioun *n.* agreement (MQ 44 69), a meeting of the nobility (MQ 58 24)
Convoy *v.* guide (MQ 42 182)
Cord *n.* hangman's rope (MQ 60 72)
Corps *n.* body (MQ 47 27)
Cors *n.* market cross (MQ 70 38), *see also* **Croce**
Cot *n.* coat (MQ 77 9)

Coulpit *pa. t.* traded, exchanged (MQ 62 37)
Coup *n.* basket (MQ 71 28)
Courches *n. pl.* kerchiefs (MQ 2 93)
Cours(e) *n.* passage in water (MQ 44 22); course (MQ 81 11, MQ 93a 3)
Courtes *adj.* courteous (MQ 49 11, MQ 62 22)
Courtingis *n. pl.* curtains (MQ 63 2)
Cousing *n.* kinsman (MQ 23 30)
Covene *n.* agreement (MQ 44 69)
Crab, Craib *v.* anger, annoy (MQ 29 52, MQ 39 74)
Craft *n.* sly cunning (MQ 11 75)
Craftines *n.* cunning, artfulness (MQ 35 30)
Craib *see* **Crab**
Craif *v.* crave, desire (MQ 37 117, MQ 42 173)
Crak *n.* boast (MQ 70 105)
Crame-craikeris *n. pl.* pedlars, stallholders (MQ 4 87)
Credence *n.* faith, trust (MQ 22 12)
Credit *n.* trust (MQ 44 8)
Crepusculein *adj.* evening (MQ 49 2)
Cryme *n.* crime, transgression of the law, wrongdoing (MQ 16 43, MQ 29 21, MQ 55 10)
Croce *n.* cross (of the crucifixion, MQ 46 26), market or boundary cross (MQ 6 22, MQ 11 47). *See also* **Cors**
Crope *n.* top, head of plant (MQ 69 57)
Croft *n.* field, pasture (MQ 70 39)
Croun *n.* gold coin (MQ 2 4, MQ 61 34); royal crown (MQ 6 44); royal majesty or estate (MQ 59 22); crown of the head (MQ 12 18); garland (MQ 85 16)
Crudelitie *n.* cruelty (MQ 29 13, MQ 33 23)
Cruikit *adj.* lame (MQ 21 39)
Cuill *v.* grow cool (MQ 5 9)
Cuir *pr. t.* cares (MQ 29 10, MQ 30 31)
Cuir(e) *n.* care (MQ 11 82); charge (MQ 44 22)
Cuiris *pr. t.* cares (MQ 29 10, MQ 30 31)
Cullouris *n. pl.* colours (MQ 76 22)
Cummer *n.* trouble, hardship (MQ 9 15, MQ 51 60)
Cummer *v.* hinder or harass (MQ 5 59, MQ 41 10)
Cunnand *n.* covenant (MQ 46 52)
Cunning *n.* knowledge or learning (MQ 43 58)
Cupititie *n.* greed (MQ 29 2)
Curall *n.* coral (MQ 48 60)
Cuschingis *n. pl.* cushions (MQ 2 44)

D

Daill *n.* dealing (MQ 44 42)

GLOSSARY

Dainser *n.* dancer (MQ 2 73)
Daingeir *n.* risk of harm (MQ 2 73)
Dayis *n. pl.* slatterns (MQ 43 55)
Dastard *n.* coward (MQ 83 51)
Debait *v.* defend (MQ 19 21); make defence (MQ 30 11)
Decoir, Decore *v.* embellish, adorn (MQ 48 29, MQ 59 15, MQ 94 3 9)
Decres *v.* diminish (MQ 52 18)
Dees *n.* goddess (MQ 48 89)
Defigurat *adj.* disfigured (MQ 81 1)
Degrie *n.* rank, station (MQ 4 91, MQ 23 39)
Deid *n.* death (MQ 12 8, MQ 16 65, MQ 49 64)
Deill *n.* ?part, dealing (MQ 35 63)
Deill *v.* act, deal (MQ 11 15, MQ 72 21)
Deilling *n.* manner of acting (MQ 43 10)
Deir *adj.* expensive (MQ 4 68, MQ 21 8)
Deir *n.* harm (MQ 35 32, MQ 53 30)
Deir *v.* harm (MQ 4 17, MQ 37 92, MQ 54 30)
Deitie *n.* deity (MQ 49 55)
Dekit *pa. t.* arrayed finely (MQ 43 55)
Delicat *adj.* refined or fastidious (MQ 2 56)
Deloyaltie *n.* disloyalty (MQ 44 2)
Deming *n.* the act of forming a judgement (MQ 43 4, BM 67)
Deme *v.* judge (MQ 43 33, MQ 62 5)
Denude *ppl. adj.* deprived (MQ 65 60, BM 192)
Depaint *v.* depict (MQ 63 31, MQ 69 9)
Depart *n.* departure (MQ 63 24)
Dependeris *n. pl.* dependants (MQ 51 32)
Depois *v.* put away (MQ 46 4)
Deray *n.* revelry (MQ 39 85)
Derf *adj.* cruel, bold (MQ 46 97)
Derthe *n.* high price of food as a result of scarcity (MQ 12 7)
Desaue, Desave, Dissave *v.* deceive (MQ 22 17, MQ 59 42, MQ 65 24). **Dissauit** *pa. p.* (BM 64)
Detract *v.* disparage (MQ 61 79)
Detractioun *n.* disparagement (MQ 55 32)
Devyce *n.* project, plan (MQ 80 34)
Devine *adj.* divine (MQ 49 7)
Devoir *v.* swallow (MQ 49 39)
Dewlie *adv.* properly (MQ 35 1)
Diffamit, *ppl. adj.* disgraced (MQ 11 22)
Digest *adj.* composed (MQ 64 21)
Digne *adj.* worthy (MQ 68 55)
Digressouris *n. pl.* those who digress (MQ 50 26)
Dyissar *n.* dice player (MQ 11 25)

GLOSSARY

Ding *v.* beat (MQ 6 27)
Disait *n.* deceit (MQ 11 69, MQ 48 127)
Disestimatioun *n.* lack of esteem (MQ 61 37)
Disestimit *pa. t.* condemned (MQ 62 4)
Dispair *v.* to be in a state of despair (MQ 7 10, MQ 49 19)
Dispyte *n.* spite, contempt (MQ 43 4, MQ 55 32)
Dispyitfull *adj.* malicious (MQ 55 39)
Dispryis *n.* disparagement (MQ 35 189)
Dissait *see* **Disait**
Dissave, Dissauit *see* **Desaue**
Dissembill *v.* to employ dissimulation (MQ 41 44)
Dissemblit *ppl. adj.* dissembled, false (MQ 11 18, MQ 25 91)
Dissever, Disseuer *v.* separate (MQ 46 38, MQ 49 70)
Dissimulatioun *n.* dissembling (MQ 12 36)
Dyte *v.* compose, indite (MQ 45 34)
Divelische *adj.* devilish (MQ 43 4, MQ 61 13)
Dyuers *adj.* separate, distinct (MQ 22 13, MQ 31 37)
Dyuouris *n. pl.* bankrupts (MQ 4 69)
Docht *see* **Dow** *v.*
Doleance *n.* sorrow (MQ 38 9)
Dolent *adj.* mournful (MQ 65 4)
Dolphin *n.* dauphin (MQ 6 9)
Douce *adj.* sweet (MQ 48 80)
Douchtellie *adv.* valiantly (MQ 44 83)
Doull *n.* grief (MQ 46 114)
Doulful(l) *adj.* mournful (MQ 64 51, MQ 65 55, MQ 76 19)
Doun-thring *v.* suppress, force down (MQ 35 126, MQ 59 7, BM 121)
Doutfull *adj.* uncertain (MQ 62 46)
Doutsum *adj.* difficult (MQ 11 58)
Dow *n.* dove (MQ 35 224)
Dow *v.* be able to do something (MQ 43 33, MQ 46 4). **Docht** *pa. t.* were of use (MQ 26 11)
Draucht *n.* scheme (MQ 62 98)
Drawin *pa. t.* ornamented with a band of a different material (MQ 2 27)
Dreid *v.* have fear of / fear for (MQ 2 46, MQ 25 105)
Dres *n.* attire (MQ 39 85)
Dres *v.* to turn, direct (MQ 16 49, MQ 28 28); maltreat (MQ 50 5); arrange (MQ 52 8)
Drie *v.* endure (MQ 35 58)
Dryiff *v.* drive (MQ 28 37)
Dryue *v.* ~ **ouer** to live out (one's life) (MQ 93a 8)
Droggis *n. pl.* spices used as a sweetmeat (MQ 2 62)
Drouth *n.* drought (MQ 65 50)
Drunking *adj.* drunken (MQ 62 60)

Duill *n.* sorrow (MQ 46 29, MQ 66 15)
Duire *v.* endure, last (MQ 65 68)
Dulcour *n.* sweetness (MQ 66 73)
Dunge *pa. p.* beaten (MQ 80 2)
Dure *n.* door (MQ 3 12)
Dwyine *v.* waste away (MQ 38 50)

E
E *n.* eye (MQ 54 19)
Eane *num.* one (MQ 95 38)
Efface *v.* obliterate (MQ 49 49)
Effectiouslie *adv.* earnestly (MQ 51 23)
Effeir *n.* respect (MQ 2 48)
Effeird *ppl. adj.* afraid (MQ 95 32)
Effray *v.* alarm (MQ 37 33)
Eik *v.* to increase (MQ 2 7)
Ein *n. pl.* eyes (MQ 20 49)
Eindill *v.* to become jealous (MQ 20 39)
Eir *n.* ear (MQ 41 58, MQ 59 41)
Eistclap *n.* after-clap, a blow following a major event (MQ 44 80)
Eithe *adj.* easy (MQ 35 28)
Elyde *v.* do away with (MQ 11 38)
Ellis *pr. t.* troubles (MQ 41 5)
Elusioun *n.* delusion (MQ 12 29)
Embrayis *v.* inflame (MQ 48 116)
Enorme *adj.* heinous, wicked (MQ 44 38)
Ennuy *n.* annoyance (MQ 46 28)
Enteir *adj.* sound, entire (MQ 39 60)
Entres *n.* opportunity to enter (MQ 52 38)
Enuy *v.* annoy, vex (MQ 46 118)
Enuironit *pa. t.* surrounded (MQ 41 18)
Ernand *n.* errand? (MQ 38 67)
Eschape *v.* escape (MQ 7 15)
Eschew *v.* refrain from, avoid (MQ 54 16, MQ 57 14)
Esperance *n.* hope (MQ 71 12)
Esteme *v.* to hold in high regard (MQ 6 53, MQ 46 131)
Eterne *adj.* eternal (MQ 12 1)
Eternise *v.* make eternal (MQ 94.3 6)
Ethnik *adj.* pagan (MQ 42 93)
Ettill *v.* to direct one's course (MQ 38 37)
Euerilk *adj.* each, every (MQ 4 42, MQ 6 19)
Eventour, Eventuire *n.* adventure, chance (MQ 17 1, MQ 27 5)
Execrabill *adj.* detestable (MQ 42 132)
Exerced *pa. t.* performed (MQ 53 14)

GLOSSARY

Exerceis *n.* exertion, activity (MQ 42 17)
Excitat *v.* rouse, stir up (MQ 69 67)
Expeditioun *n.* furtherance of a matter, active assistance (MQ 4 41, MQ 51 78)
Expell *v.* drive out (MQ 18 2)
Expert *adj.* experienced (MQ 59 4)

F
Fais *n. pl.* enemies (MQ 10 48, MQ 25 30, MQ 41 39)
Fa *v.*[1] fall (MQ 27 14)
Fa *v.*[2] befall (MQ 5 83)
Facil *adj.* easy (MQ 25 54)
Fact *n.* deed, action (MQ 44 89), wicked act (MQ 60 87)
Fay *n.* religious faith (MQ 16 4)
Faill *n.* failure, fault (MQ 7 43)
Fail3ie *n.* failing (MQ 58 27)
Fail3ie *v.* fall short, be defective (MQ 9 31)
Fain(e) *adj.* glad, satisfied (MQ 42 75, MQ 51 15, MQ 80 11)
Fairlie *adj.* strange, wonderful (MQ 44 28)
Fairlie *n.* wonder (MQ 61 45)
Fairlie *v.* marvel, feel wonder or surprise (MQ 2 8)
Falset *n.* falsity, falsehood (MQ 11 69, MQ 47 26)
Far *v.* go (MQ 19 49)
Farder *adj.* further (MQ 43 68)
Farland *adj.* belonging to far away countries (MQ 44 36)
Fartigard *n.* hooped petticoat (MQ 70 126)
Fauld *n.* enclosure for keeping animals (MQ 20 3)
Fauld *v.* to yield, bend (MQ 66 63, 68)
Fautles *adj.* faultless (MQ 92 12)
Fect *n.* value (MQ 95 4)
Fedder *n.* feather (MQ 35 43)
Feding *vbl. n.* eating, partaking of food (MQ 2 57)
Feis *n. pl.* wages, remuneration (MQ 51 66, MQ 59 19)
Feid *n.* feud (MQ 18 26, MQ 47 44)
Feidis *pr. t.* fades (MQ 65 86)
Feill *n.* understanding (MQ 5 67)
Feill *v.*[1] fail (MQ 35 37)
Feill *v.*[2] feel (MQ 41 69)
Fein3eit, Fein3it *ppl. adj.* feigned (MQ 11 9, MQ 19 54)
Feir *n.*[1] companion (MQ 46 42), spouse (MQ 6 43), equal (MQ 16 11)
Feir *n.*[2] dread (MQ 42 2, 8)
Feir *v.* fear (MQ 4 23, MQ 5 21)
Fekill *adj.* fickle (MQ 42 16)
Feminein(e) *n.* the female sex (MQ 39 90, MQ 40 2)

GLOSSARY

Ferce *adj.* fierce (MQ 66 65)
Fercis *n. pl.* stage plays, farces (MQ 6 20)
Fering *vbl. n.* fearing (MQ 39 101)
Ferme *n.* rent for land, sometimes paid in grain (MQ 21 8)
Ferrie *n.* ferry (MQ 13 26)
Fersnes *n.* fierceness, fury (MQ 42 43)
Feruencie *n.* zeal (MQ 49 62)
Feruent *adj.* passionate (MQ 35 35)
Fyne *n.* end, conclusion (MQ 66 144)
Fit *n.* base or support (MQ 46 151)
Fleing *adj.* flying (MQ 85 11)
Fleitschour *n.* one who flatters (MQ 68 158)
Flemit *pa. t.* banished (MQ 62 7)
Flesche *n.* meat (MQ 3 32)
Fleschouris *n. pl.* butchers (MQ 70 19)
Flit *v.* change (MQ 35 11)
Flyite *v.* argue violently, wrangle (MQ 20 18, MQ 95 43)
Flitting *ppl. adj.* fleeting (MQ 65 135)
Flouris *v.* flourish (MQ 43 68)
Flourishit *adj.* blossoming (MQ 69 43)
Fluid *n.* flood, overflow (MQ 71 5)
Foirbearis *n. pl.* ancestors (MQ 5 38, MQ 46 99)
Foirbeir *v.* refrain from, abstain from (MQ 2 18, MQ 4 13)
Foirpast *adj.* already past (MQ 80 13)
Foirsein *pa. p.* overlooked (MQ 16 104)
Foirskirt *n.* front skirt of a dress (MQ 2 13)
Foirthink *v.* regret (MQ 25 33)
Fond *adj.* foolish (MQ 73 50)
Forcet *ppl. adj.* forced (MQ 43 20)
Fordor, Furder *v.* further, advance (MQ 50 45, MQ 51 35)
Fordwart *adv.* forward. **help** ~ advance, promote (MQ 23 4)
Forfair *v.* to perish (MQ 3 82, MQ 25 4)
Forfaltis *n. pl.* offences (MQ 25 106)
Forleit *v.* to abandon or forsake (MQ 72 19)
Forlorne *pp. adj.* lost, completely destroyed (MQ 7 19)
Formis *n. pl.* long benches (MQ 5 47)
Forraine *adj.* foreign (MQ 44 62, MQ 60 8)
Forsien *pa. p.* overlooked (MQ 16 104)
Forsuith *adv.* truly (MQ 46 147)
Forthink *v.* to regret (MQ 12 28, MQ 55 15)
Found *v.* establish (MQ 51 9)
Fow *adj.* full (MQ 23 38, MQ 55 2)
Fra *conj.* as soon as (MQ 44 44)
Fray *prep.* from (MQ 38 10, MQ 45 15)

GLOSSARY

Fray v. frighten (MQ 5 70)
Frainis pr. t. requests (MQ 37 22)
Fraternitie n. brotherliness (MQ 6 67)
Fraward adj. adverse (MQ 46 99)
Freindfullie adv. in a friendly manner (MQ 30 13)
Freit v. fret (MQ 43 11)
Fremmidnes n. strangeness (MQ 41 88)
Fret v. rub (MQ 48 61)
Frivoll adj. of little worth (MQ 65 113)
Fuilhaist n. foolish haste (MQ 67 13)
Fuilʒeit pa. t. trampled on (MQ 44 63)
Fuk-saillis n. pl. a foresail, used figuratively of a woman's billowing skirt (MQ 2 14)
Fulfill v. fill up, bring to completion (MQ 68 105)
Fundatioun n. the church as institution (MQ 51 65); foundation of a building (MQ 68 90)
Furder see **Fordor**
Furie, Furye n. frenzy, desire to avenge (MQ 38 39, MQ 94.1. 11)
Furrit ppl. adj. lined or trimmed with fur (MQ 2 16)
Furteouslie adv. furtively, stealthily (MQ 63 42)
Furthset v. advance, set forward (MQ 9 17)

G

Ga v. go, walk, move (MQ 3 13). **ʒeid** pa. t. (MQ 23 21)
Gadge n. pledge (MQ 72 15)
Gailʒeounis n. pl. galleys, galleons (MQ 4 89)
Gaine n. profit (MQ 70 14)
Gaine v. be fitting (MQ 70 108)
Gaine pa. p. gone (MQ 45 29)
Gainestand v. withstand, oppose (MQ 14 12, MQ 21 20)
Gairdein, Gardein n. garden (MQ 19 1, MQ 40 66)
Gaist n. guest (MQ 60 75)
Gait n. way or road, or town (as in MQ 2 71, MQ 3 9); method of doing something (MQ 25 92, MQ 28 25)
Galeyis n. vessels, ships (MQ 6 26)
Ganand ppl. adj. convenient, suitable (MQ 41 136)
Gang v. go about (esp. on foot) (MQ 7 59); to depart (MQ 17 36?)
Gar v. to cause (MQ 16 63, MQ 55 4)
Gardein see **Gairdein**
Gartennis n. pl. garter (MQ 2 28)
Gasing-stok n. a spectacle (MQ 62 91)
Geill-poikkis n. pl. jelly bags (MQ 2 17)
Gein pa. p. given (MQ 35 20)
Geir n. personal possessions, clothes, equipment, money (MQ 2 15, MQ 70 69)

GLOSSARY

Geked *pa. t.* mocked (MQ 43 50)
Gent *adj.* good, gracious (MQ 41 62)
Gers *n.* grass (MQ 70 16)
Ges *n.* guess (MQ 41 130)
Gyde, Guyde *v.* show the way (MQ 3 7); direct, order something, behave (MQ 11 8, 16)
Gyding *n.* self-direction, management of one's affairs (MQ 42 52)
Giglettis *n. pl.* wanton women (MQ 2 52)
Gysaris *n. pl.* mummers, players (MQ 5 13)
Gyse, Guys *n.* fashion (MQ 60 1, MQ 39 42)
Glaid *adj.* glad, joyful (MQ 14 21)
Glaid *v.* gladden (MQ 17 32, MQ 66 97)
Glaidlie adv. willingly (MQ 54 31)
Glaidnes *n.* contentment, happiness (MQ 46 132)
Glaikis *n. pl.* mocking deception, trickery (MQ 70 78)
Glancis *n. pl.* flashes of light (MQ 43 32)
Glansing *ppl. adj.* bright, gleaming (MQ 73 12)
Gle *n.* joy (MQ 39 31)
Gleid *n.* ember, spark (MQ 30 41, MQ 43 20)
Gleit *v.* glitter, shine (MQ 69 2)
Glemis *pr. t.* gleams (MQ 43 20)
Gleting *ppl. adj.* glittering (MQ 46 35)
Glydis *n. pl.* old horses (MQ 70 56)
Glistering *ppl. adj.* glittering (MQ 77 15)
Gloise *v.* to cover up with deception (MQ 41 73)
Gloriositie *n.* boastfulness (MQ 41 127, MQ 42 59)
Gob *n.* a large or ugly mouth (MQ 3 66)
Gorgit *ppl. adj.* choked (MQ 43 19)
Gospellaris *n. pl.* preachers of the gospel (MQ 12 62)
Gouketlie *adv.* foolishly (MQ 35 67)
Graith *n.* the means of doing something, the equipment needed for something (MQ 13 30); household furnishings (MQ 26 5)
Gratuitlie *adv.* gratuitously (MQ 62 137)
Grauitie *n.* serious rather than frivolous bearing (MQ 4 52)
Grave *adj.* sober, dignified (MQ 92 2)
Grein *v.* yearn (MQ 45 39)
Greit *v.* weep (BM 161)
Grethed *pa. t.* prepared (MQ 46 35)
Grewhoundis *n. pl.* greyhounds (MQ 38 93)
Grie *n.* degree, step (in line of descent) (MQ 44 76); place of pre-eminence (MQ 48 18)
Grie *v.* settle, agree (MQ 19 78, MQ 51 15)
Gryit *adj.* great (MQ 40 13)
Grip *n.* control, power, hold (MQ 19 72)

Groundis *n. pl.* foundations (MQ 68 61)
Grudgeing *vbl. n.* lack of generosity (BM 151)
Guberne *v.* govern (MQ 12 3)
Gudmen *n. pl.* men who are good in some way, or husbands (MQ 2 24)
Guyde *see* **Gyde**
Guyder *n.* one who guides or controls (used of God) (MQ 10 22)
Guydingis *n. pl.* practices (MQ 60 12)
Guyle *n.* guile (MQ 35 55)
Guys *see* **Gyse**

H
Habill *adj.* able (MQ 9 57)
Habul3ment *n.* apparel, clothing (MQ 4 56)
Hace *adj.* hoarse (MQ 69 31)
Had, Hauld *v.* hold, observe (MQ 5 31, MQ 7 60). *refl.* keep oneself, remain (MQ 15 9, MQ 37 19)
Haill *adv.* completely (MQ 3 19)
Haillalie, Hallalie *adv.* wholly, completely (MQ 12 15, MQ 23 32)
Haimlines *n.* friendship (MQ 41 86)
Hairbour *n.* harbour (MQ 46 32)
Hairtlie *adv.* earnestly (MQ 34 25)
Hairtlines *n.* sincerity (MQ 6 56)
Haistallie *adv.* quickly, speedily (MQ 7 21)
Hait *adj.* hot (MQ 41 32)
Hallow *n.* hollow (MQ 92 1)
Hals *n.* neck (MQ 2 36)
Hals-beiddis *n.* necklace of beads (MQ 2 36)
Hant *v.* to practise or engage in (MQ 4 27); be associated with (MQ 41 95)
Hap *n.* fortune, luck (MQ 9 42, MQ 49 41, MQ 71 33)
Hardie *adj.* valiant, brave (MQ 1 2, MQ 5 10)
Hardines *n.* courage (MQ 44 15, MQ 62 30)
Harlot *n.* low or unchaste woman (MQ 2 78)
Harlatrie *n.* immoral, unchaste conduct (MQ 15 11)
Hasart *v.* hazard (MQ 35 173)
Hauld *n.* imprisonment (MQ 61 32)
Hauld *see* **Had**
Haunt *v.* engage with, frequent (MQ 15 11)
Haut *adj.* high, noble (MQ 85 12)
Hawtie *adj.* high, lofty (MQ 1 2)
Hectis *pr. t.* promises (MQ 71 24)
Heiche *n.* pride (MQ 41 2, 108)
Heichlie, Heichtly *adv.* proudly, haughtily, highly (MQ 41 108, BM 13)
Heicht *adj.* high up (MQ 2 37)
Heid *n.* governing principal (MQ 46 26)

Heid *v.* behead (MQ 5 62)
Heild *v.* incline submissively (MQ 47 41)
Heilland *adj.* highland (MQ 70 20)
Heirschip *n.* violent raid, theft of cattle (MQ 30 6, MQ 58 30)
Heisit *pa. t.* raise up (MQ 70 119)
Helsum *adj.* wholesome, healthy (MQ 35 79)
Hent *v.* seize (MQ 41 111)
Herar *n.* auditor, one who listens to the recitation of a text (MQ 55 36)
Hereit *see* **Her(r)ie**
Her(r)ie *v.* plunder, ravage, ruin (MQ 13 25. **Hereit** *pa. t.* (MQ 3 19)
Heroicis *poss.* hero (MQ 49 21)
Hest *v. pr. t.* (= contracted **hes it**) have it (MQ 83 24)
Hewit *adj.* coloured (MQ 2 21)
Hy *n.* haste (MQ 69 21)
Hiche *adj.* high (MQ 38 100)
Hyire *n.* servant (MQ 46 39)
Hyire-wemen *n. pl.* hired female servants (MQ 70 6)
Hyne *adv.* in the next world (MQ 16 79)
Hint *pa. t.* seized (MQ 23 28)
Ho *n.* cessation (MQ 38 13)
Hois *n.* a long stocking for the leg (MQ 2 26)
Holit *pa. p.* dug with holes (MQ 68 99)
Homiceid *n.* a murderer (MQ 89 14)
Honest *adj.* worthy or of good moral character (MQ 2 76, MQ 15 9)
Hostleris *n. pl.* innkeepers (MQ 70 22)
Houbeid *conj.* although (MQ 95 55)
Houke *v.* dig out (MQ 68 89)
Houp *n.* hope (MQ 71 23)
Hourdome, Hurdome *n.* harlotry (MQ 42 65, MQ 57 19)
Hous *n.* lineage (MQ 44 9)
Houshaulding *n.* the act of maintaining a household (MQ 5 12)
Huik *n.* fishing hook (MQ 45 29)
Huire *n.* prostitute (MQ 70 32)
Hulie *adv.* slowly (MQ 50 11)
Humlie *adv.* humbly (MQ 48 124)
Humanitie *n.* human nature (MQ 42 60)
Hurdome *see* **Hourdome**
Hurt *ppl. adj.* wronged (MQ 70 27)

I

Ilkane, Ilkon *pron.* each one (MQ 19 75, MQ 48 2)
Illuster *adj.* illustrious (MQ 9 10)
Imbecillitie *n.* feebleness (MQ 42 130)
Imps *n. pl.* offspring, successors (MQ 91 14)

GLOSSARY

Impyire *v.* govern (MQ 69 63)
Impyire, Impyre *n.* empire (MQ 35 201); rule (MQ 42 120)
Impute *v.* ascribe a fault to (MQ 61 80)
Inamitie *n.* enmity (MQ 38 108)
Inburied *pa. p.* interred (MQ 93a 1)
Inclusit *pa. p.* shut up, imprisoned (MQ 62 84)
Inconvenient *n.* trouble, danger (MQ 25 72)
Indewed *pa. t.* endowed, invested (MQ 44 12, MQ 49 7)
Indifferentlie *adv.* impartially (MQ 50 46)
Indigence *n.* poverty (MQ 40 30)
Indigent *n.* a pauper (MQ 41 104)
Indyit *n.* enditing (MQ 95 41)
Inding *adj.* undeserving (MQ 66 38)
Indwellaris *n. pl.* residents, inhabitants (MQ 70 3)
Infame *adj.* infamous (MQ 62 124)
Inferiouris *n. pl.* inferiors, those of low status or with little authority (MQ 7 33)
Ingyne *n.* intellectual ability, talent (MQ 35 103, MQ 68 52)
Ingraitlie *adv.* ungratefully (MQ 52 27)
Ingraitnes *n.* ingratitude (MQ 52 24)
Inimitie *n.* emnity (MQ 25 12, MQ 42 26)
Iniure *v.* injure (MQ 41 116)
Inlaik *v.* be deficient, be wanting (MQ 26 2, MQ 64 50)
Inner-mair *adv.* further in (MQ 44 37)
Inordinat *adj.* irregular, excessive (MQ 62 105)
Insensative *adj.* unfeeling (MQ 66 76)
Institutioun *n.* a law or custom, established law of the country (MQ 5 89, MQ 51 80)
Inteir *adj.* complete, whole (MQ 44 9)
Intercessouris *n. pl.* those who intercede on behalf of another (MQ 4 39)
Interpryis *v.* undertake (MQ 39 39)
Interteney *v.* entertain (MQ 6 45)
Intervall *n.* ?space, interval (MQ 48 64)
Intestine *adj.* domestic, inter-country (MQ 56 9)
Intromet *v.* to handle (money or property) (MQ 57 4)
Intromissioun *n.* the act of intromitting, assuming possession or management of someone's property (MQ 18 14)
Intrusioun *n.* unwarrented entry into (possession, authority), interference (MQ 12 28)
Inveccyde *adj.* invective (MQ 62 15)
Inveccyde *n.* piece of invective (MQ 62 title)
Invent *v.* conceive (MQ 42 104); contrive (MQ 67 5)
Invyaris *n. pl.* those who envy (MQ 43 24)
Invocat *v.* invoke (MQ 81 4)

GLOSSARY

Involent *adj.* unwilling? (MQ 65 99)
Ipocreitis *n. pl.* hypocrites (MQ 19 54)
Irk, Yrke *v.* to become bored, weary of something (MQ 4 82); irritated, troubled (MQ 41 80)
Yron *n.* iron (MQ 49 10)
Ithinglie *adv.* without remission, constantly (MQ 65 45)
Yuore, Yvoire *adj. and n.* ivory (MQ 40 89, MQ 48 63)

I = J
Iak *n.* a jerkin, a defensive garment (MQ 5 69)
Ianetflour *n.* yellow flower (MQ 40 69)
Iawis *n. pl.* waves (MQ 65 33)
Ieme *n.* gem (MQ 35 187)
Iouk *v.* bow humbly (MQ 41 37)
Iust *adj.* just, equitable (MQ 7 61, MQ 87 4)
Iust *v.* to fight/joust on horseback (MQ 6 12)

K
Kaip *n.* cloak (MQ 49 2)
Kaist, Kest *pa. t.* cast (MQ 28 44, MQ 62 146)
Kein *adj.* bold, fierce, sharp (MQ 38 75, MQ 42 43)
Ken *v.* to know, acknowledge, recognise (MQ 3 55, MQ 52 7). **Kennyng** *pr. p.* (BM 25)
Kest *see* **Kaist**
Ky *n. pl.* cows (MQ 70 20)
Kyithis *pr. t.* reveal, make known, disclose (MQ 16 23)
Kyndnes *n.* kinship (MQ 19 105)
Kinrik *n.* kingdom (MQ 58 46)
Kirk-men *n. pl.* churchmen (MQ 4 27)
Kist *n.* a large chest (MQ 3 52)
Kitchingis *n. pl.* kitchens (MQ 5 9, MQ 62 115)
Kittill *adj.* delicate, difficult to deal with (MQ 44 22)
Kna *v.* know (MQ 27 13)
Knappis *n. pl.* tassels (MQ 70 102)
Knottis *n. pl.* formal, ornamental gardens (MQ 68 127)
Knottit *pa. t.* tied with a knot (MQ 70 97)
Kow *n.* cow (MQ 18 8, MQ 58 47)

L
Labour *v.* plough (MQ 4 82)
Laid *v.* put out of action (MQ 3 28)
Laif, Lave *n.* the rest, the remainder, those things or people that remain (MQ 3 63, MQ 42 170, MQ 46 116), all the others (MQ 95 20)
Lair *n.* tuition, lesson (MQ 71 30)

GLOSSARY

Laith *v.* to be reluctant (MQ 84 6)
Lak *n.* fault, deficiency (MQ 61 38)
Lak *v.* deride, blame, find fault (MQ 39 92, MQ 43 14, MQ 44 2)
Landwart *adj., adv. phr.* of or in the country rather than the town (MQ 2 107, MQ 5 2)
Langsumnes *n.* protractedness (MQ 51 33)
Langwiss *v.* languish (MQ 48 109)
Lasoris *n. pl.* pastures (MQ 69 34)
Latter-meit *n.* food set at the table? A set meal? (MQ 41 137)
Lattin *pa. p.* let (MQ 16 66)
Laud *n.* commendation (MQ 44 81)
Lave *see* **Laif**
Lave *v.* bathe (MQ 48 7)
Law *adv.* low down (MQ 69 64)
Lawtie n. honesty (MQ 4 63), loyalty (MQ 6 48, MQ 72 29)
Lear *n.* liar (MQ 11 5)
Led *pa. p.* produced (MQ 21 28)
Leyis *n. pl.* lies, untruths (MQ 43 13)
Leid *v.* direct? (MQ 55 23)
Leif *adj.* dear (MQ 76 17)
Leif *v.*[1] cease to do something (MQ 2 86); leave (MQ 3 13)
Leif *v.*[2] live (MQ 2 68, MQ 39 10)
Leig *n.* alliance (MQ 60 68)
Leigis *n. pl.* subjects (of the realm) (MQ 7 5)
Leill *adj.* just, lawful (MQ 4 64); loyal, trustworthy (MQ 11 19)
Leip *v.* rush, jump (MQ 22 9)
Leir *v.* learn (MQ 2 68)
Leis *n.* lying (MQ 78 28)
Lekis *n. pl.* leakages (MQ 44 30)
Lekand *ppl. adj.* leaking (MQ 13 27)
Lemmand *n.* lover (MQ 66 98)
Lenth *v.* lengthen (MQ 31 62)
Lesing *n.* lie (MQ 20 37, MQ 55 3, MQ 59 46)
Lesioun *n.* hurt (MQ 19 71)
Lest *n.* permanence (MQ 35 21)
Lesume *adj.* morally or legally permissible (MQ 53 15)
Lesumlie *adv.* properly, rightly (MQ 17 27)
Let *n.* end, stop (MQ 35 176)
Leueray *n.* distinctive clothing, livery, often bestowed on servants (MQ 6 16)
Leving *n.* financial means, maintenance (MQ 59 24)
Ly *v.* lie, lie low (MQ 7 25). **Lyand** *ppl. adj.* lying, remaining (MQ 14 10).
   Lyne *pa. p.* (MQ 6 42)
Lyart *adj.* hoary (MQ 13 18)
Libellis *n. pl.* defamatory publications (MQ 55 11)

Libertie *n.* freedom (MQ 42 9)
Licence *n.* permission (MQ 39 62)
Lichlie *adv.* lightly (MQ 35 24)
Lichtlie *v.* disparage (MQ 43 13). **Lichtleit** *pa. p.* insulted, treated with contempt (MQ 5 73, MQ 41 180)
Lichtliest *adv.* with most flippancy (MQ 36 1)
Lidderlie *adv.* slothfully, cowardly (MQ 35 152)
Lyflie *adj.* vivacious (MQ 85 8, MQ 92 4)
Lyif *n.* means of support, livelihood (MQ 41 181)
Lyire *n.* complexion (MQ 48 65)
Limmer *n.*, a villain, a lawless person, a raider (MQ 4 13, MQ 19 27, MQ 51 49)
Lyne *n.*[1] line (of descent) (MQ 1 6)
Lyne *n.*[2] practice (MQ 93a 4)
Lyne *see* **Ly**
Ling *v.* dwell (MQ 70 54)
Lippin *v.* trust (MQ 42 180)
List *n.* will (MQ 39 10)
List *v.*[1] listen (MQ 74 18)
List *v.*[2] please, care, wish (MQ 60 1)
Lyvelie *adj.* vivacious (MQ 48 35)
Loif *v.* praise (MQ 64 1)
Lose *n.* loss (MQ 65 106, MQ 79 3)
Lote *n.* fate (MQ 46 23)
Louf *v.* love (MQ 33 27)
Loun *n.* ruffian, rogue (MQ 4 86, MQ 60 49); lecher (MQ 20 34)
Loup *v.* flee, leap (MQ 77 3)
Lout *v.* go down (MQ 68 74)
Loving *ppl. adj.* friendly, well disposed (MQ 62 25)
Lowse *adj.* unprincipled (MQ 61 18)
Lucent *adj.* luminous (MQ 90 9)
Luid *n.* song or verse (MQ 93a and 93b titles)
Luifsum *adj.* pleasing (MQ 69 52)
Luik *v.* pay attention (MQ 35 64)
Luit *pa. t.* let (MQ 46 165)
Luk *n.* luck (MQ 62 56)
Lurdane *adj.* base, wretched (MQ 40 108)
Lurk *v.* to hide oneself out of cowardice, sloth (MQ 7 25)

M

Magistrat *n.* secular ruler, including the monarch or regent (MQ 57 7)
Magnanime *adj.* magnanimous (MQ 46 90)
Magnanimit *adj.* magnanimous, noble (MQ 46 86)
May *adj.* more (MQ 35 167)

Maik *n.* spouse, beloved (MQ 48 46, MQ 79 3); equal (MQ 66 8, MQ 68 150)
Maikles *adj.* peerless (MQ 63 8)
Maill *n.* rent (MQ 21 9)
Maine, Mane *n.* complaint (MQ 42 161, MQ 95 40)
Maist *adj.* great (MQ 30 8)
Maister-steik *n.* a masterpiece, a work of craftsmanship (MQ 62 113)
Maistred *pa. t.* mastered (MQ 46 86)
Maistreis *n.* force (MQ 42 52)
Mait *see* **Meit**
Makdome *n.* stature, beauty (MQ 64 13)
Makeris *n. pl.* poets, writers (MQ 55 1)
Malhourous *adj.* unfortunate (MQ 38 54)
Maling, Melein *n.* rented land, a tenant farm (MQ 13 29, MQ 21 23)
Maling *v.* malign (MQ 35 124)
Malitiouslie *adv.* maliciously (MQ 14 4)
Man *v.* be obliged to, must (MQ 2 21, MQ 41 46)
Mane *see* **Maine**
Maner *n.* the state of affairs, the way things are or the way in which something is done (MQ 2 23)
Manerlie *adj.* polite, modest (MQ 64 20)
Manheid *n.* the qualities fitting for a man (MQ 6 52)
Mansuetud *n.* mildness, gentleness (MQ 46 92, MQ 64 11, MQ 71 7)
Mantenaris *n. pl.* those who uphold something (MQ 4 37, MQ 55 14)
Manuire *v.* work (MQ 13 30)
Mar *v.* go astray, hinder or obstruct something (MQ 85 19)
Marbre *n.* marble (MQ 48 68)
Mard *pa. t.* crazed, injured (MQ 71 3)
Mark *v.* observe, take note (MQ 77 7)
Marrowis *n. pl.* neighbours (MQ 44 93)
Marrowit *ppl. adj.* entered as a worthy competitor (MQ 64 38)
Mas *n.* sum total (MQ 73 42)
Mater *n.* subject of a dispute or litigation (MQ 51 7)
Maucles *adj.* feeble (MQ 65 25)
Maveis *n.* song-thrush (MQ 69 5)
Meid *n.* reward (MQ 35 117)
Mein *n.* agency, influence (MQ 6 62, MQ 15 16, MQ 50 15)
Mein *v.* declare, speak of, indicate (MQ 2 46, 49, MQ 5 5, MQ 41 152)
Meinʒie *n.* a body of people (MQ 70 11)
Meir *n.* mare (MQ 70 67)
Meit *adj.* suited (MQ 20 29); well-fitting (MQ 70 85)
Meit *n.* food (MQ 2 69, MQ 5 26, MQ 69 42); livelihood (MQ 60 76)
Meit *v.* meet (MQ 39 71)
Mekill *adj.* large, or when applied to God/Devil great in power (MQ 3 8)

Meladie *n.* malady, sickness (MQ 39 69, MQ 89 43)
Melein *see* **Maling**
Mell *v.* have dealings with (MQ 19 81, MQ 57 11); meddle (MQ 52 34)
Melling *vbl. n.* mixing (MQ 15 18)
Memberis *n. pl.* parts of the body (MQ 47 3)
Mending *n.* recompense, redress (MQ 51 14)
Merchis *n. pl.* borders (MQ 10 52)
Merle *n.* blackbird (MQ 69 5)
Mesour *n.* means of measuring (MQ 4 64)
Metar *comp.* more fitting (MQ 48 55)
Metest *superl.* most appropriate or fitting (MQ 1 5, MQ 62 113)
Midage *n.* middle age (MQ 13 17)
Myite *n.* a thing (coin) of small value (MQ 41 75)
Mint *v.* aspire (MQ 44 81)
Myris *n. pl.* swampy grounds (MQ 3 59)
Mis, Miss *n.* sin, error (MQ 33 10, MQ 42 125)
Mischance *n.* misfortune, disaster (MQ 8 15)
Mischeant *adj.* wicked (MQ 62 121)
Mischeiff *n.* misfortune, distress, or hardship (MQ 3 6)
Misforme *adj.* shapeless (MQ 46 33)
Misken *v.* to be ignorant of (MQ 37 43)
Misknaw *v.* fail to recognise, overlook (MQ 41 132, MQ 43 9)
Mislyking *pr. p.* being displeased with (MQ 61 86)
Miss *see* **Mis**
Missforme *ppl. adj.* misformed (MQ 46 33)
Missiue *adj.* written, authoritative, formal (MQ 30 46)
Mistemperit *adj.* disordered (MQ 41 3)
Mister *n.* need (MQ 20 27, MQ 70 99)
Misteris *pr. t.* needs (MQ 37 90, MQ 68 114)
Misterie *n.* something difficult to comprehend, a religious truth (MQ 84 15)
Mold *n.* earth (MQ 46 33)
Mone *n.*[1] mourning (MQ 37 8). *See also* **Maine**
Mone *n.*[2] moon (MQ 11 63)
Monyest *superl.* most, the greatest number (MQ 29 49)
Monifauld *adv.* manifold (MQ 40 10)
Monische *v.* admonish (MQ 42 125)
Monissing *vbl. n.* admonishing, warning (MQ 42 80)
Moveris *n. pl.* instigators (MQ 4 38, MQ 27 9)
Mow *n.* mouth (MQ 38 64)
Muid *n.* spirit (MQ 46 90)
Muile *n.* a mule (MQ 5 11)
Muillis *n. pl.* slippers (MQ 2 41, MQ 70 96)
Muire *n.* moorland (MQ 3 59)
Mumschancis *n. pl.* mummings (MQ 2 72)

GLOSSARY

Mundane *adj.* of the world (MQ 63 8)
Murne *v.* mourn (MQ 31 15, MQ 41 6)
Murning *n.* sorrow (MQ 31 33)
Murther *n.* murder (MQ 62 136)
Murtherar *n.* murderer (MQ 16 10)
Mutine *n.* rebellion (MQ 30 56)

N

Nar *adv.* near (MQ 38 69)
Nauchtie *adj.* wicked (MQ 60 10)
Nawayis *adv. phr.* in no way (MQ 35 195)
Neid *n.* necessity, compulsion (MQ 38 54, MQ 46 28)
Neif *n.* possession, keeping (MQ 23 28)
Neir-hand *adv.* near at hand, close by (MQ 3 19)
Nemmyng *pr. p.* naming (BM 25)
Nepotis *n. pl.* grandsons (MQ 46 127)
Nichtbour *n.* neighbour (MQ 5 63)
Niest *adj.* nearest (MQ 87 2)
Nyice *adj.* foolish, misguided (MQ 15 7)
Nil *v.* will not (MQ 41 82)
Noy *v.* annoy (MQ 37 112)
Noysum *adj.* troublesome, harmful (MQ 44 38)
Nolt *n.* cattle (MQ 3 4)
Nonage *n.* minority (MQ 59 78)
Notit *pa. t.* marked out for infamy or blame, reproached (MQ 52 23)
Nuik *n.* point, corner (MQ 32 note)
Nummer *n.* number (MQ 21 54)

O

Ocht *n.* anything (MQ 26 15)
Ocht *pa. t.* owed (MQ 26 15)
Oftymis *adv.* repeatedly (MQ 46 170)
Onbocht *ppl. adj.* something acquired for nothing (MQ 70 71)
Oncled *pa. t.* unclothed (MQ 35 30)
Onfreindis *n. pl.* enemies (MQ 14 20)
Onmolest *adj.* untroubled (MQ 37 38)
Onperfyite *adj.* imperfect (MQ 35 68)
Onset *v.* attack (MQ 3 9)
On-socht *pa. p.* unexplored (MQ 29 12)
Ornis *pr. t.* grace by one's presence (MQ 95 42)
Our *adv.* over, excessively (MQ 2 110)
Ourfleit *v.* overflow (MQ 64 46)
Our-gang *v.* to overrun (MQ 3 79, MQ 5 63)
Ourgo *v.* let pass (MQ 42 150)

GLOSSARY

Our-harle, Ourharle *v.* oppress (MQ 34 3), overturn (MQ 44 47)
Oursie *v.* neglect, overlook (MQ 34 22, MQ 51 36)
Outtrance *n.* extremity of injury (MQ 38 60)
Outwair *v.* spend (MQ 41 54)

P

Pace *n.* Easter (MQ 5 31)
Page *n.* a boy in service, an attendant (MQ 5 44)
Pairtlie *adv.* pertly (MQ 43 42)
Pak *n.* fortune, wealth (MQ 2 64)
Pallat *n.* head (MQ 55 28)
Pan *v.* correspond, agree (MQ 60 30)
Pance *v.* think (MQ 44 23), **pansis** *pr. t.* worry (MQ 14 19)
Pand *n.* pledge of security (MQ 72 15)
Pansis *see* **Pance**
Pansivnes *n.* pensiveness (MQ 37 2)
Pape *n.* Pope (MQ 12 41)
Papingo *n.* parrot (MQ 35 89, MQ 43 56)
Paramour *n.* passionate love, desire (MQ 64 27). *pl.* (MQ 38 90)
Parqueir *adv.* by heart, word for word (MQ 9 20, MQ 70 131)
Participat *adj.* sharing, in conjunction with (MQ 46 27)
Pasmentis *n. pl.* strips of gold or silver braid (MQ 2 22)
Passing *ppl. adj.* preeminent (MQ 74 6)
Pastouris *n. pl.* clergymen (MQ 4 21)
Pat *n.* paw (MQ 66 65)
Patent *adj.* open (MQ 35 29)
Patrone, Patroun, Patren *n.* example (MQ 62 21, MQ 90 6)
Pauchtie *adj.* arrogant (MQ 41 107)
Pawne *n.* peacock (MQ 35 92)
Peceablie *adv.* peacefully (MQ 30 95)
Peculiar *adj.* chosen, distinguished (MQ 46 50)
Perchance *conj.* perhaps (MQ 68 41)
Peregall *n.* equal (MQ 39 6, MQ 64 15)
Peres *v.* perish (MQ 44 94)
Perforce *adv.* of necessity (MQ 74 7)
Perhaps *adv.* by chance (MQ 65 26, MQ 69 19)
Periurd *ppl. adj.* guilty of perjury (MQ 83 2)
Perles *adj.* unmatched, peerless (MQ 9 2)
Perpend *v.* consider (MQ 35 73)
Pers *v.* pierce (MQ 48 100, MQ 66 20, MQ 68 98)
Persaif, Persaue *v.* observe, perceive (MQ 14 5, MQ 38 19)
Persew *v.* pursue, harass (MQ 16 28, MQ 25 19, MQ 39 57); **persewand** *pr. p.* (MQ 25 14)
Pertaker *n.* one who shares something, a participant (MQ 66 101)

GLOSSARY

Pertlie *adv.* expertly (MQ 3 2); boldly (MQ 71 35)
Perturbers *n. pl.* those who cause trouble or disorder (MQ 4 19)
[Perversit] *adj.* untrue, stubbornly evil (MQ 61 53)
Pest *n.* plague (MQ 12 6, MQ 37 55, MQ 46 111)
Py *n.* pie (MQ 61 17)
Pygrall *adj.* petty (MQ 62 126)
Pyne *v.* torment (MQ 66 87)
Pith *n.* virility (MQ 52 17)
Play *n.* joke, amusement (MQ 41 116)
Plaine *adj.* unpretentious, candid (MQ 35 29)
Plant *v.* establish (MQ 91 5)
Plat *adj.* lying flat (MQ 70 90)
Pleinȝie *v.* lament, complain (MQ 66 17)
Pleit *pa. t.* troubled, got the better of someone (MQ 25 63)
Plenand *pr. p.* complaining (MQ 51 4)
Pleneist, Plenist *ppl. adj.* well stocked (MQ 14 15, MQ 26 21)
Plenische *v.* furnish (MQ 68 105)
Plent *n.* statement of complaint (MQ 41 69)
Plie *n.* litigation (MQ 11 12, MQ 51 9)
Ply *v.* bend, comply (MQ 47 42)
Pleuche *n.* plough (MQ 13 33)
Plowis *n. pl.* ploughs (MQ 3 28)
Poise *n.* an amount of money set by for safe-keeping (MQ 5 28)
Poleist *ppl. adj.* polished (MQ 48 68)
Policie *n.* system of government, law and order (MQ 6 63)
Pomellis *n. pl.* breasts (MQ 48 63)
Port *n.* demeanour, conduct (MQ 48 12, MQ 62 29)
Portend *v.* ?grant as a favour (MQ 46 196)
Portratour *n.* a representation, painting (MQ 64 25)
Posseid *v.* possess (MQ 64 47)
Posteritie *n.* descendants (MQ 46 141)
Pour, Puir *adj.* poor, wretched (MQ 3 34, MQ 73 41, MQ 81 8)
Practiciens *n. pl.* practitioners of the law (MQ 51 27)
Prattick *n.* custom (MQ 46 77)
Preast *pa. p.* striven (MQ 93a 13)
Precellis *pr. t.* surpasses (MQ 49 2)
Preclair *adj.* illustrious, noble (MQ 9 1, MQ 35 86, MQ 65 31)
Predicessouris *n. pl.* ancestors, forebearers (MQ 1 1)
Preif *v.* prove (MQ 39 103)
Prein, Pryne *n.* pin, thing of little value (MQ 16 94, MQ 80 40)
Preis *v.* hasten (MQ 27 3, MQ 37 99, MQ 54 5); press (MQ 71 35)
Preitche *v.* exhort (MQ 46 74)
Prent *v.* print (MQ 35 110, MQ 55 4)
Prenteis *n.* apprentice (MQ 40 15)

GLOSSARY

Prenteisboyis *n. pl.* apprentices (MQ 70 24)
Preordinat *ppl. adj.* preordained (MQ 62 107)
Prepone *v.* set before, put forward, offer as an example (MQ 46 59, MQ 90 6)
Presage *n.* sign (MQ 46 189)
Prescryve *v.* preserve (MQ 65 133)
Prest *adj.* eager (MQ 91 5)
Pretence *n.* intention, purpose (MQ 31 37); justification (MQ 73 50)
Pretend *v.* intend (MQ 21 53); aspire to? (MQ 37 70); lay claim to (MQ 51 9)
Pretious *adj.* costly, valuable (MQ 35 197)
Prettie *adj.* fitting (MQ 42 65)
Prevein *v.* prevent, forestall (MQ 16 102)
Pryce *n.* prize, honour, distinction (MQ 44 95)
Pryis *v.* value (MQ 58 8)
Pryne *see* **Prein**
Pryss *v.* praise (MQ 35 212)
Professioun *n.* a dedicated way of life, including the religious vocation (MQ 5 55)
Propagat *v.* reproduce (MQ 46 141)
Proper *adj.* special (MQ 46 50); characteristic, distinctive (MQ 48 12)
Properlie *adv.* finely (MQ 69 44)
Propernes *n.* excellence (MQ 69 55)
Propyne *n.* gift (MQ 39 82)
Propyne *v.* present (MQ 39 74)
Propone *see* **Prepone**
Protest *v.* declare (MQ 75 25)
Prove, Pruif *n.* test, trial (MQ 46 37); evidence, means of verification (MQ 61 25, MQ 80 37)
Prove, Pruif *v.* put to the test (MQ 46 20, MQ 48 125)
Provyide *v.* prepare, make ready (MQ 11 86)
Provoike *v.* urge, rouse (MQ 49 17)
Prow *n.* advantage, good (MQ 25 74, MQ 71 36)
Prowes *n.* prowess, excellence (MQ 1 1)
Pruif *see* **Prove**
Pruinȝeis *pr. t.* preens (MQ 43 56)
Pudicitie *n.* chastity (MQ 42 66)
Puir *see* **Pour**
Puire *v.* impoverish (MQ 13 25)
Pulchritud *n.* beauty (MQ 48 113, MQ 64 9)
Puneis *v.* punish (MQ 12 25, MQ 29 67)
Punitioun *n.* punishment (MQ 4 19)
Punkis *n. pl.* beliefs? (MQ 22 51)

GLOSSARY

Q
Queir *n.* choir or chancel of a church (MQ 5 15)
Quell *v.* oppress, overcome (MQ 18 3)
Quelling *vbl. n.* melting (MQ 46 34)
Quent *adj.* sly (MQ 48 128, MQ 63 38)
Quentance *n.* acquaintance, associates (MQ 17 19)
Querrell *n.* a law suit (MQ 4 47, MQ 7 34)
Quhairas *adv.* in the place where (MQ 69 25)
Quhein *adj.* not many, few (MQ 16 30)
Quheit *n.* wheat (MQ 4 83)
Quhyllis *adv.* sometimes, from time to time (MQ 67 11)
Quhylome *adv.* formerly (MQ 45 10)
Quhodder *conj.* whether (MQ 41 74)
Quin *v.* know (MQ 2 83)
Quyetnes *adj.* peace (MQ 9 48)
Quyite *v.*[1] leave, renounce (MQ 37 98)
Quyite, Quyte *v.*[2] repay (MQ 48 135); reward (MQ 62 23)
Quyte *adj.*[1] free from (MQ 7 49)
Quyte *adj.*[2] peaceful (MQ 9 15)
Quyte *v. see* **Quyite**

R
Ragment *n.* composition (MQ 83 62)
Ralit *pa. t.* abused, scorned (MQ 62 13)
Raige *n.* passion, frenzy, excess of feelings (MQ 13 5)
Raill *v.* scold (MQ 43 69)
Railleris *n. pl.* those who talk without restraint (MQ 43 23, MQ 55 19)
Rak *v.* care about (MQ 23 48)
Raknit *pa. t.* regarded, thought to be (MQ 41 76)
Rancour *n.* ill feeling, hatred (MQ 4 17)
Rander *v.* render (MQ 37 3, MQ 66 56)
Range *v.* traverse, search through (MQ 20 2)
Rascall *adj.* low, knavish, poor in quality (MQ 41 172, MQ 43 69)
Rasche-bus *n.* clump of rushes (MQ 58 47)
Rasit *pa. t.* caused (MQ 62 80)
Rauk *adj.* hoarse (MQ 65 37, MQ 69 31)
Raveris *n. pl.* those who speak maliciously (MQ 43 69)
Ravis *v.* ravish (MQ 49 16)
Rax *v.* to stretch (MQ 16 39); hold sway or wield power (MQ 18 10)
Reave *see* **Reif**
Reciproc *adj.* mutual (MQ 49 19)
Recoird, Record *v.* speak, relate (MQ 61 61); consider, remember (MQ 75 17); meditate (MQ 73 14)
Recompanse *n.* reward, payment (MQ 49 54, MQ 72 26)

GLOSSARY

Record *see* **Recoird**
Red *adj.*[1] active (MQ 35 77)
Red *adj.*[2] fearful (MQ 25 64)
Red *n.* a clearance (MQ 4 79)
Rediviue *adj.* revived (MQ 49 8)
Redolent *adj.* fragrant (MQ 38 64)
Redound *v.* turn (MQ 46 48)
Refound *v.* repair (MQ 40 33)
Refraine *v.* restrain (MQ 16 38)
Refudge *n.* protection (MQ 48 48, MQ 60 57)
Regioun *n.* part of the world, country (MQ 19 38)
Registrat *pa. p.* recorded in writing (MQ 89 39)
Regnis *pr. t.* prevails, holds power over (MQ 12 16). **Regnand** *pr. p.* reigning (MQ 17 14). *See also* **Ring.**
Regrait *n.* complaint (MQ 51 1)
Regrateris *n. pl.* those who buy to resell for profit (MQ 4 67)
Reif, Reave *v.* to plunder (MQ 3 2, MQ 90 2). **Reft** *pa. t.* (MQ 26 10). **Reuin** *pa. p.* (MQ 95 15)
Reif *n.* robbery (MQ 7 58)
Reik *v.* to fill with smoke from a fire (MQ 62 115)
Reill *n.* spool, bobbin (MQ 3 46)
Reill *n.* a disturbance (MQ 37 93)
Relaxit *pa. p.* set free (MQ 47 27)
Remeid *n.* redress, cure (MQ 2 97)
Remoird, Remord *v.* to examine one's thoughts, reconsider (MQ 42 134, MQ 80 21); to feel regret (MQ 75 18)
Remorce *n.* cause for compunction (MQ 47 19)
Remord *see* **Remoird**
Renoumit *pa. p.* famous (MQ 68 151)
Rent *n.* landed property, source of income (MQ 14 27, MQ 41 181); payment made by a tenant to the owner of land or property (MQ 16 13)
Rent *pa. p.* torn (MQ 83 5)
Repair *n.* opportunity for trade (MQ 70 22)
Repair *v.* go (MQ 44 34)
Repyne *v.* complain (MQ 42 107)
Repledge *v.* redeem (MQ 89 27)
Repremis *pr. t.* represses (MQ 43 23)
Reset *v.* give shelter to (MQ 52 36)
Resing *v.* relinquish, give up (MQ 48 105, MQ 72 9)
Ressaif *v.* receive (MQ 3 65)
Resset *n.* shelter, succour (MQ 62 48)
Restitutioun *n.* compensation for injury, restoration of something wrongfully taken (MQ 4 42)
Reuin *pa. p.* torn (MQ 95 15)

GLOSSARY

Revar *n.* reaver, thief (MQ 18 39)
Rewis *n. pl.* roads (MQ 6 21)
Rewleris *n. pl.* those in charge of another (MQ 35 68)
Ryatous *adj.* wanton, unrestrained (MQ 54 29)
Ryfe, Ryff *adj.* numerous (MQ 18 8); widespread (MQ 30 15)
Rigour *n.* severity, strictness (MQ 6 72, MQ 81 14)
Ryme *n.* verse (MQ 41 171, MQ 55 9)
Rin *v.* ride on horseback (MQ 6 12); to be involved in (MQ 42 83); turn (MQ 42 85)
Ring *v.* reign, govern (MQ 9 33)
Ringis *n. pl.* realms (MQ 62 51)
Rinning *vbl. n.* running (MQ 14 16)
Rypis *pr. t.* ransacks (MQ 3 52)
Rod *n.* chastisement (MQ 46 48)
Roy *n.* king (MQ 59 57)
Roist *n.* roast meat (MQ 2 89)
Rok *n.* distaff (MQ 3 46)
Rounder *n.* a gossip, one who passes on confidential information (MQ 11 10)
Rout *n.* retinue (MQ 37 54)
Rowyne *n.* ruin (MQ 45 31)
Rowme *n.* landed estate, chamber, apartment (MQ 20 2, MQ 51 18); place (MQ 25 46, MQ 62 118)
Ruffian *n.* scroundrel, an immoral person (MQ 41 60, MQ 42 67)
Ruffiaris *n. pl.* scoundrels (MQ 5 16)
Ruffit *adj.* furnished with ruffs (MQ 70 88)
Rug *v.* to take something away violently (MQ 16 13)
Ruid *adj.* ignorant, uncivilised, offensive (MQ 35 224)
Ruit *n.* root, base of plant (MQ 69 50)
Ruse *n.* boast (MQ 25 43)

S

Say *v.* declare (MQ 41 27)
Sais *n. pl.* sayings, utterances (MQ 43 39)
Saikles *adj.* innocent (MQ 62 117)
Saillis *n. pl.* sails, skirts, headdresses? (MQ 70 119)
Sailȝeis *pr. t.* assails, assaults (MQ 41 170)
Sair *adj.* severe, painful, bitter (MQ 51 1)
Sair *n.* sore, injury (MQ 71 30)
Sait *n.* court of justice, court of session (MQ 51 76)
Sampillis *n. pl.* examples (MQ 35 144)
Sark *n.* shirt, shift (MQ 3 50, MQ 70 88)
Satefie *v.* satisfy (MQ 83 41)
Sawis *n. pl.* sayings, utterances (MQ 30 37, MQ 43 12)
Saweris *n. pl.* those who spread something about (MQ 4 16)

GLOSSARY

Scafrie *n.* obtaining money with threats or cheating (MQ 58 10)
Scairis *adv.* barely (MQ 16 34)
Scayth *n.* harm, damage (MQ 19 71, MQ 51 14, MQ 58 29)
Scambillis, Skambillis *n. pl.* butchers' benches, meat stalls (MQ 61 94, MQ 62 40, MQ 70 19)
Scand, Skan *v.* examine closely (MQ 73 48, MQ 85 8)
Scant *adj.* scarce, few in number (MQ 16 33)
Scant *adv.* hardly, scarcely (MQ 30 16)
Scant *n.* scarcity (MQ 12 8)
Scantlie *adv.* hardly (MQ 52 7)
Scarpenis *n. pl.* shoes (MQ 70 95)
Scauld *n.* one who quarrels (MQ 20 18)
Sceill *n.* reason or discrimination, skill (MQ 4 61, MQ 5 71)
Schairpe *adj.* intelligent (MQ 42 39)
Schamfastnes *n.* propriety (MQ 41 128)
Schank *n.* lower leg (MQ 70 129)
Schap *n.* shape, form (MQ 49 43)
Schaw *n.* grove (MQ 68 28, MQ 69 17)
Schedull *n.* written document, epistle (MQ 39 66)
Schein *adj.* bright (MQ 40 4)
Schent *v.* destroy, put to shame, disgrace (MQ 4 16, MQ 37 64); *pa. p.* (MQ 11 5, MQ 65 51); slashed (of a garment) (MQ 70 121)
Schersit *pa. p.* sought out (MQ 43 59)
Schift *n.* course of action (MQ 48 105); livelihood (MQ 70 14)
Schyire *n.* chair (MQ 63 22)
Schiller *comp.* more resonant (MQ 94.3 2)
Schreudis, Schrowis *n. pl.* evil people (MQ 3 27, MQ 46 38)
Schuif *pa. t.* shaved (MQ 12 18)
Science *n.* knowledge (MQ 35 104)
Sckayth *n.* harm (MQ 51 37)
Sclaue *n.* slave (MQ 47 31)
Scoir *n.* a unit of twenty (MQ 16 18)
Scorner *n.* one who mocks (MQ 11 9)
Scroll *n.* piece of writing (MQ 61 5)
Scrudgeing *vbl. n.* flogging (BM 151)
Scuile *n.* place of learning, school, university (MQ 5 8)
Scurge *n.* suffering, hardship (MQ 7 1)
Scurrilitie *n.* mocking invective, slander (MQ 41 87)
Secours *n.* assistance (MQ 46 139)
Seid *n.* offspring, family (MQ 16 77)
Seige *v.* beseige (MQ 10 19, MQ 25 90)
Seill *n.* happiness (MQ 17 39)
Seindill *adv.* seldom (MQ 44 46)
Seir *adj.* different (MQ 2 13)

GLOSSARY

Sekest *pr. t.* seek (MQ 81 13)
Semble *adj.* similar (MQ 90 7)
Semying *vbl. n.* judgement (BM 67)
Sen *prep. and conj.* after, since, because (MQ 6 43, MQ 39 1)
Sens *n.* perception, feeling (MQ 45 2)
Sensyne *adv.* from then on (MQ 38 16, MQ 46 178, BM 166)
Sentens *n.* meaning (MQ 45 5)
Sersit *pa. p.* searched (MQ 68 100)
Seruituire *n.* servant (MQ 40 27)
Sessoun *n.* a period of time (MQ 46 79, MQ 61 67); the appropriate time (MQ 15 19)
Seueir *adj.* severe, cruel (MQ 48 119)
Sewit *pa. p.* sewn, stitched decoratively (MQ 2 22)
Sibnes *n.* relationship by kinship, affinity (MQ 23 20)
Siching *vbl. n.* sighing (MQ 65 1)
Sicht *n.* eyes (MQ 65 8); vision, thing seen (MQ 65 183)
Sicht *pa. t.* sighed (MQ 65 139)
Sichtis *n. pl.* sighs (MQ 38 3)
Sicker *adj.* assured, reliable (MQ 66 142)
Sickernes *n.* stability (MQ 69 50)
Siclyik *adv.* in the same way (MQ 22 40)
Sies, Sysis *n. pl.* times (MQ 16 99, MQ 83 42)
Syild *pa. p.* blinded, deceived (MQ 44 91)
Sylit *pa. t.* deceived (BM 111)
Sillie *adj.* foolish, helpless (MQ 66 87)
Sinderit *pa. p.* parted, separated (MQ 38 12)
Sindill *adv.* seldom (MQ 70 8)
Sindrie *adj.* different, various (MQ 6 22)
Sindring *vbl. n.* parting (MQ 38 9)
Sing(e) *n.* sign (MQ 11 28, MQ 46 22, MQ 69 45)
Single *adj.* sincere (MQ 77 14)
Sysis *n. pl.*[1] *see* **Sies**
[Sysis] *n. pl.*[2] assizes (MQ 16 71)
Syt *n.* distress (MQ 46 83)
Skambillis *see* **Scambillis**
Skan *see* **Scand**
Skift *v.* skip (MQ 2 71)
Skrepis *pr. t.* scratches, scrapes (MQ 75 19)
Sla *v.* slay, kill (MQ 3 18)
Slaik *v.* satisfy (MQ 80 24)
Slauchter-mairt *n.* a cow fattened for slaughter (MQ 62 117)
Sleuth *n.* sloth (MQ 25 9, MQ 32 7, MQ 62 88)
Slicht *n.* cunning trick (MQ 11 46, MQ 62 88, MQ 63 38)
Slidder *adj.* unreliable, inconstant (MQ 19 72, MQ 70 58)

GLOSSARY

Sliddin *pa. p.* subsided (MQ 46 147)
Slip *v.* to evade justice, escape quietly (MQ 62 64)
Slumring *n.* sleep (MQ 65 9)
Smart, Smert *v.* to experience pain (MQ 47 3, MQ 64 28)
Smelling *adj.* perfumed (MQ 69 22)
Smert *see* **Smart**
Smittit *ppl. adj.* infected, tarnished (MQ 16 43, MQ 22 5)
Snapper *v.* trip (MQ 11 54)
Snyte *v.* to wipe the nose (MQ 70 99)
Socht *pa. p.* assailed, ravaged (MQ 3 25)
Soddis *n. pl.* saddles made of two stuffed sacks (MQ 21 40)
Soir *v.* soar (MQ 16 21)
Soirnaris *n. pl.* those who live off others by threatening them or by extortion (MQ 4 88)
Sonkin *pa. p.* sunk (MQ 65 147)
Soppit *ppl. adj.* consumed by, steeped in (MQ 12 13)
Sott *n.* fool (MQ 85 18)
Soucy *n.* the object of one's concern (MQ 38 109)
Soune *n.* sound (MQ 68 80)
Soup *v.* eat (MQ 71 32)
Souppis *pr. t.* sweeps away, overwhelms (MQ 45 2)
Sowme *n.* sum (MQ 21 19)
Spair *v.* to spare, to refrain from harming (MQ 3 23); desist (MQ 41 51)
Spauld *n.* shoulder (MQ 20 48)
Speid *n.* success (MQ 3 85)
Speid *v.* obtain (MQ 16 60)
Speir, Sper *n.* spear, jousting spear (MQ 6 17, MQ 21 35)
Speir *v.* to ask, to enquire about (MQ 2 23, MQ 23 8, MQ 94.1 3)
Speit *n.* a spit for cooking meat (MQ 3 49)
Sper *see* **Speir**
Spyit *pa. p.* noticed (MQ 29 47)
Spyice *n.* spice (MQ 2 62)
Spill *v.* destroy (MQ 65 66)
Spindill *n.* spindle (MQ 3 49)
Spray *n.* a living stem or shoot (MQ 69 66)
Spuilȝie, spoilȝie, spoyle *v.* to plunder, despoil (MQ 3 43, MQ 95 35).
    Spuilȝit *pa. t.* (MQ 14 4)
Spunk *n.* spark (MQ 51 42)
Spurne *v.* resist (MQ 65 114)
Stabilleris *n. pl.* livery keepers (MQ 70 25)
Stay *adj.* stern (MQ 43 47)
Stay *v.* stop, prevent a course of action (MQ 28 27); to reside or rest (MQ 73 67); depend? (MQ 78 18)
Staig *n.* a young horse (MQ 4 84)

GLOSSARY

Staik *n*. the stalk (or support) of a plant (MQ 65 50)
Staikis *pr. t.* satisfies (MQ 70 76). **Staikit** *pa. p.* (MQ 3 35, MQ 21 15, MQ 26 1)
Stainche *v.* to stop, bring an end to (MQ 5 20, MQ 8 37, MQ 16 101)
Stait *n*. social estate, circumstances (MQ 2 49, MQ 4 57)
Staitlie *adj.* noble, dignified (MQ 74 24)
Starnis *n. pl.* stars (MQ 40 53)
Sted *pa. p.* settled (MQ 35 28)
Steding *n.* farm (MQ 28 63)
Steid *n.* estate or farm (MQ 28 24); place (MQ 48 52)
Steif *adj.* rigid, stable (MQ 13 28)
Steik *v.* close or block (an entrance) (MQ 75 6)
Steill *n.* a weapon (MQ 5 69)
Steinȝie *v.* obscure, stain (MQ 40 101)
Steip *v.* soak (MQ 46 183)
Steir *n.* control, government (MQ 18 23)
Steir *v.* move, stir (MQ 21 26, MQ 35 151)
Stent *n.* assessment for taxation or form of tax (MQ 59 31)
Stering *vbl. n.* stirring, rousing (MQ 45 11)
Sterue *v.* die (MQ 40 58, MQ 60 58)
Stewin *n.* voice, noise (MQ 43 18)
Stirk *n.* a bullock or heifer (MQ 4 84)
Stock *see* **Stok**
Stoir *n.* provisions, livestock (MQ 25 100); sufficient content or evidence (MQ 41 162, MQ 61 54). **in** ~ in keeping, stored up (MQ 73 58). **set ...** ~ **in** regard as precious (MQ 79 2)
Stok, Stock *n.*[1] lineage (MQ 94.2 6, MQ 95 8)
Stok *n.*[2] possessions (MQ 21 26)
Stound *n.* pang (MQ 65 72)
Stouppis *n. pl.* pillars (MQ 46 152)
Stour *n.* conflict (MQ 46 94)
Stout *adj.* Courageous, proud (MQ 14 22, MQ 62 22, MQ 94.2 6)
Stouth *n.* theft (MQ 3 25)
Strainge *adj.* unfamiliar (MQ 5 89); unfriendly (MQ 38 106, MQ 43 47)
Straingeris *n.pl.* foreigners, incomers (MQ 25 32)
Stranglie *adv.* with strength, securely (MQ 10 19)
Stryind(e) *n.* nature (MQ 35 131, MQ 52 24)
Studie *n.* state of thoughtfulness (MQ 65 58)
Stuid *pa. t.* grew upright (MQ 69 50). ~ **na aw** were in no fear (MQ 30 28). **in studie** ~ stood in contemplation (MQ 65 58)
Sturt *n.* trouble (MQ 18 7, MQ 46 131, MQ 59 70)
Sturte *v.* feel troubled (MQ 38 44)
Sturtsum *adj.* quarrelsome (MQ 28 56)
Suaige *v.* subside (MQ 88 7)

GLOSSARY

Suave *adj.* sweet smelling (MQ 48 9)
Subiec *v.* subject (MQ 44 72)
Substance *n.* the means to do something (MQ 10 20)
Suddartis *n. pl.* soldiers, mercenaries (MQ 19 23)
Sueir *see* **Sweir**
Sueirnes *n.* idleness (MQ 53 10)
Suelting *adj.* fainting (MQ 38 3)
Suerue *v.* turn away (MQ 47 12)
Sufferance *n.* endurance (MQ 41 117)
Suir(e) *adj.* safe (MQ 8 22, MQ 73 44); secure or firm (MQ 18 35)
Suirlie *adv.* safely (MQ 7 59)
Suith(e) *n.* truth (MQ 5 22, MQ 43 6)
Suithlie *adv.* surely (MQ 35 129)
Sunʒeis *n. pl.* excesses (MQ 43 54)
Supercelestiall *adj.* of a nature higher than the celestial (MQ 42 101)
Supernaturall *adj.* transcendent, divine (MQ 48 86)
Supplie *n.* assistance, reinforcement, provision of funds or food (MQ 10 20)
Supplies *pr. t.* fill a vacant place (MQ 91 14)
Suppon *v.* believe (MQ 74 18)
Suspence *n.* uncertainty (MQ 46 79, MQ 47 18)
Suspitioun *n.* suspicion (MQ 4 17, MQ 55 42)
Suspitious *adj.* disreputable (MQ 2 77)
Sussie *n.* care, concern (MQ 14 23)
Sussie *v.* to care about (MQ 43 39)
Sussious *adj.* anxious (MQ 46 84)
Sustein *v.* endure (MQ 16 6)
Sute *n.* supplication (MQ 39 83)
Sutteltie *n.* treachery (MQ 42 40)
Sweir, Sueir *adj.* lazy, tardy (MQ 4 88, MQ 7 22, MQ 20 51)
Sweit *n.* perspiration, life blood? (MQ 38 66)
Swuning *vbl. n.* fainting, swooning (MQ 65 9)

T

Tafteis *n. pl.* taffetas (MQ 2 27)
Taill *n.*[1] narrative, account (MQ 13 35, MQ 28 30). **Taillis** *pl.* (MQ 13 8, MQ 20 36)
Tailis, Taillis, Teillis *n. pl.*[2] the trains on a garment (MQ 2 12, MQ 70 120); lower parts or *fig.* genitalia (MQ 13 9 and 33, MQ 20 36?)
Taine, Tane *pa. p.* taken, captured (MQ 2 74, MQ 10 8)
Tak *n.* farm, leased property (MQ 28 24, 63)
Takin *n.* a sign, and indication of something (MQ 46 24)
Taking *vbl. n.* the action of involving oneself in a relationship (MQ 39 102)
Tane *see* **Taine**
Tapeis *n. pl.* tapestries (MQ 68 109)

GLOSSARY

Tarie *n.* trouble (MQ 13 11)
Tareis *pr. t.* lingers (MQ 39 86)
Tauld *see* **Tell**
Taxit *pa. p.* accused of a crime, reproved (MQ 47 25)
Teare *pa. t.* tore (MQ 65 42)
Teastis *pr. t.* tastes (MQ 76 10)
Teilling *vbl. n.* the action of tilling or cultivating the land (MQ 13 31)
Teillis *see* **Tailis** *n. pl.*[2]
Tein *n.* offence (MQ 30 1, MQ 37 37); sorrow (MQ 46 82, MQ 49 69)
Teynd *pa. p.* emptied (MQ 20 3)
Teynd *n.* tithe (MQ 21 17, MQ 28 34)
Tell *v.* relate, inform, recount (MQ 16 44, MQ 43 48). **Tauld** *pa. t.* revealed (MQ 40 12)
Tent *n.* **tak ~**, pay attention (MQ 11 4). *pa.t.* (MQ 66 125)
Tent *v.* pay attention (MQ 28 30)
Tenty *adj.* careful (MQ 11 29)
Thocht *conj.* though (MQ 14 1), if, in the event that (MQ 41 14)
Thoill, Thol *v.* to tolerate, to endure, to suffer (MQ 2 98, MQ 55 39)
Thresour *n.* treasure (MQ 70 110)
Thrift *n.* good fortune, a way of thriving (MQ 42 52)
Tichter *comp.* more perfectly shaped (MQ 48 67)
Tyice *v.* entice (MQ 15 1)
Till *conj.* while (MQ 72 14)
Till *v.* tell (MQ 65 67)
Tyne *v.* lose (MQ 28 33, MQ 90 4); abandon (MQ 42 110)
Tinsell *n.* loss (MQ 14 19)
Tint *pa. p.* lost (a battle) (MQ 10 27)
Tyrit *ppl. adj.* exhausted (MQ 65 31)
Tytillis *n. pl.* titles (MQ 64 6)
Toy *n.* fancy (MQ 80 33)
Tonis *pr. t.* tunes (MQ 66 83)
To-name *n.* a nickname (MQ 3 38)
Toons *n. pl.* tunes (MQ 94.3 2)
Tossit *ppl. adj.* pitched, tossed (MQ 44 18)
Trace *n.*[1] those of one kind (MQ 48 26)
Trace, *n.*[2] path, way (MQ 37 79)
Traffique *n.* commerce, trading (MQ 70 13)
Traist *adj.* trusty, faithful (MQ 35 26 and 221, MQ 49 26)
Traist *v.* trust (MQ 22 6)
Traitling *ppl. adj.* gossiping (MQ 59 56)
Transing *pr. p.* traversing (MQ 80 6)
Tratourouslie *adv.* treacherously (MQ 62 85)
Travell *n.* difficulty, effort (MQ 6 80, MQ 19 34)
Tred *n.* custom (MQ 60 10, MQ 61 46)

GLOSSARY

Treit *v.* consider, show kindness and respect to (MQ 5 27, MQ 6 61, MQ 64 54)
Treitting *vbl. n.* the way of treating someone (MQ 68 110)
Tress *n.* hair (MQ 48 57)
Trew *v.* trust (MQ 17 16). *See also* **Trow**
Trewis *n.* truce (MQ 60 68)
Triffillis *n. pl.* matters of little importance (MQ 37 71)
Trim *adj.* smart, elegant (MQ 70 100)
Trimbling *adj.* quivering (MQ 65 33)
Trimlie *adv.* smartly, finely (MQ 2 11)
Triumphe *n.* (with **mak**) a public festivity or celebration, including pageantry (MQ 6 39)
Trone *n.* throne (MQ 44 97)
Trouboulous, Troublous *adj.* troubled, disordered (MQ 34 24)
Trow *v.* believe, accept (MQ 7 25). **Trowit** *pa. t.* trusted (MQ 62 60). *See also* **Trew**
Tuill *n.* trouble (MQ 60 59)
Tuilʒie *n.* strife, violence (MQ 59 70)
Turse *v.* to pack up, load with baggage (MQ 5 44); to transport (MQ 3 37)
Turtill *n.* turtle dove (MQ 35 42)
Twiche *v.* touch (BM 38)

V = U
Vnderlye *v.* submit to (MQ 31 23)
Vneis *n.* trouble, distress (MQ 78 26)
Vnfauld *v.* unfold, reveal (MQ 73 48)
Vnfet *adj.* unfit (MQ 80 35)
Ungenand *ppl. adj.* unfitting (MQ 39 75)
Vnhappie *adj.* ill-fated, wretched (MQ 49 46)
Vnkyndlie *adj.* lacking concern for kinship (MQ 19 15, MQ 25 15)
Vnperfyte *adj.* imperfect (MQ 40 38)
Vnreft *adj.* free from being robbed (MQ 7 40)
Vnsarit *pa. p.* unhurt (MQ 7 15)
Vnsatiabill *adj.* insatiable (MQ 52 2)
[Vnwrape] *v.* reveal (MQ 65 65)
Vpset *ppl. adj.* raised (MQ 80 31)
Vp-weir *v.* defend (MQ 3 75)
Vre *n.* **put in** ~, apply (MQ 75 5, MQ 85 10)
Vtilitie *n.* good, benefit (MQ 6 33)

V
Vaill *n.*[1] worth, ability (MQ 49 44)
Vaill *n.*[2] valley, vale (MQ 65 93)
Vaill *n.*[3] wail? (MQ 65 95)

GLOSSARY

Vaill *v.* to be of use or help (MQ 11 12, MQ 14 27)
Vaine *adj.* worthless (MQ 2 2, MQ 65 19)
Vanqueis *v.* vanquish (MQ 67 18)
Vant *v.* boast (MQ 66 42)
Vassal(l)ege *n.* valour, honourable conduct (MQ 42 45, MQ 44 82)
Veluot, Veluous *n.* velvet (MQ 2 12, 92)
Veritie *n.* truth (esp. religious truth) MQ 4 21
Vermell *adj.* vermillion (MQ 40 87)
Vesture *n.* clothing (MQ 48 81)
Vyilde *adj.* wild, uncivilised (MQ 44 85, MQ 61 66)
Vyile *adj.* despicable (MQ 61 69)
Vyile *n.* trickery (MQ 35 55)
Vitious *adj.* full of vice (MQ 35 217)
Vituper *n.* abuse (MQ 44 85)
Vocatioun *n.* one's station in live (MQ 10 46)
Voltis *n. pl.* archways (MQ 68 63)
Volue *v.* consider, turn in one's mind (MQ 65 17). **Voluing** *pr. p.* (MQ 65 25)
Voluptie *n.* pleasure (MQ 42 15)

W

Waige *n.* outcome, reward (ironic) (MQ 44 85)
Waild *see* **Weild**
Waill *adv.* very (MQ 18 14)
Waill, Weill *n.* choice (MQ 39 99, MQ 48 50)
Waill *v.*[1] choose (MQ 3 24)
Waill *v.*[2] mourn the loss of (MQ 91 13)
Waine *n.* hope (MQ 46 171)
Wair *v.*[1] to spend money (MQ 2 4)
Wair, Weir *v.*[2] to wear (MQ 2 3 and 25)
Waird *n.* fate (MQ 41 1)
Waird *v.* keep in custody (MQ 43 37)
Wairlie *adj.* made in a warlike manner (MQ 65 13)
Wais *n. pl.* walls (MQ 3 41, MQ 43 37)
Waist *adj.* ruined, desolate (MQ 16 96)
Waistouris *n. pl.* spendthrifts, useless individuals (MQ 4 66)
Waistrie *n.* extravagance (MQ 41 55)
Wait *v.* know (MQ 2 3, MQ 8 22)
Wak *v.* to keep watch, to be on the lookout (MQ 19 27)
Walkin *v.* waken (MQ 38 57, MQ 42 124)
Walter *n.* water (MQ 3 36)
Walter *v.* toss, surge (MQ 46 101).
Walterit *ppl. adj.* overturned (MQ 44 55)
Wand *n.* rod or staff as a symbol of authority or instrument of punishment (MQ 31 23); a sapling (MQ 35 34)

GLOSSARY

Wanhap *n.* bad luck (MQ 42 94)
Wanlukis *n. pl.* mishaps, accidents (MQ 44 30)
Wanthrift *n.* lack of thriving (MQ 5 49)
Wanwerdis *n. pl.* ill fortunes (MQ 46 101)
War *adj.* wary, aware (MQ 5 92)
War *comp.* worse (MQ 62 103)
War *n.* a worse outcome or situation (MQ 44 43)
Warie *v.* curse (MQ 42 95, MQ 44 78, MQ 66 91)
Warlie, Werlie *adv.* carefully, cautiously (MQ 11 53, MQ 65 117)
Warit *pa. p.* expended (MQ 6 89, MQ 7 12)
Wark *n.* activity, behaviour (MQ 3 53)
Waw *n.* wave (MQ 44 31)
Wax(e) *v.* to grow or become (MQ 3 17, MQ 16 36)
Wecht *n.* weight (MQ 68 96, MQ 71 18)
Wechtie *adj.* serious (MQ 76 39)
Wedder *n.* weather (MQ 44 31)
Weid *n.* apparel, clothes (BM 89)
Weild *v.* govern, control (MQ 49 15). **Waild** *pa. t.* controlled (MQ 65 119)
Weill *adv.* well, properly (MQ 11 8); carefully (MQ 6 79)
Weill *n.*[1] good (MQ 4 62); the communal good (MQ 11 8); happiness, good fortune (MQ 46 78)
Weill *n.*[2] *see* **Waill**
Wein *v.* to suppose, believe (MQ 16 46). **Wend** *pa. t.* (MQ 23 15)
Weir *n.* war, hostility (MQ 4 9, MQ 8 1, MQ 71 14)
Weir *v.*[1] to make war (MQ 35 199)
Weir *v.*[2] *see* **Wair**
Welthines *n.* happiness (MQ 42 5)
Wend *see* **Wein**
Werye, Werie *adj.* weary, exhausted (MQ 65 155); miserable (MQ 70 43)
Werlie *see* **Warlie**
West *adj.* wasted, ruined (MQ 65 55)
Westouris *n. pl.* good for nothings, squanderers (MQ 29 32)
Widdie *n.* the hangman's rope (MQ 16 39)
Wie *v.* consider, weigh up (MQ 71 17)
Wyile *n.* trick, deception (MQ 22 7, MQ 41 46)
Wyit, Wyte *n.* blame (MQ 27 9, MQ 35 66, MQ 51 16)
Wyit, Wyite *v.* blame (MQ 39 36, MQ 45 24, MQ 35 135)
Wyite *n.* wise person (MQ 5 79)
Wylicot *n.* petticoat (MQ 2 32). **Wylie-coittis** *n. pl.* (MQ 2 21)
Willie *adj.* weak, pliable (MQ 35 34)
Wink *v.* turn a blind eye, tolerate (MQ 41 94)
Wirk *v.* work, do good (MQ 4 81, MQ 43 30). **Wrocht** *pa. t.* (MQ 23 16)
Wis *n.* wish (MQ 46 12)
Wis *v.*[1] wish (MQ 35 3, MQ 48 95)

Wis v.² advise, counsel (MQ 49 33)
Without *conj.* unless (MQ 41 130)
Wittie *adj.* wise (MQ 35 71)
Wo v. lament (MQ 66 23)
Wob n. a piece of woven cloth (MQ 3 62)
Wode *adj.* mad (MQ 42 46)
Wogue n. vogue, fashion (MQ 44 99)
Wone v. to be accustomed to be something (MQ 41 55)
Workand *ppl. adj.* energetic (MQ 42 39)
Wosdome n. wisdom (MQ 39 49, MQ 42 30)
Wow v. woo (MQ 83 32)
Wowaris *n. pl.* wooers, lovers (MQ 6 10)
Wrachitnes n. meanness, greed (MQ 11 75)
Wrack, Wraik, n. retribution, punishment (MQ 7 21, MQ 48 47); suffering (MQ 64 52, MQ 87 2)
Wrack, Wraik, Wrak v. damage, injure, destroy (MQ 3 33, MQ 22 41)
Wraik *adj.* destined to be ruined (MQ 39 98)
Wrangous *adj.* used of things wrongfully or illegally acquired (MQ 4 43)
Wratch n. wretched person (MQ 41 104)
Wratched *adj.* unhappy, cursed (MQ 41 1)
Wreath n. wrath (MQ 94.4 6)
Wrocht *see* **Wirk**

3

3ad n. an old horse or mare (MQ 70 75)
3aird n. yard (MQ 21 25)
3airne v. yearn (MQ 35 3, MQ 45 20)
3eid *see* **Ga**
3eis *pron.* + v. you shall (MQ 35 64)
3eistrein n. yesterday evening (MQ 37 36)
3eit *pa. t.* poured (MQ 65 56)
3emen *n. pl.* yeomen (MQ 70 5)
3et n. gate (MQ 3 11)
3ouldin *pa. p.* yielded (MQ 48 122)
3ounkeir, 3ounkour n. young nobleman (MQ 2 38, MQ 70 8)
3uile n. Christmas time, the period of Christmas and New Year festivities (MQ 5 7)

Index of Names

Abigaal, MQ 35 1, 63
Achab, MQ 35 122
Achates, MQ 49 29
Achilles, MQ 49 27
Aenee, MQ 49 30
Andro Bell, MQ 62 100
Anna, MQ 35 155
Annas, MQ 16 49
Antechrist, MQ 12 42
Apelles, MQ 48 29
Aspasia, MQ 35 187
Attyla, MQ 66 67
Augustus, MQ 94. 4, 4, 6, 9

Baquhidder, MQ 7 39
Berrie, MQ 13 23
Berwik, MQ 7 39, MQ 10 52
Blyith(e), Blythe, MQ 14 2, 4 etc
Borace, MQ 95 49
Boreas, MQ 44 25, MQ 12, 36 65
Briton, MQ 44 53
Bruse, MQ 25 44, 47
Brutus, MQ 49 40, 42, 45
Buchane, MQ 62 77
Burges, MQ 13 23

Caballein, MQ 48 3
Caiphas, Cayphas, MQ 16 25, MQ 62 120
Calice, MQ 10 5
Canarianis, MQ 35 169
Castor, MQ 49 50
Catullus, MQ 68 5
Ceres, MQ 35 113
Charles the Maine, MQ 62 99
Christ, Chryist, MQ 16 52, 55, MQ 22 19 etc.
Christindome, MQ 61 57
Cleisch, MQ 61 16

Clementis Hob, MQ 2 61
Cleo, Clio, MQ 69 60, MQ 94.3 4
Corduba, MQ 68 3
Cornelia, MQ 35 185
Creusa, MQ 65 29
Cupid, MQ 38 36, 72, MQ 66 18, 20, MQ 89 2

Dakeris, Leonard MQ 61 56
Dalila, MQ 35 124
Dauid, MQ 35 165, MQ 49 31
Debora, MQ 35 149
Deip, MQ 13 24
Diana, MQ 40 60, MQ 63 17, MQ 69 61, MQ 86 5
Dido, MQ 66 17
Douglassis, MQ 61 13, 21, MQ 62 124
Dumfermling, MQ 61 17, MQ 62 61

Eckie of the Hairlaw, MQ 3 101
Edee, MQ 74 15
Edward [I], MQ 25 44
England, MQ 8 14, MQ 10 54, MQ 19 64, 80, MQ 60 title, MQ 61 44, MQ 68 152
Englis, Englisch MQ 10 7, MQ 44 34, MQ 60 65, MQ 61 title, MQ 66 title
Englismen, MQ 25 42, 53
Ettrik Forest MQ 3 20
Europe, MQ 63 35
[Euterpe], MQ 94.3 3

Fergus first, MQ 44 74
Flaunderis, MQ 60 80
Flora, MQ 69 15
France, MQ 6 9, MQ 8 14, MQ 10 1, MQ 19 74, 80, MQ 60 79, MQ 61 43, MQ 70 94

INDEX OF NAMES

Frenchemen, MQ 8 6
Fyfe, MQ 18 9

Ganʒelon, MQ 61 43, MQ 62 99
Greikis, MQ 35 107
Gretia, MQ 68 18
Grissell, MQ 35 192
Guise, Duik of MQ 10 5

Hab of the Schawis, MQ 3 40
Hairlaw, MQ 62 101
Handwarpe, MQ 13 23
Hary, King, MQ 61 31
Helene, MQ 48 46, 52
Helicon, MQ 48 1, MQ 64 34, MQ 74 16
Hemene, MQ 63 43, MQ 64 49
Henrie, King of France, MQ 6 9, MQ 10 1
Henrie the sext, MQ 61 49, MQ 62 53
Herodias, MQ 35 123
Heroid, MQ 16 9
Hester, MQ 35 161
Home, Lord, MQ 61 55
Homer, MQ 68 53, MQ 94.2 10
Hymen, MQ 49 48, 59
Hypocrene, MQ 68 24

Iacob, MQ 46 66
Iacobus Rex, MQ 67 attribution
Iephe, MQ 46 66
Iesabell, MQ 35 121
Iesus, MQ 12 2, MQ 16 26, 58, MQ 24 32, MQ 37 116, MQ 42 172, MQ 66 145
Iewis, MQ 16 4, 81, MQ 62 145
Ihone of the Park, MQ 3 51
Ihone of the Syide, MQ 3 55
Iob, MQ 46 2, 66, 153
Iok, the lairdis, MQ 3 47
Ionathan, MQ 49 31
Iosip, MQ 49 32
Ioue, MQ 49 41, MQ 82 1

Iuda, MQ 35 149
Iudas, MQ 16 41, MQ 22 21, MQ 61 7, 19, MQ 62 97, 119, 146
Iudith, MQ 35 158
Iuno, MQ 69 59
Iupiter, MQ 63 34

Lawderdaill, MQ 3 20
Lethingtoun, MQ 2 attribution, etc., MQ 11 title, MQ 68 49
Liddisdaill, MQ 3 1, MQ 34 11
Lindsay, Lyndsay, MQ 61 18, MQ 62 63
Lochlevein, MQ 60 title, MQ 61 14, MQ 62 38, 56, 73, 125
Lothe, MQ 46 183
Lowtha(i)ne, MQ 3 22, MQ 34 5
Lucane, MQ 68 3
Lucretia, MQ 35 177
Luke, Sanct, MQ 70 41

Mackgill, Mcgill, MQ 61 15, MQ 62 60
Maitland, MQ 2 attribution, etc., MQ 46 122, MQ 68 141, MQ 90 title, 6, MQ 91 1, MQ 95 10
Maitland, Iohne, MQ 94 title
Maitland, Richard, MQ 46 105, 121, 128
Mald, MQ 20 28
Mantua, MQ 68 1
Mar, Lord of, MQ 44 title, MQ 61 13, MQ 62 57
Margareit (Montgomerie), MQ 63 8, MQ 64 8, 16, 24, 32, 40, 48, 56
Marie (Maitland), MQ 69 41, MQ 85 9
Marie, Queen, MQ 9 64
Marie (Virgin), MQ 35 146
Meg, MQ 20 28
Menelaus, 48 46
Mical, MQ 35 165
Minerue, MQ 35 105, MQ 69 60
Moabites, MQ 49 35

Mont Edee, MQ 74 15
Montgomerie, Margareit, MQ 64 8
Morpheus, MQ 49 23
Mortoun, MQ 60 47, MQ 61 14, 25, 29, 35, MQ 62, 65, 125
Murray, MQ 60 47

Naball, MQ 35 164
Nature, MQ 48 23, MQ 69 10
Neptune, MQ 65 34
Noe, MQ 46 182
Nohemie, MQ 49 36
Northumberland, Erle of, MQ 60 title, 41, MQ 61 7, MQ 62 title, 16

Olimpia, MQ 85 6
Oliphern, MQ 35 157
Orest, MQ 49 28
Orient, MQ 40 90
Orknay, MQ 61 15
[Orpheus], MQ 66 70
Ouid(e), MQ 68 7, MQ 94.4 1

Pallas, MQ 35 107, MQ 49 8, MQ 65 97, MQ 69 59
Paris, MQ 48 45, 51, 56, MQ 64 34
Patroclus, MQ 49 27
Paul(l), Sanct, MQ 19 113, MQ 37 88
Pegasus, MQ 74 16
Penelope, MQ 35 182, MQ 49 33, MQ 89 34
Perithous, MQ 49 25
Permessis, MQ 68 25
Pernassus, MQ 48 2, MQ 68 21, MQ 74 15
Persie, Lord, MQ 62 93, 118
Peter, MQ 16 49
Phaeton, MQ 65 30
Phaetusa, MQ 65 30
Phoebe, MQ 49 3,
Phoebus, MQ 38 75, MQ 40 52, 78, MQ 43 22, MQ 48 57, MQ 49 1, MQ 63 23, 27, MQ 68 70, MQ 69 2, 14
Phoebus, Dame, MQ 63 27
Pigmalion, MQ 64 25
Pilades, MQ 49 28
Pilat, Pylat, MQ 16 17, 57 65, MQ 60 32
Pluto, MQ 66 69
Polhymina, MQ 94.3 7
Pollux, MQ 49 50
Pontus, MQ 94.4 2
Porcia, Portia, MQ 35 179, MQ 49 37
Priam, Priamus, MQ 46 110, MQ 48 51
Proserpina, MQ 69 61
Protestantis, MQ 12 33, 65

Richard, King, MQ 62 53
Richard, Sir, MQ 68 145
Romaine, MQ 49 38
Rome, MQ 66 67
Ruglintoun, MQ 70 2
Ruth, MQ 49 35
Ruthven, MQ 60 47

Samson, MQ 46 66
Sapho, MQ 66 24, MQ 85 1
Saul, MQ 35 166
Saxonis, MQ 44 51
Scot, MQ 62 8
Scotland, MQ 9 39, MQ 30 4, MQ 44 73, MQ 60 59, 61, MQ 61 47, MQ 62 33, 52, MQ 68 144, 151
Scottis, MQ 6 2, MQ 7 2, 17, MQ 19 65, MQ 61 1
Scottis, Scottisch(e), MQ 10 33, MQ 34 19, MQ 60 10, MQ 61 15, 46
Scottismen, MQ 30 90
Sicilia, MQ 68 20
Sirens, MQ 48 73
Socrates, 35 189
Spartanis, MQ 39 171
Sulmon, MQ 68 8

INDEX OF NAMES

Susan, MQ 46 182
Susanna, MQ 35 153
Sussix, Erle of, MQ 61 61

Tempe, MQ 68 28
Tersiphone, MQ 69 60
Thalia, MQ 94.3 5
Theseus, MQ 49 26
Thirlstaine, MQ 94 title
Thisbe, Tisbe, MQ 35 184, MQ 76 33
Titan, MQ 48 99
Titus, MQ 49 32
Tobias, MQ 46 161

Tobie, MQ 46 1, 66
Troy, MQ 46 110, MQ 48 48
Tyne, MQ 68 50

Venus, MQ 22 24, 26, MQ 41 61, MQ 48 30, 70, MQ 52 18, MQ 64 35, MQ 65 6, MQ 69 59
Verone, MQ 68 5
Virgil(l), MQ 68 1, 53
Vlisses, MQ 49 34

Will of the Lawis, MQ 3 39

3orke, MQ 60 title

Index of First Lines

Amang foleis ane greit folie I find (MQ 13) p. 75
Ane new fairweill, a strainge gudnicht (MQ 83) p. 258
As absence is the greatest fo (MQ 89) p. 266
As Phoebus, in his spheris hicht (MQ 49) p. 182
At morning, in ane gardein grein (MQ 19) p. 88

Before my face this nyght to me appeird (MQ 94) p. 273
Blind man, be blyithe, thocht that thow be wrangit (MQ 14) p. 77

Ceis hairt, and trowbill me no moir (MQ 37) p. 133

Declair, ʒe bankis of Helicon (MQ 48) p. 178
Dreid God and luif him faythfullie (MQ 53) p. 191

Eternall God, tak away thy scurge (MQ 7) p. 60
Excellent Princes, potent and preclair (MQ 9) p. 65

Gif bissie branit bodyis ʒow bakbyit (MQ 43) p. 160
Gif faithfulnes ʒe find (MQ 72) p. 242
Gif it be trew that storeis doe rehers (MQ 45) p. 167
Gif thow desyire thy hous lang stand (MQ 57) p. 196

Gif trowbill cummis be eventour (MQ 17) p. 84
God be his word his work began p. 457
Greit paine it is now to behauld and sie (MQ 29) p. 113
Ground the ay on gudnes (MQ 54) p. 192

He that luifis lichtliest (MQ 36) p. 132
How sould our commoun weill induire (MQ 27) p. 109

If Sapho saige, for saphic songe so sueit (MQ 85) p. 262
In this new ʒeir, I sie bot weir (MQ 8) p. 63
Intill ane morning, mirthfullest of May (MQ 69) p. 234
Is thair in erthe, or hes thair euer bene (MQ 66) p. 224
It is ane mortall paine to heir and sie (MQ 28) p. 110
It is greit pitie for to se (MQ 21) p. 94

Loe heir tuo wights inburied be (MQ 93a) p. 271
Looke to thy self by vs (MQ 93b) p. 272
Lord God, how lang will this law lest (MQ 50) p. 184
Loue vertew over all, and all vyces flie (MQ 32) p. 122
Luiffaris, leif of to loif so hie (MQ 64) p. 216

INDEX OF FIRST NAMES

Luik that na thing to sine the tyice (MQ 15) p. 79

Mair mischevous and wicked warld (MQ 34) p. 124
Maist loyall lord, ay for thy lawtie lovit (MQ 44) p. 163
My ladyis pulchritude (MQ 71) p. 240
My lordis all, sen abstinence is taine (MQ 58) p. 197
My sone, in court gif thow plesis remaine (MQ 11) p. 69

O blissed bird brichtest of all (MQ 40) p. 144
O Deith, allace! with dairt so dolours (MQ 95) p. 275
O gratious God, almichtie and eterne (MQ 12) p. 72
O hie eternall God of micht (MQ 4) p. 49
O leving Lord, that maid bayth hevin and hell (MQ 18) p. 86
O Lord in heavin above, that rewlis all (MQ 73) p. 243
O Lord, our sin hes done the tein (MQ 30) p. 116
O michtie Iove that rewlis all (MQ 76) p. 248
O wratched waird, O fals fein3it fortoun (MQ 41) p. 148
Of God the misknawlege (MQ 56) p. 195
Of Liddisdaill the commoun theiffis (MQ 3) p. 46
Our souuerane lord, into thy tender aage (MQ 59) p. 199

Pastyme with godlie companie (MQ 24) p. 101

Quha dewlie wald decerne (MQ 35) p. 125

Quhair is the blyithnes that hes beine (MQ 5) p. 53
Quhat faithfull hairt dois not for sorrow burst (MQ 62) p. 209
Quhen houp and hap, and weill and health bene heist (MQ 87) p. 264
Quhen I haue done consider (MQ 31) p. 119
Quho list to mark the Scottisch gyse (MQ 60) p. 202

Reioyis, Henrie, maist Christiane King of France (MQ 10) p. 67
Religioun now is reknit as ane fabill (MQ 42) p. 154

Sair is the recent murmour and regrait (MQ 51) p. 186
Sen Fortoun hes now randerit me subiect (MQ 39) p. 141
Sen that eine that workis my weilfair (MQ 38) p. 137
Sen thocht is frie, think quhat thow lykis (MQ 67) p. 228
Sinneris, repent that 3e haue spent (MQ 33) p. 123
Sum of the poetis and makeris that ar now (MQ 55) p. 193
Sumtyme to court I did repair (MQ 23) p. 99
Sum wyfes of the borroustoun (MQ 2) p. 42

The beatin bark with bloistrous blastis (MQ 80) p. 254
The greit blyithnes and ioy inestimabill (MQ 6) p. 57
The Lord that raise from lyif againe (MQ 16) p. 80
The lyon for hir tender whelpis dois roir (MQ 79) p. 253
The piteous plaint of heavie hairt (MQ 78) p. 251

INDEX OF FIRST NAMES

The slyding tyme so slylie slippes away (MQ 90) p. 268
This buik, who taikis in hand to reid (MQ 84) p. 261
This hallow grave within her bounds dois close (MQ 92) p. 270
This warld so fals is and vnstabill (MQ 52) p. 189
Thocht raging stormes movis ws to schaik (MQ 88) p. 265
Thocht that this warld be verie strainge (MQ 20) p. 92
Thy surname Maitland shewes thyne antient race (MQ 91) p. 269
To michtie Ioue above that ringis (MQ 82) p. 257
To prais that perfyte is, the labour wer but vain (MQ 74) p. 246
To 3ow, my lordis of renoun (MQ 70) p. 236
Tobie most trew, in monye troubillis tryit (MQ 46) p. 169
Treasone is the maist schamfull thing (MQ 22) p. 97

Virgil his village Mantua (MQ 68) p. 229

Vnto a freind I proferd once gud will (MQ 75) p. 247
Vp hairt! Thow art the pairt (MQ 47) p. 176

Who takis in hand by pen (MQ 77) p. 250
With siching sad and surging sorrow soir (MQ 65) p. 218
With weippin eis and face defigurat (MQ 81) p. 256

3e heauinlie goddis and goddessis (MQ 86) p. 263
3e hevinis abone, with heavinlie ornamentis (MQ 63) p. 214
3e nobillis all that sould this countrie guyde (MQ 25) p. 103
3e that sumtyme hes bene weill staikit (MQ 26) p. 107
3our predicessouris prayse and prowes hie (MQ 1) p. 41
3ow that doe wryte aganis the Scottis (MQ 61) p. 206

Bibliography

Andreadis, H. 2001. *Sappho in Early Modern England: Female Same-Sex Literary Erotics, 1550–1714* (Chicago and London).
Arbuthnot, P. S.-M. 1920. *The Memoirs of the Arbuthnots of Kincardineshire and Aberdeenshire* (London).
Amours, F.J. ed. 1903–14. *The Original Chronicle of Andrew of Wyntoun*, 6 vols, STS, 50, 53–54, 56–57, 63 (Edinburgh).
Armstrong, R.B. 1883. *History of Liddesdale* (Edinburgh).
Bain, J. ed. 1830. *The Poems of Richard Maitland of Lethington*, Maitland Club (Glasgow)
Barrow, G.W.S. 1980. *The Anglo-Norman Era in Scottish History* (Oxford).
Baskerville, Charles Read. 1922. 'English Songs of the Night Visit', *PMLA*, 36, 565–87.
Bawcutt, Priscilla. 1986. 'Dunbar's Use of the Symbolic Lion and Thistle', *Cosmos*, 2, 83–97.
Bawcutt, Priscilla. 1990. 'The Commonplace Book of John Maxwell', in *A Day Estivall: Essays on the Music, Poetry and History of Scotland and England and Poems Previously Unpublished in Honour of Helena Mennie Shire*, ed. Alisoun Gardner-Medwin and Janet Hadley Williams (Aberdeen), 59–68.
Bawcutt, Priscilla. 1991. 'The Earliest Texts of Dunbar', in *Regionalism in Late Medieval Manuscripts and Texts*, ed. Felicity Riddy (Cambridge), 183–98.
Bawcutt, Priscilla. 1992. *Dunbar the Makar* (1992).
Bawcutt, Priscilla. 1998. 'Scottish Poetry and English Readers in the Sixteenth Century', in *The Rose and the Thistle: Essays on the Culture of Late Medieval and Renaissance Scotland*, ed. Sally Mapstone and Juliette Wood (East Linton), 59–76.
Bawcutt, Priscilla. ed. 1998. *The Poems of William Dunbar*, 2 vols, ASLS 27 & 28 (Glasgow).
Bawcutt, Priscilla. 2001. 'French Connections? From the *Grand Rhétoriques* to Clément Marot', in *The European Sun: Proceedings of the Seventh International Conference on Medieval and Renaissance Scottish Language and Literature*, ed. Graham Caie, R.J. Lyall, Sally Mapstone and K. Simpson (East Linton), 119–28.
Bawcutt, Priscilla, ed. 2003. *The Shorter Poems of Gavin Douglas*. STS 5th Ser. (Woodbridge).
Bawcutt, Priscilla. ed. 2005. 'Manuscript Miscellanies in Scotland from the Fifteenth to the Seventeenth Centuries', in *Older Scots Literature*, ed. Sally Mapstone (Edinburgh), 189–210.
Bellenden, John. [1821] The History and *Chronicles of Scotland written in Latin by Hector Boece and translated by John Bellenden* (Edinburgh).
Benson, Larry D. ed. 1987. *The Riverside Chaucer*, 3rd edition (Oxford).

Bentham, William. ed. 1818. *Ceremonial at the Marriage of Mary Queen of Scots with the Dauphin of France*, Roxborough Club (London).

Berry, Lloyd. E. intro. 1969. *The Geneva Bible. A Facsimile of the 1560 Edition* (Madison, Milwaukee and London).

Beveridge, E. ed. 1924. *Fergusson's Scottish Proverbs*, STS, new ser., 15 (Edinburgh).

Black, G.F. ed. 1932. *The Seuin Seages ... by Ihone Rolland*, STS, 3rd ser., 3 (Edinburgh).

Blakeway, Amy. 2014. 'Kinship and Diplomacy in sixteenth-century Scotland: the earl of Northumberland's scottish captivity in its domestic and international context, 1569–72'. Historical Research, 87, no. 236, 229–50.

Blamires, Alcuin, ed. 1992. *Woman defamed and Woman defended: An Anthology of Medieval Texts* (Oxford).

Bland, James, 1984. *The Common Hangman: English and Scottish Hangmen Before the Abolition of Public Executions* (Sparkford).

Boardman, S. 1996. *The Early Stewart Kings: Robert II and Robert III* (East Linton).

Boffey, Julia. 2001. 'The Maitland Folio Manuscript as a Verse Anthology', in *William Dunbar the Nobill Poyet: Essays in Honour of Priscilla Bawcutt*, ed. Sally Mapstone (East Linton), 40–50.

Boffey, Julia, ed. 2003. *Fifteenth-Century English Dream Visions: An Anthology* (Oxford).

Boffey, Julia and A.S.G. Edwards. 2005. *A New Index of Middle English Verse* (London).

Bonner, Elizabeth A. 1992. Continuing the "Auld Alliance" in the Sixteenth Century: Scots in France and the French in Scotland', in *The Scottish Soldier Abroad, 1247–1967*, ed. Grant G. Simpson (Edinburgh), 31–46.

Borris, Kenneth, ed. 2003. *Same-Sex Desire in the English Renaissance: A Source Book* (London).

Brewer, D.S. 1955. 'The Ideal of Feminine Beauty in Medieval Literature, especially "Harley Lyrics", Chaucer and some Elizabethans', *Modern Language Review*, 30, 257–69.

Brown, Keith M. 2000. *Noble Society in Scotland: Wealth, Family and Culture, From Reformation to Revolution* (Edinburgh).

Bullen, A. H. 1889. *Lyrics from the Song-Books of the Elizabethan Age* (London).

Cameron, James. 1998. *James V: The Personal Rule, 1528–1542*, ed. Norman Macdougall, The Stewart Dynasty in Scotland (East Linton).

Campbell, L.B. ed. 1938. *The Mirror for Magistrates* (Cambridge).

Chambers, R.W. and Edith C. Batho, eds, 1936, 1941. *The Chronicles of Scotland. Compiled by Hector Boece. Translated into Scots by John Bellenden, 1531*, 2 vols, STS, 3rd ser., 10 and 15 (Edinburgh and London).

Child, F.J. ed. 1861, repr. 1957. *The English and Scottish Popular Ballads*, 5 vols (repr. New York).

Cormack, Ian L. 1983. *Old Rutherglen with Burnside* (Keighley).

Cowan, Ian B. 1982. *The Scottish Reformation: Church and Society in Sixteenth-Century Scotland* (London).
Cowling, David. 1998. *Building the Text: Architectural Metaphor in Late Medieval and Early Modern France* (Oxford).
Craigie, J. ed. 1955–58. *The Poems of James VI of Scotland*, 2 vols, STS 3rd ser., 22, 26 (Edinburgh and London).
Craigie, W.A. ed. 1919–27, *The Maitland Folio Manuscript*, 2 vols, STS, NS, 7, 20 (Edinburgh and London).
Craigie, W.A. ed. 1920. *The Maitland Quarto Manuscript*, STS, NS, 9 (Edinburgh and London).
Craigie, W.A. ed. 1923–25. *The Asloan Manuscript: A Miscellany in Prose and Verse*, 2 vols, STS, NS, 14, 16 (Edinburgh and London).
Craigie, W.A. ed. 1919–27. *The Maitland Folio Manuscript,* 2 vols, STS, NS, 7 (Edinburgh and London).
Cramsie, J. 2002. *Kingship and Crown Finnance under James VI and I* (Woodbridge).
Cranstoun, James. ed. 1887. *The Poems of Alexander Montgomerie*, 2 vols, STS (Edinburgh and London).
Cranstoun, J. ed. 1891–93. *Satirical Poems of the Reformation*, 2 vols, STS, 1st ser., 20, 24 (Edinburgh and London).
Crockett, Thomas. ed. 1913. *Poems of John Stewart of Baldyenneis*, STS, NS, 5 (Edinburgh and London).
Davidson, P. 1995. 'The Entry of Mary Stewart into Edinburgh, 1561, and Other Ambiguities', *Renaissance Studies*, 9, 416–29.
Dawson, Giles E. and Lactitia Kennedy-Skipton. 1981. *Elizabethan Handwriting, 1500–1650: A Manual* (New York).
Dawson, Jane. 2002. *The Politics of Religion in the Age of Mary Queen of Scots: The Earl of Argyll and the Struggle for Britain and Ireland* (Cambridge).
Dawson, Jane E.A. 2007. *Scotland Reformed, 1488–1587*, The New Edinburgh History of Scotland (Edinburgh).
Dickinson, William Croft. ed. 1949. *John Knox's History of the Reformation in Scotland*, 2 vols (Edinburgh).
Donald, A. K. ed. 1902. *The Poems of Alexander Scott*, STS, e.s. 85 (London).
Donaldson, Gordon. 1965. *Scotland James V to James VII*, The Edinburgh History of Scotland (Edinburgh and London).
Donaldson, Gordon. 1970. *Scottish Historical Documents* (Glasgow).
Donaldson, Gordon. 1985. *Scottish Church History* (Edinburgh).
Dunnigan, Sarah. 1997. 'Scottish Women Writers, c. 1560–1650', in *A History of Scottish Women's Writing*, ed. Douglas Gifford and Dorothy McMillan (Edinburgh), 15–43.
Dunnigan, Sarah. 1999. 'Female Gifts: Rhetoric, Beauty and the Beloved in the Lyrics of Alexander Montgomerie', *Scottish Literary Journal*, 26, 59–78.
Dunnigan, Sarah. 2003. 'Undoing the Double Tress: Scotland, Early Modern

Women's Writing, and the Location of Critical Desires', *Feminist Studies*, 29.2, 298–319.

Dunnigan, Sarah. 2005. 'Feminising the Early-Modern Erotic: Female Voiced Lyrics and Mary Queen of Scots', in *Older Scots Literature*, ed. Sally Mapstone (Edinburgh), 441–66.

Edington, Carol. 1994. *Court and Culture in Renaissance Scotland. Sir David Lindsay of the Mount* (East Linton).

Edwards, A.S.G. 2010. 'Lydgate in Scotland', *Nottingham Medieval Studies*, 54, 185–94.

Edwards, Peter. 1988. *The Horse Trade of Tudor and Stuart England* (Cambridge).

Elliott, Kenneth and Helena Mennie Shire, eds, 1957. *Music of Scotland, 1500–1700* (London).

Ewan, Elizabeth. 2004. 'The Dangers of Manly Women: Late Medieval Perceptions of Female Heroism in Scotland's Second War of Independence', in *Women and the Feminine in Medieval and Early Modern Scottish Writing*, ed. Sarah M. Dunnigan, C. Marie Harker and Evelyn S. Newlyn (Basingstoke), 3–18.

Ewan, Elizabeth and Maureen M. Meikle, eds, 1999. *Women in Scotland, c. 1100–c.1700* (East Linton).

Fairbank, Alfred and Berthold Wolpe. 1960. *Renaissance Handwriting. An Anthology of Italic Scripts* (London).

Farnsworth, Jane. 1996. 'Voicing Female Desire in Poem "XLIX"', *Studies in English Literature*, 36, 57–72.

Fein, Susanna Greer. 1989. 'Haue Mercy of Me (Psalm 51): An Unedited Alliterative Poem from the London Thornton Manuscript', *Modern Philology*, 86, 223–41.

Fowler, Alastair, ed. 1994. *The Country House Poem: A Cabinet of Seventeenth-Century Estate Poems and Related Items* (Edinburgh).

Fox, Denton. ed. 1980. *The Poems of Robert Henryson* (Oxford).

Fox, Denton and William A. Ringler. 1980. *The Bannatyne Manuscript. National Library of Scotland Advocates' MS 1.1.6* (London).

Frye, Susan. 2002. 'Materializing Authorship in Esther Inglis's Books', *Journal of Medieval and Early Modern Studies*, 32.3, 469–91.

Fullarton, J. ed. 1829. *The History of the House of Seytoun to the Year M.D.LIX. By Sir Richard Maitland of Lethington, Knight with the continuation by Alexander Viscount Kingston to M.D.C.LXXXVII* (Glasgow).

Girvan, R. ed. 1939. *Ratis Raving and Other Early Scots Poems on Morals* (Edinburgh and London).

Glenn, Duncan. 1995. *Sir Richard Maitland: Selected Poems*. Akros Pocket Classics Series (Edinburgh).

Goodare, Julian. 1999. *State and Society in Early Modern Scotland* (Oxford).

Goodare, Julian. 2004. *The Government of Scotland, 1560–1625* (Oxford).

Goodare, Julian and Michael Lynch. 2000. 'The Scottish State and its Borderlands, 1567–1625', in *The Reign of James VI*, ed. Julian Gooodare and Michael Lynch (East Linton), 186–207.

Goodman, Anthony and Anthony Tuck, eds, 1992. *War and Border Societies in the Middle Ages* (London).

Gray, Douglas. 1998. 'The Royal Entry in Sixteenth-Century Scotland', in *The Rose and the Thistle: Essays on the Culture of Late Medieval and Renaissance Scotland*, ed. Sally Mapstone and Juliet Wood (East Linton), 10–37.

Gregor, Walter. Ed. 1884. *Ane Treatise Callit the Court of Venus ... be Ihone Rolland*, STS, 3 (Edinburgh).

Gribben, Crawford and David. G. Mullan. 2009. *Literature and the Scottish Reformation* (Aldershot and Burlington).

Grummitt, David. 2008. *The Calais Garrison: War and Military Service in England, 1436–1558* (Woodbridge).

Hamer, Douglas. 1932. '*The Marriage of Mary Queen of Scots to the Dauphin: A Scottish Printed Fragment*', *The Library: The Transactions of the Bibliographical Society*, s4-XII, 420–28.

Hamer, Douglas. ed. 1931–36. *The Works of David Lyndsay of the Mount 1490–1555*, 4 vols, STS, 3rd ser., 1, 2, 6, 8 (Edinburgh).

Hamlin, H. 2004. *Psalm Culture and Early Modern English Literature* (Cambridge).

Hammond, N.G.L. and H.H. Scullard, eds, 1970. *The Oxford Classical Dictionary*, 2nd edition (Oxford).

Hanna, Ralph. ed. 1974. *The Awntyrs off Arthure at the Terne Wathelyn* (Manchester and New York).

Harker, C. Marie. 2005. 'Skirting the Issue: Misogyny and Gender in Lyndsay's *Ane Supplication Direct ... To the Kingis Grace, in Contemptioun of Syde Tallis*', in *Older Scots Literature*, ed. Sally Mapstone (Edinburgh), 266–82.

Hebron, Malcolm. 1997. *The Medieval Siege. Theme and Image in Middle English Romance* (Oxford).

Hewison, James King. ed. 1887–88. *Certain Tractates ... by Ninian Winzet*, 2 vols, STS, 1st ser., 15 and 16 (Edinburgh and London).

Hobbs, Mary. 1992. *Early Seventeenth Century Verse Miscellany Manuscripts* (Aldershot).

Hume, D. 1657. *General History of Scotland from the Year 767 to the Death of King James* (London).

Jamieson, T.H. ed. 1889. *Alexander Barclay, The Ship of Fools* (Edinburgh and London).

Kamington, Johne [1830], *The Genealogy of the House and Surname of Setoun, by Sir Richard Maitland of Lethington, Knight with the Chronicle of the House of Setoun, compiled in metre by John Kamington alias Peter Manye* (Edinburgh), 39–50.

Kelly, Christopher. 2008. *Attila the Hun: Barbarian Terror and the Fall of the Roman Empire* (London).

Klausner, David N. 1972. 'Exempla and *The Awntyrs of Arthure*', *Medieval Studies*, 34, 307–25.

Kolve, K.A. 1966. *The Play Called Corpus Christi* (Stanford).

Laing, David. ed. 1846–64. *The Works of John Knox*, 6 vols (Edinburgh).

Lee, Maurice. 1953. *James Stewart, Earl of Moray: A Political Study of the Reformation in Scotland* (New York).

Lee, Maurice. 1959. *John Maitland of Thirlestane and the Foundation of the Stewart Despotism in Scotland* (Princeton).

Lennoxlove House, East Lothian. 1960. *The History and Treasures of Lennoxlove House* (London).

Loughlin, M. 1994. '"The Dialogue of the Twa Wyfeis": Maitland, Machiavelli and the Propaganda of the Scottish Civil War', in *The Renaissance in Scotland. Studies in Literature, Religion, History and Culture*, ed. A.A. MacDonald, M. Lynch and I.B. Cowan (Leiden), 226–45.

Love, Harold. 1993. *Scribal Publication in Seventeenth-Century England* (Oxford).

Lowers, J.K. 1953. *Mirrors for Rebels: A Study of the Polemical Literature Relating to the Northern Rebellion of 1569*, University of California English Studies, 6 (Berkeley).

Lucas, Peter J. 1982. 'The Growth and Development of English Literary Patronage in the Late Middle Ages and Early Renaissance', *The Library*, 6th ser., 4, 219–48.

Lyall, Roderick J. 2000. 'James VI and the Sixteenth-Century Cultural Crisis' in *The Reign of James VI*, ed. Julian Goodare and Michael Lynch (East Linton), 55–70.

Lyall, Roderick J. 2005. *Alexander Montgomerie: Poetry, Politics, and Cultural Change in Jacobean Scotland*, Medieval and Renaissance Texts and Studies (Tempe, Arizona).

Lynch, Michael, ed. 2001. *The Oxford Companion to Scottish History* (Oxford).

Lythe, S.G.E. 1960. *The Economy of Scotland in its European Setting, 1550–1625* (Edinburgh and London).

MacDonald, A.A. 1972. 'The Poetry of Sir Richard Maitland of Lethington', *Transactions of the East Lothian Antiquarian and Field Naturalists Society*, 13, 7–19.

MacDonald, A.A. 1986. 'The Bannatyne Manuscript. A Marian Anthology', *Innes Review*, 37, 36–47.

MacDonald, A.A. 1991a. 'The Sense of Place in Early Scottish Verse: Rhetoric and Reality', *English Studies*, 72, 12–27.

MacDonald, A.A. 1991b. 'Mary Stewart's Entry into Edinburgh: An Ambiguous Triumph', *Innes Review*, 42, 101–10.

MacDonald, A.A. 1997. 'Early Modern Scottish Literature and the Parameters of Culture', in *The Rose and the Thistle: Essays on the Culture of Late Medieval and Renaissance Scotland*, ed. Sally Mapstone and Juliet Wood (East Linton), 77–97.

MacDonald, A.A. 2001. 'Sir Richard Maitland and William Dunbar: Textual Symbiosis and Poetic Individuality', in *William Dunbar, 'The Nobill Poyet'*: *Essays in Honour of Priscilla Bawcutt*, ed. Sally Mapstone (East Linton), 134–49.

MacDonald, A.R. 1997. 'The Triumph of Protestantism: the Burgh of Edinburgh and the Entry of Mary Queen of Scots', *Innes Review*, 48, 73–82.

Mapstone, Sally, ed. 2005. *Older Scots Literature* (Edinburgh).

Martin, Joanna M. 2008. *Kingship and Love in Scottish Poetry, 1424–1540* (Aldershot).

Martin, Joanna M. 2009. 'Responses to the Frame Narrative of John Gower's *Confessio Amantis* in Fifteenth- and Sixteenth-Century Scottish Literature', *The Review of English Studies*, 60/3, 561–77.

Martin, Joanna. 2012. 'The Border, England and the English in some Older Scots Lyric and Occasional Poems, c. 1420–1603', in *The Anglo-Scottish Border and the Shaping of Identity, 1350–1600*, ed. Mark P. Bruce and Katherine H. Terrell (Basingstoke and New York), 87–102.

Martin, Joanna. 2013a. 'The Maitland Quarto Manuscript and the Literary Culture of the Reign of James VI', in *James VI and I, Literature and Scotland: Tides of Change, 1567–1625*, ed. David Parkinson (Leuven), 65–81.

Martin, Joanna. 2013b. 'The Presentation of the Family in Maitland Writings', in *Fresche Fontanis: Studies in the Culture of late Medieval and Early Modern Scotland*, ed. Janet Hadley Williams and Derrick McClure (Cambridge), 319–30.

Martin, Joanna M. and Katherine A. McClune. 2009. 'The Maitland Folio and Quarto Manuscripts in Context', in *Tudor Manuscripts, 1485–1603*, ed. A.S.G. Edwards, English Manuscript Studies, 1100–1700, 15 (London), 237–63.

Marotti, Arthur F. 1995. *Manuscript, Print and the English Renaissance Lyric* (Cornell).

Mason, Roger. 1998. *Kingship and Commonweal: Political Thought in Renaissance and Reformation Scotland* (East Linton).

McBride, Kari Boyd. 1991. *Country House Discourse in Early Modern England: A Cultural Study of Landscape and Legitimacy* (Aldershot).

McClune, Katherine A. 2006. 'The Poetry of John Stewart of Baldynneis (?1540–?1607)'. Unpublished D.Phil. thesis (Oxford).

McClune, Kate. 2010. 'Depictions of Experience in Three Older Scots Poems', in *The Apparelling of Truth: Literature and Literary Culture in the Reign of James VI: Essays Presented to Roderick J. Lyall*, ed. Nicola Royan (Cambridge), 48–61.

McClung, William. 1977. *The Country House in English Renaissance Poetry* (Berkeley).

McGavin, John. 2007. *Theatricality and Narrative in Medieval and Early Modern Scotland* (Aldershot).

McNiven, P. 1994. 'Rebellion, Sedition and the Legend of Richard II's Survival in the Reigns of Henry IV and V', *Bulletin of the John Rylands Library*, lxxvi, 93–117.

Meier, Nicole. ed. 2008. *The Poems of Walter Kennedy*, STS, 5th ser., 6 (Woodbridge).

Meikle, Henry W. ed. 1914. *The Works of William Fowler*, STS, NS, 6 (Edinburgh and London).

Mill, A.J. 1927. *Medieval Plays in Scotland* (New York and London).

Mitchell, A.F. ed. 1896–97. *A Compendious Book of Godly and Spiritual Songs Commonly Known as 'The Gude and Godlie Ballatis'*, STS, 39 (Edinburgh).

Mitchell, William Smith. 1955. *History of Scottish Bookbinding, 1432 to 1650* (Edinburgh).

Mueller, Janet. 1992. 'Lesbian Erotics: the Utopian Trope of Donne's "Sappho to Philaenis"', in *Homosexuality in Renaissance and Enlightenment England: Literary Representations in Historical Context*, ed. Claude J. Summers (London), 103–24.

Mullan, David G. 2000. *Scottish Puritanism, 1590–1638* (Oxford).

Mullan, David G. 2010. *Narratives of the Religious Self in Early-Modern Scotland* (Farnham and Burlington).

Newlyn, Evelyn S. 1999. 'Images of Women in Sixteenth-Century Scottish Literary Manuscripts', in *Women in Scotland, c. 1100–c.1700*, ed. Elizabeth Ewan and Maureen M. Meikle (East Linton), 56–66.

Newlyn, Evelyn S. 2004. 'A Methodology for Reading Against the Culture: Anonymous Women Poets, and the Maitland Quarto Manuscript (c. 1586)', in *Women and the Feminine in Medieval and Early Modern Scottish Writing*, eds Sarah M. Dunnigan, C. Marie Harker and Evelyn S. Newlyn (Basingstoke), 89–103.

Norton-Smith, J. and I. Pravda, eds.1976. *The Quare of Jelusy*, Middle English Texts, 3 (Heidelberg).

Ovid [1998]. *Metamorphoses*, trans. A.D. Melville, intro. E.J. Kennedy (Oxford).

Owst, G.R. 1966. *Literature and the Pulpit in Medieval England* (Oxford).

Parker, Holt M. ed. 2003. *The Complete Writings of Olympia Morata* (Chicago).

Parkinson, David. ed. 2000. *The Poems of Alexander Montgomerie*, 2 vols, STS, 4th ser., 28, 29 (Edinburgh).

Pinkerton, John. ed. 1786. *Ancient Scotish Poems Never Before in Print*, 2 vols (London).

Potter, David. 1983. 'The Duc de Guise and the Fall of Calais, 1557–1558', *The English Historical Review*, 388, 481–512.

Powell, Jason. 2009. 'Marginalia, Authorship and Editing in the Manuscripts of Thomas Wyatt's Verse', in *Tudor Manuscripts, 1485–1603*, ed. A.S.G. Edwards, English Manuscript Studies 1100–1700, 15 (London), 1–40.

Preston, Jean F. and Laetitia Yeandle. 2002. *English Handwriting 1400–1650. An Introductory Manual*, Medieval and Renaissance Texts and Studies (Binghamton, New York).

Raber, Karen and Tucker, Treva J. eds, 2005. *The Culture of the Horse: Status, Discipline, and Identity in the Early Modern World* (Basingstoke).
Rae, T.I. 1966. *The Administration of the Scottish Frontier 1513–1603* (Edinburgh).
Reed, James. 1973. *The Border Ballads* (London).
Reid, David. ed. 2005. *David Hume of Godscroft's The History of the House of Angus*, 2 vols, STS, 5th ser., 4 and 5 (Edinburgh).
Reid, Steven. J. 2001. *Humanism and Calvinism. Andrew Melville and the Universities of Scotland, 1560–1625* (Farnham).
Rickard, Jane. 2007. *Authorship and Authority in the Writings of James VI and I* (Manchester).
Ridley, Jasper. 1968. *John Knox* (Oxford).
Ritchie, Pamela E. 2002. *Mary of Guise In Scotland, 1548–1560: A Political Career* (East Linton).
Ritchie, R.L. ed. 1921–29. *The Buik of Alexander or The Buik of the Most Noble and Valiant Conquerour Alexander the Grit*, ed. R.L. Ritchie, 4 vols, STS, NS, 12, 17, 21, 25 (Edinburgh).
Robson, Michael. 1971. 'Notes on the Historical Background and Sources of Jock o' the Side', *Transactions of the Hawick Archaeological Society*, 11–16.
Rose, Susan. 2008. *Calais: An English Town in France, 1347–1558* (Woodbridge).
Royan, Nicola. 2008. 'Some Conspicuous Women in the Original Chronicle, Scotichronicon and Scotorum Historia', *Innes Review*, 59, 131–41.
Royan, Nicola. Forthcoming. 'Scottish Psalm Translations'.
Ryrie, Alec. 2006. *The Origins of the Scottish Reformation* (Manchester and New York).
Saul, Nigel. 1997. *Richard II*, Yale English Monarchs (New Haven and London).
Scase, Wendy. 2007. *Literature and Complaint in England, 1272–1553* (Oxford).
Scattergood, V.J. 1996. 'Fashion and Morality in the Late Middle Ages', in his *Reading the Past: Essays on Medieval and Renaissance Literature* (Dublin), 240–57.
Shapiro, Norman R. ed. and trans. 2002. *Lyrics of the French Renaissance: Marot, Du Bellay, Ronsard* (New Haven).
Shaw, F.J. 1979. 'Sumptuary Legislation in Scotland', *Judicial Review*, 24, 81–115.
Shire, Helena Mennie. 1969. *Song, Dance and Poetry at the Court of Scotland under King James VI* (London).
Shrewsbury, J.F.D. 1970, repr. 2005. *A History of the Bubonic Plague in the British Isles* (Cambridge).
Sibbald, James. ed. 1802. *A Chronicle of Scottish Poetry from the Thirteenth Century to the Union of Crowns*, 4 vols (Edinburgh).
Simpson, Grant G., ed. 1992. *The Scottish Soldier Abroad, 1247–1967* (Edinburgh).

Skeat, W.W. ed. 1865, repr. 1965. *Lancelot of the Laik: A Scottish Metrical Romance*, EETS, OS, 6 (Oxford and London).
Skeat, W.W. ed. 1884, repr. 1911. *The Kingis Quaire, together with a Ballad of Good Counsel*, STS, NS, 1 (Edinburgh and London).
Small, J. 1833. *Castles and Mansions of the Lothians* (Edinburgh).
Smith, G. Gregory. ed. *The Poems of Robert Henryson*. STS, 3 vols (Edinburgh and London).
Smith, Janet M. 1934. *The French Background of Middle Scots Literature* (Edinburgh and London).
Sobecki, Sebastian I. 2008. *The Sea and Medieval English Literature* (Cambridge).
Spiller, M.R.G. 1974. 'The Country House Poem in Scotland: Sir George Mackenzie's *Caelia's Country House and Closet*', *Studies in Scottish Literature*, 12, 110–30.
Sternfield, Frederick W. and David Greer. 1967. *English Madrigal Verse, 1588–1632*. 3rd edition. (Oxford).
Stevens, J. 1961, repr. 1979. *Music and Poetry in the Early Tudor Court* (Cambridge).
Stevenson, David. 1990. *King's College Aberdeen, 1560–1641: From Protestant Reformation to Covenanting Revolution* (Aberdeen).
Stevenson, Jane. 2005. *Women Latin Poets. Language, Gender and Authority from Antiquity to the Eighteenth Century* (Oxford).
Stevenson, Jane and Peter Davidson, eds, 2001. *Early Modern Women Poets: An Anthology* (Oxford).
Stevenson, Katie. 2006. *Chivalry and Knighthood in Scotland, 1424–1513* (Woodbridge).
Stewart, A.M. ed. 1979. *The Complaynt of Scotland (c. 1550) by Mr Robert Wedderburn*, STS, 4th ser., 11 (Edinburgh).
Stewart, I.H. 1955. *The Scottish Coinage* (London).
Strauss, P. 1995. *In Hope of Heaven: English Recusant Prison Writings of the Sixteenth Century* (New York).
Strohm, P. 1996. 'The Trouble with Richard: The Reburial of Richard II and Lancastrian Symbolic Strategy', *Speculum*, 71, 87–111.
Sutherland, Robert. ed. 2007. *The Practiques of Sir Richard Maitland of Lethington, from December 1550 to October 1577* (Edinburgh).
Todd, Margo. 2002. *The Culture of Protestantism in Early Modern Scotland* (New Haven and London).
Tucker, Marie-Claude. 2002. 'Scottish Students and Masters of the Faculty of Law of the University of Bourges in the Sixteenth and Seventeenth Centuries', in *Literature, Letters and the Canonical in Early Modern Scotland*, ed. Theo van Heijnsbergen and Nicola Royan (East Linton), 111–20.
Turnball, W.B. ed. 1858. *William Stewart. The buik of the cronicilis of Scotland*, 3 vols, Rolls series 6 (London).
Turville-Petre, Thorlac. Forthcoming. 'The Vocabulary of the *Morte D'Arthure*'.

Utley, F.E. 1944. *The Crooked Rib: An Analytical Index to the Argument about Women in English and Scottish Literature to the end of the year 1568* (Columbus, Ohio).
van Heijnsbergen, T. 1992. 'The Love Lyrics of Alexander Scott', *Studies in Scottish Literature*, 26, 366–79.
van Heijnsbergen, T. 1996. 'The Sixteenth-Century Scottish Love Lyric', in *Sacred and Profane: Secular and Devotional Interplay in Early Modern British Literature*, ed. H. Wilcox, R. Todd and A.A. MacDonald (Amsterdam), 45–61.
van Heijnsbergen, T. 2001. 'Dunbar, Scott and the Making of Poetry', in *William Dunbar the Nobill Poyet: Essays in Honour of Priscilla Bawcutt*, ed. Sally Mapstone (East Linton), 108–33.
van Heijnsbergen, T. 2002. 'Masks of Revelation and the "female" Tongues of Men: Montgomerie, Christian Lyndsay, and the Writing Game at the Scottish Renaissance Court', in *Literature, Letters and the Canonical in Early Modern Scotland*, ed. T. Van Heijnsbergen, and N. Royan (East Linton), 69–89.
van Heijnsbergen, T. 2005. 'Modes of Self-Representation in Older Scots Texts', in *Older Scots Literature*, ed. Sally Mapstone (Edinburgh), 314–45.
van Heijnsbergen, Theo. 2008. 'Advice to A Princess: The Literary Articulation of a Religious, Political and Cultural Programme for Mary Queen of Scots, 1562', in *Sixteenth-century Scotland: Essays in Honour of Michael Lynch*, ed. Julian Goodare and A.A. MacDonald (Leiden), 99–122.
Walther, Hans., ed.1963–69. *Proverbia Sententiaeque Latinitatis medii aevi*, Lateinische Sprichwörter und Sentenzen des Mittelalters in alphabetischer Anordnung, 6 vols (Göttingen).
Watson, G., ed. 1943. *The Mar Lodge Translation of the History of Scotland by Hector Boece*, STS, 3rd ser., 17 (Edinburgh and London).
Whitehead, Christina. 2003. *Castles on the Mind: A Study of Medieval Architectural Allegory* (Cardiff).
Whiting, B.J. 1941–51. 'Proverbs and Proverbial Sayings from Scottish Writings before 1600', *Medieval Studies*, 11, 123–205; 13, 87–164.
Whiting, B.J with Whiting H.W. 1968. *Proverbs Sentences and Proverbial Phrases from English Writings Mainly before 1500* (London).
Williams, Janet Hadley, ed. 2001. *Sir David Lyndsay: Selected Poems*, ASLS, 30 (Glasgow).
Willetts, Pamela J. 2000. *Catalogue of Manuscripts in the Society of Antiquaries of London* (Cambridge).
Wilson, James Alexander. 1936. *A Contribution to the History of Lanarkshire*, 2 vols (Glasgow).
Winchester, Angus J.L. 2000. *The Harvest of the Hills: Rural Life in Northern England and the Scottish Borders, 1400–1700* (2000).
Wingfield, Emily. 2012. 'The Familial, Professional and Literary Contexts of

Edinburgh, National Archives of Scotland RH 13/35', *Textual Cultures*, 7:1, 76–96.

Wolffe, B.O. 1981, new ed. 2001. *Henry VI*, Yale English Monarchs (New Haven and London).

Wormald, Jenny. 1985. *Lords and Men in Scotland: Bonds of Manrent, 1442–1603* (Edinburgh).

Wormald, Jenny. 1988, repr. 1991. *Court, Kirk and Community. Scotland, 1470–1625* (Edinburgh).

Wright, Thomas, ed. 1838. *Queen Elizabeth and her Times*, 2 vols (London).

Wright, Thomas. ed. 1859–61. *Political Poems and Songs Relating to English History*, 2 vols (London).

Ziegler, Georgianna. 2000. '"More than Feminine Boldness": The Gift Books of Esther Inglis', in *Women, Writing and the Reproduction of Culture in Tudor and Stewart Britain*, ed. Mary E. Burke, Jane Donawerth, Linda L. Dove and Karen Nelson (Syracuse, New York).